D1440903

From 1789 to 1914 the shape of Christianity as a modern world faith began to emerge. Intellectual and social revolutions effected by the European Enlightenment and industrial revolutions sowed the seeds of secularity in the West. At the same time expanding missionary horizons stimulated currents of indigenous church growth beyond Europe which would in the long run prove even more important for the future of the faith. Ian Shaw's book gives a sure and illuminating guide to these multiple processes of revolutionary change which began to redraw the contours of world Christianity.

BRIAN STANLEY,
Professor of World Christianity, University of Edinburgh,
editor of *Cambridge History of Christianity: World Christianities 1815-1914*

It is crucial for contemporaries to understand how the religious tone of Western society was challenged and adapted during the recent past. It is equally important to appreciate how the faith of the West was exported to other lands so that it could grow over subsequent years into the nation-building force it is today. Ian Shaw's account of Christianity over the long nineteenth century achieves both goals in a way that calls for no previous specialist knowledge, and yet at sufficient depth to make the study thoroughly informative. The book is clear, well arranged and up-to-date in its absorption of recent research. It covers the full range of denominations across the globe, setting religion firmly in its socio-political context and so addressing central historical issues such as empire and national identity. It is likely to command a wide readership in universities, theological colleges, ministers' studies and private homes. It well deserves to be widely read.

DAVID BEBBINGTON,
Professor of Modern History, University of Stirling

This book by Ian Shaw has risen to the challenge confronting writers treating the history of Christianity in the light of the rapid increase of Christian adherence outside the western world. It is clear, comprehensive, well-informed about the history of western churches, unusually perceptive about Christian developments elsewhere in the world, and throughout written in entirely accessible prose. Students and experienced readers should both welcome this most helpful volume.

MARK NOLL,
Francis A. McAnaney Professor of History, Notre Dame University,
Notre Dame, Indiana

I think this is a most impressive book. A book like this should become a standard work in the way that Alec Vidler's *Church in an Age of Revolution* used to be."

IAN RANDALL,
Director of the Institute of Baptist and Anabaptist Studies,
International Baptist Theological Seminary, Prague

We have long known that the Nineteenth Century was a crucible of revolution that produced the modern West. What was not as clear until Dr Ian Shaw's extraordinary *Churches, Revolutions and Empires* was how the events of the nineteenth century sowed the seeds for the rise of a new world Christianity and a new world order that would transcend modernity. I have long been looking for a text that would help my students in Africa understand the double development of a post western Christianity as well as a post Christian west. With Ian Shaw's new book, that search is over.

MARK SHAW,
Director of the Centre for World Christianity,
Africa International University, Nairobi, Kenya

The period from 1789 to 1914 was the crucible in which the modern world was born. A time of revolution, upheaval, empire and war, it shaped Europe and thus the rest of the world. As a result, any understanding of the world today must be built on a clear grasp of what happened during this time. Ian Shaw is a first-rate historian and this is a first-rate book which should take its place as a standard account of the period.

CARL R TRUEMAN,
Paul Woolley Professor of Church History,
Westminster Theological Seminary, Philadelphia, Pennsylvania

Churches, Revolutions, and Empires: 1789–1914

Ian J. Shaw

This book is dedicated to my son Timothy.

Copyright © Ian J. Shaw 2012

ISBN 978-1-84550-774-9

First Published in 2012
by
Christian Focus Publications
Geanies House, Fearn, Ross-shire
IV20 1TW, Scotland
www.christianfocus.com

Cover design by moose77.com
Printed by MPG, Cornwall, England

CONTENTS

Preface   ix

1   The Legacy of the Revolutionaries:
the American War of Independence and its consequences   1

2   Crush 'l'Infâme':
The French Revolution and its Legacy   35

3   Churches and the Industrial Revolution
Britain: 1780s-1820s   63

4   'To Use Means for the Conversion of the Heathen':
The Revolution in Protestant Overseas Mission, c. 1790–1840   95

5   Moral Revolutionaries:
The Abolition Of The Slave Trade And Slavery   131

6   Revolutions of the Theological Mind: Nineteenth-
Century Germany   165

7   Building Jerusalem, or Redeeming Babylon? Churches in
the Industrial Age: Britain 1820s to 1870s   197

8   Revolutions in Modern Social and Political Thought:
Protestant and Roman Catholic Responses   233

9   The Rising Tide of World Mission: the 1840s to 1880s   271

10   Religious Responses to Revolutions in Science   305

11   Revolutions in American Religion and Society:
the Shadow of Civil War   337

CONTENTS

12 Christianity and Emerging National Identities   371

13 Missions in the Age of Imperialism   403

14 Mission at the Heart of Empires:
    Crisis in Late Nineteenth-Century Cities   439

15 Old Defences, New Expressions: Nineteenth-Century
    American Christian Thought and Expression   475

16 Conclusion: The Dawn of the World Church   509

    Subject Index   541

PREFACE

During the period 1789–1914 Christianity faced some of the most profound challenges since the time of the apostles, engaging with issues of great significance, many of which the contemporary church continues to wrestle with. It was a hugely eventful period dominated by the theme of revolution. In the wake of the Enlightenment and the Industrial Revolution, social, political, economic, and religious contexts were transformed in revolutionary ways. Although in the late eighteenth century witches were no longer burned, millions were enslaved, and millions of others remained under the bondage of feudal serfdom. By the beginning of the twentieth century, most of these systems had been swept away, monarchies had been toppled, and the powers of others severely constrained. Europe and North America saw the rising social and political dominance of the middle classes with their bourgeois values. Christianity adjusted in such diverse ways to these changes that by 1914 it begins to be possible to speak of World Christianities.

As the first chapter of this book shows, revolution overturned the established order in the United States, and posed profound questions as to the religious identity of the new nation, the enigmatic results of which Christians and non-Christians continue to debate. Hot on its heels came Revolution in France, overturning not only a political regime, but also the richest of Roman Catholic Churches, and temporarily replacing it with a civil religion. Eventually France was subject to a policy of widespread religious persecution and de-Christianisation, such as had not been experienced since the early centuries of the church,[1] and which pointed ahead to similar state-sponsored policies in the

---

1 For the purposes of this book the broad definitions of 'church' and 'Christianity' widely utilised in historical writing are employed, but the use of these terms does not imply any judgement as to whether these general understandings are theologically accurate or not.

twentieth century. Revolutionary upheavals of a different order took place in Britain, as churches were forced to deal with a new, rapidly changing, industrial, and urban world that left many areas unrecognisable from how they had been a few decades previously.

The geographical scope of Christianity began to undergo revolutionary changes between 1789–1914. Three chapters consider the major advances in world mission which took place, from the inspirational example of William Carey in India, to the pioneering work of David Livingstone in Africa, and Hudson Taylor in China, and the sacrificial labours of the Roman Catholic White Fathers. The complex role of Imperialism in the advance of Christianity is explored. This was an era in which the seeds of a truly world church were sown, and the final chapter explores these developments. The beginnings of an indigenous, non-white Christian leadership, from Bishop Samuel Crowther to the itinerant West African prophet Wadé Harris, was of profound significance for twentieth century churches.

Christianity also had to wrestle with revolutionary issues of a very different order, and separate chapters in *Churches, Revolutions and Empires* are devoted to the significant internal tensions these produced. Philosophy in the wake of the Enlightenment impacted theological expression, producing the profound reconstruction attempted by theological liberalism, emerging especially in Germany, but influential across the Christian West, especially amongst Protestants. Such significant challenges to Christian orthodoxy provoked strong defences, and the ultimate reaction of fundamentalism. Advances in the realm of science were equally profound. Charles Darwin produced what was effectively a new book of Genesis with an alternative account of cosmic and human origins. The theological implications were tremendous, posing fundamental questions about Biblical authority, and of the relationship between faith and science.

Christians wrestled over the role they should take in politics, with the formation of political parties with Christian identities in some countries, but conscious avoidance of this in others. Notable political success was secured in Britain with the campaigns against the slave trade, and in favour of emancipation, the subject of chapter five, although this success raised issues over the shape future political engagement should take. On these significant questions of social ethics there was no easy consensus, as the American Christian community was to find when they bitterly disagreed, and supported both sides in the Civil War in the United States over the issue of slavery.

The development of modern liberal democracies, with the deeper challenges of socialism and then Marxism and communism posed further challenges for Christian thinking, and chapter nine considers responses which varied from Christian Socialism, to the retrenchment and reaction of the papal condemnation of the modern world expressed in the Syllabus of Errors.

Christianity continued to be a profoundly shaping force in matters of national identity, as chapter twelve shows.

Although the period 1789 to 1914 saw rapid growth in the size of the world church, evidence suggests that by the end of the nineteenth century churches in the cities of Western Europe were not thriving, although more generally North America followed a different trajectory. The concept of secularisation is assessed in chapter thirteen, as are a series of responses by churches to this growing sense of urban crisis. With over 50% of the world population now urban, the engagement of Christianity with the urban world has great significance for contemporary churches. The scope of religious liberty in the United States in the nineteenth century produced a context in which a range of religious expressions flourished. Some tested the boundaries of traditional Christian practice and belief, others sought to reinforce them. Developments such as theological liberalism, holiness, Pentecostalism, Mormonism, fundamentalism, and major growth in the largest Christian body, Roman Catholicism, are considered in chapter fifteen, together with the strong conservative evangelical defence of orthodox doctrine which arose from Princeton.

The final chapter assesses the closing decades of the era. As imperial powers carved up the remaining parts of the globe, doing huge damage to established tribal patterns of existence, the World Missions Conference in Edinburgh reflected hope for the evangelisation of the world in its generation. Yet, Christianity was forced to develop a coherent response to other world religions, and the first World Parliament of Religions was held in the 1890s. Racism remained a deeply pervasive issue, and the seeds of widespread anti-Semitism were sown with horrifying consequences in the middle of the twentieth century. Meanwhile storm clouds were gathering over Europe, which were to erupt into two horrific world wars at the cost of millions of lives.

This book is written for all those with an interest in the history of Christianity, whether students, church leaders, or general readers. Rather than attempting encyclopaedic comprehensiveness, *Churches, Revolutions and Empires* concentrates on significant individuals, themes, and events in major chapters, in an attempt to convey a representative impression of significant developments, and also to open up debate and discussion about key issues. Short quotations from a number of primary sources are included to assist with this, and to help draw the reader into the thinking of the participants in the events under discussion. Although as a Christian historian the writer believes that debates about the nature of God's working in the historical development of Christianity are important, in order to facilitate the use of the book in as wide a range of religious and non-religious contexts as possible, these issues are not discussed directly in the text. Instead, the book presents the raw materials that enable general readers and students to open these debates up. The author also believes that the different forms in which Christianity has been expressed have been significantly influenced by historical events, and to understand the issues churches face in the contemporary world, a clear understanding of their past is needed. This is necessary for both religious and secular historians. The material covered in the following chapters allows scope for further debates about the degree to which different Christian expressions were shaped by wider social and intellectual trends.

The book is also written with the conviction that the complex of individual and institutional beliefs and activities which are found in Christianity have also been significantly shaped by the context in which they have developed. Often this has taken place unintentionally, without conscious recognition that this was the case, and sometimes despite attempted resistance to such trends. At times this process has created significant movements away from orthodox understandings of Christianity, and the factors behind this need to be carefully assessed. For this reason many chapters include some discussion of wider social, economic, and political matters, which might otherwise be reserved to the works of social historians, in an attempt to place developments in Christianity within the totality of events. *Churches, Revolutions and Empires* recognises that the history of Christianity includes the history of individual religious belief and experience, rather than just of churches and institutions, and that this belief and practice was still interwoven with most aspects of life in the late eighteenth century, and continued to be so during the nineteenth century, even if its significance was declining in Europe. The approach taken in the book also allows trajectories within Christianity to be assessed within their global context, a matter of considerable significance as it began to be a truly global religion in the twentieth century.

In writing this book I have incurred many debts. First of all, thanks are due to the International Christian College, Glasgow, for the periods of study time they permitted in the twelve years I taught there. I am also thankful for the constantly insightful and challenging questions and discussion points raised by my students over the years as I have lectured in a range of countries and academic contexts. My gratitude also goes to my current employers, Langham Partnership, for their encouragement to continue to write and teach in the midst of my work with doctoral scholars from the Developing World. Appreciation is especially due to many academic colleagues who have encouraged me on in this all-too-lengthy task, and who have spared portions of their precious time to read and comment on chapters. Special mention should be made of Mark Elliott, John Jeacocke, Brian Stanley, David Bebbington, Ian Randall, Jay Brown, and Ken Stewart for their generous efforts. Thanks are also due to my family, who have shown willing forbearance whilst 'the book' has been completed.

1

THE LEGACY OF THE REVOLUTIONARIES:
THE AMERICAN WAR OF INDEPENDENCE
AND ITS CONSEQUENCES

When on October 19, 1781 Lord Cornwallis surrendered with his troops to the Americans at Yorktown, Virginia, the British army band played '*The World Turned Upside Down*'. The choice was entirely appropriate, for this was the first of two cataclysmic events that were to hit North America and Europe in the late eighteenth century. The second storm broke in 1789 in France, ironically an ally of the Americans in their struggle against their colonial masters. Yet the two revolutions came to nations at very different points in their histories—the French revolution came to a nation in its Autumn years; in America to one in its Spring. In the decades following these momentous events, the pattern of religious life was to take very different courses in the two nations.

ORIGINS OF THE WAR OF INDEPENDENCE
As the American colonies during the eighteenth century developed identities that were local and separate from that of Britain, the seeds of the American War of Independence were sown. The rule of the British, although more loosely organised and allowing more indigenous social structures than in French, Spanish or Portuguese colonies, was increasingly seen as oppressive in the years after British-American victory in the French-Indian War (1754–63). The American colonists' confidence in their own military ability grew, as did resentment at British attempts to raise taxes to pay off the war debt. The cry of 'no taxation without representation' was justified, even though taxes were lower in America than in England.

Christianity in North America was transplanted from Europe, but into different soil and into different circumstances. The form which took root and flourished in the United States was very different to that in Latin America where the Roman Catholicism of the colonists became the dominant religious form. Although the different waves of immigrants to North America brought the multiplicity of European Christian expressions, the religious radicalism and separatism that had led them to seek a better life and religious freedom away from the restrictions of the Old World brought an openness to new practice and new ideas. The rich Puritan heritage of the New England colonies was rooted in the piety of the early British and European Protestant settlers, and included a deep-set fear of return to the religious oppression from which the founding fathers had escaped. New England Puritanism had been renewed through the Great Awakening earlier in the eighteenth century. With roots in the Reformation, Puritanism and European pietism, the evangelicalism which lay at the heart of the Awakening, brought an emphasis on personal conversion as the root of Christian experience, the Bible as the source of authoritative teaching, and the atoning death of Christ on the cross as the means by which salvation was accomplished. Evangelicals believed that faith in Christ was the gift of God, but that it was also to be lived out actively in obedient, faithful service. This was evidence of the personal, inward, heartfelt religion which was the characteristic of evangelicalism. It was a form of religious expression more suited to the expanding, market oriented societies of the eighteenth century, and was to have a profound influence on post-Independence America.

The Great Awakening also contributed to the growing cultural and religious cohesion of the American colonies. When the itinerant British Anglican minister, George Whitefield, preached to crowds of whomsoever would listen, heedless of denominational identities, he broke down boundaries. So too did his message of the new birth, spiritual liberty, for those who repented and believed. The Awakening was a distinctively national event, making Americans aware of their common identity. Those who experienced spiritual liberty from the oppression of sin and Satan, also began in time to think about liberty from other forms of oppression (especially during the French and Indian War of the 1750s). The existence of any direct link between the theological developments of the revival era of Jonathan Edwards, and the later revolution, has been extensively debated by a wide range of historians.[1] Whatever the nature of

---

1   e.g. Alan Heimert, *Religion and the American Mind from the Great Awakening to the Revolution*, Cambridge, Mass,., Harvard UP, 1966; P. Miller, *The New England Mind: The Seventeenth Century*, New York, Macmillan, 1939; and *Jonathan Edwards*, New York, Sloan, 1949; M. Noll, *Christians in the American Revolution*, Washington D.C., Christian University Press, 1977; H. Stout, *The New England Soul: Preaching and Religious Culture in Colonial New England*, New York, Oxford UP, 1986; T. Kidd, *The Great Awakening: The Roots of Evangelical Christianity in Colonial America*, New Haven, Yale University Press, 2008.

the connection, the growing imperial crisis between Britain and a significant section of the colonists descended into open war in the 1770s.

THE CHURCHES AND THE WAR OF INDEPENDENCE

For a number of years it had seemed unlikely that the revolt of the thirteen American colonies against their British rulers would succeed. Against the British army were ranged groups of farmers, tradesmen and mechanics, skilled at shooting for their food, good at skirmishing and defending themselves against native American Indians, but not as experienced soldiers. George Washington spent the bitter winter of 1777–78 holed up in Forge Valley watching his makeshift army being decimated by illness, hunger, and the cold, until the French intervened in support of the patriots, and broke the British blockade of American ports. Of the 2.5 million white population of the colonies, one third supported the revolution (a further third were neutral, and a third were Loyalists), buoyed by confidence in the progressive course of history, believing that God was on their side, Britain was identified with tyranny, wickedness and selfishness. Conversely the British, including John Wesley, believed God was on theirs.

Many preachers interpreted the struggle for independence as a religious act. Others agonised over what stance to take over the war, and some were outrightly pacifist. Once it was over, most sought to demonstrate their solidarity with the new nation. Some were definite in seeing the hand of God at work in their struggles. To Ezra Stiles, President of Yale, the victory over

---

Ezra Stiles on The Religious Implications for the World of American Independence

Already does the new constellation of the United States begin to realize this glory. It has already risen to an acknowledged sovereignty among the republicks and kingdoms of the world. And we have reason to hope, and I believe to expect, that God has still greater blessings in store for this vine which his own right hand hath planted, to make us high among the nations in praise, and in name, and in honour.

Liberty, civil and religious, has sweet and attractive charms…It may have been of the Lord that Christianity is to be found in such great purity in this church exiled into the wilderness of America; and that its purest body should be evidently advancing forward, by an augmented natural increase and spiritual edification, into a singular superiority—with the ultimate subserviency to the glory of God, in converting the world. [1]

1   E. Stiles, *A Sermon Preached Before Governor Jonathan Trumbull and the Connecticut General Assembly…* (2nd edition, Worcester, Mass: Isaiah Thomas, 1785, 58–62; 95–98, quoted in K.J. Hardman, *Issues in American Christianity*, Baker, Grand Rapids, Michigan, 1993, 78–81.

---

the armies of George III was portentous of freedom and knowledge spreading across the world. To others the success of the republic was laden with millennial significance. Not all agreed, but certainly success in the War of Independence instilled democratic values in religious organisations, and deepened the conviction that God had a special purpose for America.

THE AMERICAN CONSTITUTION—1787

The victorious United States sought to establish stable government, and an environment in which economic growth could take place. The primary focus was upon defence, revenue raising, and promoting commerce: the need to pay off the war debt was urgent. It was quickly apparent that the initial articles of confederation were too loose as the states failed in their financial obligations to support Congress. When the members of the constitutional convention, which met for seventeen weeks through the long hot Philadelphia summer of 1787, drew up a Constitution for the new nation they produced a document which contains almost no mention of religion. The work of Congregational divines, Quakers, Anglican lawyers, freethinkers, landowners, planters and merchants, it was a compromise document, designed carefully to draw some powers away from the individual states, but leave them with control of highways, education, banking, taxation, divorce, alcohol laws, and civil and criminal codes. This meant that the states were left with considerable latitude to determine policy concerning the religious life of their inhabitants.

The role of the Christian faith in the debates remains uncertain, not helped by the decision not to publish accounts of the various contributions to the deliberations until long after they were over. A story circulated in the 1820s that at one crucial point in the debates of 1787 Benjamin Franklin, who had in the same year written to Ezra Stiles doubting the deity of Christ, urged the Assembly to apply to 'the Father of Lights to illuminate our understandings'—but the exact circumstances are unclear. Amongst the founding Fathers, the Scottish Presbyterian John Witherspoon (the only clergyman to sign the declaration of independence), held views that came close to being recognisably evangelical, but others displayed reticence over speaking publicly about their beliefs, or were Deists. The Declaration of Independence, the Articles of Confederation, and the Constitution of the United States were respectful of the deity, but were largely secular documents. References to religion are couched in negative terms: 'No religious test shall ever be required as a qualification to any office or public trust under the United States' (Article 6). The American historian Mark Noll has concluded that evangelicalism 'played at best a negligible role in the founding era of the 1770s and 1780s,' the time when the basic guidelines for religious-social interaction in the new nation were established.[2]

---

2   M. Noll, *American Evangelical Christianity: An Introduction*, Oxford, Basil Blackwell, 2000, 191.

Nonetheless, the influence on popular ideology of the earlier eighteenth century evangelical revivals had not been lost by the time of the revolution. What the founding Fathers laid down could be readily built upon. The section of the religiously minded among the population who adapted themselves best to the values of the new America, and in the early nineteenth century baptised the constitution as their own, were the evangelicals.

Between 1787 and 1788 the constitution was gradually ratified by the states— North Carolina did not accept until 1789, Rhode Island in 1790. The Founders agreed on the need to promote religious liberty, but that religious belief or practice should not be dictated. Behind this lay the growing denominational pluralism of America. Throughout much of the eighteenth century Congregationalism and Anglicanism had dominated the largely nominally Protestant America—in 1775 these denominations numbered 580,000 and 500,000 respectively, with Presbyterians totalling 410,000. By this time, these denominations were less dominant than they had been in 1700, although still one-third of all churches were Congregational or Anglican. Rapid population growth, in part fuelled by high levels of immigration from different parts of Europe, brought a diversity of population, language and Christian expression, such that one church community could not dominate a particular area. The implications of such changes took time to be worked through.

Established churches in some states continued until the nineteenth century, but they were a dying breed—Connecticut's Congregationalist establishment continued until 1818. That in Massachusetts lingered until 1833, although when it was abolished the state made the point of affirming that 'the public worship of God, and instructions in piety, religion, and morality, promote the happiness and prosperity of a people, and the security of republican government'.[3] Numbering only around 25,000 at the time of the Declaration of Independence, Roman Catholics found significant resistance to the granting of their full civil rights in the following years. Pennsylvania led the way in allowing freedom of religious worship to all theists, including Roman Catholics. Generally, the position of Roman Catholics in the United States was in significant contrast to that experienced across the border in Canada. In Quebec in 1774, where Roman Catholics were in the majority, the Roman Catholic hierarchy was granted many of the prerogatives of an established church by the British government. War in 1812 between Britain and America over Canada encouraged Canadian Protestants to draw closer to the British model of church life—Canadian Presbyterians looked to the Presbyterianism of Scotland; Canadian Anglicans looked for state-church comprehension; Canadian Methodists remained loyal and balanced in their evangelicalism. In Canada, the democratic, entrepreneurial,

---

3 Article 11, amending Article 3 of the 1780 Massachusetts Constitution, in ed. F.N. Thorpe, *The Federal and State Constitutions*, 7 volumes, Washington D.C, 1909, vol 3: 1914.

anti-traditionalism of American evangelicalism was rejected in favour of a 'quasi-establishmentarian evangelicalism'.[4]

THE RELIGIOUS VIEW AT THE TIME OF THE FOUNDING FATHERS

The birth certificate of the new nation, the 1776 Declaration of Independence, announced in ringing tones that: 'all men are created equal, that they are endowed by their Creator with certain unalienable rights, that among these are Life, Liberty and the pursuit of Happiness'. The full implications of the declaration seem to have eluded the Founding Fathers. For many decades those who were black, female, or Roman Catholic, would have genuine cause to doubt just how seriously such profound assertions were to be taken.

Exactly what some of the Declaration's authors, such as Thomas Jefferson and Benjamin Franklin, intended by using the word 'Creator' remains a topic of much debate. Both stressed virtue and morality as being essential for the well-being of society, and in the promotion of morality the role of the churches was seen as important, but Jefferson believed that common moral philosophy rooted in human reason rather than a God-centred life, could provide the foundation for public morality. George Washington, first President of the United States, similarly emphasised the duty of life and disinterested service, and preferred to speak of God using names derived from Nature rather than the Bible—such as Supreme Being, Grand Architect, Great Ruler of Events, and Great Creator.

The influence of Deism on the Founding Fathers and early political leaders of the nation cannot be ignored. Of these, Thomas Jefferson was the pre-eminent representative. To him religion was more about having a moral code than believing in divine revelation, and he argued that much of the Bible was unclear, in which case he preferred ignorance to error. Nonetheless, the teaching of Jesus remained important to him, although he couched it within the framework of Deism. He argued that true religion was the 'sublime doctrines of philosophy and deism, taught by Jesus Christ'. Without this, life would 'indeed be a hell'.[5]

That both those with heterodox views, and those who were orthodox in their theology, could positively embrace the new constitutional arrangements was in part due to their common debt to Scottish Common Sense Philosophy. Thinkers such as Francis Hutcheson (1694–1746) and Thomas Reid (1710–1796) argued that Enlightenment thinking was compatible with the broad outline of received Christianity, by means of appeal to 'universal' (common) 'experience' (sense). Humans everywhere presupposed basic realities, such as the connection

---

4 M. Noll, *The Rise of Evangelicalism: The Age of Edwards, Whitefield, and the Wesleys*, Apollos, Leicester, 2004, 189–201.

5 Thomas Jefferson letter to John Adams, 14 September, 1813, quoted in E. Gaustad, *A Documentary History of Religion in America to the Civil War*, 2nd Edn, Eerdmans, Grand Rapids, 1993, 297.

between causes and effects. Behind Creation lay a First Cause—a Creator; most humans presupposed the existence of a God who would one day judge good and evil; most accepted that a Perfect Morality lay behind moral judgements. There was a natural sympathy in people that united them to others, a natural sense of right and wrong in all, regardless of education or social position. Such 'Common Sense' thinking shaped the basis upon which the new nation was constructed: they were vital concepts for a democratizing society in which ordinary people were now ranked equal with their 'betters'. The nation's social order was to be based on observable facts concerning human conduct. It was also widely believed that throwing off the truths of Christianity and their attendant moral structure, would result in a collapse of morality.

Scottish Common Sense Philosophy deeply influenced the colleges of the late eighteenth century. It also had a part in reshaping the evangelical Puritanism of the Jonathan Edwards tradition, placing increasing store on the use of logically compelling arguments to draw human minds to faith, rather than a reliance on prevenient grace,[6] and asserting the importance of scientific reasoning in demonstrating the truth of revelation. Those who stood in the Edwardsean tradition, Samuel Hopkins (1721–1803), Jonathan Edwards junior (1745–1801), and Timothy Dwight (1752–1817)—grandson of Jonathan Edwards—came to articulate an evangelicalism which was in part shaped by the wider context of the early republic. Edwards (junior) sought somewhat inflexibly to maintain his father's principles. Hopkins', *System of Doctrine Contained in Divine Revelation* (1793), the most comprehensive work of theology from an American evangelical since Edwards, became a key text for many Congregationalists espousing the 'New Divinity'. It was Calvinism, but adjusted to the rationalism of the American enlightenment. In an America which had rejected the 'tyranny' of Britain, a softer view of the sovereignty of God seemed more appropriate, together with an emphasis on the need for a voluntary response to the gospel. Joseph Bellamy sought to avoid any conception of God as a 'tyrant', by teaching a governmental view of the atonement, rather than the traditional penal substitutionary view. Although there were revivals among the student body at Yale after Hopkins became president in 1795, and other New England churches were reporting further episodes of revival, and becoming interested in mission, on the whole New England Congregationalism could not shake itself free of theological dispute, which limited its effectiveness.

Presbyterians moved in varying directions. Whilst some journeyed towards Enlightenment latitudinarianism, others consolidated their evangelical emphases, and engaged in urgent efforts to extend Presbyterianism further westwards. It was only after 1800 that American Presbyterianism was clearly

---

6   The idea that God's grace is at work before an individual's religious conversion, preparing the way for a later reception of the Christian message.

set on a path within evangelicalism that would encompass historic Calvinism, and voluntarism.

Although the open doubt of David Hume or Voltaire found less acceptance in America, the radical thought of Thomas Paine (1737–1809) was influential. An Englishman from Norfolk, Paine sailed to America in 1774, and encouraged the cause of independence. When he left America for Europe in 1787, he remained a correspondent of Thomas Jefferson and George Washington, and in his latter years he returned to the United States. His works, particularly *The Rights of Man* (1787), and *The Age of Reason* (1794), were sold in cheap popular editions, encouraged by a post-revolutionary French government determined to export its underlying philosophy to the New World. In the *Age of Reason* Paine asserted that he believed in God, but not in the church, 'My own mind is my own church'. He dismissed the Bible as being more than half filled with 'obscene stories', and that it would be more consistent to call it, 'The word of a demon than the word of God. It is a history of wickedness that has served to corrupt and brutalise mankind; and for my part I detest it'.[7]

In the social flux at the end of the War of Independence the addition of these ideas produced a potentially volatile combination. There was evidence of people ceasing to honour their debts, and increasingly disregarding the Sabbath. Anti-clerical sentiment grew, and church attendance was believed to be falling. In the 1780s the new nation was nearly bankrupt; some believed that this was not just the case financially, but also morally. Pastors who had likened victory in the war of independence to Moses leading the people out from oppression in Egypt, now extended the image: there were those 'who despised the promised land, and desired to return to Egypt'. In his election sermon of 1785, William Symmes of Andover, Massachusetts, called for a constitution which would act by 'curbing the lusts, and bounding the riotous appetites of men'.[8] There was a deep fear that the republican dream would vanish in the cold light of morning.

The period of the revolutionary war appeared to have only served to promote a civil religion of independence that sustained the patriot cause, but did little to promote the personal Christian life. The victory of the colonists did little for the colonial Anglicans, who suffered much loss of property, and although re-organised in 1785 as the Protestant Episcopal Church of the United States of America, took many years to regain momentum. However, meltdown was avoided, and before long prayers for the king were replaced by prayers for the president.[9]

---

7   T. Paine, *The Age of Reason*, 1794, quoted in K. Hardman, *Issues in American Christianity*, Grand Rapids, Baker, 1993, 97.

8   Quoted in N. Hatch, *The Sacred Cause of Liberty: Republican Thought and the Millennium in Revolutionary New England*, New Haven, Yale, 1977, 113.

9   Noll, *Rise of Evangelicalism*, 198–99.

WIDER THEOLOGICAL TRENDS

The new theological approaches of some led them to a supreme stress on divine goodness, human rationality, and the power of culture. In New England, Charles Chauncy, one-time opponent of Jonathan Edwards, became the first to declare himself Unitarian. Some Massachusetts congregational churches drifted in the same direction. The trend towards liberal and Unitarian thought was particularly strong at Harvard, where Henry Ware, Professor of Divinity, held liberal theological views. One of the ablest proponents of Unitarian theology was William Ellery Channing (1780–1842). In his famous sermon, *Unitarian Christianity,* delivered in Baltimore, Channing set out his view that the Bible was to be interpreted according to reason: the Trinity was declared an 'irrational, unscriptural doctrine'. He rejected the teaching that Jesus Christ was 'the one God'; rather, he was distinct from, and inferior to God. The work of Jesus Christ was to bring moral and spiritual deliverance through his teaching, to bring pardon to the penitent, and shed light on the path of duty.[10] The issue of Unitarianism was to open up fissures especially within Congregationalism in the years after 1820.

The fight against Unitarianism was led by the grandson of Jonathan Edwards, Timothy Dwight. Through his powerful and energetic presidency of Yale, he inspired a renewed emphasis on high standards of scholarship and morality in the college, and saw revival of religion amongst the students after 1802, with many inspired to enter the Christian ministry. The torch he laid down in 1817 was taken up by others such as Lyman Beecher, Nathaniel Taylor, and Asahel Nettleton.

The colourful assortment of new religious groups which flourished in the new American context of liberty and resistance to authority, were typically anti-Calvinist, millenarian, perfectionist, and often rural. They included the Shakers, who arrived in New York State from Britain in 1774, led by Mother Ann Lee (1736–1784). She had suffered greatly in childbirth, and all four of her children had died young. This helped shape her religious views which included the importance of community living, allowing a wide range of economic roles for women, and religious perfection and sexual celibacy. The Universalists, who were led by John Murray, came to New England in 1770, and rejected notions of eternal punishment, believing in the eventual salvation of all.

THE FIRST AMENDMENT—1791

The written Constitution of the United States has proved remarkably robust, and has proved in need of amendment only on rare occasions. One such came in 1791, just four years after the writing of the constitution, when ten amendments came into force as the Bill of Rights. The first amendment, concerning the

10   E. Channing, *The Works of William E. Channing*, 6th edition, Boston, Munroe & Co., 1846, 69–78.

religious life of the nation, declared that 'Congress shall make no law respecting an establishment of religion, or prohibiting the free exercise thereof'; it also set out the right of free speech, and of free peaceable assembly. The second amendment enshrined the right of the people to keep and bear arms, but that, as they say, is another story. The first amendment mentioned neither church nor state, but between them Thomas Jefferson believed a 'wall of separation' had been erected: at national level there was to be no formal connection between religion and society. He was convinced that the privileged status of established churches led to corruption of both the church and of the state, and that when free of it churches would follow a pattern of rationality and restraint. The policy of religious toleration emerging in Europe was not enough; religious liberty was required. It was George Washington's opinion that individuals were accountable to God alone for their religious opinions, and freedom of worship according to religious conscience should be protected. Furthermore, any person should be able to sit in national councils without inquisition into their faith or mode of worship.

The Founding Fathers recognised that common moral precepts for the nation were required, to prevent social collapse, as Thomas Jefferson wrote: 'The practice of morality being necessary for the well-being of society, he [the Creator] has taken care to impress its precepts so indelibly on our hearts that they shall not be effaced by the subtleties of our brain.'[11] Yet they also recognised that religion was a potentially explosive matter, and that to favour one denomination above another could trigger violent protests.

There has been much disagreement over what the First Amendment actually meant, or still means, but at its root lay the creation of a broadly Christian republic, without the creation of a legally established church. Religious policy was left to the individual states, allowing Congress to concentrate on government for the nation. The results, in practice, were ambiguous to say the least. In 1791, five out of the then fourteen states made provision for ministers to receive tax support, and twelve states still placed religious tests on those intending to hold public office. Restrictions on non-Protestants and non-Christians therefore remained. Legislation to assist Sabbath observance, restrict atheism, and protect public morals, was passed. The amendment also did not stop Congress or President from calling for National Days of Prayer, or provide funding for military chaplains.

POST WAR RELIGIOUS LIFE—DECLINE AND GROWTH

The War of Independence claimed lives, scattered population, and disrupted established patterns of piety. It is not surprising that religious life in the new

---

11   Thomas Jefferson Letter to Thomas Fishback, 27 September 1809, quoted in M. Noll, *Christianity in America: A Handbook*, Eerdmans, Grand Rapids, 1983, 137.

The First Amendment
First Amendment of the United States Constitution: *'Congress shall make no law respecting an establishment of religion, or prohibiting the free exercise thereof; or abridging the freedom of speech, or of the press; or of the right of people peaceably to assemble, and to petition the Government for redress of grievances'.*

George Washington on Religious Liberty
'If I could have entertained the slightest apprehension, that the constitution framed in the convention, where I had the honour to preside, might possibly endanger the religious rights of any ecclesiastical society, certainly I would never have placed my signature to it... I have often expressed my sentiments that every man, conducting himself as a good citizen, and being accountable to God alone for his religious opinions, ought to be protected in worshipping the Deity according to the dictates of his own conscience.'[1]

1 G. Washington, Reply to an Address Sent by the General Committee of the United Baptist Churches In Virginia, May 1789, quoted in N. Cousins, *'In God We Trust': The Religious Beliefs and Ideas of the American Founding Fathers*, New York, Harper Brothers, 1958, 58-59.

United States was thought to have reached a low ebb between the 1770s and 1800. Although the figures do not truly represent all who attended church, church membership was reckoned to be less than 10% of the population. The General Assembly of the Presbyterian Church in 1798 lamented 'a general dereliction of religious principles and practice', and 'a visible and prevailing impiety and contempt for the laws and institutions of society'. Apart from the dislocations occasioned by war, the problem was also in part due to structural change within the churches themselves between 1750 and 1800. Territorial Protestantism dominated by establishmentarian Congregationalism, Episcopalianism, and Presbyterianism, began to give way to a more dynamic structure, led by Methodists, Baptists, and voluntary religious organisations.

Post-war America was more socially open, committed to republicanism, and freedom of opportunity. It was a rapidly expanding society, with few structures of institutional control, few distinctions of class, and with the physical and social space to dynamically adapt and develop. Republicanism, viewed with suspicion by many European Christians, and often associated with theological heterodoxy, was embraced positively by American evangelicals late in the eighteenth century. The controlling influence of establishment or social culture, so significant in Europe, was no restraining force in North America.

Although connections with the 'Old World' remained, the 'New World' was to be separate and free, its religious expression more heterogeneous. Most of the national European expressions of Christianity found themselves replicated within one nation, but the years after 1781 gave an opportunity to explore and develop a religious practice that was truly 'American.' And America was a rapidly changing nation, with a population which reached 4 million in 1790, and 13 million in 1830. In such times of transition, churches with dynamic structures able to appeal in 'go-getter' style to the masses, were more likely to succeed. What evolved tended to be voluntary and evangelical.

Settled order and form gave way to the dynamism of individual leadership, and more democratic structures. The new vocabulary of voluntary and democratic thought, was readily adopted and utilised by evangelical religion. Whilst strongly individualistic (with a stress on personal conversion), at the same time there was also a strong sense of community (expressed in church membership, or membership of voluntary societies). The evangelicals appeared to have become heirs of the new society, with rapid growth amongst the Methodists, Baptists, and new denominations such as the Disciples and the Churches of Christ. Their religion was small town or rural, emotional, conversionist, and apocalyptic. It was less a matter of inherited right, and more an issue dictated by market forces. Leaders were possessed of personal charisma, confident of their ability to interpret and preach the Bible without resort to lengthy periods of scholarly education. Jefferson's hopes that the first amendment would create religion characterised by rationality and restraint were far from fulfilled.

Recent studies of these radical religious groups in the post-revolutionary period have challenged the traditional picture of an overall post-war decline in religion. Although in traditional denominations the trend may have been a negative one, in the new groups congregations were rapidly increasing. This suggests a greater degree of continuity between the first and second Great Awakenings.[12] However, the evangelicalism that came to the fore was by no means united, but was divided by class, region, denomination, and attitudes to slavery.

This fundamental shift in the denominational structure of America was marked. In 1776, 55% of American churchgoers were Congregational, Episcopalian, or Presbyterian; by 1850 the figure was just 19%, with Methodists and Baptists at 55%. It was Methodism that did most to harvest the seed sown by the Great Awakening. In 1771, Francis Asbury (1745–1816) responded to John Wesley's call for volunteers to work in America.[13] Although Wesley had opposed the revolution, a stand so unpopular amongst patriots that most Methodist leaders had to return to England, when the war was over Asbury commenced a ministry parallel to that of Methodism's founder. He travelled over 270,000

---

12   See S.A. Marini, *Radical Sects in Revolutionary New England*, Cambridge, Mass., 1982; and R. Finke and R. Stark, *The Churching of America, 1776–1990*, New Brunswick, New Jersey, 1992.

13   The nature of Methodism as a transatlantic, and then trans-national, force is explored in D. Hempton, *Methodism: Empire of the Spirit*, London, Yale University Press, 2005.

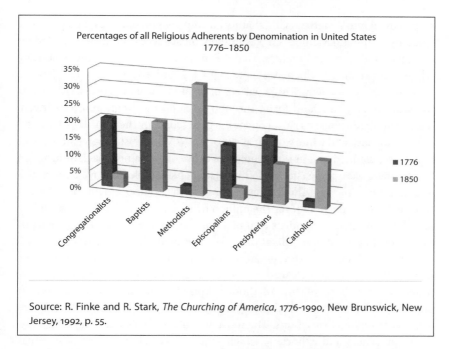

Percentages of all Religious Adherents by Denomination in United States 1776–1850

Source: R. Finke and R. Stark, *The Churching of America*, 1776-1990, New Brunswick, New Jersey, 1992, p. 55.

miles across the colonies, and into the new states of Tennessee and Kentucky, preaching 16,500 sermons and ordaining 4,000 preachers. Wesley had made all the world his parish, and Asbury urged, 'Go into every kitchen and shop; address all, aged and young, on the salvation of their souls'. He ensured Methodism was to be the leading religious force in America for the next century. As with Wesley, Asbury was a fine organiser, and alongside him laboured dedicated preachers, such as Freeborn Garretson (1752–1827), a hugely effective itinerant preacher in the southern states, and in the Canadian Maritimes and New York State.

A boost to Methodism came in 1784 when Wesley ordained clergy for North America. At a meeting in Baltimore in that year a formal structure for Methodism in America was drawn up, mixing the control of preachers and discipline through Asbury, with democratic and egalitarian forms in the class meetings, local churches, and lay preachers. Inherent was a series of creative tensions. The movement was capable of dynamic expansion, and local self-direction, yet was governed closely by a strong authoritarian structure. Liberty of expression and spiritual freedom was exercised through the ordered structure of class meetings. The result was, as with British Methodism, the potential for schism. The Republican Methodists of 1792 were a product of James O'Kelly's demands for more democracy in the naming of preachers for circuits, and a reaction against the authoritarian style of leadership. The majority of Methodists, however, remained loyal to Asbury.

Methodist structures proved well suited to the post-Independence era, and helped instil into American Christianity an emphasis on openness and personal sincerity. Although Methodism was initially most successful in areas settled by Anglicans and European Pietists, Methodism was also shaped by the American religious context, to which it adapted quickly and effectively, and where it took on a life of its own, with a variety of local forms and expressions—from the steadier New England form, through to camp meetings, and its African-American dimensions. Its social openness gave scope for the ministry of a small number of black and white women as exhorters to Methodist congregations, and one source claimed that in 1810 there were at least 13 ordained black ministers.[14] In 1784 there were some 15,000 Methodists, a considerable improvement on the less than 1,000 of 1771. This was as nothing to the 200,000 Methodists by the time of Asbury's death in 1816. The million mark was passed before 1850, and by 1855 the 1.5 million Methodists (out of a population of 23 million) were part of the largest Protestant denomination—over 30% of all church members.

Methodist preachers were urged to seek out the poor and dispossessed, of which slaves were the clearest example. In 1786, there were 1,890 African-American members of the Methodist Episcopal Church, and 20,000 in 1800, a rise from 10% of total membership to over 30%, although there were significant regional variations. The most able black slaves were encouraged to act as preachers and exhorters, which was a powerful statement of spiritual equality, as well as being the best way of successfully reaching other slaves, Methodist religious practice, with extemporary spiritual preaching and prayer meetings, hymn-singing, and the love-feast, seemed well-adapted to African-American culture.

Home and abroad, Methodism was also significantly a movement of women, especially with the domestic locus of many of its gatherings. Women could play significant roles in class meetings, although they rarely exercised a public ministry beyond that realm. It was not the practise of Francis Asbury and his successors to recognise calls, extraordinary or otherwise, to women to preach, and most denominations followed this policy in the early nineteenth century.[15]

Through its circuit system, and practice of itinerancy, the Methodist system was flexible, and fast-moving, following early settlers, and incorporating new areas into circuits, stations, and classes. Not all endeavours were successful, and sometimes expansion was too rapid, but there was a ready supply of income and personnel to meet new challenges.[16] Only in the later years of the nineteenth

---

14   N. Hatch, 'The Whirlwind of Religious Liberty in Early America', in ed. R. Helmstadter, *Freedom and Religion in the Nineteenth Century*, Stanford, Stanford University Press, 1997, 49.

15   M. Westerkamp, *Women and Religion in Early America, 1600–1850*, London, Routledge, 1999, 109–118.

16   Hempton, *Methodism: Empire of the Spirit*, 159; 152–154.

The Circuit Rider

century was this dynamism and spontaneity to slow, as ministers became more upwardly mobile, and urban congregations demanded a 'settled' ministry.

The Baptists, emphasising individual profession of faith, with its public sign—baptism by immersion—similarly fitted well with the dynamics of post-revolutionary society. In rural areas 'farmer-preachers' combined agricultural work during the week with the role of pastor-preacher at the weekend. The 460 Baptist churches of 1780 had become 12,000 by 1860, with over 1 million members. Free of the restrictions that had constrained them in the Old World, Baptists in regions in the mid and southern regions were able after the 1760s to organise freely, and they expanded rapidly. By 1790 half of all American Baptists lived in the southern states. In the 1780s they were founding fifty new churches every year.

Other new 'American' denominations also flourished. Their Restorationist vision of a return of Christianity to the purity of the New Testament era, produced an anti-traditional, lay oriented, self-starting religion that appealed to many disillusioned with the traditional churches. With baptism by immersion for adults, and autonomy for local congregations, they offered an indigenous expression of Christianity for the new era. By 1860 there were 2,100 Disciples

Churches, compared with 2,150 Episcopalian and 2,240 Congregationalist churches. An ongoing feature of American Christianity was to be its dynamism and huge diversity.

AFRICAN-AMERICAN CHRISTIANS

Another significant element of cultural and religious diversity in the new United States was the presence of some 500,000 African-Americans. The fact that most of them were enslaved to white owners was to tax political and religious thinkers for the next century, once an attempt in the 1787 constitutional convention to commit the new Republic to the abolition of slavery had been quashed by southern opposition. In the late seventeenth century, and early eighteenth century, the first efforts were made to bring Christian instruction to slaves by the colonial government and the churches, but this was often in the face of hostility from slave owners who argued that the provision of religious instruction made slaves neglectful, or rebellious, and that slaves only expressed interest in Christianity in order to gain their freedom.

The Great Awakening of the 1730s and 1740s saw a number of conversions amongst slaves, and later in the century slaves were notable for their responses to Methodist and Presbyterian evangelistic preaching, and then that of the Baptists. In the North, African-Americans generally worshipped with white Christians, and subscribed to the same religious beliefs and forms. However, this did not necessarily mean equality within the churches—segregated seating was to be found, and restrictions upon participation in worship. This encouraged free African-Americans to establish their own churches.

The first 'continuing' black church, in Aiken County, Southern Carolina, was established through the work of David George (1742–1810) in 1773–74. George's connection with this work was brief, for in 1776 he fled Savannah with the British and settled in Nova Scotia where he established further black churches. The move was to prove of lasting significance in terms of world mission, for in 1793 a small number of free black Nova Scotian converts returned to the new colony of Sierra Leone in West Africa, established as a free land for freed slaves. They were to play a significant role in the evangelisation of that area of West Africa, where their original cultural roots lay.

A number within the evangelical tradition spoke out against the practice of slavery. Samuel Hopkins (1721–1803) of Newport Rhode Island, where merchants made a fortune from the slave trade, courageously added his voice to those of the Quakers. They expressed their horror that black slaves were treated as if they were 'quite another species of animals, made only to serve us and our children'. Such attitudes violated the benevolent values of loving 'our neighbours as ourselves', and were believed to be utterly inconsistent in the face of a war fought in the name of winning civil liberties. Slavery was a crime, provoking in God's sight. In 1776 the leading American Methodist John Fletcher combined loyalist and anti-slavery rhetoric, deploring the 'hypocritical friends of liberty, who buy, and sell, and whip their fellow men as if they were brutes' whilst complaining they were 'enslaved' by the British parliament.[17]

In the South, resistance to such thought was deep-set. In 1784, the newly constituted Methodist Episcopal Church added to its fierce anti-slavery preaching, rules that would rid its societies of slave-holders, but this brought such strong objections from the white laity in the south, that the leadership were forced to back down. Slavery was an entrenched part of regular family order in a hierarchical social structure. Between 1800 and 1820, amongst both Baptists and Methodists, racial politics progressively undermined the stress on spiritual and personal equality that lay at the heart of evangelicalism, and the white leadership came to predominate in both mixed race, and black majority churches.

On the whole, black Christians found more sympathy from the British 'oppressors' than in the new land of 'liberty', as Andrew Bryan (1737–1812), founder of the Ethiopian Church of Jesus Christ in Savannah (later the First African Baptist Church), was to find. In 1790, he and fifty members of his congregation were imprisoned for refusing to heed the guidelines of the slave system. When they were eventually able to purchase their freedom, they established a church outside Savannah, which had a congregation of 700 by 1800.

Despite the fact that by 1800 around one in three American Methodists was black, the religious discrimination they faced could be severe and humiliating. In St George's Methodist Episcopal Church, Philadelphia, as the number of African American worshippers increased, they faced growing hostility from white members of the congregation, who required them to sit in separated areas of the church. In November 1787 a number of black worshippers found themselves pulled from their knees because they were praying in the wrong part of the crowded church. Incidents like these spurred the formation of separate churches for African Americans, such as the African Methodist Episcopal Church, the African Methodist Episcopal Zion Church, and independent African-American Baptist churches, which served as centres for free African communities, and proved the first decisive steps towards freedom by African Americans. They were the fruits not of doctrinal division, or disputes over church organisation, but of a quiet rebellion against the bitterness of racial discrimination and the failure of Christian expressions of faith to match up to professed teachings. To African Americans, white churches appeared to be instrumental in upholding the social and political policies behind slavery.

The African Methodist Episcopal Church grew out of the demeaning incident in Philadelphia in 1787. One of those pulled from his knees was Richard (1760–1831) a slave who had been converted through the itinerant

17   J. Fletcher, *The Bible and the Sword*, 1776, quoted in E. Sandoz (ed.), *Political Sermons of the American Founding Era, 1730–1805*, Indianapolis, Liberty Press, 1991, 567.

Richard Allen

Discrimination Against Black Christians

'A number of us usually attended St George's church in Fourth street; and when the coloured people got numerous in attending the church, they moved us from the seats we usually sat on, and placed us around the wall, and on Sabbath morning we went to church and the sexton stood at the door, and told us to go to the gallery. He told us to go, and we would see where to sit. We expected to take the seats over the ones we had occupied below, not knowing any better. We took those seats. Meeting had begun, and they were nearly done singing, and just as we got to the seats the elder said, "Let us pray". We had not been long upon our knees before I heard a considerable scuffling and low talking. I raised my head up and saw one of the trustees, H__ M___, having hold of Rev. Absalom Jones, pulling him up off his knees, and saying, "You must get up – you must not kneel here". Mr Jones replied, "Wait until prayer is over"... we all went out of the church in a body, and they were no more plagued with us in the church... my dear Lord was with us, and we were filled with fresh vigor to get a house erected to worship God in...'[1]

1   R, Allen, *The Life Experience and Gospel Labours of the Rt. Rev. Richard Allen,* Nashville, Abingdon, 1960, pp. 24-35, quoted in Hardman, *American Christianity*, p. 70.

---

preaching of Methodists, as were many others. Despite his status, he began to preach, and around 1780 his master was challenged over holding slaves by the Methodist preaching of Freeborn Garrettson. Allen and his family were allowed to purchase their freedom, and he engaged in itinerant preaching to both black and white audiences before settling in Philadelphia, where he ministered to the black members of St George's Methodist Episcopal Church. He saw such success that he was often required to preach five times a day. Despite this, the hostility from whites remained, and after the incident in St George's, Allen and other blacks withdrew to form churches which attempted to combine loyalty to Methodism with African-American self-government. The attempt was not successful, and by 1816 the movement had become an independent entity, the African Methodist Episcopal denomination. Within two years it had grown to number 7,000 members, and 20,000 by 1860.[18] The church was African in name and membership, and helped to promote strength and unity amongst African-Americans in the face of racial discrimination. It was also part of a search, shared by other dissident groups, for an authentic, scriptural, form of Christianity; it was a search that meant tradition needed to be challenged.

---

18   Allen's account of these events is in R. Allen, *The Life Experience and Gospel Labours of the Rt. Rev. Richard Allen*, 2nd edn, Nashville, 1960; see also C.V.R. George, *Segregated Sabbaths: Richard Allen and the Emergence of Independent Black Churches, 1760–1840*, New York, 1973.

There is evidence that the first African-American Baptist congregation was in existence in Virginia as early as 1758; another was formed in South Carolina in 1777. By 1800, there were some 25,000 African American Baptists. The African Baptist Missionary Society of Richmond was organised by two black ministers, and in 1821 one of them, Lott Carey, became the first black Baptist missionary to Africa, travelling to Liberia under the auspices of the American Colonization Society, a society which sought to facilitate sending free black Americans back to Africa. Much black Baptist missionary endeavour was limited to Liberia and the West Coast of Africa in the nineteenth century. There were more African-American preachers amongst the Baptists than the Methodists and Presbyterians—black ministers were known to have pastored white Baptist churches in Virginia in the late eighteenth century. However, there remained only small numbers, in good part due to the desire to maintain an educated clergy, and there were few well-educated African-Americans.

In the South the concentration of African Americans was far larger than in the North, and most were enslaved. Whites in the South were suspicious of black-led churches for their encouragement of the anti-slavery cause, although they were mostly congregations of free blacks. Slaves were usually required to attend either white churches, where they often outnumbered the white congregation, or black churches pastored by white clergy. African-Americans who were permitted to preach in white churches in the South were not allowed to administer the sacraments of baptism or the Lord's Supper.

Part of the mechanism slaves adopted for survival and seeking to make meaning for life in oppressive circumstances was the maintenance of elements of African culture and customs. Although they originated from very different African countries and societies, they drew from their traditions elements that were blended with aspects of European culture, to produce new cultural and belief systems that helped them be reconciled with their new situation. Traditional ideas of kinship, naming offspring, diet, and language, were adapted to their new environment. It seems to have been the urgent, experiential, evangelical preaching of the Second Great Awakening of the later eighteenth century that proved decisive in drawing large numbers of African Americans to Christianity—by 1800 there were up to 15,000 black Methodists, and some 20,000 black Baptists in the South. Christian teaching, particularly of the evangelical variety was powerfully attractive to slaves. The message of awakening to personal sinfulness, conversion and spiritual rebirth, assurance of forgiveness and acceptance before God through the work of Christ, spiritual liberation and the promise of eternal life, brought to the dispossessed a sense of dignity and self-worth that transcended social status—in short they were important to God. The egalitarian implications of such evangelical doctrine were not lost on African Americans, even if they were not always realised. Nor were its revolutionary social aspects lost: any system built upon brutality and degradation could not have the favour of God. The deliverance of the people of Israel from slavery in Egypt was a powerful motif. If liberation did not come in this life, it would come in eternity. The community ethos of evangelical Christianity was also an important attraction: congregations, class meetings, prayer meetings, social support mechanisms, all proved strongly attractive to slaves.[19] African-American Christianity merged with African cultures forced together by the oppression of slavery to produce a spontaneous, and often exuberant, expression of Christianity. In the words of Eugene Genovese, 'The slaves shaped the Christianity they had embraced; they conquered the religion of those who had conquered them'.[20]

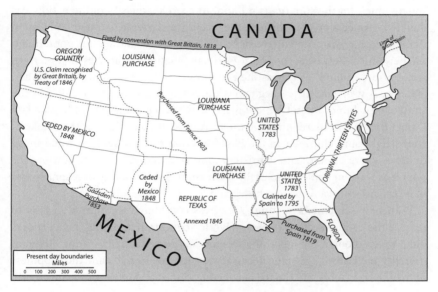

The Formation of the United States in the Nineteenth Century

Opposition to slavery in America depended on the work of voluntary societies to petition Congress. Such societies demanded, but also unleashed, tremendous energy. In the 1790s evangelical voices were raised against slavery amongst the Methodists, and the Congregationalists. Yet the rapid expansion of the gospel in the South, with slave-owners as well as slaves professing conversion, led evangelists to be more constrained in their complaints against slavery. Slavery remained as an entrenched, and often unquestioned, part of the

19   W.E. Montgomery, *Under their Own Vine and Fig Tree: The African-American Church in the South, 1865–1900*, Baton Rouge, Louisiana State University Press, 1993, 1–23; D.G. Mathews, *Religion in the Old South*, Chicago, 1977, 1–38.

20   E.D. Genovese, *Roll, Jordan, Roll: The World the Slaves Made*, New York, 1972, 212.

prevalent social system. In the South, the property owning and middle classes, the powerhouse of the voluntary anti-slave societies so influential in Britain, had no interest in changing the social framework, despite their religious profession. American evangelicalism was flexible, assertive, people-centred, but not necessarily a force to re-shape prevalent worldviews.

'GO WEST YOUNG MAN'

America was expanding. Between 1791 and 1819, nine new 'frontier' states joined the original thirteen. In 1803 the American government bought from the French government Louisiana and all of its lands further west, some 828,000 square miles, for the sum of $15 million. At a stroke, the size of the nation was doubled. Pioneers pressed through the recently discovered Cumberland Gap in the Appalachians, opened up overland trails westward, and settlers poured into the new lands. Between 1795 and 1835, the population of the West soared from 150,000 to 5 million. Here was life in the raw: as Emerson put it, the United States was European to the Alleghenies, but America lay beyond. Typified by the simple log cabin of the settler, the lifestyle encouraged a robust individualism. Daniel Boone considered the landscape crowded if you could see the smoke of your neighbour's chimney. In the East fears rose that the settlers would move to areas where there was no Christian influence, and revert to paganism. The populace was too scattered to easily form churches. Flexibility of response was to be crucial, itinerancy a key strategy.

With new settlement in mind, Congress considered a proposal in 1785 to reserve the central section of each town for education and religious purposes, but a watered down version of the scheme was passed in 1787, stating 'Religion, morality and knowledge being necessary to good government and the happiness of mankind, schools and the means of education shall forever be encouraged'.[21]

NATIVE AMERICANS

The rapid expansion into the West of Americans of a European background from the eastern seaboard was not into virgin territory. It involved encroachment into the traditional lands of the native American Indians. Settlers removed American Indians, some by treaty, others by force. Others sought to assimilate the indigenous tribes, and encourage education, and the adoption of settled European patterns of agriculture, with an expectation that Western attitudes and lifestyles should be adopted. Attempts to Christianise Native Americans were a part of this endeavour, and efforts towards this had been undertaken from early periods of colonisation by Protestant churches, with government support. The policies were of limited success in the nineteenth century in

---

21 Quoted in E.S. Gaustad, *Neither King Nor Prelate: Religion and the New Nation, 1776–1826*, Grand Rapids, Eerdmans, 1993, 116.

the face of periodic military conflicts, and government policies of relocation, broken treaties, land confiscations, and tension and violence at the hands of local white settlers, who also brought diseases against which native peoples had limited resistance. Attempts by Thomas Coke and Francis Asbury to reach Native Americans enjoyed limited success, but between 1819 and 1844 the Methodists established missions amongst 35 tribes, sent out 200 preachers, and organised some 4,000 converts into membership of the societies. Methodists only tended to stay in a missionary role in such areas for a few years, which gave little incentive for language study, or attempts to understand local culture, severely limiting their effectiveness.[22]

Most success in missionary activity amongst native Americans was seen in the south eastern states. In North Carolina, Tennessee, and Georgia, many Cherokees embraced the Christian gospel, and blended its teachings with their own cultural traditions. Several were ordained as Baptist and Methodist ministers. The American Board of Commissioners for Foreign Missions sent Presbyterian and Congregationalist ministers amongst the Native Americans. Under their influence, Cherokees built churches, adopted European agricultural patterns, and laws modelled on the US constitution. Tragedy was to befall what had appeared a triumph of Christian mission. After gold was discovered in Georgia in 1828, claim was laid to Indian lands, and President Andrew Jackson, who had little time for Indian rights, pushed through the Indian Removal Bill, forcing Native Americans to relocate West of the Mississippi. Despite resistance from missionaries, and in defiance of a ruling of the US Supreme Court, the relocations were pushed through, and Cherokees and other Native Americans forced West along the 'Trail of Tears'. White American antipathy to the presence of Indians was, in the early nineteenth century, not weakened by the presence of a shared Christian faith. By 1838 the American Board was reporting of its American Indian mission, 'little else than disappointment.'[23]

THE 'SECOND GREAT AWAKENING'
Whereas the first 'Great Awakening' had helped to establish a more cohesive identity amongst scattered New England colonies, the 'Second Great Awakening' was shaped by a nation conscious of its newly won independence, and which was being rapidly transformed as it outgrew its previous confinement to the Eastern seaboard. It was a means by which Americans made religious and cultural meaning in their transformed context. Whilst some argue that it was a predominantly conservative force, Nathan Hatch has emphasised that it was moulded by the populism of the Revolution, through which the Puritan

22 Hempton, *Methodism: Empire of the Spirit*, 155–156.
23 Hutchison, 46, 62–63; Annual Report, 29, (1838), American Board of Commissioners for Foreign Mission, 138, quoted in Hutchison, 69.

social and religious model was eroded, with a reduction in deference to clerical authority, tradition and social station. The capacity to interpret the Bible was democratised; one person's reading of the Bible, whether lay or ordained, began to be viewed as equal to another's, the preaching of laymen and women equally anointed with that of the clergy. Even revival was re-interpreted in populist fashion: no longer was it exclusively seen as a sovereign dispensation, but was capable of being produced by the faithful and zealous activity of ordinary Christians.[24]

The Second Great Awakening produced church growth of astonishing levels, and helped Christianize institutions and social habits in the new nation. It started in the 1780s in the South, and rural New England, initially through the work of Methodists, Baptists, and radical evangelicals: a large number of those affected were black. It was later experienced amongst New England Congregationalists in the 1790s, and developed into large-scale revivalism in upstate New York in the 1820s. Revivalism was to become a distinctive feature of late eighteenth and early nineteenth century American Christianity. It was a diverse phenomenon. One of its most striking expressions were the camp meetings, during which up to thirty thousand people could assemble for four days over a weekend, in the woods or the outback to hear robust preaching, engage in prolonged worship sessions, and seek new or renewed spiritual experiences. During the most famous of these at Cane Ridge, Kentucky, in August 1801, which lasted six or seven days, some 20,000 people attended what was arranged as a Presbyterian 'communion season', but at which Presbyterian, Methodist and Baptist pastors preached. In this intense religious environment, with evocative preaching and urgent exhortation, the most exuberant results were reported, including not only people screaming out loud or swooning into trances, but also laughing, jerking, dancing, running, and barking. A personal encounter with God was expected to produce an emotional response, and such signs were considered evidence of the power of the Holy Spirit. Two-thirds of those so affected were women and children, but no race or class was untouched, and those involved included some ministers and professional people.[25] The camp meeting became a regular feature of frontier life, a helpful antidote for both pastors and congregations to the isolation in which they lived. It was embraced by Baptists and Methodists, although it was many years before such gatherings could be tamed and domesticated. Denominations came eventually

24 On these themes see W.G. McLoughlin, *Revivals, Awakenings and Reform: An Essay on Religion and Social Change in America, 1607–1977*, Chicago and London, University Chicago Press, 1978; N.O. Hatch, *The Democratization of American Christianity*, New Haven and London, Yale University Press, 1989.

25 P. Conkin, *Cane Ridge: America's Pentecost*, Madison, University of Wisconsin Press, 1990, 103–104. On camp meetings see also D.D. Bruce, *And they All Sang Hallelujah: Plain-Folk Camp-Meeting Religion, 1800–1845*, Knoxville, University of Tennessee Press, 1974.

The Cane Ridge Meeting

'In the woods, ministers preaching day and night; the camp illuminated with candles, on trees, at wagons, and at the tent; persons falling down, and carried out of the crowd... If they speak, what they say is attended to, being very solemn and affecting – many are struck under such exhortations. But if they do not recover soon, praying and singing is kept up, alternately, and sometimes a minister exhorts over them... Now suppose ten of these groups around, a minister engaged in preaching to a large congregation, in the middle, some mourning, some rejoicing, and great solemnity on every countenance, and you will form some imperfect idea of the extraordinary work'.[1]

1 James Paterson letter to John King, 25 September 1801, quoted in Paul Conkin, *Cane Ridge: America's Pentecost*, Madison, University of Wisconsin Press, 1990, 93.

---

to co-ordinate camp meeting schedules, and advertise events; outpourings of the spirit were replaced by well-organised and managed human events.

Revivalism was key in the evangelisation of the trans-Appalachian West; it typified the Christianity of the new era in America. Its aim was converting sinners to faith in Christ, and through reformed behaviour to improve society. It was voluntary (tied to no particular denomination), democratic (experience was open to all), egalitarian (clergy and laity, sometimes including women, could preach), and individualistic although operating within a communal setting. It was therefore a highly contextualised expression of the gospel. The further West you went, the more rugged the lifestyle, and the hotter the gospel became. Preachers coupled what learning they had with plain speaking, an all-consuming passion for soul-winning, and appeal to the emotions.[26] Looser theological and ecclesiastical structures emerged, allowing a role for women to operate as exhorters, if not preachers. Theology shifted in an anti-intellectual and Arminian direction. This emphasis was received with approval in parts of a nation which had exerted itself to shake off oppression, and deference, and in which human endeavour to tame a hostile physical environment was constant: individuals were urged to exert themselves for God. Amongst rootless, opportunity-seeking, egalitarian-minded men and women, here was a religion that could be experienced, and expressed in enthusiastic singing. As revivalism was absorbed into folk-culture, the barriers between religious orthodoxy, superstition, and magic could become blurred.

More traditional revival patterns were continued, especially in the East. At Hampden-Sydney College, in the late 1780s, a revival outpouring was reported

---

26 For the life story of one famous frontier preacher see R. Bray, *Peter Cartwright: Legendary Frontier Preacher*, Urbana, University of Illinois Press, 2005.

as a result of students reading the Puritan Joseph Alleine's '*Alarm to the Converted*'. Between 1798 and 1803, 150 churches in New England experienced 'special effusions of the Holy Spirit. Operating within the framework of the New Divinity, with a greater emphasis on human agency and the importance of moral reform, Timothy Dwight, ceaselessly urged his students at Yale to experience evangelical conversion, and to settle as pastors of ordered churches. He saw significant success through his endeavours, with several outpourings of revival reported amongst the students.[27] Yale graduates, who were to play a key role in the Second Great Awakening in the North, included Asahel Nettleton (1783–1844), through whose ministry over 25,000 people were thought to have been converted, and Lyman Beecher (1775–1863). From his base in Cincinnati, where Beecher moved in 1832, he sought to train ministers who would respond to the challenge of the westward flow of settlers. He pleaded the need for churches, schools, seminaries, churches and pastors to train this 'young empire of mind, power, and wealth, and free institutions, rushing up to giant manhood'.[28]

Charles Finney (1792–1875) has been seen as a transitional figure in the religious life of the United States.[29] He was not the inventor of the revivalism, but he proved its great innovator and systematiser. He brought the exuberant revivalism of the frontier states to the North-East, but reshaped it for a more settled context. His conversion in 1821 came after a period of deep conviction of sin, which lasted about a week, followed by an overwhelming joy, and sense of call to preach. Declining the offer of theological training at Princeton, he received private tuition from a local Presbyterian minister, George Gale, who sponsored his ordination as a Presbyterian minister. In his preaching for conversion he saw great success. He was an imposing figure, over six feet tall, with penetrating eyes, and abilities that could not be denied. He preached passionately, and directly, without the use of notes, and people were readily persuaded.[30]

Finney saw revival through his preaching in towns by the Erie Canal, then in Philadelphia and New York State. His revivalist preaching at Rochester, New York, a centre of the distillery industry, between September 1830 and March 1831 was believed to have added 10,000 members to the churches, and the town converted to temperance. Over time, and indifferent to subtleties of doctrine,

---

27   Dwight's life is explored in J.R. Fitzmeir, *New England's Moral Legislator: Timothy Dwight, 1752–1817*, Bloomington, Indiana, 1998.

28   L. Beecher, *A Plea for the West*, 2nd ed., Cincinnati, Truman and Smith, 1835, 11–40, quoted in K. Hardman, *Issues in American Christianity*, Grand Rapids, Baker, 1993, 82. On Beecher's life see B.M. Cross, ed, *The Autobiography of Lyman Beecher*, 2 vols, Cambridge, Mass., 1961.

29   N. Hatch, *The Democratization of American Christianity*, New Haven, Yale University Press, 1989, 196–200.

30   On Finney see C. Hambrick-Stowe, *Charles G. Finney and the Spirit of American Evangelicalism*, Grand Rapids, Eerdmans, 1996.

Eng.ᵈ by H.B.Hall & Sons. 11 Fulton S.N.Y.

C. G. Finny.

Æ.T. 80.

he introduced the revivalist techniques of the West into the East, despite stern resistance from Nettleton and Lyman Beecher. A daily series of 'protracted' meetings would be held, carefully choreographed to build to a climax at the end of the week; some lasted late into the night. These were thoroughly planned, prayed for, and widely advertised. Those who were affected spiritually were invited to come forward and sit upon the 'anxious bench.' Those who were uncertain found themselves prayed for by name, and God earnestly invoked to break them down to contrition. Some hearers collapsed as he preached. A catalogue of sins were roundly denounced—smoking, drinking, gambling, dancing, fashion: 'It seemed to myself as if I could rain hail and love upon them at the same time; or in other words, that I could rain upon them hail, in love.'[31] Finney's *Lectures on Revival* (1835) were to prove a hugely influential handbook, setting out their 'promotion.' He asserted that 'Almost all the religion in the world has been produced by revivals', but he strongly countered the view that revival was a sovereign act of God, 'revival is not a miracle'. Revivals could be promoted, and produced by the right use of 'the constituted means'. These included self examination amongst Christians, concerted 'prevailing' prayer, urgent, direct preaching, that would 'hunt after sinners', the regular series of meetings in succession through a week, and the invitation of those under spiritual concern to the 'anxious seat'.[32]

Finney moved from the Calvinism of his background, even though he was ordained a Presbyterian, and articulated an Arminian, and at times semi-Pelagian, theology. Gone was the long period of conviction and soul-searching before conversion; conversion might be accomplished in only a few minutes. The agency of the individual in this was stressed: 'God will never yield nor grant you his Spirit, till you repent'. Such action was also required in the moral dimension: slave owners, and anyone involved in the slave trade, were excluded from communion: 'Let Christians of all denominations meekly but firmly come forth and pronounce their verdict, let them clear their communions, and wash their hands of this thing... and there would not be a shackled slave, nor a bristling, cruel, slave-driver in this land'.[33]

Here was a ready-made, and readily adopted, respectable pietistic religious system, with few intellectual barriers to acceptance. It was designed for the needs of the new era. Women tended to make up the majority of church members, often 60–70% in the North-East, and the work of the revivalists saw the highest levels of response amongst them, up to 72% of the total in places. Amongst

31   C. G. Finney, *An Autobiography*, Old Tappan, NJ, Fleming H. Revell, 1876 (repr. 1908), 101.

32   C. G. Finney, *Lectures on Revivals of Religion*, New York, Boston, Leavitt, Lord; Crocker and Brewster, 1835, 2–5.

33   C. Finney, *Lectures on Revivals of Religion*, ed. W.G. McLoughlin, Cambridge, Mass., 1960, 107–108; 112, 302.

Finney's converts were the women's rights activist Elizabeth Cady Stanton, and Antoinette Brown Blackwell, the first woman ordained in the USA.[34] Despite his successes, Presbyterians were deeply divided by his approach.

The emotional intensity of revivalism could not be sustained indefinitely by preacher or congregation. By 1828, the fire had largely burned out of Eastern revivalism, which had become everyday and systematic. Religious life slipped into a more usual course. Finney sensed the day of the revivalist was passing, and after a short pastorate in New York, took up a post at Oberlin College, Ohio. Although Finney had preached to segregated congregations, Oberlin was after 1830 to become a key centre of abolitionist sentiment. One strong theme of Finney's teaching was the need for conversion to have an outcome in terms of desire to fight sin, not only personally, but also in society. If a person was truly converted, it should make a demonstrable difference to their lifestyle. Finney strongly advocated the temperance movement, and the abolition of slavery: some of those influenced by his teaching in the pulpit and at Oberlin College, became strong advocates of moral reform, a number of whom were women.

The revivalism of Finney and others produced a less-doctrinally aware, more easily accessible and personally adaptable, religious framework. Between the more dynamic developments in the West, and a more conservative course of events in the East, an evangelical culture was formed that although divided, was vibrant. The Second Awakening was to last well into the nineteenth century; it became the dominant religious vision of the young republic. Over time the excesses of outback revivalism were tamed. Disorder was eschewed, and although tumult was still required, it was to be inward and spiritual, managed according to the textbook 'new measure' system Finney had outlined. The next major revival in the United States, that which took place in 1858, was to be ordered, solemn, and lay-led.

VOLUNTARY BODIES

The first amendment to the constitution had ruled out any religious establishment, rendering religion personal, and voluntary. People were free to change their religious adherence if they so wished, and, as many chose to do so, denominations began to fragment. However, a powerful link between individual piety and public life was forged through the range of voluntary, and often pan-denominational, societies, formed largely by Protestants, to address specific issues. In 1810 the American Board for Foreign Missions was formed, followed by the American Sunday School Union (1824), and the American Anti-Slavery Society (1833).

By 1830, each American drank on average over five gallons of distilled spirits each year; a thousand distilleries operated in New York in the 1820s. Excessive

---

34   Westerkamp, *Women and Religion*, 138–140.

drinking was linked to domestic violence, public disorder, and poverty. In 1826 the American Society for the Promotion of Temperance was founded, and was to become the largest reform organisation, emphasizing individual reform, in which conversion was a key component. By 1834, millions of Americans had taken the pledge to avoid strong drink. The American Temperance Union followed in 1836, advocating total abstinence, and campaigning for restrictions in the sale of alcohol. Strong evangelical sentiment, and self-help impulses to improve the lot of families, proved an attractive combination. In 1851, Maine became the first state to prohibit the sale or manufacture of alcoholic beverages, and others were to follow suit and go 'dry'.

Education was another area in which reformers were actively engaged. In 1827, Massachusetts passed the first law allowing public schools to be supported by taxes. In a matter of a few years, children aged from five to nineteen were able to obtain a free education in various subjects, although continued employment opportunities for children meant that many left school at age fourteen. By the late 1830s, most towns in the north and west had a school. In 1837, Oberlin College, Ohio, founded by religious leaders who were also abolitionists, began to admit women, and African-Americans were also admitted. Single women teachers became the backbone of the educational system in the schoolhouses of isolated communities

Churches were places where the established patterns of community and intellectual authority could be challenged, and proved attractive to the dispossessed and marginalised, including the poor, slaves, and especially women. Throughout the nineteenth century, the majority of church members were women, and a 'feminization of religion' has been discerned, evidence by their increased levels of active participation in religious life in the domestic sphere, in churches, and in the rapidly developing range of voluntary organisations designed to promote religious, missionary, and benevolent work.[35] Religion became a route by which women could gain access to greater participation in the public sphere.

The emphasis in the type of theology made popular by Charles Finney was for individuals to make responsible choices, and to persuade others to do the same. For women, as for others, this offered new opportunities to take control of their lives and destiny, and to shape the lives of others. Within the domestic sphere, a pattern of female moral guardianship and reform was encouraged by churches. The responsibility of women as upholders of the religious and moral well-being of their families, with a special mission to reclaim unbelieving husbands, was promoted. For the benefit of wider society, women began welfare organisations, relief societies, Sunday Schools, maternal associations, or visiting neighbouring

---

35   A. Douglas, *The Feminization of American Culture*, New York, Kopf, 1977.

homes to advise and exhort.[36] The Female Moral Reform Society was established by middle class evangelical women to address issues presented by prostitution, rather than simply blaming prostitutes for their activities. Attempts were made to offer practical support to prostitutes through running soup kitchens, and provide alternative work, and these were coupled with attempts to name and shame their male clients. Other reformers targeted their efforts at the plight of prisoners, or the treatment of those with mental illness.

The voluntary bodies organised were powerful demonstrations of a functional ecumenicity amongst churches, and also gave significant opportunities for women to take an active, and sometimes prominent, role. This was especially the case in the campaign against slaveholding, where Sara and Angelina Grimké, who became Quakers, conducted Sunday schools for black children, and joint prayer meetings with slaves, and mounting an active abolitionist campaign through writing and public speaking.[37]

Although amongst the Quakers there was a tradition of women preaching, in general, restrictions on women preaching, or even praying in public, were maintained. However, early nineteenth-century revivalism allowed a greater role for individual inspiration from the Holy Spirit, and opened opportunities for women to participate. Women who did preach emphasised that they felt constrained by God to speak, and claimed an exceptional call from God to do so, believing that they were not doing so on their own authority. Although there were only small numbers of women speakers, their presence gradually became more evident at the camp meeting, on the lecture hall of the moral reform campaign, and eventually in the church.

The American Bible Society, founded in 1816, was to prove a key voluntary body, ensuring the Bible was cheaply printed, widely distributed and significantly present across the nation. By 1830 it was distributing over 300,000 copies of the Scripture, in whole or in part. Martin Marty has claimed that the Bible became 'America's Iconic Book'[38]: it was personally central, read for comfort and guidance, and of such cultural significance that it was produced for Presidents to swear their oath of office upon.

THE LEGACY OF THE PERIOD

The American revolution left the newly independent states with a Constitution that acknowledged no God, and a First Amendment that permitted no national church. That there were to be no religious tests left office holding open to

---

36   T.K. Wayne, *Women's Roles in Nineteenth-Century America*, Westport, Conn., Greenwood Press, 2007, 50–53.

37   K.K. Sklar, *Women's Rights Emerges Within the Anti-Slavery Movement, 1830–1870*, Boston, Bedford/St Martin's, 2000, 5–6.

38   Martin Marty, quoted in Gaustad, *Neither King Nor Prelate*, 129.

people of any denomination, indeed there was no requirement that they be Christians at all. Attempts in the early nineteenth century by the National Reform Association to add a Christian element to the 'atheistic' constitution proved futile. The constitution placed power ultimately in the hands of the people, rather than the hands of the states; similarly the churches belonged to the people, not the states. The denominations that adapted to this new state of affairs most readily, were those which prospered most.

The gaps left by the constitution were filled in various ways by individual states. In 1790, Pennsylvania decreed that no person would be disqualified from public office as long as they acknowledged 'the being of a God, and a future state of rewards and punishments'. Massachusetts went further and gave towns authority to make provision, 'at their own expense, for the institution of the public worship of GOD, and for the support and maintenance of public Protestant preachers of piety, religion and morality'.[39] In 1817 Pennsylvania upheld Sunday closing laws, and expected that there be a decent observance of the Sabbath. Yet, state impositions in the area of religion were declining in the early nineteenth century—in 1818 the citizens of Connecticut voted to disestablish the state's Congregational churches. It was a distressing decision to many, but provoked urgent efforts to extend the Congregational cause by voluntary means.

Neither the war of independence, nor the constitution, Christianised America; that task was instead accomplished by the wave of popular religious movements that swept across the new country in the late eighteenth century. Early nineteenth century American society emphasised talent, native intelligence, and opportunity, rather than inherited status and privileges, success came to those willing to test their mettle. Religion became a mass enterprise—the 1,800 ministers of 1775, serving a population of 2.5 million, had become 40,000 ministers serving a population of 20 millions in 1845. Many were zealous young men, skilled in communication, possessed of abundant energy, operating with an ethic of toil, a vision for expansion. Theirs was a popular Christianity for a new democratic society. Their message appealed to the common people, who were welcomed without any regard to their social standing, and offered a message of self-respect and self-confidence. Untutored in deep theology and irregular in practice, in a way that would have been unacceptable in the middle of the eighteenth century, they were populist to the core. This was the new order of things post 1776, an age when deference, patronage and orderly succession were pushed aside. Their preaching was received with a mixture of credulity and scepticism, but largely the former. American congregations wanted their leaders unpretentious, their doctrine plain, self-evident and practical, their music lively and sing-able, and that is usually what they got. Ironically, the more

---

39   Quoted in Gaustad, *King Nor Prelate*, 114–115.

their leaders enjoyed the democratic acclaim of the people, the more they were inclined to don an authoritarian mantle.

In 1800 as Thomas Jefferson stood for President, there were fears that he would prove to be a dangerous infidel: in fact he proved highly moral, attending of Christian services in the Capitol, and approving of military chaplains and Christian missions to native Americans. The doubts over his religious position were no bar to his election in 1800, but so successful was the evangelical campaign to grab the soul of the nation that by the 1830s Presidential candidates needed to stress their godly character to win the votes of Christians. On an individual level, many Americans were convinced that vigorous faith was not only compatible with the pursuit of happiness and freedom, it was also indispensable to the maintenance of republican institutions.

Between the events in America in the years after 1776, and those in France in 1789, there were undoubted connections. In 1790 Thomas Paine was given the key to the Bastille, and asked to forward it to President George Washington. In his covering letter, Paine referred to the key as the first fruits of American principles transplanted into Europe. Yet, as events in the revolution in France unfolded, not all shared his confidence. In 1798 Rev. Jedidiah Morse made astounding revelations of a plot by the French anarchists to extend their operations to America. Another denounced the French Revolution as a counterfeit millennium, 'the millennium of Hell'.[40] By the early nineteenth century, liberty was to Americans a sacred cause, one closely intertwined with, and inseparable from, notions of Christianity: it had become impossible to imagine one without the other.

---

40   N. Hatch, *Sacred Cause of Liberty*, 132.

FURTHER READING

S.A. Ahlstrom, *A Religious History of the American People*, New Haven, Yale, 1972.

E. Gaustad, *A Documentary History of Religion in America to the Civil War*, Grand Rapids, Eerdmans, 1993.

E. Gaustad, *Neither King nor Prelate: Religion and the New Nation 1776–1826*, Grand Rapids, Eerdmans, 1993.

K. Hardman, *Issues in American Christianity*, Grand Rapids, Baker, 1993.

H. Mitchell, *Black Church Beginnings*, Grand Rapids, Eerdmans, 2004.

N.O. Hatch, *The Sacred Cause of Liberty; Republican Thought and the Millennium in Revolutionary New England*, New Haven and London, Yale University Press, 1977.

N.O. Hatch, *The Democratization of American Christianity*, New Haven, Yale University Press, 1989.

M. Noll, *The Old Religion in the New World: A History of North American Christianity*, Grand Rapids, Eerdmans, 2002.

M. Noll, *American Evangelical Christianity: An Introduction*, Oxford, Basil Blackwell, 2000.

M. Noll, *America's God: From Jonathan Edwards to Abraham Lincoln*, Oxford, Oxford University Press, 2002.

H. Stout and D.G. Hart (eds), *New Directions in American Religious History*, Oxford, Oxford University Press, 1997.

M. Westerkamp, *Women and Religion in Early America, 1600–1850*, London, Routledge, 1999.

P.W. Williams, *America's Religions, Traditions, and Cultures*, New York, Macmillan, 1990.

2

CRUSH 'L'INFÂME':
THE FRENCH REVOLUTION AND ITS LEGACY

War is an expensive business, and between 1689 and 1815 Britain and France engaged in war with each other five times, placing considerable strain on the economies of both nations. With its growing industrial and mercantile wealth, Britain was more able to finance these war efforts than France. The French decision to intervene on the side of the American colonists in their war against their British rulers proved crucial in helping the Americans win their conflict, but it brought the French economy to its knees. The success of the American revolutionaries also opened the eyes of radical thinkers in France to the possibilities of what could be achieved against oppressive rulers. What happened exceeded by far the expectations of the most radical of thinkers. The social and political change that was so desperately needed in France came through revolution.

PRE-REVOLUTIONARY FRANCE

That this revolution took place in the most populous, and probably most powerful, state in Western Europe—one in five Europeans was French—was remarkable. But France lived far beyond its means, and national expenditure exceeded income by 20%. Although the extravagance of the court at Versailles was a problem, and accounted for 6% of spending, it was the servicing of the national debt, particularly the war debt, which crippled the economy by eating up half of national expenditure, and disrupting trade. With much conspicuous consumption, there was little surplus for re-investment. The lack of an established banking and credit system greatly compounded matters.

France was predominantly agricultural, and its social relations still bore the legacy of feudalism. Its population of some 23 million people was dominated by the 0.4 million who belonged to the nobility. There were huge inequalities of wealth. Faced by falling agricultural incomes, the landed class reacted by extracting further income from their feudal tenants. The large peasant section of the population was also required to bear the heaviest burden of taxation. Fluctuations in harvests and prices brought food shortages, and drained peasant incomes as a growing crisis loomed. One cleric reported that of 2,200 in his parish, 1,800 were asking for bread: he wept at his inability to help owing to his own poverty. Bad weather, poor harvest, high taxes crippled the most needy. A tinderbox of suffering and resentment was being created: violence was never far from the surface.

When Louis XV died of smallpox in 1774, one priest wrote, 'it was high time, for France was in despair'.[1] The lower clergy raised their voices in protest at injustices suffered by the poor, but suffered themselves from inadequate and insecure incomes—some were to become radical voices for reform in the early years of the revolution. Ironically, those who suffered most, the agricultural peasantry, were probably to achieve the least through the revolution—lands confiscated from the church ended in the hands of those who already had wealth, or the urban bourgeoisie. Wholesale redistribution of land to the land-hungry peasantry never occurred, and the lack of primogeniture meant that existing landholdings continued to be divided on the death of the owner. Small, inefficient, farms multiplied.

The *ancien régime* not only faced social and economic problems, but was also confronted by strong challenges to traditional patterns of faith and understanding.

THE ENLIGHTENMENT LEGACY

The Enlightenment[2] was born of great optimism in the human spirit and its achievements. Watchwords of the Enlightenment were 'reason', 'liberty', 'happiness', and 'nature': the 'superstition' of previous ages was to be set aside. Emphasis on rationality and empirical methodology encouraged strong opposition to the assumptions of the pre-Enlightenment church, and any appearance of religious intolerance. In the spirit of open, critical enquiry, Enlightenment thinkers in France and other parts of Europe began to dismiss Biblical revelation and the supernatural in Christianity as mystical obscurities. The dominant French Roman Catholic Church was an obvious target.

1   Quoted in J. McManners, *Church and Society in Eighteenth Century France, Volume 2: The Religion of the People and the Politics of Religion*, Oxford, Clarendon, 1998, 709.
2   It has been argued that the term 'The Enlightenment', misleadingly suggests a single unitary process, and that the definite article should therefore be dropped. 'Enlightenment' more properly refers to the variety of phenomena that appear to be similar, interrelated, and the product of a shared history. (J.G.A. Pocock, 'The Enlightenment and Revolution: The Case of English Speaking North America', in *Transactions of the Seventh International Congress on the Enlightenment*, Oxford, 1989, 252.)

To Voltaire (François-Marie Arouet (1694–1778)), the church was the enemy of progress: John Locke's philosophy and Isaac Newton's science had banished mystery from human affairs. Together with Jean Jacques Rousseau (1712–78) he rejected the tenets of orthodox Christian theology, especially the divinity of Christ and the revealed religion of the Bible. He praised the theologians who had rejected superstition and embraced Socinianism (a non-Trinitarian view of God). Although Voltaire emphasised the evidence of the Creator in nature, his view was of a God who did not intervene, who had no particular concern for the affairs of men, and to whom humans owed no obligations. God was rendered an impersonal force, an abstraction, with little meaningful place in a rather cold and empty world. Christian ethics had value insofar as they agreed with elements found in other religions. Using methods that were to foreshadow later historical criticism, Voltaire attacked the historicity and ethics of the Old Testament. He was also unsparing in his criticism of the Roman Catholic Church, which was to him a self-interested conspiracy to perpetuate superstition. His exhortation to the 'chapel' of *philosophes* was to crush 'l'Infâme'. Yet, his enlightenment thinking led him to speak out for the rights of individuals, and he publicised the cruel persecution to which some Protestants were subjected. Voltaire hated the control of the Roman Catholic Church over the minds of the intelligent. His radical religious views were not matched in the political realm: although a man of great social concern, Voltaire was no egalitarian. His was the Enlightenment of the elitist and the paternalist. Voltaire's pessimistic Deism[3] appealed little to the Roman Catholic clergy, but among a significant section of the educated classes seeds of critical enquiry and doubt were being sown.

Jean-Jacques Rousseau similarly rejected Biblical revelation. He attempted to replace it with a version of 'natural religion', based on the Christian gospels, and Jesus Christ as a virtuous but unsung prophet. To Rousseau, the dogmatism of traditional Christian belief was unhealthy: God was to be found in nature, and in the noblest sentiments of the human heart. He stressed ethical integrity, and his optimistic view of human potentiality reduced the Fall into merely a wrong turning, with humans being inherently good, but pushed into vice and selfishness by the failings of society's customs and institutions. Rousseau argued that theologians had lost sight of the central Christian doctrine that God is love, and that rightly ordering human affairs would put right the mistakes of the past. This optimism and warmth of human feelings feature in his novels, which were widely read by Christians, who appreciated their emphasis on ethical conduct. This humanistic, optimistic faith, devoid of the supernatural and revealed

---

3   Deism is a rationalistic understanding of God's relationship to the world, which sees God as involved in giving initial impetus to the world, but then withdrawing from special interventions in it. Deism emphasised human rationality, and questioned divine providence, revelation, and any supernatural scheme of salvation.

element of Christianity, foreshadowed the approach of theological liberalism later in the century.

Although far from Christian orthodoxy, Rousseau realised that for society to continue to function it needed moral machinery, some form of *religion civile*, by which the worst vices of civilisation would be eradicated, or at least controlled. It was the same conclusion the founders of the new-born United States had come to, and it remained influential during the post 1789 revolutionary era in France, and during the rule of Napoleon Bonaparte.

The *Encyclopédie* (Encyclopaedia) compiled by Denis Diderot (1713–84) and Jean Le Rond d'Alembert (1717–83), exemplified enlightenment confidence in human reason. It was arranged on a functional alphabetic basis, with no presupposition of a hierarchy of knowledge which would have placed God as the first entry. It was largely Deist in tone, permeated by rationalistic attitudes, although it did include some contributions from Roman Catholic priests and Reformed pastors.

Such writings were certainly known by the clergy, and some were deeply attracted to such thinking. Loménie de Brienne, Archbishop of Toulouse, appointed by Louis XVI in 1787 to sort out the financial affairs of the church just before the revolution, was one such. He belonged intellectually to the party of the *philosophes*[4], and was reputed to have spent more time leaning on his billiard cue than saying mass. When it was suggested he be a candidate for the arch-episcopate of the French capital, Louis retorted 'At the very least, the Archbishop of Paris must believe in God'.[5] Although Brienne called for financial sacrifices from the church, on exiting from his short period in office he awarded himself large compensation, and promotions and preferments for his relatives.

The anticlerical writing of the *philosophes* was at times scurrilous, but some of its content not without foundation. Although the hard work of many parish priests continued to be held in high regard, respect for those in authority in the church and state began to erode. No wholesale or widespread de-sacralization should be claimed for the decades before 1789, and anticlerical feeling was far from universal, but legitimate questions began to be asked about aspects of the church, and its strict adherence to the teaching of the Council of Trent. Some hoped for a renewed society, still Roman Catholic in form, but with an emphasis on morality and the removal of superstition. Among urban élites Rousseauian-style moralizing became fashionable. For a growing number of others, Freemasonry offered a 'reasonable' variant on Christianity, and the membership of lodges in France increased.

---

4   The *philosophes* were eighteenth century literary men, thinkers and scientists were united in their belief in the supremacy and efficacy of human reason.

5   N. Aston, *Religion and Revolution in France 1780–1804*, Macmillan, 2000, 86–92, J. McManners, *The French Revolution and the Church*, London, SPCK, 1970, 1, 16.

THE CHURCH BEFORE THE REVOLUTION

The French Roman Catholic Church in the decades before 1789 defies easy categorisation. It was not hopelessly corrupt, but there were problems. It was much spoken against, but much loved; there were clergy who lived scandalous lives, there were others who were faithful to their duties. Some served for the wrong motives, others for the right. Moves to reform clerical life in the eighteenth century had borne some fruit—priests were more moral and better educated; Easter communicant levels remained high until the 1770s, religious endeavour in education and the care for sick was earnest and sincere. Liturgical observance and church music were more splendid than ever. Yet it was the gold of autumn before the fall. Calls for change became irresistible, and anticlerical feeling became a significant strand of public opinion.

A major cause of complaint was the huge wealth and privilege of the Gallican church, in an increasingly impoverished France. Its income was somewhere between 170 and 250 million livres per year, and some estimate that one third of land was owned by the church or clergy. Such wealth, bolstered by the church's exemption from taxation, made it a ready target for the cash-strapped state in the late eighteenth century. Yet it was a church filled with inequalities between the income of the lower clergy and the élites which matched those in wider society. The high ranks of the clergy were dominated by the offspring of aristocratic families, with considerable nepotism. The lower clergy were far less affluent, dependent as they were on income from tithes which became increasingly difficult to collect as agricultural incomes fell: 'as beggarly as a threadbare priest' was a proverbial saying. Such inequalities opened up divisions amongst the clergy during the revolution, as the *curés* (parish priests) offered their protests against the privilege and wealth of the higher clerical orders. *Curés* were popularly seen as men of the people, often locally born and from the middle classes and below of society, in contrast to excessively wealthy, and tax avoiding, higher ranks of the clergy. As with other forms of absolutism in eighteenth-century France, episcopal absolutism, which could be accompanied by harsh and uncaring attitudes, was increasingly thrown open to question. The calls of the clergy for change did not result in the reforms in the Gallican church they sought, but rather, to everyone's surprise, a dismantled church.

France was an overwhelmingly Roman Catholic country, ruled over in absolutist fashion by the Bourbon monarchy. Louis XVI (1752–93) ascended the throne in 1774 as a young man of deep Roman Catholic piety, in contrast to Louis XV. He regularly attended church, and one of his sisters became a nun. An effective alliance had been forged between throne and altar, with Roman Catholic religious ideology dominating the monarchical state. Across Europe, Roman Catholic states were progressively reducing the influence of the pope to that of a figurehead. Whilst accepting the spiritual authority of the papacy, the French king took a leading role in ecclesiastical affairs, and after 1682 the pope was effectively excluded from intervening in the Gallican church without his approval. In return the monarch ensured the preservation of Roman Catholicism as the state church. From the enthronement of a monarch to the execution of a criminal, the church was formally present. The registration of births, marriages, and deaths, was in the hands of parish priests; education was effectively a clerical monopoly. In the eighteenth century, three First Ministers of the Crown were high ranking ecclesiastics, all of whom later became cardinals.

Evidence suggests that by the second half of the eighteenth century the influence and authority of the church over a substantial portion of the laity was declining. The suppression of Jansenism robbed the Gallican church of one stream of spiritual vitality. Pietism and Methodism, streams of renewal in Germany and Britain, passed Roman Catholic France by. Bland latitudinarianism and lukewarmness replaced the rigors of Counter-Reformation orthodoxy. By the 1770s and 1780s there is some evidence of religious observance declining in popularity—Easter communicant attendance at Bourdeaux in 1772 was under 50% of the population. Church attendance on Sunday began to fall in the 1780s; how 'pure' the faith of those who attended might have been debatable. Religious teaching, folklore, and superstition blended together. Piety and successful female domesticity merged—a housewife might place a crucifix on the bread dough to encourage the bread to rise. Adherence remained strongest amongst artisans and the working classes, but amongst the middle classes and professional classes the work of the *philosophes* gained an influence. Religious indifference tended to increase the higher up the social scale one progressed.

The moral state of the nation was also deteriorating, a decline fuelled by deepening poverty. At the start of the eighteenth century, only around 1% of births were illegitimate; by the end of the century the figures in the towns ranged from 4% to 17%. Marital breakdown increased, as did prostitution; infanticide and the abandonment of children became a growing problem. The ranks of the clergy, numbering some 170,000 (0.6% of the population), were not immune from wider trends in society. Between 1755 and 1764, 2,500 monks and clergy were reported to the local authorities and arrested for debauchery. The Commission des Réguliers, which sat from 1765–84, brought some reform to religious orders, shutting down 426 religious houses, and numbers in religious orders fell from 22,500 in 1768 to 15,000 in 1790.

Within the French Roman Catholic Church there were moves for reform against the corruptions and inadequacies of the pre-Enlightenment church. One such was Jansenism. Taking its root from the writings of Cornelius Jansen (1585–1638), bishop of Ypres, it was a rigorous, ascetic and intensive form of Roman Catholic spirituality, with an Augustinian emphasis on grace and predestination. It stressed the supremacy of church councils over popes and kings (conciliarism), an approach that proved attractive to many in the lower clerical orders. It also offered a robust reaction to enlightenment religious thinking, arguing that natural religion was an alternative 'pagan' system to Christian faith and morals. In France the Jansenists became locked into bitter conflict with the Jesuit order, whom they considered too lax. Condemned by papal decree in 1713, Jansenism became subject to severe persecution in France, particularly in the years 1730 to 1732, when prophecies, miracles, and convulsions were reported in their midst. By the 1750s and 1760s, Jansenism was more tolerated, especially after the Jesuits were expelled from France in 1764.

France was overwhelmingly Roman Catholic, but not all belonged to the Gallican Church. After the appalling massacres of French Protestants on and after St Bartholomew's Day in 1572, France had descended into civil war. This was ended in 1598 with the Edict of Nantes, which allowed Protestants to maintain an existence in certain areas of the country. When in 1685 this Edict was repealed, Roman Catholicism was given a legal monopoly on the religious life of France. To be French was to be Roman Catholic; to be outside the Roman Catholic Church was to be a non-person, as the 2% of the population who were Protestants found in the severe persecutions they faced. Most were Calvinists, but 200,000 were Lutherans living in Alsace, once under German control. Attempts at their forced conversion, with the *dragonnades* of Protestants after 1685, led some 200,000 Huguenots to flee the country by 1720, although the armed response of the French Protestant resistance fighters, the Camisards, did little to help their cause. Outright aggression against Protestants gave way to steady, but cruel, repression. In 1737 the 89 year old Anne Maret died in a convent to which she had been consigned 50 years previously for refusing to recognise Roman Catholic observances. A mother found singing psalms in her house with her neighbours was sent to a convent for life, leaving behind seven children. Some children were forcibly removed from Protestant parents, and re-educated in Roman Catholic convents or schools. Such persecution rarely led to genuine conversion to Roman Catholicism, but created a secret 'church of the desert', or individuals cowed into occasional outward conformity for fear of losing their children. Although repression was formally in the hands of the state, it was the Roman Catholic clergy, especially the bishops, who often called for stern measures against such 'heretics'. Unless they were held in a Roman Catholic Church, marriages were not legal, nor were baptisms. In the years to 1762, two to three thousand Huguenots were sent to the galleys where they were subject to appalling cruelties often for decades. The last of the Protestant galley slaves were not released until 1775; pastors could face imprisonment or the gallows—the last to do so died in prison in 1771.

Ironically, the *philosophes* who so opposed the Roman Catholic Church campaigned vociferously for better treatment of Protestants on the grounds of freedom. Only in 1787 did the 'Edict Concerning those who do not Profess the Catholic Religion' allow Protestants to marry, and leave property to fellow Protestants, although their churches were not allowed to own property, or pastors wear clerical dress. They remained second-class citizens, but had not been wiped out. Assisted by the Treaty of Westphalia (1648), the Lutherans in Alsace generally fared better than the Huguenots, although they were subject to aggressive Jesuit endeavours at proselytism, which yielded limited success. The plight of the 40–50,000 Jews was little better, subjected as they were to periodic 'Jew-hunts'. For these religious minorities, the events of the French Revolution were to prove more beneficial than for the once dominant French Catholic church.

THE CALLING OF THE ESTATES GENERAL

As an absolute monarch, Louis XVI believed his sovereign power in the kingdom was to be shared with no-one, and that he was accountable only to God. Louis XVI was generally respected, but his brothers and Queen Marie Antoinette were hated for their extravagance. By the mid 1780s, bankruptcy faced the French state: the budget deficit reached 161 million livres in 1788. Emergency loans were raised, but the harvest of 1788 was the worst for decades. In early 1789, riots broke out as the lowest classes of society responded to hardship in the way they had done many times before, but now there was talk of popular rights, and utopian hopes. With crisis looming, Louis was forced into desperate action, and he took the extraordinary step of calling a meeting of the Estates-General, the ancient feudal assembly which had not sat since 1614.

One of the constituent bodies that made up the Estates-General consisted of ecclesiastical representatives. The system adopted for selection yielded a majority from the lower orders of the clergy: in all there were 49 bishops, 208 curés, and 35 monks. At a stroke, the grip of the bishops and higher ecclesiastics on the affairs of the church was broken. Many of the deputies were strong advocates of clerical reforms.

The absence of a national assembly in post-Enlightenment France created pent up forces waiting to be unleashed. Louis XVI contributed to this by his hesitancy, and mismanagement of matters, which fostered a sense of grievance and suspicion, and events took on momentum of their own. The Estates General met in Versailles in May 1789. Early debates concerned whether the representatives of the First Estate (the church) should debate separately, or join with the Second Estate (the nobles), and the Third Estate (largely the bourgeoisie including many from the financial, commercial, and professional classes). It was a crucial issue for the clergy—where did their allegiance lie, with the nobles or the ordinary people? In late May, the Third Estate called on the curés to join them in common cause: the challenge divided the ranks of the clerical delegates. On June 17th 1789, the Third Estate declared themselves the National Assembly, and within five days, in opposition to the wishes of the bishops and cardinals, 150 priests had joined the self-styled National Assembly, together with fifteen Protestants. The Estates General, simply called to offer the king advice, had within six weeks declared itself a sovereign parliament. Unexpectedly, power had fallen to the Third Estate, who drew in the support of the urban poor, the revolutionary peasantry, and a number of clerical deputies. The presence of the clergy was to be fraught with irony, for they had opted to join cause with those who were about to bring about the church's downfall.

In the early days, however, great respect was shown to the church: the first President of the Assembly was an archbishop. Control rapidly slipped from the crown to the Assembly; as the leader of the National Assembly, Mirabeau famously declared to the king, 'Sire, you are a stranger in this assembly, you have not the right to speak here'.[6] Away from Versailles, the economic crisis deepened. The price of bread almost doubled, and the people of Paris rose. On the 14th July the Bastille, a state prison and symbol of royal oppression and despotism, was stormed by a crowd of around eight thousand, and the prisoners inside released. The crowd was largely made up of artisans and shopkeepers, but when a number of soldiers joined the act of liberation it became clear that the army could no longer be relied upon to halt revolt. Across Europe, governments and thinkers were shaken. Even Immanuel Kant, so regimented in his personal habits, postponed his afternoon walk for an hour on hearing the shattering news. Others sympathetic towards the early stages of the French Revolution included the poets Wordsworth and Blake, the composer Beethoven, and the philosopher Hegel.

Within weeks the old social structure of France was turned upside down. Paris set up its own municipal authority and National Guard, with defensive militias against the 'aristocratic conspiracy', and the lower orders who might threaten property. The Sanscoulottes, an urban movement of artisans and the labouring poor, organised demonstrations, riots, and barricades. In the countryside, peasants rose against the aristocrats, destroying symbols of their previous servitude.

The church was quickly sucked into the vortex of events. On 4 August the clerical delegates, fearing church property would be confiscated, belatedly agreed to reforms including the abolition of the tithe. Within six months of the Estates General being called, the Assembly had voted to put the vast wealth of church property at the disposal of the bankrupt nation, leaving a residue for the support of the clergy, and the care of the poor. On 26 August 1789 a 'Declaration of the Rights of Man and the Citizen' was adopted by the Assembly. It was a critique of the privileged and hierarchical nature of the *ancien régime*: its preamble stated: 'ignorance, forgetfulness or disregard for the rights of man are the sole causes of public misfortunes and of the corruption of governments'. The 'Declaration', which changed European discourse about liberty, became

---

6   Honoré Gabriel Riqueti, comte de Mirabeau (1749–91), quoted in E.J.Hobsbawm, *The Age of Revolution 1789–1848*, New York, Mentor, 1962, 82.

The Declaration of the Rights of Man and of the Citizen, August 1789

Article 1: Men are born and remain free and equal in rights...

Article 4: Liberty consists in being able to do anything that is not harmful to others. Thus, the only limits to the exercise of the natural rights of each man are those that ensure the enjoyment of the same rights for other members of society...

Article 5: The law has the right only to forbid acts that are harmful to society. Anything that is not forbidden by the law may not be prevented, and no one may be constrained to do what it does not command.

Article 6: The law is the expression of the general will. All citizens, or their representatives, have the right to work solemnly towards its formulation... All citizens, being equal in its eyes, are equally admissible to all public dignities, posts and employment, according to their abilities, and without any distinction other than that of their virtues and their talents.

Article 10: No man may be harassed for his opinions, even religious ones, as long as their manifestation does not trouble the public order established by law.

Article 11: The free communication of thoughts and opinions is one of the most precious rights of man; thus any citizen may speak, write, and print freely...[1]

1 Source: *Gazette nationale ou le Moniteur universel*, n. 44, 20 August 1789, vol. 2, pp. 362-3, in Philip. G. Dwyer and Peter McPhee (eds), *The French Revolution and Napoleon*, Routledge, London, 2002, pp. 26-28.

---

one of the great statements of the universal principles of liberalism. It asserted that 'men are born free and live free and equal under the laws'; that liberty, property, security, and resistance to oppression are 'natural' rights of man; and that the source of all sovereignty was located in the nation rather than the king or the church. People were not to be detained unless they had infringed the law; individuals were to be presumed innocent until declared guilty. Although the focus of the statement was civil liberty, the position of religion was not ignored. Its articles recognised the need for the freedom to communicate personal opinions to others, 'even religious ones'; this was 'one of the most precious rights of men'.[7] However, two bitter years were to follow before the Constitution of 1791 decreed freedom for all men to speak, write and print their thoughts and to practise the religion to which they were attached.

Initially the king refused to sanction the declaration, but once again the people of Paris stepped forward to safeguard the revolution. As at other key moments of the revolution, women took a prominent role—as 7,000 of them,

---

7 *Gazette nationale ou le Moniteur universel*, n. 44, 20 August 1789, vol. 2, 362–3, in Philip. G. Dwyer and Peter McPhee (eds), *The French Revolution and Napoleon*, Routledge, London, 2002, 26–28.

followed by the National Guard, marched to Versailles, where they invaded the National Assembly. The king capitulated, and accepted the measures. Under pressure from the protestors, on the 6th October, the king and the National Assembly moved to Paris, and the anarchy and disorder of the 'October days' followed. Through the winter of 1789 to 1790 most of the clergy deputies stayed at the National Assembly, hoping to act as voices of moderation, but the once inviolable religious framework of France was being dismantled around them. In February all monasteries and convents, except those dedicated to educational and charitable work, were dissolved, and two months later a proposal that Roman Catholicism be declared the religion of the state, with the exclusive right of public worship, was defeated. To some this was 'national apostasy'. The Gallican church, a cornerstone of the ancien régime, had lost its privileged status, and most of its finance. Soon its very existence was to be threatened.

THE CIVIL CONSTITUTION OF THE CLERGY

In the celebrations of the anniversary of French revolution on 14th July 1790 the clergy took a prominent role, saying masses and preaching sermons, but the moment of national consensus in the new France was not to last. The mood of the Assembly was turning decisively against the Roman Catholic Church. By April 1790 it had voted to dispossess the clergy of their property, and in the summer of 1790, a plan was drawn up by a committee of the National Assembly to fundamentally restructure the church. Although it could make representations to the lay politicians of the Assembly, the church had no veto over decisions relating to its own affairs.

Under the plan, the boundaries of the dioceses were redrawn to mirror the 83 new *départements*, each of which was to have a bishop (a severe reduction from the previous 140), and the post of archbishop abolished. Parish size was to be rationalised; clergy promotion was to be based on merit and experience, and patronage was to be abolished. Priests were to be elected locally, and paid a salary of 1200 livres (an increase on the 700 livres of the old *congrué*): as Mirabeau declared, now 'religion belonged to everyone'.[8] Roman Catholic doctrine was to be retained, and communion maintained with the pope, but he had no say in the reforms, a decisive blow against his influence over the Roman Catholic Church. France's place as the 'eldest daughter of the church', was no longer assured.

Louis XVI, long used to power and prestige in the church, was plainly embarrassed by the plan for the Civil Constitution of the Clergy, but fearing the loss of his crown felt forced into accepting it. The dilemma for the existing Roman Catholic clergy was even greater, for the measure included a requirement that the clergy should swear an oath to the nation, the law, the king, and

8   Quoted in N. Aston, *French Revolution*, 142.

Decree on the Civil Constitution of the Clergy, 12 July 1790

TITLE 1   *On ecclesiastical duties*
Article 1. Each department will be comprised of one diocese only, and each diocese will have the same area and the same boundaries as the department… Article 5. All churches and parishes in France, and all French citizens, are forbidden from recognising, in any case and under any pretext whatever, the authority of a … bishop whose see is established under the domination of a foreign power… all of this without prejudice to the unity of the faith and the communion that will be maintained with the visible head of the universal Church…

TITLE 2   *Nomination to ecclesiastical positions*
Article 1. Counting from the day of publication of the present decree, only one manner of filling bishoprics and cures will be known, that is through elections. Article 2. All elections will be conducted by ballot and absolute plurality of votes. Article 21. Before the consecration ceremony begins, the elected bishop will, in the presence of the municipal officers, the people and the clergy, make the solemn promise to watch with care over the faithful of the diocese that is entrusted to him, to be faithful to the nation, to the law and to the king, and to maintain to the best of his power the Constitution decreed by the National Assembly, and accepted by the king…[1]

1   Source: *Archives parlementaires,* 12 July 1790, pp. 55-60, in Dwyer and McPhee (eds), *The French Revolution and Napoleon,* pp. 45-47.

'the Constitution decreed by the National Assembly'; those who failed to do so were deprived of their salary, pension, and rights as French citizens. The requirement inextricably linked church reform to loyalty to the new political order, especially the national assembly. In January 1791, the clerical deputies to the assembly were summoned individually to take the oath: about two-thirds of the clerical deputies, together with forty-four bishops, refused. These non-jurors chose the loss of their livelihood, and a pension of only 500 livres. Even those who accepted the need for reform could not accept the measure, insisting that the state could not legislate for the reform of the church without its consent. The requirement of the oath drove a wedge between the church and the revolution, and alienated the majority of the clergy: the choice appeared to be 'pro-Revolution' or 'pro-Catholic'.

If the National Assembly believed that the transition between the old church and the new Constitutional Church would be seamless, they were much mistaken. The elections for the new clergy were unsatisfactory in places; not all who voted were faithful Roman Catholics—some mockingly cast votes for the devil. The newly elected clergy received a mixed response: some were incompetent, others heroic; some were stoned by hostile congregations, others agreed that non-juring clergy could work alongside them. In reality two churches were created—a Constitutional one, and a refractory one. Although evidence suggests some were willing to attend the services of both, it became increasingly dangerous to attend worship conducted by refractory priests.

The Constitutional Church was a child of both the revolution and the enlightenment. Its supporters believed that the gospel and the Declaration of the Rights of Man could co-exist. God was preached as the 'God of liberty, tolerance, and fraternity'; the hand of God was to be seen in the revolution. Exactly how many churchgoers attended the new Constitutional Church is uncertain, but perhaps a little over 50% became adherents. Roman Catholicism in partnership with the progressive political cause, Tridentine and Enlightenment influences, seems an unlikely combination, but it was an attempt at post-1789 contextualised spirituality. Some dreamed of a return to primitive Christian piety, shorn of papal interference and vested hierarchical interests. Its clergy were to be citizen-priests in the heart of the community. However, although freed of ties to the monarchy and the papacy, the church was now wedded to the revolutionary state: its clergy were public officials bound by oath to the state, and to preach public virtues.

To the adherents of the 'refractory' church of those who had refused the oath, such pollution was abhorrent. Opposition to the new clergy and bishops could be intense—services were noisily interrupted, effigies of Constitutional clergy burned, some priests were stoned. Protests were often led by women. In some areas it was so intense that churches lay empty. The refractory bishop of Limoges declared of the Constitutional clergy: 'The sinners they absolve will not be absolved... the marriages they bless will not be blessed and will count as nothing in the eyes of religion'.[9]

In all around 18,000 clergy, some 52–55% of the total, chose the non-juring path and became refractories. It was a conscientious stand that cost them their parishes, their ministry, their income, and often their liberty. It was a radical stance for those who were inherently conservative. In August 1792, the National Assembly gave all non-juring priests two weeks to leave France; those who refused were to be deported to French Guyana; any who returned would face ten years of detention. Many of the refractory clergy fled over the borders, others continued their ministries in secrecy in abandoned churches, or barns or homes. Some hid in the same caves in which the Protestants they had previously persecuted had once taken refuge. The refractory church responded in various ways theologically to its plight: some saw it as a call to repentance; others willingly embraced suffering, or viewed events in apocalyptic terms.

9   Quoted in Aston, *French Revolution*, 223.

For Protestants and Jews, some of whom had taken part in the Estates-General, the revolution brought early benefits. A law of 1790 brought compensation for those who had been forced to flee abroad, or lose property. For French Jews, the Declaration of the Rights of Man was a means by which they could call for the freedoms they had for so long been denied. In 1790 the National Assembly abolished the requirement that the Jews wear the yellow hat, and in September 1791, Jews were granted equality as citizens.

In April 1791, Pope Pius VI, who had already condemned the Declaration of the Rights of Man, published his denunciation of the Civil Constitution of the Clergy. He declared that the required oath of allegiance overthrew 'absolutely the authority of the Church and annihilates all its rights.' In the pope's view, the Constitutional Church was a 'secular sect', its bishops and priests 'usurpers'. He drew a line between faithful Roman Catholics and the new church, calling on the faithful to ensure that there was, 'nothing in common between you and them, especially in divine matters'. He added the solemn warning: 'no-one can be in the Church of Christ unless he is unified with the visible head of the Church itself and is strengthened in the cathedral of Peter'.[10] The publication of the pope's views was fraught with danger for the Gallican church. Up to 10% of the clergy who had taken the new oath retracted their consent. Amongst the revolutionaries, hostility towards the refractory church intensified. The close link between the church and the crown meant that the refractories were increasingly considered counter-revolutionaries, and associated with the king as enemies of the new state.

For Louis XVI, the skies were rapidly darkening. The Estates General he had convened to offer him advice was now a sovereign parliament that had sharply limited his powers. When in April 1791, he tried to attend a service held by a non-juror priest, his way was blocked by crowds. His relatives began to slip over the borders to safety. In June, Louis, his wife Marie-Antoinette, and their children, made the fateful decision to follow their example. He was captured en route, and was returned to Paris under guard, his days now numbered. As South and South East France descended into turmoil, the clergy were seen as instigators of opposition to the new order by the newly formed Legislative Assembly. Far less tolerant of opposition to the Civil Constitution of the Clergy, in November 1791 the Assembly declared that non-jurors had just 8 days to take the oath, or they would be 'suspected of sedition', and removed from their homes.

Nonetheless, in 1791 France was still officially a Christian state, with a Constitutional Church, Roman Catholic in form, operating as the religious arm of the new order and proclaiming its new legislation from their pulpits. Yet, within three years of its origin, the Constitutional Church itself had been

---

10   Papal Bull, *Charitas*, 13 April, 1791, in Augustin Theiner, *Documents inédits relatifs aux affaires religieuses de la France*, Paris, 1857, 75, 85, 88, in P.G. Dwyer and P. McPhee (eds), *The French Revolution and Napoleon*, Routledge, London, 2002, 49–50.

disowned by the very state which had created it. In all it lasted just ten years, caught between the compromise necessary in its creation, the opposition of the refractory clergy, and the increasingly radical agenda of the revolutionaries. Chilling and brutal events were to follow swiftly.

THE STORM BREAKS—DE-CHRISTIANISATION

The major source of opposition to revolutionary events was believed to come from outside France, particularly Austria supported by the papacy, in alliance with the internal forces of the ancien régime, including the refractory church. In April 1792, war was declared against Austria. Now non-juring clergy were clearly seen as potential fifth-columnists, and faced deportation, ten years in prison, or worse—on Bastille Day 1792, a refractory priest was seized in Bordeaux, and beheaded. Before long, hatred of non-juring clergy had become hatred of Roman Catholicism as a whole: by the end of August priest hunts had started.

On 2nd September 1792, word reached Paris that the fortress of Verdun, just 250 km away, had fallen to the Prussians. As waves of volunteers left the capital to join the war, panic spread fears that those deemed 'counter-revolutionaries' would break out of the prisons where they were detained and welcome the invaders. Hastily convened popular courts sentenced to death some 1,200 out of the 2,700 prisoners brought before them; many were horribly butchered by mobs. Some 240 were priests, together with three bishops, who had failed to leave France as required. That month the Roman Catholic monarchy was abolished, and the Republic founded. The king was sent to the guillotine on 21 January 1793: his last confession made to a non-juring Roman Catholic priest.

In 1792, the commune in Paris attempted to close the churches on Christmas Eve, although pressure from the laity forced the services to go ahead. In 1793, hostility was renewed, and by the end of that year Christianity as a whole had been equated with opposition to the revolution. The changed policy came in part from philosophical motives—'fanaticism and religious superstition' were to be removed from the soil of liberty. More significantly, as with many waves of persecution from the earliest days of Christianity, it was the fruit of a nation externally threatened, seeking internally to keep control of the minds of people. The resistance of the papacy, and the Gallican church, to earlier measures for reform had placed them in the camp of opposition to the revolution.

In the American Revolution the state had declared itself neutral towards every religious denomination, whilst maintaining that freedom of religious worship was one of the 'rights' of Man. In France, the Jacobin view that all clergy were suspect gained ground, and that Christianity should be exterminated in the name of revolutionary humanism. An attempt was made to overturn a Christian nation in the name of rationalism. Although the de-christianisation policy was conducted by a minority, and did not last long, a powerful blow had been struck against the seeming inviolability of the church. It was a chilling foretaste of what was later to come elsewhere in the twentieth century, when again Christians were to face persecution by totalitarian regimes which sought to deny to people the right to autonomous personal thought or religious life.

In April 1793 a Committee of Public Safety began to encourage attacks on manifestations of traditional Roman Catholic Christianity—the crucifix, icons, images of Christ, the cross: church lands and buildings were confiscated and desecrated. The aim was to rid the nation of Roman Catholic religious practice, and liberate the Republic from the 'yoke of theocracy'. 1,400 streets were renamed to eliminate all references to kings or saints. Even the very framework of time was to be reshaped in the name of revolution. In October the Gregorian calendar was abolished, and replaced with a new calendar. It included a ten-day week, with Sunday replaced by the tenth day or 'décadi', and new names given to the months; it was enforced by law. Harvesters who stopped work on a Sunday in Toulouse were arrested; failure to keep the tenth-day could lead to individuals being denied bread, flour, or grain supplies. Although it was claimed that the ten day week would be more efficient, it was not a success; farm production fell, and some workers took both Sunday and the 'décadi' off. The leaders of the revolution believed that Reason had dethroned the Created order: the new calendar was dated, not from the birth of Christ, but from 22 September 1792, the day of the first proclamation of the French Republic. Education was taken from the church and placed in the hands of the state: children were to be trained to be citizens of the republic. The teaching of Christianity in schools was banned, replaced by 'la morale républicaine', inculcating a few cardinal beliefs neutral in religious tradition—belief in God, the immortality of the soul, and humanity. The wording on the civic cemetery in Paris was changed to the bleak 'Death is an eternal sleep'.

Responsibility for registration of births, marriages and deaths was taken from the church. The religious ceremony of marriage was replaced by 'rational' civil ceremonies of marriage and divorce. Sexuality was celebrated, and liberated; vows of abstinence abhorred as selfishness. Through a mixture of ridicule, intimidation and violence, people were encouraged to renounce the faith. Everything was done to get priests to break their vocation: by August 1794 around 20,000 had married or resigned. In September 1794, the state stopped paying clergy salaries. Of 85 Constitutional bishops, 23 renounced the faith; in Paris 27% of priests abdicated: in other areas the number reached 70%. Some clergy joined the revolt against the Jacobins: its failure led to further mass imprisonments and executions of clergy.

The 'Terror' raged through the winter of 1793–94, with an orgy of stabbings, lynchings, drownings, or guillotinings. Those killed included most of the royal family, aristocrats and others deemed enemies of the new regime. In all, two to three thousand clergy were executed, around 2% of their total number. To be a priest, whether refractory or Constitutional, was to be liable to arrest and execution; killings were justified as being in the 'general interest'. Although with significant regional variations, 'the Terror' was a mass crime against the church in the name of the state. By Spring 1794, the policy appeared successful—only 150 of the 40,000 pre-1789 parish churches were still celebrating mass: churches were locked, or turned into temples of reason. Christian worship, if it was to take place, was to be private, or held in secret. Some 40% of the refractory clergy fled from France—to Belgium, Italy, Spain, Portugal, Germany, Britain, and even Russia. Starved of the oxygen of state support, and facing the continued bitter hostility of those who remained faithful to the old Roman Catholic Church, the Constitutional church struggled. This new established church in a revolutionary society was not to succeed.

European alarm grew as Jacobins sought to spread revolutionary ideas across the continent: what had started as a protest against the excesses of the government of the day, had become a movement aiming to revolutionise European society. Christendom, which had prevailed in Europe since the medieval period, was believed to be on the verge of collapse. For French Protestants, persecution for their beliefs was nothing new. They had little fondness for the Bourbon monarchy, and tended to lie low, and keep out of the major power struggles in Paris and the larger towns. Some pastors threw their lot in with the revolutionaries, others could not see the revolution as compatible with the teaching of the Gospels.

During the period of de-christianisation, traditional Christian festivals were replaced by those celebrating attributes such as Genius, Work, and Virtue. A statue of the Goddess Nature was placed on the site of the Bastille, and on 10 November 1793, the 'goddess of Reason' was enthroned in Paris's former Cathedral of Notre Dame. It was hoped that in place of Christianity, a natural religion would emerge, civic, domestic, and patriotic. Maximilien Robespierre, one of the best known of the revolutionary leaders, recognised the danger to public morality if there were no belief system at all. For a short period in 1794, he attempted to introduce his own alternative civic religion– the cult of the Supreme Being. This was a mixture of classical mythology, symbolism, and human reason. In place of traditional Roman Catholic worship were opened Temples to Reason, or Liberty. Although there was professed belief in God, the system was Deist, believing in the immortality of the soul, and the moral goodness of humanity. It was little different from what was believed by the Free Masonic Order. The scheme did not long outlast Roberspierre's overthrow some months later.

The new religious cult attracted little grass-roots support. Man-made moral abstractions had little to offer those facing the harsh realities of revolutionary France. Some women had played a key role as agents of the revolution. Yet, learning from their example, other women took a key role in resisting the de-christianisation policy, by perpetuating the symbols of Roman Catholic piety—

ensuring their children were baptised, and teaching children the rosary and the catechism. They picketed churches to stop their desecrations, and tipped ashes on those who opposed them. Simple domestic piety was a powerful force against state and military opposition.

THE DIRECTORY (1795–99)

By February 1795 the worst of the excesses were over, although the guillotine continued to work steadily, reminding all that nobody was truly safe. Although the Directory, a feeble civilian regime which ruled with the support of the army for the next four years, found France scarcely governable, official religious repression was formally over. The republic and the churches were to co-exist, but worship was limited to designated places, no clerical dress was to be worn, and no confiscated property was returned. Religion was to be a private matter, and churches were to stay out of politics. Non-juring priests and nuns were released from prison, and as long as priests submitted to the laws of the state, they could minister in public without coercion. Easter 1795 saw people flocking back to church, but the buildings in which they met bore the marks of the ravages of the previous years—some looted and burned, others with crosses, pulpits, altars, statues and confessionals destroyed. Some churches had been used as Temples of Reason, others as prisons, grainstores, or military hospitals. Calvaries and statues were restored, Corpus Christi festivals re-instated.

The religious policy of the Directory was uneven—renewed bouts of persecution of refractory priests occurred in 1795 and 1797, followed by the Second Terror of 1797–98, which sought to purge France of royalist sympathisers. Priests returning to their parishes and attempting to restore traditional Tridentine observance found lay religious life had developed a pattern of its own—the rosary had attracted an intense significance. The Constitutional church, shorn of state support, was greatly reduced: by 1795 of 85 dioceses, 44 were vacant. It sought to adapt to changed times, taking the controversial step of allowing mass to be said in French. The formal separation of church and state in 21 February 1795 allowed Protestants to re-open their churches, although later that year they had to endure the 'White Terror' of vengeful Catholics who hunted down any they suspected of support for the Jacobins, and into their net they drew hundreds of Reformed Protestants. The recovery of the Reformed churches from the persecutions of the century was slow. In 1799, only 120 pastors were in active ministry; the figure had been 150 in 1789. A declaration of toleration in 1795 brought easier conditions for the Jews, but they remained scattered, and still faced prejudice and hostility.

Attempts at creating a state sponsored version of religion were not over. One such venture in the period of the Directory was 'theophilanthropy'. Based on a minimum level of religious content, it focussed on God, the immortality of the soul, and the moral goodness of humanity. Imitations of Roman Catholic devotion were retained—with an altar, sermons and saints: it was a religion of common morality based upon universal maxims. Readings from Socrates, Seneca, Confucius, the Koran, and Pascal were offered. Granted the use of ten churches in Paris, it never became the state religion, and never took a place in the heart of the French people. Instead, the Directory placed greater emphasis on replacing traditional religion with moral education.

The rest of Europe looked askance at the wholesale destruction of Christian heritage in France, with its accompanying regicide. Neighbouring countries were flooded with refugees, relating the horrifying story. Nowhere before had the machinery of central government been directed against an overwhelmingly Christian majority. The French church survived the onslaught, but it was never to be the same again: relations between church and state were affected throughout the nineteenth century. There is also evidence that religious zeal was noticeably slackening by the end of the century, especially amongst men.

1799–1804—THE CONSULATE

The revolution left a power vacuum. No pattern of government seemed to fit. The very unstable years of the Directory (1795–99) were replaced by the Consulate (1799–1804) and then the Empire (1804–14), before restored monarchy, republic, and empire all followed in the nineteenth century. Yet, revolution had made France a successful military force of surprising vitality: hostility to outside influence turned it into a nation in arms, a remarkable force of 30 million citizens. Much success was owing to the skill of revolutionary generals. In November 1799, one young revolutionary general, Napoleon Bonaparte, stepped onto the domestic political scene. The 'little corporal' had risen through the ranks of the artillery to become the general leading the revolutionary armies in Italy. He took power through a *coup d'état* in November 1799, and was endorsed as First Consul in a plebiscite the following year. He was later to become Consul for life, and after a further plebiscite in 1804 was granted the title of Emperor. Until his military defeats in 1813–14, he was extremely popular in France. Posing as a representative of the conservative wing of the revolution, Napoleon Bonaparte's advent brought more settled times internally for France, but not for the rest of Europe. An assiduous supporter of the revolution, he was a military and administrative genius. He brought centralised, vigorous, efficient government, a lasting system of public education; he promoted economic prosperity and improved the finances of the state. Napoleon symbolised the transformation from the *ancien régime*—born a commoner, he became more powerful than those born to crowns, with an empire that stretched from Germany to Rome and the Atlantic coasts of Spain and Portugal. From 1805 to 1812 his army appeared irresistible. Only the might of Napoleon could control and channel the energy of the revolution, but under him it changed course, and the ideals of liberty, equality and fraternity were constrained.

The campaigns in which Napoleon had won his spurs had brought him into contact with wider European Roman Catholicism. In 1796–97 he had driven the Austrian armies from Italy, and occupied most of the papal states. In 1798 the French revolutionary armies entered Rome, and proclaimed a French style republic. The pope and his cardinals were forcibly removed: Pius VI was to die in French captivity in 1799. The Directory had proclaimed him the 'Last Pope', but prematurely, for Pius VII was subsequently elected in Venice.

When he became First Consul, and Head of State, Napoleon turned to address the religious needs of France. He realised that the revolution had been weakened by making an enemy of the church, and that it was necessary for the state to come to terms with Christianity. He also saw that the possession of some form of faith was politically advantageous: 'If I had not believed in God, who would have been willing to negotiate with me?'[11] The extent to which Napoleon was a Roman Catholic believer is very much open to question, for he was attracted to the religious approach of Rousseau, and spoke of the 'mystery of religion'. As people returned to Roman Catholic observances after the revolution, he saw no need to seek to dissuade them. As with other revolutionary leaders in America and France, he saw the social utility of religion. Although not all his colleagues in government agreed with his policy, Napoleon sensed that Roman Catholicism retained a hold on the lives and emotions of ordinary people, and that influential, intellectual, opinion, had begun to swing back in its favour in the late 1790s. In 1800 he declared, in a speech to the priests of Milan, that 'Catholicism is the only religion which can procure true happiness for a well-ordered society'. He distanced himself from the forced repression and restructuring of the church, which as a 'simple agent of government' he had been unable to prevent. It was the consummate pragmatism of the politician:—'My policy is to govern as the majority wish to be governed. That is the way, I believe, in which one recognises the sovereignty of the people'.[12] He quickly undid much revolutionary policy, returning church buildings to churches, releasing priests from prison: only the revolutionary calendar survived until 1806.

Napoleon Bonaparte's assumption of power created a dilemma for the Roman Catholic Church. His rule was certainly an improvement on what had gone before, but dealing with him shut the door on prospects for the return of the Roman Catholic monarchy. The election of Pius VII in 1800 brought to Roman Catholicism a pope more willing to concede that democracy and equality could be reconciled with Christianity. Napoleon famously told Cardinal Martiniana, 'Go to Rome and tell the Holy Father that the First Consul wishes to make him

---

11   J. McManners, *The French Revolution and the Church*, Westport, Conn., Greenwood Press, 1969, repr., 1982, 141.

12   Bonaparte's speech to the priests of Milan, 5 June 1800, in Dwyer and McPhee (eds), *The French Revolution and Napoleon*, 142–44; and McManners, *French Revolution and the Church*, 141–42.

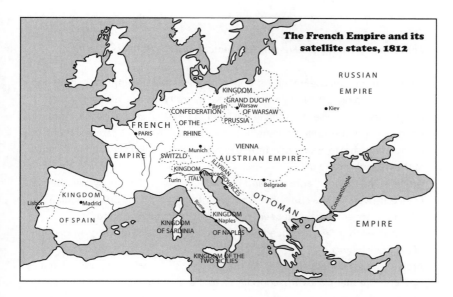

a gift of thirty million Frenchmen',[13] but in the negotiations that followed, the First Consul, with his armies which had overrun much of Italy, held the whip hand. The loss of the papal territories had to be accepted, as had the fact that church property sold off during the revolution would not be returned.

The Concordat drawn up between Napoleon and Pius VII was to govern relations between the papacy and France for the next 100 years, and provide a model for future agreements between the papacy and other world governments. The papacy was granted the leading role in religious matters, and although forced into many concessions, a chance to restore Roman Catholicism in France was won, although only as the religion of 'the great majority of French citizens,' rather than the state religion of France. Bishops were to be selected by the head of state, but 'canonic institution' (authorisation to perform spiritual functions) was to be provided by the pope. The lower clergy were chosen by the bishops from lists of names approved by the government, with the controversial election system abandoned. The link between the church and the Bourbon monarchy was broken: the pope recognised Napoleon as head of state with the same 'rights and prerogatives' of former governments. Bishops were to declare their loyalty to the government of the French Republic, and pray for the Republic and the Consulate, and in return clergy were paid from the public purse.

Napoleon was intent on rewarding the Constitutional Church for its loyalty to the principles of the revolution, even though it was in places now only attended by a handful of worshippers. He insisted that the orders of the Constitutional clergy should be accepted by the pope, with no humiliation or retraction of

13   McManners, *French Revolution*, 143.

The Concordat, 1801
Convention between the French Government and His Holiness Pius VII

The government of the French Republic recognises that the Roman Catholic and apostolic religion is the religion of the great majority of French citizens.

His holiness recognises that this same religion has derived and at this moment again expects the greatest benefit and grandeur from the establishment of Catholic worship in France and from the personal profession which the Consuls of the Republic make of it...

Article 1. The Catholic, apostolic and Roman religion shall be freely exercised in France. Its worship shall be public, and in conformity with the police regulations which the government shall deem necessary for the public tranquillity...

Article 2. The Holy See, in concert with the government, will make a new division of the French diocese.

Article 3. His Holiness declares to the holders of French bishoprics that he expects from them, with firm confidence, for the good of peace and unity, every sacrifice, even of their sees.

Article 6. Before entering upon their functions, the bishops shall directly swear, at the hands of the First Consul, the oath of loyalty...

'I swear and promise to God, upon the holy scriptures, to obey and remain loyal to the government established by the Constitution of the French Republic. I also swear not to have any correspondence, nor to assist by any counsel, nor to support any league, either within or without, which is contrary to the public tranquillity; and if, within my diocese or elsewhere, I learn that anything to the prejudice of the State is going on, I will make it known to the government.'[1]

1   Source: Buchez and Roux, *Histoire parlementaire de la Révolution française,* Vol. 38, pp. 465-70, in Dwyer and McPhee (eds), *The French Revolution and Napoleon,* pp. 149-152.

---

errors being demanded. In consequence, Napoleon and the pope effectively created a new church; Pius negotiated for the French Church over the heads of the French episcopate. It was a huge shift for a body once so proud of its independence. The hierarchies of both refractory and Constitutional churches were removed: bishops from both bodies were to step down. Refractory bishops who refused to resign were deprived of office by the pope.

This re-formed Église de France took elements from both the old Gallican Church and the Constitutional Church. It had ten archbishops, and sixty bishops, with dioceses modelled on the local government boundaries: of these, twelve were former Constitutional bishops. Only about one in ten parishes were given to former Constitutional priests (Napoleon had hoped for one-third), and locally there were some forced re-baptisms and remarriages of those previously conducted in Constitutional churches. France gained a re-united church, legally recognised, and free to worship, with the widespread support of both refractory and Constitutional church camps, but it was not the pre-1789 Gallican Church. In some areas only a quarter of pre-revolution clergy were back in post by 1801, and priests were in short supply (36,000 compared to the 60,000 of 1789). A great work of rebuilding and renewal was required to reverse what had been done in the previous twelve years: even in 1816, 15% of parishes were still vacant. Not all could accept the new arrangements, and the Petite Église was born in 1801 of those who refused to accept the Concordat. This survived through the nineteenth century, maintaining the independent spirit of the pre-1789 Gallican church.

Napoleon proved the saviour of the French Roman Catholic Church, but he donned that mantle for his own purposes. The restored church was socially useful, but subordinated to the rule of the state. Even the pope was used by Napoleon for his own purposes, as a way to lever public opinion: the pope could help him to a religious settlement that would end counter-revolutionary forces. Napoleon retained a close oversight over church matters, and required to be consulted on most policies; bishops were to foster loyalty to him. In 1802 he added to the Concordat the Organic Articles, drawn up without the pope's knowledge or consent, which contained regulations for Roman Catholic ecclesiastical affairs, and bound French clergy to be loyal to the state, but not the monarchy. They also limited the exercise of papal power in France: the 'liberties, franchises and customs of the Gallican church' were to be protected, but 'police regulations' set out laws for the maintenance of 'public tranquillity'. The authority of the French national state over education at all levels was also consolidated by Napoleon. In 1806 he created the *Université de France*, which sought to create a state monopoly of education at all levels, and to prevent the Roman Catholic Church regaining its ascendancy in schooling. The uniform instruction it promoted included the precepts of the Roman Catholic religion.

Conditions for faith communities other than the Roman Catholic Church in France also improved. The 480,000 Calvinists and 200,000 Lutherans were given freedom to worship. These Protestant groupings had proved remarkably resilient in the face of persecution (remaining around 2% of the population), although there had been significant losses, including many wealthy and influential supporters. In a parallel measure to that for the Roman Catholic Church, Protestant Organic Articles were introduced by which the state gained control of the Protestant churches in return for freedom to worship, and even state funding of salaries. The number of churches and ministers was regulated, and state consent required for the doctrines and creed to be taught. Such relative freedoms brought a renewal of life for these long repressed churches, their spirituality infused with pietistic fervour. French Protestantism was later to benefit from *Le Réveil* (The Awakening), which spread from French speaking Switzerland to the Netherlands by 1825.

For the Jews, freedom of worship had to wait until 1808, although Napoleon's military exploits in Egypt and the Middle East, brought a bout of Messianic and apocalyptic speculation. Many Jews in Europe hoped his conquests would permit their return to Palestine. Others wondered what a general, who ate bacon and sausages, had to do with their religious hopes. The state only took on the payment of the salaries of rabbis in 1831.

In 1804 Napoleon created a ministry of religious affairs. Considerable liberties and freedoms were granted at the price of an element of state control, but for the regime to work, it had to be permissive rather than authoritarian. The first holder of the post was a loyal Roman Catholic who helped protect the church from the hostility of anticlerical prefects. A symbiotic relationship between religions and the state was created, and on the whole held, to the advantage of both sides.

Pius VII travelled to Paris to witness Napoleon's coronation as Emperor in December 1804. It was a scene in which he was merely a spectator, for the new Emperor was to place the crown which Pius had previously blessed upon his own head—demonstrating that he yielded authority to none. The popular welcome the pope received from the crowds on his journey to the French capital irritated Napoleon, but helped strengthen the hold of Roman Catholicism and the papacy on the popular mind. However, such gestures of support did not guarantee Pius' security. In 1806, Francis II resigned as Holy Roman Emperor, ending over eight centuries of the role's existence. Napoleon expected the pope to sanction the re-ordering of Europe to reflect his military conquests, but when Pius refused to agree relations broke down. In 1809 the French annexed the Papal States. Pius VII was seized, and held captive: he was not to return to the Vatican until 1814. It was a far cry from the negotiations leading to the Concordat, but even then Pius had negotiated under duress. The pope bore his trials with dignity, and as French officials pushed for a harder line against the church, Roman Catholics looked increasingly in ultra-montane (over the mountains) fashion to Rome for guidance. The tensions intensified when, in an attempt to consolidate his position in Europe as Emperor, Napoleon divorced his first wife Josephine (they had turned their union into a Christian marriage just before the coronation, at the pope's insistence), and married Marie-Louise of Austria, daughter of the Habsburg emperor. Pius VII was reluctant to recognise this marriage, and in response Napoleon forced a new Concordat on the French church, its assaults on traditional Roman Catholicism reminiscent of earlier days in the revolution. The imprisoned pope was forced to sign this in January 1813, but Napoleon's position was rapidly weakening militarily, and

Napoleon Crowns Himself Before the Pope

the new Concordat was only patchily enforced before his abdication as emperor the following year. The papal states were restored to the pope at the Congress of Vienna in 1815.

It took time for the Restored Roman Catholic Church of 1801 to overcome the bitter divisions of the revolution. It was clearly no longer the First Estate of the *ancien régime*: its vast wealth and privileges were gone. Efforts went into improving the seminary education for priests, but the church was ill-equipped to offer an intellectual challenge to Voltaire or Rousseau. Its adherents, particularly women, simply wanted a return to the traditional observances of the church. Many men had been affected by their conscription into the militantly anti-Christian revolutionary army. The social atmosphere of the tavern, so important during the republican era, became more acceptable than attendance at the mass. Attendance became confined to major religious festivals and rites of passage, and even then attendance at Easter communion, and the confessional, become more infrequent. However, Roman Catholicism remained particularly pervasive in the home, where women continued to take a vital role in its maintenance. When Napoleon returned female education to the religious orders, they instilled in girls a lifelong devotion to the Virgin Mary and the rosary, and helped retain the adherence of women to the church. Marian shrines became a focus for popular devotion, and claims of miracles were widely circulated. French Roman Catholicism became increasingly rural, and priests found the need to accommodate themselves to local religious practices, which had taken root during the revolutionary years. These folk practices were allowed to co-exist with traditional Roman Catholicism.

The lasting impact of the French Revolution on adherence to Roman Catholicism in France varied greatly. In some areas of South-Eastern and Central France, together with Paris, the percentage of those who accepted the Civil Constitution of the Clergy was high—touching 100% in places. In Provence and Aquitaine, where anti-clericalism was strong and religious observance was already at a low level by the mid-eighteenth century, the closure of churches, and the imposition of secular ceremonies, was widespread. However, in the West of France, especially Brittany, together with Flanders, the Massif Central, Flanders and the Payes Basque, Roman Catholicism remained strong. Here priests stubbornly resisted the radical advances and the creation of a civic religion, and enjoyed strong support from the laity. The differences were not just between regions, but also within localities. Post-revolution Roman Catholicism was strongest in rural areas, amongst women, older people, with a group of elite noble families retaining a dominant role. If there were already two Frances religiously before 1789, the revolution drove an even firmer wedge between the two.

Many found it hard to forget the cruel persecutions of the church in the name of national unity. Only after 1815 did Roman Catholicism attain new vigour, but it was of an ultramontane variety. Although many flocked back to monasteries and convents (there were 12,500 nuns in 1814, and 25,000 in 1830), no radical injection of spiritual energy was to follow. The revolution brought a break between the government and personal beliefs and values. If the values of individuals were in the way of government, the individuals were to be removed: even under Napoleon, the state had a say in private beliefs. In America, religion had no part in the laws of the nation, but grew rapidly in significance in the hearts of its citizens. In France the church's position had eventually been confirmed, but its hold over hearts and minds had begun to waver.

CONCLUSIONS

Borne out of impending financial disaster for the nation, grinding poverty for the peasantry, and lack of political rights, through the French Revolution fundamental human rights were declared, and in its aftermath the standard of living for the poorest improved. Between 1789 and 1830, France was effectively dragged from the middle ages to the modern era. Every individual was affected, male, female, soldier or civilian, clergy or lay person, Jacobin or royalist. Social, economic and political causes for the revolution must be given their due place, but the *philosophes* offered a rationale for change. The revolution demonstrated the enlightenment conviction that humans are responsible for their own destiny, and should have a chance to achieve it. Yet, enlightenment ideals were tempered by the horrors of revolution and war; many had faced a stark choice between the Revolution and Christianity, sometimes on the pain of death. The collapse of the monarchy brought an end to the idea of rule by divine right. When, in 1815, the monarchy was restored it was a constitutional monarchy, but with the rights of 1789 confirmed. The king only ruled through the law, and such rule required the consent of the people, or the military.

In the decades between 1789 and 1804 every aspect of traditional religious life was also subject to change. For a period Christianity had to operate as a persecuted and struggling minority religion, and even as an underground movement. The Gallican church was brutally divested of its wealth, power, and influence. Its survival was testimony to the force of popular, lay belief; in homes and local communities. It was especially Roman Catholic women who operated as a vital counter-revolutionary force, maintaining traditional beliefs. Nationally, the church was shunted from being a partner with the state, to a subordinate position: religion began to be moved from the public to the private sphere. Seeds of doubt were sown. Male religious adherence began to decline after the revolution, and the thinking of the *philosophes* gained increasing ground amongst the intelligentsia. By the 1790s, a significant number of the middle class in French cities were Voltairians, prefiguring the spread of secularism in other cities in the nineteenth century.

The revolutionary watchwords 'liberty, equality, fraternity' were to echo across Europe. They were words filled with tremendous potential, but also fraught with danger: the nineteenth century was to be profoundly shaped by their resonance.

FURTHER READING

N. Aston, *Religion and Revolution in France, 1780–1804*, Macmillan, Basingstoke, 2000.

N. Aston, *Christianity and Revolutionary Europe, 1750–1830*, Cambridge, CUP, 2002.

E. Duffy, *Saints and Sinners: A History of the Popes*, New Haven, Yale University Press, 1997.

G. Dwyer and Peter McPhee (eds), *The French Revolution and Napoleon*, Routledge, London, 2002, 26–28.

C.T. McIntire, 'Changing Religious Establishments and Religious Liberty in France, 1787–1879', in R. Helmstadter, ed, *Freedom and Religion in the Nineteenth Century*, Stanford, California, Stanford University Press, 1997.

J. McManners, *Church and Society in Eighteenth-Century France: Volume 1*, Oxford, Clarendon, 1998.

J. McManners, *Church and Society in Eighteenth-Century France: Volume 2*, Oxford, Clarendon, 1998.

J. McManners, *The French Revolution and the Church*, London, SPCK, 1969.

A. Vidler, *The Church in an Age of Revolution*, Penguin, Harmondsworth, 1974.

W.R. Ward, *Christianity Under the Ancien Régime 1648–1789*, Cambridge, Cambridge University Press, 1999.

3

Churches and the Industrial Revolution
Britain: 1780s-1820s

O bservers in Britain watched proceedings in America and France with a keen eye. In America they witnessed not only defeat of the British army, but also a collapse in the exercise of sovereign authority by the established powers. Events in France in 1789 shook the establishment not only in Britain, but *ancien régimes* across Europe. To Edmund Burke, the great principle of liberty was being disgraced: 'what is liberty without wisdom, and without virtue? It is the greatest of all possible evils; for it is folly, vice, and madness, without tuition or restraint'.[1] The Church of England was the most alarmed: its clergy lined up to denounce the spirit of democracy, and the blasphemous character of the revolutionary movement. Preaching in Plymouth in December 1792, in the wake of the massacres in Paris, the Anglican Robert Hawker announced his text, as Proverbs 24:25, 'My son, fear thou the Lord and king, and meddle not with them that are given to change'. His sermon against political revolution 'attempted by tumult and clamour' was not untypical, although he added, he 'was not unmindful of the poor'.[2]

Yet not all regarded events in France with horror. For many the fall of the Bastille in July 1789 portended the downfall of feudal despotism and absolutism, the dawn of a new and better age. They hoped that civil and political equality, free of dependence on social or religious distinction, would follow. Many Dissenters in Britain, who keenly felt the oppressive hand of a state church which merely tolerated their existence, greeted the early phase of the revolution

---

1 E. Burke, *Reflections on the Revolution in France*, (1790), Harmondsworth, Penguin, 1969, 373.

2 R. Hawker. Sermon on 27 December 1792 before the 'Lodge of Unity', in J. Williams, *Memoirs of the Life and Writings of the Rev. Robert Hawker, D.D.*, London, 1831, 35–37.

positively. 1789 appeared a Gallic equivalent of the revolution of 1688: they watched with approval as an oppressive Established church, this one Roman Catholic, fell away, and as political equality was given to non-Roman Catholics. The Baptist Robert Hall rejoiced that an empire of darkness and despotism had been 'smitten with a stroke which sounded through the universe': full of hope he penned his work 'Christianity Consistent With a Love of Freedom'.[3] Such early optimism was later to prove an embarrassment as the French Revolution changed its course, persecution was directed at the church, and Europe was plunged into decades of war. Hall drew back from his advocacy of civil and religious liberty, fearing the loss of energy and sanctity to the Christian ministry that would ensue from engaging in political debate.

Nonetheless, by the time Napoleon was deposed and exiled, movements for reform and the recognition of individual rights, were gaining a momentum across Europe that was to prove unstoppable. Despite the inevitable, and often harsh, conservative reaction against such change, it became clear that the relationship between church and society, and the concept of Christendom, would have to change. Religious establishments, and their long cherished ideologies and practices, could not go on as they were. The days of confessional religious settlements, in which the religion of the populace was decided by social and political elites, were numbered. Voluntarist sentiment was abroad: freedom to make conscientious choices was high on the agenda. This eventually included the choice not only to change one's religion, but also to abandon religious profession completely. Denominations were moving into uncharted territory.

BRITAIN AND REVOLUTION

That Britain did not have a revolution in the late eighteenth century may appear surprising. On occasions some believed it very close, and that the authorities had every right to fear social explosion. In 1807 the poet and social commentator Thomas Southey wrote 'revolution in England inevitably must come, and in its most fearful shape'.[4] Yet, the political example of France was not followed, and the reasons for this are complex. In the range of factors, the role of the churches cannot be ignored. Whether Christianity, and in particular Methodist evangelicalism, saved England from revolution and created an environment of social and political stability is a question that has intrigued historians. The classic statement of this theory is that of Elie Halévy, in his work *England in 1815*.[5] If the Halévy hypothesis is correct, it would indicate that religion, in the form of the eighteenth-century evangelical revival, could be productive of the most profound of social and political consequences.

---

3   R. Hall, *Works of Robert Hall, Vol. 1*, London, 1839, Memoir by Dr Gregory, 38–41.

4   R. Southey, *Letters from Spain*, 1807, (ed. J. Simons), London, 1951, 375.

5   E. Halévy, *England in 1815*, 2nd Revised English Edition, London, 1949.

The Halévy Hypothesis

'Why was it that of all the countries of Europe England has been the most free from revolutions, violent crises and sudden changes? We have sought in vain to find the explanation by an analysis of her political institutions and economic organization. Her political institutions were such that society might easily have lapsed into anarchy had there existed in England a bourgeoisie animated by the spirit of revolution. And a system of economic production that was in fact totally without organization of any kind would have plunged the kingdom into violent revolution had the working classes found in the middle class leaders.... a definite ideal, a creed, a practical programme. But the *élite* of the working class, the hard-working and capable bourgeois, had been imbued by the evangelical movement with a spirit from which the established order had nothing to fear'.[1]

1   E. Halévy, *England in 1815*, Second Revised English Edition, London, 1949, 424–5.

Halévy asserted that the Evangelical Revival developed in the context of economic crisis. The distressed proletariat, suffering economically and socially, could easily have vented their frustrations in revolutionary fervour, especially in a nation with a potentially volatile level of political, economic and religious freedom. However, their distress was of a malleable form, and the forces of anarchy and social revolution were moderated and re-directed by the influence of the Evangelical Revival. The antidote to revolutionary Jacobinism was therefore Methodism, assisted by the free organisation of sects permitted in England. Although committed to the radical evangelical message of repentance and the new birth, the early Methodists were socially conservative, emphasising biblical teaching on obedience to rulers and authorities. John Wesley's evangelicalism, with its seriousness about the centrality of scripture, including its teachings on passive obedience to authorities appointed by God, was crucial.

Working-class Methodists shared Wesley's views because they shared his biblical conservatism, his emphasis on the immediate urgency of soul-winning, the comforts of the believer after death, and on the importance of care for the poor. Radical social or political restructuring was no part of Wesley's agenda, or of his immediate successors. As France descended into chaos, the Wesleyan Conference in 1792 warned that no-one should 'speak lightly or irreverently of the Government;' Methodists were to 'observe the oracles of God' which commanded Christians 'to be subject to the highest powers; and that honour to the King is connected with the fear of God'. Halévy argued that efforts that might have been directed towards challenging oppressive conditions were re-channelled into efforts for personal spiritual experience and transformation.[6]

6   E. Halevy, *England in 1815*, 427.

Others have followed Halévy in arguing that Methodism was a negative force, placing limits on necessary and legitimate class conflict. It bred saints, not citizens, and did not call for the violent redress of injustice.[7] It was therefore especially influential as a force of social control on the lower working classes—the classic 'opium of the masses'. Although the historian E.P. Thompson recognised that the 80,000 Methodists of 1791 would not have in themselves been sufficient to stem the tide of revolution, he still argued that Methodism was a politically stabilising, or regressive, influence. Religious revivalism became the channel for disaffection and hopelessness. When political radicalism was at the point of defeat: 'Energies and emotions which were dangerous to the social order... were released in the harmless form of sporadic love-feasts, watch-nights, band-meetings or revivalist campaigns'. To Thompson, Methodism was, between 1790 and 1830, the 'chiliasm of despair.' In compensation for the lack of improvements on the social front, Methodists directed their longings towards the return of Christ. Sunday Schools proved strong forces for the cultural indoctrination of the lower orders with the values of the higher. Through them the working classes were rendered a disciplined, obedient, willing, workforce suited to the needs of capitalist businessmen, some of whom sponsored the schools.[8]

Some have modified Halévy's approach, arguing that Methodist doctrine was largely a progressive ideology, a religious embodiment of enlightenment liberalism, through which many of the egalitarian and libertarian aspirations of the French Revolution could find an outlet. Wesley promoted religious toleration, opposed persecution, violence, and slavery, and held the Arminian view that the atonement of Christ was general in its scope, which left salvation open to all who strove to attain it. These factors rendered Methodism a democratic social and spiritual revolution, in which people had individual liberty to decide their own spiritual destiny, and proved an important component in the transition from a traditional to a modern society. The Methodist system allowed for lay preachers, class leaders from the labouring orders, and even for a short period, women preachers, all tangible expressions of the ideals of liberty and equality. Ultimately, however, the real revolution was a personal one: evangelical conversion was believed to change lives, bringing decency, frugality and industry where previously these had been absent.[9]

The view that popular evangelicalism made English society less violent, and more ordered and disciplined than would otherwise have been the case, has some merits, but there remain significant weaknesses to Halevy's hypothesis, and its later variants. One obvious reason for a lack of revolution in Britain

---

7   J. L. and B. Hammond, *The Town Labourer*, London, 1920, 268–282.

8   E. P. Thompson, *The Making of the English Working Class*, New York, Gollancz, 1980, 412–419.

9   See B. Semmel, *The Methodist Revolution*, London, Heinemann, 1973.

in the late eighteenth century was that two had already occurred in the seventeenth century, in both of which religion had taken a prominent role. They left the monarchy with its powers progressively reduced, only able to rule with the consent of parliament and people. These political readjustments brought a stability which meant that England's *ancien régime* was never again sufficiently weak or insecure for revolution to be probable. Nor was Methodism, with, in 1811, only some 110,000 members out of a population of 10 million, ever of sufficient size and influence to have decisive importance in the outcome of wider political developments. Britain had a stable and growing middle class from the late eighteenth century onwards, and the establishment remained sufficiently flexible to concede some elements of power when serious pressure for change built up. In contrast to Halévy's assertions, social unrest was often greatest in areas where Methodism was also strongest. The start of some revivals appears to have preceded the political setbacks that Thompson says aided recruitment, rather than following them.

Methodism was the outcome of a radical religious dynamic in the nation, rather than a political one. Its radicalism was expressed through an eclectic array of causes such as itinerant preaching, campaigning for the abolition of slavery, and opposition to Roman Catholic emancipation. Within Methodism itself there was an internal dynamic of radicalism of such strength that it was eventually riven by schism, all of which absorbed energies that might have been directed elsewhere. Indeed, rather than being an antidote to radicalism, Methodism itself was viewed by the establishment itself as a radical threat. The activities of non-ordained preachers, with little or no theological education, regularly fell under the suspicions of local magistrates, who sought to curtail their activity by a variety of legal means: exuberant preaching could look all too much like rabble rousing. In 1811 Lord Sidmouth sought, through Parliament, to restrict the activity of itinerant preachers, fearing their potential to spread sedition, or undermine the religious establishment. In the face of protests, the measure was dropped, but in the febrile post-1789 atmosphere, such alarms were never far away, and the Methodist leadership duly made expressions of loyalty and obedience out of an instinct of self-preservation.

Historians generally remain unconvinced by Halévy's analysis. Evangelicalism may certainly have played a role as a force for social stability, and the similarity between the world-view of the working classes and the middle classes owed something to this. The experience of revival can also produce social solidarity and reduce social tensions; evangelical Christians did seek to be a 'leavening' force in society, and their work was a means of extending humanitarian care. However, evangelicalism was too dynamic and socially diverse to support simple theories about social and political outcomes. In its ranks were artisans and labourers, members of the middle class, together with wealthy industrialists and aristocrats. Halévy's thesis raises significant issues, but fails as a single cause explanation for the absence of revolution in Britain, which was far more stable than France in the eighteenth century.[10]

THE 'INDUSTRIAL REVOLUTION'

Whilst no violent political earthquake rocked Britain, revolutionary change of a different order was taking place, but it unfolded gradually and often unremarkably. Since Arnold Toynbee's use of the phrase, this period of social and economic change during the late eighteenth and early nineteenth century has been known as the 'Industrial Revolution', although scholars have questioned the appropriateness of the term. Certainly it was a process rather than a single event, but by the 1820s economic change had become irreversible, and by 1850 the results were as momentous as those of the Bastille in 1789. It was a movement that absorbed many radical frustrations: a 'self-made man' could progress from rags to riches in one generation, and through newly acquired wealth, break through barriers of privilege and vested interest.

Economic change accelerated during the eighteenth century. Agriculture, industry, transport, were all transformed; the population became increasingly urban. Labour began to shift from the land to industry. In attics, upstairs rooms, cellars, and sheds, agricultural incomes were supplemented by small-scale domestic industry. Better industrial organisation led to economies of scale, which, coupled with technological breakthrough, brought significant rises in productivity. Manufacturing output accelerated rapidly after 1750. Similar trends were to follow in the eastern United States and France in the 1830s, and then Germany, where dramatic economic growth was experienced later in the century. In 1780, 25% of Britain's population were engaged in manufacturing, mining, and building; by 1851 this was 42%. The cotton industry led the way in industrial production, but iron and woollen textiles were not far behind. The rate of growth in industrial production accelerated from 22% in the decade after 1800, to 47.2% in the 1820s. Agricultural production increased by 40% during the eighteenth century, helping to feed the growing industrially-employed population, which was increasingly centred in urban areas. A transport revolution was also under way. Improvements in road construction reduced travel times, and assisted the transport of agricultural goods to urban areas. It took four days to travel from London to Shrewsbury in 1753; one and a half days in 1772; and in 1835 a little over 12 hours. By the late eighteenth century a network of inland waterways crossed Britain, facilitating the transport of raw materials, building materials, and heavy finished products. In the eighteenth

---

10   See J. Walsh, 'Elie Halévy and the Birth of Methodism', *Transactions of the Royal Historical Society*, 5th Series, 25, 1975; D. Hempton, *Methodism and Politics in British Society 1750–1850*, London, Hutchinson, 1987.

century steam power had been used to pump water, but in 1804 Richard Trevithick developed a steam locomotive capable of pulling wagons along nine miles of railway in Wales. Others perfected what Trevithick had pioneered—in 1829 George Stephenson's 'Rocket' attained the dizzying speed of 35 miles per hour. The development of the steam railway brought faster, and more flexible, transport. When applied to water transport, the impact of the new technology of steam was also dramatic—by 1819 paddle steamers were crossing the Atlantic. The world was becoming a smaller place.

The British population rose rapidly, from 10.5 million in 1801, to 20.8 million in 1851, with a further doubling by 1911. A rapidly growing population was also an increasingly young population; 49% were aged under 19 in 1821. The full scale of the urban revolution only became clear during the nineteenth century, but by the late eighteenth century it was well under way. In 1801 around a third of people were classed as 'urban': London had over 1 million inhabitants, and was twice the size of Paris. By 1851 the 'Age of Equipoise' between town and country was passed, with the decennial census revealing 54% of Britain's population was urban. The rate of urban growth was twice that found in any other European country. Manchester was a market town of 17,000 in 1760, and industrial city of 180,000 in 1830. Bradford's population rose by 65.5% between 1821 and 1831. With industrialisation came the creation of a working class, to which some 64% of Manchester's population belonged by 1836, and over 90% in smaller surrounding industrial settlements. Nonetheless, even in 1838, less than half a million out of a labour force of seven million worked in factories.

Whether industrialisation brought improved standards of living is much debated. Wages in general followed an upward trend between 1790 and 1850, prices were stable or falling after 1815, and employment became more stable, although it may have involved working 12 hours or more in a hot cotton factory, the air filled with choking dust. One witness to a Parliamentary enquiry in 1834 declared, 'no man would like to work in a power loom shed ... there is such a clattering and noise it would almost make someone mad'.[11] The dirt and darkness, in which women and children worked alongside men, was notorious. Returning home each evening to a crowded, and unsanitary, home was for many an unhealthy and depressing existence. Some children suffered horrific accidents at work, or succumbed to diseases brought on by poor working conditions. Only after the mid 1840s can sustained improvements in standards of living be clearly demonstrated. Benefits did come, but they tended to be in the long term: certainly by 1850, the population were taller, and healthier, than they were in 1750—whether they were happier is more open to debate.

The system of welfare support, known as the Poor Law, which had been in

---

11   'Evidence to Select Committee on Handloom Weavers, 1834', *Parliamentary Papers*, 1834 [556], X, 432.

existence since the sixteenth century, was ill adapted to the social dislocation of the new industrial age. Its cost rose, placing a heavy burden on local rates. Harsher attitudes towards the poor became evident. Fears rose that indiscriminate relief was creating a class of paupers perpetually dependent on the state. The Rev. Thomas Malthus in his *Essay on the Principle of Population* (1798) set out what he saw as God-given laws of population, in which a series of checks (of which moral restraint was one of the chief) would operate to stop numbers rising beyond increases in the food supply. Intervention to support the incomes of the poor only interfered with this system. The economic theories of the Deist, Adam Smith, stressed the importance of free trade and minimal government interference in economic life.

Political reform was held back by the fearful and repressive reaction to the French Revolution. Between 1815 and 1820 social and political tensions increased during the economic hardship in the aftermath of the Napoleonic Wars. Calls for reform became emphatic. Change, when it arrived with the Reform Act of 1832, proved a very moderate concession. Around one in five Englishmen, mainly from the middle class, obtained the vote, one in eight in Scotland and one in twenty in Ireland—a 50% increase on previous levels, but it was not widespread democracy.

RELIGIOUS LIFE IN THE INDUSTRIAL REVOLUTION

The frontiers of economic growth were the English Midlands, Lancashire, the West Riding of Yorkshire, South Wales, and Lanarkshire. Areas of wealth creation were often on the margins of traditional authority structures. As traditional social structures began to break down, the new order presented major challenges for churches within the establishment, but for those organised on a freer, voluntary basis, it offered huge potential. The Act of Union with Ireland in 1801 created a United Episcopal Church that embraced England, Wales, and Ireland. Scotland's establishment had been finally determined in 1690 as Presbyterian, a settlement which the Act of Union of 1707 affirmed. By 1801 the United Kingdom was a semi-confessional Protestant state in which subjects were expected to conform to the worship and discipline of the established church of the kingdom in which they resided. Each square mile was part of the parish system of the established churches, through which baptisms, marriages and burials, were administered, and which was the locus of most educational and social relief. Religious dissent was tolerated, but not granted absolute liberty.

Beneath this ordered surface, all was not well. Lay patronage was restored to the Church of Scotland in 1712, and in consequence disputes over appointment of ministers and the control of local churches could be bitter. In England, Wales and Scotland, the richest livings fell into the hands of the sons of the gentry and the privileged. The eighteenth century saw a widespread, tepid latitudinarianism, in which Deism made inroads. Theology was reduced to arguments over the existence of a Supreme Being, sermons focussed on formal morality. In Scotland, Moderatism prevailed, an orthodox, but dry, Calvinism married with civilising enlightenment emphases: clergymen could be little distinguished from the local gentry.

Yet the eighteenth century brought signs of deepening interest in personal spirituality, both within the High Church tradition, and amongst the evangelical heirs of the Reformers and Puritans. Indeed, the two were not unconnected. At the heart John Wesley's Evangelical Arminianism was a fusion of the High Church mysticism of William Law, the European influences of Pietism and the Moravians, and the residual Puritan tradition. Wesley's experience of evangelical conversion at a Moravian meeting in London, where he felt his heart 'strangely warmed', brought him into a movement that was already well under way, and in which he became a pivotal figure. For many thousands of others, the freer atmosphere of religious dissent, or Nonconformity, proved increasingly attractive.

THE CHURCH OF ENGLAND

The Anglican Church of the late eighteenth and early nineteenth century was most definitely the national church of England, with the country divided into over 10,500 parishes. Until 1828, members of Parliament were required to be communicants of the Established Church, and Anglican bishops sat in the House of Lords. To many, it was a force for social stability, and, between 1790 and 1830, Established Church and State closed ranks to snuff out any hint of sympathy with the French Revolution. The Church of England acted as an agency not only for Christianising, but also for controlling, people—by 1820 some 22% of magistrates were clergymen, a fact which did little to stem the growing undercurrent of anticlericalism. On 16 August 1819, at a mass meeting on St Peter's Fields in Manchester, a peaceful crowd of up to 100,000 listening to speeches calling for reform, and wider political representation, and carrying banners such as 'Liberty and Fraternity', was ineptly cleared by the Yeomanry Cavalry who were attempting to arrest the speaker. Eleven people were left dead (including a child), and hundreds injured. Few in the working class would forget that it was a clerical magistrate who read the Riot Act on the fateful day, nor could they ignore the fact that the bishops voted against the second Reform Bill, which was defeated in the House of Lords in October 1831. The financial exactions of the Anglican church—tithes, church rates, even on those who never attended their churches, added to their unpopularity.

The Church of England in the eighteenth century proved remarkably resistant to major reform in its hierarchy and financial provisions. Numerically it did not do well: the period between 1740 and 1830 has been called 'an era of disaster', in which Anglicanism moved from a religious position of near-monopoly, to one of near minority.[12] However, local studies of places such as Oldham have questioned the over-pessimistic assessment, and have highlighted the work of some assiduous pastors, and their attempts to extend church accommodation and extend education.[13] Nonetheless, religious provision remained patchy. Rural parish clergy could enjoy a modest but significant place in the social hierarchy. Many were diligent, but the 'huntin', shootin', and fishin'' parson was no mere caricature.

Two-thirds of England's parishes were situated in the south, leaving the Church of England weakest in areas of most rapid social change, and leaving the door open for the advance of Dissenting churches. In 1831, the parish of Halifax contained 109,899 inhabitants—far beyond the capacity of a vicar and curate to give pastoral support. For some, a pattern of religious indifference was inculcated through the absence of a local church or chapel. Change was needed, but the structure of the Established churches of late eighteenth and early nineteenth century Britain was ill-adapted to respond to the new industrial age: the parish unit performed both ecclesiastical and civil social functions. The solution was the erection of chapels of ease, together with other churches built by subscription, and proprietary chapels operating within the establishment, under bishop's license, which extended the amount of church accommodation in newly industrial areas.

The financial disparities found amongst the clergy of the French church were replicated in the Anglican church. Whilst average clerical income was £387 per year, 4% of clergymen earned between £1,000 and £2,000, and in 1810 the Bishop of Durham received over £19,000. In contrast, 3,300 livings were worth less than £150 per year; and 860 were worth less than £50 per year. The plight of curates, with low incomes and even lower job-security could be bleak. Pluralism, non-residence and neglect of pastoral work followed—of 10,558 livings in 1813, just 4,183 had a clergyman resident within them. Even in 1831, 33% of clergymen held more than one living, 6% held three or more livings.

After the Act of Union in 1801, the Episcopalian Church of Ireland became the Established church of Ireland, but it was an anomaly, a minority church attracting only around 10% of the Irish population, mainly located in Ulster and Leinster. With four archbishops and eighteen bishops it was also top-heavy, although attempts at its reform were to spark controversy in the 1830s. Its 2,400 parishes were streamlined into 1,200 livings, served by only 1,133 clergy, but 561 of these were non-resident. Its support came through exacting tithes from a reluctant, largely Roman Catholic, population. Episcopalianism in Ireland

---

12   A.D. Gilbert, *Religion and Society in Industrial England: Church, Chapel, and Social Change 1740–1914*, London, Longman, 1976, 27.

13   e.g. M. Smith, *Religion in Industrial Society: Oldham and Saddleworth 1740–1865*, Oxford, Clarendon, 1994.

was not missionary minded, and was estimated to have won less than 6,000 converts from Roman Catholicism throughout the entire eighteenth century.

Yet for Anglicanism change did start to come. After 1808, more money was released to supplement the incomes of the poorest clergy. In 1818, the law on the creation of new parishes was simplified, and £1 million was granted by the government for the building of new churches, followed by a further £500,000 in 1824. This was more than matched by voluntary giving—in the 1820s, 308 new churches were consecrated; 929 in the 1840s. Reforms in the hierarchy of the Church of England, with the creation of new bishops in industrial areas, such as Manchester in 1836, were to follow in the 1830s and 1840s. A bill for the division of this vast, and extremely wealthy, parish was finally published in 1850.

The High Church party were a significant factor in Anglican church life long before the advent of Tractarianism. In the aftermath of the French Revolution, loyalty to the state began to be seen as a part of theological orthodoxy, of which a sacral theory of monarchy was part. Nonetheless, the spiritual authority of the Established Church within this equation was asserted, and unwanted reforming intrusions by Parliament were resisted. The High Church clergy were orthodox, although inclined to Arminianism, in their belief and practice (only later in the nineteenth century did 'High Church' become synonymous with Anglo-Catholic ceremonialism). Leading High Churchmen were figures of deep learning, and often of devotional piety, who considered the maintenance of its established church order, and the offices of bishops, priests and deacons essential to its health. They believed that the sacraments, especially the eucharist, properly administered by a priest standing in an apostolic succession which transmitted spiritual authority to the clergy, was central to the life of the Christian community. In devotion there was a strong emphasis on mystery, and a high respect for tradition, especially the writings of the early church fathers. High Churchmen tended to dominate the episcopate; others were archdeacons, deans, or held significant positions at Oxford and Cambridge Universities. After William van Mildert (1765–1836) became Bishop of Durham, he diverted some of the great wealth of the See to founding Durham University.

At the heart of High Church thinking in the early nineteenth century was a tightly knit group known as the 'Hackney Phalanx' (numbering somewhere between fifty and a hundred lay and ordained men). They took an active role in social, philanthropic, and educational projects, and encouraged the building of new churches. The National Society, which promoted education amongst the poor according to the principles of the Church of England, won their strong support. Founded in 1811, within four years it had attracted 100,000 children to its schools, and nearly a million in the early 1830s. The quiet devotion of High Church spirituality was consistent, but it was also narrowly focussed—salvation outside of the true Catholic church, of which the Church of England was a branch, could not be conceived of. The emotional connotations of evangelicalism were strongly resisted, and many of the developments associated with it, such as the Church Missionary Society, were treated with suspicion. Association with religious Dissenters was discountenanced: they were considered to be in a state of schism, and without a properly constituted clergy, their sacraments were considered null and void. There were elements of continuity with the Oxford Movement of the 1830s, which was clerical, academic and reformist, but also points of fundamental difference. The Hackney Phalanx was lay, practical and conservative.

A broader stream of theology within Anglicanism was represented by 'Liberal Churchmen' such as William Paley (1743–1805), well-known for analogy of the watchmaker in his argument from design approach in natural theology. The most distinguished group of academics in this party were to be found at Oriel College, Oxford, in the second and third decades of the nineteenth century. Their devotion to knowledge led to them being known as the Noetics. Richard Whateley (1787–1863), later Archbishop of Dublin, typified the Noetic emphasis on the all-sufficiency of reason. Thomas Arnold (1795–1842), who was to become Headmaster of Rugby School, was another leading figure: his noble ideal was of Christianising the nation, and introducing the principles of Christianity into social relations. To him Christianity was not a creed or speculative system, but primarily a way of life: his moral earnestness was a practical embodiment of his views.

The Evangelical Revival brought a new dynamic to the eighteenth-century religious landscape, and infused life into parts of the Establishment, both in England and Scotland. Alongside John Wesley, another key figure was George Whitefield, also an Anglican clergyman, who attracted huge crowds when he preached, often in the open air, whether in Britain or North America. He formed strong alliances with revival leaders such as Howell Harris and Daniel Rowland in Wales, who initially operated within the Anglican tradition before helping to found Calvinistic Methodism, and the Independent Jonathan Edwards in America. The revival was strongest in closely knit communities where there was a strong degree of social interaction, a pattern repeated in the cottage meetings and local societies which drew people together on a geographical basis, and consolidated social and spiritual cohesion. There were exceptions, such as London, where the crowds drawn to Moorfields and Kennington Common were less locally defined. Those most affected appear to have come from the lower middle, skilled artisan and working classes.

Evangelicalism emphasised the Reformation doctrinal heritage of justification by faith alone, the atoning work of Christ upon the Cross, the grace of God in salvation, and the Bible as the source of Christian teaching, and a daily devotional tool. The central, and initiatory, evangelical experience was a deep awareness of personal sin, followed by a sense of forgiveness brought through the saving work of Christ. This conversion experience, or 'new birth', was to be followed by a life of devotion to Christ, with a commitment to growth in personal holiness, and good works as the outward confirmatory sign of an inward spiritual change. It was an antidote both to Deism, emphasising the immanence of God in the world and the believer's life, and to high Calvinism, found in some Baptist, Independent and Anglican circles, which so stressed the sovereignty of God, that preachers had become fearful of calling the unregenerate to believe lest they presumed on the divine purposes in election.

By the early nineteenth century, although numbers were not large, the influence of evangelicalism had penetrated deeply. Yet it still met with institutional resistance: 'serious' ministerial candidates could be denied training, ordination, parish settlement, or promotion. In 1789 there were perhaps forty or fifty Evangelical clergymen. However, the scene was changing. By 1800 they numbered around 500; and by 1833 they were between an eighth and a quarter of the clergy. Although some early evangelical Anglicans such as Henry Venn in Huddersfield, William Romaine in London, and Samuel Walker in Truro, preached within their parishes an evangelical message that owed much to Methodism, others, such as John Berridge of Everton, Bedfordshire, and William Grimshaw of Haworth, Yorkshire, undertook extensive itinerancy in other parishes. In the later eighteenth century, a growing sense of the importance of respect for Established church order developed amongst Evangelicals, and an aspiration to deepen the credibility of Evangelicalism within Anglicanism. A desire to operate as model parochial clergy emerged, shifting the focus from Wesley's emphasis on 'the world is my parish', to 'the parish is my world'.

Charles Simeon lamented, 'the clergyman beats the bush, the dissenters catch the game.' In order to prevent this leakage of converts to other churches, and in order to maintain the 'vital religion' of their parishioners, activities more commonly associated with Methodism were introduced. At Olney in Buckinghamshire, in addition to regular Sunday services, John Newton introduced a weekly lecture, a catechism class, a twice-weekly prayer meeting, and he visited his parishioners diligently. In association with William Cowper, Newton produced the Olney Hymnal, including hymns expressive of the profoundest devotion.[14]

Most Anglican evangelicals were not Arminians, but rather moderate Calvinists who rejected a number of the emphases of Methodism. Charles Simeon (1759–1836) declared himself a Bible Christian: 'though strongly Calvinistic in some respects, I am as strongly Arminian in others. I am free from all trammels of human systems'.[15] Simeon was appointed curate-in-charge of Holy Trinity Church, Cambridge, in 1782, where he served until his death in 1836, and he held Deanships at King's College on three occasions between 1788

14   On Newton see B. Hindmarsh, *John Newton and the English Evangelical Tradition: Between the Conversions of Wesley and Wilberforce*, Oxford, Clarendon Press, 1996.

15   R. Carus, *Memoir of Rev. Charles Simeon*, London, 1847, 563.

and 1830. After a period of strong opposition from churchwardens and pew holders, he began to exercise a profound influence through his steady biblical expositions, organisation of parochial visitation schemes, and provision of help to the poor. Simeon's influence was probably greater than that of any bishop, with large numbers of students attending his ministry at Holy Trinity. Around half of the undergraduates at Cambridge were preparing for Anglican ministry, making Simeon's sermon classes, conversation parties at which he discussed matters ranging from theology to politics, and his preaching and pastoral practice at Holy Trinity, vital training resources.[16]

Placing love for the Prayer Book second only to love for the Bible, Simeon did much to make Evangelicalism and loyalty to Anglicanism compatible, and helped establish a credible Evangelical and loyal party within the Church of England. He sought to consolidate evangelical influence in parishes through purchasing the rights of presentation to forty-two livings and perpetual curacies: the Simeon Trust was formed to assist this process in 1833. Evangelicalism gradually broadened in its appeal: some leading aristocratic families identified with the movement, and even a Prime Minister, Spencer Perceval. The first Evangelical bishop, Henry Ryder, was appointed in 1815.

Anglicans influenced by evangelicalism also included a group of influential, and wealthy, laymen, a number of whom were associated with the parish of Clapham, where John Venn (1759–1813) was the vicar of Holy Trinity Church from 1792 until his death. Noted for their capable minds, and pious devotion, they attracted the label 'the Clapham Sect.' Men such as William Wilberforce (1759–1833) and Henry Thornton (1760–1815) saw it as their Christian duty to use their considerable wealth and influence (a number were members of parliament and colonial administrators) for the betterment of wider society. They are most famous for their role in the campaigns against slavery and the slave trade, and to improve moral standards in Britain.[17] In 1787 the king was persuaded to issue a royal Proclamation Against Vice, which condemned Sabbath breaking, blasphemy, drunkenness, obscene literature, and immoral amusements, and a society to vigorously campaign for the enforcement of the proclamation was founded. This aspect of their work has attracted much criticism, for being particularly directed at the vices and failings of the poor, whilst paying too little attention to those of the rich.[18] Yet their campaigns did something to improve the moral tone of the nation, and they were men of great personal generosity: in 1793 Henry Thornton gave away £6,680 to charity, whilst

---

16   Simeon's ministry is discussed in Hopkins; C. Smyth; M. Hennell and A. Pollard, *Charles Simeon (1759–1836)*, London, SPCK, 1959.

17   These are discussed fully in chapter five.

18   see F.K. Brown, *Fathers of the Victorians: The Age of Wilberforce*, Cambridge, Cambridge University Press, 1961.

spending only £1,988 on his own needs. The 'Saints' also promoted Sunday Schools, and day schooling for the poor. Wilberforce was among the founder members of the RSPCA in 1824.

Wilberforce experienced an evangelical conversion in the mid 1780s, and at first he considered a career in the Church, but was persuaded by Evangelicals such as John Newton to continue to be of service to God in parliament. In 1797 he published *A Practical View of the Prevailing Religious System of Professed Christians in the Higher and Middle Classes in this Country Contrasted with Real Christianity*, which created a sensation. In it he criticised the formal, nominal, Christianity of many in his day, and pleaded for more seriousness in matters such as prayer, Bible reading, acknowledging personal sinfulness, a sense of accountability before God for each aspect of daily life, and for social responsibility. When Christianity prevailed, he argued, moral standards were raised to a height

---

Wilberforce—'A Practical View'

The main object...is...to point out the scanty and erroneous system of the bulk of those who belong to the class of orthodox Christians, and to contrast their defective scheme with a representation of what the author apprehends to be real Christianity. Often it has filled him with deep concern, to observe in this description of persons scarcely any distinct knowledge of the real nature and principles which they profess. (p. iii)

Essential Principle of the Gospel

Christianity is a scheme for "justifying *the ungodly*," by Christ's dying for them *"when yet sinners;"* a scheme for reconciling us to God *"when enemies;"* and for making the fruits of holiness *the effects*, not *the cause*, of our being justified and reconciled. (p. 97)

Nominal and Real Christians

The main distinction between real Christianity and the system of the bulk of nominal Christians, chiefly consists in the different place which is assigned in the two schemes to the peculiar doctrines of the gospel. These, in the scheme of nominal Christians...appear but like the stars of the firmament to the ordinary eye. Those splendid luminaries draw forth...a transient expression of admiration, when we behold their beauty...and...have no influence on human happiness, or any concern with the course and order of the world. But to the real Christian, on the contrary, these doctrines constitute the centre to which he gravitates! The very sun of his system! The origin of all that is excellent and lovely![1]

1 W. Wilberforce, *A Practical View of the Prevailing Religious System of Professed Christians, in the Higher and Middle Classes in this Country, Contrasted with Real Christianity*, London, 1886 edition, 270.

---

previously unknown. Wilberforce touched a nerve: the French Revolution had opened the eyes of the higher orders to what might happen if they were perceived to have little regard for religion and its moral and social obligations.

Between 1784 and 1832 there were some 112 or so MPs who can be identified as Evangelicals. Most of them were Tories, and although the 'Saints' sought to remain independent of party alignment, and follow conscience, their social and political background could not always be forgotten. They believed in a divinely ordered society, were fervent anti-Jacobins, and had no vision for dealing with the structural causes of poverty by re-ordering social and economic structures or by wealth redistribution. They simply dealt with the worst symptoms of poverty on an individual basis. In all this they replicated the prevalent views of a hierarchical society. Critics have demonstrated their blind spots—Wilberforce has been accused of knowing more about what went on in the hold of a slave ship than at the bottom of an English mineshaft.[19] Their vision for amelioration was based on a pre-industrial, rural, voluntary, paternalistic model of face-to-face charity which was increasingly ill-suited to the burgeoning and constantly shifting urban populations. Yet through their assiduous efforts, much good was accomplished.

THE CHURCHES OF SCOTLAND

William III's decision in 1690 that the religious establishment in Scotland should be Presbyterian largely ended over a century of bitter, and often bloody, conflict over the matter. Episcopalianism, the Established Church south of the border, was thereby rendered a small, Dissenting minority in Scotland. Indeed, in the aftermath of the Jacobite uprisings of 1715 and 1745, penal restrictions were imposed on the Episcopalians who had supported the cause, although in 1792 these were repealed, as were restrictions on Roman Catholicism the following year.

The parochial system of the Church of Scotland was more efficient than that found in England. Ministers were to be resident in each of the 970 parishes, where they were to preach, visit, and catechise the young. Clerical incomes could be low—28% of livings in 1750 yielded less than £50 per year, with up to half of the teind (tithe) income being retained by the landed classes. As in England, the parish system was inflexible: by 1815 some urban parishes had populations of up to 12,000, rendering meaningful contact between the local minister and the local populace almost impossible. In contrast, Highland parishes, with small populations scattered over many miles, saw a shortage of ministers and church buildings. The Scottish parochial educational system, largely run by the church, was more egalitarian than that in England. With 942 parish schools in 1816, Scotland had one of the highest literacy rates. Education offered the 'lad o'pairts'

19   E. Williams, *Capitalism and Slavery*, Chapel Hill, 1944, 182.

from poor families a chance to rise in social status. University entrance was more open than at Oxford or Cambridge, and afforded opportunities to enter the professions or Christian ministry. Those who benefited from a Presbyterian parish school, were imbued with its characteristic values: the pervasive sense of the divine presence behind everything, deep respect for education, a sense of the importance of consecrating one's life to greater service, a determination to extract maximum profit through their own industry from whatever intellectual endowments they possessed, and a distrust of superficial pleasures.

The Moderate Party, strongly influenced by a Scottish Enlightenment ethos, was in the ascendancy in the late eighteenth century. Although adhering to the Westminster Confession, Moderates downplayed teaching on predestination and the atonement, and emphasised morality and human reason. They endorsed lay patronage, believing that this was the means to preserve a high quality Scottish clergy, refined, well-mannered, and intellectual. The fruits of the Evangelical Revival were experienced in the North-East of Scotland, and then in lowland parishes such as Cambuslang and Kilsyth in 1742. George Whitefield was reported to have addressed crowds of up to 20,000 in the Cambuslang 'Wark.' In the revival's wake, an Evangelical Party emerged in the Church of Scotland, which so grew in size and influence that it won control of the General Assembly in 1834, promoting policies such as opposition to patronage and slavery, support for mission and voluntary agencies such as the British and Foreign Bible Society, and ardent pastoral ministry. Others drawn to evangelicalism left to join the burgeoning Secession Churches. In the Calvinist soil of Presbyterian Scotland, the Arminianism of Wesleyan Methodism did not take strong root, despite the regular visits of John Wesley north of the border. The pluralism and absenteeism which Methodism had exploited in England, were little known in Scotland.

When patronage was restored in 1712, a major cause of grievance and division entered Scottish ecclesiastical politics. Presbyterianism became increasingly fragmented as the eighteenth century progressed. Major secessions from the Church of Scotland occurred in 1733 and 1761, and by 1801 the combined forces of the Secession and Relief churches numbered over 300 congregations, with around 150,000 adherents, almost 10% of Scotland's population. Enlightenment influences encouraged people to move in individualistic, voluntary, democratic, and reformist directions. By the 1820s, 30% of Scotland's population were Dissenters, with the highest numbers in towns and cities. This placed the Established Church, with its parish system, upon which poor relief and educational provision was based, in an increasingly anomalous position. It became untenable after the Disruption of the Church of Scotland in 1843.

The influence of evangelicalism was also seen in the work of James and Robert Haldane, who conducted a successful home mission subsequent to their conversions in 1795. After leaving the Church of Scotland, they founded the

Society for the Propagation of the Gospel at Home (1797), and their evangelistic work was to considerably boost the Independent churches, the numbers of which grew from 14 in 1800, to 85 in 1807. In 1810 the Haldanes became Baptists, and took a large number of their supporters with them. Their itinerancy saw significant success in the Highlands and the Islands. From being a mission field in the eighteenth century, these remote regions had become bastions of evangelical Presbyterianism by the mid-nineteenth century—98% of the population of Lewis left the Established Church for the Free Church at the Disruption in 1843.

METHODISM

Born in the fire of the early Evangelical Revival, with strong influences from Europe and America, Wesleyan Methodism drew on High Church, Pietist, and Moravian traditions. The Protestant tradition of grace and its emphasis on preaching, were fused together with a range of holiness influences, and given practical expression by the organisational genius of John Wesley. In many ways Wesley was a man of the enlightenment with a concern for religious toleration, deploring violence, slavery, and emphasising rationality when enquiring after Christian truth. His teaching on Christian perfection (which Wesley believed could be an instantaneous experience) could be seen as a product of enlightenment optimism. His Arminianism stressed personal responsibility and freedom of choice. Yet he was also deeply indebted to the theology and traditions of the Protestant Reformation—he owed his conversion experience to the public reading of Luther's work.

The reality of 'vital religion,' with its bible-based certainties, tales of divine intervention in ordinary lives, and awareness of the struggles with temptation and the devil, met a ready response from people whose world-view had not yet been shaped by enlightenment rationalism, fearful as they were of evil spirits, ghosts, boggarts, the future, or the prospect of their own mortality. Encounters with evangelical preaching in the eighteenth century could be dramatic—some wept, cried out, or fell to the ground overwhelmed by the sense of their own sins or the glory of God. Other preachers were met by rioting mobs; many were injured, some imprisoned, a few were killed. Opposition ranged from drunken crowds, to local clergymen incensed at the invasion of their parishes, and magistrates who suspected preachers of subversive activities.

Wesley, who repeatedly asserted that he lived and died an Anglican, nonetheless allowed the laity a distinct role in preaching, and providing mutual pastoral support. Class membership was opened to men and women. In 1739 he declared 'I look upon the world as my parish,'[20] and through his policy of unrestricted open air preaching he was prepared to push the church order of the

---

20   J. Wesley, Letter to James Hervey, 20 March 1739, in *Letters of John Wesley*, Vol. 1, 286.

establishment to it limits, cutting across parish structures and challenging the authority of incumbents. Designed to supplement the work of the Established Church, Methodism proved both a movement for renewal from within Anglicanism, and also a decisive movement away from it. As premises were acquired, Methodism began to look like a denomination, especially after the need during the 1780s to register its buildings as dissenting houses of worship under the Toleration Act. A decisive step came in 1784 when the Bishop of London refused to ordain Methodist ministers to administer the sacraments in America, and Wesley himself performed the ordinations.

In 1791, the year of the death of its founder, Wesleyan Methodists numbered over 56,600, and over 230,000 by 1830, around 1.5% of the population.[21] Some historians believe that for every member there were at least three adherents to Methodist and Dissenting causes, suggesting it had a much greater numerical impact. Methodism seemed well adapted to the increasingly flexible social and economic world. In the second half of the eighteenth century, over half of its members were skilled artisans, craftsmen, textile and manufacturing operatives, or miners, about one-sixth were labourers, servants, or paupers; nearly 58% of Methodists were women.[22] It flourished in places where Anglicanism was at its weakest and struggling to respond to social and demographic change. Methodism advanced at the moment when the Established Church's role as the agent of Christianising the poor was coming most under threat, in the aftermath of the French Revolution. The religious Establishment lost control of the minds of the masses not through riot and revolt, but through the more prosaic work of itinerant lay preachers, Sunday School teachers, and cottage prayer meetings.

Methodism was also highly adaptable. Although preachers were required to undertake a rigorous course of reading, a high-grade education, or university degree, was not required. Sermons were idiomatic, accessible, attuned to local contexts. The circuit system readily drew in towns, new industrial villages, fishing villages, isolated hamlets, linking together groups of believers who could not survive independently. Its numerical strength was greatest in Yorkshire, the East Midlands, County Durham, and Cornwall. The Evangelical Revival also brought Methodism to Ireland, especially Ulster. Here there were 3,124 Methodists in 1770 and 29,357 in 1815.

In Wales, at least fifteen revivals were reported between 1762 and 1862, and the 1817 Beddgelert revival exercised a wide influence across the north of Wales. Wesleyan Methodism made less impact than in England: the Welsh preferred Calvinistic Methodism, which stayed within the Establishment until it formally became a denomination in 1811. Great leaders of the Evangelical Revival in

21 A.D. Gilbert, *Religion and Industrial Society in England*, London, Longman, 1976, 31.

22 C.D. Field, 'The Social Composition of English Methodism to 1830: A Membership Analysis', in *Bulletin of John Rylands Library*, Spring, 1994, 153–169.

Wales passed from the scene in the late eighteenth century: Daniel Rowland died in 1790, and William Williams (Pantycelyn) in 1791. A key leader in the new denomination was Thomas Charles (1755–1814), converted through Rowland's preaching. After study at Jesus College, Oxford, and a curacy in Somerset, he became a Methodist minister in Bala, North Wales. He helped re-establish circulating schools in Wales, and promoted Sunday Schools. His call for Bibles in Welsh was important to the formation of the British and Foreign Bible Society. Other notable Welsh preachers of the era were the Calvinistic Methodist John Elias (1774–1841) in Anglesey, and the Baptist Christmas Evans (1766–1838).

Methodism was riven by division during the lifetime of John Wesley and George Whitefield, and especially after the latter's death in 1770, largely over doctrinal matters. Whilst Whitefield and his Welsh and Scottish associates were Calvinists, as were most of the Anglican ministers who became Evangelicals, the Wesley brothers and their associates were strongly Arminian. Whitefield's aristocratic patron, the Countess of Huntingdon (1707–91), appointed a number of his associates as chaplains, and established 60 proprietary chapels where they officiated. In 1779 she was forced to register her chapels as Dissenting chapels under the Toleration Act, after bitter legal disputes from local Anglican clergy. Other supporters moved into Independency, which began increasingly to be shaped by the characteristics of evangelicalism.

The interaction of Methodism with developing industrial society had a number of outcomes. Opportunities in trade and commerce allowed many members to rise in the social scale: some became modestly prosperous, others made considerable fortunes. Wesley's dictum, 'Gain all you can, save all you can; give all you can', led to considerable giving to charities and chapel building, but rising wealth created social demarcations in the chapels. Preachers became reluctant to say anything that might offend prosperous donors. Wesley's urgings to avoid laziness, sloth and indolence, had an economic outcome. Methodists were promoted to positions of trust through their reliability and probity. The Methodist system was well-suited to development within the urban proletariat.

With the death of his brother Charles in 1788, and John himself in 1791, Methodism passed into uncharted waters. In the rapidly changing post-1789 political and social context, organisational tensions within Methodism surfaced. In 1796 Alexander Kilham was expelled from the Wesleyan Connexion for criticising its leadership, calling for lay representation in its governance, and for matters to be decided by a majority of those voting. To his detractors Kilham was a Methodist Roberspierre; to his defenders little more than a reforming Whig. The following year he formed his followers, who numbered around 5,000 (5% of the Wesleyan membership), into the New Connexion.

The Wesleyan leadership strove to keep members from adherence to radical political causes, and removed from membership any who were openly associated with them. Kilham's secession served to push Methodism to affirm

---

The Mow Cop Camp Meeting

About noon the congregation was so much increasing that we were obliged to erect a third preaching stand... I had not conceived that such a vast multitude were present; but to see thousands hearing with attention solemn as death, presented a scene of the most sublime and awfully pleasing grandeur my eyes ever beheld. The preachers seemed to be fired with an uncommon zeal ... numbers were convinced and saints were uncommonly quickened, and the extraordinary steadiness and decorum... seemed to make a great impression. ... Persuasion dwelt upon their tongues, while the multitude were trembling or rejoicing around.

... To see thousands of people all in solemn attention... and four preachers dealing out their lives at every stroke—these things made an impression on my mind not soon to be forgotten...About seven o'clock in the evening the meeting was finally closed. A meeting such as our eyes had never beheld; a meeting for which many will praise God in time and eternity.... [1]

1   *Observations on Camp Meetings, With an Account of a Camp Meeting held on Sunday May the 31ˢᵗ, 1807, at Mow, near Harriseahead*, Newcastle-under-Lyne, 1807, in J.T. Wilkinson, *Hugh Bourne 1772-1852*, London, 1952, pp. 46-48.

---

more strongly its loyalty to the King, and to present itself as no threat to the stability of society. The result was a movement divided within itself, split between a conservative leadership allied with a wealthy laity, determined to expel from its ranks any who were politically disaffected, and a large part of its local membership who were calling for improved social and political conditions. The class conflict, which Methodism was supposed to have resisted, was played out in its midst. A whole series of secessions followed in the early decades of the nineteenth century. The redoubtable Jabez Bunting, elected President of the Methodist Conference in 1820, oversaw Methodism during this period of transition. Autocratic, Tory, combative and controversial, he saw Methodist membership grow from 143,311 in 1811; to 435,591 in 1840, when its relative strength in English society was at its peak. [23]

The bleak moorland hill of Mow Cop, on the borders of Staffordshire and Cheshire, was in 1807 the scene of a revival meeting, based on the 'camp meetings' so significant in America. Thousands were drawn to hear fervent preaching, prayer, exhortation, and personal testimony. Hugh Bourne, a 29 year old lay Methodist, who had already led a revival in local villages, was a key

---

23   On Bunting see J. Kent, *Jabez Bunting, the Last Wesleyan. A study in the Methodist ministry after the death of John Wesley*, London, Epworth Press, 1955; W.R. Ward (ed), *Early Victorian Methodism: The Correspondence of Jabez Bunting, 1830–1858*, Oxford, Oxford University Press, 1976.

figure. The event challenged existing Methodist structures, and after Bourne and William Clowes were expelled from the Wesleyan body for their involvement in these and subsequent events, they formed their supporters into the Primitive Methodist Connexion, in which revivalism was institutionalised. In a time of political and social instability, Wesleyan Methodism struggled to relate such calls for a return to early, or 'primitive', Methodism, to the well-functioning orderliness of a formalised denomination.

The early Primitive Methodists owed much to the work of American revivalists. Lorenzo Dow arrived in 1805, the asthmatic, epileptic, son of a Connecticut father. With his long hair and unkempt dress, he was certainly a remarkable figure and a hugely dramatic preacher. Drawing on local revivalist movements such as the 'Magic' Methodists of the Delamare Forest in Cheshire, who specialised in visions, and other groups of prophets and seers in Cheshire and North Staffordshire, Primitive Methodism expanded rapidly to number 62,306 members in 1836. The movement was more democratic than the Wesleyans, allowing equal status to laymen within the movement, and their politics were more radical, in sympathy with the industrial workers.

Other Methodist groups in the primitivist tradition departed from the Wesleyan parent body. In 1805, the first conference of Independent Methodists was held in Manchester. In the South-West of England, the Bible Christians, who emerged through the work of William O'Bryan after 1810, numbered 10,499 by 1836.

ROMAN CATHOLICISM

In Scotland, there were around 30,000 Roman Catholics in 1779, a figure soon to be swelled by Irish migrants into the West of Scotland. In England and Wales the Roman Catholic community numbered some 80,000 in 1770. The continued presence of Roman Catholics in post-reformation England owed much to the support of a number of aristocratic families, who employed priests as their chaplains. Although Roman Catholic public worship was formally prohibited, the laws were not rigorously enforced. Roman Catholicism was, on the whole, fairly well assimilated into society, but English Roman Catholicism retained a European focus, with its priests trained in Europe, and a spiritual leadership derived from the papacy. The community could still be subject to hostility, as in the Gordon Riots of 1780 when angry crowds pillaged Roman Catholic homes, leaving a trail of devastation, in protest at the Roman Catholic Relief Act of 1778. A further Act of 1791 eased restrictions on Roman Catholic worship, and brought an influx of several thousand priests from Europe, especially in the wake of the French Revolution. Awareness of their sufferings during the revolution generally brought a more tolerant attitude to the newly permitted Roman Catholic worship.

Between 1778 and 1793, legal penalties against Roman Catholicism in Ireland were also eased, but an Irish uprising in 1798, inspired by the examples of America and France, drew support from both Roman Catholic priests and revolutionary France. It descended into sectarian bloodletting and massacre, leaving some 30,000 dead. Political union between Britain and Ireland in 1801 was a response to this, giving Westminster direct responsibility for Irish affairs. Union with an overwhelmingly Roman Catholic country changed perceptions and realities. With some four or five million Roman Catholics in Ireland, 80% of the population, they were no longer a small minority in Britain. Irish Protestants were only in a majority around Belfast. Union in 1801 also paved the way for the Roman Catholic Emancipation Act of 1829, which owed much to the need to govern Ireland better in the face of a mounting agrarian crisis, growing political protest in which the Roman Catholic clergy took a role, and the threat of civil war. It was stoutly resisted by defenders of Protestantism and the Protestant constitution in Britain, but many who had argued for toleration and freedoms for Dissenters found it hard to deny these to Roman Catholics, and some members of the Clapham Sect, including Wilberforce, offered the measure their support.

The Irish Catholic church, with 26 dioceses, four archbishops, twenty-two bishops, and some 1,000 priests and 800 curates, drew its support from the giving of the congregations, and hence was largely poor. To assist with the training of priests, the government voted a grant of £8,000 to the new seminary at Maynooth, hoping that this would also end their interest in fomenting rebellion. In later decades the renewal of this grant was to become increasingly controversial, attracting strong opposition.

Between 1800 and 1850, the size of the Roman Catholic community in England, Wales and Scotland changed rapidly. A large influx of Irish migrants swelled numbers from under 100,000 to around 750,000. English Roman Catholicism became more Ultramontane in outlook, with a growing respect for the office of the Roman Catholic priest. In areas of major Irish migration, such as Lancashire, and Western Scotland, significant sectarian tensions arose. In times of economic and social hardship, Irish migrants were blamed for taking jobs and houses, and spreading disease and crime. Not only Roman Catholics, but also Protestants migrated from Ireland, and the divisions between the two communities of their homeland were carried into the areas in which they settled.

OTHER DENOMINATIONS

After 1689, Protestants who did not conform to the religion of the state were tolerated, although their activities were restricted, and in the early nineteenth century to be a Dissenter was still to hold a form of second-class citizenship, and to inhabit a different culture from the privileged position of the Establishment.

Until 1828 it meant political exclusion, and enduring bigotry and discrimination from the establishment that ran close to persecution. Campaigns to secure Dissenting civil and religious liberties continued into the 19th century. Although excluded from social and political leadership, a number of Dissenters became successful businessmen.

The repeal in 1828 of the Test and Corporation Acts, some of the restrictive laws against Nonconformists, represented a huge challenge to the Established church system. Parliament, whose approval for formal legislation for the Established church was required, was no longer comprised entirely of Anglicans. This challenge to the Establishment was deepened by Roman Catholic Emancipation the following year. The result was a profound, but peaceful constitutional revolution: no longer was the United Kingdom a semi-confessional state in which political rights were restricted to those who adhered to a particular confession.[24] However, it took an often bitter campaign through succeeding decades to redress other restrictive laws on Dissenting life, which drove a wedge between Anglican and Dissenter. Key issues in the acrimonious debates included those over whether the Church of England should be disestablished, and over who should control educational provision.

Although tolerated, eighteenth century English Dissent was generally in a state of decline, albeit modest. The total number of Independents, Baptists and Presbyterians slipped from some 5% of the population in 1715 to 4% in 1773.[25] Around two-thirds of all English Dissenting congregations in 1714 were Presbyterian, but during the eighteenth century many adopted Socinian and Arian views, and in 1774 the first formally Unitarian congregation was formed in London, stressing the humanity of Jesus, and rejecting Trinitarian formularies. Other Presbyterians remained orthodox, and their numbers were strengthened by evangelical Presbyterian migrants from Scotland. In Ireland, Presbyterianism largely took root through migration from Scotland in the seventeenth Century: by the 1780s there were 515,000 Presbyterians in Ireland, with some 432,000 in Ulster. In the late eighteenth century these churches increasingly came under the influence of evangelicalism.

Other forms of 'Old' Dissent in 1800 included around 20,000 Quakers in England and Wales, but these were only half the numbers of 1700. Quakers took a key role in the campaigns to end slavery, and the slave trade, and moves for prison reform. Other Dissenters, such as Baptists and Independents drew fresh life from the Evangelical Revival, gaining converts who could not settle in local Anglican or Methodist churches. Ministers were infused with a new evangelistic

24   S.J. Brown, *Providence and Empire: Religion, Politics and Society in the United Kingdom, 1815–1914*, Harlow, Pearson, 2008, 62.

25   K. Hylson-Smith, *The Churches in England from Elizabeth I to Elizabeth II, Vol II 1689–1833*, London, SCM, 1997, 54.

vision, lay and itinerant preaching flourished, and societies for home evangelism were formed. In Particular Baptist Churches high Calvinism was generally supplanted by evangelical Calvinism, and some Quakers adopted a more outward-looking, evangelical approach, with a stronger focus on the Bible.

The late eighteenth century proved a vital stage in the development of Protestant Dissent into Victorian Nonconformity. The number of Dissenting congregations in England rose from just under 1,700 in the 1770s, to a little over 17,000 in 1851, with particularly rapid growth between 1790 and 1815. The membership of Congregational churches grew from just 15,000 members in 1750, to 35,000 in 1800, and 127,000 in 1837. On the whole theologically orthodox, the Evangelical Revival infused new vigour into these churches. The formation of the Congregational Union in 1831, preceded by county-wide associations which had fostered evangelism and the support of small congregations, allowed for a formal national expression of sentiment and identity. The main Baptist groupings saw similar growth. Particular Baptists, who numbered around 10,000 members in 1750, and 17,000 in 1790, had grown to 86,000 in 1838. The Arminian Baptist New Connexion was founded in 1770, and counted just under 14,000 members by 1838.[26] Andrew Fuller (1754-1815), who embraced the evangelical Calvinism of Jonathan Edwards, helped bring amongst Particular Baptists a new stress on the necessity of offering the gospel to the unconverted, active itinerant evangelism and home mission in Britain, and a deepening interest in world mission, as shall be seen in the case of William Carey. High Calvinists who opposed Fuller's views, such as the redoubtable Strict Baptist William Gadsby, could nonetheless be active in itinerancy, and attract large congregations. Early attempts at union amongst Baptists eventually led to the formation of the Baptist Union of Great Britain and Ireland in 1831, initially for mutual acquaintance and ministerial support, as the Baptists developed their own denominational identity.

THE JEWISH COMMUNITY

By 1830, there were between 20,000 and 30,000 Jews resident in England, with their numbers increasing, fuelled by migration from Portugal and Germany. Much of the discrimination they had faced was declining, although their full emancipation did not come until later in the century. New synagogues were built, occupying increasingly prominent places, such as those built in Liverpool in 1808, and in Birmingham the following year. The role of Jews in trade and banking brought increasing acceptance and support from the nation's political and social leadership. Notable members of the Jewish community included Nathan Rothschild, an important figure in the Stock Exchange, who arranged

---

26   A. Gilbert, *Religion and Society in Industrial England: Church, Chapel and Social Change, 1740–1914*, London, Longman, 1976, 36–37.

financial transactions between Britain and Continental Governments. Others, such as David Ricardo, the leading economist of his day, together with the Disraeli family, from whom came a future Prime Minister, responded to the challenges of assimilation by choosing to convert to Christianity.

THE RISE OF VOLUNTARY SOCIETIES

A characteristic device in Evangelicalism, which cut across barriers of denomination and church tradition, was the formation of trans-denominational voluntary societies, with similarities to Anglican and Pietist religious societies. Notable examples were the Religious Tract Society (1799), the British and Foreign Bible Society (1804), and the Sunday School Union (1812), all of which grew rapidly in size and influence. By 1816 the Bible Society had 541 branch societies.

The role of education in promoting the Christian message had been demonstrated by Griffith Jones with his eighteenth-century Welsh circulating schools. Although the beginnings of Sunday Schools can be traced to the 1760s, the man most associated with their early development was Robert Raikes (1735–1811) of Gloucester, a newspaper publisher whose famous letter promoting them appeared in the *Gloucester Journal* in November 1783. After this date the Sunday School concept spread rapidly. Initially formed to provide basic education for the children of the urban poor who did not attend school, Sunday Schools came to combine educative, philanthropic, and evangelistic intent, with a significant aspect of social control of the behaviour of children, especially on a Sunday. The schools could grow to a very large size, with their own premises, and operate partially, or entirely, independent, of local churches to which they were associated. The Bennett Street Sunday School in Manchester attracted 1,766 children in 1818, and paid its teachers, who were often from the working class, a small allowance. The Stockport Sunday School was independent, and attracted 6,000 scholars at its peak. Although managers and trustees were often of a higher order than the children, Sunday Schools proved to be significantly more than an imposition of the middle classes and their values upon the working class. Some were strongly proletarian organisations.[27]

Early Sunday Schools in places like Manchester ran on non-sectarian lines, with Roman Catholic Churches initially involved, although a more denominational outlook gradually emerged, and schools increasingly operated

---

27 The debate over whether Sunday Schools were examples of social control by the middle class upon the working class is set out in T.W. Laqueur, *Religion and Respectability: Sunday Schools and Working-Class Culture, 1780–1850*, New Haven, Yale University Press, 1976, and M. Dick, 'The Myth of the Working Class Sunday School', *History of Education* 9/1 (1980), 27–41. There was a significant variety of experience, and evidence can be produced to support the claims of both sides.

Robert Raikes on Sunday Schools

'Could you take a view of this part of the town on a Sunday, you would be shocked indeed; for then the street is filled with multitudes of these wretches, who, released on that day from employment, spend their time in noise and riot, playing at "chuck," and cursing and swearing in a manner so horrid as to convey to any serious mind an idea of hell rather than any other place… I then enquired… if there were any decent well-disposed women in the neighbourhood who kept schools for teaching to read…to these I applied, and made an agreement with them to receive as many children as I should send upon the Sunday, whom they were to instruct in reading and in the Church Catechism. For this I engaged to pay them each a shilling for their day's employment…

… It is now about three years since we began… From being idle, ungovernable, profligate, and filthy in the extreme, they say the boys and girls are become not only cleanly and decent in their appearance, but are greatly humanised in their manners—more orderly, tractable, and attentive to business, and, of course, more serviceable than they ever expected to find them…

… You will understand that these children are from six years old to twelve or fourteen. Boys and girls above this age, who have been totally undisciplined, are generally too refractory for this government. A reformation in society seems to me to be only practicable by establishing notions of duty and practical habits of order and decorum, at an early age'. [1]

1   R. Raikes, letter in *Gentleman's Magazine*, June 1784, in J.H. Harris (ed), *Robert Raikes: A Man and His Work*, London, 1899, pp. 304-311

as adjuncts of churches and chapels, with the clear intention of recruitment. The educational agenda also shifted, from wider instruction, to a narrower focus on reading, especially of the Bible. By the 1840s most Wesleyan Sunday Schools no longer taught writing on Sundays, seeing it as an infringement of the Lord's Day (although it was often taught in other classes during the week). The practice continued amongst the Primitive Methodists, Methodist New Connexion, and the Unitarians.

The Sunday School movement grew at a phenomenal rate. In 1800, some 200,000 children were enrolled (2.5% of the population); over one million in 1831 (8.4% of the population); and 2 million by 1851—around half children aged between five and fifteen, and 75% of working-class children. Although the educational approach adopted was frequently limited and unsophisticated, delivered by ill-trained teachers of limited education ability, the attendance of such large numbers of children made Sunday Schools in the years before 1850, probably the most crucial institution in widening popular literacy amongst the working classes. Population increased by 100% in the fifty years after 1780,

ORKNEY

ZETLAND

CAITH-
NESS

SUTHERLAND

ROSS AND
CROMARTY

MORAY-
SHIRE

NAIRN

BANFFSHIRE

ABERDEEN-
SHIRE

Aberdeen

INVERNESS-SHIRE

1	KINCARDINESHIRE
2	DUMBARTONSHIRE
3	STIRLINGSHIRE
4	CLACKMANNANSHIRE
5	KINROSS-SHIRE
6	RENFREWSHIRE
7	WEST LOTHIAN
8	MIDLOTHIAN
9	PEEBLES-SHIRE
10	SELKIRKSHIRE
11	CAERNARVONSHIRE
12 }	FLINTSHIRE
13	
14	MONTGOMERYSHIRE
15	RUTLAND
16	HUNTINGDON
17	CAMBRIDGESHIRE AND ISLE OF ELY
18	BEDFORDSHIRE
19	MONMOUTHSHIRE
20	WORCESTERSHIRE

ANGUS

Dundee

PERTH

FIFE

ARGYLLSHIRE

Edinburgh

EAST
LOTHIAN

BERWICK-
SHIRE

Greenock
Glasgow
Paisley

BUTE

LANARK-
SHIRE

ROXBURGH-
SHIRE

AYRSHIRE

NORTH
SEA

DUMFRIES-SHIRE

NORTHHUMBERLAND

Newcastle-upon-Tyne

KIRKCUD-
BRIGHTSHIRE

WIGTOWN-
SHIRE

CUMBERLAND

DURHAM

WESTMOR-
LAND

ISLE OF
MAN

YORKSHIRE

York

Kingston-upon-Hull

IRISH SEA

Preston Blackburn
Bolton
Salford
Manchester Oldham
Liverpool
Stockport

Leeds

Sheffield

ANGLESEY

CHESHIRE

DENBIGH
SHIRE

DERBY-
SHIRE

LINCOLNSHIRE

NOTTINGHAM-
SHIRE

MERIONETH-
SHIRE

Nottingham

STAFFORD-
SHIRE

LEICESTER-
SHIRE

Leicester

Norwich

CARDIGANSHIRE

RADNOR-
SHIRE

SHROPSHIRE

Birmingham
Coventry

NORTHAMPTON-
SHIRE

NORFOLK

PEMBROKE-
SHIRE

BRECKNOCK-
SHIRE

HEREFORD-
SHIRE

WARWICK-
SHIRE

SUFFOLK

CARMARTHEN-
SHIRE

GLOUCESTER-
SHIRE

OXFORD-
SHIRE

BUCKINGHAM-
SHIRE

HERTFORD-
SHIRE

ESSEX

GLAMORGAN

Bristol

BERK-
SHIRE

MIDDX
London

Bath

WILTSHIRE

SURREY

KENT

SOMERSET

HAMPSHIRE

SUSSEX

DEVONSHIRE

DORSET

Portsea

Brighton

Exeter

CORNWALL Plymouth

0   km   120
0   Miles   80

Map of Britain in 1831 with Towns Over 25,000 People

but literacy increased by 500%. By the 1830s, some 60–75% of working class children could read, and 30% could write. The achievements of the limited day schooling provision cannot alone explain this achievement, and the role of the Sunday School movement must be acknowledged. The Sunday School was the one religious institution which the working classes of the nineteenth century were keen to make use of. As recruitment agencies for local churches, their success is less certain. Nonetheless, large numbers were drawn into the sphere of influence of local churches, and many converts of revivals in the 1830s onwards were drawn from Sunday Schools and Bible classes. In reality, Sunday Schools were 'the only religious institution which the nineteenth-century public in the mass had any intention of using'.[28]

CONCLUSIONS

The rapid social, economic, and demographic changes in Britain between 1750 and 1830 were truly revolutionary. Whether this transition produced, as some have argued, a rootless proletariat, destabilised by the collapse of traditional community life, thrust into an urban wilderness, alienated by the capitalist means of production, and left socially fragmented, without the comforting trappings of familiar institutions, such as the Established church, is open to debate. The sharpness of the transition from rural idyll to urban wilderness has certainly been overplayed—most migrated only short distances, and many worked in industrial villages, before reaching the towns. The process of urbanisation did not always destroy community, but served to create new communities, often more socially uniform than the ones they replaced.

In Britain, the assault on the *ancien régime* was often led by religious forces. With the lines of demarcation between Established church and chapel sharply etched both in religious discourse, and in social and political life in the late eighteenth and early nineteenth century, the fact that those who did not conform to the Established churches in Britain comprised 30% of the population in 1815 is remarkable. The pattern varied across the country, but the traditional hold of Anglicanism on the countryside was slipping, as itinerancy extended the influence of Nonconformity. In the developing urban areas Dissent initially prospered, but when growing industrial towns became major urban centres, it experienced more difficulties. Despite political emancipation in 1828, the ecclesiastical gulf between Establishment and Dissent yawned as wide as ever.

In the context of dramatic social change, religious structures proved capable of rapid and significant adaptation, as with the birth and rapid rise of the Sunday-School movement, and other voluntary religious societies for charity and evangelism. Confronted by rapid population growth, industrialisation, and urbanisation, some Christian churches and organisations responded

---

28   W.R. Ward, *Religion and Society in England 1790–1850*, London, Batsford, 1972, 135.

with remarkable vitality and adaptability in the new circumstances. Although the Established churches, with their inflexible territorial systems, responded least well, and for some individuals the new economic context brought social dislocation and an associated weakening of ties with traditional religious structures, there was no inevitable link between industrialisation and secularisation in the early nineteenth century. There was too much vigour in the churches for that. Christianity frequently operated not so much as the opiate of the masses, but as an expression of radicalism in a religious guise.

Between 1789 and the 1830s there was a marked change in the moral tone of Britain. Movements for the reform of prisons, the abolition of slavery, the relief of debtors, improvements in the care for the poor, and improvements in hygiene and sanitation in towns, all emerged. They owe something to both the enlightenment, with its growing conviction of the power of individuals to control their environment and to alter their worlds, and to the distinct, although contested, influence of evangelicalism on the national conscience. By the 1820s there was a growing sense of seriousness, of the importance of 'vital' Christianity, of heightened moral and religious sensibility. Even amongst those who had lapsed from formal Christian profession, there remained a desire to retain the values associated with it, and their humanitarianism remained informed by the Christian principle of love. But then, between 1831 and 1836, there came a passing of the old guard with the deaths of William Wilberforce, Hannah More, and Charles Simeon. In the following decades new faces and new issues were to dominate the religious scene.

FURTHER READING

N. Aston, *Christianity and Revolutionary Europe, c. 1750–1830*, Cambridge, Cambridge University Press, 2002.

I. Bradley, *The Call to Seriousness: The Evangelical Impact on the Victorians*, London, Cape, 1976.

F.K. Brown, *The Fathers of the Victorians: The Age of Wilberforce*, Cambridge, Cambridge University Press, 1961.

S.J. Brown, *The National Churches of England, Ireland and Scotland*, Oxford, Oxford University Press, 2001.

S.J. Brown, *Providence and Empire: Religion, Politics and Society in the United Kingdom, 1815–1914*, Harlow, Pearson, 2008.

R. Furneaux, *William Wilberforce*, London, Hamish Hamilton, 1974.

A. Gilbert, *Religion and Society in Industrial England: Church, Chapel and Social Change 1740–1914*, London, Longman, 1976.

D. Hempton, *Methodism and Politics in British Society 1750–1850*, London, Hutchinson, 1987.

M. Hennell, *John Venn and the Clapham Sect*, London, SPCK, 1957.

E.M. Howse, *Saints in Politics: The 'Clapham Sect' and the Growth of Freedom*, London, Allen & Unwin, 1953.

K. Hylson-Smith, *The Churches in England from Elizabeth I to Elizabeth II: Volume II: 1689–1833*, London, SCM, 1997.

T. Laqueur, *Religion and Respectability: Sunday Schools and Working Class Culture 1780–1950*, New Haven, Yale University Press, 1976.

D. Rosman, *The Evolution of the English Churches 1500–2000*, Cambridge, CUP, 2003.

E. Royle, *Modern Britain: A Social History, 1750–1985*, London, Edward Arnold, 1987.

4

'To Use Means for the Conversion of the Heathen': The Revolution in Protestant Overseas Mission, c. 1790–1840

In 1792 a young Baptist minister from the English Midlands compiled statistics suggesting that the world population was 731 million people, of whom 130 million were Muslims, with 174 million in the Roman Catholic, Orthodox, and Armenian churches; 44 million people had access to Protestant teaching. The rest remained in 'pagan darkness'. Christianity was a predominantly white religion, largely confined to Europe, and North America. Many Christian countries were reported as being filled with scenes of 'ignorance, hypocrisy, and profligacy', with 'baneful, and pernicious errors... in almost every part of Christendom'. The compiler of the statistics, the young William Carey (1761–1834), lamented that the 'vast proportion of the sons of Adam... yet remain... utterly destitute of the knowledge of the gospel of Christ, or of any means of obtaining it'.[1] There were few Christians in vast parts of Asia; missionary efforts had been largely driven out of China; the small band of Christian believers in Japan had almost been persecuted out of existence. In Korea there were a few thousand Roman Catholics, and no Protestant missionary reached that country until 1865. Little progress in promoting the gospel had been made in India, and no missionary had yet reached the Pacific Islands. Muslim areas were largely untouched by missionary endeavours. In Africa, apart from the historic churches in Egypt and Ethiopia, Christian influence was largely confined to the coast.

---

1 W. Carey, *An Enquiry into the Obligations of Christians to Use Means For the Conversion of the Heathens*, Leicester, A. Ireland, 1792, facsimile edition, Didcot, Baptist Missionary Society, 1991, 64–87, 91, 88.

Carey stitched together a leather globe of the world, and prayed for the vast lands where the Christian message was unknown. He believed Christians had profound obligations to such areas: 'Humanity, and much more Christianity, call loudly for every possible exertion to introduce the gospel among them.'[2] Over the next two centuries a truly Copernican revolution in the make-up of world Christianity was to take place. By 1910, only Afghanistan, Tibet and Nepal were closed to missionary effort; from Tierra del Fuego to Greenland, from North America to Australasia and the South Pacific, Christian churches were to be found. By the late twentieth century six out of every ten Christians were to be found in Africa, Asia, South America and the Pacific.

William Carey argued that mission had lain at the heart of Christianity from the time of the Apostles. Although the sixteenth-century Reformers believed they had recovered an apostolic purity of doctrine, there was no commensurate return to apostolic zeal for world-wide mission, despite the boldness of their preaching within Europe,[3] and a short-lived mission from Geneva to Brazil.[4] Criticism of the Reformers should be tempered by an awareness of the social and political reality of the sixteenth-century world, which restricted many opportunities for mission. When the Pope granted the Spanish and Portuguese exclusive rights in the New World, this militated against successful Protestant endeavours there. Most of Europe was controlled by Roman Catholic authorities hostile to Protestantism. Turkish military strength left any doors to the Islamic world well guarded.

CHRISTIAN MISSION AFTER THE REFORMATION

Within the Roman Catholic Church there were those who responded to the overseas opportunities presented during and after the Reformation period with missionary earnestness, and willing self-sacrifice. In India, the East Indies, Japan, and China the work of the Jesuits was notable, as was their readiness to develop contextually appropriate methods of missionary strategy, with attempts at sensitivity towards local culture, and dress, although the degree to which this lapsed into accommodation and dilution of their message to local culture is debated.[5] How genuine the conversions of those subject to mass baptisms at the order of a chief or ruler were, and whether adherence to a few ceremonies and simple rote-learned truths, would constitute a genuine Christian conversion, are also matters open to question. Carey himself criticised the Jesuits for allowing

---

2   Carey, *Enquiry*, 40–41.

3   Carey, *Enquiry*, 42–63.

4   See David Smith, 'The Forgotten 'Grandfather' of Protestant Mission: Perspectives on Globalization from Jean de Lery', *Missiology*, Vol. XXXIV, no. 3, July 2006, 349–359.

5   On Jesuit missions and methods see A. Ross, *A Vision Betrayed: The Jesuits in Japan and China, 1542–1742*, Maryknoll, New York, Orbis, 1994.

their converts to retain former religious customs and beliefs.[6] Nonetheless, the significance of the efforts of Roman Catholic missionaries from Spain and Portugal in South America and South-East Asia, cannot be underestimated. The religious geography of the world was significantly shaped by their work, and remains so to this day.

When Protestant missionary efforts developed, they were influenced by wider political factors, being initially concentrated where access was possible because of the rule or influence of Protestant nations, such as in North America. Settlement brought contact with indigenous peoples, and a number of the charters for the new colonies included the intention that the colonists would seek to win the native peoples to the Christian faith. The Puritan John Eliot's work in Massachusetts between 1633 and 1690 saw 3,600 Native Americans gathered into fourteen settlements, indigenous preachers trained, with the Bible translated into the 'Moheecan' language by 1663.[7] David Brainerd also worked amongst the Native Americans, and although he died aged just 29 in 1747, he had seen significant fruit from his labours, including some 130 converts in 1745–1746. When his diary was published by Jonathan Edwards, it became a spiritual classic, inspiring later missionaries such as William Carey and Henry Martyn.[8]

Other societies such as the Society for Promoting Christian Knowledge (founded between 1696 and 1699), and the Anglican Society for the Propagation of the Gospel in Foreign Parts (founded 1701), also included in their remit missionary concern amongst British colonies in America, the West Indies, and India.[9] The three hundred and fifty missionaries sent out by the SPG during the eighteenth century included in their number John Wesley, whose short, but unsuccessful, period of ministry in North America took place before his evangelical conversion. In 1751, Thomas Thompson, who had worked as a missionary for the SPG in New Jersey, moved his sphere of labour to the Gold Coast (Ghana). The fruits of nearly five years of work there were limited, but one of the three boys he sent to England for education was baptised. Philip Quaque became the first African to be ordained into Holy Orders in the Church of England, and served for fifty years as a missionary and teacher of Africans in the Gold Coast before his death in 1816.[10]

6   Carey, *Enquiry*, 90.

7   On John Eliot see O. E. Winslow, *John Eliot, Apostle to the Indians*, Boston, Houghton Mifflin, 1968. On Puritan missions see S.H. Rooy, *The Theology of Missions in the Puritan Tradition*, Grand Rapids, Eerdmans, 1965.

8   J. Edwards, *Life of David Brainerd* (ed. N. Pettit), in *Works of Jonathan Edwards*, Vol 7, New Haven, Yale, 1985.

9   On the SPG see H.P. Thompson, *Into All Lands: The History of the Society for the Propagation of the Gospel in Foreign parts 1701–1950*, London, 1951; D. O'Connor, *Three Centuries of Mission*, London, Continuum, 2000.

10   S. Neill, *History of Christian Missions*, 2nd edition, Harmondsworth, Penguin, 1986, 203.

Through the Dutch East India Company, missionaries from the Netherlands worked in the Dutch colonies in Malaya, India, Sri Lanka (Ceylon), and for a short period Taiwan, and were allowed to work for the conversion of the local people. At the end of the seventeenth century, the Dutch claimed 100,000 Christians in Java, although the sincerity of some converts was far from what was desired. In 1776 there were still only 22 missionaries in the whole of Indonesia, only five of whom could speak an indigenous language.

The Lutheran Pietist tradition influenced the Protestant missionary movement well before the rapid growth of evangelicalism in Britain in the mid-eighteenth century. Inspired by August Francke (1663–1727), Pietism found a strong base at Halle, in Germany, where there was a university and an orphan house. The Pietist dynamic of Christian philanthropy, commitment to learning, and the promotion of the gospel, inspired huge sacrifices in the endeavour to share the Christian message. Missionaries fanned out across and beyond Europe, in co-operation with the king of Denmark.[11]

The Danish-Halle mission reached Tranquebar in 1706, the first non-Roman Catholic missionaries from Europe to India. Led by the inspirational Bartholomew Ziegenbalg, a former Halle student, the mission's work focussed upon education, Biblical translation, understanding local culture with the goal of seeking personal conversions, and the establishment of an indigenous Indian church. A New Testament in Tamil was completed in 1714, but Ziegenbalg's death after thirteen years in India meant that progress in translation work slowed, and it was 1796 before the whole Bible in Tamil was completed. Nonetheless, by 1732 the mission consisted of 1,478 members, and in the following year the first Indian pastor, a convert from Hinduism, was ordained. Extensive use was made of indigenous catechists, and schoolmasters.[12] The mission eventually passed into the control of the English SPCK, but Lutheran Pietists continued in the work until 1825.

The Evangelical Revival of the eighteenth century also had roots in the displaced, persecuted minorities of Central Europe, whose spirituality was deepened in the face of attempts to impose Roman Catholicism on them, and by reaction against the confessional absolutism of early-eighteenth-century Europe. This was the experience of the small community of Moravian refugees who in the years after 1722 found shelter from Count Nikolaus von Zinzendorf in Saxony, and settled at Herrnhut on his Berthelsdorf estate. Hernnhut was to rank alongside Halle as one of the twin engines of eighteenth century Protestant

11 W.R. Ward, *The Protestant Evangelical Awakening*, Cambridge, CUP, 1992, 61–63; A.F. Walls, 'The Eighteenth-Century Protestant Missionary Awakening', in B. Stanley (ed), *Christian Missions and the Enlightenment*, Grand Rapids, Eerdmans, 2001, 30–32.

12 D.D. Hudson, *Protestant Origins in India: Tamil Evangelical Christians, 1706–1835*, Grand Rapids, Eerdmans, 2000, 1–29.

missionary endeavour. In 1727 they reported: 'a great grace was amongst them and in the whole district', and one of the most intense periods of revival witnessed in the eighteenth century followed, with profound emotions displayed, and spontaneous prayer meetings held by the children of the community.[13] Already living as refugees, and fired by deepened spiritual experience, the impulse to overseas mission was strong. Some were willing literally to become slaves in order to preach to other slaves.[14]

Moravianism became a missionary movement: between 1732 and 1740, 70 missionaries were sent out from a community of just 600. By 1760 the number was 226, and by the 1880s it was over 2,100. They reached Danish colonies in the Caribbean in 1732, and the following year Greenland, where they built on an earlier Danish Lutheran Mission. Lapland was reached in 1735, and by 1737 Georg Schmidt was pioneering work in South Africa.[15] Their work in London was a significant factor in the evangelical conversion of John Wesley in 1738. The Moravian strategy was to create small communities of volunteers, which served as largely economically self-sufficient mission stations connected to the home base, with clear spiritual goals, strong principles of doctrine and discipline, and an avoidance of political involvement. This model, together with a network of personal connections, was to significantly influence the formation and approach of later missionary organisations such as the Baptist Missionary Society (1792), the London Missionary Society (1795), and the Church Missionary Society (1799).[16]

The British East India Company, formed in 1600, appointed chaplains for British settlers, but operated on the principle of non-interference with the customs of the country, fearing that propagation of the Christian gospel might provoke the inhabitants, and prove harmful to the development of commerce. However, in South India the British authorities allowed the missionaries of the Danish-Halle mission, which had been taken over by the Anglican SPCK, to preach the gospel amongst the non-Christian populace, whilst acting as chaplains to British regiments and communities. The most notable of these was the German Christian Friedrich Schwartz (1726–98), who after work at Tranquebar, moved to Trichinopoly, and then Tanjore where he worked for twenty years until his death. The Tanjore church grew to some 2,000 members during the period of Schwartz's ministry, although after his death the

13   W.R. Ward, *Protestant Evangelical Awakening*, 118–28.

14   Walls, 'Eighteenth-Century Protestant Missionary Awakening', 30–32.

15   J.E. Hutton, *A History of Moravian Missions*, London, Moravian Publication Office, 1922; J.C.S. Mason, *The Moravian Church and the Missionary Awakening in England, 1760–1800*, Woodbridge, Boydell, 2001. On the Moravians in South Africa see B. Krüger, *The Pear Tree Blossoms: A History of Moravian Mission Stations in South Africa, 1737–1869*, Genadenal, Moravian Book Depot, 1967.

16   A. Walls, *The Cross-Cultural Process in Christian History*, Maryknoll, New York, Orbis, 2002, 202–206.

congregations fell into severe decline. A significant advance between 1795 and 1805 around Cape Comorin led to the baptism of some 5,000 people by the Tanjore missionaries and their Indian co-workers. This became the foundation of the Tinnevelly Church, which some 100 years later produced the first Indian Anglican bishop.[17]

The extent of these early Protestant endeavours have led to a questioning of the traditional narrative that modern missions started with the pioneering work of Roman Catholic missionaries between the fifteenth and eighteenth centuries, followed by a lull associated with the suppression of the Jesuit order, before a revival in the early nineteenth century, inspired by the work of William Carey. The significant continuity between the efforts of earlier Protestantism and those in the nineteenth century is now recognised, as is the need to discuss both Roman Catholic and Protestant movements as aspects of European interaction with peoples of the non-Western world.[18] Carey and other British pioneers joined a well-established continental tradition at a time when the logistical facility of the British mercantile and maritime empire was becoming available. The significant upsurge in Protestant missionary endeavour in the decades after Carey's call to duty in 1792 built upon what had gone before, and he in turn set a pattern followed by many modern Protestant voluntary missionary societies.

WILLIAM CAREY AND THE PARTICULAR BAPTIST MISSIONARY SOCIETY

William Carey may have left a significant mark on world Christianity, but there was little in his early life to indicate that this would happen. Born in humble circumstances in an obscure village, he enjoyed little formal education, and most of what he learned he taught himself. Converted through the efforts of a fellow apprentice, Carey worked as a shoemaker between the ages of sixteen and twenty-eight. That he progressed from artisan to missionary statesman is testimony to his natural genius, and deep spirituality.[19] When he became the pastor of a village Baptist church he came into association with a vibrant group of Baptist ministers in the English Midlands, including Andrew Fuller (1754–1815). Influenced through reading Jonathan Edwards, they had come to believe that Calvinism and evangelicalism were compatible, and that the task

---

17   S.H. Moffett, *A History of Christianity in Asia, Volume II: 1500–1900*, Maryknoll, New York, Orbis, 2005, 236–244; S. Neill, *History of Christian Missions*, Harmondsworth, Penguin, 1986, 197–200.

18   Walls, 'The Eighteenth-Century Protestant Missionary Awakening', in Stanley, *Christian Missions and the Enlightenment*, 22–44.

19   For first hand accounts of Carey see E. Carey, *Memoir of William Carey, D.D*, London, 1836; J.C. Marshman, *The Life and Times of Carey, Marshman and Ward*, 2 vols, London, 1859. For more recent studies see S.P. Carey, *William Carey D.D.*, 7th edn, London, 1926; B. Stanley, *The History of the Baptist Missionary Society 1792–1992*, Edinburgh, T&T Clark, 1992, 1–68. M. Haykin, *One Heart and Soul: John Sutcliff of Olney, His Friends and His Times*, Darlington, Evangelical Press, 1994.

William Carey: An Enquiry Whether the Commission Given by Our Lord to His Disciples Be Not Still Binding On Us

Section I ... It seems as if many thought the commission was sufficiently put into execution by what the apostles and others have done; that we have enough to do to attend to the salvation of our own countrymen; and that if God intends the salvation of the heathen, he will some way or other bring them to the gospel... It is thus that multitudes sit at ease and give themselves no concern about the greater part of their fellow sinners, who to this day, are lost in ignorance and idolatry... To the consideration of such persons I would offer the following observations.

'FIRST. If the command of Christ to teach all nations be restricted to the apostles, or those under the immediate inspiration of the Holy Ghost, then that of baptising should be so too...
SECOND... then all such ordinary ministers who have endeavoured to carry the gospel to the heathens, have acted without warrant, and run without sent...
THIRDLY, If the command of Christ to teach all nations extend only to the apostles, then, doubtless, the promise of the divine presence in this work must be so limited; but this is worded in such a manner as expressly precludes such an idea. *Lo, I am with you always, to the end of the world.'* [1]

1   W. Carey, *An Enquiry into the Obligations of Christians to use Means for the Conversion of the Heathens*, Leicester, A. Ireland, 1792.

of evangelism was not solely confined to Britain. This led to a move away from high Calvinism, with its conviction that once the message of the gospel had been declared, God would sovereignly draw to himself those who were his elect, without the need to make direct calls for repentance and faith. As the impact of the Evangelical Revival began to be felt amongst English Nonconformists, evangelical Calvinism,[20] with a stress on the autonomy and capacity of the individual human will, brought a deepened sense of the necessity to preach the gospel for conversion, and an emphasis on the duty of people to believe. In 1784 the Midlands Baptists also took up the call to concerted prayer that Edwards had issued, starting a monthly prayer-meeting for revival, and 'the spread of the Gospel to the most distant parts of the habitable globe.'[21]

20   For the distinctions between 'evangelical Calvinism', 'high Calvinism' (sometimes referred to as hyper Calvinism), and 'moderate Calvinism' see I. J. Shaw, *High Calvinists in Action*, Oxford, OUP, 2002; 10-25.

21   E. Carey, *Memoir of William Carey*, London, 1836, 18.

In 1789, Carey, inspired by reading the accounts of the Pacific explorations of the English explorer, Captain James Cook, and his discoveries of previously unknown peoples, proposed a discussion at a local Baptist minister's fraternal. The subject was whether the Commission of Jesus to his disciples in Matthew 28, 18–20 was still binding on the church. He was reportedly dismissed as a 'most miserable enthusiast' by the senior minister present, J.C. Ryland, who declared that 'nothing could be done before another Pentecost, when an effusion of miraculous gifts, including the gift of tongues, would give an effect to the Commission of Christ as at first.' Carey's enthusiasm was undiminished.[22] In 1792 he published his 'Enquiry into the Obligations of Christians to Use Means for the Conversion of the Heathens', which included statistics concerning the progress of Christianity across the world. The 'means' to be used included prayer, and every 'lawful method' to spread the knowledge of Christ's name. He also offered an answer to the question on Christ's commission he had proposed for discussion three years earlier. That same year he preached his famous missionary sermon on Isaiah 54, 2–3, stressing the 'spacious promises' of the new covenant, and the confidence that should accompany the preaching of the gospel: 'Expect great things, attempt great things.'[23]

Carey expressed what other local Baptist pastors had become convinced of, and at Kettering in October 1792, the 'Particular Baptist Society for Propagating the Gospel Among the Heathen' was formed. The small group of men who gathered that day collected in a snuff box the small, but significant, sum of £13. 2s 6d. It was to be a voluntary society, influenced by the prevailing commercial form of organisation, with rules, subscribers, and a governing executive committee, but no major denominational backing. In 1793, it was Carey himself who volunteered to become the first missionary sent out by the society, along with John Thomas, a surgeon who had previously worked in India. It was an extraordinary decision for a journeyman artisan and his family, who had probably never even seen the sea before. For his young family, especially his wife Dorothy, the decision that they should accompany him on the perilous journey was a traumatic step, which eventually placed her under unbearable mental strain.

The poorly-financed project seemed destined to end in abject failure. Carey's attempts to preach to the Indians in Calcutta were frustrated by official opposition, and his lack of command of the local languages. As a Dissenter from the artisan classes, Carey was used to the barriers of social discrimination, but he was ill prepared for the obstacles to the evangelism created by the strength

---

22 Stanley, *History of BMS*, 6–7. There is some debate as to what exactly was said by Ryland.

23 The original form seems to have been this shorter version, the expansion 'Expect great things from God, attempt great things for God' being a later addition (A.C. Smith, 'The Spirit and the Letter of Carey's Catalytic Watchword', *Baptist Quarterly* 33 (1989–90), 226–37.

William Carey

of the Hindu caste system. In 1800 he relocated the base of his missionary work to Serampore, a Danish colony near Calcutta and away from the restrictions of British rule. This was to remain his missionary base for the last thirty-four years of his life. Operating in India with neither a formal licence nor the official sanction of the East India Company, Carey proved an inspirational figure and motivator of others, his vision and gritty determination undiminished. In 1800, the self-educated shoemaker, often plagued with depression and a sense of his own inadequacy, was appointed Professor of Sanskrit, Bengali, and Marathi, at the government established College of Fort William, Calcutta.

Carey gathered around him a team of able workers, forming the Serampore Trio along with William Ward (a printer), and Joshua Marshman (a skilled linguist and educator). Following the Moravian example, living as a community, sharing leadership, and holding goods in common, the Serampore Trio stressed the importance of educating and training Indian preachers. A vast work of translation was undertaken to support this. Serampore College was established initially for the training of future Christian leaders, but the curriculum included studying Hindu culture, and Indian languages, and eventually Hindu and Muslim students were admitted.

Success in the mission was hard won. It was seven years before the first Indians, Krishna Pal and his friend Gokul, renounced the caste system, and professed conversion. Although such Indian converts and their families were to face great opposition and persecution for their faith, a steady flow of baptisms followed that of Krishna Pal in the River Ganges on 28th December 1800. Records suggest that between 1800 and 1821, 1,407 persons were baptised at Serampore, over half of whom were Indians, with a significant number being higher caste Brahmins. It was a major accomplishment for a pioneer missionary work with slender resources.[24]

Amidst the successes were tragedies aplenty. John Thomas and Dorothy Carey sadly descended into insanity. Between 1811 and 1812 ten of the missionary party died, including five of their children, and in 1812 fire swept through buildings in Serampore, destroying some of Carey's important manuscripts, and printing equipment. Unshakeable in his conviction of the sovereignty of God, he simply resolved to do the translations again, and better.[25] Yet, as the community of workers grew, the presence of younger missionaries who found it hard to share the ideals of the pioneering Trio, created significant tensions. The trusteeship of the complex of buildings at Serampore which the Trio had constructed largely from their own finances became bitterly contested, and acrimonious controversy rumbled on from 1816 to Carey's death in 1834, resulting in painful division. In typically far-sighted fashion, Carey saw the work of a mission society as being

24   Stanley, *BMS*, 37, 56–57.
25   W. Carey to Andrew Fuller, 25 March 1812; 30–31 July 1832, cited in Stanley, *BMS*, 38.

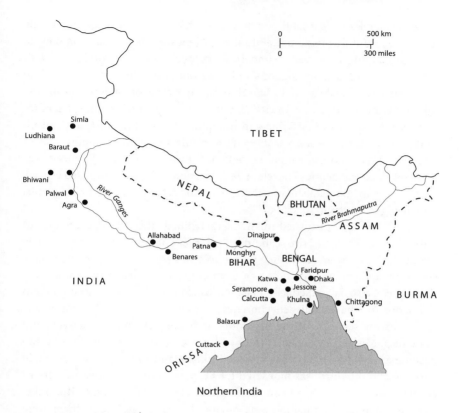

Northern India

to recruit personnel and raise funds, with the heart of its control vested in the field, and a strong place for national workers, but this led to conflict with the attempts of the BMS committee to retain control in Britain.[26]

Carey and his colleagues soon realised that because of the linguistic and cultural barriers between Europeans and Indian peoples, the evangelisation of India was most likely to be achieved through the work of indigenous converts who had the Christian scriptures in their own languages. Carey's translation work was prodigious: the whole Bible was eventually translated into six languages, and parts of it into 29 other languages. The translations had many weaknesses, but were foundations upon which others could build. He added to these grammars in seven Indian languages, and dictionaries in Bengali, Sanskrit, and Marathi.[27] Carey also stressed the value of understanding local life and culture, and a number of great works of Indian literature were translated. His steady perseverance reaped a remarkable harvest of Bible translation and printing, evangelism, education, and medical relief work.

26 The controversy is fully discussed in Stanley, *BMS*, 57–67.
27 Stanley, *BMS*, 48–51.

Key principles were established by Carey which were to prove significantly formative for future missiological thinking. Alongside the emphasis on Biblical translation, indigenous pastors undertook evangelism and pastoral work, with a network of missionary stations radiating out from the central base. The intention was to establish an Indian church, largely free of foreign control. The role of the missionary was formative, but temporary, initiating new churches, and setting patterns of doctrine and discipline. By the time of Carey's death in 1834, nineteen missionary stations were connected with Serampore, staffed by fifty workers, most of whom did not come from Britain. The intention was to establish an indigenous church in each location. Education was also crucial: Joshua Marshman established a network of schools; by 1818, some 10,000 pupils were being educated in 92 schools.[28]

Carey, the artisan-turned-missionary, typified the first generation of missionaries. The first two candidates of the London Missionary Society, founded in 1795, were craftsmen, whose role was primarily to provide simple education and training in crafts as a form of pre-evangelism. This meant that they were of a social and educational level which would not have secured them ordination in the established churches, nor in some other denominations. It was a risky strategy: of the first four candidates sent by the Glasgow and Edinburgh Missionary Societies (founded in 1796), one abandoned his task to become a slave trader, another returned to Scotland to become a lecturer in atheism, and the third was murdered for his possessions.[29] The use of artisans attracted the famous barb from the Anglican cleric Sydney Smith 'if a tinker is a devout man, he infallibly sets off for the East'.[30] Although there were undoubtedly some who disappointed amongst these early missionary recruits, the sacrificial efforts of many cannot be overstated. Whilst church leaders at home fretted over whether those who had served as missionaries overseas for a few years should be allowed to return and take-up a comfortable ministry in Britain, most embraced the missionary call for life. All too frequently it proved a very brief life.

Early disappointments led to attempts to bring missionary candidates closer to the standards expected of the general ministerial candidates. Colleges for their training were established, with the missionary vocation increasingly seen as one branch of the ordained ministry: ministerial status became the norm for missionaries until 1870. Scottish missions so emphasised education, especially at higher levels, that a full university degree in arts with further training in divinity, became normal. Lay and artisan personnel were still sent to the mission fields, often to work in industrial or agricultural projects, but often to serve

28   Stanley, *BMS*, 53, 51.

29   A. Walls, *The Missionary Movement in Christian History*, 167–68.

30   S. Smith, 'Indian Missions', *Edinburgh Review*, 12 (April 1808), 180.

Resistance to Overseas Missions

'We admit it to be the general duty of Christian people to disseminate their religion among the Pagan nations who are subject to their empire… We believe that we are in possession of a revealed religion… and the possession of that religion can alone confer immortality and best confer present happiness. [169–170]… [yet] there is scarcely a parish in England or Ireland, in which the zeal and activity of any one of these Indian apostles would not have done more good… than can be expected from their joint efforts in the populous regions of Asia [171]… the duties of conversion appear to be of less importance, when it is impossible to procure proper persons to undertake them and when such religious embassies, in consequence, devolve on the lowest of the people… The wise and rational part of the Christian ministry find they have enough to do at home… But if a tinker is a devout man, he infallibly sets off for the East. Let any man read the Anabaptist missions… without feeling that they are little detachments of maniacs, benefiting us much more by their absence, than the Hindoos by their advice.' [179–80]¹

1   Rev. Sydney Smith, 'Indian Missions', in *Edinburgh Review*, 12, (April 1808), 169–70, 171, 179–80, voicing the opposition of many to the approach to mission being adopted early in the nineteenth century.

---

as auxiliaries under the direction of clerical missionaries, and their allowance levels remained below those of the ordained missionaries.[31]

The radical nature of what Carey, and other pioneers of his time, were attempting must be recognised. To Sydney Smith, they were 'little detachments of maniacs'. Far from being the handmaiden of imperialism, the Protestant missionary movement of Carey's day was considered as potentially subversive to European overseas trade interests. Carey himself entertained politically radical sentiments, initially welcoming the French Revolution for its overthrow of the corrupt French regime and the Roman Catholic Church. Although believing that much of Indian culture need attract no opposition from Christian evangelists, some of his radical egalitarianism was channelled into opposing Brahmin teaching, priestcraft and superstition: his opposition to *sati*, the practice of widows being burned alive on their husband's funeral pyres, was implacable. A protracted campaign was conducted by the missionaries, before the practice was declared illegal in Bengal in 1829.[32]

The decision to adopt the voluntary society format, rather than the

---

31   A. Walls, 'The Missionary Movement: A Lay Fiefdom?', in *The Cross-Cultural Process in Christian History*, Maryknoll, NY, Orbis, 2002, 226–228.

32   Stanley, *BMS*, 45.

denominational one, was similarly radical, and helped the mission to draw on the growing pan-evangelical interest in foreign missions.[33] Carey's vision was also radical, not confined to India, but drawing in most of East Asia: Afghanistan, Nepal, Tibet, Assam and China were unfulfilled aspirations, but there were connections between his work and that begun in Bhutan, Burma, Sri Lanka, and the East Indies. Within fifty years of Carey's death in 1834, there were half a million Protestants in India.[34]

THE LONDON MISSIONARY SOCIETY

Another product of the deepening of interest in overseas mission amongst Protestants in the late eighteenth century was the London Missionary Society. From its foundation it aspired to be a truly ecumenical missionary society, involving Churchmen and Dissenters, in promoting the gospel rather than denominationalism. Started in 1795 as simply the 'Missionary Society,' and designed to unite Calvinists and Arminians, its founders were in fact predominantly Calvinists from Anglican, Independent, Calvinistic Methodist, and Presbyterian churches. The society gradually lost its denominational breadth, and by the 1820s it was largely the missionary organ of congregational churches.[35] David Bogue, one of the founders, was an Independent minister in Hampshire. As an evangelistically-minded Calvinist he engaged in itinerancy, trained young men for ministry, and took a keen interest in overseas mission. Many of the early London Missionary Society candidates were trained at his Gosport Academy, imbued with zeal and confidence in their evangelism, and encouraged to see that the first task of the missionary was to civilise, and use reason to support the claims of revelation. Mission work involved effective partnership between gospel proclamation, education and social improvement.[36]

Within four years of its foundation, the LMS had sent out sixty-seven missionaries.[37] It shared a considerable debt to the pre-existing European missionary movement: by 1850, around sixty out of 506 LMS missionaries came from Europe.[38] Its policy of sending out candidates with limited training and experience, alongside ordained clergy, was fraught with difficulties. Most of its early endeavours were focussed upon the islands of the South Pacific. In 1796

33 Stanley, BMS, 20–21; W. Hanna, *Memoirs of Thomas Chalmers, D.D*, Vol 1, Edinburgh, Constable, 1854, 162, 236–238.

34 Stanley, *BMS*, 55, 68–105.

35 On the founding of the LMS see R.H. Martin, *Evangelicals United: Ecumenical Stirrings in Pre-Victorian England, 1795–1830*, London, 1983, 40–60; R. Lovett, *History of the London Missionary Society 1795–1895*, London, H. Frowde, 1899.

36 Stanley, 'Christian Missions and the Enlightenment: A Re-Evaluation', 17–18.

37 J. Sibtree, *London Missionary Society: A Register of Missionaries, Deputations, etc, from 1796–1923*, 4th edn, London, LMS, 1923, in Walls, *Cross-Cultural Process*, 226.

38 Walls, *Cross-Cultural Process*, 207

four ordained missionaries set out for Tahiti, Tonga and the Marquesas Islands, along with a party of twenty-six others possessed of practical artisan skills, including those of bricklayer, weaver, tailor and shoemaker, together with six wives and three children. They were to live as a community, preach, and teach European trades. The physical, mental, moral and spiritual challenges involved in this pioneer cross-cultural work quickly took their toll. After five years, only a handful were left. One of the party, together with his wife, abandoned the journey at Portsmouth; three returned home soon after arrival; eleven left when violence erupted and three were killed. Two gave up profession of Christianity, and married local women. Their missionary ship, the Duff, was captured by the French together with a further party of missionaries. Yet, Tahiti was in time to become one of the great missionary success stories. The conversion of the principal chief, Pomare, on the island of Tahiti in 1819 heralded a movement amongst the local population with the majority of the island embracing Protestantism by the 1830s.[39] French imperialist expansion significantly re-shaped the long-term religious complexion of Tahiti after they controversially took over the island in the 1840s, and favoured a Roman Catholic religious system. The Protestant church survived on Tahiti, but no longer as the jewel in the crown of evangelical missionary endeavour it had once been.

There was a succession of martyrs in the early years of the LMS. John Williams (1796–1839) was to prove an inspirational leader, and through his policy of placing as many native teachers on as many islands as possible, he succeeded in widespread evangelisation. In 1830 he established eighteen teachers on Samoa, and within a generation most of the islanders had professed conversion. By 1834 every major island within 2,000 miles of Tahiti had been visited. Williams was an example of the heroic life and sacrifice of pioneering men and women who lived in isolation and constant danger to their lives, sharing the Christian faith, translating the scriptures, and seeking to build churches. Although he was martyred on the island of Erromanga in 1839, and his body eaten by cannibals, he was one of many Europeans and native Polynesians whose blood was to become the seed of the church in the South Pacific—there were five missionary martyrs on Erromanga alone, together with other Polynesian teachers. Through their devoted labours, churches grew, and strong indigenous leadership was established.[40]

Whilst the LMS vision of evangelical union in overseas mission was never realised, it became one of the largest missionary societies in Britain. By 1820 it

39   Lovett, History of the LMS, 46–47; 57–64; C.W. Newbury (ed), The History of the Tahitian Mission, 1799–1830: Written by John Davies Missionary to the South Sea Islands, Cambridge, Cambridge University Press, 1961.

40   On John Williams see J. Glutch, Beyond the Reefs: John Williams, Missionary to the South Seas, London, Macdonald, 1974.

had fifty stations manned by 140 missionaries, and in 1830 it was operating on every continent. It was to greatly influence other pan-evangelical ventures—the Religious Tract Society owed its foundation directly to the LMS, and the British and Foreign Bible Society indirectly.

The pattern for Protestant missionary expansion through voluntary societies had been set. In 1796, the New York Missionary Society was formed, and other societies in Europe followed, with close fraternal links to the LMS. The Basel Mission was founded in Switzerland in 1815, and the Berlin Missionary Society in 1824. Other societies followed in Denmark (1821), Paris (1822), Sweden (1835), and Norway (1842). The interdenominational spirit operative in the foundation of the LMS was often replicated on the mission field, and created an environment in which union churches could later be formed, in places such as North and South India.[41]

ANGLICAN MISSIONS

As a national established church, the Church of England was a parochial system for maintaining the faith within a Christendom context, rather than a strongly missionary-minded body, although the efforts of the Anglican SPG and SPCK have already been noted. However, it was drawn into the developing missionary movement, partly because, as the established church, it had the responsibility for appointing chaplains to serve expatriates in British territories, especially in India.

Members of the Clapham Sect used their influence to promote Christian mission in India. Charles Grant (1746–1823) experienced evangelical conversion whilst working in India for the East India Company, and rose within its ranks to serve as director, and then chairman. He began to campaign against the Company's prohibition of Christian outreach amongst the Indian population. When he returned to England in 1792 he won the support of William Wilberforce in a campaign to open India to missionary endeavour.

Although his personal ministry was limited to Britain, the influence of Charles Simeon on undergraduates at Cambridge University made him of far wider significance. Simeon encouraged a number of students to work in India as chaplains of the East India Company. They were missionaries in all but name, and included Claudius Buchanan (1766–1815), who arrived in India in 1797, and worked hard to promote the cause of mission in the country, David Brown (1763–1812), and Henry Martyn (1781–1812). A first-rate scholar who won academic prizes at Cambridge University, Martyn served as Simeon's curate before setting out as chaplain to the East India Company in 1805. In Calcutta he consulted with William Carey and after he was stationed at Dinapore (1806–09) began the work of translating into Urdu the New Testament and the Book of

---

41   R.H. Martin, *Evangelicals United*, 53–55; N. Goodall, *A History of the London Missionary Society 1895–1945*, London, Oxford University Press, 1954, 3ff.

Common Prayer—a work of such merit that in the 1960s it was still the basis of the version in use. He also, controversially, sought opportunities to share the Christian faith with Hindus and Muslims. In 1810, with his health failing, Martyn was advised to take a sea voyage, and he travelled to Shiraz, where he consulted Persian scholars, and discussed with them his Persian and Arabic translations of the New Testament. He died in Armenia on his journey home to Britain, aged just 31. His *Journals* were preserved, and are classics of devotional literature, revealing the intensity of his commitment to both Christ, and the cause of Christian missions.[42] His policies of ecumenical missiological co-operation, rejection of imperialistic attitudes towards Indians, and achievements as a missionary scholar, were far sighted.[43]

Charles Simeon regularly met with other Evangelicals in the Eclectic Society. Challenged by the example of the Particular Baptist Missionary Society, one topic of significant debate in the 1790s was the lack of opportunities for Anglicans to take the gospel overseas. The failure of the London Missionary Society to attract widespread Anglican support, and the SPG's lack of sympathy for evangelicalism, led the members of the Eclectic Society to resolve in 1799 to form a voluntary missionary society of Anglicans, with the intention of promoting missions in Africa and the East, without infringing the order of the Anglican Church. Along with Simeon, John Venn, vicar of Holy Trinity Church, Clapham (where members of the Clapham Sect attended), took a leading role in forming the 'Society for Missions to Africa and the East,' which became known after 1812 as the Church Missionary Society.[44] John Venn helped lay down the society's principles, and draft its rules. His son, Henry Venn (1796–1873), served as the society's secretary from 1841–72. Yet, the relationship of the society to the Anglican Church remained uncertain. No bishop joined its committee until the Evangelical Henry Ryder in 1814.[45]

The CMS, as with other British missionary societies, drew heavily in its early days on the already active European missionary movement, particularly the Missionary Seminaries in Berlin. For the first five years of its existence the CMS had little to report, before in 1804 the first two candidates, both from Berlin, were sent to Sierra Leone. Out of the first twenty-four CMS missionaries,

42 H. Martyn, *Journals and Letters of The Revd. Henry Martyn. B.D,* (ed. S. Wilberforce), London, Seeley, 1837.

43 C. Bennett, 'The Legacy of Henry Martyn', *International Bulletin of Missionary Research,* January 1992, 10–14.

44 On the history of the Church Missionary Society see E. Stock, *History of the Church Missionary Society,* 4 vols, London, 1899–1916; recent analysis is in the collection of essays edited by Kevin Ward and Brian Stanley, *The Church Mission Society and World Christianity 1799–1999,* Grand Rapids, Eerdmans, 2000.

45 A. Porter, *Religion Versus Empire? British Protestant Missionaries and Overseas Expansion, 1700–1914,* Manchester, Manchester University Press, 2004, 53.

seventeen were from Europe, mostly Lutherans, and only three were ordained Englishmen. Although after 1815, the balance began to change, even by 1830, forty-nine out of the first 166 missionaries of the Anglican CMS were Europeans, including Germans, Swiss, Dutch and Danes. The use of already ordained Lutherans circumvented the problem of securing ordination for candidates with Evangelical principles, who were unacceptable to most bishops. Often they came from humble backgrounds, but had demonstrated great academic potential.[46]

The CMS had strong links with the Clapham Sect's project in Sierra Leone, where a number of Anglican ministers served as chaplains. They encountered an already existing church, comprised of resettled African Christians from Nova Scotia and Britain. It was the first modern church of tropical Africa created without missionary input, and included growing congregations of Baptists and Methodists. After 1807, the British naval squadron operating off the West African coast also began to settle those it had liberated from slave ships in Sierra Leone, and the CMS concentrated its African operations amongst them. Early work by Baptists, Wesleyans, and Presbyterians from Europe was beset by problems amongst the missionaries, and saw minimal success.[47] The work of the CMS was also slow and uneven, and the society had significant difficulty in recruiting missionaries. The commitment and self-sacrifice of those who went was extraordinary—of the twenty-seven missionaries sent by the mission to Sierra Leone after 1804, fifteen had died before the end of 1820. In 1822 alone, twelve CMS missionaries or missionaries wives died. West Africa was truly the white man's grave.[48] Sierra Leone itself struggled for existence, with its mixed and conflict ridden population of freed and re-settled slaves, increasingly mistrustful of the policy of the authorities who seemed to support European above African interests. Early hopes that the settlement might prove self-sufficient and self-governing were disappointed.

The Sierra Leone colony for freed slaves embodied what were to become the three pillars of the nineteenth century missionary movement: the attempt to establish legitimate commerce in place of slave trading; Christianisation, through the work of chaplains; and civilisation—imparting education, and thereby improved moral standards. The CMS made determined efforts to promote education amongst the former slaves, although to do this it depended

46 Walls, *Missionary Movement in Christian History*, 168–170.

47 The disastrous divisions and failures amongst the missionaries, and their unwise policies, together with later Wesleyan successes are set out in A.F. Walls, 'The Early Sierra Leone Colony', in ed. G.J. Cuming, *The Mission of the Church and the Propagation of the Faith*, Cambridge, CUP, 1970, 107–129.

48 P.D. Curtin, 'The White Man's Grave: Image and Reality 1780–1850', *Journal of British Studies* 1 (1), 1959, 94ff.

upon government grants. After disappointing early results, in 1827, the Church Missionary Society established the 'Fourah Bay Institution' primarily to serve missionary requirements, but also to educate liberated Africans, who were equipped to be future indigenous leaders for the Anglican church in West Africa. Despite significant set-backs CMS work was also established in India and New Zealand.

The East India Company, with its legal monopoly of trade and patronage of Hindu temples, effectively recognised Hinduism as the de facto established religion in India. This placed missionaries, some of whom operated without formal licence, constantly under threat. A mutiny amongst sepoy [Indian] troops at Vellore in 1806 was blamed on their efforts, and severe restrictions were placed on their work. The East India Company depended on a charter granted by the British government, and a major campaign was launched to achieve recognition of a place for Christianity in India. The calls for missionary access by Nonconformists were one part of their campaign for toleration and liberty for religion in Britain, and full use was made of the language of natural rights in their appeals for missionaries to operate freely in India. Anglicans looked instead for an extension of the religious establishment to India. Skilful political manoeuvring by Wilberforce and his friends, and mass petitioning of the government, especially by dissenters, resulted in 1813 in the insertion of a 'Pious Clause' in the Charter of the East India Company, allowing for measures for the religious and moral improvement of the peoples of India. It was a victory, but a limited one. Missionaries still found restrictions on both their access into India, and on their activities within the country.[49] Ironically, although the 'Pious Clause' was designed to ease the work of voluntary mission agencies, an Anglican episcopate in Calcutta was also created and a religious establishment for Anglicans. Bishops of Calcutta included the High Church Thomas Middleton (1814–23), the hymn-writing Reginald Heber (1823–26), and the Evangelical Daniel Wilson (1832–57).

As British influence extended into the South Pacific, Australia was established as a penal colony, where social undesirables and criminals were dumped, gulag-style, as far as possible from their homeland. John Newton and William Wilberforce lobbied William Pitt to appoint a chaplain for New South Wales, and Richard Johnson (1755–1827) was sent out with the fleet in 1787. He was joined in 1794 by Samuel Marsden (1765–1838). In his role as chaplain, Marsden encouraged the founding of churches and voluntary societies, and in 1813 he promoted a mission to the Maoris of New Zealand, with a missionary party

---

49   A. Porter, *Religion Versus Empire? Protestant Missionaries and Overseas Expansion, 1700–1914*, Manchester, Manchester University Press, 2004, 73–75; On this campaign see A.K. Davidson, *Evangelicals and Attitudes to India, 1786–1813: Missionary Publicity and Claudius Buchanan*, Sutton Courtenay, 1990, esp. chapters 13–14.

The Pious Clause for India

'And whereas it is the Duty of the country to promote the Interests and the Happiness of the Native Inhabitants of the British Dominions in India and such Measures ought to be adopted as may tend to the introduction among them of useful knowledge and of religious and moral improvement, and in furtherance of the above objects, sufficient facilities ought to be afforded by Law to persons desirous of going to and remaining in India, for the purpose of accomplishing those benevolent designs so long as the authority of the Local Governments respecting the Intercourse of Europeans with the interior of the Country be preserved, and the Principles of the British Government, on which the Natives of India have hitherto relied for the free exercise of their religion be inviolably maintained.'[1]

1 Act of Parliament 53 Geo.3. c.155, Section 33, in Porter, *Religion Versus Empire?*, 74.

---

arriving in 1814. Although it was 1825 before the first baptism was reported, the mission expanded to embrace other South Pacific islands. Although showing little regard for Australia's aborigines, Marsden was far more sensitive towards the indigenous peoples of the Pacific islands, and did much to establish the Evangelical character of the Church of England in Sydney.[50]

METHODIST MISSIONS

Although spoken initially in justification of itinerant preaching in Britain, John Wesley's dictum, 'I look upon the whole world as my parish,' lent to Methodism a missionary character from its inception. A leading figure in Methodist mission was Thomas Coke (1747–1814). Educated at Oxford, and taking deacons orders in the Anglican church in 1770, he became associated with John Wesley from 1777 onwards. Driven out of his curacy on account of his evangelical preaching, he approached Wesley for guidance as to what he should do. The reported retort was: 'Brother, go out, go out and preach the Gospel to all the world!' Coke was true to this directive, and became a tireless itinerant preacher. In 1783 he drew up his 'Plan of the Society for the Establishment of Missions among the Heathens', and the following year he and Francis Asbury were set apart by Wesley as superintendents for America. This committed Coke to prolonged journeys across the Atlantic, which took him away from his cherished missionary schemes. Coke rejected the distinction between 'home' and 'foreign' missions, and tirelessly raised funds, sent out missionaries, and proposed new fields, and staunchly opposed slavery.

50 On Samuel Marsden see J.R. Elder (ed), *The Letters and Journals of Samuel Marsden, 1765–1838*, Dunedin, 1932; A.T. Yarwood, *Samuel Marsden: The Great Survivor*, Carlton, Victoria, 1977.

Some of Coke's schemes were held back by John Wesley himself, who preferred to concentrate efforts on the harvest in Britain. When Duncan McCallum offered himself to serve in Africa, Wesley's response, was 'Convert the heathen in Scotland'.[51] Similarly the plan for Asia was placed on hold, Wesley considered it too much of a hazard to the health of missionaries at the time. Nova Scotia, Newfoundland, and the West Indies offered opportunities for quicker and safer results. Nonetheless, Coke consistently promoted mission amongst the Methodist societies, sending missionaries to the West Indies, West Africa, and North America. The fruits of these labours were significant. Methodist missionaries first arrived in the West Indies in 1787, and by 1813 Methodists there numbered 6,570. Mission work in areas where slavery persisted needed to be undertaken with caution. Missionaries were to focus on religious and moral improvements, but questions relating to civil matters were to be left unaddressed. Faced by a barrage of harassment and even persecution from slave-owners and local officials, such strictures proved hard to maintain.

Coke was an inspirational figure, although an impulsive one. For all his lack of administrative gifts, Methodist missionary effort significantly advanced. At the age of sixty-six Coke himself volunteered for the first Methodist mission to India, but he died on the outward journey before he reached his destination. A national Methodist missionary society was formed in Britain in 1818.

The missionary spirit amongst Methodists in Britain was replicated in North America. The first 'foreign' missionaries sent out by Protestants of the New World were Freeborn Garretson, and James Cromwell, sent to Nova Scotia in 1784 by the Methodist Episcopal Church.[52] Here they ministered to contacts from different denominational backgrounds, including the group of black Africans who subsequently moved to the newly founded Sierra Leone, where they were joined in 1811 by George Warren, the first English Wesleyan Methodist missionary to West Africa.[53] In 1820 the constitution of the Missionary Society of the Methodist Episcopal Church was formally adopted by the General Conference in America. This gave Methodism its own niche in the missionary market from which it could promote the distinctive emphases of Methodism, and attracting funds that might otherwise have gone to other societies.

THE CHURCHES OF SCOTLAND AND MISSION

The promotion of mission from the Church of Scotland developed more slowly than in other denominations. The territorial system of presbyteries created difficulties, prompting great debates as to which presbytery the Scottish

---

51   *Letters of John Wesley, Vol. VI.,* 316.

52   D. Hempton, *Methodism: Empire of the Spirit*, New Haven, Yale University Press, 2005, 151.

53   On Sierra Leone see C. Fyfe, *A History of Sierra Leone*, Oxford, 1962, 25–58, 139–81; J. Peterson, *Province of Freedom: A History of Sierra Leone, 1787–1870*, London, 1969, 123–74.

Presbyterian churches in England should belong, let alone those overseas. Scotland also had its own mission field—the Highlands and Islands, which were the scene of extensive endeavours to promote the gospel in the eighteenth century. The difficulties of the Church of Scotland in sanctioning home mission are witnessed by its resistance to the itinerant endeavours of James and Robert Haldane, who were forced into Independency. The General Assembly of 1796 managed to both approve of mission work, and yet effectively prevent any practical action. Debates were caught in tensions between moderates, who identified mission with the work of radicals, and evangelicals who sought a wide extension of the gospel. It was 1824 before the Assembly instituted its own mission. Most early endeavours from Scotland were therefore promoted through small voluntary societies, as in England, such as the Glasgow Missionary Society, founded in 1796. There were also strong links with the London Missionary Society, which between 1795 and 1845 sent out eighty-one Scottish missionary candidates.

Thomas Chalmers was to lead the way in challenging the thinking of the Kirk. One fruit of his evangelical conversion whilst in pastoral ministry in Kilmany, Fife, was an interest in overseas mission, and Chalmers was an early supporter of William Carey. After his pioneering urban mission work in Glasgow, Chalmers accepted a lecturing post at St Andrews University, where he encouraged a group of students who were interested in overseas mission, including Alexander Duff (1806–78), sent out as the first Church of Scotland missionary to India (see ch. 9).[54] Chalmers' ideas and practice moulded their missiological thinking, drawing on the model of mission practised in the Highlands, where alongside preaching, and Bible distribution, the Scottish Society for the Promotion of Christian Knowledge had given a central role to education as a means of cultural transformation.[55] Chalmers' urban mission scheme placed elementary education at the heart of efforts to promote the Christian faith,[56] and the school and the Bible were to be central to the work of mission home or abroad. Through education people could gain access to the Bible and Christian literature, and 'civilised' society, raising its intellectual and moral tone, and preparing the way for the reception of the Christian message.

MISSIONS TO THE SOUTH OF AFRICA
When the British took over the Cape of Good Hope from the Dutch in 1795, Moravian missionaries were already active. Johannes van der Kemp (1747–1811),

---

54   S. Piggin and J. Roxborogh, *Thomas Chalmers and the St Andrews Seven*, Edinburgh, Banner of Truth, 1985.

55   D.E. Meek, 'Scottish Highlanders, North American Indians, and the SSPCK: Some Cultural Perspectives', *Records of the Scottish Church History Society*, 23, 3 (1989): 378–96.

56   G. Smith, *The Life of Alexander Duff*, London, Hodder and Stoughton, 1879.

a medical doctor from Holland, arrived in Cape Town in 1799 under the auspices of the LMS, and in time attracted a large Khoi (Hottentot) congregation. He helped a sister society to the LMS, the Netherlands Missionary Society, based in Rotterdam, and the South African Missionary Society. He worked in partnership with a Xhosa evangelist Ntiskana (1760–1820), who proved remarkably effective amongst his own people, and demonstrated the significance that indigenous teachers and evangelists were to have in the future work of mission. Van der Kemp was significantly more successful than other LMS workers in the area, but proved a controversial figure. He vigorously denounced the behaviour of the Boer settlers to the native peoples, refusing to see the black population as inferior. In turn, he was criticised for the condition in which he allowed those who settled at his missionary station to live. He further alienated a number of European colonists, especially after he married an African wife.[57] Mission work, and conflict with local colonial authorities, often went together.

John Philip arrived in the Cape Colony, later to become South Africa, in 1819, where he became superintendent of the London Missionary Society. Leaving his home country at the age of 44, this Scotsman was to hold the post for the next thirty years. Philip insisted that the expansion of Christianity was to be a catalyst for raising the moral and social standards of the colony, and he set himself to defend the interests of the black population. Whilst emphasising the high spiritual status of the individual, Philip placed an enlightenment emphasis on natural human rights alongside the attempt to seek evangelical conversion. The equality of black and white people was asserted. Indeed his personal convictions that at times black Africans showed a higher level of moral virtue than the supposedly civilised whites led him to being dismissed as a negrophile by many European settlers. Nonetheless, Philip's representations to the British authorities helped secure the adoption of a non-racial constitution. Through education and commerce, Philip also sought to oppose the inroads of slave traders into the colony, and his revelations as to the ongoing slave trade had a profound affect on Thomas Fowell Buxton and David Livingstone. He challenged oppressive attitudes amongst European settlers, insisting that with equal opportunities, Africans would match the achievements of the white population. This controversial stance was a factor behind the Great Trek, or Voortrek, of Boer settlers who rejected British rule, and after 1830 formed communities across the Orange River in what became the Orange Free State and the Transvaal. Philip championed humanitarian imperialism against those who sought white-settler led colonialism free from control from London, and

---

57 Studies of early mission work in South Africa are found in R. Elphick and R. Davenport (eds), *Christianity in South Africa: A Political, Social, and Cultural History,* Oxford, James Currey, 1997; H. Bredekamp and R. Ross (eds), *Missions and Christianity in South African History,* Johannesburg, Witwatersrand University Press, 1995.

provided a model of missionary engagement with South African authorities and imperial policy makers that continued into the 1890s.[58]

AMERICAN MISSIONS

The War of Independence, and further war with England in the early nineteenth century turned American thinking inward. Nation-building became the dominant theme. As with Scotland, the country had its own mission field, amongst the native Americans. American foreign missions was therefore small-scale in the early nineteenth-century and it was not until the 1830s that overseas mission was widely embraced by Protestant denominations. Here voluntary bodies again led the way, but as was the case with missionary efforts from other countries, the interweaving of religious impulses with expressions of national identity and political thinking, could be hard to separate.

The largest missionary sending organisation in the early nineteenth century was the American Board of Commissioners for Foreign Missions, set up in Boston in 1810. It was primarily inspired by East Coast Congregational churches, although it operated outside formal denominational structures. The well-established transatlantic evangelical network quickly brought it into contact with British societies, and early growth was impressive, with income reaching $114,000 in 1828.[59] The American Baptist Missionary Board followed in 1814, and focussed its early efforts on Burma and India. West Africa was later to be an arena for missionary efforts from Presbyterians, Methodists, and Episcopalians, with especial concentration upon Liberia.

The American Board concentrated its small, but determined band of missionaries, on a few fields, notably the Sandwich Islands (Hawaii), the Middle East, and the Indian subcontinent. Between 1810 and 1850 there were mixed results in South Asia, but success was enjoyed on Hawaii. A party of two missionaries, five assistants, three native teachers, and seven women, led by Rev. Hiram Bingham, sent by the American Board, reached the islands in 1819. Some significant chiefs were converted in 1825, although widespread conversions did not take place until ten years later. By 1837, the mission had ninety Americans, and several hundred native workers. After a series of revivals, there were, in the late 1830s, some 18,000 communicants out of a population of 100,000. Between 1839 and 1841 a further 20,000 were received into the church.[60]

American missions were impelled by conviction of the absolute lostness of those held by the 'vain superstitions' of heathen religion, but also by the need

58   On Philip see A. Ross, *John Philip (1775–1851), Missions, Race and Politics in South Africa*, Aberdeen, Aberdeen University Press, 1986.

59   W.R. Hutchison, *Errand to the World: American Protestant Thought and Foreign Missions*, Chicago, University of Chicago Press, 1993, 44–45.

60   Hutchison, *Errand to the World*, 69–70, Neill, *Christian Missions*, 254.

Adoniram Judson—Parting Challenge to Missions on his Last Departure from America, July 5th 1846

'In the missionary enterprise, the work to be accomplished is the universal preaching of the gospel, and the conversion of the whole world to the Christian faith; and in order to do this, some must go, and some must send and sustain them that go… Those who remain at home, and labour to send and sustain those that go, are as readily employed in the work, and as really obey the Saviour's command as those who go in their own persons. See you not, then, that the great command can be obeyed, and is actually binding on every soul?… It is possible there is some one in this assembly to whom it may be said, You will find, on examination, that you have not done your utmost… How is it possible that you love the Saviour, and yet feel no interest in that object on which his heart is set?'[1]

1   A. Judson, Letter from Moulmein, 6 May 1835, in F. Wayland, *A Memoir of the Life and Labours of the Rev. Adoniram Judson*, London, James Nisbet, 1853, Vol. II, 418.

---

to respond appropriately to the grace of God. Adoniram Judson (1788–1850) urged the students of Waterville College in 1846, 'if any of you enter the Gospel ministry in this or other lands, let not your object be so much to 'do your duty', or even to 'save souls,' though these should have a place in your motives, as to *please the Lord Jesus*. Let this be your ruling motive.'[61] Alongside this sat a conviction that the final work of God would begin in America, and spread to the world. To fail to use the wealth, talents and influence of America to extend the cause of Christ would be gross disobedience.[62]

Judson was to prove an inspirational figure for the American missionary movement. Son of a Massachusetts Congregationalist minister, he was ordained in 1812, and with five friends was sent out by the American Board of Commissioners for Foreign Missions to India. He married Ann Hasseltine just thirteen days before departure, Ann having ignored the advice of friends not to throw her life away on the 'wild, romantic undertaking' of Christian missions. The lengthy journey gave Judson and Ann opportunity to re-examine their theology of baptism, and they were baptised by immersion on arrival in Calcutta by William Ward, of the Serampore Trio. This step cost them Congregationalist support, but the Baptist Triennial Convention took them on in 1814. On the advice of William Carey, Judson settled in Burma, to promote the gospel in a Buddhist context. In the years after their arrival in 1813, the Judsons suffered from intense physical privations, with frequent bouts of ill health. It

61   Adoniram Judson, in E. Judson, *Life of Adoniram Judson*, New York, Randolph, 1883, 473, quoted in Hutchison, *Errand to the World*, 49.

62   Hutchison, *Errand to the World*, 53–59.

Adoniram Judson

was six years before the first convert was baptised. Judson sought with great difficulty to master Burmese, at which he eventually excelled, that he might preach in the language, and understand Buddhist culture and religious thought. He completed a Burmese dictionary in 1826. When his Burmese translation of the Bible was completed in 1834, he believed the key component of his work was done:

> I have knelt down before him, with the last leaf in my hand, and imploring his forgiveness for all the sins which have polluted my efforts in this department....

May he take his own inspired word, now complete in the Burman tongue, the grand instrument of filling all Burma with songs of praise to our Great God and Saviour Jesus Christ. *Amen.*[63]

Other translations of the Bible into Karen, Peguan, and Pali were to follow. Working in Rangoon, Ava, and later Moulmein, Judson set up a *zayat*, a shelter open to anyone for rest and engagement in debate about the merits of Christianity. His approach proved successful, and slowly a Burmese church began to grow. The attitude of the Burmese government to foreigners varied from toleration to hostility, and Judson had to endure some seventeen months in prison, part of the time under the sentence of death. By 1826, his wife Ann together with two of their children had died, and Judson's second wife was to die in 1845, after which he married for a third time. His wives played vital roles in his thirty-seven years of missionary work in Burma.[64]

Ann Hasseltine on Receiving a Proposal of Marriage from Adoniram Judson
'An opportunity has been presented to me, of spending my days among the heathen, attempting to persuade them to receive the Gospel. Were I convinced of its being a call from God, and that it would be more pleasing to him, for me to spend my life in this way than any other, I think I should be willing to relinquish every earthly object, and, in full view of dangers and hardships, give myself up to the great work.'
[two months later]... 'O, if he [God] will condescend to make me useful in promoting his kingdom, I care not where I perform his work, nor how hard it be. *Behold, the handmaid of the Lord; be it unto me according to thy word.'* [1]

1   Ann Hasseltine, Diary Entry on 10th September, 1810, quoted from J.D. Knowles, *Memoir of Mrs Ann H. Judson*, Boston, Lincoln and Edmands, 1831.

His stress on linguistic work, and his emphasis that language training and education should be a key part of missionary training, was a key contribution to missiological thought. So too was his emphasis on the use of native assistants in evangelism, with whom he spent time each day in prayer and training. To Judson, their achievements were outstanding:

---

63   Quoted in C. Anderson, *To the Golden Shore: The Life of Adoniram Judson*, Grand Rapids, Mich., Zondervan, 1972, 411.

64   On Judson see F. Wayland, *A Memoir of the Life and Labors of the Rev. Adoniram Judson, D.D.* Boston, Phillips, Sampson, 1853; C. Anderson, *To the Golden Shore: The Life of Adoniram Judson*, Boston, Little, Brown, 1956. On the significant role of his wives see J.J. Brumberg, *Mission for Life: The Story of the Family of Adoniram Judson*, New York, Free Press, 1980.

These men penetrate every lane and corner of this place and the neighbouring villages; … Now, ten such persons, half-students, half-assistants, cost no more than one missionary family; and for actual service they are certainly worth a great deal more. This is the way in which I think missions ought to be conducted. One missionary, or two at most, ought to be stationed in every important central place, to collect a church and an interest around him; to set the native wheels at work, and to keep them at work'[65]

The publication of Judson's letters, his mission work, his sufferings and his imprisonment, afforded Judson a revered and inspirational status. Although Burmese Buddhists remained resistant to the Christian message, Judson attracted other missionaries to Burma, who found significant success amongst the tribal peoples. He reported 74 baptisms during 1834, 21 of whom were Burmese, 44 were Karens, and 9 foreigners, totalling 666 since the mission started.[66] George Boardman (1801–1831), working with Ko Tha Byn (1778–1840) a convert of great humility from the Karen people whom Judson helped rescue from a criminal past, saw great success in the work amongst the Karens. By 1851, there were some 10,000 baptised believers in Burma, which had a total Christian population of around 30,000 people—far larger than the Christian community in India at the time.[67]

REASONS FOR THE EXPANSION OF PROTESTANT OVERSEAS MISSION

The Enlightenment

A new world order began to emerge in the late eighteenth century as old regimes and structures crumbled. Events in America after 1776, and France in 1789, cast a shadow over the concept of Christendom, centred upon Europe and North America. The Christian encounter with the Enlightenment was undoubtedly important, and was to influence missions. The rights of the individual and the validity of individual religious expression were increasingly recognised. Yet the factors shaping the church were not solely Western. Through the work of mission, new non-Western expressions of Christianity independent of both Christendom and Enlightenment influences were to emerge.

---

65   A. Judson, Letter from Moulmein, 6 May 1835, in F. Wayland, *A Memoir of the Life and Labours of the Rev. Adoniram Judson*, London, James Nisbet, 1853, Vol. II, 81.

66   F. Wayland, *A Memoir of the Life and Labours of the Rev. Adoniram Judson*, London, James Nisbet, 1853, Vol. II, 73.

67   W.H. Brackney, 'The Legacy of Adoniram Judson', *International Bulletin of Missionary Research*, July, 1998, 122–127; Neill, *History of Christian Missions*, 248–250.

The links between the upsurge in Protestant missionary interest in the late eighteenth century, and the rise of evangelicalism, are undeniable. It is no longer possible to view evangelicalism as simply an experiential, anti-intellectual, reaction to the Enlightenment emphasis on reason: indeed scholars have claimed a significant debt owed by evangelicalism to the Enlightenment.[68] David Bosch argued that the Enlightenment period was one of the 'paradigm shifts' in the history of mission, or at least the second stage in the Protestant paradigm, claiming that 'the entire modern missionary enterprise is, to a very real extent, a child of the Enlightenment.'[69]

Whilst Roman Catholicism remained the Christian tradition that was numerically dominant, and most widely spread geographically, Roman Catholic missions did not prosper after the suppression of the Jesuit order in 1773, nor were they assisted by the loss of papal influence and wealth through the French Revolution and the subsequent Napoleonic era, together with the decline in Iberian power and influence. In Britain and America, much Roman Catholic missionary endeavour was absorbed by the needs of 'home' mission, seeking to reclaim those who in the process of migration to urban areas or new countries, had lapsed from the Mass. As chapter nine will show, after 1840 there was a marked recovery of Roman Catholic missionary and ecclesiastical expansion, but for the century after the French Revolution, Roman Catholicism set itself to resist modernity, in contrast to Protestant openness to at least some aspects of the post-Enlightenment intellectual climate.

Although some features of Christian mission within the modern Protestant tradition appear to have a root in Enlightenment thinking—such as confidence in the regenerative capacity of knowledge (if this was linked to Christian proclamation), and the stress on addressing the Christian message principally to individuals, other aspects demonstrate continuity with earlier Reformation and Puritan thinking.[70] These included the conviction that non-Western peoples were lost in the degradation of sin, and capable only of salvation through the atoning work of Jesus Christ, the portrayal of other religious systems as heathen idolatry or superstition, and belief in the Bible as the supernatural revelation of God. The Enlightenment may have shaped the way missionaries reworked these

---

68   See D. Bebbington, *Evangelicalism in Modern Britain: A History from the 1730s to the 1980s*, London, Unwin Hyman, 1989, 40–42; 50–74; M. Noll, *A History of Christianity in the United States and Canada*, London, SPCK, 1992 154–57.

69   D. Bosch, *Transforming Mission: Paradigm Shifts in Theology of Mission*, Maryknoll, New York, Orbis, 1991, 262–64; 274. Following Hans Küng he sees each era as commensurate with a paradigm shift in theology.

70   The essays in K. Stewart and M. Haykin (eds), *Continuities in Evangelical History*, Leicester, IVP, 2007 critically evaluate the extent of evangelicalism's debt to the Enlightenment.

ideas, but they were not simply the product of the Enlightenment paradigm.[71] What Protestant missionaries saw and did was moulded by what they read and believed from the Bible. The lost state of the heathen and their need of salvation through Christ was shaped by reading Romans 1, and entailed a repudiation of Enlightenment optimism about the state of humanity.[72] The Protestant missionary model was therefore something of a hybrid. Enlightenment confidence in individual responsibility and human capacity, with a shift in religion from the public to the private sphere, in the wake of the confessional conflicts of post-Reformation Europe, was mixed with a Pietist emphasis on the gathered fellowship of believers, and adherence to Reformation doctrine with particular emphasis on personal conversion, the cross, and scripture.

Debates about missionary methods reflected the tensions within the Enlightenment context. Were activities such as preaching, evangelism, and translating the Bible, reliant on the work of the Holy Spirit sufficient, or should a prior work of civilising take place? Thomas Chalmers, whilst believing that even the rudest barbarians had a moral sense upon which missionaries could build, and that civilisation was a vital accompaniment of mission, still saw that the primary aim of mission was to preach Christ.[73] The debate as to the role of legitimate commerce in replacing the evils of defective commerce such as the slave trade, also gradually began to feature increasingly in discussions as to missions policy.[74]

Missionary zeal was tempered with recognition of the practical needs of sound organisational structures and logistical support. The establishment of regular maritime trade routes made the world a smaller place, opening travel opportunities for missionaries, and providing avenues by which supporters in Europe and America could send funds and materials for their support, and relaying news of their work. The emergence of the voluntary missionary society in Britain in the late eighteenth century was a pragmatic rather than ideological development, owing much to the developing business practices of the time, with the establishing of committees, raising subscriptions, creating income and expenditure flows. Surplus wealth created through industrial expansion, especially amongst the developing nonconformist community,

---

71   See B. Stanley, 'Christian Missions and the Enlightenment', in *Christian Missions and the Enlightenment*, ed. B. Stanley, Grand Rapids, Eerdmans, 2001, 8–11. The essays in this book offer a thorough assessment of Bosch's case.

72   A.F. Walls, 'Romans One and the Missionary Movement', in A.F. Walls, *The Christian Movement in Christian History: Studies in the Transmission of Faith*, Edinburgh, T&T Clark, 1996, 55–67.

73   T. Chalmers, *The Utility of Missions Ascertained by Experience*, Edinburgh, 1815, 25.

74   A. Porter, *Religion Versus Empire? British Protestant Missionaries and Overseas Expansion, 1700–1914*, Manchester, Manchester University Press, 2004, 94–97.

became available to fund missionary expansion. Evangelical networks, both formal and informal, bound key players together through family ties, personal friendships, correspondence, and geographical proximity, as was the case with the Particular Baptist Missionary Society, the London Missionary Society, and later the Church Missionary Society.[75]

Missions, Western Influence and the anti-slavery campaign
The nineteenth century was pre-eminently the century in which Europe imposed its will and ideas on the world. Despite the growing weakness of European Christianity itself, the extension of Christianity was to become increasingly inseparable from the extension of European civilisation. Technological developments in the military sphere meant that it was possible to dominate large numbers of people with a small armed force. Holland occupied much of Indonesia. The strengthening of the British navy, which helped to eradicate the slave trade, also served to support the expanding British overseas empire in the years after the loss of America, and fostered conditions in which foreign missionary efforts could take hold. Conflict between Britain and France in the late eighteenth and early nineteenth centuries helped to expand British interests into Canada, and the West Indies. International interests also drew Britain into India, West Africa, South Africa, Australia and the South Pacific, offering opportunities for trade, and the expansion of Protestant missions. Cultural supremacy, and military and political authority lay in the hands of white Europeans and later Americans. This pushed European Christian influence into previously strongly Islamic areas. In 1830 France occupied Algeria, and later Tunisia; Britain went on to establish control of Egypt.

In the early nineteenth century, missionary expansion tended to follow in the wake of the extension of European influence. This, Christian writers believed, was simply following the unfolding of God's providence. It created a culture of dependence,[76] but the dangers of entanglement with the state, and state aid, were readily appreciated: Moravian missions had been seen to flourish without any such connection. Concerned Christian voices in the British Parliament insisted that overseas rule should be wise, as well as profitable, and opened official doors for a Christian presence in the colonies. It was believed that if a nation held overseas possessions, it was that nation's duty to Christianise them. However, to conclude that missionary expansion in the early nineteenth century was a tool of colonialism is too simplistic. Overseas authorities were reluctant to encourage the spread of missionary activity, as William Carey found, for fear of

---

75   M. Hennell, *John Venn and the Clapham Sect*, London, Lutterworth Press, 1958, 227; B. Stanley, *History of the BMS*, 1–20.

76   Porter, *Religion Versus Empire?*, 64.

unsettling relationships with local people, and disturbing trade. In the period 1789 to 1830, direct links between colonialism and missions are limited.[77]

The late eighteenth century was an age of exploration and discovery. Knowledge of the world was expanding, typified by the accounts of the voyages of discovery of James Cook, and raised awareness that there were many peoples in the world as yet unreached by the gospel. There was an element of romanticism in the idea of heroic self-sacrifice to serve 'noble savages' not yet affected by the progress of civilisation. In 1796, the London Missionary Society sent the first missionaries to the South Pacific. There also were strong links between the rise of mission in the early nineteenth century, and the campaigns to abolish slavery and the slave trade, which awoke the conscience of religious people to the moral responsibilities that came with expanding European influence. Christian missionaries became strong opponents of the horrors of slavery they encountered. Anti-slavery supporters, many of whom also supported mission societies, were in turn outraged at the restrictions placed upon missions for their opposition to slavery, and the further suffering felt in consequence by slaves. Support for missions was buoyed by a tide of humanitarian sentiment.[78] Missionary activity was much more than a moral salve in recompense for the involvement of white Europeans in slavery, but the sense of a need to make reparation for past wrongs cannot be ignored. Much missionary endeavour was directed at West Africa, and the West Indies, where slavery had been prominent, but much energy was also invested in Asia and the South Pacific where European slavery had not been an issue.

Theological Influences
The sense of optimism about the progress of the Christianity in parts of Europe and North America during the Evangelical Revival, inspired hope for the spread of the gospel, and a sense of moral responsibility and urgency in the light of the fate of the lost. Expectation grew of a time coming when the earth 'would be filled with the knowledge of the glory of the Lord as the waters cover the sea.' [Habbakuk 2, 14], reflected in Isaac Watts' hymn of 1719:

> Jesus shall reign where'er the sun
> Doth its successive journeys run,
> His kingdom stretch from shore to shore
> 'Till moons shall wax and wane no more.

---

77   B. Stanley, *The Bible and the Flag: Protestant Missions and British Imperialism in the Nineteenth and Twentieth Centuries*, Leicester, Apollos, 1990, 33–110.

78   Porter, *Religion Versus Empire?*, 138–39.

Jonathan Edwards looked for the time when 'religion and true Christianity shall in every respect be uppermost in the world.'[79] He believed that the revival in New England was 'the dawning, or at least the prelude, of that glorious work of God, so often foretold in Scripture, which in the progress and issue of it, shall renew the world of mankind.'[80] Many holding a post-millennial world view believed that they were witnessing the time when the fullness of the Gentiles was coming in. Some were convinced that Romans 11:25 indicated that the conversion of the Jews would follow, and then the return of Christ, others that the millennium would follow the Second Coming. The 'signs of the times' in the mid and late eighteenth century appeared portentous. Wars in North America, the Lisbon earthquake, the French Revolution with the overturn of the Roman Catholic monarchy and Church in France, and followed by the capture of the pope, appeared a prelude to the end of the papacy (popularly viewed by Protestants as the anti-Christ), and the end-times. When a Republic was proclaimed in Rome itself, people questioned whether this was the death-wound of Babylon the Great.[81] In 1807 Thomas Coke declared: 'the great period of the consummation is at hand,—that is even at the door.'[82] The hardships missionaries faced, and the slowness with which the gospel advanced overseas, brought, by the late nineteenth century, a significant re-evaluation of this thinking.

In the Evangelical Revival, preachers such as George Whitefield and Jonathan Edwards proclaimed an evangelical Calvinism that held in creative tension the sovereignty of God, the responsibility of the preacher to preach the gospel, and that of the hearer to believe it. This moulded thinking about mission within the trans-Atlantic evangelical network, as was seen with the founders of the Baptist Missionary Society. John Wesley transformed Arminianism, which had been associated with High Church orderliness, into a free ranging evangelical Arminianism.[83] The evangelical emphasis on assurance of salvation brought

79   J. Edwards, *The Works of Jonathan Edwards*, Vol. 2, London, Westley and Davies, 1834, 297–98. Edwards' writings on the end times are found in S.J. Stein (ed) *Works of Jonathan Edwards Vol. 5: Apocalyptic Writings*, New Haven, Yale, 1977.

80   J. Edwards, *Thoughts on the Revival of Religion in New England* (1740), in E. Hickman (ed), *The Works of Jonathan Edwards*, Vol. 1., repr. London, Banner of Truth, 1974, 380.

81   See R.H. Bloch, *Visionary Republic: Millennial Themes in America Thought, 1756–1800*, Cambridge, CUP, 1985. On millennial expectations and mission see J.A. de Jong, *As the Waters Cover the Sea: Millennial Expectations in the Rise of Anglo-American Missions 1640–1810*, Kampen, J. H. Kok, 1970.

82   T. Coke, *The Recent Occurrences of Europe Considered in Relation to Such Prophecies as are Either Fulfilling or Unfulfilled. First Published in 1807, in an Appendix to his Commentary on the Bible*, London, 1809, 314, quoted in Porter, *Religion Versus Empire*, 34.

83   On Wesley's Evangelical Arminianism see H.D. McGonigle, *Sufficent Saving Grace: John Wesley's Evangelical Arminianism*, Carlisle, Paternoster, 2001.

a sense of responsibility to share this experience with others, which coupled with a view that all humans, no matter where located, were equal in God's sight, and had a right to hear the gospel, provided an urgent impetus to action. Interest in foreign missions served to draw Protestant denominations closer together at the end of the eighteenth century, and render theological differences of less significance.[84]

The conviction that prayer was crucial in the latter-day expansion of the gospel worldwide was emphasised by Jonathan Edwards.[85] Similarly, in his *Enquiry* Carey argued that 'an universal conjunction in fervent prayer' would come before the outpouring of the Spirit on the mission of the church in the last days, but that such prayer was to be combined with 'exerting ourselves in the use of means'.[86] The belief in the spiritual lostness of those who had not yet received the Christian message also served as a powerful motive force towards mission to rescue them, along with a strong sense of the love of God for those to whom they went.

Undoubtedly, therefore, the reasons for the expansion of Protestant mission are complex. No single, coherent theology promoting missions existed, although the millennial incentive was strong. Nor was there a single practical strategy for promoting Christian mission. Much activity was the product of inspired and enthusiastic individuals, with each often motivated by a unique combination of personal forces.

Conclusions

It is clear that William Carey was not the founder of missions, nor even the founder of modern Protestant missions; the cradle of the movement was more truly Halle, or Herrnhut, than the parlour of the Baptist manse in Kettering. Nor should Carey be seen as working in isolation from his contemporaries. However, his work represents a significant turning point for Christian mission. The vehicle chosen to promote it was the voluntary society, giving full reign to entrepreneurial, inspirational leadership, and on the whole, mission societies developed free of the restrictions of denominational controls. The CMS prided itself on being both an independent and a 'church society'. The LMS and ABCFM were formed before the existence of national Congregational structures in either England or the United States, indeed they contributed towards their later formation. Wesleyan missions were more closely connected to their newly formed denomination.

84   Stanley, *Missions and the Enlightenment*, 15.

85   J. Edwards, *An Humble Attempt to Promote Explicit Agreement and Visible Union of God's People in Extraordinary Prayer for the Revival of Religion and the Advancement of Christ's Kingdom on Earth*, Boston, New England, 1747.

86   Carey, *Enquiry*, 104, 107.

It is only in retrospect that the 1790s can be viewed as momentous events in the history of mission. A series of missionary societies were established at the time, but no unstoppable wave of missionary enthusiasm swept Britain, Europe, or the United States. The societies formed were small, and had difficulty in recruiting missionaries. They were held together by a series of, sometimes fragile, personal international networks, drawing in Britain, Continental Europe, and North America, through which they shared information, news, prayer networks, and even personnel, rather than denomination frameworks.[87] Only by 1830 was the fruit of these small, but determined, endeavours to promote Christianity around the globe beginning to be seen. Missionary agencies were becoming significant forces. After a slow and uncertain start, the annual income of the CMS rose from £3,046 in 1813, to £54,010 in 1829. It was sending out 10 workers per year between 1820 and 1830. Income to Wesleyan Missions reached £40,000 in the 1820s, and doubled again in the 1830s.[88] Although not a truly global faith until the twentieth century, Christianity at least began to be present during the nineteenth century in the southern hemisphere amongst black and Asian populations. There is no doubt that mixed into the presentation of the Christian message there was a sense of the cultural and educational superiority of the West, a vision reinforced by scientific advance. To Europeans, non-Western religions appeared steeped in idleness, polygamy, human sacrifice, witchcraft, superstition, and the demonic, indeed through the century the 'darkness' of Africa was painted in successively darker terms. Carey's interest in non-Christian culture was all-too-often replaced by a blanket condemnation of it.

Nonetheless, Western Protestant mission in the first half of the nineteenth century was not simply a product of imperialism, nor were its agents determined advocates of the advantages of empire. Early missionaries in places such as the West Indies or South Africa found a 'no politics' rule impossible to sustain—at times local authorities were opposed, at others, their support was fostered to win their defence against other opponents. The argument that missions should follow into the areas God had providentially opened up through colonial expansion, created linkages between the two, but slavery, colonial ill-treatment of indigenous peoples, widow burning, idol worship, and the opium trade, all drew missionaries into conflict with governmental authorities. The social background of Carey and his co-pioneers in the artisan or lower middle classes, added to the radicalism of mission, giving it a role in promoting social egalitarianism, offering opportunities for people with limited social opportunity, wealth, or status, including many women. The late eighteenth century Protestant missionary movement was a child of mixed parentage, but the dominant gene was evangelicalism.

87   See A. Porter, *Religion Versus Empire?*, 116–135
88   Porter, *Religion Versus Empire?*, 91.

FURTHER READING

D. Bosch, *Transforming Mission: Paradigm Shifts in Theology of Mission*, Maryknoll, New York, Orbis, 1991, 262–64; 274.

W.R. Hutchison, *Errand to the World: American Protestant Thought and Foreign Missions*, Chicago, University of Chicago Press, 1993.

S.H. Moffett, *A History of Christianity in Asia, Vol. II, 1500–1900*, Maryknoll, Orbis, 2005.

S. Neill, *History of Christian Missions*, Harmondsworth, Penguin, 1986.

A. Porter, *Religion Versus Empire? British Protestant Missionaries and Overseas Expansion, 1700–1914*, Manchester, Manchester University Press, 2004.

B. Stanley, *History of the Baptist Missionary Society 1792–1992*, Edinburgh, T&T Clark, 1992.

B. Stanley, *The Bible and the Flag*, Leicester, Apollos, 1990.

B. Stanley (ed), *Christian Missions and the Enlightenment*, Grand Rapids, Eerdmans, 2001.

A. Walls, *The Missionary Movement in Christian History: Studies in the Transmission of Faith*, Maryknoll, Orbis, 1996.

A. Walls, *The Cross-Cultural Process in Christian History*, Maryknoll, New York, Orbis, 2002.

5

Moral Revolutionaries:
The Abolition Of The Slave Trade And Slavery

Between the fifteenth century and the late nineteenth century, one of the most appalling and barbaric episodes in world history took place. Some 18 million black Africans were forcibly transported as slaves to the Americas and Asia, where they faced cruel oppression. A further 10 million people had by 1850 been subjected to domestic slavery by their fellow Africans.[1] Slavery was a complex phenomenon, fuelled by the pressures of European colonisation in the New World, the demands of developing industry and the mercantile economy in Europe, and the internal political and social structures of Africa. It was motivated by human greed and conducted with indescribable cruelty. Although not occurring primarily in Europe, and often involving ruthless exploitation by African tribal chiefs and traders of their own indigenous peoples, many of the events took place in European ships and colonies, or through the work of traders from the Middle East. Trade in the flesh of Africans helped bring prosperity and economic development to other parts of the world, but left areas of Africa despoiled and divided, with serious population imbalances.

Although the relationship between slavery and racial prejudice is complicated, there is little doubt that the slave trade both reflected, and contributed to, racist attitudes amongst white Europeans and Americans. It fuelled, and was fuelled by, belief in a hierarchy of different peoples, in which black slaves occupied

---

1   H.S. Klein, *The Atlantic Slave Trade*, Cambridge, CUP, 1999, 129; P. Manning, *Slavery and African Life: Occidental, Oriental and African Slave Trades*, Cambridge, CUP, 1990, p.171. Statistics and studies on 27,000 voyages are found in D. Eltis, S. Behrendt, D. Richardson, H. Klein, *The Transatlantic Slave Trade 1562–1867: A Database*, Cambridge, CUP, 1998.

the lowest place. However, one by-product of such cruelty was that out of the repression and denigration which slavery brought, Africans began to construct a common identity for themselves.

The trade in slaves from Africa for the Arab and Eastern markets was well established before the Atlantic dimension of the trade developed. In the years from 800 to 1500 AD somewhere between 3.5 and 10 million Africans were taken by Islamic slave traders from North Africa and the sub-Saharan regions, a trade which continued in the nineteenth century.[2] However, this chapter concentrates upon the Atlantic dimension of the trade and especially upon the campaign for its abolition, and then the emancipation of slaves in Britain. The abolition movement in the United States is dealt with in chapter 11.

In 1452, Pope Nicholas V, in a move that was to profoundly affect black Africans, authorised the Portuguese to conquer and enslave the peoples of Guinea. The vast African slave trade that developed after that fateful decision was spurred by European colonisation, particularly Spanish and Portuguese, in Central and South America. Here they encountered harsh conditions relative to those in Europe, and were unable to supply from their own resources a suitable manual workforce. In the face of this constant shortage, the eyes of the colonists turned to Africa to secure a labour force, but it was a forced one.

To facilitate this, what was in effect a triangular trade route developed in which manufactured products were taken to the West coast of Africa, slaves were transported on the 'middle passage' from Africa to the slave colonies of the Americas, and raw materials such as sugar, cotton, tobacco and rum were transported from slave colonies to Europe. The voyage from the Americas to Europe was the least profitable leg, and many ships returned in ballast, or with only a small cargo. Slavery was a profitable, but risky, business. It could take six years for all accounts to be settled, some never were.

THE SIZE AND SCOPE OF THE SLAVE TRADE

It has proved impossible to calculate for certain how many Africans were enslaved, or died as a result of enslavement. The main years of the westward Atlantic slave trade were between 1650 and 1850, with a peak in the 1780s, when the number of African slaves arriving in the Americas was around 75,000 per annum. Using backward projections from known population figures, it has been suggested that between 1700 and 1850, the population of Africa actually declined, from 25 million people to 23 million. At the time, the natural growth rate of the population was about 0.5% per annum. This would mean that Africa's net population loss was 16.3 million by 1850, for which the slave trade was significantly responsible, and the trade was by no means over by the mid-nineteenth century. In total it is likely that some 18 million Africans had been

2   Klein, *Atlantic Slave Trade*, 9.

exported as slaves by 1900.[3] Of these, over 6 million were taken on the Atlantic route between 1700 and 1808, and by 1900 the total exceeded 10 million. Arab slave traders took a further seven million slaves from the north and east of Africa between 1500 and 1900, with numbers peaking sometime around 1850.[4] Although the Atlantic slave trade had begun to decline even before its abolition in 1807, continuing slave exports to other destinations meant that the number of slaves taken from Africa actually peaked in the middle of the nineteenth century at around 120,000 per year. Mortality directly related to the slave trade and slavery is hard to calculate. Probably around 4 million people died as a direct result of the slave trade itself, and the harshness of subsequent slave life contributed to further high mortality levels.[5] By 1914 the African slave trade itself was largely ended, but by then profound damage to the continent had been done. The Atlantic slave trade has rightly been called the 'Rape of Africa.'

The resultant slave populations produced by this trade were vast. In 1790, the slave population of the British West Indies was around 600,000, similar in size to that of the French West Indies, and growing. The world's largest producer of sugar until the 1830s was Jamaica, which had in 1810 over 350,000 African slaves. By 1800 there were nearly 1 million slaves in Brazil, at the time the largest slave population in the Americas. Significant numbers were engaged on sugar and cotton plantations, and in mining for gold and diamonds, but coffee was to prove Brazil's major nineteenth-century slave crop. After Brazil, the next largest concentration was to be found in the newly formed United States, with 698,000 slaves in 1790, 94% living in the states south of Maryland. A further rapid upturn between 1801 and 1808 was fuelled by the demands for labour for tobacco and especially cotton growing. By the time the slave trade into the United States was abolished in 1808, the country already possessed some 1.2 million slaves. Their numbers were also beginning to grow steadily through natural reproduction: 85% of America's slave population was already native-born by 1820. In 1860 there were some 4 million slaves in the country.[6]

The regions of Africa from which the slaves were sourced changed over time. In early years, large numbers came from West African regions such as Senegambia and Gold Coast. The Congolese and Angolan coasts were then developed as a source, providing 48% of all Africans taken for the Atlantic slave trade in the nineteenth century. The trade from Mozambique, on the East coast of Africa, largely serving Brazil, was not developed until early in the nineteenth

---

3   Klein, *Atlantic Slave Trade*, 127–129; P. Manning, *Slavery and African Life*, 84–85. The much higher estimates of earlier studies are now questioned by scholars. The latest revisions are in D. Eltis, *The Transatlantic Slave Trade Database*.

4   Klein, *Atlantic Slave Trade*, 45, 129.

5   Manning, *Slavery and African Life*, 171.

6   Klein, *Atlantic Slave Trade*, 37–44, 196, 70.

century. As late as the 1830s, nearly 11,000 slaves were annually being shipped from Mozambique on the long Atlantic crossing.[7]

THE MECHANISMS OF THE SLAVE TRADE

The slave trade depended on a complex series of interconnected arrangements with local agents who sold on both slaves and goods. Some Africans profited significantly from the trafficking of their own peoples, including West African chiefs who sold permissions to purchase slaves at high prices, and African slave traders who brought the slaves from inland regions to the slave trading post. Many slaves were prisoners of war taken in the course of inter-tribal conflict, and by being sold into slavery they may have been saved from immediate slaughter.

Device to stop captured slave from escaping

Although a third of those slaves captured probably stayed in Africa, those exposed to the march from inland areas to the coast were subject to extreme cruelties. Some of the most evocative images from the abolitionist campaign are of manacled slaves, or slaves joined to each other by means of yokes made from logs, or being anchored to the ground to prevent escape. The process of transportation from internal regions to the coast, and then whilst slaves were held prior to embarkation on the trans-Atlantic journey, could take up to six months, and produced high mortality rates. The abolitionist campaigner Thomas Fowell Buxton estimated that 71% of deaths occurred before slaves left

7   Klein, *Atlantic Slave Trade*, 196, 70.

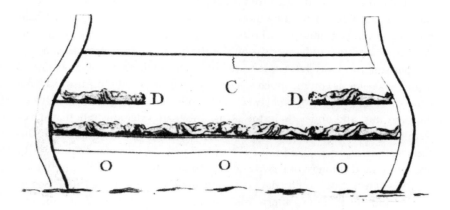

Coffin-like conditions below deck on a slave ship

the African coast, although recent studies suggest that the figures were between 18% and 30%.[8]

Once the slaves embarked on the Atlantic crossing, the cruelties they faced were far from over. The horrors of the 'Middle Passage' were those which attracted the greatest outrage from abolitionists. Often between 450 and 600 slaves were packed together on a wooden sailing vessel, and shackled together at night. They were kept for long periods on lower decks, or on shelves between the decks, which were just two metres wide, with severely restricted head room. Each slave was allowed some five to seven square feet for the journey (a British Act of 1799 increased the figure to 8 square feet per slave). With minimal air, light, and space in which to move, slaves were afforded a space about the size of a coffin, and for significant numbers that is what it literally became. At sea, with slaves shackled together at night, and diseases such as dysentery, which accounted for some 30% of deaths, or smallpox, sweeping through those below decks, and many suffering from seasickness, conditions were horrific. When they were allowed on deck, some slaves were so traumatised that they committed suicide by throwing themselves into the sea.

Death rates in the middle passage were undoubtedly very high. The anti-slave trade campaigner Thomas Clarkson gathered statistics for 20 slave-ship voyages: of 7094 slaves who embarked, 2053 died on the journey. Recent assessments indicate a mean figure of 12% mortality during the Atlantic crossing between 1750 and 1807, falling to 8.8% between 1808 and 1829, then rising to 11.5% between

---

8   T. Buxton, quoted in Klein, *Atlantic Slave Trade*, 130. Buxton argued that a further 18% of deaths took place during the Atlantic crossing, and the rest in the process of adjusting to the conditions in the New World. For revised figures based on Dutch West India Company ships see Klein, 157.

1830 and 1867. Longer voyages produced higher mortality rates—30% mortality was on average experienced by those crossing the Atlantic from East African ports between 1700 and 1749. This fell to 25% in the following half century to 1807, compared to a little over 9% on the shorter route from Sierra Leone. In comparison, mortality rates amongst convict ships taking prisoners (some of whom were elderly) on the much longer voyage from Britain to Australia have been calculated to be 10.4% between 1787 and 1800, falling to 4.1% between 1810 and 1815, and under 1% in the 1830s. The figures demonstrate that slaves were treated worse than criminals. When the average annual death rate in late-eighteenth-century England was 29 per thousand, a death rate of up to 250 in every thousand amongst otherwise healthy young African adults on an Atlantic crossing of just thirty to fifty days is an appalling statistic. The fall after 1807 to around 100 per thousand afterwards was hardly much better.[9] Even amongst the crews of slave ships mortality was very high: in the 1770s Liverpool slave crews experienced mortality of 28% a month during the middle passage, and up to 45% whilst off the African coast.[10]

Anti-slave trade campaigners brought to light some of the worst examples of the treatment of slaves during transportation. In 1783 the *Zong*, a slaver on its journey across the Atlantic, lost sixty slaves and seven crew in an epidemic. Sailing off course, it found its water supplies dwindling. The rest of the slaves were in poor health, and reckoning the survivors would fetch a low price, the slave-ship captain chose to throw the remaining 132 slaves overboard to claim the higher sum that would be obtained from the insurance underwriters if the cargo were lost. Amazingly, in a subsequent court case the captain escaped sanction for his actions.

SLAVE LIFE IN THE AMERICAS

Those who survived the Atlantic crossing still faced great inhumanities. Although the healthiest were usually sold in small lots soon after arrival, those who were unwell could remain unsold for weeks. The abolitionist Buxton claimed that a further 11% of slave deaths occurred in this process of adjusting to life in the New World, although the trend in scholarship has again been to significantly reduce these figures. Evidence from Dutch slaving ships in the early eighteenth century record just 0.6% mortality in the period between arrival and disembarkation of the slaves. Nonetheless, the figures recorded by Jamaican officials between 1655 and 1787 indicate that 4.6% of Africans died whilst the ships were in harbour before even landing.[11]

9   Klein, *Atlantic Slave Trade*, 134–140.

10   R. H. Steckel and R.A. Jensen, 'New Evidence on the Causes of Slave and Crew Mortality in the Atlantic Slave Trade', *Journal of Economic History*, 46, no. 1, 1986, 57–77.

11   Klein, *Atlantic Slave Trade*, 157.

In the eighteenth century slaves were predominantly male and young: 65% were male, and 23% under 15 years old. There was a tremendous range in the prices they fetched. Those with skills could be valued at several hundred pounds, others who were unwell, or disabled, just a few shillings. Human life had been reduced to a commodity, and a cheap one at that. Women, although commanding a lower price in slave markets, worked in the field gangs of American plantations, with little differentiation in their work from that of male slaves.[12]

The long-term life-expectancy of slaves after settlement is hard to ascertain—the oft quoted figure that 25% of all Africans died within 18 months of arriving in America remains unproven, as is the average seven years of life for a slave. Life-expectancy for slaves appears to have been longer in temperate zones such as North America. Figures from Cuba suggest that twenty years survival after arrival was more likely, with slaves living into their forties or fifties. This meant that life expectancy was more in line with Europeans in America.[13]

Slaves were subject to a process of systematic dehumanisation during the 'Middle Passage,' designed to render them fit for slavery at the end of the journey. Slaves conditioned in this way were deemed ready for work, and were more valuable than newly captured slaves. They were forbidden to speak their own language, and on British ships had to learn a simple 'pidgin' English. Yet for all the efforts of the slave masters, African culture and language was not erased during this process, and in places it was re-enforced. Those who gained their freedom were able to progress economically and socially, especially in South America. For some, the adoption of Christianity was a part of the process of cultural adaptation, although it was often mixed with elements of African beliefs. Such residual patterns often emerged in the post-emancipation periods, especially in Roman Catholic countries, as accepted parts of folk belief. Cults such as candomblé, voudou, and santería survived as part of the African element of slave identity, although these influences became less evident as the work of Christian missionaries increased.

SLAVERY, THE INTERNATIONAL ECONOMY, AND EARLY ABOLITIONISM

The impact on the African economy of such dislocation and loss of population can only have been detrimental, for unlike other labour movements of the

---

12 See B.W. Higman, *Slave Populations of the British Caribbean 1807–1834*, Cambridge, Cambridge University Press, 1979.

13 H.S. Klein and S.L. Engerman, 'Fertility Differentials Between Slaves in the United States and the British West Indies: A Note on Lactation Practices and Their Implications', *William and Mary Quarterly*, 35, no. 2 (1978): 357–74. On the lives of Caribbean slaves see K.F. Kiple, *The Caribbean Slave: A Biological History*, Cambridge, CUP, 1984. On Cuba see J.E. Eblen, 'On the Natural Increase of Slave Populations: The Example of the Cuban Black Population, 1775–1900', in eds. S.L. Engerman and E.D. Genovese, *Race and Slavery in the Western Hemisphere: Quantitative Studies*, Princeton, Princeton University Press, 1975.

period, there was no net inflow of savings to Africa from migrants sending money 'home'. The slave trade created conditions for long-term economic decline in Africa, and appears to have increased the prevalence of major internal conflict within the region: some wars were waged for the purpose of obtaining slaves. Traditional patterns of government were affected, and viable areas of agriculture were abandoned as a result of the activities of slave raiding parties. Rising demand for slaves pushed prices higher, and internal trade routes for slaves became longer, drawing more of West and East Africa into the trade.

The consequences for European economies of the slave trade have been widely debated. In 1944, Eric Williams argued that British industrialisation owed significantly to the high level of profits made from the slave trade. These provided the capital necessary for funding large scale economic growth. Others have argued that because the system was so inefficient, and the wastage so high, the net economic benefit was negligible.[14] Certainly, ports at the hub of the trade routes, such as Nantes, Liverpool, Bristol and London, benefited from profits from slavery and sugar, and economic activity in their surrounding areas was stimulated through supplying goods for export, such as guns, knives and axes, and cotton textiles. The cotton industry was provided with its basic raw material, cotton, produced by slave labour. Indeed almost all major American plantation crop exports to Europe, from basic necessities to luxuries, were produced by enslaved Africans.[15] Nations had a vested interest in the continuation of slavery, for between 1750 and 1780, 70% of British government income came from taxes on goods from the colonies, including £1.5 million from taxes and duties from Jamaica alone in 1770, much of it the product of slave labour.[16] Those who opposed the slave trade were therefore faced by a phalanx of concerted opposition, from merchants, to MPs and governments, who contended that mercantile and maritime strength would be jeopardised by abolition. However, although vast sums could be made from a very successful slave trading voyage— on one journey in July 1803, the 'Enterprise' made a profit of £6428— returns to investors in slave trading, at around 10%, remained solid, but not outstanding.[17] The Williams thesis has therefore been subject to significant challenge and modification by scholars.[18] Although there were undoubted linkages between slavery and economic growth, access to capital from Europe, or the profits

---

14   E. Williams, *Capitalism and Slavery*, Chapel Hill, North Carolina, 1944. Those who have challenged Williams include R. Anstey, *The Atlantic Slave Trade and British Abolition, 1760–1810*, London, Macmillan, 1975; and S. Drescher *Econocide: British Slavery in the Era of Abolition*, London, Feffer and Simons, 1977.

15   N. Grant, *The Savage Trade*, Harmondsworth, Kestrel, 1980, 108.

16   Grant, *Savage Trade*, 113.

17   Klein, *Atlantic Slavery*, 83, 98–100; Grant, *Savage Trade*, 108;

18   For discussion of approaches to Williams' work see B.L. Solow and S.L. Engerman, *British Capitalism and Caribbean Slavery: The Legacy of Eric Williams*, Cambridge, 1987, 1–23.

from agriculture, seem to have been a more important source of investment for industrial growth than profits from the slave trade.[19]

THE BEGINNINGS OF THE ABOLITION MOVEMENT

In the eighteenth century, a diverse range of opinion began to be ranged against slavery, not all of it with an explicitly Christian motivation. The eighteenth-century enlightenment has generally been considered as significant and beneficial in the campaign against the institution of slavery. Its emphasis on the solidarity of the human race, and the natural right of individuals to liberty and happiness, were significant, as was the growing sense that deep-rooted evils were no longer to be viewed as irremediable. The economist Adam Smith argued that making slaves work by physical coercion was uneconomic, creating an unwilling workforce which offered the least amount of work, whereas the liberal reward of labour 'increases the industry of that people,' and therefore encouraged industrialisation.[20] Yet the enlightenment contribution was not entirely positive. With it came assumptions that Western culture, in which reason was seen to have reached its fullest stage of development, was superior to non-European cultures, which were racially inferior or even savage. Such concepts of cultural and intellectual supremacy helped foster strong anti-Jewish sentiment (of which Voltaire was a proponent), a racial justification for slavery, and eventually Aryan thinking. It has led to the suggestion that 'Eighteenth-century Europe was the cradle of modern racism.'[21] The Scottish philosopher David Hume opposed slavery, but in a work of 1753 revealed his inclination to 'suspect the negroes, and in general all other species of men (for there are four or five different kinds) to be naturally inferior to the whites.'[22] Others, such as James Beattie, Professor of Moral Philosophy and Logic at Marischal College, Aberdeen, argued strongly against the racism of Hume's view, convinced that there was nothing in the physical or spiritual make-up of black people to suggested they were of a different family to white people. Beattie believed that on the subject of slavery it was not easy to preserve the 'coolness of argument which philosophy recommends', and declared slavery: 'inconsistent with the dearest and most essential rights of a man's nature… it is utterly repugnant to every principle of reason, religion, humanity, and conscience. '[23] The Enlightenment could

19   Klein, *Atlantic Slave Trade*, p.99.

20   A. Smith, *Inquiry into the Nature and Causes of The Wealth of Nations*, ed. R.H. Campbell and A.S. Skinner, Oxford, Clarendon, Book I, 1976, viii, 98–100.

21   G.L. Mosse, *Towards the Final Solution: A History of European Racism*, London, Dent, 1978, 1–3.

22   D. Hume, 'Of National Characters', in *Essays, Moral, Political and Literary*, ed. E.F. Miller, Indianapolis, Liberty Classics, 1987, 208 fn 629–30.

23   J. Beattie, *Elements of Modern Science (1790–93)*, Vol. II, Edinburgh, 1793, reprinted New York, Georg Olms Verlag, 155–56.

therefore produce both a 'de-Christianised form of scientific racism', and also a clearly articulated ethnology shaped by Scottish Common Sense Philosophy and the Bible, which saw all humans with the same capacity for civilisation and development, and as suitable objects for Christian mission.[24]

In France, Montesquieu, and then Rousseau opposed slavery. The principles enunciated in the French Declaration of the Rights of Man and of the Citizen of 1789, proved of major significance to the abolition cause, asserting that men are born free, and that liberty was a 'natural' right of man. The 1794 National Convention abolished slavery, a move well received in France, but which produced unrest in the French dominions. This culminated in the only successful slave rebellion, which took place in Haiti, where an independent government had been established by 1804. Slavery was abolished amongst the island's half a million black inhabitants, shocking other slave-holding areas of the Caribbean. However, the economic consequences for Haiti were serious, as the country eventually dropped out of sugar production, and coffee production was greatly reduced. Its mantle as the world's primary sugar cane producer was taken by Cuba, the largest slave colony in Spanish America. Cuba had, by the middle of the nineteenth century, developed a mixed labour force of African and creole (native-born) slaves, together with Indian and Chinese labourers.

When the United States Declaration of Independence of 1776 asserted that 'all men are created equal', it appeared to sound the death-knell of slavery in America: holding a fellow human being as a slave was hardly commensurate with the statement. Tom Paine questioned how an American colonist could claim the right to freedom from Britain, whilst remaining a slave owner. Opinion amongst the founding fathers was mixed: George Washington owned slaves, but Benjamin Franklyn was staunchly opposed. Several North American states abolished slavery in the wake of the revolution, but when delegates from Georgia and South Carolina declared they would refuse to join the Union if their right to hold slaves was interfered with, it was pragmatically decided that maintaining the Union was the paramount need. The 1787 Constitution defined a slave as three-fifths of a person for the purpose of counting the population.[25] Religious voices opposing slave-holding and the slave trade were led by the Quakers, who made it a basic policy by the 1770s.[26] The slavery issue festered in America for nearly a century before culminating in civil war.

The abolition campaign in Britain is the one best documented, and the most influential, and is the primary focus of the rest of this chapter. Campaigners came to believe that Britain had been providentially set apart to take a moral

---

24   C. Kidd, *The Forging of Races: Race and Scripture in the Protestant Atlantic World, 1600–2000*, Cambridge, Cambridge University Press, 2006, 120.

25   Manning, *Slavery and African Life*, 152.

26   See D.B. Davis, *The Problem of Slavery in Western Culture*, Ithaca, Cornell University Press, 1966.

lead on the issue, and their success in persuading a large section of society to oppose slavery drew British governments into demanding and enforcing the abolition of the slave trade in the role of 'moral policeman' for much of the nineteenth century.

Slave-owning had been abolished in Britain as early as 1772, but, with small numbers of slaves in the country at the time, the task was considerably more straightforward than that of abolishing either the slave trade, or the institution of slavery in British colonies. As in America, there had been opposition to slavery from the Quakers since the mid-eighteenth century. In 1774, London Quakers declared that any Friend who had dealings with the slave trade would be expelled. In 1781 a Quaker abolition petition was presented to Parliament, and in 1783 they formed a small group to mobilise abolition sentiment, which proved a key foundation for the involvement of others.

John Wesley abhorred what he witnessed of the practice of slavery on his visit to America. In his *Thoughts on Slavery* (1774) Wesley argued for abolition on the basis of both Christian teaching and enlightenment humanitarianism. He declared liberty as 'the right of every human creature, as soon as he breathes the vital air.' A slave should be acknowledged as 'thy brother:' slaves had immortal souls. Wesley appealed on the basis of common humanity to the slave traders, 'Do you never feel another's pain? Have you no sympathy, no sense of human woe, no pity for the miserable? When you saw the flowing eyes... or the bleeding sides and tortured limbs of your fellow-creatures, was you a stone or a brute... when you threw their poor mangled remains into the sea, had you no relenting'. He addressed the slavers with the starkest of Christian images: 'there must be a state of retribution, a state wherein the just God will reward every man according to his works. Then what reward will he render to you?'[27] Wesley's views helped to mobilise Methodist opinion against slavery.

In 1785 Thomas Clarkson produced his prize-winning essay *On the Slavery and Commerce of the Human Species*, and two years later joined with Quakers and others in the 'Great Cause'. Clarkson, who was to expend most of his fortune on the campaign, played a vital role in gathering information that could be used to oppose the slave trade. After the outbreak of the French Revolution he extended his work to France, and presented his ideas to the European Congresses of 1815.

Alongside enlightenment influences, and early Quaker efforts, the contribution of evangelicalism in the heightened humanitarian concern towards the end of the eighteenth century was also significant. Whilst not the sole reason for success in the abolition campaign the link between the Evangelical Revival and opposition to slavery is unmistakeable. An all-too easily ignored dimension

27   John Wesley, *Thoughts Upon Slavery*, 1774, in Wesley, *Works* (3rd ed: 1872), repr. Peabody, Massachusetts: Hendrickson Publishers, 1984, Vol 11, 79f.

Olaudah Equiano

of the campaign is the role of slaves and former slaves, and in their actions evangelicalism also played an important role. The publication of Olaudah Equiano's account of his early enslavement and later release and evangelical conversion, greatly assisted the anti-slavery cause.[28] Similarly, the challenge of

28   O. Equiano, *The Interesting Narrative of the Life of Olaudah Equiano, or Gustavus Vassa, the African*, London, 1789.

enslaved Africans to the institution of slavery from within the British colonies was also to be of vital importance in the emancipation campaign.

WILLIAM WILBERFORCE AND THE CLAPHAM SECT

The figure most synonymous with the anti-slavery campaign was William Wilberforce (1759–1833), Member of Parliament for Hull from the age of 21. As a close friend of the brilliant young William Pitt, who became prime minister at the age of just 24, Wilberforce appeared destined for high political office. However, after his evangelical conversion, he was approached by abolition campaigners who urged him to become a parliamentary advocate in the cause. The significance of such a recruit was recognised by John Wesley, who six days before his death in February 1791, wrote to Wilberforce with a faltering hand: 'Unless God has raised you up for this very thing, you will be worn out by the opposition of men and devils. But if God be for you, who can be against you?' Wesley's hatred of slavery, 'that execrable villainy, which is the scandal of religion', came to be shared by Wilberforce.[29] The 'Clapham Sect', a group of evangelical thinkers, writers and MPs, who gathered around him, operated at the heart of the abolition cause. Some, such as Zachary Macaulay and James Stephen, had been turned against slavery by witnessing at first-hand the horrors of the system.

The Clapham Sect worked together with Methodists and Nonconformists (including Quakers and Unitarians) in the first popular mass movement that used widespread propaganda techniques. These included letter writing, delivering lecture tours, fund raising, the distribution of large numbers of tracts, and even boycotts of the produce of slave labour, especially sugar. Strenuous efforts were made to persuade Parliamentary candidates to oppose slavery. The publication of the drawings of the slave ship *Brookes*, and the inhuman conditions in which its cargo of 450 slaves were kept, created an image that shocked the public.

Wilberforce was convinced he had divine sanction for what he was doing, declaring 'God has set before me two great objects, the suppression of the slave trade and the reformation of manners'. Although evangelicals remained in a religious and political minority in the early nineteenth century, Wilberforce made it a badge of evangelicalism to oppose slavery, an achievement not matched in the United States. The widespread dissemination of Enlightenment concepts of individual liberty, and the right to personal happiness, also provided a broad basis of the humanitarian thinking to which the campaigners frequently appealed. Key to the success of Wilberforce and his colleagues was their ability to win the support of a cross-section of Parliament, including those who did not share their faith perspective, such as the Whig leader Charles

---

29   John Wesley Letter to William Wilberforce, 24 February 1791, *Letters of John Wesley, Vol. VIII.*, ed. J. Telford, London, 1921, 265.

John Wesley to Wilberforce on Slavery

'Dear Sir,
Unless the Divine Power has raised you up to be as *Athanasius contra mundum*,
I see not how you can go through your glorious enterprise in opposing that
execrable villainy, which is the scandal of religion, of England, and of human
nature. Unless God has raised you up for this very thing, you will be worn out by
the opposition of men and devils. But if God be for you, who can be against you?
Are all of them stronger than God? O, be not weary of well-doing! Go on, in the
name of God and in the power of his might, till even American slavery (the vilest
that ever saw the sun) shall vanish away before it.'[1]

1   Extract from John Wesley, Letter to William Wilberforce, 24 February 1791, *Letters of John Wesley*, Vol. VIII, ed. J. Telford, London, Epworth, 1931, 265.

Fox, and Pitt himself. For politicians such as Wilberforce, who were politically
and socially conservative, such tactics were extremely radical, and have been
termed 'holy worldliness': seeking, through alliance with the forces of the
world, to achieve a greater Christian good.[30] The tactics adopted were to set
a pattern for subsequent crusading campaigns on issues of moral and religious
concern to evangelicals. The number of public petitions signed in the campaign
against slavery in the fifty years after 1785 was greater than for any other issue
in British politics, exceeding even the numbers gathered in the campaign for
parliamentary reform in the 1830s.

The complex political processes in the late eighteenth century, where the
British parliament was dominated less by party systems, and more by interest
groups, delayed the success of the abolition campaign. Wesley's 'Athanasius
contra mundum' analogy was apt. West Indian plantation owners, with a strong
voice in Parliament, claimed their interests were vital to the national economy,
as did merchants involved in the Atlantic trade. Wilberforce's first bill against
the slave trade was introduced in 1787, amidst high hopes that the campaign
would secure a speedy victory, and by 1792 the abolition campaign seemed on
the verge of success. Yet it took twenty years of persistent campaigning, and
resilience in the face of a series of defeats for successive bills, before abolition
was finally achieved. Growing political turmoil in Europe, and war with France,
made the British government increasingly reluctant to do anything that might
hinder trading relationships, and threaten the national economy. Opponents
sought to draw parallels between the Jacobins in France and abolitionists.

30   H. Willmer, 'Holy Worldliness in Nineteenth-Century England', in D. Baker (ed), *Sanctity and Secularity: The Church and the World*, Oxford, Blackwell, 1973, 200.

Wilberforce on Christian Attitudes to Slavery

'But they who thus urge on us the Divine toleration of slavery under the Jewish Theocracy, should remember that the Jews themselves were expressly commanded not to retain any of *their own nation*, any of their *brethren* in slavery, except as a punishment, or by their own consent; and even these were to be set free on the return of the sabbatical, or the seventh year. Inasmuch therefore, as we are repeatedly and expressly told that Christ has done away all distinctions of nations, and made all mankind one great family, all our fellow creatures are now our brethren; and therefore the very principles and spirit of the Jewish law itself would forbid our keeping the Africans, any more than our own fellow subjects, in a state of slavery... fraud, and rapine, and cruelty, are contrary to that religion, which commands us to love our neighbour as ourselves, and to do to others as we would have them do to us'. [1]

1 W. Wilberforce, A Letter on the Abolition of the Slave Trade: Addressed to the Freeholders and Other Inhabitants of Yorkshire, London, Cadell and Davies, 1807.

Although acts were passed in 1788 and 1799 to improve the conditions in which slaves were transported, they were hardly what the campaign ultimately desired.

CHRISTIAN ARGUMENTS AGAINST SLAVERY

The reasons why Christians in general, and evangelicals in particular, were constrained to embrace radical tactics in the abolition campaign were complex. Using Acts 17:26 as a basis, Quakers stressed the universal brotherhood of mankind. Evangelicals, with their strong emphasis on the biblical text, had to deal with the apparent toleration of slave holding in both Old and New Testaments, but Wilberforce was convinced that the Bible provided the principles upon which slavery was to be abolished. Texts such as Exodus 21:16 and 1 Timothy 1:9–10 were used as a basis for opposition to slave trading, as was the claim that Old Testament slavery, surrounded as it was with humane provisions, was very different to that found in the Americas. It was claimed that in the New Testament social order Christ had done away with previous distinctions and made of all nations one family guided by the principle of love to one's neighbour. [31]

The evangelical theological emphasis on redemption, which stressed deliverance from the slavery of sin, was an important motivation—freedom from the physical bondage of slavery appeared an external representation of the inward spiritual experience of evangelicals. This theological dynamic of liberation drew evangelicals into the political arena in the abolition cause

31 W. Wilberforce, *A Letter on the Abolition of the Slave Trade: Addressed to the Freeholders and Other Inhabitants of Yorkshire*, London, Cadell and Davies, 1807.

An Attempt to Justify Slavery from the Bible

'The slave trade appears… in perfect harmony with the principles and decisions of the Word of God… once the practice of Slavery, or the SLAVE-TRADE, had been expressly declared by the FATHER essentially just and lawful in the Sacred Writings of the Old Law, which the SON *did not come to destroy, but to fulfil*, it was absolutely impossible, that either HE or his Disciples should declare it unlawful and unjust in the Writings of the New, the principles of both the Laws respecting the intrinsic nature of *Right* and *Wrong, Justice* and *Injustice*, being invariably the same.

It follows then, that the argument drawn in favour of the SLAVE-TRADE from the constant silence of the Inspired Writers of the New Testament respecting the pretended illicitness of that Trade …. [is] a most powerful positive argument, showing in the strongest light, that the nature of the SLAVE-TRADE is perfectly consonant to the principles and tenets of the Christian Law'…

[After quoting from 1 Timothy 6, 1–2 Harris adds] … 'It is likewise evident from the Apostle's doctrine, that the primitive Christians were not only not forbidden, but expressly allowed by the principles of our Religion the purchasing of slaves, and keeping their fellow-creatures, nay, even their fellow-Christians, under the yoke of bondage of Slavery'. [1]

1   Rev. Raymund Harris [Raimundo Hormoza], *Scriptural Researches on the Licitness of the Slave-Trade, shewing its conformity with the principles of natural and revealed religion, delineated in the Sacred Writings of the Word of God*, Liverpool, 1788.

Harris' work is reprinted in P.J. Kitson, (ed) *Slavery, Abolition and Emancipation: Writings in the British Romantic Period, Vol. 2: The Abolition Debate*, London, Pickering and Chatto, 1999, 300, 302–03, 309. Harris dedicated it to the city of Liverpool, which had profited so much by the slave trade, and in return paid the author £100. At least six replies to his work appeared within the same year. It emerged that Harris was the 'nom de plume' of Raimundo Hormoza, a Spanish Jesuit who had been expelled from Spain in 1767, and moved to Liverpool where he had quarrelled with his bishop, and been suspended as a priest.

with a zeal and perseverance few could match.[32] Once slave trading was ended, the same theological argument was turned against the institution of slavery itself. Depicting it as a 'sin', absolutely wrong biblically, and which inhibited the spread of the gospel to slaves, turned abolition into a religious and moral duty for evangelical Christians. The tactic helped to overcome scruples as to challenging public authority, and becoming involved in what was considered the dubious world of politics. So too did the sense that Christians should do

32   R. Anstey, *The Atlantic Slave Trade and British Abolition 1760–1810*, Atlantic Highlands, New Jersey, Humanities Press, 1975, 406.

their utmost to avoid being implicated in a trade that sold humans into bondage. The Quaker Joseph Woods expressed the fear of many that the entire nation was a participant in the crime taking place in British ships and colonies. The loss of the American colonies was seen as a sign of God's disfavour, and urgent action was needed to avert the consequences of the nation further falling under the wrath of God, and to bring a restoration of God's grace and favour.[33]

However, not all from within the churches opposed slavery.[34] Some claimed biblical authority for the practice, a line of argument which was to be repeated far more vehemently in the United States in the nineteenth century. Others, hoping to gain preferment from wealthy merchants involved in the trade, maintained a discreet silence. Many seemed unaware that there was a problem: the practice was simply part of the way things were. The image of the slave-ship captain John Newton, newly converted to evangelicalism, reading his Bible in his cabin, and thanking God for having given him 'an easy and creditable way of life,' whilst below decks on his ship slaves suffered the horrors of the middle passage, is particularly evocative, although Newton later came to repent deeply of his involvement in the practice. Several years after his conversion he left slave trading, and was ordained as an Anglican clergyman. Newton added his own first-hand testimony to the anti-slavery campaign, and from his enlightened evangelical conscience denounced 'a commerce so iniquitous, so cruel, so oppressive, so destructive', and which contradicted 'the common sense of mankind.'[35] Yet the trumpet blast of opposition from official Christianity certainly sounded an uncertain note. Bishop Porteus of London only became a supporter of abolition in 1806, and he was one of a very small number of bishops who took such a step. The General Assembly of the Church of Scotland also came out against the slave trade, but would not endorse the policy of petitioning parliament on the subject. Nor should it be suggested that the abolitionists argued entirely for the equality of black Africans with themselves—

---

33   J. Woods, *Thoughts Upon the Slavery of Negroes*, London, James Phillips, 1784, p23; see also the Anglican Granville Sharp's, *The Law of Retribution: Or a Serious Warning to Great Britain and Her Colonies; Founded On Unquestionable Examples of God's Temporal Vengeance Against Tyrants, Slave Holders and Oppressors*, London, W. Richardson, 1776.

34   In 1772 an Anglican missionary to Africa with the Society for the Propagation of the Gospel published *The African Trade For Negro Slaves Shown to be Consistent With the Principles of Humanity and with the Laws of Revealed Religion*.

35   J. Newton, *The Journal of a Slave Trader*, in B. Martin and M. Spurrell (eds), London, Epworth Press, 1962, xii; J. Newton, *Thoughts Upon the African Slave Trade*, London, 1788, repr. in ed. P.J. Kitson, *Slavery, Abolition and Emancipation: Writings in the British Romantic Period, Vol. 2: The Abolition Debate*, London, Pickering and Chatto, 1999, 117. The *Journal* of the ship's surgeon, James Irving, from Liverpool similarly reveals a man engaged in slave trading and able to reconcile his involvement in the trade with his Christian faith. See ed. S. Schwarz, *Slave Captain: The Career of James Irving in the Liverpool Slave Trade*, Wrexham, Bridge Books, 1995.

after all, many were distinctly hesitant about affording political equality to white working-class Britons.

Finally, in 1807 the force of moral argument could no longer be denied, and amidst scenes of mounting excitement, during a debate in which MPs spontaneously gave Wilberforce a resounding three cheers, the House of Commons voted by 283 votes to 16 for the Abolition of the Slave Trade in British ships. After 18 years of campaigning, and eleven earlier defeated bills, Wilberforce attributed the victory to the hand of God. The bill became law in March 1807. The challenge became, how to enforce it?

ENFORCING ABOLITION

The abolition act of 1807 brought slave trading to an end in areas controlled by the British Crown, and in the years after 1808 a British anti-slavery squadron patrolled the West African coast intercepting ships involved in slave trading. However, until other nations embraced abolition, especially the Spanish and Portuguese, the trade continued, and disputes arose when ships from other nations carrying slaves were intercepted. Advances in the war against France made the task easier, and at the second Treaty of Paris in 1814, the abolition of the slave trade was agreed by European powers, a decision confirmed after the final defeat of Napoleon at Waterloo in 1815.

In France an abolition law was promulgated in April 1818. Nine weeks later three French warships arrived off the coast of Africa to inspect French ships suspected of being slave traders, although they proved far less effective in their task than the British squadron. Dutch involvement in slave trading collapsed before it was formally ended in 1818, although slave imports into the colony of Surinam continued until 1826. Britain pressed its case hard on other nations, negotiating in 1815 a treaty with Portugal to prohibit slave trading north of the equator. However, the slave trade was not halted by such measures. Brazil separated from Portugal in 1822, and defiantly maintained the slave trade into the 1850s before succumbing to British pressure. Spain also maintained the slave trade with Cuba until the 1860s, when combined British and American efforts brought it to an end.

From a peak of some 80,000 per annum in the 1780s, the number of slaves shipped fell to around 53,000 per annum in the 1810s, and after a temporary revival, dropped again to 55,000 per annum in the 1830s, when the trade had become formally illegal in most places. By the 1860s, less than 4,000 slaves per year were being transported.[36] The British squadron seized around 1,600 slave ships, and liberated some 160,000 Africans from them. Their work rescued about one in ten of potential slaves from crossing the Atlantic.[37] For all the

36   Klein, *Atlantic Slave Trade*, 187–197
37   Klein, *Atlantic Slave Trade*, 199.

efforts of the abolitionists some 3 or 4 million Africans were still shipped across the Atlantic after 1807.

Greater success was enjoyed by the British in framing world opinion that the slave trade was an immoral traffic in human life, and no longer defensible. Yet the failure to bring an effective end to the trade until the 1860s reveals how subtle and persistent slave traders were in defying sanctions against them, and how unenthusiastic some governments were about enforcing abolition. It also reflects the unending growth of European demand for the products of the American plantations, the engine that drove the whole mechanism.

SIERRA LEONE

Abolitionists did not solely focus their attention upon the slave trade, but also on conditions in Africa itself. One practical measure to assist slaves who had been liberated was the development of the Sierra Leone colony. In 1787 Granville Sharp, a leading figure in the anti-slave trade campaign, was approached by the leaders of a group of emancipated slaves in London who had been unable to secure employment in the city. Sharp conceived of a plan to send them back to Africa to settle on the small mountainous peninsula of Sierra Leone. The scheme was endorsed by Wilberforce, who believed that legitimate commerce could replace that of trade in human flesh. With his financial backing, and that of other Clapham friends, including Henry Thornton, the Sierra Leone Company was established in 1791. Under its flag, all who settled were to be free and equal, regardless of colour, with education for children, and protection under English common law.

Early arrivals in Sierra Leone were boosted by a group of slaves who had escaped from the American South, and had fought with the British in the war of independence. They were led by David George, a slave who had purchased his freedom, and had helped to start congregations of Black Africans in South Carolina and Georgia. After the war the ex-slaves had temporarily settled in Nova Scotia, an area of British control, where George founded a black church. Ten years later, George embraced the opportunity to take part of his congregation to Sierra Leone, where he became the leading black minister in the new British colony. Indeed, much of the pioneering work of Christian ministry within Sierra Leone was done by African ex-slaves. The young Zachary Macaulay was sent from Britain, and proved a fine early administrator for the colony. He later brought some of the sons of chiefs from Sierra Leone back to Clapham for education and training with the hope that they would return as civic leaders and missionaries. The African children shared lessons with the children of the Clapham Sect families, and they played together freely.

Sierra Leone was a brilliant dream, conceived by deep Christian compassion. It was to be the morning star of Africa, a model settlement devoted to peaceful commerce, designed to inspire the foundation of similar colonies elsewhere in

West Africa. However, it struggled against huge odds. Established well before the abolition of the slave trade, it faced opposition from the slave traders; the cost of the settlement's defence was high; and it was ravaged by a French invasion force in 1794. The colony ran at a huge commercial loss, and Wilberforce, Thornton, and friends were constantly required to supplement public funds from their own resources. Yet the example inspired others. A small American naval squadron also operated in the area, depositing slaves liberated from the slave trade at Monrovia, in Liberia, which was started in 1821, and declared itself a republic in 1847. The French followed suit after 1848 with the establishment of Libreville in Gabon.

A significant aspect of the Sierra Leone scheme was the hope that it could be used as a base for promoting the extension of education, farming, industry, and Christianity, into West Africa. This was fraught with considerable difficulties. European missionaries struggled to survive in the West African climate: many died, others returned home. The task of educating the freed slaves was not easy: one promising pupil lost his temper, and burned his school down![38] Only after the abolition of the slave trade, and the creation of Sierra Leone as a British colony, did the scheme begin to show signs of succeeding. By 1820 it had over 10,000 free slaves, most of whom had been rescued from the holds of slave ships, and who were receiving education, training in skills for life, and Christian instruction. In 1823, Wilberforce pronounced Sierra Leone a success: Africans had acquired the virtues of citizens, and demonstrated that they were capable of great industry and productivity without the requirement to use physical brutality. The goal of using Sierra Leone as a base for future Christian mission into West Africa was far sighted. Here was a living language laboratory, with freed slaves from many different tribes, gathered in one place. Amongst the converted, educated, slaves, was a labour force well suited to the task of mission in West Africa, able to withstand the climate, and take the gospel to their own tribes, without the need to learn a new language, or spend time understanding different cultures. Over a sixty year period later in the nineteenth century, Sierra Leone produced over 100 clergy for the Church Missionary Society from a population of around 50,000, in addition to many other catechists, teachers and mission workers.[39]

THE CAMPAIGN FOR EMANCIPATION FROM SLAVERY

Some had urged that the ending of the slave trade should not be accepted without the abolition of slavery itself, but Wilberforce believed it was not in the

---

38   On Sierra Leone see A. F. Walls, 'A Christian Experiment: The Early Sierra Leone Colony', in ed G.J. Cuming, *The Mission of the Church and the Propagation of the Faith: Studies in Church History 6*, Cambridge, Cambridge University Press, 1970, 107–130.

39   A Walls, *The Missionary Movement in Christian History: Studies in the Transmission of Faith*, Edinburgh, T&T Clark, 1996, 86–87, 102–109.

power of the initial campaign to heal both wounds at once. The continuance of War in Europe until 1815 further delayed progress, but by the early 1820s, some of the newly established republics in South America had begun to abolish slavery. It had been hoped that the Colonial Assemblies in the West Indies would do the same in the aftermath of the abolition of the slave trade.

When it became clear that this was unlikely to happen, in 1823 the second phase of this moral crusade for the soul of the British nation and its colonies was launched, with the formation of what became known as the Anti-Slavery Society. From the outset it was a significant body, but with a Duke as its president, and vice-presidents that included five peers of the realm and fourteen MPs, it was disinclined to radical strategies. Two months later, Wilberforce issued an *Appeal* expressing his fear that it was presuming upon the favour of God for a nation blessed with Christian light and civil freedom, to keep Africans in the colonies in 'their present state of unexampled darkness and degradation.' Slaves were treated as an inferior race, mere chattels, part of the owner's estate with no independent rights, driven to work with the whip like animals, with females punished in indecent ways. Slaves were denied the Christian ordinance of marriage, and not allowed to work on their own land on any other day than Sunday, effectively denying them access to religious worship. Slavery had, to Wilberforce, left on Britain's character 'the deepest stain of dishonour'. His demand that slaves have access to education, especially in Christian teaching, was a key strategy in a campaign for both the temporal and the eternal welfare of slaves.[40]

Wilberforce was by then ageing and infirm, and his mantle in the anti-slavery crusade passed to Thomas Fowell Buxton (1786–1845), known for his concern for the London poor, an interest in penal reform, and in missionary societies. Buxton was an Evangelical Anglican, born into a wealthy family. With a Quaker mother, and Elizabeth Fry as his sister-in-law, he had close connections with strongly abolitionist Quakers, especially the Gurney family.[41] Buxton served as MP for Weymouth from 1818 until his defeat in 1837, claiming his political views were independent of party—'I vote as I like'.[42] Buxton delivered the opening salvo of the emancipation campaign in the House of Commons in May 1823 with his resolution 'That the state of Slavery is repugnant to the principles of the British Constitution and the Christian Religion; and that it ought to be gradually abolished'. The reaction was varied, but predictable. Buxton found little immediate support, but nonetheless, the battle lines were drawn.[43] Slave-

---

40   W. Wilberforce, *An Appeal to the Religion, Justice, and Humanity of the Inhabitants of the British Empire, in Behalf of the Negro Slaves in the West Indies*, London, J. Hatchard and Son, 1823, 77, 53–54.

41   On Buxton see C. Buxton (ed.), *Memoirs of Sir Thomas Fowell Buxton*, London, 1850.

42   On Buxton see T.F. Buxton, *The African Slave Trade and Its Remedy*, London, 1838; C. Buxton, ed, *Memoirs of Sir Thomas Fowell Buxton*, London, 1855.

43   *Parliamentary Debates (1786–1838), Vol. IX*, London, 1823, 275, 286.

Slavery and Racist Attitudes

'A writer of the highest authority on all West India subjects, Mr Long, in his celebrated History of Jamaica, though pointing out some of the particulars of their ill-treatment, scrupled not to state it as his opinion, that in the gradations of being, Negroes were little elevated above the oran outang, "that type of man." Nor was this an unguarded or a hastily thrown-out assertion. He institutes a laborious comparison of the Negro race with that species of baboon; and declares, that, "ludicrous as the opinion may seem, he does not think that an oran outang husband would be a dishonour to a Hottentot female". When we find such sentiments as these to have been unblushingly avowed... we are prepared for... the practical effects of these opinions.'[1]

1   An appalled William Wilberforce quoting Long's 'History of Jamaica', in *An Appeal to the Religion, Justice and Humanity of the Inhabitants of the British Empire, in Behalf of the Negro Slaves in the West Indies*, London, J. Hatchard and Son, 1823, 10–11.

---

holders dug in to resist change, free blacks called for the establishment of their civil rights, and the slave population expressed their growing longing for freedom with stirrings of rebellion. The Anglican clergyman, G.W. Bridges, serving a Jamaican parish, and not averse to flogging his own slaves, responded to Wilberforce that West Indian slaves lived in better conditions than the working classes in Europe. Attempts at change, he darkly warned, would only end in bloodshed.[44] A small, but generally non-vocal body of evangelicals, such as Edward Irving and Henry Drummond, argued that slavery was part of the providential order of the world.

The key focus of the debate was the British colonies in the West Indies, where some 67,000 Europeans lived, with 140,000 of mixed race, and 695,000 of African origin. Slavery was generally conducted on the principle that the maximum labour should be extracted for the minimum expenditure on food and subsistence. The ugly racism that lay behind the practice was vividly depicted in sources such as Long's *History of Jamaica*.

The anti-slavery campaign was fought on both sides of the Atlantic, and the role of missionaries in the West Indies proved important, especially after the British government adopted a policy of amelioration, which placed an emphasis on the provision of religious instruction for slaves. As key providers of education, missionaries were placed in a strategic, but controversial position, especially as amelioration won limited support from the local colonial assemblies. From being at first heavily dependent on the patronage of planters, they increasingly took on the mantle of reformers who were closely engaged in the anti-slavery

---

44   G.W. Bridges, *A Voice from Jamaica: In Reply to William Wilberforce*, London, 1823.

campaign, playing a vital role in convincing the British public that slavery was a denial of not only civil, but also religious, liberty to slaves, and that abolition, rather than reform, was the only solution. They found themselves increasingly cast in the role of defenders of the rights of slaves, and those who played an increasingly prominent role in promoting the investigation of cases of abuse. As with the campaign against the slave trade, Christianity again proved a significant weapon by which slavery could not only be challenged, but be overthrown.

Colonial power exercised from England brought with it an Established Anglican Church, with bishops of Jamaica and Barbados appointed in 1824, but recruitment of clergy for the colonies proved difficult, and little work was done amongst the slave population. Despite the CMS having leading members who were abolitionists, such as Wilberforce and Buxton, there was no mission in the British West Indies until 1823, held back by the presence of the Anglican Establishment, and tensions with Anglican bishops over matters such as education. Into this gap stepped dissenting missionaries. The first significant missionary presence in the West Indies was that of the Moravians, whose work started as early as 1732, on the Danish colony of St Thomas. They had reached Dutch Guiana (Surinam) by 1738. Their work in Antigua was particularly successful, where 7,700 members, or about one in five slaves, belonged to one of its four congregations by 1820. Methodist missionary efforts in the West Indies were organised by Thomas Coke in 1784: his seven visits between 1786 and 1803 have seen him hailed as the Wesley of the West Indies. Despite opposition, by 1793 the Methodist society in St Vincent included some 1,000 slaves. In 1823, there were fifty Methodist missionaries in the West Indies, the societies had over 26,000 members, of whom 95% were slaves, and membership reached 48,000 in 1840,[45] welcomed by the Wesleyan Conference as 'brethren'. Coke was carefully neutral on the social and legal issues related to slavery, but such a policy could not last in the face of what the missionaries encountered. During the 1820s, the voice of official Methodism became stronger in its opposition to slavery, and in 1830 the Wesleyan Conference called for petitions against the practice, condemning the 'violent prejudices of caste, founded upon the colour of the skin'.[46] That year, a speaker at the Wesleyan Missionary Society urged his audience, 'We cannot care for the salvation of the negro, without caring for his emancipation from bondage'.[47]

After the American War of Independence, a number of English settlers moved to the West Indies from the United States, taking with them their slaves,

---

45   Report of the Wesleyan Methodist Missionary Society, London, 1823, 40, and London, 1840, 84.

46   Minutes of the Wesleyan Conference, 1830, Collected Edition, vi, 613–15, in ed. D. M. Thompson Nonconformity in the Nineteenth Century, London, Routledge and Kegan Paul, 1972, 69–71.

47   Richard Watson, quoted by R. Anstey, 'Religion and Slave Emancipation', in D. Eltis and J. Walvin (eds), The Abolition of the Atlantic Slave Trade, Madison, Wisconsin, 1981, 47.

including a number of Baptists. By 1813, they numbered some 8,000. After the first British Baptist missionary for the West Indies was appointed in 1813 there followed a story of steady success. By 1830, there were 10,000 Baptist members and 20,000 enquirers.[48] Baptist missionaries were instructed not to oppose the system of slavery, in order not to endanger the mission, but new recruits in the 1820s brought with them the growing anti-slavery sentiment from Britain, and they were to take an increasingly prominent role in the West Indian dimension of the anti-slavery campaign. Missions were to play a key role in the extension of education, and especially religious instruction, by means of Sunday Schools.

Evangelical missionaries, especially nonconformists, did all they could to promote the official policy of amelioration of the condition of the slaves through the 1820s, but increasingly they took on the role of supporters and defenders of the individual rights of slaves, and assisting them in seeking legal redress. Their role in bringing cases of abuse and serious cruelty against slaves in the West Indies to the attention of the authorities, and the British public, deepened the conviction that slavery was a denial of civil and religious liberty, and strengthened the abolition cause. This set them in opposition to not only the local colonial assemblies, who proved resistant to improving the conditions of the slaves, but also the Anglican Church, with whom the authorities were in close association. Their actions reflected growing Dissenting access to political influence after the repeal of the Test and Corporation Acts in 1828. Dissenters were turned from being a tolerated group on the margins of society, into individuals with civil and political rights. Dissenting missionary engagement in the emancipation campaign served as a dimension of the Dissenting Grievances campaign against the privileges and religious dominance of the Anglican Establishment, which attracted a vehement response on both sides of the Atlantic.

It was the actions of the slaves themselves, with the slave rebellions in the years 1823 and 1831, which eventually proved pivotal in the emancipation campaign. Reaction to the former probably delayed the advent of emancipation; the latter made it inevitable. As news reached the West Indies in 1823 of the renewed parliamentary debate on emancipation, rumours circulated amongst the slaves that emancipation had in fact been granted by parliament, but was being withheld by the plantation owners. Amidst growing frustration over the harshness of their treatment a number of slaves resolved to refuse to work, seize what firearms they could, and lay claim to the freedom which they believed was theirs. Some 13,000 out of 74,000 slaves took part in a rising in Demerara, but the rebellion was quickly put down. Although two white settlers were killed, 200 slaves were shot, and 47 were later hanged. Hundreds of others were imprisoned, and some brutally flogged.

48 *Annual Report, Baptist Missionary Society 1830*, London, 1830, 38–39.

Missionary engagement in the anti-slavery cause was highlighted through the death of the London Missionary Society's John Smith, accused of involvement in the Demerara rising. Smith was already unpopular with the authorities for publicising the excessive punishments meted out against some slaves, sometimes of up to 200 lashes, which proved fatal to some. He had also ignored instructions not to teach slaves to read, and had appointed a number of slaves as deacons in his church. On slender evidence, part of which included his reading the book of Exodus to the slaves, he was charged with fomenting the 1823 rebellion, and tried by a local court-martial. In a verdict clearly designed to strike a blow against the work of the missionaries, Smith was sentenced to death by hanging. Already in frail health, he died in prison whilst waiting for the sentence to be carried out. Smith's death created a martyr for the anti-slavery cause, and hardened the convictions of the abolitionists that they were involved in a religious crusade. Planter suspicion of the missionaries and abolitionists mounted, and the backlash against their work was severe. They asserted that further talk of emancipation would only encourage further rebellion. The Wesleyan mission in Bridgetown, Barbados, was destroyed in 1823, and the missionary, John Shrewsbury, driven from the island. Magistrates became increasingly obstructive over providing missionaries with licences to operate, and there were real doubts as to whether missionary work would be allowed to continue. Antipathy towards all that missionaries, and abolitionists such as Wilberforce, stood for was vented on the slaves. In Jamaica in 1824 three slaves were transported and fourteen given sentences in the workhouse simply for hurrahing Wilberforce.[49]

The campaign for the abolition of slavery was much more than a product of white humanitarian and benevolent concern, it was also significantly a movement from below on the part of black slaves and former slaves. Their demands for, and expression of, religious freedom, was an aspect of their demand for personal liberty, indeed some colonial authorities viewed attendance at a missionary church as subversive. Fervent, experiential, religion was considered unorthodox and potentially rebellious: in 1829, the slave Sam Swiney was punished for attending a late night prayer meeting and crying out 'O Lord, Lord God, Jesus, my Saviour', an exclamation judged a mockery of religion by the Anglican dominated authorities.[50]

In 1824, William Knibb, one of the best known of the early Baptist missionaries, arrived in Jamaica where he served until his death in 1845. Knibb typified the new missionary recruits to the West Indies who were convinced that all Christians should be abolitionists. He became a tireless champion of

---

49   M. Turner, *Slaves and Missionaries*, 107.

50   S. Jakobsson, *Am I Not a Man and a Brother? British Missions and the Abolition of the Slave Trade and Slavery in West Africa and the West Indies 1786–1838*, Uppsala, Gleerup, 1972, 436.

the black slaves, certain that neutrality was not an option: those silent in the face of injustice and inhumanity shared the guilt of the crime. He was appalled that in Barbados the murder of a slave by his owner might only result in a small fine. His work highlights the significance of the colonial dimension of the emancipation campaign, as he wrote to the BMS in 1831, 'While you are exerting all your energies at home, ought we to sit all day idle?'[51]

The changing political context in Britain in the late 1820s made discrimination against missionaries and black Christian slaves increasingly untenable. Success in achieving Dissenting political rights in 1828, and Roman Catholic Emancipation the following year, released reforming energies which could be diverted into further campaigns to extend religious liberty, of which slave emancipation was one dimension. The Anti-Slavery Society had through the 1820s adopted a gradualist approach of conciliation and negotiation, at first seeking mitigation and amelioration of the conditions of the slaves. Others urged a more radical campaign, which eventually split the society. In 1830 the Anti-Slavery Society changed its policy, and re-launched its campaign, now demanding immediate emancipation, and a petition of 170,000 signatures was presented to Parliament. The Dissenting contribution was powerful: of the 2,600 petitions, 2,000 were believed to have originated with them. In 1833, a further 5,020 anti-slavery petitions were sent to Parliament: in all, more than one in five males over the age of fifteen signed the petitions.[52] As with the anti-slave trade campaign, the movement was a coalition of liberal humanitarian sentiment, through the formation of alliances with wider groups to strengthen the appeal of their cause. This involved making compromises, and using economic as well as humanitarian arguments, rather than simply quoting Biblical texts to assert their case. Similar tactics to the earlier campaign were employed: abolitionist lectures in the 1830s were attended by packed audiences, often with large numbers turned away. Many who attended were associated with local churches, convinced that slavery was repugnant to their religion, and profoundly anti-Christian: slavery was a crime against God. Up to date facts were reported in the monthly *Anti-Slavery Reporter*, and the voting habits of MPs on the issue were publicised.

Abolitionism proved attractive not only to middle class evangelicals including many nonconformists who opposed slavery on religious and moral grounds, but also urban artisans who embraced the cause as part of their wider protest against the forces of social oppression. When congregations signed anti-slavery petitions they were moving into the overtly political territory they

51 Letter 6 July, 1831, quoted in Hinton, *Memoir of William Knibb*, 114.

52 R. Anstey, 'Religion and British Slave Emancipation', in D. Eltis and J. Walvin (eds), *The Abolition of the Atlantic Slave Trade*, Madison, Wisconsin, 1981, 51; and J. Walvin (ed.), *Slavery and British Society 1776–1846*, London, 1982, 26.

generally hesitated to tread. An important role in the anti-slavery cause was also taken by women, who established ladies' anti-slavery associations after 1825, concentrating on raising mass petitions, and house-to-house canvassing of support for the cause, rather than public meetings. From the 1830s these groups formed important links with abolitionists in the United States. Their campaign drew particular attention to the sufferings of female slaves, especially the sexual exploitation to which they were subject, the cruelties faced when pregnant, or their enforced separation from husbands and children. Although the campaign was led by middle-class women, they were able to draw on the support of working-class women. This engagement in anti-slavery campaigning and charitable work gave women vital early experience of self-organisation and political activity.[53]

Yet not all within the churches were comfortable with mass campaigning. In 1833, the Wesleyan Methodist leader Jabez Bunting declared that the 'Holy cause of Anti-Slavery has already been disgraced and prejudiced in some quarters by the system of "agitation".[54] The Tractarian Hurrell Froude's reaction was extreme: 'I cannot get over my prejudice against the niggers; every one I meet seems to me like an incarnation of the whole Anti-Slavery Society and Fowell Buxton at their head'.[55]

Although an abolition motion was defeated in the House of Commons in April 1831, news of the anti-slavery campaign in Britain circulated amongst the slaves, and excitement at the prospect of emancipation intensified. As in 1823, and despite missionary assertions to the contrary, many believed that emancipation had already been granted but was being denied by the West Indian authorities. A long period of drought followed by heavy rains, and epidemics of smallpox and dysentery deepened unrest amongst the slaves. Rebellion followed in 1831. A key figure in this was the slave Sam Sharpe, who united skills gained as a leader in his local Baptist church, with the principles of English radical nonconformists, and the Christian tradition of resistance to oppression. Passionate, eloquent, and literate, he was not willing to remain a 'Daddy' or 'Ruler' among black Baptists, but argued that the Bible taught the natural equality of all men, that slaves were entitled to freedom, and that whites had no right to hold blacks in slavery. He became convinced that slaves could play a pivotal role in the overthrow of the system. Sharpe was made a 'General' by the rebels, and under his leadership members from mission churches and independent sects, took a key role in the desperate bid for freedom. There

53 The role of women in the campaign is covered in C. Midgley, *Women Against Slavery: The British Campaigns, 1780–1870*, London, Routledge, 1992.

54 W.R. Ward, *Early Victorian Methodism: The Correspondence of Jabez Bunting, 1830–58*, Oxford, Oxford University Press, 1976, 29.

55 Quoted in M. Hennell, *The Sons of The Prophets*, London, SPCK, 1979, 21.

they had gained skills of self-organisation, been educated, and informed of the growing emancipation cause. Of ninety-nine slaves later tried for their role in the Jamaican rebellion, it was believed that twenty-five were connected with the Baptists. Sharpe believed that the work of proclaiming freedom was God's work, and would enjoy his favour and assistance.

Sharpe's rebellion began at Christmas 1831, with a refusal to work, as part of a movement of passive resistance, but plans had also been laid for armed revolt if the government troops failed to rally to support their cause. A lack of organisation and effective communication meant that the passive resisters were soon quelled, but estates were burned, and a Black Regiment took over areas of the country. Slave support for the rebellion was not unanimous, but was widespread. Between 20,000 and 50,000 slaves were believed to have been involved in the rebellion, and in it fourteen white settlers were killed, and 201 slaves. The official death toll did not take account of the brutality of the white militia. Slave property was destroyed, some suspected of involvement were shot out of hand. Three hundred and twelve slaves were executed on minimal evidence through the actions of hastily convened courts-martial that followed quashing the rebellion. Most died with quiet dignity, believing they had struck a blow in the cause of both emancipation and religious freedom. Their claims were solidly founded in the social ideology of the homeland of their oppressors— the belief in individual liberties sanctioned by law.[56]

In the aftermath of the Jamaican rebellion, attempts were made to suppress the work of Dissenting missionaries. Despite their denials, they were believed to be complicit in the rising. Knibb, amongst others was arrested, but released on bail. The missionaries were left with a stark choice between supporting the rebels and slaves, who had identified their claims with the cause of Christian freedom and had claimed missionaries as their allies, and the uncertain patronage of the planters. Their decision was made clearer by the reprisals they faced. Missionary homes were attacked, and missionaries threatened by white mobs: fourteen Baptist chapels and six Methodist chapels were demolished, and others were closed. Local Assemblies and magistrates showed little interest in protecting their rights and property. Missionaries were cast into the role of spokesmen for the slaves, and even the rebels, asserting their intellectual and spiritual equality. Their campaign for the freedom to preach to the slaves became inextricably linked with the freedoms of the slaves not only to receive religious instruction, but also exercise individual rights.

Such ongoing repression afforded the cause of the slaves with the oxygen of publicity. After order was restored, missions sent delegates to Britain, and the reports of Knibb and others proved a vital boost to the emancipation

---

56 M. Turner, *Slaves and Missionaries: The Disintegration of Jamaican Slave Society, 1787–1834,* Urbana, University of Illinois Press, 148–173.

movement. Their arrival coincided with the passing of the Reform Act in 1832, which gave the emancipation cause further impetus. The subsequent election returned 134 candidates pledged to the abolition of slavery, ranging from Anglicans, to Independents, Quakers, and Roman Catholics, spanning the political spectrum from conservative to radical, but most were liberals. Calls had been made by the Wesleyan Conference in 1830, and the Protestant Deputies in 1832, for votes only to be cast for candidates pledged to abolition. There is evidence of significant tactical voting: in Manchester, loyal Tories switched their support to Whig anti-slavery candidates when the Conservative candidates refused to support immediate emancipation of the slaves.[57] The alliance of Tory landowners and West Indian planter and merchant interests was decisively weakened by the Reform of Parliament, which gave increased representation to the growing manufacturing districts. Slave labour appeared not only immoral, but also outdated and, uneconomic, the antithesis of free trade sentiment. Emancipation could no longer be denied.

The abolition of slavery bill passed its second reading in the House of Commons on 26 July, 1833, and 'emancipation' took place on 1st August 1834. Religious freedom was proclaimed: missionaries were able to work freely, government grants made available to support education, and permissions granted for former slaves to become lay preachers and even ministers. Three days before his death, Wilberforce heard the news. His response was characteristic: 'Thank God that I should have lived to witness a day in which England is willing to give twenty millions sterling for the abolition of slavery.'[58] However, it was a gradualist, compromise, measure with full emancipation to be granted only after up to six years of 'apprenticeship', in which slaves were required to work for their masters for 45 hours a week. Compensation was paid to planters for their loss of slaves, their 'property', set at about half their market value.

The final stage of emancipation fell largely to the actions of the local Assemblies in the West Indies. Those in Bermuda and Antigua freed slaves immediately, but in other areas the condition of the apprentices was considered worse than slavery. Further anti-slavery agitation followed, but whilst the British government hesitated over ending the system, local assemblies in the West Indies decided to do so of their own accord. In August 1838, the apprenticeship system was over. Former slaves were set free, although left at the mercy of planters who controlled the local legal and legislative system.

Aspirations amongst slaves for freedom, which had been expressed through adherence especially to Wesleyan and Baptist missions before emancipation, resulted in thousands flocking to the churches on Emancipation Day. It was

---

57   I.J. Shaw, *High Calvinists in Action: Calvinism and the City, Manchester and London, c. 1810–60*, Oxford, Oxford University Press, 107–108.

58   R.I and S. Wilberforce, *Life of William Wilberforce*, London, John Murray, 1838, Vol V, 370.

an expression of their belief that Christianity and the missionaries had played a vital role in the cause of freedom. William Knibb was welcomed as a hero when he returned to Jamaica in October 1834. Mission churches were significantly boosted. Chapels destroyed in reprisals after the rebellion were quickly rebuilt, extended, and multiplied. Opportunities to advance the education of the 'apprenticed' slaves were freely embraced. By 1839 there were some 34,000 in day, evening, and Sunday schools. Also important was the role of the free black and mixed race populace, especially after they were granted full civil rights in 1830. Mission churches gave them opportunities to develop skills in preaching, and social organisation. Missionaries had taught slaves to read and write, that they were made in the image of God, and that they had rights —to learn Christian truth and the way of salvation in a context of religious freedom, and self-expression. Not all embraced the missionary version of Christianity. Some, conscious of disparities with their own traditions, formed their own Native Baptist sects, with black leaders.

ABOLITION AND EMANCIPATION IN PERSPECTIVE

The process of abolishing slavery took a century and a half from the abolition of slave holding in Britain in 1772. As Spanish territories in South and Central America gained their independence, some such as Chile in 1823, and Mexico in 1829, abolished slavery at once. The French only granted emancipation in their territories in 1848, and full emancipation in the United States had to wait until the 1860s and a civil war [chapter 11]. Argentina, Peru, and Bolivia waited until the 1850s. Only in 1888 did Brazil end slavery. Slavery in the East took longer to abolish. It was made illegal in India under British rule in 1843, in Egypt in 1882, and in Morocco (under French rule) in 1912. After success in the emancipation campaign in 1833, Buxton redirected his attentions to the internal slave trade of Africa, seeking to tackle the problem of slavery at its root. The resultant Niger Expedition will be discussed in chapter nine. Anti-slavery campaigning was also a component of the widespread missionary strategy of the French Roman Catholic monks whose work was superintended by Cardinal Lavigerie. They strongly challenged the stubborn persistence of slavery in North Africa. With most of Africa under European colonial rule by 1914, further enslavement was prohibited, although many of those previously enslaved were not released. Only when countries such as Turkey, Iran and Saudi Arabia, sought admission to the League of Nations after 1920 did they make slavery illegal.[59]

Alongside evangelical and enlightenment humanitarian influences, other powerful forces were at work in the ending of slavery. Peace in Europe after 1815 reduced the need to narrowly defend British overseas interests, and the growth of the British economy made it far less dependent on trade with the

59   P. Manning, *Slavery and African Life*, Cambridge, Cambridge University Press, 1990, 12.

colonies.[60] New-found wealth rested increasingly in the hands of liberal minded industrialists and the middle class after the passing of the Reform Act in 1832, which dealt a crippling blow to the old West India lobby. Free-trade, including free labour, became the dominant economic philosophy, to which slavery was antithetical, and did not make economic sense.[61] Paradoxically, the cotton industry which flourished under free trade philosophy and applied the most modern of industrial techniques, relied for its raw materials on slavery, the most primitive and exploitative of production methods.

Success in the two campaigns had a significant influence on the moral tone of the British government's foreign policy, which thereafter included ensuring implementation of abolitionist promises made by foreign governments, and enforcing abolition where no such promises were forthcoming. Victory also affected the evangelical psyche throughout the nineteenth century. Campaigning had been seen to work when it was targeted against specific issues, which could be portrayed as 'sins.' One consequence was a piecemeal evangelical political theology. Rather than creating a comprehensive alternative world-view and policy for reform of society as a whole, periodic crusading moral outrage was instead raised, sometimes targeted very effectively at a narrow range of causes, followed by lengthy periods of inactivity.[62]

Contrary to popular opinion, the Clapham Sect did not abolish the slave trade, nor did it abolish slavery in the British colonies. The British Parliament did. Yet behind the parliamentary acts lay a complex series of influences, religious, economic, social, humanitarian, and political, as Europe adapted to the post-enlightenment and post-French Revolution world. Evangelical religion, both lay and clerical, but rarely official, was an absolutely central component in the mix. It provided, to a degree not matched by other factors, the spiritual and moral drive required to persevere in the 'great cause.' Campaigners attributed their success to the hand of God. They held no monopoly on Christian thinking about slavery, especially where it was closely allied to white settler interests. Nonetheless, Christianity in general led the way towards shifting opinion from the acceptance of slavery, to condemning it: Islam and African religions later followed suit.[63]

Simplistic understandings of the nature of slavery, and how it was ended,

---

60   On debates about economic influences behind abolition see R. Anstey, *The Atlantic Slave Trade*, 1975, and S. Drescher, *Capitalism and Anti-Slavery*, London, Macmillan, 1986. The interconnection between religious, business and social factors in abolition is discussed in J. Jennings, *The Business of Abolishing the British Slave Trade 1783–1807*, London, Frank Cass, 1997.

61   On the economic dimension to debates over emancipation see S. Drescher, *The Mighty Experiment: Free Labour Versus Slavery in British Emancipation*, Oxford, OUP, 2002.

62   For criticisms of the approach of evangelicals see F.K. Brown, *Fathers of the Victorians: The Age of Wilberforce*, Cambridge, CUP, 1961.

63   Manning, *Slavery and African Life*, 173–74.

should be avoided. Slavery involved far more than Africans being subject to barbaric treatment by evil Europeans, although this certainly happened. Africans and Islamic slave traders were heavily involved. Slavery harmed, but did not destroy the economies of Africa, and even brought wealth to cities such as Kano, in Nigeria. But the trade which had previously existed for a long time, was massively accelerated by external demand. Slavery left an ugly legacy outside Africa. It reinforced the domination of men over women, and sanctioned the abuse of children; it cost millions of lives. Racism had existed from before the eighteenth century, but slave-owning promoted the dominance of one race and culture above another as the natural order of things, and asserted that African slaves were not fit for freedom. As ideas of evolutionary human progress took hold in the nineteenth century, corresponding theories of human backwardness were conceived, placing Africans on the bottom rung. The late nineteenth century was to see a huge upsurge in racism, against black ex-slaves in the Americas, and against Jews in Europe. The poverty and racial discrimination suffered by black people in Africa and the Americas today owes much to the past practice of slavery.

FURTHER READING

R. Anstey, *The Atlantic Slave Trade and British Abolition, 1760–1810*, London, Macmillan, 1975.

R. Brent, *Liberal Anglican Politics: Whiggery, Religion and Reform 1830–41*, Clarendon, Oxford, 1987.

T. F. Buxton, *The Slave Trade and Its Extinction*, London, 1839.

T. Clarkson, *The History of the Rise, Progress and Accomplishment of the Abolition of the African Slave Trade by the British Parliament*, 2 vols, 1st edn 1808, repr. Frank Cass and Co. 1968, Vol 1, 167.

D. Eltis and J. Walvin (eds), *The Abolition of the Atlantic Slave Trade*, Madison, Wisconsin, University of Wisconsin Press, 1981.

R. Furneaux, *William Wilberforce*, London, Hamish Hamilton, 1974.

S. Jakobsson, *Am I Not a Man and a Brother? British Missions and the Abolition of the Slave Trade and Slavery in West Africa and the West Indies, 1786–1838*, Uppsala, Gleerup, 1972.

C. Kidd, *The Forging of Races: Race and Scripture in the Protestant Atlantic World, 1600–2000*, Cambridge, CUP, 2006.

P.J. Kitson, (ed) *Slavery, Abolition and Emancipation: Writings in the British Romantic Period, Vol. 2: The Abolition Debate*, London, Pickering and Chatto, 1999.

H.S. Klein, *The Atlantic Slave Trade*, Cambridge, CUP, 1999.

P. Manning, *Slavery and African Life: Occidental, Oriental, and African Slave Trades*, Cambridge, Cambridge University Press, 1990.

C. Midgley, *Women Against Slavery: The British Campaigns, 1780–1870*, Routledge, London, 1992.

H. Thomas, *The Slave Trade: The History of the Atlantic Slave Trade 1440–1870*, London, Phoenix, 2006.

M. Turner, *Slaves and Missionaries: The Disintegration of Jamaican Slave Society, 1787–1834*, Urbana, University of Illinois Press, 1982.

J. Walvin (ed.), *Slavery and British Society, 1776–1846*, London, Macmillan, 1982.

J. Walvin, *The Slave Trade*, Stroud, Sutton, 1999.

J. Walvin, *England, Slaves and Freedom 1776–1838*, Basingstoke, Macmillan, 1986.

6

REVOLUTIONS OF THE THEOLOGICAL MIND:
NINETEENTH-CENTURY GERMANY

The late eighteenth century brought shattering social and political change. Revolutions in the United States and France, and industrial revolution in Britain, undermined traditional structures of the past. The concept of European Christendom was shaken. Political, social, and economic change was to follow in nineteenth-century Germany, shaped by events in the United States and France, and profound in its own right with moments of high drama, but spread over a longer time frame. Germany was also the heartland of transformation in another sphere—that of philosophical and theological thought. The cradle of the European Protestant Reformation was to become the cradle of radical, and for some faith shattering, theological reformulation.

GERMANY IN THE WAKE OF THE FRENCH REVOLUTION
The struggle of the American colonies for liberty and equality was carefully noted in Germany. America was to prove a land of liberty and promise for millions of German emigrants in the nineteenth century. Yet, America was far away, whereas events in France after 1789 took place on the German doorstep. The Napoleonic wars helped to define what Germany was to become, as well as accelerating a process of intellectual debate and change. Some Germans travelled to France to witness revolutionary events for themselves, believing the world was moving towards a new social, political, and intellectual future as *ancien régimes* crumbled. Progress in reason, justice, freedom, and happiness, so long talked about, appeared to be at hand. Beethoven's opera *Fidelio* (1805) ends with the victims of tyranny being released from their dungeons into

the light of freedom. Others drew parallels between events in France and the Reformation, a symmetry that was to have highly significant implications for theological developments.

State control of religious affairs had been strong since the eighteenth century. In Würtemberg, state law included 24 rescripts governing 83 aspects of clerical life—such as the length of sermons (with penalties for preaching too long), and prohibitions on using Greek and Hebrew quotations. Church attendance was obligatory, but complaints over low attendance at parish churches recurred. In Saxony, communion attendance was also falling, especially after the suppression of Pietism, and growing rationalist tendencies in the 1740s. Between 1700 and 1800, communion attendance was thought to have fallen by half, and it had halved again by 1880.

Those who advocated Enlightened Absolutism as a means of governance were little troubled by the early years of the French Revolution, before it descended into regicide and the reign of terror. Frederick William II of Prussia was unsympathetic to the Enlightenment, and to events in France. He expected the French would be consumed with their own domestic conflagration, and the idea that revolution would be exported by France seemed unlikely. Those suspected of unorthodoxy—whether in the political or theological realm—were subjected to hostility and censorship, as had happened in Britain. As the French Revolution descended into chaos, intellectual sympathy for it waned in Germany. Romantic writers stopped speaking of the dawn of universal humanity, and looked instead to what was traditional and natural in Germany itself.

Through a good part of the nineteenth-century, Germany was in a process of becoming a nation, rather than being one. In 1800 it was not a nation with precise boundaries, but was, as it had been since the Treaty of Westphalia in 1648, a complex series of some 350 separate jurisdictions, ruled over by a mixture of princes and nobles and private dynasties, or which were the hinterlands of large commercial cities. On the whole it proved politically viable, although Prussia and Austria were dominant. Economically, it was a hindrance: simpler government was needed to bring unification of the law, and regularise excise duties, tariffs, tolls on the roads and rivers, and currency systems. The sense that Germany had economically fallen behind other parts of Europe provoked forces of patriotism and nationalism, seeking political change. The actions of Napoleon Bonaparte simplified the process.

The conquering armies of Napoleon swept away the small jurisdictions of Electors and Imperial Knights that had sustained the Holy Roman Empire. The Holy Roman Emperor was forced to abdicate in 1806, although he responded by declaring himself emperor of Austria. The power and influence of Prussia and Austria, the two largest states, were curtailed. Yet out of Napoleon's devastating military advances, and then humbling retreats, defeats, and peace treaties in 1814 and 1815, a Confederation of the Rhine emerged, and later a German

Confederation (*Bund*) of states, dominated by Prussia and Austria, which also controlled territories outside the Confederation. It was not political union, although Prussia was rewarded for its role in the defeat of Napoleon with control over large parts of northern Germany, including the Rhineland and Westphalia. German nationalism grew in succeeding years, closely linked to Lutheranism, with Martin Luther depicted as a national hero. Economic union was furthered by the creation of the Prussian-dominated Zollverein in 1834, a German customs union and unified market comprising over 23 million consumers, and stretching from the south to the Baltic and the borders of Russia.

In 1850, the population of Prussia was 16 million and rising, but still less than the 17 million in the German part of the Habsburg Empire. Large flows of population from overpopulated rural areas, and from eastern Germany towards the West, saw cities mushroom in size. Others migrated overseas: between 1847 and 1914, 4.5 million Germans left their homeland, the vast majority, around 4 million, for the USA. The population of Berlin grew from 172,000 in 1800, to 0.9 million in 1871, and over 2 million in 1910; Hamburg's from 175,000 in 1850 to 931,000 in 1910. Yet by 1860, Prussia's share of world manufacturing output was still only 5%, compared to Britain's 20%.

PROTESTANTISM, ROMAN CATHOLICISM AND THE *KULTURKAMPF*

Voices calling for liberal reform reached their peak with a popular revolution in 1848, counterpart to other European revolutionary movements that year, and fuelled by poor harvests, inflation, overpopulation, and economic downturn. Demands rose for civil rights, a free press, the right of free assembly, trial by jury, and a national Parliament. Revolts shook Baden, Hesse, and Thuringia. Although the unrest was suppressed, sometimes viciously, by the army, Germany was changing. After 1850, most German princes, including Frederick William in Prussia, ruled constitutionally, and Roman Catholic and Protestant churches were given significant autonomy to run their own internal affairs. In Austria, a concordat of 1855 freed the Roman Catholic Church from the state's control over clerical nominations and its own internal administration, until defeat in war against Prussia brought a distinct change of policy. Between 1868 and 1874, laws to grant religious freedom, and end the Roman Catholic Church's monopoly over education, were passed. In 1870 the concordat was declared void, although state support and patronage for the church continued.

Between post-enlightenment calls for change in traditional political structures, and a willingness to challenge the philosophical and theological presuppositions of previous centuries, there was a connection, but it was a complex one. The government maintained strong control over the Lutheran state church. Many Prussian clergymen and academics were removed from their positions in the 1840s after they called for political liberalisation, and theological freedoms. The lesson was quickly learned, and in the revolutionary period of 1848–49 a growing consensus against political and social revolution emerged within the German Protestant Church, although this served to alienate many middle-class liberals. Rulers across Germany wanted churches to serve as bastions of authority and order, with clergy effectively working as agents of the state to enforce this. In turn, churches looked for state help in the battle to re-Christianise Germany, and against rationalistic unbelief.

In some areas, such as Westphalia, Protestantism was of a predominantly Reformed rather than Lutheran form. Roman Catholicism, especially in the South, remained strong in the late eighteenth century, appearing to be little affected by the Enlightenment. In 1799, the Munich diocese reported that barely 1% of parishioners missed mass. As the century progressed, a pattern emerged of lower attendance at mass in the cities than in rural areas, but it nonetheless remained appreciably higher than urban church attendance patterns amongst Protestants.[1] A number of Romantic writers, including Friedrich Schlegel converted to Roman Catholicism in search of the emotional and traditional they felt was lacking in Lutheranism. Gothic was rediscovered as part of the idealized portrait of the German Middle Ages, and found expression in the project to complete the medieval Cologne Cathedral. After 1850, German Roman Catholicism took on an ultramontane dimension, stressing the importance of hierarchy (especially obedience to the Pope), and discipline. Pope Gregory XVI made loyalty to Rome a requirement for being a German bishop, and German seminaries were increasingly influenced by the Jesuit Collegium Germanicum in Rome. Monasteries and convents flourished: the 27 monasteries of 1825 had multiplied to 441 in 1864. Religious societies were established to increase popular involvement in religious life.

Yet within Germany, there was considerable denominational pluralism. Although ways of working together were developed, there were significant tensions, such as the imposition of the law in Roman Catholic Rhineland and Westphalia in 1825 which required that children of mixed Protestant and Roman Catholic marriages should be reared in the religion of the father. This aroused great opposition from the Roman Catholic hierarchy and laity in the region. Conversely, a Bavarian edict of 1838 required all soldiers, whether Roman Catholic or Protestant, to kneel when the Sacrament passed by during a religious procession.

The ultramontane tendency in German Roman Catholicism fuelled Protestant suspicion that what passed as Roman Catholic devotion was really superstitious, and non-German. It brought a notable increase of inter-confessional hostility. Protestant writers argued that German culture was particularly Protestant, and sought to undermine Roman Catholic Austrian claims to leadership in the German region. This identity was re-affirmed with the Prussian defeat of

---

1 H. McLeod, *Religion and the People of Western Europe*, 58.

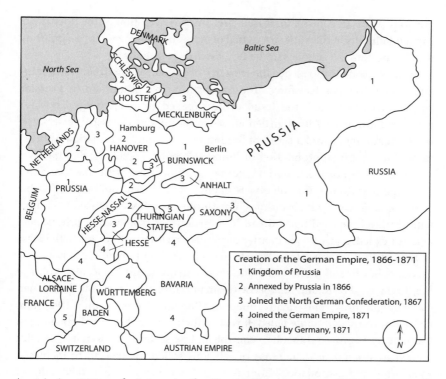

Austria in 1866, and victory in the Franco-Prussian war of 1870. The result was a largely Protestant German Empire (*Kaisereich*), including southern German states, headed by the King of Prussia. It was the largest state in size and population in Europe, Russia excepted, numbering 64.9 million people in 1910. In 1871, Adolf Stoecker, a future Prussian court preacher, proudly proclaimed, 'The holy Protestant empire of the German nation is now completed.'[2] Despite the rhetoric, it extended over territory that included many people who did not consider themselves 'Germans,' and there were great differences between Roman Catholics and Protestants, Prussians and Rhinelanders. About 35% of the population were Roman Catholics, concentrated largely in the South and West. Protestantism itself was not united politically or theologically.

The *Kulturkampf*, or 'struggle for civilisation,' which began in 1871, grew in intensity until 1878, and then continued with less force to 1887. It was part of the authoritarian reaction of the German Chancellor, Otto Von Bismarck (1815–98), against forces which were believed to be a threat to the newly unified German Reich, including Poles, socialists, and Roman Catholics. Distrust of Roman Catholicism in Protestant Germany, already strong because of association with

2   Quoted in A.J. Steinhoff, 'Christianity and the Creation of Germany', in *Cambridge History of Christianity, Vol. 8, World Christianities*, 282.

previous Austrian control, increased after the promulgation of the doctrine of papal infallibility at the Vatican Council of 1870, and the election of a significant number of Roman Catholics in the 1871 *Reichstag* elections.

Bismarck sought to restrict the capacity of Roman Catholicism to become established as a political force. The role of Roman Catholicism in Prussian education was reduced, the Jesuit order expelled from Germany, and civil marriage introduced. Although denounced by the pope as a 'massive persecution', the *Kulturkampf* proved a series of limitations and controls on religious belief, rather than a formal prohibition of Roman Catholic worship. It did, however, produce an atmosphere of anti-Roman Catholicism, with the pervasive suspicion that Roman Catholics were enemies of the state and therefore liable to oppression. Led by their bishops, most Roman Catholics refused to comply with the laws imposed upon them. In the late 1870s, some 1,800 priests were jailed or exiled, and 4,600 (a quarter of) parishes left vacant. Access to the mass, or the last rites and burial was denied to over a million Roman Catholics.

As a policy to end Roman Catholicism as a major factor in German political life, impose a Protestant version of German national identity on the Roman Catholic minority, and finally integrate Roman Catholics into Protestant Germany, the *Kulturkampf* failed. It was inefficiently implemented, the Roman Catholic press proved difficult to control, and persecution of Roman Catholics tended to strengthen their sense of religious solidarity. Instead of increased integration and assimilation, Roman Catholics developed their own cultural, charitable, and sporting institutions to meet the needs of their own community. A sense of German national Roman Catholic identity emerged. Many Protestant churches also refused to endorse the policy, which Bismarck began to reverse after 1878. By the time of Bismarck's resignation in 1890 most *Kulturkampf* legislation was repealed or redundant.[3] After 1900, the Centre Party defended Roman Catholic interests in the legislature, and became an influential party of government.

THE GERMAN ENLIGHTENMENT AND ROMANTICISM

Levels of literacy in nineteenth-century Germany were high and rising: only 15% of Prussians were illiterate in the 1830s, although the active reading public remained predominantly middle class or aristocratic.[4] German governments progressively sought to control education, but confessional schools, and the influence of Protestant and Roman Catholic Churches on public education

---

3 On the *Kulturkampf* see R.J. Ross, *The Failure of Bismarck's Kulturkampf: Catholicism and State Power in Imperial Germany, 1871–1887*, Washington D.C., Catholic University of America Press, 1998.

4 J. Breuilly, *The Formation of the First German Nation State 1800–1871*, London, MacMillan, 1996, 91–92.

remained after reforms in the 1810s, and were strengthened after the events of 1848. Art grew in significance, with a deepening sense of respect for the Creator who lay behind it. Royal operas and court theatres were replaced by National theatres in Berlin (1807), Munich (1836), and the German Opera in Dresden in 1841. Music increasingly demonstrated national characteristics—Richard Wagner's operas *Rienzi* and *Tannhaüser* were premiered in Dresden in 1842 and 1845. Music associations and public festivals allowed for performance of a wide range of folk songs, often with characteristic patriotic and nationalist sub-texts. There was a deepening interest in the study of history, German literature and language, and a growing belief in the supremacy of German cultural life, which transcended the individualism of the German states, contributing to the growing conviction of a need for a united German nation.

In the late eighteenth-century some reacted strongly against the rationalism of the Enlightenment. Religion was driven more firmly into the realm of human feeling; religious experience was privatised. A new emphasis on otherness, the supernatural, developed. In Germany, it found expression in the idea of 'spirit', or *geist*, a rich concept referring to the whole person in every aspect of their being, with associations not only to the New Testament, but also to paganism and pantheism. Spiritual significance was sought in the everyday world, the supernatural in the natural. The Romantic revolt of the early nineteenth century placed intuition and perception, emotion and imagination, tradition and history, above a mechanistic emphasis on rationality. Romanticism was strong in Germany before England: art, music, philosophy and science began to complement, or even replace, religious life, with a highly subjective emphasis on feelings, and the correspondence between humanity and nature. Romanticism sought a more all-encompassing vision of reality than that offered by reason alone. Artists of various backgrounds—poets, playwrights, novelists, historians claimed the right to make theological comment. The greatest of the German Romantics, Johann Wolfgang von Goethe (1749–1832), rejected the traditional idea of God found in the Judaeo-Christian tradition, believing that this was a God who only acted from outside the world. Instead he proposed a divine spirit which indwelt all creation and life. His multi-chrome religious view is summarised in his statement: 'In the study of nature we are pantheists. When we write poetry we are polytheists. Morally we are monotheists'.[5]

That the German Enlightenment, and then the rise of Romanticism, occurred in the context of political change and industrial advance, demonstrates the complexity of social and intellectual currents in the eighteenth and early nineteenth century. Yet the currents worked together in forging an increasingly

---

5   Quoted in G.R., Evans, A.E. McGrath, A.D. Galloway (eds), *The Science of Theology*, Vol. I, Basingstoke, Marshall Pickering, 1986, 236.

self-confident German political and cultural identity. In this fertile milieu also emerged philosophical and theological developments that were to profoundly influence Western religious and secular thought during the nineteenth and twentieth centuries.

Wider European Enlightenment themes were repeated in Germany, especially the emphasis that the workings of the universe could be understood through rationality, observation, and measurement. Keywords of the German enlightenment were virtue, utility, harmony, humanity, patriotism, and above all, reason. Its ambitious and optimistic intent was to let the human spirit, through the use of reason, illuminate everything in the world of ideas. In Germany, Protestantism, especially Pietism, was also to be central to the Enlightenment, and it was more closely connected to universities and churches than in France or Britain. German Enlightenment writers were less likely to be unbelievers, or Deists, but were often Protestant clergymen, or their close relations or students. Yet, although it was an age of enlightenment thinking, it has been noted that it was not necessarily an enlightened age.

Christianity remained a vital component of German life during the nineteenth century. Church and state were not separated as liberal voices had hoped. A preference for state authority over churches remained, and a carefully regulated relationship between government and religion. Yet, by the end of the century, despite intervention by the state to protect Christian standards of morality, the active practice of religion in Germany was significantly declining. In this political and cultural factors were significant, but the role of theological change and development, which was in many ways revolutionary, also made an important contribution, as the rest of this chapter explores.

REVOLUTIONARY THEOLOGICAL CHANGE AND RECONSTRUCTION

Kant and his Legacy

Immanuel Kant (1724–1804) was the fourth of nine children born into a devout, but impoverished, Lutheran Pietist home, at Königsberg in East Prussia. Kant was taught at home and at school that religion was more than a set of doctrinal propositions, it was a personal living relationship with God. Scripture, which contained the truth of God, stood above the authority of human reason, and was to be read for spiritual inspiration and edification. Conversion was the transforming work of God's grace, which led to a life of moral uprightness. This latter emphasis Kant retained through his life, but he became increasingly unconvinced by the emotional fervour of the religious activities amongst the Pietists, and their anti-intellectual and inspirationalist attitude to scripture. He also rejected the use of catechisms and creedal formulations because they restricted the intellectual integrity of faith. He argued that much religious service was in fact 'counterfeit service' (*Afterdienst*). True service of God instead consisted of nothing but morally good conduct in life. Prayer was good as long as it brings about a morally good lifestyle.[6]

Kant went on to teach at the University of Königsberg, eventually becoming Rector. Over time he ceased to attend religious services, and he declared himself 'indisposed' when officially required to participate. In 1781, at the age of fifty-seven, he produced his *Critique of Pure Reason*, which began the Kantian "Copernican Revolution." Kant argued that when it came to questions of theology, such as the existence of God, which are issues of *noumena*—the very inner essence of things—human mental capacity cannot cope. The mind can only deal only with *phenomena*—the outside of things. Reality beyond sense impression cannot be reached by the human mind. Therefore pure reason cannot lead to certainty about the existence of God.

The impact of German Romanticism on developments in philosophy, and then theology, in Germany was to be highly significant. In his *Critique of Pure Reason* (1781), Kant challenged the reign of reason alone, emphasising the need of feeling, the heart, for perceiving the good. Yet Kant was himself shaped by wider European enlightenment thinking. Although following the Scottish philosopher David Hume's (1711-1776) rejection of empirical knowledge as a basis for knowing God, Kant does not end up with scepticism, or a state of simply not knowing. Setting aside the view of Hume and other empiricists that the mind at the start of life was an empty vessel, receiving ideas as a result of empirical experience, Kant believed that the mind is in fact active, shaping and ordering those experiences. Humans possess moral autonomy, and this, whilst not proving the existence of God, makes it a very real possibility. The mind shapes experience according to rules, or 'Ideas', which exist before any sense experience has taken place. These are beyond the possibility of experience, and therefore beyond traditional proof, but are necessary to giving sense and order to what we see. There needed to be a cause adequate to explain this effect. Kant believed that conscience, or this sense of moral law, is not something imposed from without, from the Bible or the church, yet it was something that people universally, allowing for certain cultural differences, voluntarily obeyed, often without access to Christianity. These vital Ideas, beyond traditional proof, Kant called God, Freedom and Immortality. Conscience forces humans to regulate their lives according to its dictates—its presence drives humans to the idea of a giver and upholder of the moral law—to God. The presence of a moral nature opens the way for faith. Kant draws a distinction between the realms of

---

6   For Kant's views on religion see his *Religion Within the Boundaries of Mere Reason*, 1793, in *Works of Immanuel Kant: Religion and Rational Theology*, ed. A.W. Wood and G.D. Giovanni, Cambridge, CUP, 1996, 57–215.

knowledge, or pure reason, and belief or faith. In his famous phrase, 'I had to remove knowledge to make room for faith.'[7]

Kant had little time for much of popular religious culture, religious ceremonies, and ecclesiastical authority. He still believed in a role for the church, imperfect as it was, as the vehicle for genuine religious faith and the best hope for moral progress, yet his negative critique was not matched by a positive prescription of what true religious life should look like.[8] Despite rejecting the rule of reason, his religion was deeply shaped by Enlightenment presuppositions. There is a God in his system, but his existence is not provable on theoretical grounds. The mystical and the miraculous were rejected. His belief in God was not based on the evidence of Biblical revelation, but the inner voice of conscience calling the individual to stretch out towards God. Religion was possible only in the realm of belief, or faith experience, rather than in the realm of theoretical argument. His system had no need for the incarnation, or the Cross, or resurrection.

Kant's thought was not without its opponents: strong protests were uttered against his rejection of the traditional. Thinkers steeped in Lutheranism and Pietism declared Kant as mistaken, and guilty of subverting true religion. Yet Kant was not alone amongst holders of university professorships, and even church pulpits, in entertaining ideas that deviated significantly from Lutheran orthodoxy in the 1780s. Whilst none matched the freethinking of the French Enlightenment, there were those who openly questioned the literal truth of scripture, the Trinity, the incarnation, the bodily resurrection, and the reality of miracles. Karl Friedrich Bahrdt, a popular lecturer at Leipzig university, denied the divinity of Christ, and rejected the Biblical miracles. To this no official objection was raised during the reign of the anti-clerical Frederick the Great (1740–86), but the accession of Frederick William II brought a conservative reaction, led by officials such as the Minister of Education and Religious Affairs, J.C. Wöllner. Clergy were tested on their adherence to the creed of the Lutheran church, and state observers sent to listen to sermons. The orthodoxy of theology students was assessed. The policy met with stiff resistance from large parts of the Lutheran clergy, who had embraced religious rationalism. Kant was outraged by Wöllner's approach, which struck at the system he had promoted. In 1794, the seventy-year old Kant was called to give an account of his teachings, or face 'unpleasant measures.' Kant denied criticizing the scriptures, or harming religion in the land, arguing that his writings were in the realm of philosophy, rather than biblical theology. However, he pledged not to discourse in the future on religious matters in lectures or writings. The death of the king in 1797 freed Kant from his promise.

---

7   I. Kant, *The Critique of Pure Reason*, 2nd edn, trans N.K. Smith, London, 1958, 29.

8   An assessment of Kant's religious views is found in A.W. Wood's Editors Introduction to *Works of Immanuel Kant: Religion and Rational Theology*, xi–xxiv.

Friedrich Schleiermacher (1768–1834)

Kant's influence on subsequent philosophers and theologians was immense, especially on two giants of German theology, Friedrich Schleiermacher and Albrecht Ritschl. In Karl Barth's words, 'Schleiermacher determined the nineteenth century.'[9] His work was the watershed in theology, providing the classic statement of the Romantic and liberal understanding of the Christian faith. Ritschl's role was to firmly root that in the German Protestant church.

The son of a chaplain in the Prussian army, Schleiermacher was born in the town of Breslau in Silesia, now in Poland. He was reared by his father in the Reformed rather than the Lutheran tradition, to which was added Pietist influences, leading to the decision by his father to send him to a Moravian school. His mother's death a few weeks after he started at the school, and his father's journeys with his regiment, meant that he and Friedrich never met again, although they frequently corresponded. Instead, the Moravian community became his home and family during his formative adolescent years. Here he encountered warm devotion to Christ, and 'that mystic tendency developed itself, which has been of so much importance to me, and has supported and carried me through all the storms of scepticism.' Although as he grew into adulthood Schleiermacher was to leave the Moravians, the understanding that religion was to be an inward, personal, experience of Jesus encountered in community remained core to his theology and spirituality. The mature Schleiermacher believed he had become a 'Hernhutter' again, 'only of a higher order.'[10] Years later he wrote of his Moravaian experiences: 'while absorbed in heavenly faith and love, I could not but feel deeply how far behind them we are in our church, where the poor sermon is everything, and even this is hampered by meaningless restrictions.'[11] Yet doubts began to surface in his mind, especially about the doctrine which lay at the heart of the Moravian system—the atonement of Christ for sin, belief in which was expected to bring liberating, peace-bringing bliss to the soul. He began to draw a line between correct doctrinal religious formulation, which was an external thing and of secondary importance, and religion that was felt inwardly.

Against his father's wishes, Schleiermacher chose in 1787 to study at the University of Halle, where he encountered a far wider range of influences. He had been sent to the Moravian school to protect him from the corrupting influence of the Enlightenment, and his father was distressed to see him turn from Moravianism. Kant's argument that humans possess moral autonomy,

9   K. Barth, *The Theology of Schleiermacher: Lectures at Göttingen, Winter 1923–24*, ed. D. Ritschl, Grand Rapids, Eerdmans, 1982, 274.

10   *The Life of Schleiermacher as Unfolded in his Autobiography and Letters*, Transl. F. Rowan, Vol. II, London, Smith, Elder and Co, 1860, 125.

11   Quoted in B.M.R Reardon, *Religion in an Age of Romanticism*, Cambridge, CUP, 1985, 4.

through the forms and categories of the mind by which the world as it is experienced is shaped into something that makes sense, helped Schleiermacher give the 'spirit' primacy over the material world. 'Spirit' became the key concept for interpreting and expressing the fullness of the human condition.

In 1790 Schleiermacher qualified as a minister of the Reformed Church, and after four years as a tutor in East Prussia, and a short pastoral ministry, he was in 1796 appointed a preacher at Berlin's leading hospital, the Charité. Here, he moved in a circle of writers, artists and thinkers taken up with Romanticism's stress on the capacity of imagination, passion, and action to shape events, as well as thought. Its appeal to inward feelings, as opposed to things formal and rationalistic, was influential. Yet, whilst enjoying their company, Schleiermacher did not simply create a theology of religious subjectivity—the sense of dependence remained strong.

At Berlin, Schleiermacher formed deep intellectual and spiritual friendships with a number of women, who became his confidantes and encouragers, but when he fell in love with Eleonore Grunow, the issue was far more complicated. Eleonore was already married, albeit in a childless and unhappy marriage, to a Berlin pastor. Schleiermacher argued that their feelings should over-ride convention, and that she should divorce and marry him, but Eleonore refused to dissolve her original union. Marital happiness was eventually to come for Schleiermacher in 1809, when he married Henriette, the widow of a close friend. Schleiermacher felt far more able to express his deepest religious feelings and thoughts to women, than men, believing that they were more capable of experiencing and retaining inner feelings of love.

After a period of three years as professor of theology at the University of Halle, he moved to the Prussian capital, where he became preacher at Holy Trinity Church in Berlin. Here his preaching became famed throughout Germany and Europe. In 1810 Schleiermacher accepted the chair of theology at the new University of Berlin, and became the first Dean of the theological faculty, formed as part of the programme of Prussian renewal under King Friedrich Wilhelm III. In 1815 he became Rector of the University. His demands for political reform were delivered in both his writings and his pulpit, and, in a society where censorship was frequent, he was viewed with some suspicion. Nonetheless, this small man with penetrating and sonorous voice, continued to hold forth on vital religious and political questions before Berlin's students and educated citizens. One such was Bismarck, who was to play a vital role on the creation and consolidation of the Prussian Empire.

The most significant works of Schleiermacher are his *On Religion: Speeches Addressed to Its Cultured Despisers* (1799), and *The Christian Faith*, which came out in two parts in 1821 and 1822, and was revised again in 1830. In the former work Schleiermacher sets out his new conception of religion. He argued that the rejection of religion by the cultured and educated of his time was in fact a rejection of its external shell—'these systems of theology... wherein everything runs to cold argufying... this is certainly not the character of religion'.[12] Influenced by Moravianism and Romanticism, he argued that religion was more than just a code of conduct or character (which is where Kant's approach had tended), nor was it just a matter of faith or contemplating the world, nor is it just knowledge. The sum total of religion was, to Schleiermacher, 'to feel that... our being and living is a being and living in and through God'.[13] In this reality doctrine is located.

The Christian Faith, with its extended title the 'Connected Exhibition of the Christian Faith, according to the Principles of the Evangelical Church' was designed to be a unifying theology for the united Church of Prussia, with a scale and systematic form to match John Calvin's *Institutes of the Christian Religion*. Here he explains religious emotion, or feeling, in a way which distinguishes it from other feelings. It is 'the consciousness of absolute dependence, or, which is the same thing, of being in relation with God'.[14] To Schleiermacher 'True religion is *sense and taste* for the infinite,' which does not spring from doctrines, or institutions, or codes of action.[15] Because God exists, he argued, people have ideas about God, and doctrine follows. Thus doctrine comes, not from the Bible or Christian tradition, but as a result of reflection upon feeling, as a putting into words of prior Christian feelings. Theology is personal confession of belief, an act of self-analysis by a Christian community, but is not to be apologetic. True religion cannot be taught.

F. Schleiermacher, The Christian Faith

On Scripture: 'As history shows, the sense for the truly apostolic is a gift of the Spirit that is gradually increasing in the church; hence at an early stage much may have crept into the sacred books which a later age can recognise as uncanonical and definitely prove to be so. '[1]

1   F. Schleiermacher, *The Christian Faith*, trans. H.R. Mackintosh and J.S. Stewart, Edinburgh, T&T Clark, 1928, 130.

Although, to Schleiermacher, religion begins with this innermost contemplation, it is not simply self-awareness and subjectivism. It needs the sympathetic

12   F. Schleiermacher, *On Religion: Speeches to Its Cultured Despisers*, (1831 final edition), trans. J. Oman, New York, 1958, 15.

13   Schleiermacher, *On Religion*, 49–50.

14   F. Schleiermacher, *The Christian Faith*, ed. H. R. Mackintosh and J.S. Stewart, Edinburgh, 1948, 12.

15   Schleiermacher, *On Religion*, 39.

contemplation of others, particularly in close friendships where one can share the sense of one's heart stirred by God: 'If there is religion at all, it must be social, for that is the nature of man, and is quite peculiarly the nature of religion'.[16] However, this sharing was not with the intention of proselytising, but as mutual contemplation amongst persons who already have some kind of religion. The Church was to offer pure spiritual fellowship of the type of Moravian piety he knew as a child, and not of the 'school-mastering, mechanical nature' he had experienced as an adult.[17] The balance between inwardness in religion and human interdependence in church and society found in his theology was not always repeated by later followers. Schleiermacher called on the Church to give less attention to subscription to creeds, to break down distinctions between priest and laity and to free itself from external interests, such as union with the civil state.

To Schleiermacher, the sense of feeling, the consciousness of God, lay behind the foundation of all religions, which reflect a feeling that is 'great and common.' In this sense 'there is but one religion'.[18] However, he still saw Christianity as the most sublime of the religions, and distinguished from other faiths because everything in it 'is related to the redemption accomplished by Jesus of Nazareth'.[19] This is where, to Schleiermacher, Christian theology begins. Sin was infinite distance in consciousness from God. Redemption is a passage out of evil by another agency than the one who is redeemed. It is a passage from a state of God-forgetfulness to God-consciousness, an inward, experiential change. This is the one miracle, the essential truth. Christ's redeeming work imparts God-consciousness to the believer as the dominant principle of life. Jesus represented the most perfect consciousness of God that there could be, and the Christian is dependent on him for his or her religious consciousness. Jesus Christ is, to Schleiermacher, more than a moral example, more than the perfect Christian: in this sense it is possible to speak of his perfection and sinlessness. He embodied the new human race, and became the medium for the communication of God's redemptive power, which must be appropriated as a gift, for humans lack the power to match the example of perfected humanity found in the person of Christ.

Christ is presented with a human life as ours, but who also is divine—his life was at every moment the activity of God in the world. Schleiermacher criticised the classical formulae of the divinity of Christ. Elements in the Christian faith such as miracles, or fulfilments of prophecy, are expressions of faith in Jesus which is already held, rather than evidence to support that faith. These were of

---

16   Schleiermacher, *On Religion*, 148.
17   Schleiermacher, *On Religion*, 161.
18   Schleiermacher, *On Religion*, 217–18.
19   Schleiermacher, *The Christian Faith*, 52.

F. Schleiermacher, The Christian Faith

On the resurrection of Jesus Christ: 'I gladly waive any claim to understand Christ's second life as a historical event with a beginning and an end. On the contrary, I regard this second life appearance of Christ just as I do every individual miracle. There is something in it that is wholly factual, but the genesis of it is incomprehensible to us because it is connected with something that in its way is unique and for which there is no analogy... Therefore much that I have presented in our description of the life of Christ will be quite uncongenial to those who want to assume in the Gospels an inspiration of the letter and a completely settled unity'.[1]

1 F. Schleiermacher, *The Life of Jesus, Lectures at the University of Berlin*, 1832, edited. 1864, transl. S.M. Gilmour, Fortress Press, Philadelphia, 1975, Lecture 71, 470–481.

---

lesser significance than the truth of Christ. In this Schleiermacher was paving the way for later thinkers who distinguished essential truth from symbolic expressions of that truth, which could be stripped away, or demythologized, to reveal the kernel at the heart.

Religious experience is made the root of authority by Schleiermacher, rather than the external authority of the Bible or Christian doctrine. The Bible still had a role for Schleiermacher, with his belief that doctrine was the true expression of the Christian consciousness in the Church, which should genuinely reflect the piety found in the New Testament. Religion was therefore of varied types: 'nothing is more unchristian than to seek uniformity in religion'.[20]

Schleiermacher had produced a way of expressing Christianity that seemed to resolve some of the problems raised by Enlightenment thinking. If truth was the symbolic rendering of religious feeling and experience, belief in God came not through intellectual activity, as the traditional proofs had suggested, but by religious experience of that which was holy and dependable and to be loved, God himself. A distinction between feeling and intellect, between intuitive piety and reflective theology had been created. When King Friedrich Wilhelm III desired a union of Reformed and Lutheran churches in Prussia, Schleiermacher welcomed this, but he objected to Lutheran demands that there should be precise agreement on doctrine and liturgy before such a union could take place—theological or doctrinal formulae were secondary to religion as feeling. This emphasis was to lie at the heart of liberal Protestantism. It laid Schleiermacher open to the accusation of producing a theology for a bourgeois society with the time, space, and freedom to cultivate inner 'feelings.'

His work was hugely popular. When he died in 1834, thousands lined the

20 Schleiermacher, *On Religion*, 251–52.

streets as his funeral procession passed. Schleiermacher's thought was also immensely significant for post-Enlightenment theology. It was relieved of the need to seek scientific verification in an age when theologians were struggling to respond to new developments, and from the need to defend traditional doctrinal formulations in the face of the Enlightenment critique. It brought a God who could be personally experienced into the world of history and nature, and challenged the radical separation between the natural order and supernatural intervention that was central to Deism. His was a spacious understanding of the Christian faith, emphasising generosity and tolerance, but it opened the door to a more critical attitude to the Bible and the creeds. Where doctrine and practice did not find a place in Christian experience, they could be set aside. The traditional foundations of the Christian faith—the virgin birth, the Trinity, the second coming of Christ, the Bible, were beginning to be shaken. Karl Barth, the leading figure in the twentieth-century neo-orthodox reaction to this approach, argued that through Schleiermacher theology had shifted into the anthropological horizon: 'I have no reason to conceal the fact that I view with mistrust both Schleiermacher and all that Protestant theology essentially became under his influence'.[21]

In 1817, a Roman Catholic theological faculty was established at Tübingen, which became one of the German universities where the Roman Catholic and Protestant faculties existed side by side. Some Roman Catholic scholars began to seek to do for Roman Catholicism what Schleiermacher had done for Protestantism, arguing that reason and revelation, liberty and authority, were complementary. Their attempt to show that Roman Catholicism could match the challenge of Protestant historical criticism, science, and philosophy drew significant criticism from conservative Roman Catholics.

G. W. F. Hegel (1770–1831)

Another intellectual giant of the hugely fertile post-Enlightenment German intellectual context was Georg Hegel. In 1818, Hegel was offered the chair of philosophy at the University of Berlin, where he stayed until his death in 1831. Although an academic colleague of Schleiermacher, the two apparently had little time for each other's views—if religion was simply about a feeling of absolute dependence, Hegel argued, the best Christian is a dog who absolutely depends on its master. Hegel's German Idealism has been subject to a variety of interpretation, and there is a lack of agreement on exactly what he meant in some of his writings. Like Schleiermacher, he was influenced by the Romantic movement, aspects of which he sought to combine with the intellectual rigour of the Enlightenment. They also both sought to show that there is an essential

---

21 Barth, *Schleiermacher*, xv.

relationship between the human and the divine spirit, and that in Christianity is the best expression and fullest realisation of that relationship.

Hegel remained a Lutheran all his life, but he was never moved by the personal religious emotion that Schleiermacher had drawn from Moravianism. Unlike Kant, he denied that anything in the universe was beyond the knowledge capacity of the mind—if there is *noumena* that is unknowable, how can we ever know it is there? Our consciousness is instead in progress towards knowledge of the Absolute, the Spirit. To Hegel, religion was not simply feeling God's presence, or doing his will. Religion was to know the Christian God—whom he identified with his idea of the Absolute, the Spirit. In world history, progress comes about through reason: everything that is real is reasonable. To Hegel, the world and its history was the working out of a rational principle, the Absolute Idea, led by the 'world spirit', perfecting itself in stages through history, each moving to higher levels of freedom. In the evolving process of nature and history, spirit realizes itself through a dialectic process. It develops into forms that conflict with each other: thesis is countered by antithesis, before resolution is found in synthesis, which moves the idea or process on to a higher level. Progress continues in a series of upward steps, or an upward spiral. The Hegelian approach proved to be very influential on the thinking of Charles Darwin.

In seeking to understand the essence of Christianity, Hegel drew a distinction between objective religion, located in the understanding, and subjective religion, which was the awe and presence of God found in the heart. Hegel wrestled with the traditional form of Christianity, which he came to reject, and yet he found himself unable to dismiss the faith held by millions for centuries as 'bare nonsense'. He argued that the historical, dogmatic, presentation of Christianity should not be lost, but set on one side, to allow its truth to be more fully seen. God has revealed himself in representational ways. Now 'thinking spirit' must move from this to grasp in thought that which had first been revealed in representation. Instead of speaking of God as person, or a transcendent Being 'out there', the Christian God was an image of the Absolute Spirit.

The foundation of Christianity was, to Hegel, laid on the historical fact of the incarnation of Christ. He argued that Jesus not only taught the truth, in his historic person he is the truth. Only in spiritual unity with the divine is the human spirit fully realised, and only in Jesus Christ was such a unity present, making Jesus divine as well as human. Yet Hegel was more interested in the symbolic truth of the doctrine of the divine-human union in Christ, than in the historical life of Jesus of Nazareth, which he thought could not be established by historical research. Stories about God in the Bible were seen as images of greater truths that lay behind them. The virgin birth, and the miracles, are just symbols of that truth, not reports of events. The truth behind them is that Man who is God, God who is Man, appeared in the world. In the incarnation God passed from abstract idea into historical individuality, and hence full reality. The crucifixion of Christ is seen as the destruction of finitude, but this was a transitional happening, for through the crucifixion the personal transcendence of the God of traditional theism dies, to be replaced by the universality of Spirit. The resurrection and ascension show that the death of Christ is the death of death, and are a pictorial representation of the coming of the Holy or Universal Spirit: 'only after the death of Christ could the Spirit come upon his friends… only then they were able to conceive the true idea of God, viz., that in Christ man is redeemed and reconciled…. Only by stripping himself of his finiteness and surrendering himself to pure self-consciousness does [Christ] attain the truth.'[22] This is the pattern for his followers, but what Christ has accomplished is passed on to them: for the Kingdom of God '*is* the Spirit'. The people of God are the 'community of Spirit', where all external distinctions of power, position, sex, and wealth are given up—'Before God all persons are equal'.[23]

Hegel sought to understand the human condition through his dialectic approach. His idea of antithesis allowed justice to be done to the frustration, suffering, conflict, sorrow over transgressions, and estrangement found within the self-consciousness, alongside longing for righteousness and holiness. Although to Hegel, the biblical story of the Fall was only a poetic representation, it did reveal the truth of the human condition. It was a movement from innocence to loss of natural happiness, but also a movement from innocence to consciousness and knowledge, which brought alienation, but also a 'prediction of reconciliation'.[24]

In the dialectic process, it may be that only the philosopher or theologian can understand the synthesis, so religions are an expression of higher truths to those less capable of understanding them. Fixing religion in terms of images and dogmas in an authoritarian way spoils it. In changing times and circumstances, the images and doctrines in which religion is expressed must develop; they need to be integrated with the spirit and culture of the society of which they are a part. Although Hegel believed that all religions gave an image of the truth, Christianity was the most perfect because its inner meaning corresponded most closely to true (i.e. Hegelian) philosophy.

Hegel attempts to transform Christianity from religion into philosophy, to elevate it from the level of imagination to conceptual universality. Religion only represents the truth; philosophy states the truth. But the question remains as to whether this is religion at all, or just a philosophical replacement for Christianity? To some, Hegel was Christianity's arch-critic, destroying the positive content

22   G. Hegel, *Lectures on the Philosophy of History (1827)*, ed. P.C. Hodgson, Berkeley, 1985, 328.

23   G. Hegel, *The Christian Religion*, ed. P. Hodgson, Missoula, MT, Scholars Press, 1979, 238, 235.

24   G. Hegel, *The Philosophy of History*, trans. J. Sibtree, New York, 1944, 321.

of the Christian faith. To others he was its philosophical saviour, offering a scientific tool by which Christianity could be expressed in a form relevant to modern experience. His followers in the Left-Wing Hegelian school, the so-called 'Young Hegelians' saw his ideas as a way of overcoming the Christian tradition. They included radical thinkers such as D.F. Strauss, Ludwig Feuerbach, and Karl Marx. Hegel's influence on Arthur Schopenhaur (1788–1860) and Friedrich Nietzsche (1844–1900) was also significant. German thought began to be characterised by radical criticism of Christianity. Radical Hegelians, willing to sacrifice their academic positions for their views, were behind one of the most devastating historical and philosophical critiques Christianity has ever faced, the results of which continue to shape debate about religion.

David F. Strauss (1808–74)

One young Lutheran pastor and lecturer at the University of Tübingen attended Schleiermacher's lectures, and drew on Hegel's philosophical approach. David Strauss made explicit what was already present in Hegel, believing that his approach enabled him to consider the historical claims of the New Testament without being influenced by the religious and dogmatic presuppositions that bound most theologians. He followed Hegel's idea that the stories about God in the Bible were images or vehicles of eternal, universal, truths which lay behind them, which function in narrative form as the myths of other great religions did. Strauss now applied this approach rigorously to the New Testament in his *The Life of Jesus Critically Examined (1835)*.

In the nine months the young Strauss spent as a curate, he decided that although he could not embrace traditional doctrinal views, he could express the philosophical concepts he understood in traditional language. Therefore he felt no need to resign from the ministry, or to disturb the faith of his congregation. Meanwhile he sought to raise their understanding to a level where they could embrace the new concepts. Strauss believed he wrote without presuppositions, but in setting aside the presupposition that there was supernatural activity in the world, he was in effect arguing from the opposite presupposition that there was no supernatural activity in the world, apart from the laws of nature. God, if he existed, was not free to break into history.

Whereas some had seen myth as evidence of superstition and falsehood, Strauss argued that this was the natural thought-form of the pre-scientific, pre-historical mind. Many new ideas were started by Jesus, and old ideas were also applied to him, but these could only be expressed by a community of unlearned people in the form of concrete stories and sacred narratives that encapsulated these new ideas. From the human person Jesus, who believed himself to be the Messiah, arises the divine and supernatural Christ as a product of myth-making imagination. Strauss applied 'the notion of the mythus to the entire history of

---

D.F. Strauss, On the Resurrection of Lazarus

'We, nevertheless, distinctly declare that we regard the history of the resurrection of Lazarus, not only as in the highest degree improbable in itself, but also destitute of external evidence... theologians of more enlarged views have long ago remarked, that the resurrections in the New Testament are nothing more than mythi, which had their origin in the tendency of the early Christian church, to make her Messiah agree with the type of the prophets, and with the messianic ideal.'[1]

1   D.F. Strauss, *Life of Jesus Critically Examined*, 4th edn, trans. G. Eliot, London, Swan Sonnenschein and Co, 1902, 495.

---

the life of Jesus' and recognized 'mythi or mythical embellishments in every portion.'[25] He ended with a Jesus who was a great teacher, whose followers retold his life drawing on legends from the Old Testament, or the popular hope of the Messiah. The New Testament was portrayed as a sincere work of theological symbolism, rather than eye-witness accounts of historical fact. The thinking of the writers of the New Testament was circular—if the Messiah had come, these things would have happened; therefore, because Jesus is the Messiah, these things did happen.

The decision as to whether an event in the Bible was historical or not depended, to Strauss, on whether it was reconcilable 'with the known and universal laws which govern the course of events.' When an event or phenomenon was presented as 'produced immediately by God', or 'by human beings possessed of supernatural powers', including miracles or prophecies, Strauss argued that 'such an account is *in so far* to be considered as not historical.'[26] Strauss did not identify his work of historical criticism with attempts in the eighteenth century to undermine the historicity of Christianity in order to destroy its religious truth, but rather as an attempt to make it acceptable to reasonable men. Although he believed that the faith of the Church is the product of the historical Jesus, Strauss's presentation concentrates almost entirely on how the Christ of the Gospels is the product of the faith of the Church. Strauss believed there was only limited historical material in the New Testament, but he argued that there remained an historical core even if the real facts could not be determined. What was more important to Strauss was that: 'The supernatural birth of Christ, his miracles, his resurrection and ascension, remain eternal truths, whatever doubts

25   D.F. Strauss, *The Life of Jesus Critically Examined*, 4th edn, trans. by George Eliot, London, 1906, 64–65.
26   Strauss, *Life of Jesus*, 87.

may be cast on their reality as historical facts… the dogmatic significance of the life of Jesus remains inviolate'.[27]

In response to those who feared that the foundations of Christianity would be lost by this approach, Strauss attempted a task of dogmatic reconstruction in his closing essay in the book. He wanted to leave the church with what he believed was eternally true. Truth needed to move from past to present, from external event, to intimate experience. The result is the transformation of Christian faith, under Hegelian influence, into logical and metaphysical categories, representing the relations of the human race to the Absolute, the Infinite to the Finite. The connection between these and the person of Jesus is at times tenuous. In the stories of the birth, miracles, resurrection, and ascension of Jesus Christ, the universal truth is the essential unity of God and man.

D.F. Strauss, The Real Essence of Christianity

'So long as Christianity is considered as something given from without, its Author as literally heaven-descended, the Church as a machinery for procuring the expiation of human offences through his blood, Christianity, though claiming to be the religion of the Spirit, must remain unspiritual, and in fact Jewish. Only when it is seen that in Christianity man did but become more deeply conscious of his own nature, that Jesus was the individual in whom this deeper consciousness first became a supreme all-pervading influence, that redemption means but the advent of such a disposition and its inward adoption as our very life-blood, then only is Christianity really and thoroughly understood.'[1]

1   D.F. Strauss, *The Life of Jesus for the People*, Second Edition, London, Williams and Norgate, 1879. Preface, xiv, xv.

In his later work, *The Life of Jesus for the People* (1864), Strauss sought to focus less on criticism of the gospel traditions, and more on the personality of Jesus. Nonetheless, a similar approach is taken. In Christ he discerned 'a supernatural or divine element: not indeed as a special nature distinct from the human, but only as we conceive the agency of the divine spirit to exist in the faithful Christian, namely as an inward influence, in the case of Christ absolutely controlling his whole being'.[28] Strauss believed that the church of his day had moved on from the time when things were accepted as valid and obligatory because they are

---

27   Strauss, Preface to First Edition (1835), in *The Life of Jesus Critically Examined*, 4th edition, London, Swan Sonneschein and Co, 1902, xxx.

28   D.F. Strauss, *The Life of Jesus for the People*, Vol. 1, 2nd edition, London, Williams and Norgate, 1879, 20.

'supernaturally revealed to us in the Bible'. Rather, a matter was to be accepted 'because it is seen to be true in itself, because reason and experience show it to be imperishably established in the laws and constitution of our nature'. There was a need to break free from traditional conceptions and outward acts which are deemed essential to salvation, and from the 'chief offence of all ancient religion, namely belief in the miraculous.' He offered the devastating critique, 'So long as Christianity is considered as something given from without, its Author as literally heaven-descended, the Church as a machinery for procuring the expiation of human sins through his blood, Christianity, though claiming to be the religion of the Spirit, must remain unspiritual, and in fact Jewish'.[29]

Strauss argued that the Christ of mythical tradition, a person of power and supernatural nature, grew out of the religious consciousness of the Christian community. Because religious writing always functioned in the realm of myth, Strauss sought to put an end to the possibility of miracles as matters of historical fact. The New Testament could not be used as a historical source for the life of Jesus in the way that the Roman histories of Livy could be used as sources for the life of Roman Emperors. When the mythical and poetic material is stripped back, in Strauss's eyes the only Jesus who emerges clearly is that of the mythical God-man.

The impact of Strauss's *Life of Jesus* was profound. It opened a new era in the history of theology, which laid out the ground for modern critical study of the New Testament. Yet Strauss's influence was probably greatest on intellectual circles outside the Church. Some believed Strauss had produced a weapon for the destruction of the faith. For others it assisted in the destruction of their own faith. Friedrich Engels' turn from Lutheranism was influenced by his enthusiasm for Strauss's book. The English novelist George Eliot produced a translation of *Leben Jesu*, which had confirmed her rejection of Christianity.

Strauss's career was ruined by what he had written, and he was removed from his lecturing post at Tübingen. In the third edition of his book in 1838–39, Strauss adopted a more concessionary tone, but that was not sustained. In his disillusionment, he gradually moved further from orthodox Christianity, towards a secular Hegelian theology of Absolute Spirit. In the instructions he left for his burial, he instructed that the Church should be excluded from participation in his burial service, and no minister should participate.[30]

Ferdinand Baur

Another significant figure in promoting the new theological ideas emerging from Germany, and in particular Tübingen University, was Ferdinand Christian Baur (1792–1860). He was more interested in the origin, dating, composition,

---

29 Strauss, *Life of Jesus for the People,* Vol 1, Preface, xv.

30 H. Harris, *David Friedrich Strauss and His Theology*, Cambridge, CUP, 1973, 257.

and relationships between the New Testament documents than Strauss. Using the Hegelian dialectic approach he argued that the understanding of Idea, or Divine Spirit, had been developed to full expression in history through a series of opposing movements. He saw, in the earliest expressions of Christianity, a pattern of conflict, and resolution, between the Judaising attitude of Peter and the older disciples, and Paul's universal Gentile mission. He saw the book of Acts as a second century synthesis created to resolve the thesis and antithesis of this conflict. The development of the Christian doctrines of the Trinity and the Incarnation were also a result of the dialectic working out of ideas of God-manhood, and reconciliation between the divine and the human, within Christian history. This made theology a very historical discipline, which required penetrating the thoughts of 'the eternal Spirit' as they became evident in Christian history.

Baur found this historical dimension in Christianity lacking in Schleiermacher, and even in his own pupil Strauss. Baur emphasised that the Christ of faith must be linked to Jesus the historical founder of Christianity: 'the self-subsisting truth, the unity of the divine and human nature, must first become in Christ a concrete truth, a self-conscious knowledge, and was expressed and taught by him as truth.'[31] However, his historical-critical study took him away from traditional dogmatic, or supernatural, understandings of Jesus Christ assumed by orthodox theologians. He argued that the task of the historian was to uncover the true tradition which would be able to withstand critical investigation.

Baur moved the study of the New Testament back into its historical context, arguing that debate and personal issues played an important role in theological formulation. It was far more than the product of the mythologizing activity of Christian imaginations drawing on Old Testament images. Nonetheless, over both Strauss and Baur, Hegel's shadow loomed large, as they saw Christianity as the product of a dialectic, evolutionary, process.

Ludwig Feuerbach
Radical Hegelians went much further than Baur or Strauss. Ludwig Feuerbach (1804–72) studied for two years under Hegel in Berlin. He devoted himself to philosophy, but his lecture 'Thoughts on Death and Immortality' destroyed his hopes of academic advancement, and he spent much of the rest of his life in private scholarship. Unlike Hegel, he did not believe that the purpose of philosophy was to restore a lost Christianity. Instead he proposed a materialist view. He believed that humans are different from the animals by reason of their awareness of self, which is what religion expresses: 'If it is only in human feelings and wants that the divine "nothing" becomes something, obtains qualities,

---

31   F.C. Baur, *Die Christliche Gnosis*, cited in R. Morgan, 'Ferdinand Christian Baur', in N. Smart (ed), *Nineteenth Century Religious Thought in the West*, Vol. I, Cambridge, CUP, 1985, 279.

then the being of man is alone the real being of God –man is the real God....
then the human consciousness is, *per* se, the divine consciousness.'[32] Thus, to
Feuerbach, religion can be explained in terms of how humans understand their
own essential nature. God is a projection by humans of their higher qualities,
purified and made objective, into the creation of an infinite divine Being who
embodies these qualities, and who is worshipped. Theology has shifted into
the realm of anthropology: a person's religion is the human self-consciousness
externalised and objectified. This is a form of projectionist theory of religion,
which was to be developed by Sigmund Freud.

Feuerbach saw himself as a new Luther, bringing to birth a new religion of
humanity. Christian doctrines were expressions of profound human truths,
which reveal human hopes and ideals: 'The resurrection of Christ is therefore the
satisfied desire of man for an immediate certainty of his personal existence after
death.'[33] Feuerbach argues for a religion of love as the basis for true community
and the root of a purposeful life. The result is a form of secular Christianity.
Themes from Feuerbach's thinking were to recur in the philosophical writings
of Friedrich Nietzsche (1844–1900), and in twentieth-century existentialism.
His influence on Karl Marx was also to prove decisive (see ch. 8).

Albrecht Ritschl (1822–1889)
Whilst some took Hegel's approach in ever more radical directions, Ritschl,
who taught at Bonn and Göttingen Universities, was notable amongst those
who reacted against Hegelian thinking. Son of a leading Lutheran preacher, he
had started out as a promising recruit to the Hegelian school at Tübingen, but
he began to argue that harm had been done to theology by pushing it into the
mould of philosophical systems. Working from the perspective of a historical
theologian, he rejected Hegel's abstraction and pietism as a return to Roman
Catholic piety. With Germany appearing on the brink of new Reformation in
the social and political realm, Ritschl followed other German theologians in
believing that he was continuing the work of theological reconstruction of the
Reformers. Their ideas needed to be creatively re-interpreted in a way suitable
for the modern world. Schleiermacher's view of Christianity as rooted in the
individual's consciousness, a sense of 'absolute dependence,' was too subjective,
mysticism and pietism were too individualistic and deficient of moral impulse,
and Hegelian Idealism was too speculative.

Ritschl instead sought to root theology in the historical fact of the revelation of
God in Jesus Christ. Arguing against Baur's view that most of the New Testament
documents were the product of the second century, he dated the Gospels in
the first century and accepted the authenticity of most of the Pauline Epistles.

32   L. Feuerbach, *The Essence of Christianity*, trans Geo. Eliot, repr. New York, 1950, 230.
33   Feuerbach, *The Essence of Christianity*, 135.

Nonetheless, Ritschl did not think that the gospel pictures of Jesus Christ should be accepted uncritically. Doctrines, such as the traditional Christological formulae, which went beyond verifiable history and immediate Christian experience, were to be subject to historical judgement and questioned. He argued that the Virgin Birth, the miracles, the resurrection were not integral to understanding the historical Jesus. Ritschl believed that God could not be known in himself, but only in his 'effects' upon humans, 'we know the nature of God and Christ only in their worth for us. For God and faith are inseparable conceptions; faith, however, does not consist in abstract knowledge which deals with merely historical facts.'[34] Religion was to Ritschl a response of faith, resting on 'value judgements,' based on feelings produced by actions. The Divinity of Christ was, to Ritschl, not to be understood as a historical statement of fact, for it could not be objectively demonstrated. It was rather an expression of 'Revelational-value,' based on the Christian community's experience of the saving work of Christ. In consequence, Jesus has the 'value' for us of God. Through inclusion with the unique Christ, people are brought into communion with God: 'union with God is to be thought of as the forgiveness of their sins, as the ending of their separation from God… the community which belongs to Christ has imputed to it His position towards the love of God, in which He maintained Himself by His obedience.'[35]

A great stress in Ritschl is the kingdom of God, founded by Christ, set in motion by his death, and over which he maintains ethical lordship. Salvation is a social fact: 'The individual believer… can rightly understand his position relative to God only as meaning that he is reconciled by God through Christ in the community founded by Christ.'[36] Forgiveness of sin, or justification, is achieved in and through the community for whom Christ died, rather than simply in the heart of the believer. Christ came to redeem a community, not individuals. Divine redemption finds practical application 'only on the condition that the believer takes at once an active part in the recognised purpose of the kingdom of God.'[37]

Here was a very different theology to Hegel's metaphysics of Absolute Spirit. Faith was to be distinguished from other forms of mystical experience, which Ritschl distrusted. Speculative, dogmatic, or pietistic Christianity fell under suspicion. Ritschl portrayed a view of a welcoming, loving God, to whom devoted service should be given in the Kingdom, which was immensely influential in late nineteenth-century Germany. His hope was that the ethical

---

34 A. Ritschl, *The Christian Doctrine of Justification and Reconciliation*, Vol III, transl. H.R. Mackintosh and A.B. Macaulay, Edinburgh, 1900, 212.

35 Ritschl, *Justification and Reconciliation*, 546–47.

36 A. Ritschl, *Instruction in the Christian Religion*, in *The Theology of Albrecht Ritschl*, trans. A.M. Swing, New York, 1901, 235.

37 Ritschl, *Instruction*, 200.

implications of this practical and moral Christianity would underpin the rapidly developing industrial-urban German society. As humanity evolved towards new realms of progress and prosperity, with enormous confidence in human ability and potential, religion would give ethical guidance to society, as well as meeting the spiritual needs of humans. This was the golden age of liberal Protestantism. Ritschl's theology, with its emphasis on the kingdom of God, was a bridge to the moral optimism of the American liberal social gospel in the twentieth century. Yet the values of the kingdom of God he presented looked little different from the cultural values of the bourgeois in Bismark's Germany. The Ritschlian school were quick to support the declaration of war in 1914, believing that they were defending the values of German civilisation.

Julius Wellhausen

In the field of biblical criticism, Julius Wellhausen (1844-1918) was another German theologian to exert a powerful influence. He served as professor of Old Testament at Griefswald from 1872 to 1882, but was forced to resign when he cast doubts on the inspiration of Scripture. He switched to the teaching of oriental languages, at Halle, and Marburg, before moving to Göttingen in 1892. He came to believe that there was little known of the Old Testament law before the Babylonian exile, and that there was a discontinuity between the religion traditionally associated with Moses and Sinai, and the experience of Israel in the period of the Judges. Between the Law, and the historical and prophetical books, he believed there was 'all the difference that separates two wholly distinct worlds'.[38] The position was not new. Karl Heinrich Graf (1815–69) had earlier dated the Law after the Prophets, but the position was known even earlier in the early nineteenth century through the *Contributions to Old Testament Introduction* (1806–07) of Wilhelm DeWette (1780–1849). Wellhausen argued that the Pentateuch, with its priestly code, lay not at the foundation of Israelite religion, but it was in fact, together with the Psalms, the youngest part of the Old Testament. The Prophetic books were the oldest. The Hebrew religion had gradually developed from a nomadic form, through the prophets, until it became a religion of the Law. Wellhausen's *History of Israel* (1878) was translated into English in 1883, and produced shock waves in the field of biblical studies similar to those created by Darwin's work. In his Documentary Theory he summed up and developed much scholarship that had gone before, proposing that the Pentateuch was a skilful combination of originally independent narrative sources undertaken by various editors. For his advocacy of Higher Criticism Wellhausen encountered widespread opposition, but his views transformed

---

38   J. Wellhausen, *Prolegomena to the History of Israel (1878),* English translation, Edinburgh 1885, 3.

Old Testament studies, and were adopted by many Protestant biblical scholars in Germany, Britain and America in the early twentieth century.

CONSERVATIVE RESPONSES

The rise of liberal and radical theology and philosophy was not without its opponents. The subjectivism of Schleiermacher in particular, was challenged by those who appealed to the objective basis of theology in Scripture and the Church and its traditional teachings. A stout conservative defence was mounted by evangelical theologians such as E.E. Hengstenberg (1802–69), against the rationalist and idealist approaches of progressive liberalism. Theirs was a theology of 'repristination', seeking to restore Lutheranism to its original doctrine and order, coupled with an adherence to biblical inerrancy, and the verbal inspiration of scripture. Hengstenberg also coupled conservative doctrine with conservative politics, dismissing the revolutions of 1848 as acts of sinful rebellion against the legitimate authority of powers appointed by God. Religious and political themes remained closely related—proponents of liberal theology often advocated liberal politics. Attempts to revive evangelicalism in Germany in the face of Enlightenment advances were furthered by the efforts of Friedrich Krummacher (1796–1868), pastor of Holy Trinity Church, Berlin, where Schleiermacher had preached twenty years before, and also preacher to the Prussian court.[39] Friedrich Tholuck (1799–1877), professor at Halle from 1826 onwards, exercised a powerful influence in calling students back to the scriptural emphasis of pietism, and the fervent, devotional preaching of Claus Harms (1778–1855) called people back to classical Lutheranism.

CONCLUSIONS

That German theologians confidently produced new and radical approaches to Christianity at the time when the German nation was emerging and consolidating into an economic, and then political empire is significant. Increasing confidence in the merits, and supremacy of their culture, allowed German theologians to present themselves as in the unchallenged vanguard of theological developments. Yet the results reflected the context in which they emerged. Ritschl's expression of Christianity accorded well with the values of the German middle class. Hegel's philosophic abstraction appealed to radical intellectuals. The thinking of Marx and Feuerbach came at a time when advances in the social and natural sciences were already beginning to undermine confidence in religious revelation as the means for understanding life and its meaning. Atheism began to have an impact on German intellectual circles: for some, science would become their religion.

---

39   On Krummacher see *Friedrich Wilhelm Krummacher: An Autobiography*, (trans. M. G. Easton), Edinburgh, T&T Clark, 1869.

The direct impact of these profound theological debates and the rise of theological liberalism upon the patterns of belief and practice of the majority of German Christians was mixed. However, an overall impression emerges that the new Reformation, with its work of major theological reconstruction, did not succeed in persuading the majority of German Christians to increase their levels of religious adherence, or even to retain existing patterns. Indeed, evidence suggests that the opposite was happening. By the 1830s and 1840s German religious life was changing. Shops and bars were open on Sunday mornings, bands played in the parks. In the 1850s, pastors in Central Germany were complaining that faithful Lutherans had little understanding of doctrines such as the Fall, the Eucharist, and life after death.[40] The rise of political liberalism and Social Democracy later in the century was also symptomatic of declining church influence on society. In 1848 the church had been used by the government as a force for conservatism in society, with an increased religious component in education, and a strong reaction against radicals and liberals. Such measures did little to increase affection for it. Although few had formally left the church by the 1860s and 1870s, its authority was weakening, theological conservatism was often ridiculed, and a large market for books that popularised the new scientific world-view developed. Opportunities for leisure and recreation increased, further affecting church attendance patterns.

By the end of the century, levels of church attendance across Germany were very low. The working classes were joining the professional and commercial middle classes as the most secularised sections of society. In Hanover in 1891–95 the average Sunday morning attendance at the Lutheran state church was just 6% of the population, in Berlin just 2%. Even amongst church members, levels of practice were extremely uneven—ranging from 80 out of 100 members attending communion in Schaumburg-Lippe, to 10 per hundred members in Hamburg. In 1882, Nietzsche proclaimed 'God is dead.' His statement was undoubtedly premature, but religious practice did appear to be on the wane. The increase in Social Democracy and militant secularism was pronounced between 1890 and 1914, with the socialists winning 75% of the votes in Berlin in 1912. Social Democracy offered a world-view with mass appeal, social provisions and support structures. In the years 1908–09, and 1912–13, some eight to ten thousand people left the church every year. Anti-clerical and anti-religious feeling grew amongst the working classes. In the home-land of Pietism, the role of the laity in the task of biblical interpretation was lost to a scholarly community, dominated by liberal theological emphases. Confidence in the Bible declined, and the ability of Christianity to provide answers that would deal with the issues of life and death was doubted.

Yet Germany did not become wholly irreligious or secular. Germans were not

40   H. Macleod, *Religion and People*, 59.

necessarily less religious, but many became more comfortable with expressing their faith in less traditional, and more nominal ways. The clergy remained busy with baptisms, funerals, weddings, and confirmations. Craftsmen, clerks, and minor officials of the state appeared to retain adherence to Protestant culture most strongly as the century progressed. The adherence of women to religion remained stronger than that of men. Churches that stayed strongly theologically conservative often did well, such as the fashionable Matthäikirche, the best attended church in Berlin. For the middle classes, religious attendance remained a way of maintaining an appearance of respectability, and it continued to be an important part of family celebrations. Home-based piety remained strongly rooted in the petite bourgeoisie, characterised by religious orthodoxy, patriotism, political conservatism, hard work, and thrift. Such devoted adherents of Protestantism were often by no means uneducated, and often widely read.

In 1914, 95% of Berliners were still affiliated to some form of religious group. Whilst the percentage of Protestants in the capital fell from 89% to 83% of the population between 1871 and 1905, Roman Catholics increased from 6% to 11%, and Jews from 4% to 5% of the population. Roman Catholicism, despite facing serious political and practical restrictions, displayed resilience to the pressures of the modern world.

Although the outbreak of war in Europe in 1914 saw different religious groups rally together in common cause, as Kaiser Wilhelm II urged Germans to defend the fatherland 'without difference of race or religion,' the impact of the theological revolution that took place in nineteenth-century Germany remained. It had sent shock waves across established patterns of thought and practice during the nineteenth century, and the impact continued into the twentieth. For churches, the implications were as great as the French Revolution, and the development of the Darwinian world-view.

Across Europe some had little problem in readily adopting the new patterns of liberal theological thought that developed in Germany. In France, Joseph Ernest Renan, at one time intent on the Roman Catholic priesthood, in 1863 produced his own *La Vie de Jésus*, placing Jesus Christ 'at the highest summit of human greatness,' but rooting the foundation of Christianity with the first Christians, 'not with him whom legend has deified.'[41] This combination of German textual criticism with the assumptions of sceptical thought proved extremely popular amongst a readership drawn to rationalism. In England, the acceptance of advanced critical views amongst leading Anglican theologians was reflected in *Essays and Reviews* (1860), which drew forth official censure from Anglican authorities. The liberal Protestant writings of John Colenso (1814–83), Bishop of Natal, were another part of the attempt to make Christianity relevant to

---

41   E. Renan, *The Life of Jesus*, London, Trübner and Co, London, 1864, 250–51, 305.

humanity 'come of age', and provoked a similar reaction. Colenso had already questioned a number of key doctrines before raising questions of the historicity and authorship of parts of Scripture in his *The Pentateuch and Book of Joshua Critically Examined* (1862). Compared to developments in Germany, Colenso's views were moderate, and he championed a progressive missionary policy that defended Africans against colonial injustices, but he spent the last two decades of his life mired in controversy.

The reconstruction of Christianity in the form of religious subjectivism or conceptual universality, together with the radical critique offered by biblical criticism and scientific naturalism, was believed by conservative defenders of orthodoxy to be undermining the foundations of the faith. For some the response was to seek to return to an ideal vision of the Christian past, which saw expression in the Oxford Movement, and ultra-montane Roman Catholicism. From others, such as Presbyterians in North America, came staunch defences of confessional orthodoxy.[42] In the 1870s and 1880s, conservative Congregationalists and Baptists in England sought to resist theological downgrade in their denominations, although with limited success.[43] The battles were not easily won. Although William Robertson Smith was in 1870 removed from his post at the Aberdeen Free Church College for propounding views similar to those of Welhausen, by the end of the century broader theological views were being tolerated in Presbyterian colleges in Scotland that had once been bastions of evangelical orthodoxy. The ground rules of theological debate for most participants had fundamentally shifted.

42   Discussed more fully in chapters 8 and 15.

43   See M. Hopkins, *Nonconformity's Romantic Generation: Evangelical and Liberal Theologies in Victorian England*, Carlisle, Paternoster, 2007.

FURTHER READING

D. Blackbourn, *History of Germany 1780–1919: The Long Nineteenth Century*, Oxford, Blackwell, 2003.

J. Breuilly, *The Formation of the First German Nation State 1800–1871*, London, MacMillan, 1996.

K. Clements, *Friedrich Schleiermacher: Pioneer of Modern Theology*, London, Collins, 1987.

M.B. Gross, *The War Against Catholicism: Liberalism and the anti-Catholic Imagination in Nineteenth-Century Germany*, Ann Arbour, University of Michigan Press, 2004.

J.C. Livingston, *Modern Christian Thought: Vol I, The Enlightenment and the Nineteenth Century*, Upper Saddle River, NJ, Simon and Schuster, 1997.

H. McLeod, *Piety and Poverty: Working Class Religion in Berlin, London, and New York 1870–1914*, London, Holmes and Meier, 1996.

B.M.G. Reardon, *Religion in the Age of Romanticism: Studies in Early Nineteenth-Century Thought*, Cambridge, CUP, 1985.

R.J. Ross, *The Failure of Bismarck's Kulturkampf: Catholicism and State Power in Imperial Germany, 1871–1887*, Washington DC, Catholic University Press of America, 1998.

J.J. Sheehan, *German History 1770–1866*, Oxford, Oxford University Press, 1989.

N. Smart, J. Clayton, P. Sherry, S.T. Katz (eds) *Nineteenth Century Religious Thought in the West*, 3 vols, Cambridge, CUP, 1985.

H.W. Smith, *German Nationalism and Religious Conflict 1870–1914*, Princeton, Princeton University Press, 1995.

7

Building Jerusalem, or Redeeming Babylon?: Churches in the Industrial Age—Britain: 1820s to 1870s

When the novelist Daniel Defoe visited Glasgow, Scotland, in the 1780s, he described it as 'a very fine city; the four principal streets are the fairest for breadth, and the finest built that I have ever seen in one city together.'[1] One hundred years later Lord Shaftesbury's impressions of the same city were very different:

'I did not believe until I had visited the wynds of Glasgow that so large an amount of filth, crime, misery and disease existed in one spot in a civilised country... Health would not be possible in such a climate ... is moral propriety and moral cleanliness, so to speak, more probable? Quite the reverse?'[2]

By 1820, the impact of the Industrial Revolution in Britain was deeply, and irreversibly, etched onto the face of town and cities like Glasgow, and the next decades saw continued rapid change. The years 1850 to 1870 were times of mid-Victorian prosperity, when Britain was seen to lead the world in commerce and manufacturing. The factory increasingly became the dominant form of industrial enterprise: by 1851 only 21% of the population worked in agriculture, with 42% in manufacturing, mining, and building. The urban area became the dominant residential location, and in towns an organised proletariat emerged.

---

1 D. Defoe, *A Tour Thro' the Whole Island of Great Britain, Divided into Circuits or Journies* (1724–27), London: J.M. Dent and Co, 1927, Letter 12.

2 Lord Shaftesbury, 1839, quoted in S. Laidlaw, *Glasgow's Common Lodging Houses and the People Living in Them*, Glasgow, Glasgow Corporation, 1956, 20–21.

Leafy suburbs appeared on urban fringes; arcadian ideals found a place in city-centre streets; civic pride inspired the construction of grand public buildings. Agricultural change continued apace, with technical and mechanical advances reducing the cost of food production. Transport improvements speeded the flow of cheap and plentiful food imports, sustaining large urban populations. Confidence in the beneficent power of economic forces fostered the attitude that state or local intervention in society was best avoided: help for social needs should come from religious institutions, charities, or self-help.

Yet, beneath the confident and prosperous appearance of Mid-Victorian Britain, social investigators found growing evidence that the welfare of much of the urban populace was far from satisfactory. Their studies of urban life, replete with copious statistics and detailed descriptions of room sizes, widths of streets, capacities of sewers, the numbers of earthen closets and other sanitary facilities, provided ammunition for social problem novelists, and social reformers, to prick the conscience of the nation.

Britain's population continued its seemingly inexorable growth, from 14.4 million in 1821, to 26.1 million in 1871. Yet the hold on life of most remained short and tenuous: in the years 1838–54 life expectancy was around 40 for men, and 42 for women. Environment proved a highly significant factor: the life span of a child born in Manchester in 1840 was half that of a child born in Surrey. The death rate, which had fallen from around 25 per thousand of the population in 1800, to 22 per thousand in the 1830s, changed little until the 1870s. Population rose mainly because of the high birth-rate, which stood at around 35 per thousand between the 1840s and the 1880s. Scarlet fever and typhus remained major killers, and cholera epidemics struck periodically in each decade from the 1830s to the 1860s, with the outbreak of 1832 killing 31,376 people. The suddenness and virulence of the onset of cholera made it a headline grabber, and a catalyst for much urban and sanitary reform. Yet mundane diseases, such as diarrhoea, still claimed 19,000 lives in 1849. Tuberculosis, fuelled by cramped housing conditions, and bad hygiene, remained the greatest killer, reaping a death toll of around 59,000 lives in 1838.[3]

The two million people who worked in factories in 1871 enjoyed regular, and often high wages, but at significant social cost. The noise, heat, and dust, created by spinning and weaving machines in close environments produced unpleasant working conditions in which men, women, and children laboured for up to sixteen or seventeen hours a day. Yet those employed in domestic industry, weaving, dress-making, or simple metal-working, fared little better: The conditions of the handloom weaver John Harrop were not untypical, as a report at the time noted.

---

3   Relevant statistics as to life expectancy and conditions of living are set out in F. Le Crouzet, *The Victorian Economy*, London, Methuen, 1982, 19–30.

He earns on average six shillings a week, out of which he pays all his loom expenses, more than one shilling per week…He is thin, pale, hollow-cheeked and looks half-starved. He works from five in the morning until nine at night, and often longer in winter.[4]

Unemployment fluctuated during these decades, with peaks and troughs as trade cycles ebbed and flowed: in 1858 it stood at 12% of population. Alongside those in regular employment existed many unskilled casual labourers, employed as need arose in employment sectors such as dock working, the building industry, and agriculture, producing an uncertain and harsh lifestyle. Poverty remained a real, and recurring, spectre haunting the lives of many working people. The 'Hungry Forties' brought high bread prices, and political protest movements, notably Chartism, which called for proper democratic representation, of men at least, and wider political reform. Yet whilst some existed on the margins of starvation, others joined the ranks of the growing middle class—in 1851 some 5.4 million people earned more than the respectable income of £200 per annum, and in 1871 this was 6.6 million.

Rapid urbanisation accompanied industrial growth. In 1841, fifty-four towns in Britain had populations of over 20,000 people; in 1871, seventeen cities had more than 100,000 residents. London's population was almost 4 million people. Urban centres were swamped by migrants from rural areas, boosted during the 1840s by a large migratory inflow from Ireland. People crammed into the existing housing stock, which was divided up, and gardens built over, creating damp, airless conditions. In Liverpool in 1840, 86,000 people lived in 2,400 overcrowded courtyards. Population densities could reach 1,000 per acre. Sewerage, drainage, and cleaning, was provided along the main roads, but not in the poorest quarters away from key thoroughfares. One observer in Manchester described courtyards with one privy (a bucket toilet) for fifty people, which was often 'in a short time completely choked with excrementitious matter. No alternative is left to the inhabitants but adding this to the already defiled street.'[5] Many families were restricted to living in a room eight feet by ten feet, with broken windows stuffed with sacks, the property riddled with vermin, and lice infesting bedding and clothing. Such living conditions led inevitably to such a high rate of death and disease. The highest mortality was experienced amongst children under the age of ten, which rose from 13.33 per 1,000 in 1821, to 20.8 per 1,000 in 1838.[6] In the

---

4   P. Gaskell, *Artisans and Machinery: The Moral and Physical Condition of the Manufacturing Populace*, London, 1836, repr. London, Cass, 1968, 40.

5   Gaskell, *Artisans and Machinery*, 78.

6   M. Flinn, ed., *Scottish Population History from the Seventeenth Century to the 1930s*, Cambridge, CUP, 1977, 19–20, 377–79; 'Report to the Select Committee on the Health of Towns', in H.J. Dyos and M. Wolff, *The Victorian City: Images and Realities*, Vol. I, London, Routledge and Kegan Paul, 1973, 389.

poorest urban areas, children were noticeably several inches smaller than others in less crowded areas.[7]

A mixed range of provision was available for those who suffered poverty, ranging from the formal provisions of the Poor Law, to the large number of charities, and the kindness of friends, and neighbours. In the early 1860s in London alone, charities were estimated to be distributing up to £7 million each year, whereas the cost of the Poor Law nationally was just £5.8 million.[8] This ancient parish-based provision for the care and support of poor people, was changing. Fears grew that the system of 'outdoor relief,' by which the Poor Law authorities topped up the incomes of impoverished residents to an agreed minimum from the poor rates, only propagated the problems of idleness and poverty, and discouraged employers from increasing wages. Poor Law reform, when it came in 1834, proved drastic, in an attempt to encourage self-help. The New Poor Law sought to abolish outdoor relief; those who sought assistance were required to enter the workhouse, where living conditions were deliberately kept at minimal levels, making seeking parish assistance an absolutely last resort. Those receiving support became stigmatized as 'paupers', which was particularly harsh for those forced to seek help owing to factors beyond their control, such as the elderly, the disabled, and children left orphaned or uncared for by their parents. The rigor of the application of the system varied according to area. The mixing on the workhouse wards of the elderly, children, and those suffering from learning disabilities, with vagrants, and those who lived by petty criminality, occasioned great concern.

Rapid urbanisation created administrative dislocation, and an increased sense of anonymity and social disconnection amongst urban dwellers. The social reformer Edwin Chadwick estimated that in the 1830s 11,000 people died each year as a result of acts of violence.[9] Only gradually were new forms of social control established. In London, the employment of constables to support the magistrates—the Bow Street Runners—paved the way for the formation of the Metropolitan police force in 1829. Other cities followed in the following decade. High birth rates, coupled with high parental death rates, created a preponderance of unsupervised children and juveniles living on the streets of cities. In 1859, around one crime in ten was committed by those under the age of sixteen. Most towns had at least one heavily overpopulated quarter where a criminal fraternity existed. These rookeries became notorious 'no-go' areas, and social commentators pointed to the appearance of a clearly recognisable

---

7   R. Rodger, 'Wages and Employment' in R. Rodger and R.J. Morris, *The Victorian City : a Reader in British Urban History, 1820–1914*, London, Longman, 1993, 103.

8   M. Hartwell, *The Long Debate on Poverty*, London, Institute of Economic Affairs, 1972, 116.

9   Figure quoted in E.C. Midwinter, *Law and Order in Early Victorian Manchester*, Manchester, MUP, 1968, 123.

criminal race. Observers debated the relationship between poverty, crime, and social deprivation: periods of high unemployment appeared to bring higher levels of crime.

The strictures of free trade dictated that social problems were matters that the market would in time resolve, and that it should be left to do so unfettered. Growing evidence showed that this 'inevitable' process was not happening, and legislative solutions were needed. The 1840s saw the introduction of local authority building regulations for new houses, followed by housing acts in the 1850s and 1860s, together with the appointment of medical officers of health with powers of sanitary inspection. This pointed the way to greater state intervention on social issues, although the scope for Christian churches and individuals to be actively engaged in social concern activities remained significant.

PERCEPTIONS OF THE INDUSTRIAL REVOLUTION

The twin phenomena of industrialisation and urbanisation were viewed by contemporaries with a mixture of fascination and horror. For some, there existed an antithesis between Christianity and the newly emerging world, as described by one High Church London clergyman in 1844: '*the atmosphere of cities is essentially a worldly atmosphere... there is much in the cities that is uncongenial with a vital and pure Christianity...*'.[10] To Friedrich Engels, who was to become Karl Marx's close associate, Manchester in 1844 was a place of separation, and anonymity:

'The very turmoil of the streets has something repulsive, something against which human nature rebels... they crowd together as if they had nothing in common... their only agreement is the tacit one that each keep to his own side of the pavement.'[11]

Charles Dickens depicted the apparently bleak and monotonous social and religious life of the northern industrial town, in his novel *Hard Times* (see text below).[12] The social prophet Thomas Carlyle was, in 1843, more ambivalent: 'Sooty Manchester,—it too is built on the infinite Abysses; overspanned by the skyey Firmaments; and there is birth in it, and death in it;—and it is every whit as wonderful, as fearful, unimaginable, as the oldest Salem or Prophetic City.'[13] To the Congregationalist, Robert Vaughan, it was 'the age of great cities.'

---

10   J.S. Boone, *The Need of Christianity to the Cities, a Sermon, 1844, 10,* in B. I Coleman (ed), *The Idea of the City in Nineteenth-Century Britain,* London, Routledge, 1973, 97–101. Boone was a High Churchman in Paddington. Perceptions of the city are discussed in S. Lees, *Cities Perceived: Urban Society in European and American Thought, 1820–1940,* Manchester, MUP, 1984.

11   F. Engels, *The Condition of the Working Classes in England in 1844,* repr. Oxford, OUP, 1958, 100.

12   C. Dickens, *Hard Times,* 1854, Book I, 22.

13   T. Carlyle, *Past and Present,* 1843, Book III, 15.

Charles Dickens' Portrait of an Industrial Town in Northern England.
'Coketown... was a town of machinery and tall chimneys, out of which interminable serpents of smoke uncoiled themselves for ever and ever, and never got uncoiled. It had a black canal in it, and a river that ran purple with ill-smelling dye, and vast piles of building full of windows where there was a rattling and a trembling all day long... It contained several large streets all very like one another, and many small streets still more like one another, inhabited by people equally like one another, who all went in and out at the same hours, with the same sound upon the pavements, to do the same work, and to whom every day was the same as yesterday and tomorrow, and every year the counterpart of the last and the next... You saw nothing in Coketown but what was severely workful. If the members of a religious persuasion built a chapel there—as the members of eighteen religious persuasions had done—they made it a pious warehouse of red brick, with sometimes (but this is only in highly ornamented examples) a bell in a birdcage on the top of it...'[1]

1   C. Dickens, *Hard Times*, 1854, Book I, The Keynote, 22

The city was the fulcrum of change, 'the great effect, and the great cause, of progress.'[14] Yet, many of the more affluent remained oblivious of the fate of the 'other nation' living close by: as the novelist William Thackeray in 1850 observed, 'we had but to go a hundred yards off and see for ourselves, but we never did.'[15]

THE CHURCHES IN THE NEW INDUSTRIAL AND URBAN WORLD

The profound physical and social changes created in the new industrial world had profound implications for the churches of Britain. The country remained very religious in the mid-nineteenth century, and the form of that religion was overwhelmingly Christian. Churches were found in most neighbourhoods, and denominations appeared prosperous and expanding, although it should be remembered that this was also a time of rapid population growth. When on Sunday 30 March 1851 the government conducted a religious census, it revealed that in England and Wales over 35% of the 17.9 million population attended a service of worship on that day, or 47% of the population above the age of ten. Large numbers attended more than once, and an even larger number attended irregularly. Others would have gone, but were prevented by illness, age, or work. Local studies in the 1880s suggest that the level of church attendance

14   R. Vaughan, *The Age of Great Cities: or, a Modern Civilization Viewed in its Relation to Intelligence, Morals, and Religion*, London, Second Edition, 1843, 1, 108.
15   W. Thackeray, 'Waiting at the Station', in *Punch*, XVII, 1850, 93.

as a percentage of population remained similar to that in 1851, with a relative decline in later decades.[16]

The Anglican Church remained overwhelmingly the largest English denomination, with 14,077 places of worship in 1851, and just under 5.3 million people in attendance. It was at its strongest in rural areas, and in regions south of the English Midlands. The Religious Census proved alarming to the Anglicans, for although the Established Church of the land, its attendance level was only slightly larger than the combined total of the main Nonconformist churches (Presbyterian, Methodist, Congregationalist and Baptist) at 4.5 million. Nonconformist denominations proved particularly attractive to the upper-working class and lower middle class echelons of society. Methodism was the largest non-Anglican body, although it was an increasingly divided movement. Wesleyans numbered 288,000 in 1831, with a total of 654,000 attendances recorded in 1851. There were a further 230,000 Primitive Methodists. Independents, increasingly known as Congregationalists, grew from just 26,000 members in 1790, to 127,000 in 1838, and 165,000 members in 1851. The number of those who attended Nonconformist churches was usually significantly higher than those who embraced church membership: 515,000 attendances at Congregational churches were recorded in 1851. There were nearly 100,000 members of Baptist churches in 1837. The small but influential Society of Friends, saw 22,478 attendances at their 371 places of worship in 1851, although numbers had fallen to 13,755 in 1864, as Quakers wrestled with issues such as the retention of their distinctive style, and compulsory expulsion for marrying non-Quakers. In the 1830s, a number of evangelicals dissatisfied with the ordained ministry and liturgical forms of Anglicanism, left to form new groupings, including the Plymouth Brethren. The Unitarians, who rejected Trinitarian doctrine, had 229 congregations in 1851, with just over 50,000 individuals in attendance. Many Unitarians held highly influential roles in local religious and social elites, giving them far greater significance than their numerical size would indicate. In 1851, the 570 Roman Catholic places of worship recorded 383,630 attendances, from a Roman Catholic community thought to number around 1.5 million. The overall Roman Catholic population had been significantly boosted by the arrival of Irish migrants, especially into North-West and North-East England, parts of the Midlands, and Scotland, but many priests became deeply concerned over their low levels of religious practice, with fears that some would slip into Protestantism. As well as high levels of investment in education, homes for orphaned children, reformatories for fallen

---

16   See W.S.F. Pickering, 'The 1851 Census: A Useless Experiment?', *British Journal of Sociology*, Vol. 18, no. 4 (1963); K.S. Inglis, 'Patterns of Religious Worship in 1851', *Journal of Ecclesiastical History*, Vol. 11, No. 1, 1960. The pattern of church growth, and factors influencing this, are explored in chapter 13.

women, and ragged schools, were established. Clerical control amongst Roman Catholics deepened, with an extension of Marian devotion.

In Wales, resistance to religious change in the eighteenth century had cost the Anglican Church dear. The 1851 Religious Census suggested that 246,000 attended Calvinistic Methodist churches, 197,000 Congregationalist churches, and 135,717 Baptist churches. Anglicans numbered just 155,000. In Scotland, the dominance of the Church of Scotland was challenged by the growing strength of the Secession churches, who formed together into the United Presbyterian Church in 1847, which attracted attendances of 336,000 in 1851. Fundamental division befell the Church of Scotland in 1843 with the secession of 451 out of 1,203 ministers, with significant portions of their congregations, to form the Free Church of Scotland. In 1851, the Free Church recorded 555,700 attendances, nearly matching the 566,409 attendances of the Church of Scotland. Of growing significance in Scotland was the Roman Catholic Church, its numbers boosted by new arrivals from Ireland. By 1851 there were just under 80,000 people attending the Mass in Scotland, and their numbers were growing.

Thomas Chalmers: The Urban Parochial Model
Many believed that, with the changing social and religious geography of Britain, urgent and innovative responses were needed if the church was to remain relevant in the new context. One influential experiment was played out in the years after 1815, when the brilliant young minister, Thomas Chalmers, was called from the rural Church of Scotland parish of Kilmany, Fife, to the Tron parish on the East side of Glasgow city centre, a place of significant social need. Over the next eight years Chalmers developed an approach to urban mission, which he publicised and promoted through his writings. His ideas proved extremely influential during much of the following century.

Chalmers' conversion to evangelicalism transformed a young minister who believed that his weekly parochial work could be done in only two days, into a diligent pastor interested in the social and spiritual welfare of his parishioners, and an electrifying preacher. The Glasgow into which Chalmers arrived was enjoying rapid economic and industrial growth, but was also prone to periods of political unrest. Its population mushroomed from 43,000 in 1780, to 274,000 in 1831. Between 30 and 40% of the population lived at or below the poverty line between the 1820s and 1840s. The issue of not only Christianising the urban populace, but also civilising them, was an underlying theme in the thinking of many Christian thinkers, and Chalmers was no exception.

With a theology rooted in the rich Scottish Reformation heritage, enlivened by his evangelicalism, Chalmers' ideal of creating a Godly Commonwealth was nothing new. In a providentially ordered society, he saw family networks as the foundational social unit, which, together with the local community, was the source of much practical support. Inculcating values of sturdy independence,

Thomas Chalmers

hard work, thrift, temperance, and personal piety, would promote self-help.[17] Chalmers proceeded to visit each of his 10,000 parishioners, and discovered a 'very deep and universal ignorance on the high matters of the faith and eternity'.[18] The needful response, he argued, should be an urgent and active

17   A. C. Cheyne, 'Thomas Chalmers: Then and Now', *Studies in Scottish Church History*, Edinburgh, 1999, 89.

18   W. Hanna, *Memoirs of Thomas Chalmers, D.D*, Edinburgh, 1854, I: 432.

work of mission:[19] his motto became famous, 'a house-going minister, a church-going people.'[20] In an extensive urban parish this was beyond the ability of one minister, and Chalmers succeeded in mobilising and overseeing a large workforce of lay people to be involved in active pastoral ministry. Establishing an 'intercourse of piety' between 'men of respectable station and men of labour and poverty,' would be a means of spiritual and moral leavening, and was to be accomplished through domestic visitation. Elders were to focus on spiritual oversight of the parish, with social provision administered by deacons. At one time there were also up to fifty Sunday School teachers, including many young men of the middle and upper classes.[21] Twenty-six Sunday Schools were run by the church in the Saltmarket area of Glasgow alone.[22]

Building on his experience in a rural parish, he stressed the importance of 'locality.' When, in 1819, the new St John's parish was carved out of the old Tron parish, Chalmers divided it into twenty-five districts, or proportions, each comprising between sixty and a hundred families, overseen by an elder and deacon. Based on the Scottish reformation model, Kirk and school operated as redemptive units for society. By 1823 there were two day schools in St John's parish, with 800 pupils. The extension of urban mission through education was furthered by the provision of at least one Sabbath School in each proportion, offering the only schooling many children could afford. One of Chalmers' elders and Sunday School teachers, David Stow, went on to become a pioneer in infant school education, and the professional training of teachers.

Chalmers' scheme for parochial urban mission, set out in *The Christian and Civic Economy of Large Towns*, was truly comprehensive. Although it was Chalmers' conviction that 'the salvation of a single soul is of more value than the deliverance of a whole empire from pauperism,' he envisaged the parish church taking on responsibility for collecting and distributing all the parish relief for the poor in the area.[23] Through preaching and visitation of the poor, the more affluent were to be mobilised in their charitable concern for their fellow parishioners. Conviction as to the values of self-help, and a deep horror of pauperisation, creating a class who were dependent on charity, helped mould the scheme, encouraged by the thinking of Thomas Malthus.[24]

19   On Chalmers and mission see J. Roxborogh, *Thomas Chalmers: Enthusiast for Mission*, Edinburgh, Rutherford House, 1999.

20   Chalmers, quoted in Cheyne, 'Thomas Chalmers Then and Now', 82.

21   Chalmers, *The Christian and Civic Economy of Large Towns*, Glasgow, Chalmers and Collins, 1821, I: 275, 260, 296, 349.

22   Hanna, *Chalmers*, I, 444.

23   Thomas Chalmers to James Brown, 30 January 1819, quoted in S.J. Brown, *Thomas Chalmers and the Godly Commonwealth*, Oxford, OUP, 1982, 138. *The Christian and Civic Economy* was published in instalments between 1819 and 1826.

24   On Chalmers, Malthus, and Free Trade see B. Hilton, *The Age of Atonement: The Influence of Evangelicalism on Social and Economic Thought 1785-1865*, Oxford, Clarendon, 1988.

Thomas Chalmers –The Locality Principle

'We think that the same moral regimen, which, under the parochial and ecclesiastical system of Scotland, has been set up, and with so much effect, in her country parishes, may, by a few simple and attainable processes, be introduced into the most crowded of her cities, and with as conspicuous an effect on the whole habit and character of their population... One most essential step... in a large city parish, is a numerous and well-appointed agency... what [the minister] cannot do but partially and superficially in his own person, must, if done substantially, be done in the person of others. And he, by dividing his parish into small and manageable districts—and assigning one or more of his friends, in some capacity or other, to each of them—and vesting them with a right either of superintendence or of enquiry, will always be found to be gratefully met by the population.'

Social Separation in Urban Areas

... 'there is a mighty unfilled space interposed between the high and low of every large manufacturing city, in consequence of which... a resentful feeling is apt to be fostered, either of disdain or defiance, which it will require all the expedients of an enlightened charity effectually to do away with. Nor can we guess at a likelier, or more immediate arrangement for this purpose, than to multiply the agents of Christianity amongst us, whose delight it may be to go forth among the people, on no other errand than that of pure good-will, and with no other ministrations than those of respect and tenderness...'[1]

1　T. Chalmers, *The Christian and Civic Economy of Large Towns*, Glasgow 1821–26, I, 24–29, 95–99, 126–7.

Chalmers' attempted to recreate the Reformation 'godly commonwealth.' However, the model was ill suited to the new industrial context.[25] Although during the period of Chalmers ministry St John's church was able to assume the support of the poor within its parish, and achieve a reduction in the number of paupers, saving Glasgow's ratepayers £300 per year, when Chalmers left in 1823 so did many of his wealthy congregation. The support of the poor, without the use of public assistance, could not be sustained financially, and the parish-based godly commonwealth of interests failed.[26] The evangelistic side of the scheme also fell away, because of a waning supply of suitable middle class volunteers with the time and inclination to devote themselves to the work of

25　Cheyne, 'Thomas Chalmers: Then and Now', 105. Anstruther was the small community in Fife in which Chalmers was born and brought up.

26　Brown, *Thomas Chalmers*, is the most thorough recent study of Chalmers, and explores the godly commonwealth idea.

urban visitation. Chalmers failed to achieve a long-term reversal of the pattern of religious alienation in his parish.[27]

Chalmers perpetuated his ideas amongst the rising generation of Scottish ministers during his subsequent years of lecturing at St Andrews and Edinburgh universities. His characteristic emphasis on preaching, visitation and education was widely replicated. Most parishes in Britain were operating some form of visitation scheme by the middle of the nineteenth century, with the intention of carrying the Christian message to the homes of the uncommitted, offering discriminating charity based on knowledge of personal circumstances, encouraging self-help among the poor, improving social relationships and reducing class tensions.[28] However, Chalmers' parochial model of poor relief was not widely followed. His endorsement of political economy was more influential. Chalmers promoted the view that the self-regulating market and competition for limited resources, with the consequent inevitability of some inequalities, was consistent with a providential world order of free moral choice and individual responsibility.[29] Charles Simeon, who visited Chalmers in Glasgow, recognised his 'depth of thought, originality in illustrating, and strength in stating,' but warned, 'a Chalmers is necessary to carry into effect the plans of Chalmers... if we cannot all follow him closely, we may yet tread in his steps.'[30]

THE URBAN MISSION MOVEMENT

For some, district visitation became the panacea for urban social problems. In Glasgow, the somewhat eccentric genius, David Nasmith, devised a method for putting Chalmers' visitation plan to wider use. In 1826 he formed the first city mission in the world, the Glasgow City Mission. Nasmith went on to found a string of town and city missions, including those in Dublin (1828), New York (1830) and London (1835). Some were small and short-lived; others such as the London City Mission became bastions of evangelicalism. These missions employed full-time, often working-class, lay agents in the work of domestic visitation, reading, and discoursing on the scriptures. After 1850, an increased specialisation in the work of the missions was noted, with the development of specific ministries to soldiers, cabmen, dockworkers, and prostitutes, or to specific locations such as public houses and hospitals. City missionaries became widely respected for their labours, sometimes the only outsiders

---

27   Roxborogh, *Chalmers*, 115–116.

28   For a discussion of various visitation schemes, including those amongst Unitarians, see H.D. Rack, 'Domestic Visitation: A Chapter in Early Nineteenth-Century Evangelism', *Journal of Ecclesiastical History*, XXIV, 1973, 357–376.

29   B. Hilton, 'Thomas Chalmers as a Political Economist', in A.C. Cheyne (ed), *The Practical and the Pious*, 141–56.

30   W. Carus, *Memoir of Rev. Charles Simeon*, London, Hatchard and Sons, 1847, 552–53.

willing to venture into the darkest of slums. They became experts in their knowledge of urban deprivation. In 1860, the 375 workers of the London City Mission reported they had made nearly 1.5 million visits, and distributed over 2 million tracts.[31] Urban missions were also formed by Unitarians, including the Domestic Missions started in London (1832) and Liverpool (1836), and the Manchester Ministry to the Poor, founded in 1833. These were inspired by the work of Dr Joseph Tuckerman in Boston, Massachusetts. Their approaches included encouraging friendship across classes, educational efforts, and doing everything to prompt the poor towards self-help. If assistance was given, it was only to be to deserving causes.[32]

A further supply of workers for Anglican churches was opened up with the formation of the Church Pastoral Aid Society, in 1836, and the Additional Curates Society in 1837. The Scripture Readers Association, formed in 1844, visited the poor in their own homes, held Bible classes, read prayers, and conducted services in homes or hired halls. The Christian Instruction Society, formed in 1825, and largely supported by Independent churches, similarly utilised the practice of domestic visitation, with visitors offering a range of tracts, books, food, clothing, and on occasion, money. These means brought the churches into contact with the urban poor, but were also moulded by the social views of their active participants, which emphasised respectability, self-help, and self-improvement.

PREACHERS AND PREACHING

The Victorian period was an age of great preachers, with large congregations built on the strength of pulpit prowess. The sermon was a significant event in the spiritual and cultural world of the local congregation. The commanding pulpit ministry of Thomas Chalmers in Glasgow was a prime example, to which was attracted a large and often affluent congregation. His sermons exuded controlled passion, overwhelming in its intensity. He could hold his audience spellbound for an hour and a half. According to one hearer: 'His eloquence rose like a tide, a sea, bearing down upon you, lifting up all its waves... there was no doing anything but giving yourself up for the time to its will.'[33] A fellow Glasgow minister, the Independent Ralph Wardlaw, described Chalmers' preaching as: 'Thrilling, overwhelming. His whole soul seemed in every utterance'. Wardlaw was struck by 'the breathless, the appalling silence,' with which the sermon was

---

31   D.M. Lewis, *Lighten Their Darkness, The Evangelical Mission to Working Class London, 1828–1860*, New York, Greenwood Press, 1986, 205, 278.

32   *First Report of the Manchester Ministry to the Poor*, Manchester, 1834. On the societies in Liverpool and London see the articles by D. Steers and A. Ruston, in *Transactions of the Unitarian Historical Society*, 21/1, April, 1996.

33   Dr John Brown, *Horae Subserivae*, quoted in Cheyne, 'Thomas Chalmers, Then and Now', 81.

heard.[34] There was a tremendous range to Chalmers preaching: something of a polymath, his subjects ranged from scripture texts, to a series of Astronomical and Commercial Discourses, preached to packed lunchtime congregations. Yet he was equally effective in small gatherings in workshops and cottages in his parish.[35]

In 1822, Edward Irving, one-time assistant of Chalmers, was called to the Caledonian Chapel in London. A striking figure, standing six feet two inches tall, his scintillating preaching soon attracted a crowded congregation, which included statesmen, philosophers, poets, peers and leaders of fashionable society. After five years a new building in Regent Square was constructed to accommodate the hearers. Irving sought to break away from a logical and scholastic approach to the truths of revelation, appealing rather to the heart. He declaimed in extravagant, rhetorical, style on his subject matter, with deep veneration for the things of the past, and suspicion of matters present, especially utilitarianism. Drawn to the emotion and intuition of the Romantics, Irving's thinking was significantly moulded by Samuel Taylor Coleridge, who judged him the greatest Orator he had ever heard. From him Irving developed a deep reverence for the ideal, and a hatred of expediency. Irving's rise was meteoric, but his fall into disfavour was equally dramatic. His adoption of a premillennial theology, with stark predictions of the return of Christ after a period of profound turmoil, and stern denunciations of aspects of contemporary evangelicalism, turned many hearers away. Others were profoundly disturbed by a movement in his church that proved a precursor to Pentecostalism, including manifestations of speaking in tongues. When the trustees excluded him from the Regent Square church, the Catholic Apostolic Church was formed, although in it Irving only held the role of 'angel', not apostle. Eventually, after expressing views which suggested that, in his human nature, Christ was capable of sinning, Irving was tried and found guilty of heresy by the Church of Scotland. Beset by poor health, and personal family tragedy, he died the following year aged just 42.[36]

Other Scottish preachers influenced by Thomas Chalmers included Robert Murray McCheyne who for seven years conducted a remarkable ministry at St Peter's Church, Dundee, characterised by deeply devoted pastoral visitation, penetratingly sincere preaching, and a period of revival, before his untimely death at the age of 29.[37] Thomas Guthrie, who similarly studied under Thomas

34   Ralph Wardlaw, quoted in W. Hanna, *Memoirs of Thomas Chalmers, D.D.*, Vol. I, Edinburgh, Thomas Constable, 1854, 464.

35   H. Watt, *Thomas Chalmers and the Disruption*, London, Nelson, 1943, 67.

36   On Irving see C. G. Flegg, *Gathered Under Apostles: A Study of the Catholic Apostolic Church*, Oxford, OUP, 1992; on his theology see G. MacFarlane, (ed), *Edward Irving: The Trinitarian Face of God*, Edinburgh, St Andrews Press, 1996.

37   On McCheyne see A. Bonar, *Memoir and Remains of Robert Murray McCheyne*, Edinburgh, 1844.

Chalmers at Edinburgh University, began ministry in Edinburgh in 1837. His dramatic pulpit oratory included a strong pictorial sense, and ability to evoke a sympathetic response from his hearers, rich and poor alike. Guthrie exercised a deep social concern, and played an active role in events surrounding the Disruption of the Church of Scotland in 1843.[38] Norman MacLeod, minister of the Barony Church, Glasgow, from 1851 to 1872, was one of Queen Victoria's favourite preachers, and appointed one of her chaplains. Deeply devoted to urban pastoral ministry, he was equally at home preaching to royalty as to the crowded congregations of Glasgow's urban poor admitted to evening services on the condition that they wore working clothes. Edward Ramsay, Episcopalian minister of St John's Church, Edinburgh in the years after 1830, also an admirer of Chalmers, was another eloquent and popular preacher.

Within the more liturgical services of the Church of England, preaching held a less dominant role, yet amongst mid-nineteenth century Anglicans were those capable of wielding considerable influence through their pulpit work, not least being John Henry Newman (see chapter 8). Henry Melvill of Camden Chapel, Camberwell, attracted regular congregations of 1,500 before he became Canon of St Paul's Cathedral in 1839. Hugh McNeile, who ministered in Liverpool from 1834 to 1868, was a powerful preacher and speaker, who threw himself into the life of the city. An ardent Protestant, McNeile did much to foster a strong Evangelical tradition in the city, and to shape its public institutions. The ministry of Francis Close in Cheltenham, in the years 1824–56, was rooted in both preaching, and pastoral and public engagements. He took such intensive interest in the social and educational matters in the community, generating much charitable relief for the poor, and ensuring that shops closed on Sundays, that he was dubbed 'the Pope of Cheltenham' by the *Times*. The work of William Farquhar Hook (1798–1875), who became vicar of the vast parish of Leeds in 1837, demonstrates how an old-fashioned high-churchman could exercise a powerful parochial ministry. He laboured hard in visitation, creating new parishes, and providing much money for their endowment. Pre-eminent amongst Anglican preachers of the second half of the nineteenth century was J.C. Ryle. After spending most of his ministry in two Suffolk parishes, Ryle was appointed the first Bishop of Liverpool in 1880, at the age of 64. He was a prolific author of tracts and works of practical and devotional theology, and his writings did much to consolidate the Evangelical tradition within Anglicanism alongside the Anglo-Catholic and Broad Church alternatives.

An emphasis upon preaching was notable amongst English Nonconformists. When, in 1805, John Angell James became minister of the Independent Carrs Lane Chapel, Birmingham, its membership stood at just fifty. By 1855, it had 1,000 members, and six daughter churches had been formed. The congregation

---

38 On Guthrie, see C.J. Guthrie, *Thomas Guthrie: Preacher and Philanthropist*, Edinburgh, 1899.

also maintained four preaching stations, and employed two town missionaries. James' successor, R.W. Dale, attained equal eminence.[39] The call of Andrew Reed to New Road Chapel, Stepney, in 1811, was to a church of just sixty members. Over the next fifty years the congregation grew to number around 2,000 people, and Reed developed a wide range of philanthropic and educational ventures alongside his pulpit ministry.[40] The Congregationalist Joseph Parker's work at the City Temple, London, from 1869-1902 won him a reputation as one of the capital's masters of the pulpit. A man of impressive appearance, commanding voice, if slightly histrionic pulpit manner, he preached with great authority and much popular appeal.

The 'Prince of Preachers' of the Victorian era was undoubtedly Charles Haddon Spurgeon. From an Essex family steeped in the Puritan tradition, he underwent a period of deep spiritual struggle in his teenage years, before his conversion. As a teenager he became pastor of Waterbeach Baptist Chapel, before in 1854 he was called to New Park Street Baptist Chapel, London. Within a few months of his arrival, the building was filled to overflowing, and for a period the congregation met in the Surrey Gardens Music Hall, at which attendances of 12,000 were not uncommon. In 1859 the Metropolitan Tabernacle was constructed, holding some 6,000 people. Spurgeon's preaching was widely reported on, initially with considerable hostility, and was widely circulated by means of a weekly published sermon, and he became a household name. Although rarely offering systematic expositions of passages of scripture, his preaching was filled with Biblical texts, Calvinistic theology steeped in the Puritans, coloured by rich illustration and metaphor, and enlivened by irrepressible humour. He started a number of projects of social concern, and in 1856 the Pastor's College, for training gospel preachers. Late in life he launched a determined rearguard action against the growing influence of liberal theology in Baptist circles, known as the 'Downgrade Controversy.'[41]

Spurgeon was not the only Baptist preacher to draw large crowds. A number of Spurgeon's close Baptist associates, such as Archibald Brown at the East London Tabernacle, and William Cuff in Shoreditch, attracted congregations numbering over 1,000. Alexander Maclaren's ministry at Union Chapel, Manchester from 1858-1903, gained him the reputation of 'the prince of expository preachers.' His methods of subdivision, and illustration from the world of nature and ordinary life, became widely followed. Even High Calvinist Strict Baptist preachers could

---

39   J.A. James, *The Life and Letters of John Angell James: Including an Unfinished Autobiography*, ed. R.W. Dale, 2nd edn, London, 1861, 493-94.

40   On Andrew Reed see I.J.Shaw, *The Greatest is Charity: The Life of Andrew Reed (1787-1862), Preacher and Philanthropist*, Darlington, Evangelical Press, 2005.

41   On Spurgeon see C.H. Spurgeon, *Autobiography*, 4 vols, London, 1897-1900; G.H. Pike, *The Life and Work of Charles Haddon Spurgeon*, London, Cassell and Co, 1892-93.

draw large bodies of hearers: that of James Wells at the Surrey Tabernacle in South London reached 2,000.[42]

Despite the seeming success of the Victorian churches, there were those within the Christian community who were prepared to offer significant critiques. Evidence of the growing alienation of the poor from regular worship was already appearing in the middle decades of the nineteenth century. [See chapter 14 below] Some Dissenters, who felt keenly the religious and social discrimination against them, maintained a vigorous campaign for the Disestablishment of the Church of England. A leader of that campaign, Edward Miall, believed that maintaining an Established church harmed religious conditions for the poor. In his work *The British Churches in Relation to the British People* he argued that there was something 'seriously amiss' with churches, lamenting their lack of spiritual life, their insularity, their formalism and 'Pharisaism', with strong lines of demarcation between the rich and the poor within congregations.[43]

THE CHURCHES AND SOCIAL CONCERN

Churches and individuals engaged in a wide range of philanthropic activity as part of their wider concern to Christianise society in the mid-nineteenth century. David Bebbington has described the hundred years before the First World War as the 'Evangelical century'.[44] One estimate suggests that three-quarters of charitable organisations in nineteenth-century London were evangelical in character and control.[45] The multitude of agencies formed to meet with needs, even within a local congregation, was astonishing: societies for visiting the sick, loaning blankets to the poor, offering food and clothes to mothers and their newborn babies, providing coal in the winter. Philanthropic individuals gave significant sums to charitable causes. The wealthy Congregationalist hosiery manufacturer, Samuel Morley, supported over 100 religious and philanthropic institutions alone.[46] At St Jude's Church, Mildmay, London, the Anglican William Pennefather, started an elementary school for the poorest children, a soup kitchen for the poor and sick, a Sunday School which attracted over 1,000 children, and a training programme for women in aspects of Christian service. The Mildmay Medical Mission started in 1870.

The lack of adequate health-care in urban areas, attracted the concern of charitable individuals. The Edinburgh Medical Mission, founded in 1841,

---

42 On Gadsby and Wells see I.J. Shaw, *High Calvinists in Action*, Oxford, OUP, 2002.

43 E. Miall, *The British Churches in Relation to the British People*, London, 1849, Preface, 406–423.

44 D. Bebbington, *Evangelicalism in Modern Britain*, London, Unwin Hyman, 1989, 149.

45 K. Heasman, *Evangelicals in Action: An Appraisal of their Social Work*, London, Geoffrey Bless, 1962, 13–14.

46 E. Hodder, *Life of Samuel Morley*, London, Hodder and Stoughton, 1887, 288, 499–501.

sought the 'double cure' of the soul and the body. It provided a doctor, nurse and a free dispensary. As patients waited, the Bible was expounded to them, and prayer offered. Similar missions were started in Liverpool (1866), Glasgow (1868), Manchester (1870).[47] Concern for the social and spiritual needs of the urban poor led to the employment of working-class women in visitation in deprived areas, selling Bibles, and offering advice on domestic issues. In 1857, the London Bible and Domestic Female Mission was started, and ten years later it employed 234 'Bible Women'. Visitors often encountered people with serious medical needs during visitation, and in 1868 women began to be trained as 'Bible nurses.'[48]

EDUCATION

Rapid population growth, and an increasingly young population, saw growing interest in the needs of children. Churches were also experiencing a slowing rate of recruitment from adults of the artisan class, which had been a strong source of new members up until 1820 as a result of itinerant preaching. Instead, resources began to shift to work with children. In this trend of introversion, children already adherent to the diverse body of church and chapel organisations became the primary mission field, rather than those outside their immediate sphere of influence.[49] The result was a heavy investment in Day Schools, Sunday Schools, Ragged Schools, and Children's rescue organisations.

There was no state provision for education in England and Wales until 1870, and 1872 in Scotland. Before then, education was provided by an unsatisfactory mixture of private fee paying schools, public schools for the wealthy, charity schools, church schools, and the poor quality 'dame' schools. Some enlightened factory owners also ran schools for the children they employed.[50] Education was believed by Christian leaders to be a core part of the ministry of the church. In the view of John Venn of Clapham: 'Man cannot by education be made a real Christian; but by education he may be freed from prejudices and delivered from the dominion of dispositions highly favourable to temptation and sin.'[51] Increased literacy would particularly promote the reading of the Bible.

Building on the work of the Quaker Joseph Lancaster, the British and Foreign School Society, founded in 1814, attracted support from across the denominations, including William Wilberforce. It became increasingly

---

47   Heasman, *Evangelicals in Action*, 225–28.

48   F.K. Prochaska, 'Body and Soul: Bible Nurses and the Poor in Victorian London', *Historical Review* 60 / 143 (1987), 336–48.

49   A. Gilbert, *Religion and Society*, 159–160.

50   M. Sturt, *The Education of the People, A History of Primary Education in England and Wales in the Nineteenth Century*, London, Routledge and Kegan Paul, 1967, p6.

51   *Christian Observer*, 1804, 542.

associated with Nonconformist churches: in 1851 it was educating 123,000 children. The Anglican National Society, founded in 1811 by Andrew Bell, was by 1851, providing schooling for 465,000 children, with other Anglican schools educating a further 336,000. In the 1830s, both schemes began to receive government grants of money for school building. Other denominations— Methodist, Congregationalist, and Roman Catholic all provided day schools, but the appropriateness of accepting state funding troubled Nonconformists, which gave a considerable advantage to Anglicans in terms of resourcing—in 1861 Anglican schools were educating 76% of all day school children in England.[52] In 1847 Wesleyans decided to accept government financial assistance, and Roman Catholic schools followed suit in 1848. A combination of denominational rivalries, suspicion of Anglican domination, and fear from nonconformists that there would be little, or no, religious component in any state system, held its introduction back until 1870, which was probably to the detriment of national educational welfare.[53]

The horizons of such educational provisions were limited. In 1805, Andrew Bell feared that, through 'indiscriminate education,' those facing the 'drudgery of daily labour' would be rendered 'discontented and unhappy in their lot.' He believed that it was 'sufficient to teach the generality, on an economical plan, to read their Bible and understand the doctrines of our Holy Religion.'[54] The need for social control, and the economic utility of education, were strong driving forces, as the classical economist Adam Smith, argued: 'An instructed and intelligent people besides, are always more decent and orderly than an ignorant and stupid one.'[55] Lord Shaftesbury combined such motives as he declared that education, had 'control over and possession of the youthful mind of the country, and the temporal and eternal destiny of millions.'[56]

Nonetheless, many remained uneducated. In 1841, 26% of men and 58% of women in Manchester were unable to write their names in the marriage register, and in 1864, 57% of children in Manchester were still receiving no education at all.[57] In Scotland, the Reformation educational heritage had left a school in

52   G. Kitson Clark, *Churchmen and the Condition of England, 1832–85*, London, Methuen, 1973, 125.

53   On nineteenth century education debates in Britain see Sturt, *Education of the People*; F. Smith, *A History of English Elementary Education 1760–1902*, London, University of London, 1931.

54   A. Bell, *An Experiment in Education*, 1805, quoted in Sturt, *History of Primary Education*, 28.

55   Quoted in M. W. Flinn, 'Social Theory and the Industrial Revolution' in T. Burns and S.B. Saul, *Social Theory and Economic Change*, London, Tavistock, 1967.

56   Lord Shaftesbury, in Hansard, Parliamentary Debates, 3rd Series, XLVIII, 270, quoted in G.B.A.M. Finlayson, *Shaftesbury*, 118.

57   *The State of Education in* Manchester, in T.S. Ashton, *Economic and Social Investigations in Manchester 1833–1933*, London, P.S. King and Son, 1934, 32. A. Kidd, *Manchester*, Keele, Keele UP, 1933, 53–55.

every parish, rendering education more accessible, especially in villages and towns, although in larger urban areas access to schools was more limited.

The intention of the 1870 Education Act was to fill in the gaps left by voluntary provision for education, by creating non-denominational publicly funded schools. It reflected the failure of churches to live up to their ambitions to be the source of religious, moral and educational guidance for the nation. The new Schools provided by the Act were run by locally elected School Boards, to which many Christian leaders sought election, in often bitterly fought contests. An element of religious education was preserved, although of a non-sectarian nature.[58] The 1870 Act spurred denominations into a renewed burst of school building activity, in an attempt to out-compete the Board Schools. The number of voluntary schools peaked in 1890 at 14,479, but from then on the Board Schools with their larger financial resources and facilities, became increasingly dominant.[59]

Over the course of the nineteenth century, the efforts of churches in day-schooling were prodigious, but their level of overall success is unclear. The 'civilising' effect of their educational work seems undeniable, but their impact in inculcating individual religious sentiment is harder to assess. At the end of the century, that astute observer of social life, Charles Booth, was of the opinion that the Christian hope of planting seed through education, which would later be brought to life by the outreach work of churches, was, on the whole, unfulfilled. Workers were 'often disheartened, and sorely tried by failure, the world continually claims the children, and God's kingdom seems to come no nearer'.[60] Others claim the real, but diffuse, value of Christian education, which, according to David Bebbington, 'helps explain the continued esteem for Christianity in the non-church going population'.[61]

The Sunday-School movement continued to play a significant role in the extension of education in the middle decades of the nineteenth century. The spiritual intent of Sunday-School work became increasingly dominant, with a growing stress on Sunday, rather than school, and the Bible above other kinds of knowledge.[62] Facilities improved significantly, most erecting a building separate from the church for their activities. The number of Sunday schools reached 23,135 in 1851, with around 2 million in attendance. By 1888, around 75% of all children went to Sunday School in Britain. Thereafter, numbers rose to an absolute peak at 6 million children in 1903, although this represented

---

58   O. Chadwick, *The Victorian Church*, Vol II, London, Black, 1970, 300.

59   Chadwick, *Victorian Church*, II, 305.

60   C. Booth, *Life and Labour of the People of London, Third Series, Religious Influences, vii*, Summary, London, 1902, 12–13.

61   Bebbington, *Evangelicalism in Modern Britain*, 124.

62   P.B. Cliff, *The Rise and Development of the Sunday School Movement*, Redhill, National Christian Education Council, 1986, 73–81.

a decline to 16% of population from 20% fifteen years earlier.[63] The Anglican church was the largest provider of Sunday School education, accounting for 42% of enrolments in 1851; Methodists accounted for 29%; the Independents 13.3%, and the Baptists just 7.4%.[64]

The nineteenth-century Nonconformist politician John Bright reportedly declared: 'I don't believe all the statesmen in existence...have tended so much to the greatness and true happiness, the security and glory of this country, as have the efforts of Sunday school teachers.' The reality was that many continued to be inefficient, offering limited educational provision.[65] They did not prove the panacea for religious alienation many hoped for, and children often stopped attending in their early teens. In 1854, a Wesleyan spokesman lamented how 'beyond the possibility of doubt...vast multitudes of children are incessantly passing through our Sunday schools, and then becoming...utterly alienated from our religious fellowship.' Suggestions of less than 4% of Sunday School pupils subsequently becoming church members have been made.[66] Nonetheless, before 1870 Sunday Schools were, for many, the only avenue for educational progress available to the working classes. It was often the opportunity to gain a cheap secular education, rather than any religious grounding, that attracted working class children to the Sunday Schools, and the widening availability of free day-school education during the 1880s, corresponded with the beginnings of decline in Sunday School attendance.[67] Nonetheless, by extending literacy they brought the Bible, religious tracts, and a copy of Bunyan's *Pilgrim's Progress* into most homes. Sunday School anniversaries and outings were significant events in the calendar for many children and their parents. In 1856, 23,000 Sunday School scholars attended the Halifax 'Big Sing', accompanied by a band of 560, including eighty-three trombones. Other Sunday Schools also ran large adult Bible classes, which were often attended by working men who did not attend regular church services.

A significant non-denominational attempt to retain the religious adherence of young people was the YMCA started in 1844. Its founder was George Williams, a drapery apprentice, who began a series of Bible study groups for fellow apprentices, clerks, and shop assistants who lived away from home, exposed to the temptations of city life. From its early beginnings in London, it

63   Cliff, *Sunday School Movement*, 102, 125, 164; Chadwick, *Victorian Church I*, 256.

64   Cliff, *Sunday School Movement*, 102.

65   J. Bright, *Church Congress* Reports, 1888: 363; 1894: 393, quoted in Chadwick, *Victorian Church*, II, 257; Chadwick, *Victorian Church*, II, 258.

66   'Wesleyan Sunday Schools as they are and as they Ought to be', London, 1854, 10; T.W. Laqueur, *Religion and Respectability, Sunday Schools and Working Class Culture 1780–1850*, New Haven, Yale, 80.

67   T.W. Laqueur, *Religion and Respectability*, 148–157.

soon expanded to other towns across the country. In 1855 it added recreational, educational and social activities to its extensive programme, and became an increasingly significant international movement later in the century.[68]

Concern for Socially Deprived Children

The condition of children from the lowest social classes, the 'street Arabs', or 'ragged' children, who had been abandoned or orphaned, or had poverty-stricken or uncaring families rendered dysfunctional by problems such as alcohol abuse, were the focus of particular Christian concern. The problems created by their behaviour, lack of clothing, or filthy, vermin ridden or diseased bodies, meant that they were even excluded from many Sunday Schools. In 1810, Thomas Cranfield made early attempts to help such children in Camberwell, and in 1820 John Pounds, a cobbler from Portsmouth, began teaching a group of ragged children. Ragged Schools became an important aspect of the London City Mission's work. After visiting a Ragged School in 1843 Lord Shaftesbury became a strong supporter of the movement, and Chairman of the Ragged School Union, founded the following year. By 1861 there were 176 schools associated to it, offering education to some 25,000 children, and many other Ragged Schools operated independently of the union. The Ragged schools, which provided free education, soon found it was difficult to offer education to children who were hungry and ill-clothed, and began to offer food and clothing, alongside basic education with a strong religious component. Their unpretentious premises located near to where the children roamed, often were stables, storerooms, or under railway arches.[69] Some Ragged Schools provided children with overnight shelter. Other industrial schools were developed to help prepare children for employment. Alongside their educational work, churches were started by some schools for their children and their parents. To Shaftesbury, the Ragged Schools were the only hope to 'reclaim a wild and lawless race, unaccustomed from their earliest years to the slightest moral influence or even restraint,' offering children a chance to 'run the course set before them... as citizens of the British empire, and heirs of glorious immortality.'[70]

Thomas Guthrie, a Church of Scotland minister, began ragged schools in the poor Cowgate area of Edinburgh, and extended the provision of his schools to include breakfast, dinner and supper for the children, together with basic and religious education. Out of these schemes grew the 'Destitute Children's Dinner Society' in 1867, offering meals for hungry children in ragged schools and Christian missions. By 1888 there were sixty-four dining rooms serving 18,000

---

68   On the YMCA see C. Binfield, *George Williams and the YMCA: A Study in Victorian Social Attitudes*, London, Heinemann, 1973.

69   Heasman, *Evangelicals in Action*, 69–73.

70   Lord Shaftesbury, quoted in Finlayson, *Shaftesbury*, 251–253.

dinners each week. Many of the 132 ragged schools, which were educating 23,132 children, were taken over by the School Boards formed in 1870, bringing to an end the important role they had played when the state had been unwilling to offer free, universal education.[71]

Orphans and Orphanages
Within the Poor Law system there was provision for orphaned or abandoned children in workhouses, but there they mixed with vagrants, petty criminals, and the mentally ill, leaving them open to abuse and exploitation. Charities had been responding to the needs of homeless children since the eighteenth century. The Foundling Hospital (1739) catered for illegitimate children who were often abandoned on church doorsteps; the Marine Society (1756) was for 'destitute boys of good character', and the Orphan Working School (1758) supported 'orphans and other necessitous children'. In 1813, Andrew Reed, the minister of the New Road Independent Chapel, Stepney, founded the London Orphan Asylum as a result of pastoral needs he encountered in the East End of London. By the time of his death in 1862, that orphanage had cared for over 2,700 children, and two others had been started. Christian instruction and regular religious services were a strong component of the work.[72] The example of German Pietists and the orphanage at Halle, which admitted and educated destitute children, proved a powerful inspiration to George Müller, who in 1836 established his first orphanage in Bristol. By the 1880s, Müller's Ashley Down Orphanage cared for some 2000 children. His 'faith principle' of raising money was copied by some others, although his tracts promoting remarkable answers to prayer when in financial need also served to advertise the needs of the children.[73]

Charles Spurgeon's Stockwell orphanage was started in 1867, and the Wesleyan minister Thomas Bowman Stephenson established the National Children's Home in Lambeth in 1869. 'The Waifs and Strays Society', later to become the Church of England Children's Society, followed in 1881.[74] The Roman Catholic Church was similarly active in setting up homes and orphanages for homeless Roman Catholic children. Thomas Barnardo's extensive provision for children grew out of the East End Juvenile Mission, which he started in 1868. After two years, the mission was running day schools and Sunday schools, and a home for boys. By the time of Barnardo's death in 1905, over 8,500 children were in the care of the homes, of whom 1300 were disabled or seriously ill. A total

---

71   Chadwick, *Victorian Church*, Vol. II, 307; Heasman, *Evangelicals in Action*, 84–85.

72   On Andrew Reed see I.J. Shaw, *The Greatest is Charity: The Life of Andrew Reed (1787–1862), Preacher and Philanthropist*, Darlington, Evangelical Press, 2005.

73   R. Steer, *George Müller: Delighted in God*, London, Hodder and Stoughton, 1975, 191.

74   Heasman, *Evangelicals in Action*, 91–92.

George Müller

of around 60,000 children had been rescued, and 16,800 helped to emigrate to the colonies. Exercising a 'no destitute child refused admission' policy, in effect Barnardo maintained the largest children's hospital in London, and had pioneered innovative approaches to the fostering of children by supportive families.[75] Over the century there was considerable development in child-care facilities, which moved from spartan, barrack-like orphanages offering frugal care, into 'Homes,' with children housed in smaller cottages in family units.

CHRISTIANS AND POLITICS

There was no Christian consensus on political issues or approaches during the middle decades of the nineteenth-century. Whilst many church leaders consciously sought to maintain an apolitical stance, they quickly found that religious issues had political implications. However, any political action tended to take the form of periodic forays into the political field, and was rarely concerted.

A paternalist understanding of social responsibility shaped many attempts in the middle of the nineteenth century to remedy the social problems attendant upon rapid industrialisation and urbanisation. Paternalists saw it as the duty of those with wealth and influence in society to use this for the benefit of others. This underlay the approach of Thomas Chalmers, and was a strong emphasis in the thinking of the eminent politician and social reformer, Lord Shaftesbury (1801–1885). He was motivated by his evangelical beliefs, convinced that humans were made in the image of God and that their immortal destinies were at stake: 'the temples of the Holy Ghost, ought not to be corrupted by preventable disease, degraded by avoidable filth, and disabled for His service by unnecessary suffering.' The duty of society was to give each person 'full, fair and free opportunity to exercise his moral, intellectual, physical and spiritual energies.'[76] Shaftesbury argued that both individual philanthropy and state intervention, should be designed to raise individuals to the point at which they could help themselves. To go beyond this was to rob the individual of initiative and responsibility, rendering socialist approaches unattractive to him. Shaftesbury was an active personal philanthropist, and also promoted a range of legislation in Parliament to ameliorate social need.

Before it was taken up by Lord Shaftesbury, the mantle of Wilberforce had initially fallen to a group of paternalist-minded Tory Evangelicals, who began to direct the moral outrage engendered in the campaign against slavery towards 'white slavery', especially the plight of vulnerable industrial workers. In 1830 a group of Evangelicals from the North of England, led by the MP Michael Sadler, and the clergyman Parson G.S. Bull, of Bierley near Bradford,[77] began a campaign against the long working hours of both children and women in the

75   On Barnardo, see G. Wagner, *Barnardo*, London, Weidenfeld and Nicolson, 1979.

76   Shaftesbury, address as President of the Health Section, to Social Science Congress Liverpool, 1858 on Sanitary Legislation, in *Speeches of the Earl of Shaftesbury, K.G. Upon Subjects Having Relation to the Claims and Interests of the Labouring Class*, London: Chapman and Hall, 1868.

77   See J.C. Gill, *The Ten-Hours Parson: Christian Social Action in the 1830s*, London, SPCK, 1959; R.B. Seeley, *Memoirs of the Life and Writings of Michael Thomas Sadler*, London, 1842.

mills. Accounts were produced of children badly injured whilst working near or under machines that were running. The sheer drudgery and misery of the relentless hours worked by children was captured in a famous letter by Richard Oastler to the *Leeds Mercury* newspaper in 1830. Children working in factories tended to be smaller, and prone to bodily deformities. The campaign to reduce working hours met fierce resistance from mill-owners, some of whom were

---

Richard Oastler—Child Industrial Slavery

'thousands of our fellow creatures, the inhabitants of a Yorkshire town… are at this moment existing in a state of slavery… thousands of little children, both male and female… from seven to 14 years, are daily compelled to labour from six o'clock in the morning to seven in the evening… the very streets… are every morning wet with the tears of innocent victims at the accursed shrine of avarice'[1]

1   R. Oastler, *Letter to the Leeds Mercury*, Saturday 16 October, 1830.

Nonconformists, who rejected such government intervention in the free market.

After 1833, Shaftesbury, then known as Lord Ashley,[78] assumed leadership in the campaign. He was convinced that the task was his 'duty to God and the poor.' Reducing working hours would allow children time for education and Christian instruction. As in the struggle against slavery, the campaign required dogged persistence. Concessions were gradually won in the years after 1833, but it was 1847 before a bill was passed in parliament, limiting the hours of work of women and children to ten hours.[79] Alongside the moral impetus given to the campaign by Christian politicians, other factors were at work. There was growing recognition of the economic inefficiency of overworking and exploiting labour. As technology improved, the employment of children became less necessary. Factory owners also recognised that a more educated workforce was more efficient, and they began making opportunities for schooling available, some of it at the workplace.

Shaftesbury's paternalistic social concern was wide ranging. In 1840, he saw a bill through Parliament to stop the employment of boys to climb and sweep chimneys.[80] After further campaigning, in 1842, the Coal Mines Regulation Act was passed. This outlawed the employment of women, and children under the age of ten, in underground mines where they worked in dreadful conditions, often naked, and exposed to serious physical and sometimes sexual abuse.

---

78   Anthony Ashley Cooper, was known as Lord Ashley before he inherited his father's title of Lord Shaftesbury.

79   Gill, *Ten Hours Parson*, 82.

80   Finlayson, *The Seventh Earl of Shaftesbury*, 228–32. 249–51.

The repeal of the Test and Corporation Acts in 1828, Roman Catholic Emancipation in 1829, together with the Reform Act of 1832, had opened the door to a more representative parliament. However, by 1852 the Nonconformist population in England and Wales was still significantly underrepresented, with only 27 Nonconformist members of Parliament. Campaigns to address the deep social inequalities they still faced also absorbed much political energy, and their grievances only slowly addressed. The necessity of marriage in an Anglican church was removed in 1836, with the civil registration of births and deaths also granted that year. The campaign against the capacity of the Anglican church to levy a 'church rate' for the upkeep of the parish church, regardless of whether individuals attended a parish church or not, was only resolved in 1868 after a bitter campaign in which some who refused to pay were imprisoned. The Factory Bill of 1843, which included educational provisions that appeared to favour Anglicans, provoked a storm of protest before they were withdrawn. The consistent reluctance of the Anglican church to give ground on these issues fuelled growing, and often strident calls, for the disestablishment of the Church of England, and drove a significant wedge between Anglicans and Nonconformists. Although the Church of Ireland was disestablished in 1869, bills for the disestablishment of the Church of England failed to pass through Parliament in the 1870s.

Nonconformity found a far higher level of representation at local government level, after the 1835 Municipal Reform Act. Four out of the first five mayors of Bradford came from Horton Lane Congregational Chapel, the local 'cathedral' of Nonconformity. In the campaign for the repeal of the Corn Laws, which had been introduced to protect home agriculture by keeping the price of grain high, Nonconformists took an active political role. From their urban and industrial heartlands they took an active part in an eventually successful campaign in the 1830s and 1840s, arguing that the laws kept the price of bread high, and were effectively a tax on the poor.[81]

The political and religious advances of Roman Catholicism drew Protestants into the political arena when they discerned a threat to the Protestant basis of the British constitutional system. In the 1840s there were concerted campaigns to stop the payment of government grants to the Maynooth Seminary in Ireland, where Roman Catholic priests were trained.[82] Popular Protestant feeling against Roman Catholicism increased in 1850 when the newly appointed archbishop of Westminster, Nicholas Wiseman declared England no longer a missionary province, and the restoration of the Roman Catholic hierarchy in the country. In the middle decades of the century Roman Catholicism became more self-

---

81   See N. McCord, *The Anti-Corn Law League, 1838–46*, 2nd edn, London, Allen and Unwin, 1968.

82   On anti-Catholicism see J.R. Wolffe, *The Protestant Crusade in Britain, 1829–60*, Oxford, Clarendon, 1991.

confident, developing its own institutions, and emphasising the provision of separate Roman Catholic schools and social organisations where free association with Protestants was unlikely.

The attempt to enforce stricter observance of the Sabbath pre-occupied many Christian politicians in the middle of the nineteenth century. Whilst there was genuine concern to give workers a rest day, free of the demands of work with opportunity to attend religious services, there were deep fears that that leisure time might be used for irreligious ends, particularly the consumption of alcohol. Whilst most gladly embraced a day free of labour, they were less enthusiastic about spending a good part of it in church. Some mill girls were so exhausted from weekly labours that they spent the whole day asleep. Trade, entertainment and sport had been stopped on Sunday from as early as 1780, but the formation of the Lord's Day Observance Society in 1831 suggested that the law was being only partially observed. In 1849 Lord Shaftesbury saw a measure through Parliament to stop the collection and delivery of post on Sundays, followed in 1856 by the Sunday closure of museums and art galleries in London. More controversial was the decision in 1854 to completely close public houses on Sundays, a move so unpopular that riots followed, and the measure was rescinded.[83] Whilst it has been argued that such measures restricted the pleasures of the poor on their one day free from work, for many church and chapel goers Sunday remained the high point of each week. Judging by the readiness with which large numbers went to services, attended or ran Sunday School classes and prayer meetings, sang in choirs or undertook various outreach activities, it was not for them the monotonous, boring day, depicted by some.

Concern for public morality continued to be a theme of Christian political activity. Campaigns against obscenity led to the passing of the Obscene Publications Act in 1857. The state lottery was ended in 1826, and endeavours were made to regulate and reduce gambling. Horse racing on a Sunday was stopped, and some of the traditional street fairs, associated with much disorder and immorality, were closed or curtailed. In 1824, the Royal Society for the Prevention of Cruelty to Animals was formed, including William Wilberforce and a number of evangelicals among its founders. Legislation was passed in 1835 outlawing popular entertainment which involved cruelty to animals, including bull and bear baiting, dog fighting, and cock-fighting, although the practices continued illegally.

Prison Reform

Prison reform attracted much Quaker interest. Whilst William Allen strove for the abolition of capital punishment, T.F. Buxton believed that the eighteenth-

---

83 On the campaigns for Sabbath observance see J. Wigley, *The Rise and Fall of the Victorian Sunday*, Manchester, MUP, 1980.

century penal code, in which someone could be hanged for stealing sixpence was utterly contrary to the Christian religion. The publicity Buxton gave to bad prison conditions encouraged the Home Secretary, Robert Peel, to introduce reforms in the system in the 1820s. In 1813 Elizabeth Fry began visiting female prisoners in Newgate jail. Concentrating initially on reading the Bible to the prisoners, and offering spiritual comfort and practical help, she soon extended this to educational opportunities, and training in basic domestic skills. By the 1820s she had organised visiting male and female prisoners across the country, and was able to bring about significant improvements in their conditions. Her writings on the need for prison reform, published in the late 1820s, proved extremely influential in campaigns for more humane prison regimes.[84]

Temperance

Alcohol was a significant aspect of working-class culture, and the temperance cause originally developed as a movement of self-help amongst working people. Excessive consumption of drink was widely seen as a social problem, fuelling poverty, violence, and social dislocation. In Glasgow in 1850 there were 15,700 arrests for drunkenness—one in twenty-two of the city's population. In the 1830s the temperance cause began to be drawn into the life of churches and chapels, with alcohol consumption believed to be a major barrier to the moral and religious improvement of the people. Roman Catholicism had its own temperance movement, making use of popular lecturers. One such was the Franciscan temperance campaigner Father Theobald Mathew, who visited Glasgow Green in 1842 and was greeted by a crowd of 50,000 people.[85] The National Temperance League was formed in 1856, and the Church of England Total Abstinence Society in 1862. For some, temperance was an insufficient response to the problem, and the more radical teetotal, or total abstinence, stance was advocated. This spread significantly under the influence of American revivalists, as part of their call for radical separation from the world. Some were initially suspicious of a movement associated with dramatic preaching, and emotional calls to 'sign the pledge,' which looked all-too-like calls to conversion itself, and refused the use of their buildings for such meetings. Yet as middle-class church goers embraced the teetotal message, it attained a measure of respectability. The United Kingdom Alliance, formed in 1853, campaigned for measures to prohibit the sale of alcoholic liquors.[86] Although this proved unsuccessful, licensing laws were tightened. The teetotal cause was promoted

---

84 See J. Rose, *Elizabeth Fry*, London, Macmillan, 1980.

85 J.E. Handley, *The Irish in Scotland, 1798–1845*, Cork, Cork University Press, 1943, 247–48.

86 On temperance see B. Harrison, *Drink and the Victorians: The Temperance Question in England, 1815–72*, London, 2nd edn, Keele UP, 1994.

amongst children by bodies such as the Band of Hope, who spread their message through a lively programme of musical and recreational activities.

Part of the crusade against drink included attempts to create alternative social venues to the public house. This led in the 1850s to the establishment of coffee houses for workmen, offering a convivial social atmosphere, without the presence of alcohol. In the early 1870s, the British Workmen Public House movement started, offering cheap meals and non-alcoholic refreshments in warmth and comfort and décor that resembled conventional public houses. Cafés and dinner rooms for working men were also set up as places where respectable working people could eat without alcohol being present.

The prevalence of alcohol abuse did decline, in part through temperance campaigning, although other factors were significant—the wider availability of clean water, together with supplies of cheap tea, and coffee. Also influential were demands from employers for a disciplined and regular workforce, which did much to reduce excessive alcohol consumption. As homes became more comfortable and pleasant places in which to live, the attraction of the public house declined.

Prostitution

For all its reputation as an era of strict morality, prostitution was a significant feature of Victorian society. In 1838, the seaport of Liverpool was believed to contain 711 brothels; up to 80,000 prostitutes worked in London. The public nature of the problem was noted by the *Edinburgh Medical Journal*:

'Let anyone walk certain streets of London, Glasgow or Edinburgh of a night, and without troubling his head with statistics, his eyes and ears will tell him what a multitudinous Amazonian army the devil keeps in constant field service.'[87]

Behind this issue lay a complex array of factors, including poverty, limited employment opportunities for women, late age of marriage, alcohol abuse, and 'double standards' of morality. The public health consequences were serious. London hospital records suggested that around 7% of adults suffering from poverty had some form of venereal disease, 1.5% of children had congenital syphilis.

Concern for the welfare and reform of prostitutes began in the eighteenth century. The Magdalen Hospital had been founded in 1758 for 'penitent prostitutes', and the first Lock Hospital for women suffering venereal disease, was established a few years later. Early nineteenth-century moral welfare charities focused upon seeking penitence from prostitutes, and treating them in fairly strict fashion. The Manchester and Salford Female Penitentiary, formed in 1822, admitted 375 women in the years up to 1841, but with an estimated 1,500

---

87   *Edinburgh Medical Journal*, May 1859.

prostitutes in Manchester, it had much work to do.[88] The Female Aid Society opened a home for ex-prostitutes in Islington in the 1830s. In the 1840s, the London Moonlight Mission sent urban missionaries out onto the streets to plead with prostitutes to abandon the practice, and accept places in refuges. High Church sisterhoods formed houses of refuge and mercy in the 1850s to assist fallen women, which were linked together by the Church Penitentiary Association in 1852.

In the middle decades of the century, the tone of such work became more sympathetic, with attempts to contact prostitutes through visitation, the distribution of tracts, and late-night meetings. The Rescue Society was formed in 1853, the London Female and Reformatory Institute in 1857, and Homes of Hope in 1860. The Midnight Meeting Movement started in 1860, and the Female Mission to the Fallen, held gatherings for prostitutes, where refreshments were offered and crowds of several hundred women were urged to abandon their lifestyle.

Concern for those with Mental Illness and Learning Disabilities
Christian thinkers led the way in introducing more humane treatment for those suffering from mental illness. The Quaker William Tuke's asylum at York, pioneered treatment without the use of physical coercion. The Lunatics Act of 1845 was the beginning of modern legislation regulating the care of those with mental illness and disabilities. Behind it lay Lord Shaftesbury, who at the age of 26, after only a few months in Parliament, began to take a deep interest in the cause. He became Chairman of the Commission of Lunacy set up in 1845, and the Board of Health established in 1848, ensuring rigorous inspection of asylums, and strict medical admission procedures.

Until 1886, there was no officially recognised distinction between those with mental illness, and those with learning disabilities (mental handicaps). Pioneering work in this field was done by the Congregationalist minister Andrew Reed who in 1848 began a home in Highgate for children with severe learning difficulties. After extensive research into the issue, including visits to European care facilities, Reed became convinced that through education, physiotherapy, and occupational therapy, significant improvements in the quality of life of children were possible. He also argued that children with learning disabilities did indeed have a spiritual nature, and needed as much as others to hear the Christian message. When he opened the Earlswood Hospital near Redhill, in 1855, it was a world leader. A significant step was the appointment of Dr John Down as medical superintendent, after whom 'Down's Syndrome' is named.

Housing Reform
The way physically degrading environmental conditions sapped human

---

88   I.J. Shaw, *High Calvinists in Action*, 96–97.

potentiality was an increasing concern to Christian thinkers in the nineteenth century. In 1859, the Anglican clergyman Charles Kingsley declared, 'You may breed a pig in a sty and make a learned pig, ... but you cannot breed a man in a sty and make a learned man of him... or in any true sense of the word a man at all.'[89] The link between poor environmental conditions, immorality and crime became undeniable. In 1850, Lord Shaftesbury introduced legislation which laid down minimum standards for the lowest level of housing provision—the common lodging houses, which were usually dirty, overcrowded, and disease-ridden. He was also involved in the passing of acts allowing for the compulsory purchase and demolition of the worst housing. This dealt with the immediate problem, but without the building of replacement housing, slum residents were simply displaced, relocating the overcrowding problem elsewhere.

Some manufacturers built housing to attract and retain a stable workforce. David Dale, a member of the Scotch Independent Church, built New Lanark on the upper reaches of the River Clyde for his factory workforce of 2,000 people in 1786. New Lanark was taken over by his son-in-law Robert Owen who rejected Dale's Christian convictions and operated the village on co-operative and socialist, but strongly paternal, lines. Titus Salt, a leading manufacturer of fine woollen products, moved his workforce six miles out of the centre of Bradford to a picturesque site in the Aire Valley. A strong Congregationalist, Salt's social concern shaped his paternalistic philanthropy. He built a new factory, and housing for some 2,500 people, together with the fabric of an entire community, including a church, shops, a school, almshouses for the elderly, a public hall, an institute with reading room, library, gymnasium, a park with cricket ground, wash houses, public baths, and facilities for adult education classes A hospital and a dispensary followed. By the time Salt died in 1876, he had spent over £100,000 on the Saltaire village.[90]

CONCLUSION

In evaluating Christian responses to the industrial and urban form of Britain, the influence of other factors should not be underestimated. Utilitarianism, inspired by thinkers such as Jeremy Bentham, and J.S. Mill, was clearly highly influential in promoting social intervention. (See chapter 8) It helped shape key policies in health and sanitary reform, stressing decisions should be made upon the principle of 'utility.' On the whole, Christian responses to the new urban and industrial world tended to take the form of first aid for casualties, rather than offer fundamental criticism of the system behind the casualties. Thomas

---

89   C. Kingsley, *Sanitary and Social Lectures and Essays*, London, Macmillan, 1880, Part III.

90   See J. Reynolds, *Great Paternalist: Titus Salt and the Growth of Nineteenth Century Bradford*, London, Temple Smith, 1983.

Chalmers' comprehensive parochially-based social model was, by the middle of the nineteenth-century, outdated. The 'Christian Socialist' response to social tensions from the late 1840s onwards offered some critique of the social order, and of the individualistic nature of Christianity, (See chapter eight), but even here paternalist concerns over class-conflict and the spread of 'infidelity' remained.

The absence of a coherent, widely accepted, Christian vision of the social order meant a lack of systematic policies of social engagement towards issues such as poor factory conditions, education, the Corn Laws, temperance. For Nonconformists, Anglicans, and Roman Catholics to work together, it required an issue to be presented in terms which evoked moral outrage, allowing differences to be set aside, and common cause identified, as had happened in the campaign against slavery. But indignation could easily ebb away, to be replaced by a return to political quietism. It suggested a failure to adjust to the reality of the political world, in which a long game of compromise, half-measures, and gradualism, had to be played. This was to profoundly shape Christian political theology in Britain, and betrayed a continuing suspicion of the political process. Some Christians began to question the appropriateness of the Christendom concept in what was a very Christian society, and the propriety of pressing their system on others through the legislature.

Nonetheless, the role of Christian activity in ameliorating social need was significant. According to one writer, Wilberforce and Shaftesbury 'removed more sin and misery than any other British social reformers inside or outside Parliament.'[91] Their periodic interventions on social issues, whilst not ceding power to the oppressed, strengthened the conception that power should be used paternally, and responsibly for their betterment. After assisting with the abolition of slavery, their work in Factory Legislation and humanitarian reform helped, in the words of Charles Smyth, to heal 'the worst sores of the industrial revolution.'[92] In establishing the moral right and duty of Parliament to interfere paternally with the organisation of industry and commerce for the welfare of the citizens of the state, laissez-faire philosophy was challenged, and a significant step taken towards the creation of a welfare state. Christian paternalists were less open to measures that improved the present condition of those suffering but disregarded the eternal dimension.

Apart from periodic campaigns for government intervention, as in the United States the favoured Christian agency remained the voluntary society, hundreds

---

91   M. Hennell, *Sons of the Prophets, Evangelical Leaders of the Victorian Church*, London, SPCK, 1979, 50.

92   C. Smyth, 'The Evangelical Movement in Perspective', *Cambridge Historical Journal*, Vol. vii, no. 3, 160.

of which were formed in the nineteenth century for causes as specialised as the provision of drinking troughs for horses on the streets of London. Most had national committees, and often local auxiliaries. They were dependent on large scale benevolent giving, culminating each year with an Anniversary gathering in London. It was with some justification called 'The Age of Societies.'[93] Their significant, active agency was especially women. Prodigious numbers were engaged in regular visitation, fund raising, and the pastoral care and support of other women and children. They formed an army of Sunday-School teachers and Bible-class leaders. The social engagement of the churches in their local communities laid the foundation for future professional and statutory provision. Domestic visitation opened the way to social work, Bible nurses to district nursing, and prison gate missions and support for discharged prisoners to the probation service.

Gradually, through intense campaigning, legislative means, and the influence and activities of churches and Christian individuals, the aggressive, riotous behaviour that seemed common in the early nineteenth century, became less prevalent. Britain undoubtedly became a more stable society. Respectability became the cultural norm; family the focus of social life, and churches important social as well as religious centres. Yet questions are rightfully raised. Was too much endeavour targeted at the poor man's pleasures, and did this serve to increase their sense of alienation from the churches?[94] Illegal gambling dens were closed, but the aristocracy continued to bet lavishly at horse races; Sunday trading was stopped, but the rich still required their coachmen to drive them to church services on that day. The replacement of unruly excess, with the hypocritical behaviour that characterised some aspects of Victorian society was not an entirely attractive step.

93   J. Stephen, *Essays in Ecclesiastical Biography* (1849), London, 1907, Vol. II, 248.

94   B. Harrison, 'Religion and Recreation in Nineteenth-Century England', *Past and Present*, 38, (1967), 123–24.

FURTHER READING

D. Bebbington, *Evangelicalism in Modern Britain,* London, Unwin Hyman, 1989.

I. Bradley, *The Call to Seriousness: The Evangelical Impact on the Victorians,* London, Cape, 1976.

F.L. Brown, *The Fathers of the Victorians: The Age of Wilberforce,* Cambridge, CUP, 1961.

S.J. Brown, *Thomas Chalmers and the Godly Commonwealth in Scotland,* Oxford, OUP, 1982.

O. Chadwick, *The Victorian Church,* Vols I and II, London, Black, 1966 and 1970.

T. Chalmers, *The Christian and Civic Economy of Large Towns,* Glasgow, Chalmers and Collins, 1821–26.

G.B.A.M. Finlayson, *The Seventh Earl of Shaftesbury, 1801–1885,* London, Eyre Methuen, 1981.

K. Heasman, *Evangelicals In Action: An Appraisal of their Social Work,* London, Geoffrey Bles, 1962.

J. Roxborogh, *Thomas Chalmers: Enthusiast for Mission,* Edinburgh, Rutherford House, 1999.

J. Wolffe, *The Expansion of Evangelicalism : the Age of Wilberforce, More, Chalmers and Finney,* Leicester, IVP, 2007.

8

Revolutions in Modern Social and Political Thought: Protestant and Roman Catholic Responses

The conviction that the individual should have liberty to think and believe independently of official strictures had roots in both the Reformation and the Enlightenment. It was echoed in the watchwords of the French Revolution: liberty, equality, and fraternity. It fed into social and political ideologies which significantly shaped nineteenth and twentieth-century thinking. The advance of liberalism did not go unopposed. The events of 1789, and the aggressive exportation of revolutionary sentiment by the armies of Napoleon, provoked European governments to impose severe restrictions on political activities which appeared subversive. Yet, military campaigns are easier to win than battles of the mind. Authorities found that once religious and political concessions had been granted, such as offering civil rights to minorities like Protestant dissenters, the demands of others, such as Roman Catholics, Jews, or even, atheists, could not be long refused.

Liberalism enjoyed no formal creed. It was a set of ideas and assumptions widely disseminated in the wake of the French Revolution by lawyers, journalists, and leaders in commerce, especially by the rising middle class intelligentsia. Its stress on the autonomy of human conscience profoundly influenced nineteenth-century Europe. Liberalism meant freedom, especially from restraints. It meant constitutional and representative government, calls for free trade, easing controls on industry, and also for freedom in the market of opinion—freedom of the press, widespread education, and religious liberty. Great optimism underlay it, with a somewhat simplistic conviction as to the inevitability of progress.

These demands provoked fundamental questions about religion in Europe. How could the concept of a state church be sustained? Should there not be a free market in religion, as in everything else? To the utilitarian thinker, Jeremy Bentham, the Church of England was a remnant of the old order, using its dominant position to indoctrinate the minds of the young, maintained by corrupt systems of patronage and non-residence. He argued that Anglicanism was 'ripe for dissolution', and urged the 'euthanasia of the Church'.[1] Liberalism proved particularly popular amongst middle-class Dissenters, who won an increasing number of civil rights as the century progressed, and waged an often bitter campaign for Disestablishment in England and Scotland after 1829. Proponents argued that churches should be sustained only by the voluntary contributions of their adherents, and without state aid. However, although the logical outcome of liberal social theory was equality of political representation, the middle classes proved less than enthusiastic about sharing power with the lower orders.

Liberty of conscience, and genuine toleration, implied not only denominational pluralism, but also religious pluralism, and for some, an inevitable progression to a secular state. The Enlightenment vested confidence in the power of truth to conquer its opponents by sound argument, without the need to resort to persecution, censorship, or repression. Liberalism opened up debate as to what that 'truth' actually was, allowing liberty to disagree with and reject foundational truths. The resultant questioning of subscription to orthodox creeds and confessions led John Henry Newman to declare in 1841, 'The more serious thinkers among us are used to regard liberalism as the characteristic of the destined Antichrist.' To Pope Pius IX, in 1864, freedom to think meant freedom to doubt and disbelieve: the child of religious liberty was scepticism.[2] Charles Hodge set Princeton Theological Seminary on a determined defence of historic evangelical creedal orthodoxy, declaring in 1872, 'a new idea never originated in this Seminary.'[3] One irony was that the advance of liberalism made it possible for its opponents to gain power. Granting voting rights to the Roman Catholic majority population in Ireland, gave significant influence to a Roman Catholic Church which opposed liberalism through much of the century.

---

1 J. Bentham, *Church of England and its Catechism Examined*, London, 1818, Appendix IV, 198–99, quoted in S.J. Brown, *The National Churches of England, Ireland, and Scotland 1801–46*, Oxford, OUP, 2001, 169–170.

2 J.H. Newman, *Apologia Pro Vita Sua*, (1967 edition, ed. Svaglic), 174, and Pius IX, *Syllabus Errorum* (1864), no. 80, both quoted in O. Chadwick, *The Secularization of the European Mind*, Cambridge, Cambridge University Press, 1975, 22.

3 A.A. Hodge, *The Life of Charles Hodge*, London, T. Nelson and Sons, 1881, 521.

UTILITARIANISM

One significant expression of liberal sentiment, Utilitarianism, was formulated by Jeremy Bentham (1748–1832), the leading British philosophical radical of the early nineteenth century. Corporate social responsibility meant that the supreme end of society was to achieve the greatest happiness for the greatest number of people. Moral and ethical decisions were to be based on the principle of 'utility.' Bentham's ideas, refined and developed by others such as John Stuart Mill (1806–73), permeated the approaches of politicians, and social and religious thinkers.

The need to provide a quantitative evaluation of moral and social problems placed the collection of statistics at the heart of the utilitarian approach. Making socio-ethical decisions purely on the basis of 'facts', was bitterly satirised by Charles Dickens in his novel *Hard Times*. Thomas Gradgrind rears his children in a factual world in which there is no place for human affection, or imagination. It is a world that inevitably crashes around him. Utilitarianism offered a solution to social decision-making, but reducing social problems to moral calculus gave little sense of fellow-feeling, or community support for the vulnerable, or the needs of minorities.

Nonetheless, utilitarians were activists. They threw themselves into projects for public health and sanitary improvement, education and prison reform. This was coupled with a commitment to political economy, with its view that the state should interfere as little as possible in economic affairs, and that the market should operate freely. Social problems were seen as barriers to economic efficiency, and therefore needed removing. There were significant parallels between utilitarian policies, and those of many Christians in areas such as education, the abolition of slavery, the reform of prisons and the care

---

Utilitarianism

'Now what I want is, Facts. Teach these boys and girls nothing but Facts...You can only form the minds of reasoning animals on Facts: nothing else will ever be of any service to them.'

The scene was a plain, bare, monotonous vault of a schoolroom, and the speaker's square forefinger emphasised his observations ... The emphasis was helped by the speaker's hair, which bristled on the skirts of his bald head... all covered with knobs, like the crust of a plum pie, as if the head had scarcely warehouse room for the hard facts stored inside.[1]

1 Thomas Gradgrind in Charles Dickens, *Hard Times*, 1854, 1.

---

of those suffering from mental illness. Although each derived something from the approach of the other,[4] the rationale behind their policies was significantly different. Christians remained convinced that resolving humanity's lack of happiness could not simply be achieved by dealing with external factors.

FRATERNITY AND EQUALITY: THE RISE OF SOCIALISM AND COMMUNISM
Whilst the French Revolutionary cry of 'liberty' fed into liberalism, others asserted the claims of 'fraternity', the brotherhood of humanity. The failings of human organisations were seen to lie behind inequality, poverty, and social disorder. Only when these were dealt with, especially the worst abuses of the capitalist system, would the fullness of human potentiality and the brotherhood of humanity be achieved.

Robert Owen (1771–1858), an early British socialist, ironically made his fortune through part-ownership of the New Lanark cotton spinning mills, in Scotland. Here he extended the pattern of paternalistic, benevolent care, for the workforce that had been established by their founder, David Dale, an evangelical Christian. After Owen sold the mills, he toured Britain expounding his rationalist principles, and establishing 'Halls of Science', or 'Social Institutions.' Here lectures promoting socialism or anti-Christian themes were offered, non-religious Sunday Schools established, and temperance promoted as a way of social improvement. Owen rejected religion as superstition, and marriage as 'a Satanic device of the Priesthood to place and keep mankind within their slavish superstitions.'[5] Owenites called themselves 'Socialists,' and employed 'social missionaries,' debating the demerits of the Christian religion before public audiences. Through their work, unbelief and socialism became inseparably linked in the minds of a number of working men.

From the broader background of liberal thought came the radical social critique of Friedrich Engels and Karl Marx who formulated the doctrine of dialectical materialism, and applied it especially to politics and economics. By the middle of the twentieth century their followers were numbered in their millions. Engels (1820–95) was born into a devout middle-class German family. His childhood faith eroded, especially after reading Strauss's *Life of Jesus*, although he did not admit himself an atheist until 1842. Engels' social views were shaped through living in six European cities. His work *The Condition of the Working Class in England in 1844*, was strongly shaped by Owen's thinking, and also by two years spent in Manchester, where he observed the living and working conditions of the emerging industrial working classes. Engels argued that the only way to rid society of the inevitable abuses of the capitalist system

4   B. Hilton, *The Age of Atonement: The Influence of Evangelicalism on Social and Economic Thought 1795–1865*, Oxford, Clarendon, 1988, 245.

5   Quoted in E. Royle, *Radical Politics 1790–1900: Religion and Unbelief*, London, Longman, 1971, 42–43.

Karl Marx

was through class conflict. The existing industrial order would soon collapse and be replaced by a communist society in which rivalry between capitalists and the proletariat would disappear.[6] Although his perceptions of social conditions were distorted by being made during a period of recession, the book was widely embraced by socialists as a classic account of the evils consequent upon the

6   F. Engels, *The Condition of the Working Class in England* (translated and edited by W.O. Henderson and W.H. Chaloner), Oxford, Blackwell, 1958.

industrial revolution. One admirer was Karl Marx, with whom Engels began collaborative work after 1844.[7]

Karl Marx (1818–83) shaped socialist ideas and rhetoric into a clearly defined philosophy and ideological system. Marx's grandfather was a Jewish Rabbi, but his father converted to Protestant Christianity to obtain a post in the Prussian civil service. As a child, Marx felt alienated from the Jewish community, yet he never felt he belonged to the Christian one. He studied at the universities of Bonn and Berlin, and gained a doctorate from the University of Jena. By the age of twenty-three he had turned against all forms of religion, whether Christianity or Judaism, indeed he became strongly anti-Semitic.

The influence of Feuerbach's thought was most significant, providing a link between Hegel and Marxism. In his *Contribution to the Critique of Hegel's Philosophy of Right* in 1843, Marx depicted religion as the product of human, earthly needs, developed as a way of expressing infinite nature: 'Man makes religion, religion does not make man'. In his famous assertion: 'Religion is the sigh of the oppressed creature...It is the opium of the people...The abolition of religion as the illusory happiness of the people is required for their real happiness.'[8] Marx used Hegel's dialectical understanding of the process of change in his understanding of the progress of human history towards scientific socialism. The final radical re-ordering of society would be achieved by the overthrow of all social and economic relationships that created unhappiness, and the factors that drove people to religious illusions. Marx believed he was not attacking religion in itself, but the root problems of which it was the symptom: 'The criticism of religion is therefore *in embryo the criticism of the vale of woe*, the *halo* of which is religion.'[9] Religion was a distraction from the true response to alienation, the revolutionary task, because it preached solutions only in the hereafter. The irony of religion was that it was both a response to social needs, and also a barrier to those needs being met, an opiate dulling responses to the abuses of capitalism.

Although rejecting Christianity, Marx clearly retained an optimistic sense of purpose in history and the future. His vision for an alternative social structure also seems to have been influenced by radical Anabaptist sects who called themselves 'Christian communists,' who lived in community, and held goods in common, albeit with the social adhesive of commitment to the Christian message. Engels helped Marx draw up the *Communist Manifesto*, which contained the core elements that would make Marxism one of the great 'religions' of the twentieth century. The *Manifesto* called for communists everywhere to

7   On Engels see W. O. Henderson, *The Life of Friedrich Engels*, 2 volumes, London, Frank Cass, 1976.

8   K. Marx, *On Religion*, Moscow, n.d. p. 15, 42.

9   K. Marx, 'Contribution to the Critique of Hegel's Philosophy of Right', in K. Marx and F. Engels, *On Religion*, Moscow, Progress Publishers, 1972, 37–38, 42.

support revolutionary movements to overthrow existing social political orders, and create a classless society in which property would be owned by the state. Its closing words sent shivers through the capitalist world: 'Let the ruling classes tremble at a communist revolution. The proletarians have nothing to lose but their chains. They have a world to win. Workers of the world, unite!'[10]

When the *Manifesto* was published in 1848 it looked as if the change Marx and the Communist League called for was about to happen. In France republicans and socialists successfully toppled the monarchy of Louis Philippe, and proclaimed the Second Republic: all men were given the vote. In Italy, a Republic was also proclaimed. Mass meetings and demonstrations in Germany were followed, in March 1848, by street-fighting. Although the authorities responded with a range of liberal reforms, including an elected parliament which sat in Frankfurt, the hopes of the revolutionaries rapidly dissipated. Moderate liberals and radical democrats found agreement on policy hard to come by; the Parliament fell apart, and revolutionary governments established in parts of Germany were put down by Prussian troops. Although the French rising resulted in the election of Louis Napoleon as President of the Republic, by 1850 he had restricted the right to vote, and in 1851 declared himself emperor Napoleon III. Far from creating a dictatorship of the proletariat, the risings resulted in the installation of authoritarian régimes in France, Prussia, and Austria.

Marxism was to be the most powerful expression of growing secular attitudes across nineteenth-century Europe. In many areas the sympathy of the working classes, especially working men, towards organized religion eroded. By the 1860s and 1870s, Social Democratic activists in Germany understood the world in terms of a synthesis of Marx and Darwin: the rejection of religious beliefs as unscientific was deemed the sign of the mature intellect.[11] In France, secular liberalism attracted Jews, promising a society of equal and fair treatment, with social advance based on merit rather than professed belief. Some liberal Protestants in France progressed towards humanism, a pattern repeated in the evolution of German Free Parishes in the 1850s and 1860s. The British Labour Churches, formed after 1891, contained individuals from a range of religious backgrounds, who downplayed theological distinctives, emphasizing socialism as expressed in the Labour movement, rather than religion.[12]

The pressures of the modern world could not be ignored by the mainstream churches of Europe, but responses to the cry of liberty, fraternity, and equality, were varied. Some fought a determined rearguard action, others refused to contemplate the implications of new ways of thinking. Avoidance

---

10   See K. Marx, *The Communist Manifesto*, ed. A.J.P. Taylor, Penguin, Harmondsworth, 1967.

11   H. McLeod, *Secularisation in Western Europe, 1848–1914*, Basingstoke, Macmillan, 2000, 120.

12   McLeod, *Secularisation*, 139. On the Labour churches see S. Mayor, *The Churches and the Labour Movement*, London, Independent Press, 1967.

was unsuccessful. Some denominations split under the pressures unleashed, whilst others adjusted and accommodated, or were strengthened by embattled resistance. By the later decades of the nineteenth century, the place of Christianity in European society had changed significantly.

ROMAN CATHOLICISM AND LIBERALISM IN
NINETEENTH-CENTURY FRANCE

Many Roman Catholics saw demands for constitutions and civil liberties as a continuation of the attack of the French Revolution on religion. The fear was exacerbated by the tendency of liberals to extend calls for political reform to church reform, resistance to which led liberals to view the Roman Catholic Church as the enemy of political liberty and progress. Nonetheless, some contended that Roman Catholicism was a basis for liberty, and with it religion would thrive. Some argued that Liberal Catholicism was a positive engagement with modern society, and would win young intellectuals back to the church. Bishops blessed liberty trees and declared liberty, fraternity and equality biblical principles; even Pope Pius IX showed early sympathy. This created difficulties for John Henry Newman, who had portrayed himself and Roman Catholicism as the implacable foe of liberalism, such that he was forced to offer an explanatory note in the *Apologia* as to the attitude of European Roman Catholics.[13]

The defeat of Napoleon I brought a restoration of the Bourbon monarchy to France in the person of Louis XVIII, but the nation and church were much changed. Although the monarchy had traditionally defended the Roman Catholic Church, its restoration did not bring a return of the vast endowments lost in the revolution, nor did it end the Napoleonic concordat of 1801 that governed church-state relations. Louis XVIII proved, on the whole, wise in handling these relationships, and a revival in French Roman Catholicism followed, largely through its commitment to the basics of church life— pastoral care, worship, and the sacraments.

In 1824, Louis was succeeded by Charles X, ardent in his Roman Catholicism, and reactionary in his political views. Seeds of radicalism, rationalism and anticlericalism were well rooted in French soil after 1789, and when revolution broke out in July 1830, seeking to return France to the ideals of liberty, equality, and fraternity, Charles X abdicated. The church was again seen as overly dominant, and Roman Catholic bishops suspected of being too strong in their support for the monarchy. Pope Pius VIII acted swiftly to defuse the situation by recognising the new regime of Louis-Philippe, although it was seven years before the Archbishop of Paris could be reconciled to the new order. Roman Catholicism was acknowledged by the new constitutional charter as the religion

---

13   Newman, *Apologia*, 284–85, note 1 to 1865 edition.

of most French people, but no longer the religion of the state. Its clergy, along with those of other denominations, continued to be paid by the State.[14]

Two very different reactions to the new political context in France emerged. From the 1830s onwards Liberal Catholics, Catholic democrats, social Catholics, and Catholic Socialists sought to embrace the advances of liberalism. Others endorsed a strong anti-modernist agenda, with an increase in ultramontane devotion, appeal to traditional Roman Catholic doctrines with a high veneration for the papacy, and defence of Roman Catholic schools and religious orders.

Whilst not the founder of Liberal Catholicism, Félicité de Lamennais (1782–1854) was a key figure in its development. Lamennais became disappointed with the role played by the monarchy in the years after its restoration. He began to argue that the church should be freed from royal control, and instead look to the papacy for leadership. Ultramontane attachment to the papacy and tradition became attached to a liberal interest in freedom and liberty, which would allow the church spiritual freedom in its mission.

Lamennais took advantage of the revolution of 1830, which brought reforms including freedom of the press, to launch the paper *L'Avenir* (The Future) with his associates Henri Lacordaire (1802–61), a young priest, and Charles Montalembert (1810–70), a young peer. They argued, against reactionary and ideologically conservative Roman Catholics, that a reconciliation between the modern world and Roman Catholicism was possible. The paper, called for separation between Church and State, believing that a free church, in a free state with liberty of conscience, was possible. Truth was capable of standing on its own merits, without state support or restriction. *L'Avenir*, which ran only until 1831, took as its motto 'God and Liberty,' out of the conviction that the Roman Catholic Church would not only benefit from political liberty but also become the agent of it: the doctrine of the rights of man had Christian foundations. The papacy was urged to lead a movement for moral and spiritual regeneration rooted in support for constitutional liberty.[15]

Although the paper never sold widely, Lamennais' work attracted great interest in Belgium, Italy, Poland, Germany and England. Within France, the Roman Catholic Church, reacted negatively to the writings of a priest with sympathy for Liberalism, fearful that its progress might be de-stabilised. In November

14   On post-1830 religion in France see A. Dansette, *Religious History of Modern France*, trans. J. Dingle, 2 vols, New York, Nelson, 1961; E. Berenson, *Populist Religion and Left-Wing Politics in France, 1830–1985*, Princeton, New Jersey, Princeton University Press, 1984; R. Gibson, *A Social History of French Catholicism, 1789–1914*, London, Routledge, 1989.

15   R. Grew, 'Liberty and the Catholic Church in Nineteenth-Century Europe', in ed. R. Helmstadter, *Freedom and Religion in the Nineteenth Century*, Stanford, Stanford University Press, 1997, 196–211.

1831, with the paper almost bankrupt, and labouring under severe criticism from both the French government and Roman Catholic hierarchy, a final unsuccessful appeal for support was made to Pope Gregory XVI. The papacy, struggling to win allies in its campaign to keep the Papal States, responded to this attempted marriage of Roman Catholicism and Liberalism with hostility. In August 1832, the papal Encyclical *Mirari Vos* condemned the 'unbridled lust for freedom,' together with separation of Church and State. Lamennais and his two associates, without retracting their views, dutifully issued a statement of submission to the Pope. In the following years he gradually drew away from the church, looking for social regeneration through democracy, republicanism, and socialism, rather than the church. He served for a short period after 1848 in the republican government, but later withdrew, disillusioned with politics. He insisted that there be no religious signs at his funeral, and that he be buried in an unmarked pauper's grave.

Henri Lacordaire continued to argue that both 'liberal' and ultramontane values could be upheld. After the failure of *L'Avenir,* he went on to re-found the Dominican order in France, returning it to its original emphasis on preaching and teaching, but in a manner suited to the modern, industrial age. His intellectual, yet passionate, preaching in Paris was widely acclaimed—a Lent sermon at Notre Dame Cathedral in 1835 was reportedly attended by 6,000 people. Although a monarchist, he believed that if French people wanted a democratic republic, it remained possible to be a Roman Catholic and a loyal citizen. He was even prepared to allow himself to be elected a representative in the constituent assembly after the 1848 revolution, still wearing his Dominican habit, although the assembly lasted for only eleven days.[16]

Those who were religiously Roman Catholic and politically Liberal called for the Church to work in freedom in a society where the government was now effectively non-Christian. They demanded that Roman Catholic schools should operate freely and independently of the State system established under Napoleon Bonaparte. When the revolution of February 1848 swept away the regime of 1830, the Archbishop of Paris quickly gave his support to the new order, and clergy were treated with respect. However, during a violent proletarian uprising in Paris in June 1848, the Archbishop was killed before the insurrection was ruthlessly suppressed by the government. Out of the chaos emerged the dictatorial rule of Napoleon Bonaparte's nephew, Louis Napoleon, who was initially elected President of the new Republic. After a *coup d'état* in 1851, the second Empire was proclaimed, and he ruled as Emperor.

---

16   On Lacordaire see L.C. Sheppard, *Lacordaire: A Biographical Essay*, New York, Macmillan, 1964. His preaching is discussed in H.O. Old, *The Reading and Preaching of the Scriptures in the Worship of the Christian Church: Vol. 6, The Modern Age*, Grand Rapids, MI, Eerdmans, 2007, 8–18.

Roman Catholics struggled with the legitimacy of his rule, but they deemed his conservatism preferable to the radical republicans. For its support the Roman Catholic Church was rewarded with freedoms which helped it to prosper in the 1850s and 1860s. The number of monks and nuns burgeoned from 37,000 in 1851 to over 106,000 in 1861, and 162,000 in 1901. Many religious orders ran primary and secondary schools. New churches were built, and numbers of priests increased. The French Church became the driving force in Roman Catholic overseas mission. Religious education was maintained in public schools.[17]

Bitter disagreement between French ultramontanes and Liberal Catholics remained. The former deemed faith and reason utterly incompatible. All forms of modern thought and philosophy were to be rejected, in the hope of better days for traditional Roman Catholicism. Liberal Catholicism proved attractive to a group of intellectuals, but failed to win a widespread following amongst the lower clergy. Despite the rising tide of democratic reform, Ultramontanism moved into the ascendancy.

Defeat at the hands of the Prussians in 1870 brought the fall of Louis Napoleon as emperor, and the advent of the Third Republic. France moved in an increasingly anti-clerical direction, with a series of laws in the 1880s gradually reducing the role of Roman Catholicism in society. Although France still contained the largest body of Roman Catholics in Europe, many became nominal in their adherence, and public demonstrations of religion could be subject to violent protests. Significant numbers of working men became alienated from the church, convinced that Christianity was bad for society. The *ralliement*, attempts in the early 1890s to reconcile the Roman Catholic Church with the Republic, failed. The distrust of republicanism amongst Roman Catholics was deeply ingrained.

Increasing secularist tendencies were shown by the Republican government of France, especially in the realm of education. After 1902 religious schools began to be closed, and in 1904 monks and nuns were stopped from teaching activities, although ex-monks and ex-nuns were allowed to continue. Traditional religious expressions were prohibited in public schools. In 1905, the Concordat with the Pope, the Organic articles, and the religious settlements with the Protestants and Jews were abolished. Roman Catholicism, no longer the official religion of France, was not even acknowledged as the religion of the majority of French people. Church and State were separated: the Church in France, the eldest daughter of Rome, was effectively disestablished. Although the Pope had absolute freedom to choose bishops for the French Church, its property was sequestered by the State. Church buildings were legally 'owned' by the local communes, who then permitted the congregations to use them for

17   Chadwick, *History of the Popes*, 94–104; 161–6.

worship.[18] Between 1830 and 1908, under the pressure of the modern Liberal agenda, France had completed the transition, begun in 1789, from a state closely bound to the Roman Catholic Church, to a largely secular state.[19]

WIDER EUROPEAN ROMAN CATHOLICISM AND THE ADVANCE OF LIBERALISM

In France, Liberal Catholics had argued that Liberalism was not only compatible with Roman Catholicism, but could prove beneficial to it. Elsewhere, the rise of liberal political thought, with its emphasis on the equality of all citizens, helped remove legislation that discriminated against Roman Catholics. In Belgium an alliance of Liberals and Roman Catholics helped to win independence from Holland. The free Belgian constitution, a model for liberal Roman Catholics in the nineteenth century, gave considerable freedoms to the Roman Catholic Church, allowing it to open schools, and granted the Pope freedom to select bishops. In the United States, Roman Catholicism prospered in a context of political and religious freedom. Roman Catholic Emancipation in Britain afforded Roman Catholicism significant opportunity for advance: Daniel O'Connell, a campaigner for political liberty in Ireland, was a strong Roman Catholic. Liberty appeared good for religion, and O'Connell argued that liberal Roman Catholicism was a positive and healthy way to engage with society.

However, hopes that the papacy would widely endorse liberal Roman Catholicism were disappointed. Bible societies, other than Roman Catholic ones, were condemned, Roman Catholic theologians, especially in Germany, who sought to engage with Enlightenment thinking, and propose practical and theological reform, were strongly opposed, and their works banned. Pope Gregory and his successors became convinced that liberalism was an insidious cancer within society, spreading atheism, and overturning the established social order. There followed a full-scale campaign of resistance to the challenges of the modern liberal socio-political agenda.

The 'Catholic Revival' of the middle decades of the nineteenth century brought changes to the tone of Roman Catholicism across Europe. Attendance at confession and the mass increased in frequency, to become weekly, or even daily. There was renewed interest in the lives of the saints and the miracles associated with them, the Pope was subject to increased veneration, and the Marian focus in piety increased, with greater use of the rosary. Penitential devotion became more pronounced. Roman Catholic societies, known as

---

18 On church and state in late nineteenth century France see Chadwick, *History of the Popes*, 290–301; 377–402; R. Gibson, *A Social History of French Catholicism*, London, Routledge, 1989.

19 C.T. McIntyre, 'Changing Religious Establishments and Religious Liberty in France, Part I 1787–1879, and Part II, 1879–1908', in ed. R. Helmstadter, *Freedom and Religion in the Nineteenth Century*, Stanford, Stanford University Press, 1997, 232–301.

confraternities, sodalities, or guilds, became a feature of this devotional revival, allowing the laity to participate more fully in religious life by focussing on a particular devotional practice. Evidence suggests that a more inclusive pattern of personal and family devotion emerged, with greater opportunities for women to participate. Unsophisticated, sentimental, and eclectic it may have been, but it had tremendous folk appeal. Roman Catholic life was increasingly lived separately from that of non-Roman Catholics, especially as a result of its educational policies. Withdrawal from policies of assimilation into ultramontane, or 'Italianate,' devotion encouraged what has been termed the Catholic 'ghetto'.[20] One by-product of this was increased suspicion of Roman Catholics and a growth of anti-Roman Catholic feeling.

How much this reviving of Roman Catholic spiritual and devotional practice was the conscious policy of a politically weak and defensive Vatican, striving for some alternative expression of tangible unity, remains unclear. At times the papacy itself struggled to keep up with the pace of devotional change, which was fuelled by improved communication, and extensive publication networks which spread devotional products and literature rapidly.[21]

ROMAN CATHOLICISM AND THE ADVANCE OF LIBERALISM IN ITALY

The continued existence of the Papal States appeared a symbol of the failure of the papacy to adapt to the modern world, and an obstacle to attempts to unify Italy into a nation. These territories allowed the Papacy to preserve its independence from secular rulers, although they often caused popes to act in similar fashion to them. In 1846, a known supporter of liberal movements for a democratic federation of Italian states, was elected pope. The fifty-five year old Cardinal Giovanni Maria Mastai-Ferretti took the name Pius IX,[22] and set up a consultative assembly with lay representatives to help him govern the papal states, and added an elected municipal government in Rome.[23] He introduced railways to the papal states, gas street-lighting to Rome, and an amnesty for political prisoners.

Pius IX, or Pio Nono as he was widely known, regularly preached, visited schools and hospitals, and celebrated the Mass in out-of-the-way churches and chapels. He was publicly applauded wherever he went, although some feared he was unleashing forces that could not be restrained. Then in 1848, revolution

---

20   H. McLeod, *Religion and the People of Western Europe*, 36.

21   M. Heiman, 'Catholic Revivalism in Worship and Devotion', in ed. S. Gilley and B. Stanley, *The Cambridge History of Christianity: Volume 8; World Christianities, c. 1815–c.1914*, Cambridge, Cambridge University Press, 2006, 70–83.

22   On Pius IX see E. Duffy, *Saints and Sinners: The History of the Popes*, Yale, New Haven, 1997, 220–235; O. Chadwick, *History of the Popes*, Oxford, OUP, 2003, 132–273.

23   On the role of Catholicism in Italian nationalism see Chapter 12.

broke out in Italy. Rome became ungovernable, and when republican armies overran the Papal States, Pius IX fled. The revolution was put down with the help of French and Austrian troops, and Pius returned, but scarred by the experience. His interest in liberalism was replaced by outright opposition. Pius now saw himself as called to make the last heroic stand of Christian civilisation against atheism and rebellion against the rule of God.

Pius sought to counter the claims of the modern world by working for a conservative Roman Catholic renewal across Europe. He created over 200 new bishops or apostolic vicariates, and approved seventy-four new religious orders for women. In 1850 he made the controversial decision to restore the Roman Catholic hierarchy to England, appointing bishops with territorial titles, a move which provoked fierce Protestant resistance, as did a similar action in the Netherlands in 1853. Responding to Roman Catholics who argued for the need to build bridges between the Roman Catholic Church and democracy, Pius issued his *Syllabus of Errors* in 1864. Eighty 'errors' were condemned as incompatible with the Roman Catholic faith, including rationalism, socialism, communism, freemasonry, and Bible Societies. In a determined retrenchment against the forces of the Enlightenment and liberalism, it was declared impossible that a pope should ever reconcile himself to the most 'pernicious errors of the day'—'progress, liberalism and modern civilization'. Although it was prompted by events close at hand in Italy, the wider implications were great. Rome was inundated with protests from across Europe. The book was banned in France, a country closely allied to the papacy, and publicly burned in Naples. Many Roman Catholics sympathetic to liberalism left the church. John

---

SYLLABUS OF ERRORS (1864)

Propositions declared as Errors included that:

41. In the case of a conflict between the law of the two powers [civil and sacred], civil law prevails...

44. The civil authority may mix itself up in matters which appertain to religion, moral and spiritual rule. Hence it can exercise judgement. Concerning those instructions which the Church's pastors issue according to their office for the guidance of consciences.

56. The laws of morality need no divine sanction, and there is no necessity that human laws be conformed to the law of nature, or receive from God their obligatory force'

80. The Roman Pontiff can and ought to reconcile and harmonize himself with progress, with liberalism and with modern civilization'[1]

---

1   The Dublin Review, Vol. IV, 1865, 516–529, in J.F. Maclear, *Church and State in the Modern age : a Documentary History,* Oxford : Oxford University Press, 1995, 163–168.

Henry Newman believed that the Roman Catholic Church was presenting itself in a way that confirmed the worst prejudices of his countrymen against her, making their conversion all the harder.[24]

Yet Pius IX remained immensely attractive to Roman Catholics, a man of great personal courage and humour, a focal point for the defence of Roman Catholicism against threats from modernity and Protestantism. Ultramontane devotion involved an emotional, almost mystical veneration for the Italian Pope 'beyond the mountains,' to whom unconditional obedience was offered. Pictures of Pius were as popular as crucifixes or statues of the Virgin Mary, and Roman Catholics flocked to Rome to venerate him. In 1854, his enthusiasm for devotion to the Virgin Mary led to the issuing of a formal definition of her Immaculate Conception. A product of the Roman Catholic tradition of the development of doctrine, rather than arising from the Biblical text, Pius IX asserted that, when conceived, Mary had been preserved from original sin. The step also reflected changes taking place in the nature and understanding of the papacy, being proclaimed on the Pope's sole authority rather than as the result of a council of the church. Events at Lourdes in the French Pyrenees in 1858 placed the seal of approval from the Roman Catholic laity for the teaching. Here the fourteen-year-old Bernadette Soubirous reported seeing visions of Mary declaring herself 'I am the Immaculate Conception.' Lourdes quickly developed into the largest pilgrimage site of modern Roman Catholicism.

In 1869–1870, with Italian troops about to end the last vestiges of papal temporal power, ultramontane sentiment reached its pinnacle. A General Council of the Roman Church, usually referred to as the First Vatican Council, was convened. If the Council of Trent was a work of Counter-Reformation, Vatican I was a work of Counter-Enlightenment.[25] The humiliating loss of papal political influence was countered with the highest ever statement of papal spiritual authority, although supporters argued that the doctrine had been around since the Middle Ages. The council accepted a declaration of the Pope's primacy of jurisdiction over every national church and over every individual Roman Catholic, a step which significantly eroded the authority and independence of local bishops. It was further decreed that *ex cathedra* decisions, those made when the Pope was officially fulfilling his role as pastor and teacher of the Roman Catholic Church, on matters of faith or morals were infallible and unchangeable of themselves. Previously this had been understood only of decisions made by an ecumenical council. Although many of the 700 bishops who attended were deeply opposed to this, and the debates keenly argued, their affection for Pius meant that rather than appear disloyal they left Rome before the vote. In the end, 535 voted in favour of the declaration and only two against. A small number of

---

24   W. Ward, *The Life of John Henry Newman*, 2 vols., London, Longmans, Green, 1912, vol. 1, 14.

25   H. Küng, *Christianity: Its Essence and History*, London, SCM, 1995, 512.

The Promulgation of The Infallibility of The Pope

'The Roman Church has the pre-eminence of ordinary authority over all others, and that this authority of jurisdiction of the Bishop of Rome, which is truly Episcopal, is direct: to it the pastors and faithful of every rite and rank... are obligated in hierarchical submission and true obedience ... This is the teaching of the Catholic truth, from which no one can deviate without harm to faith and salvation.... If the Bishop of Rome speaks *ex cathedra*, in other words if he decides, in exercising his office as pastor and teacher of all Christians by virtue of his supreme apostolic authority, that a doctrine of the faith is to be maintained by the whole church, then, by means of the divine support promised him in blessed Peter, he possesses that infallibility with which the divine Redeemer willed to see his church equipped, in which the definitions by the Bishop of Rome are of themselves unalterable, and are not based on the assent of the church.

If anyone—which God forbid—should undertaken to contradict this our definition: let him be excluded.'[1]

1   *Constitution Pastor aeturnus of the First Vatican Council, 18 July 1870*, quoted in H. Küng, Christianity: Its Essence and History, London, SCM, 1995, 515.

Swiss, German and Dutch Roman Catholics felt so strongly about the measure that they broke away from the Roman Catholic Church, to become the 'Old Catholics'. Others, who likened the infallibility of the pope to that of Jesus Christ, and believed that when the pope 'thinks, it is God who is thinking in him,' were disappointed that infallibility was not taken further and declared to rest in the pope himself, or in his general teaching.[26] Since 1870, only one papal statement has been deemed 'infallible'—the definition of the bodily Assumption of Mary into heaven, set out in 1950. Nonetheless, it was still a striking development— even a General Council of the Church could not alter a decision of the Pope. To Newman, Roman Catholics were 'shrinking into themselves'.[27] The assertion of papal authority was used to justify the *Kulturkampf* in Germany, which sought to restrict the freedoms of indigenous Roman Catholics.

Heightened papal spiritual power stood in contrast to disappearing political authority. Within two months of the declaration of the doctrine, the troops of Victor Emmanuel took over Rome. Papal political jurisdiction was restricted to the Vatican, and the country residence of Castel Gandolfo. Pius never again set foot outside his territory, attracting popular sympathy as the 'prisoner of

---

26   C. Butler, *The Vatican Council*, London, Collins, 1962, 303; K. Schatz, *Vaticanum I, 1869–70*, 3 vols, Paderborn, Schöningh, 1992–94.

27   Küng, *Christianity*, 506–508; Gilley, *Newman and His Age*, 344.

the Vatican.' Pius died in 1878, ending a thirty-two year pontificate during which Roman Catholicism had changed out of all recognition. Traditionalism and Ultramontanism left no room for compromise with modern liberal and national notions.

Leo XIII, Pius's successor, although remaining conservative and highly authoritarian, showed a more open attitude towards liberal freedom and democracy, although he believed that political forms were relatively unimportant. He also firmly resisted advances in biblical and theological scholarship. His 1891 encyclical *Rerum novarum cupidi* ('Desirous of new things'), coming forty-three years after the publication of the *Communist Manifesto,* set out the challenges posed for the church by industrial society, and articulated the social and ethical dimensions of Roman Catholicism. Communism and socialism were rejected because they denied the God-given right to own property, damaged the family, and encouraged class warfare. However, the excesses of capitalism were also condemned, and Roman Catholics were challenged to help workers seek a living wage and decent working conditions. The right for labour to organise into trade unions was accepted, although strikes were to be avoided. The preference for a democratic form of government was not deemed in breach of Roman Catholic duty. However, another door, this time to Anglican hopes for re-union with Rome, appeared to be firmly shut with the encyclical *Apostolicae Curae* (1896). The ordinations of Anglican clergy were declared as invalid, and Roman Catholicism presented as the only true representative of Western Christianity. Hopes for Christian reunion were vested in all churches submitting to Rome.

By 1900, Roman Catholicism which had been humiliated by the forces of liberalism in the years after 1789, was left weaker in the temporal realm, but far stronger in the religious. In resisting the cry of 'liberty, equality, fraternity,' which appeared part of a wholesale attempt to undermine religion, the Roman Catholic Church found considerable strength.

PROTESTANT RESPONSES IN BRITAIN TO MODERN POLITICAL THOUGHT
Whilst Roman Catholicism largely succeeded in maintaining structural and spiritual unity in the face of advancing liberal challenges, Protestant churches in Britain were less successful. Although the full achievement of popular democracy had to wait until the twentieth century, the government was wise enough to make gradual concessions of power, especially to the middle classes, during the nineteenth. Measures such as the removal of the Test and Corporation Acts in 1828, the granting of Roman Catholic Emancipation in 1829, and the passing of the Reform Act in 1832, opened the way towards a more religiously representative and democratically elected Parliament. With political liberalism advancing, and rising opportunities for democratic representation within the British state, demands increased for the internal politics of churches and denominations to reflect such changes. Resistance from denominational

authorities to such claims meant that the first half of the nineteenth century was a period of notable division within major Protestant churches.

DIVISIONS AND DISRUPTION

John Wesley retained a strongly controlling hand over the Methodist movement until his death in 1791, although the 'Deed of Declaration' in 1784 had appointed a 'Conference' of one hundred preachers to oversee the movement, and maintain a continuity of doctrine and practice. Methodism excluded the laity from its governing body, and sought to resist the rising democratic sentiment of the time, provoking a series of major conflicts.[28] In 1795, the itinerant preacher Alexander Kilham expressed the frustration of a growing number of Methodists, who often possessed higher levels of education than their preachers, and significant financial resources, when he questioned: 'Is it not strange that any sect or party should refuse to give their brethren what the laws of the country so cheerfully allow?'[29] He protested over a number of issues including the lack of lay involvement in circuit meetings, district meetings, and the Conference of Preachers. The Methodist Conference of 1796 disagreed, and fearful that Methodists were being infected with the principles of the French Revolution and the sentiments of Tom Paine, expelled Kilham. Although he died two years later, by 1805 his Methodist New Connexion had 84 chapels.

Jabez Bunting (1779–1858), who controlled the Wesleyan Conference in authoritarian fashion in the early nineteenth century, determinedly resisted those who refused to conform to the rule of local societies, or sought a less structured system with more opportunities for charismatic leaders.[30] His famous declaration, 'Methodism is as much opposed to democracy as it is to sin,'[31] reflected the distance between the Methodist leadership and the aspirations of many of its members. Groups dissented from the leadership's position over issues as diverse as politics and education, attitudes towards Anglicanism, temperance, and even the installation of a church organ. The largest break-away group were the Primitive Methodists, who by 1850 numbered 104,762. The secessions of the Wesleyan Methodist Association, and the Wesleyan Reform movement, resulted in a vast haemorrhaging of members from Wesleyan

---

28   On the Methodist secessions see J.T. Wilkinson, 'The Rise of Other Methodist Traditions', in R. Davies, A.R. George, G. Rupp (eds), *A History of the Methodist Church in Great Britain*, Vol. 2, London, Epworth, 1978; D.A. Gowland, *Methodist Secession*, Manchester, Chetham Society, 1979.

29   A. Kilham, *The Progress of Liberty Amongst the People Called Methodists*, Alnwick, 1795, 19.

30   Fine studies of Methodism in the nineteenth century are to be found in David Hempton's books, *Methodism and Politics in British Society 1750–1850*, Hutchinson, London, 1984; and *The Religion of the People: Methodism and Popular Religion, c. 1750–1900*, London, Routledge, 1996.

31   T.P. Bunting and G.S. Rowe, *The Life of Jabez Bunting*, London, Longman, 1887, 472.

Methodism—100,000 were lost in 1849–50 alone. Nonetheless, despite the divisions, the Wesleyans remained, on the whole, a growing movement, in the nineteenth century.[32]

Presbyterianism in Scotland was also riven by dissension, culminating in the events of 1843. In 1690, the Church of Scotland had formally become Presbyterian, after over a century of bitter conflict. In the eighteenth-century, in the enlightenment context of deepening interest in individual rights, the exercise of patronage, which had been restored to the Scottish Established church in 1712, fell under question. This gave the right to a lay patron, usually a wealthy landowner, member of the aristocracy, or the crown, to appoint a minister to a local parish. However, possibly 86% of the nobility and landed classes, the ranks from which most patrons were drawn, were not even Presbyterians, but Episcopalians. The eighteenth-century secessions that led to the formation of the Associate Presbytery (1733), and the Relief Church (1761) arose largely from disputes over patronage. When they merged to form the United Presbyterian Church in 1847, they numbered around a third of Scottish Presbyterians.

Within the Established Church of Scotland, pressures continued to grow, fuelled by conflict between the Moderate and Evangelical parties over issues that were largely, although not solely, theological. When the Evangelical party achieved a majority in the General Assembly of the Church of Scotland in 1834 they passed a series of reforming measures. This raised fundamental questions about whether ultimate control in the church rested with the members, the presbyteries, the General Assembly, and ultimately 'the sole Headship of the Lord Jesus over his Church', or whether it rested with the patrons, or even the civil courts. The Veto Act, passed in 1834, allowed congregations to block a patron from appointing ministers of whom they disapproved, often on theological grounds. Some patrons viewed this as a popular libertarian attack on their authority, and as rebellion against the civil law. The 1834 Chapels Act sought to produce a more flexible parochial system, allowing chapels-of-ease (extension chapels) to enjoy full parochial status, and increasing the supply of churches and parishes, especially in Scotland's growing urban areas.

In the wider political context of a reforming Whig government beginning to dismantle the powers of ancient ruling monopolies and oligarchies, conflict became inevitable. The new Acts were not only challenged in the General Assembly, but also in the highest civil court in Scotland, the Court of Session, and ultimately the House of Lords.[33] In the resulting legal decisions, the civil

32 D. Hempton, *Religion and Political Culture in Britain and Ireland from the Glorious Revolution to the Decline of Empire*, Cambridge, CUP, 1996, p.27.

33 The Ten Years' Conflict before the Disruption of 1843 is set out in R. Buchanan, *The Ten Years' Conflict*, 2 vols, Glasgow, 1852.

Disruption—Claim of Right

'This Church, highly valuing... her connection... with the State... [must] persevere in maintaining her liberties as a Church of Christ...

THEREFORE, the General Assembly, while... they fully recognise the absolute jurisdiction of the Civil Courts in relation to all matters whatsoever of a civil nature... CLAIM, as of RIGHT, that she shall freely possess and enjoy her liberties, government, discipline, rights and privileges according to law... and that she shall be protected therein from the foresaid unconstitutional and illegal encroachments of the said Court of Session.'¹

1 *The Principal Acts of the General Assembly of the Church of Scotland, Convened at Edinburgh, May 19, 1842,* Edinburgh, 1842, 35–48.

---

courts affirmed their right to overrule the internal decisions of the church, and patrons were granted consent to act regardless of the conscientious objections of congregations. The rulings were of immense significance: the precedence of civil law above church law was something even the pope was to protest against in 1864. In 1842, the General Assembly responded with its Claim of Right, declaring that the Court of Session was forcing ministers to act contrary to the Word of God, the standards of the Church, and 'the dictates of their consciences.'[34] Huge crowds turned out to hear 'Non-intrusion' preachers. The ultimate crisis was precipitated by both the failure of the government to understand the nature and the gravity of the situation and intervene, and the loss of the Evangelical Majority in the General Assembly, in part a consequence of the court rulings. The Disruption of 1843 saw 474 out of 1195 ministers leave the Church of Scotland. Their leader, Thomas Chalmers, declared 'we quit a vitiated Establishment and would rejoice in returning to a pure one.'[35] Secession was a remarkable step for someone who had previously stoutly defended the principle of Establishment. The cause attracted huge popular support: somewhere between a third and a half of the membership of the Church of Scotland joined the new parallel church structure, free of court and state intervention, the Church of Scotland 'Free.' Its strength was particularly in the urban lowlands, amongst the upper working class and lower middle class, but there was also strong support in rural areas, particularly in the Highlands. Here there was deep resentment against landlords who had forcibly removed families from their lands in the

34 'The Claim of Right', in *The Principal Acts of the General Assembly of the Church of Scotland, Convened at Edinburgh, May 19, 1842,* Edinburgh, 1842, 35–48.

35 On the Disruption see S.J. Brown, *Thomas Chalmers and the Godly Commonwealth in Scotland,* Oxford, 1982; S.J.Brown and M. Fry, *Scotland in the Age of the Disruption,* Edinburgh, 1993.

Highland clearances, coupled with considerable evangelical strength as a result of extensive missionary work. Within ten years the Free Church of Scotland had 850 congregations and 760 ministers.

The Disruption was fuelled by rising liberal political sentiment, with its demand for extension of popular democracy into the church. It also awakened elements of Scottish nationalist sentiment. The rising wealth and educational attainments of the growing middle class was a strong factor, as was the fundamental division between the old elite gentry and professional families, and upwardly mobile commercial and industrial families. It was also a dimension of the upturn in evangelical sentiment in Scotland, boosted by the religious revivals of 1839–40, and provoked a deepened commitment to both evangelisation and mission, and to the defence of Biblical orthodoxy. This deepened the conviction that the Church of Christ should have both leadership and forms of governance decided by spiritual convictions, not by politics or expedience. The Disruption effectively ended the Scottish Presbyterian Establishment. In 1851, the Church of Scotland attracted less than a third of Scotland's churchgoers, seemingly incapable of adapting to the pressures of the modern world.

MODERNITY AND TRADITION: THE OXFORD MOVEMENT
During significant parts of the nineteenth century, the capacity of the Church of England to withstand the forces of popular liberal sentiment was also severely tested. The demands of the non-intrusionists for spiritual autonomy for the Scottish church bore parallels to those from the Oxford Movement in the Church of England, although the theological differences between the two groups were profound.

By 1832, the establishment status quo of the *ancien régime* in England was over. Emancipation for Dissenters and Roman Catholics, and then the Reform Act, broke the tightly knit monopoly on power held by a small group from the landed classes, high ranking merchantile families and the established church clergy. This elite had controlled institutions from Parliament to the civil service, the armed forces, the magistracy, the system of social relief, and the churches, through the exercise of lay patronage. When the 1835 Municipal Reform Act gave further opportunities for Dissenters in local government, many accepted them with alacrity.

Free Trade thinking, and utilitarian philosophy, made the existence of an established Church in England an increasing anomaly. The likelihood of the state undertaking major reform in the Church of England brought a number of leading Anglican thinkers at Oxford University to a point of crisis. Oxford began to see itself as the conscience of the church, a bastion for the defence of the orthodoxy and independence of the church against political interference.

In the early nineteenth century, the Anglican High Church party, led by the Hackney Phalanx,[36] viewed the Church of England as part of the universal Catholic Church, its bishops standing in a line of apostolic succession, although the Roman Catholic Church itself was viewed as being filled with false, superstitious practices. Protestant clergy without episcopal ordination were deemed of lower status, if not true clergy at all. The supremacy of scripture was affirmed, but High Churchmen believed it was to be interpreted by means of the Prayer Book, the Catechism and the Creeds. Their deep, often mystical, spirituality emphasised holiness, and distrusted anything that deviated from establishment religious practice, or was suggestive of either Calvinism or emotionalism. This produced hostility towards evangelicalism. Anglicans who were willing to co-operate in any way with Protestant Dissenters were subject to severe censure.[37] High Churchmen believed it was the duty of the state to promote the interests of the Established Church, and for the Established Church to make the state religious.

The Oxford Movement, therefore, built on forces that were already at play within Anglicanism. Its influence spread far beyond Oxford students and Anglican clergy to the educated classes. It counted amongst its supporters a future Prime Minister, W.E. Gladstone. The movement deeply divided the university authorities, for, as with the campaigns of the evangelical Clapham Sect, it involved those who were by nature conservative acting in a radical way. It sought a second Reformation in England, purging the Established church of Protestant innovations, and restoring its traditional Roman Catholic faith and practice, particularly as expressed in the medieval period. It was a movement promoted through the preaching of sermons, the delivery of lectures, the exertion of personal influence, the writing of letters. The publication of tracts aimed at the clergy and educated in society was a key tactic, giving the movement one of its names—Tractarianism. The result has been likened to a civil war within the Anglican Church, understood by Tractarian leaders as a profound battle between, not only Protestantism and Roman Catholicism, but also faith and doubt, religion and the forces of secular liberalism.[38]

36 The High Church party had existed within the Church of England from the time of Archbishop William Laud in the early seventeenth century. It had in the eighteenth century defended theological orthodoxy in the face of the abandonment of Trinitarian doctrine by some, and the adoption of Latitudinarianism by others. Latitudinarianism was the willingness to tolerate a range of theological alternatives, and a refusal to be dogmatic on any particular issue.

37 On the High Church Party see P. Nockles, *The Oxford Movement in Context: Anglican High Churchmanship 1760–1857*, Cambridge, CUP, 1994; and P. Nockles, 'Church Parties in the Pre-Tractarian Church of England 1750–1833: The 'Orthodox'—Some Problems of Definition and Identity', in J. Walsh, C. Haydon, S. Taylor (eds), *The Church of England c. 1689–c. 1833: From Toleration to Tractarianism*, Cambridge, CUP, 1993.

38 *Christian Reformer*, n.s.7 (1840), 382, in F. Turner, *John Henry Newman: The Challenge to Evangelical Religion*, New Haven, Yale, 2002, 2, 6.

Whilst being a movement for renewal, the Oxford Movement was also a response to an impending sense of crisis—its cry was 'The Church in Danger'. Everything seemed set against the Church of England, with the emancipation of Dissenters and Roman Catholics granted by, of all people, a Tory government, and then further revolution in Paris in 1830. In 1833, the Whig government, introduced much needed legislation for the reform of the Church of Ireland, in which twenty-two bishops oversaw 1,200 parishes, in some of which there were no Protestant adherents at all. In contrast, the diocese of Lincoln had just one bishop for the same number of parishes. The government proposed to reduce the number of Irish bishops by ten, to re-distribute income, and to re-organise parishes to reflect the areas where Protestants were found. Between 1835 and 1836 an Ecclesiastical Commission established by the government introduced reforms to the Anglican Church itself, reducing pluralism and the non-residence of clergy. The Anglican Church emerged leaner, and fitter, and more able to rebut the criticisms of those who called for its disestablishment. Nonetheless, the measures spoke only to the Tractarian leaders of political interference in the affairs of the church. The faith, liturgy and property of the Church of England appeared in peril.

Oxford in the 1820s had become a place for serious study, and lively intellectual debate. There was renewed understanding of the Anglican Church as a spiritual body, charged with elevating the whole of society. Of all the Oxford colleges, Oriel stood in the intellectual vanguard. Here gathered a group of brilliant scholars, Keble, Newman, Pusey, and Richard Hurrell Froude. In the words of R.W. Church, the Oxford Movement 'sprang in the consciences and character of its leaders.'[39]

On 14th July 1833, John Keble (1792–1886) preached a sermon from the University pulpit, before the Assize judges gathered for the courts sitting in Oxford. It was later published with the title 'National Apostasy,' and proved the effective launch of the Oxford Movement. The government's Erastian[40] interference in the affairs of the church was, to Keble, sacrilege, a deliberate attack by the state on the church, and its bishops who held offices instituted by Christ. It heralded the likely end of the Church of England. The sermon stirred an intellectual and religious ferment.

The shy, retiring, Keble became the father of the movement. Its early leaders united around veneration for his deep sense of religious feeling, personal holiness, and heartfelt devotion, rooted in the Prayer Book. Reared in the High Church tradition, which he believed he had been entrusted to steadfastly guard, Keble could also be unyielding, even obstinate, on matters of principle. He had little time

---

39   R.W. Church, *The Oxford Movement: Twelve Years 1833–45*, London, Macmillan, 1892, 20.

40   Erastian refers to the union of church with state, with the implication that the state can then interfere in the church, and hence spiritual authorities become subordinate to those of the state.

John Keble

for nonconformists, and distrusted Evangelicals for what he saw as their emphasis upon spiritual experience and feeling rather than duty. Keble gained a double first at Oxford, becoming a Fellow of Oriel College (1817–23), and Professor of Poetry (1831–34), yet most of his life was spent as a rural parish priest at Fairford, and then from 1836–66 at Hursley in Hampshire.[41] His absolute commitment to parish ministry, especially visitation, his championing of the Prayer Book, a restoration of the daily services of Mattins and Evensong, and regular practice of catechising, were a model for others. Church-going was presented as a duty, a service due to God, as well as a means of edification. The memorial to Keble erected by his friends was an Oxford college that bears his name.

Richard Hurrell Froude (1803–36) who studied with Keble, and revered him deeply, demonstrated Tractarian spirituality that was intense, and passionate. The posthumous publication of his journal in 1838, revealing his strongly ascetic practices and anti-Protestant polemic, proved embarrassing to the movement. Froude declared he hated 'the Reformation and the Reformers more and more.' He presented Tractarians as 'Catholics without Popery, and Church of England men without Protestantism'.[42] Froude saw the campaign as part of a Tory defence against state interference by the reforming Whig government, as well as a reactionary response to the anti-clerical sentiment of liberals and radicals.

If Keble was the founding father of the Oxford Movement, John Henry Newman (1801–1890) framed its theological perspective and distinctive ecclesiology. The son of an unsuccessful London banker, he learned from his mother a love for the Bible. Aged fifteen, he underwent a conversion experience, of which he declared nearly fifty years later, 'I am still more certain than that I have hands or feet.'[43] Although underachieving in his undergraduate degree, he performed brilliantly in the examinations that helped him secure a Fellowship at Oriel College in 1822.[44] At Oxford, Newman travelled a spiritual odyssey. His evangelical views were soon given up, replaced by reverence for the significance of tradition, and deep respect for the Church of England. In the Patristic period he believed he found the truest expression of apostolic Christianity, and the failure of the church of his day to match up to such standards troubled him deeply.

Newman's prestige and influence was enhanced in 1828 when he was instituted as the Vicar of St Mary's, Oxford, the University Church. Here Newman's preaching was simple and direct, delivered in a low, clear voice, capable of creating a profound sense of awe and mystery. His sermons could hold in rapt attention large audiences of undergraduates and senior members

41   On Keble's life see G. Battiscombe, *John Keble: A Study in Limitations*, London, Constable, 1963.

42   R.H. Froude, *Remains*, 1838–39, vol. I, 389, 404, quoted in B.M.G. Reardon, *Religious Thought in the Victorian Age: A Survey from Coleridge to Gore*, 2nd edition, London, Longman, 1980, 68.

43   J.H. Newman, *Apologia Pro Vita Sua: Being a History of His Religious Opinions*, (1865 edition), London, Longman's, Green, and Co., 1890, 4.

44   On Newman see I. Ker, *John Henry Newman: A Biography*, Oxford, Clarendon, 1988; S. Gilley, *Newman and His Age*, London, Darton, Longman and Todd, 1990. B. Martin, *John Henry Newman: His Life and Work*, London, Continuum, 2000; F.M. Turner, *John Henry Newman: The Challenge to Evangelical Religion*, New Haven, Yale, 2002, offers a revisionist interpretation of Newman's career to 1845.

John Henry Newman

of the university. He set high intellectual and moral standards, and demanded a response of spiritual commitment and holy living. Newman's travels in Europe brought him into contact with examples of Roman Catholic worship, which he found simple, warm, and possessed of a sacramental richness, giving him a sense of the reality and nearness of the spiritual world, and of continuity with the past. In September 1833, John Henry Newman published the first three of the Tracts: by the end of the year, twenty had been published.

Edward Bouverie Pusey (1800–82), ranked alongside Newman and Keble in significance for the Oxford Movement, bringing added weight by virtue of his status—some referred to the Tractarians as Ritualists, or Puseyites. Pusey had studied in Germany, rendering him well versed in developments in theological scholarship, but he set aside his early, broader, liberal views, and embraced a deeply conservative approach to theology, rooted in the Early Church Fathers, and a prodigious grasp of Semitic languages. By the age of twenty-nine he was Regius Professor of Hebrew, and Canon of Christ Church, Oxford, positions which he retained for the rest of his life. The death of Pusey's wife in 1839 proved a devastating blow from which he never truly recovered, and he spent many of his remaining years in a semi-monastic existence, living simply, fasting regularly, giving much time to prayer and confession. Though not outgoing, many students were attracted to him as a friend and confessor. Pusey was by 1835 committed to the Tractarian cause. His steadiness in the face of Newman's eventual conversion to Rome probably prevented many others from following suit, and helped ensure the continuance of a significant Anglo-Catholic party in the Church of England.[45]

THE THEOLOGICAL DISTINCTIVES OF THE OXFORD MOVEMENT

Tractarians vested authority in the Bible, but as interpreted by the writings and sermons of the early Church fathers, the early councils and creeds of the Church, and the catechism and liturgy. Continuity with the Church of the first centuries was also maintained through the doctrine of the apostolic succession of bishops, who safeguarded doctrine and the proper administration of the sacraments: the Tractarians preferred to call themselves 'Apostolicals.'[46] Moved by Romantic idealism, this belief that they were recreating the purity of the Apostolic church, brought an intense zeal for self-sacrifice, and breathed spiritual warmth into High Church thinking.

The Oxford Movement stressed how, by means of the sacraments, believers were brought into regular, tangible, contact with spiritual and eternal realities. As Newman wrote:

'Christ shines through the sacraments, as through transparent bodies, without impediment… He has touched them and breathed upon them; and thenceforth they have a virtue residing in them… till the eye of faith sees in them no element of matter at all.'[47]

---

45 On Pusey see H. P. Liddon, *Life of Edward Bouverie Pusey*, 4th edn, 4 vols, London, Mowbray, 1894; D. Forrester, *Young Doctor Pusey: A Study in Development*, London, Longmans, Green and Co, 1989.

46 J. H. Newman, *Lectures on the Prophetical Office of the Church, Viewed Relatively to Romanism and Popular Protestantism*, 2nd edn, London, 1838, 305–306 in Brown, *National Churches*, 279–281.

47 J.H. Newman, *Parochial Sermons*, iii, 302, quoted in Reardon, *Religious Thought in Victorian Age*, 71.

TRACT 1—John Henry Newman: Authority based on Apostolic Succession
'The Lord Jesus Christ gave his spirit to his apostles... they in turn laid their hands on those who should succeed them; and these again on others; and so the sacred gift has been handed down to our present bishops, who have appointed us as their assistants, and in some sense their representatives'.[1]

1 Tract 1, in E.R. Fairweather (ed), *The Oxford Movement*, New York, Oxford University Press, 1964, 55–59.

This also brought a renewed focus on the eucharistic celebrant: the wearing of distinctive vestments was introduced; stone altars with richly adorned cloths and candles, the place where the mysteries of the faith were acted out, replaced wooden communion tables with plain white cloths. These developments proved deeply controversial, as did the practice of clergymen kneeling, bowing, and crossing themselves at points in the service. Some clergymen began to refer to themselves as priests, rather than ministers, and advocate clerical celibacy. Outraged opponents viewed such practices as at odds with the Protestant heritage. Protest turned into unruly brawls in places. A series of legal challenges were provoked, which resulted in the passing of the largely ineffectual Public Worship Regulation Act of 1875 in an attempt to control both the spread of ritualism and the protests.

Because the Church was seen as a divine institution, the means by which sacramental grace was conveyed to believers, it needed to be pure, free from any unsought attempt by the government, or those who were not members of the Church of England, to interfere in its internal workings. Tractarians rejected the broad-church approach of Thomas Arnold (1795–1842), a one-time friend of Keble, who argued that the church was a human institution, which should be reorganised as the wider context changed, with traditional theological beliefs open to reinterpretation. To the Tractarians this was subjecting revealed doctrines to human judgement. The nomination of R.D. Hampden (1793–1866) as Regius Professor of Divinity was also bitterly opposed on the grounds of his political liberalism and suggestions of his theological liberalism.

The emphasis on felt experience, through personal faith of the truths propounded, brought an emotional intensity to Tractarian spirituality, suggesting the influence of Romanticism, as well as that of evangelicalism. The Oxford Movement was a form of religious revival, bringing its converts a new vision of the beauty and otherness to be found in historic Christianity, vested in liturgy and tradition. The desire to give tangible expression to the mysteries of the faith brought a deepened appreciation of poetry, architecture, and the religious art of painters such as Holman Hunt (1827–1910) or J.E. Millais (1829–96). Some chose to live out the parochial vocation in urban slums, through missionary service in distant lands, or through life in the Anglican religious orders which were formed, particularly for women, devoted to nursing, teaching, and charitable works. Architecture was brought to the service of liturgy. The eucharistic emphasis was matched by an architectural focus on the altar, rather than the pulpit. The renewal of the Gothic style of decorated stonework, heavy ornamented woodwork, and richly carved rood screens, reflected how beauty and wonder in the spiritual life were to be demonstrated in the fabric of the church. The mind and the spirit were to be drawn upward in worship, assisted by pointed arches, ceilings opened to reveal soaring roofs and richly decorated woodwork overhead. Ironically, over-enthusiastic restorations removed many traces of the medieval past to which the Tractarians so longed to return.

Augustus Welby Pugin (1812–52), who converted to Roman Catholicism in 1835 at the age of 23, led the revival of medieval Christian architecture as a part of the renewal of Christian society. In 1839, J.M. Neale (1818–38) founded the Cambridge Camden Society, a group of Cambridge undergraduates who promoted study of the principles behind medieval church architecture and its influence on worship. A wide range of Protestant churches, including nonconformist chapels, were also drawn to these influences. Into the plain, bare-walled simplicity of churches and chapels, designed so that nothing would detract from the word and worship of God, were introduced stained glass windows, ornamented stonework, with flowers and even candles.

THE END OF THE OXFORD MOVEMENT

The imminent danger of significant reform in the Anglican church was over by 1836, but, the Tractarian movement continued to strengthen. It was by 1840, according to Frank Turner, a 'quasi-schismatic or sectarian movement within the Church of England'.[48] Younger, more enthusiastic and less moderate, Oxford men were coming to the fore, less critical of what had previously been dismissed as 'popery' and superstition. Then, in 1841, Newman dropped a bombshell with the publication of *Tract 90*.[49] [See Extract below] In an attempt to prevent Tractarians from converting to Rome, Newman argued that the Thirty-nine articles of the Church of England, although flawed and in need of revision, were not 'unCatholic', and did not condemn many Roman Catholic practices. It was therefore possible to subscribe to the Thirty-Nine Articles of the Church of England in a way that was also consistent with upholding Roman Catholic teaching.

Newman's Tract was seen as an attack on the Protestant nature of the Church of England: his description of the Anglican Church as being in bondage provoked outrage. The Tract was quickly condemned by the Oxford University

48   Turner, *Newman*, 21.

49   J. H. Newman, *Remarks on Certain Passages in the Thirty-Nine Articles*, Tract 90, London, 1841.

authorities, and by numerous bishops, for whose authority and office Newman had profound regard. Even High Churchmen rejected Newman's arguments. When the Archbishop of Canterbury and his own bishop, the Bishop of Oxford, asked that no further tracts be written, Newman's confidence in the Church of England as a genuine via media between Protestantism and Roman Catholicism was over. The Oxford Movement was in crisis.

Newman had once argued that those considering conversion to Rome were lacking in patience and dutifulness,[50] and that significant elements of Roman Catholic teaching and practice were inconsistent with Scripture. Now he began to argue that the Church of Rome was the heir of Patristic Christianity, and that, because the development of Christian doctrine had been guided by the Holy Spirit over the centuries, Roman Catholic teachings were legitimate. His ideas were later set out in his *Essay on the Development of Christian Doctrine* (1845).

In 1843 Newman resigned from St Mary's Church, Oxford, and devoted himself, with a small group of followers, to a life of prayer, confession, study, and fasting, at the village of Littlemore, just outside Oxford. He now believed that were Athanasius or Ambrose alive in the nineteenth century, they would choose to worship with the Church of Rome.[51] In October 1845 Newman made his confession to Father Dominic Barberi, a Passionist Priest, and was admitted into the Roman Catholic Church. The Pope wrote to him congratulating him on his recovery from 'heresy'.

His conversion to Rome was a bitter blow to Newman's close friends. John Keble wrote to him, 'I cannot well bear to part with you… and yet I cannot go along with you'.[52] Although it marked the formal end of the Oxford Movement proper, Newman's conversion, and that of others, did not halt what had been started. Tractarianism became steadier, less Oxford-based, more widely disseminated, under the able leadership of Keble and Pusey, who remained convinced that Anglicanism was a genuine middle way between Rome and Protestantism. They were convinced that, with its teachings on the papacy, Purgatory, Indulgences, and the role of the Virgin Mary, Roman Catholicism had gone beyond the teachings of the Bible and the early Church. The cry of 'Church in danger' retained a popular resonance; Anglicanism appeared a bulwark against secularisation, industrialisation, political liberalism, and religious dissent. Although some comment on issues of social concern was

---

50   See letters in G. Tracey (ed), *The Letters and Diaries of John Henry Newman, Vol. 7, Editing the British Critic, January 1839–December 1840*, Oxford, Clarendon, 1995; also Turner, *Newman*, 9.

51   Ed., C.S. Dessein, *Letters and Diaries of John Henry Newman*, Vol. XIII, London, 1963, 295–96; D. Newsome, 'Newman and the Oxford Movement', in ed. A. Symondson, *The Victorian Crisis of Faith*, London, SPCK, 1970, 87.

52   Letter from John Keble to Newman, 11th October 1845, quoted in G. Battiscombe, *John Keble: A Study in Limitations*, London, Constable, 1963, 261.

offered,[53] in its early years Tractarian social and practical engagement amongst the urban masses was far less than that of evangelical clergy. However, by the end of the century Anglo-Catholic slum priests were devotedly working amongst the urban poor, and the mission fields of the world.

The attraction of the Oxford Movement to a significant group who had been reared in evangelicalism was notable. W.E. Gladstone discerned an evangelical note in Tractarian preaching.[54] The emphasis on holiness, the Bible, Christological and Trinitarian orthodoxy, personal felt religion and spiritual devotion were other similarities. However, by interpreting the Bible in the light of early church teaching, and maintaining a high view of episcopacy, high sacramentalism, and the stress on baptismal regeneration, meant that there were fundamental differences between Tractarianism and evangelicalism. Whilst some have stressed the natural affinities between Tractarianism and evangelicalism discerned by Pusey, it has been argued that, in the case of Newman's Tractarianism and later Roman Catholicism, there was considerable reaction against the evangelicalism which once attracted him. Indeed, a number of prominent former Evangelicals remained dissatisfied with what Tractarianism taught, and converted to Roman Catholicism.[55] They included the sons of William Wilberforce, Robert and Henry, and Henry Manning, archdeacon of Chichester.[56]

By the late nineteenth century Anglo-Catholicism had replaced the old High-Church party, becoming the third of the great strands within Anglicanism, alongside Evangelicalism and the Broad Church. Yet Anglo-Catholicism was also subject to change. *Lux Mundi*, a collection of essays published in 1889,[57] was an attempt to express Anglo-Catholic thinking in the light of contemporary issues, especially evolutionary science, and biblical criticism. That Charles Gore, a leading contributor, went on to become an Anglican bishop, demonstrated how both Anglo-Catholicism, and openness to liberal theological thinking, was no bar to ecclesiastical preferment.

After leaving Anglicanism, in 1848 Newman established an Oratory in the industrial city of Birmingham. In 1851 he was invited by Pope Pius IX to establish a Roman Catholic University in Dublin, but the project failed,

53 The social and political thought of the Oxford Movement is explored in S.A. Skinner, *Tractarians and the 'Condition of England'*, Oxford, Clarendon, 2004.

54 W.E. Gladstone, 'The Evangelical Movement', *British Quarterly Review*, 1879. The relationship between evangelicalism and Tractarianism is set out in Y. Brilioth, *Three Lectures on Evangelicalism and the Oxford Movement*, London, Oxford University Press, 1934.

55 Newman's abandonment of evangelicalism is explored in F. Turner, *Newman, The Challenge to Evangelical Religion*.

56 These secessions, and the reasons behind them, are explored in David Newsome's *The Parting of Friends: A Study of the Wilberforces and Henry Manning*, London, John Murray, 1966.

57 C. Gore, *Lux Mundi*, London, John Murray, 1889.

leaving him under the suspicion of many ultramontane Roman Catholics. The publication in 1864 of his *Apologia Pro Vita Sua*, in which he recounted his personal theological and spiritual journey from Anglicanism to Rome, helped restore his reputation.[58] In 1879, aged seventy-eight, Newman was appointed a Cardinal, his status assured as one of the greatest English theologians.[59]

CHRISTIAN SOCIALISM

Whilst the Anglicans of the Oxford Movement responded to the agenda of the modern world by resorting to a vision of the traditional past, others embraced contemporary dialogue and engagement. Observing the events of 1848, some believed that Britain had come very close to the socialist revolutions of Europe. Although still operating with a paternalist and hierarchical view of society, they sought to stem the threat of socialism through understanding the concerns of politically disenfranchised and alienated working people, and then by Christianising it. Their thinking was summed up by the Anglican clergyman, Charles Kingsley (1819–1875), who in 1848 argued that the Bible was 'the true Reformer's Guide', but had instead been used 'as if it was a mere special constable's handbook, an opium-dose for keeping beasts of burden patient while they were being overloaded, a mere book to keep the poor in order.'[60]

The intellectual force behind Christian Socialism was Frederick Denison Maurice (1805–72), who, along with Newman, was one of the most original and influential nineteenth-century theologians. The son of a Unitarian minister, his widowed mother and sister embraced evangelicalism, and received believer's baptism. Maurice himself decided on Anglican ministry, which he entered in 1834, and of which he became a staunch defender. By 1846 he was Professor of Theology at King's College, London.[61]

Maurice was a complex figure, at times radical, at others deeply conservative. He sought to express ideas in the light of his own personal thinking and experience, which led him to reject theological systems, and question elements

58 Newman, *Apologia*, 203–204. Frank Turner in *Newman, The Challenge to Evangelical Religion*, 5–13, argues that in the *Apologia*, Newman rewrote the early history of Tractarianism in his own favour as being one aspect of a battle for universal Roman Catholic truth against secular and liberal religious forces. Turner believes that Newman's account has been too uncritically accepted. Tractarianism was instead 'the most extensive, vigorous theological and intellectual assault of the century on evangelical Protestantism' (pp. 6–7).

59 R.H. Hutton, *Criticisms on Contemporary Thought and Thinkers Selected from the Spectator*, London, Macmillan, 2: 278, in Turner, *Newman*, 3.

60 C. Kingsley, *Politics for the People*, No. 4, 27 May 1848, and *Politics for the People*, No. 9, 17 June 1848.

61 On Maurice see A.R. Vidler, *The Theology of F.D. Maurice*, London, SCM, 1948; D.M. Thompson, 'F.D. Maurice: Rebel and Conservative' in ed. S. Mews, *Modern Religious Rebels*, London, Epworth, 1993; B.M.G. Reardon, *Religious Thought in the Victorian Age*, London, Longman, 1980.

of orthodox theology. In the *Kingdom of Christ*, published in 1838,[62] Maurice placed the starting point of the gospel as the love of God, stressing the Fatherhood of God, and the brotherhood of humanity. Social reform required a warming of hearts, a growth in 'feeling' for one other. Because the Kingdom of Christ was already in existence—all were already in Christ. However, in order to be set free, this truth needed to be realised: 'the condemnation of every man is, that he will not own the truth.'[63] The agent by which the discovery of God was to be made was the Church: 'The World is the Church without God; the Church is the World restored in its relationship to God, taken back by him into the state for which he created it'.[64] Writing in the *Christian Socialist* in 1850, he urged that the church be 'taken out of the sanctuary and into the world…to assert the rule of God over every act of common life and embody its gospel in forms of social organization'.[65] The existence of the Kingdom of Christ meant that the bad conditions in which many workers lived were a disgraceful blasphemy, a denial of God's intentions for his creatures.

Maurice's theology proved controversial in other ways. He rejected the substitutionary understanding of the atonement, speaking instead of Christ's work as one of absolute sympathy with mankind, his suffering being of supreme mental anguish. This oneness with humanity deals with sin and reconciles. In his *Theological Essays*, published in 1852, Maurice also questioned the doctrine of eternal punishment, hinting at universalism: 'there is something which must be infinite in the abyss of love beyond the abyss of death.'[66] When these views became known, he was in 1854 dismissed from his post at King's College, London, for unsettling the thinking of students, although his identification with 'Christian Socialism' was also contributory.

The Chartist protests of 1848 renewed Maurice's interest in social reform. Although alarming to the ruling classes, the aims of Chartism were more moderate than Marx's revolutionary ideals, focused primarily upon the extension of the electoral franchise to all males. Chartists ranged from infidel radicals to orthodox Christians. In the summer of 1839 many Chartists marched into Anglican churches, symbols of the heavy hand of state religion, and demanded sermons on passages from the Old Testament prophets or the gospels on ending oppression. Generally, the response was instead sermons on

---

62   F. D. Maurice, *The Kingdom of Christ: or Hints on the Principles, Ordinances, and Constitution of the Catholic Church*, 3 vols, London, 1838.

63   *Life of F.D. Maurice*, London, 1884, Vol. 1, 155, quoted in E.R. Norman, *The Victorian Christian Socialists*, Cambridge, CUP, 1987, 7.

64   F.D. Maurice, *Theological Essays*, London, Macmillan, 1852, 403.

65   F.D. Maurice, in *The Christian Socialist*, November 1850, quoted in O. Chadwick, *Victorian Church*, Vol. 1, 356.

66   Maurice, *Theological Essays*, 406.

submission to God-given authority. One vicar preached provocatively on 'My house shall be called the house of prayer but ye have made it a den of thieves'.[67]

Maurice was urged by J.M. Ludlow (1821–1911) to view Chartism, and the growing socialist movements across Europe, as a demonstration of brotherhood among men, the church under another name. Ludlow believed that socialism needed to be Christianised, or it would shake Christianity to its core. The lack of contact between the Anglican Church and the working class appalled Maurice, Ludlow, and Kingsley. They came to refer to themselves as Christian Socialists,[68] launching a campaign against 'unsocial Christians', and 'unChristian socialists'. They sought to harmonise relationships between different social orders, and to challenge the effects of ruthless competition, but they did not advocate economic and social equality, which, to them, was communism. In 1848, *Politics for the People* was launched as a series of tracts, part of a determined effort to turn the working people away from the claims of Marxism, and back to the church. Through a series of meetings at the London Coffee House in 1849, a dialogue with working leaders began.

Kingsley was attracted to Christian Socialism through friendship with Maurice. He was Rector of Eversley, Hampshire, and, from 1860–69 Professor of Modern History at Cambridge.[69] Writing as 'Parson Lot,' Kingsley contributed tracts to *Politics for the People*, and in his novels *Yeast* (1848) and *Alton Locke* (1850) demonstrated sympathy for some of the Chartist demands. He was deeply concerned at the image the church presented to working men. He stressed the humanity of Christ, as 'the Poor Man who died for poor men.' Rejecting anything that appeared to make Christianity effeminate—the Oxford Movement was deeply suspect to him—he presented Christianity as robust and manly: the term 'muscular Christianity' was used of his approach. Although designed to appeal to working men, this ethos proved attractive to English public schools, where high educational, ethical and moral standards, were combined with encouragement to prowess in sport, and a willingness to engage in works of public service.

The significance of Maurice, Ludlow and Kingsley lay in their willingness to open the mid-nineteenth century church up to the agenda of the modern world. Maurice's thinking prefigured much in the twentieth century and his social thinking coupled with his theological liberalism became widely accepted

---

67   E. Yeo, 'Christianity in Chartist Struggle, 1838–42', *Past and Present*, 91 (1981), 133–39.

68   On Christian Socialism see E.R, Norman, *The Victorian Christian Socialists*, Cambridge, CUP, 1987; T. Christensen, *Origins and History of Christian Socialism 1848–54*, Aarhus, 1962; D.M. Thompson, 'F.D. Maurice: Rebel and Conservative' in ed. S. Mews, *Modern Religious Rebels*, London, Epworth, 1993; P. Jones, *The Christian Socialist Revival, 1877–1914. Religion, Class, and Social Conscience in Late-Victorian England*, Princeton, Princeton University Press, 1968.

69   On Kingsley see F.E. Kingsley, *Charles Kingsley: Letters and Memories of His Life*, London, Henry S. King, 1877.

in the Anglican Broad-Church party. After 1854, the early phase of Christian Socialism came to an end. Marx dismissed it as a salve to the consciences of the upper classes. The 1870s brought renewed interest in what Maurice had attempted. Stuart Headlam (1847–1924) combined Anglo-Catholic ecclesiology, with interest in social and political engagement, a theological debt to Maurice, and a stronger commitment to genuine socialism. He founded the Guild of St Matthew in 1877, which grew to some 350 members, of whom 99 were clergy. The less radical Christian Social Union, formed in 1889, attracted leading academics such as Henry Scott Holland (1847–1918), Charles Gore (1855–1932), and the eminent New Testament scholar B.F. Westcott (1825–1901). The CSU influenced many official Church of England pronouncements between the late 1880s and the 1920s. Although Christian Socialism had been espoused by an isolated minority in the 1850s, by the end of the century the message of most British denominations had a distinctly social and political dimension.[70]

Significant numbers remained unconvinced of the need for socialism to be equated with atheism. Friendly Societies, Trade Unions, and Co-operatives, were often led by those who had gained speaking and leadership experience in Nonconformist, especially Methodist, chapels. Although most Nonconformists looked to the Liberal Party for the expression of their political sentiment, the Independent Labour Party, formed in 1893, advocated 'ethical' socialism. It attracted many who gave a Christian rationale for their socialism, claiming to follow the teachings of Jesus, even if they did not formally practice Christianity.

CONCLUSIONS

The ideological and political challenge of liberalism did not simply provoke disagreement between the religious and the irreligious. The fiercely fought debates within churches reflected its impact on the deeply religiously committed. Responses did not conform to a simple pattern. To Christian Socialists, dialogue with the representatives of popular democracy was the way forward, together with theological accommodation to a changing world. The non-Intrusionist party in the Church of Scotland campaigned for more representative and flexible church structures, but remained firm in their evangelicalism. However, the strongly evangelical leadership of the Wesleyan Methodists stoutly resisted calls for change from below. Roman Catholics and Anglo-Catholics rejected the modern agenda: the triumph of ultramontane sentiment in Roman Catholicism militated against egalitarian structures, increased papal authority made Roman Catholic practices more uniform, obedience a cardinal virtue, and placed official and international Roman Catholicism in the ascendancy above local leaderships and practices. Paradoxically, whilst the official declarations of the Roman Catholic Church affirmed its alienation from modernity, the century

---

70   See A. Wilkinson, *Christian Socialism: Scott Holland to Tony Blair*, London, SCM, 1998.

saw significant advances for Roman Catholics through political liberalisation, including widening access to the electoral franchise. Whilst resisting freedoms, such as that of the press, the Roman Catholic Church still used it to determinedly promote their agenda. Liberal Roman Catholics, such as the English historian Lord Acton, who continued to believe in the compatibility of Liberalism and Roman Catholicism, were forced to produce a Roman Catholic definition of Liberty, which was not 'the power of doing what we like, but the right of being able to do what we ought.'[71]

The growing anti-clericalism evident in Europe in the later nineteenth century, with an increased appetite for radical social democracy which had little place for formal religious practice, suggests that the efforts of the churches to resolve their relationship with the modern world were less than entirely successful.

---

71   Lord Action, 'The Church in the Modern World', *The Rambler*, Jan 1860, in J.R. Fears, ed., *Selected Writings of Lord Acton, 3, Essays on Religion, Politics and Morality*, Indianapolis, 1983, 613.

FURTHER READING

S.J. Brown, *The National Churches of England, Ireland and Scotland 1801–46*, Oxford, Oxford University Press, 2001.

O. Chadwick, *The Secularization of the European Mind in the Nineteenth Century*, Cambridge, Cambridge University Press, 1975.

O. Chadwick, *A History of the Popes 1830–1914*, Oxford, Oxford University Press, 1998.

R. Davies, A.R. George, G. Rupp (eds), *A History of the Methodist Church in Great Britain*, Vol. 2, London, Epworth, 1978.

R.J. Helmstadter (ed), *Freedom and Religion in the Nineteenth Century*, Stanford, Stanford University Press, 1997.

D. Hempton, *The Religion of the People, Methodism and Popular Religion, c. 1750–1900*, London, 1996.

I. Ker, *John Henry Newman: A Biography*, Oxford, 1988.

H. McLeod, *Secularisation in Western Europe 1848–1914*, Basingstoke, Macmillan, 2000.

K. Marx, *The Communist Manifesto*, ed. A.J.P. Taylor, Harmondsworth, Penguin, 1967.

E.R. Norman, *The Victorian Christian Socialists*, Cambridge, CUP, 1987.

F. Turner, *John Henry Newman: The Challenge to Evangelical Religion*, New Haven, Yale, 2002.

9

THE RISING TIDE OF WORLD MISSION: THE 1840S TO 1880S

By the mid nineteenth-century, Protestant missionary societies, such as those which had begun in 1792 in the parlour of an obscure Baptist pastor's house in the English Midlands, had been transformed. They had become substantial bodies, with religious, and even political influence, paid administrators, large and sometimes cumbersome committees, and administrative support structures. Networks of local auxiliaries sustained their work at grassroots level, raising funds, and organising promotional and fund-raising sermons. Women came to play an ever more important role, not only as fund-raisers, but on the mission field itself, as missionary wives, and also as single missionaries.

As the small trickle of converts to Christianity became a steady flow, optimism as to the potential results of cross-cultural mission grew. Appreciation of the inherent dignity and natural intelligence of indigenous peoples deepened. Despite the export of the worst aspects of European culture—alcohol, unscrupulous trade, and immoral behaviour by settlers, Christianity and civilization were believed to be working hand in hand, with Christianity leading the way. The role of European governments in overseas territories was generally, but not always, seen as beneficial, complementing missions by bringing peace, affirming the rights of individuals, and providing resources for the promotion of agriculture, and manufacturers.[1] Later in the century the relationship between mission and empire became increasingly troubling.

The flow of recruits and income into missionary societies saw rapid, albeit fluctuating, increases. The emancipation of slaves in British colonies, the Niger Expedition, and promotional visits to Britain from John Williams and Robert

---

1   A. Porter, *Religion Versus Empire? British Protestant Missionaries and Overseas Expansion, 1700–1914*, Manchester, Manchester University Press, 2004, 141–44.

Moffat all served to deepen British interest in mission in the 1830s and 1840s, as did the signing of the Treaty of Nanking in 1842. The late 1850s saw a further surge with Livingstone's appeal for Africa, and the aftermath of the Indian Mutiny in 1857, before a fall-off in the 1860s as theological controversies and debates over denominational education sapped energies. The CMS received 246 candidates between 1849 and 1861, but just 159 in the years between 1862 and 1872. The 1870s saw fresh momentum, with new missionaries arriving in Uganda, Tanzania, and Congo, and opportunities opening up in the Far East: the CMS saw 118 applicants in 1876.[2] Impetus was also given after 1865 with the advent of 'faith' missions.

Whilst America avoided the unseemly overseas colonial scramble that occupied Germany, Britain, Belgium and France, it was busily colonising its own Westerly and South Westerly regions. After a burst of enthusiasm for the cause of overseas mission in the early nineteenth century, attention in the middle decades focussed on this internal mission field, where population was rapidly relocating. By the 1870s the Methodist Missionary Society was providing over 3,000 domestic missionaries for the frontier communities of the West.[3] The freedom and vitality of America's voluntary missionary societies were shaped by prevailing cultural values: democracy, innovative and entrepreneurial business styles, and willingness to use the latest technological methods. This left some suspicious of the emerging 'faith-based' mission models.[4]

Methodism was by nature, especially in its early years, a missionary movement, with lines between home and overseas mission finely drawn. The remarkable career of William Taylor typifies this. He began Methodist missionary work in the Californian gold fields in the late 1840s and 1850s, before working in England and Australasia (1862–66), South Africa (1866), the West Indies (1868–69), India (1870–75), South America (1877–84), and the Congo and Liberia, where he was missionary bishop from 1884 to 1896.[5] As a missionary preacher in South Africa in eight months he claimed 8,000 converts: in one five week period, during which the theologically-liberally minded Bishop Colenso toured his diocese and baptised just two children, Taylor's missionary preaching yielded 1,000 conversions.[6]

2   E. Stock, *History of the Church Missionary Society*, Vol. II, London, Church Missionary Society, 1899,

3   Hempton, *Methodism: Empire of the Spirit*, 159; 152–154.

4   A. Walls, 'The American Dimension in the History of the Mission Movement', in J.A. Carpenter and W.R. Shenk, eds., *Earthen Vessels: American Evangelicals and Foreign Missions, 1880–1980*, Grand Rapids, Eerdmans, 1–25.

5   D. Bundy, 'Bishop William Taylor and Methodist Mission: A Study in Nineteenth Century Social History', Pt 1, *Methodist History*, 27:4 (July 1989): 197–210; Part 2, *Methodist History*, 28: 1 (October 1989): 2–21.

6   Hempton, *Methodism: Empire of the Spirit*, 168–171.

DEVELOPMENTS IN MISSIOLOGICAL THINKING

Henry Venn (1796–1873), was to develop significantly what his father had helped start. John Venn had helped to draft the rules of the Church Missionary Society, and in 1841 Henry Venn became honorary part-time secretary. In 1847 he resigned from his Anglican parish to devote himself full-time to the mission, working tirelessly until his retirement in 1872.[7] He maintained a vast correspondence, entertained many missionaries in his home, and oversaw developments on the mission field from a distance. He steered the Evangelical CMS through Anglican controversies over Tractarianism and rationalism. He sought to ensure that CMS energies were not diverted from the primary task of evangelism, which he emphasised above other strategies such as the provision of higher education.[8]

The impossibility of the whole non-Christian world being evangelised by European and North American missionaries quickly became clear to Venn. He instead conceived the role of the missionary as being primarily to establish indigenous churches which would be self-supporting, self-governing, and self-propagating. The missionary phase in the life of a church was to be only temporary. Missionary societies were instead to work towards the so-called 'euthanasia of missions'—the removal of missionaries to other unevangelized fields, leaving a national church standing unassisted.[9] Newly started churches were to be assisted to maturity by being supplied with scriptures in the vernacular, and theological literature, converts trained as teachers, catechists, and eventually pastors of indigenous churches. In time a native episcopate was to be established. Unlike some Anglican societies, Venn did not believe that a bishop was necessary from the commencement of missionary operations. However, the Anglican system made the fulfilment of Venn's scheme difficult, as he complained in 1858: 'Missionaries are too backward to trust their Native agents of all classes.' Nonetheless, he noted numerous instances where 'pressure from home had put the native forward; and that subsequently the Missionary has expressed his surprise and satisfaction at the result.'[10] Conflicts between the authority of local bishops and the CMS, and between missionaries and local church leaders, were exacerbated by the length of time it took for letters to reach the mission fields, and replies to be returned.

7   On Venn see M. Hennell, *Sons of the Prophets: Evangelical Leaders of the Victorian Church*, London, SPCK, 1979, 68– 90; W. Knight, *Memoir of Reverend H. Venn-the Missionary Secretariat of Henry Venn, B.D.*, London, Longmans, 1880; J. Venn, *Annals of a Clerical Family*, London, Macmillan, 1904.

8   Venn's strategy is explored in C.P. Williams, *The Ideal of the Self-Governing Church: A Study in Victorian Missionary Strategy*, Leiden, Brill, 1990.

9   E. Stock, *History of the Church Missionary Society*, 1899, Vol. II, 80.

10   H. Venn Letter to Rufus Anderson, 2 March 1858, cited in W. Shenk, *Henry Venn, Missionary Statesman*, Maryknoll, New York, 1983, 169.

Henry Venn

In Sierra Leone, nine out of twelve missionary districts had by 1852 become native pastorates according to Venn's plan, under the superintendence of the Bishop of Sierra Leone, a European. However, the full establishment of the native pastorate in 1860, with the complete withdrawal of missionaries, was attempted too quickly and all-but paralysed the church. A similar pattern was followed in South India, creating self-governing and self-supporting churches.

Venn followed Thomas Fowell Buxton in advocating commerce and civilisation, alongside Christianity, as the way to end slavery, and also to assist the creation of self-supporting churches. Training in basic industrial, commercial, and agricultural skills would lay an economic foundation sufficient to sustain a local church, and help transform local society. Venn particularly wanted trade to be by Africans, but finding ways by which this could be reliably and securely conducted, without some form of British military force on hand to police matters, proved taxing.

The debt owed by the CMS to Venn's depth and insight made him of enormous and lasting significance.[11] Under his secretaryship, the CMS extended its activities from West Africa, to the Middle East, India, Japan, New Zealand, Canada and Madagascar. The source of recruits also changed, with less reliance on German Lutherans. Between 1815 and 1840 sixteen graduates of Oxford and Cambridge offered their services, rising to thirty-two between 1841 and 1848, and sixty-two from 1849 to 1862, before falling back to twenty-three between 1862 and 1872.

Henry Venn's missiological significance is matched in America by that of Rufus Anderson (1796–1880), indeed the two met, and their approach had significant points of commonality. Anderson was turned down for missionary service on health grounds in the 1820s, but was given administrative employment by the ABCFM in Boston. In 1832 he was appointed one of three 'secretaries for correspondence', and served with great distinction for over forty years until the age of 70. Along with Venn, he argued strenuously for the creation of self-governing and self-supporting indigenous churches. He also advocated the 'euthanasia of mission': the missionary task was to evangelise, train workers, ordain natives, and then move on.[12]

Although convinced of the superiority of Western civilisation, Anderson made less of a connection between Christianity and civilisation than Venn, perhaps because the latter was most concerned with Africa where the elimination of slavery was so important. Instead Anderson warned that missionary activity had become too readily associated with 'education, industry, civil liberty, family government and social order.' The Christianity being propagated looked all-too-like New England society. He believed that civilisation would spread inevitably as a result of scattering the gospel seed; education was valuable only in so far as it furthered the work of evangelism.[13]

Anderson's emphases were carried into practice. By 1842, those engaged

11 This is discussed in W.A. Shenk, 'Henry Venn's Legacy', *Occasional Bulletin of Missionary Research*, April, 1977, 16–19.

12 Anderson's views are set out in R. Anderson, *Foreign Missions, Their Relations and Claims*, New York, Scribner, 1869.

13 R. Anderson, Sermon 'Theory of Missions to the Heathen', 1845, 73–74, quoted in W.R. Hutchison, *Errand to the World: American Protestant Thought and Foreign Missions*, Chicago, University of Chicago Press, 1987, 82.

The Christian Providential View of History

'Every war in Asia, for the past half-century, has been fulfilling the prophecy, that the valleys shall be exalted, and the mountains and hills made low, the crooked made straight, and the rough places plain... The great anti-Christian powers are acting under mighty restraints. ... And these providential influences are more and more evidently preparing the way for Christ's progress, with his gospel, through the unevangelized nations'.[1]

1 R. Anderson, *Memorial Volume of the First Fifty Years of the American Board of Commissioners for Foreign Missions*, 4th edition, Boston, ABCFM, 1861, 388, in Hutchison, *Errand to the World*, p. 79.

---

in preaching and direct evangelism for the ABCFM far outweighed those in auxiliary ministries. Some schools were closed in the 1850s, and by 1852 no farmers or mechanics were employed.[14] However, as Venn had found, the desire to create indigenous churches with indigenous leadership was not readily endorsed by the American missionary community. In India, mission work which had started in 1815 did not yield an ordained indigenous pastor until 1854.

Similar views to those of Anderson were set out in 1853 by Francis Wayland (1796–1865), the Baptist President of Brown University, Providence, Rhode Island: 'the son of God has left us no directions for civilising the heathen, and then Christianising them. We are not commanded to teach schools in order to undermine paganism, and then, on its ruins, to build up Christianity'.[15] Wayland argued that the apostolic injunction was rather to preach the gospel. Educational work was to focus upon the training of preachers—government grants for the promotion of education were not to be accepted. Anderson and Wayland were bolstered by evidence from the field: seventy years of mission work in India, in which huge amounts of labour had been invested, had produced a body of just 30,000 Christians, just one hundredth of one percent of the population of the country. It was a finely balanced debate. Certainly good schools filled up quickly with able pupils, many of whom were not much interested in Christianity. Yet those who rejected an educational strategy produced churches full of illiterate converts, and few candidates for future indigenous leadership, which made the establishment of churches on the three-self principle hard to achieve. This led to a greater acceptance in the later decades of the century of a civilising role for missions, as schools, hospitals, and social projects began to proliferate.[16]

---

14   Hutchison, *Errand to the World*, 78–82.

15   F. Wayland, *The Apostolic Ministry*, Rochester, Sage and Brother, 1853, 19, quoted in Hutchison, *Errand to the World*, 84.

16   Hutchison, *Errand to the World*, 83–89, 99.

MISSIONS AND CAMPAIGNS AGAINST SLAVERY

Between 1833 and 1838, slavery was brought to an end in British colonies, although the political, social and economic domination of the slave-owning class remained. However, churches established by missions during the time of slavery developed rapidly. Methodism saw significant success, and the membership of Baptist churches in Jamaica also grew from 10,838 in 1831, to 27,706 in 1840. Voices called for Baptist work in Jamaica to become self-supporting, and the work handed over to indigenous leadership. The younger churches appeared to be coming of age when in 1840 the Jamaican Baptist Missionary Society was formed, and a missionary sent to West Africa. The BMS withdrew from Jamaica as a mission field in 1842, yet in 1857 there were just 36 pastors for 77 Baptist churches. A college was established, but over fifteen years it turned out just 14 pastors. In 1842 the CMS also withdrew from Jamaica and Trinidad, again leaving churches with limited financial security. The indigenisation of church leadership was little helped by the declining post-emancipation economic situation in Jamaica, which bred social unrest. During a revolt in 1860, martial law was declared and 439 people shot, including three Baptist pastors, arousing a storm of protest. Nonetheless, the willingness of the BMS and CMS to hand these mission fields over to local leadership stands as a challenge to those who depict Western missions as dominating the churches they had established, and denying them self-governance. Instead, in these cases it could be argued that missionaries stepped back too soon from churches that were economically poor, and without sufficient local leaders.[17]

After 1850, the internal African demand for slaves rose to exceed that of the Eastern or Atlantic markets, indeed slavery within Africa peaked in the last half of the nineteenth century. Areas particularly affected included Nigeria and Bénin, much of northern Angola and southern Zaire.[18] Possibly half the population of Western Sudan was of slave status. Slavery within Africa varied: in Zanzibar slaves were allowed to marry and have their own plots of land. In other areas the slaveholding pattern began to look more like serfdom.[19]

The protests of Christian missionaries had a significant impact on the efforts of European governments to curtail the slave trade within their areas of colonial control. Slave holding flourished in Sudan until the British returned to power in 1898. In the 1870s, Tunisia and Egypt abolished the open slave trade as part of their attempt to gain European recognition; Ethiopia phased out slavery after 1918 for similar reasons.[20] The sense of moral responsibility for those subject to

---

17   Stanley, *BMS*, 83–105.

18   P. Manning, *Slavery and African Life: Occidental, Oriental and African Slave Trades,* Cambridge, CUP, 1990, 140–42.

19   Manning, *Slavery,* 142–148.

20   Manning, *Slavery,* 157–58.

the depredations of slavery profoundly influenced the work of two key figures and their attempts to promote Christianity in sub-Saharan Africa. They were Thomas Fowell Buxton and David Livingstone.

THE NIGER EXPEDITION AND ITS AFTERMATH

Buxton, who had seen to completion the anti-slavery campaigns of Wilberforce, argued for the need to deal with slavery at its root. In late 1839 he set out his scheme in *The African Slave Trade and Its Remedy*, claiming that the internal African slave trade still enslaved half-a-million Africans each year. He advocated the tri-partite solution of civilization, commerce, and Christianity. The Bible, the plough, and legitimate trade were to regenerate Africa. He proposed that the River Niger be used to open up the heart of West Africa, establishing trading posts and agricultural settlements along its banks which would also serve as centres from which Christianity would be propagated.[21] If the gains to be made from legitimate trade exceeded those from selling humans, then slavery would naturally wither away. Civilised and industrious values would be spread through educational work.

These ideas were not new. Buxton drew on the thinking of the freed slave Olaudah Equiano, an Ibo from territory which bordered the Niger, who had as early as 1789 urged that legitimate commerce replace the cruel trafficking in human flesh.[22] Wilberforce and his friends had also planned that in Sierra Leone the gospel would work with civilisation and commerce to regenerate West Africa.

On 1st June 1840, at a meeting of the Society for the Extinction of the Slave Trade and the Civilisation of Africa, with Prince Albert in the chair, Buxton launched his project for the redemption of Africa from the curse of slavery. It combined the might of the British navy with the spread of the ideas of Western civilisation, especially education, legitimate commerce, and Christianity. Commerce was embraced as part of God's providential rule in human affairs, although this did not later stop missionaries from being strongly critical of its less acceptable features, such as the opium trade with China, or trade in guns and alcohol elsewhere.

The British government, privately sceptical about the project, was persuaded to back it after pressure from the anti-slavery lobby. The role of Britain in disseminating Christian and humanitarian values, implicit in Buxton's plan, was an extension of the moral policeman role adopted when ending the slave trade. Some were unconvinced that Christianity would inevitably prosper alongside commerce; others objected to members of the proposed expedition carrying weapons. Questions were raised about the complex series of treaties, land purchases, trading and peacekeeping measures that the expedition demanded,

---

21   T.F. Buxton, *The African Slave Trade and Its Remedy*, London, John Murray, 1840, 172, 353.

22   L. Sanneh, *West African Christianity*, New York, Orbis, 1983, 55; Buxton, *African Slave Trade*, 301.

Buxton on the Niger Expedition

Legitimate commerce would put down the Slave Trade, by demonstrating the superior value of man as a labourer on the soil, to man as an object of merchandise; and if conducted on wise and equitable principle, might be the precursor, or rather the attendant, of civilisation, peace and Christianity, to the unenlightened, warlike, and heathen tribes who now so fearfully prey on each other, to supply the slave markets of the New World. In this view of the subject, the merchant, the philanthropist, the patriot, and the Christian may unite ... Let missionaries and school masters, the plough and the spade go together and agriculture will flourish; the avenues of legitimate commerce will be opened up; confidence between man and man will be inspired, whilst civilisation will advance as the natural effect and Christianity operates as the proximate cause of this happy change.'[1]

1   T. F. Buxton, *The African Slave Trade and Its Extinction*, London, John Murray, 1840, 306.

---

but nonetheless a budget of £100,000 was allocated, and expert crews equipped with the latest technology recruited.

The expedition set sail in May 1841. Alongside the naval officers, there were agriculturalists, scientists, teachers, and Christian missionaries. One was Friedrich Schön, who had worked as a linguist and CMS missionary at Sierra Leone since 1832. With him was Samuel Ajayi Crowther (1807–1891), an African whose personal story typified what the expedition was all about. Brought up in Yorubaland in what is now Western Nigeria, he had been captured by a slave raiding party, and eventually sold into the hands of Portuguese slave traders ready for shipment across the Atlantic. The ship on which he was being transported was intercepted by the British naval squadron, and he was taken to Sierra Leone, where after a few years he became a Christian, taking the name Samuel Crowther after a member of the CMS home committee. He was educated at the Fourah Bay College in Sierra Leone, and became a schoolmaster and evangelist.[23] The Niger Expedition relied heavily on Sierra Leone for interpreters and helpers in its task force.

The venture started out well, with treaties made with local chiefs at Abo and Idda to suppress the slave trade and engage in lawful commerce. At Lokoja a model farm was started. But then things began to go badly wrong. Delays in organising the expedition had meant that it sailed from Britain in May 1841, six months later than Buxton had planned. The steamers therefore entered Niger in August 1841, at the height of the rainy season, when the risk of malaria was at its greatest. As the ships progressed upstream malaria began to reap a heavy

23   Crowther's early life is discussed in A.F. Walls, 'A Second Narrative of Samuel Ajayi Crowther's Early Life', *Bulletin of the Society for African History*, 2 (1965).

toll. When the ships limped back down the Niger, 130 out of 145 Europeans had contracted malaria, and forty had died. In contrast, all the 158 Africans survived, and only eleven had been ill. The model farm at Lokoja lasted barely a year, before the British residents were evacuated over fears for their security.

The Niger Expedition appears, on the face of it, one of the great failures of mission history. The result was complete humiliation for Buxton, with the blame for the deaths of forty able men laid at his door. By January 1843, the African Civilisation Society had been wound up. Buxton died in February 1845, aged just fifty-nine, crushed by the failure of his scheme. Yet his ideas were not lost, and lived on in the work of Henry Venn and David Livingstone.[24] Indeed, what appeared Buxton's shame proved a catalyst for a large and sustained missionary advance into West Africa, from which the strength and vibrancy of churches in the region in the twentieth century in good part stemmed.

In his report on the expedition, Friedrich Schön drew vital lessons for missions strategy. He emphasised that native agency should be used to spread Christianity into the heart of Africa. Not only could Africans withstand the climate and the diseases of the area, they were those best suited by culture and language to communicate the gospel to their fellow Africans: it was Samuel Crowther's preaching in the local tongue amongst his own Yoruba people that had produced the greatest response.[25] The previous assumption of the need to teach people English, and then communicate the gospel in that medium, was now questioned. Sierra Leone, with a population in 1846 of less than 50,000 former slaves, speaking some 117 different languages, was to prove an unlikely, but vital base for the supply and training of missionary personnel. Between 1800 and 1900, Sierra Leone produced on average one ordained clergyman per year for the CMS alone, together with countless catechists, teachers, and other mission workers, and in this the Fourah Bay College played a key role. Others from the Sierra Leonean diaspora moved as migrant labour across West Africa, taking their Bibles, hymns, and the practice of family prayers, giving the small colony a missionary impact far beyond its boundaries.[26] The lessons learned from the tragedy of 1841 meant that the propagation of Christianity in West Africa in its early phase became more contextually appropriate, and less an aspect of white colonisation. The leading role in European advance fell not to commercial enterprises, but to missionary societies.[27]

24   A. Porter, 'Commerce and Christianity: The Rise and Fall of a Nineteenth-Century Missionary Slogan', *Historical Journal* 28, 1985, 597–621.

25   On Crowther see A. Walls, 'The Legacy of Samuel Ajayi Crowther', *International Bulletin of Missionary Research*, January 1992.

26   Walls, *The Missionary Movement in Christian History*, 86–87, 105–106.

27   A positive African assessment of the results of the expedition is found in C.C. Ifemesia, 'The Civilising Mission of 1841: Aspects of an Episode in Anglo-Nigerian Relations', in O.U. Kalu (ed), *The History of Christianity in West Africa*, Harlow, Longmans, 1988.

A visit to Abeokuta by the Anglican Henry Townsend led to the founding of a mission amongst the Yoruba people, staffed in good part by Yoruba Christians from Sierra Leone. A key figure was Samuel Crowther, who after his successful role in the Niger Expedition, had been sent to England for training, and was the first of Sierra Leone's indigenous ministers to be ordained. Amongst his first converts were his long-lost mother and sisters. Vital to the success of the work in Yorubaland was Crowther's involvement in the translation of the Bible into Yoruba, making it the first translation in which a native African speaker was involved on equal footing with Europeans, lending to it significant colloquial and idiomatic strengths. He also acted on Buxton's principles, introducing the growing and export of cotton to keep Abeokuta out of West Africa's slave economy. Crowther skilfully led a group of talented African clergy, allowing Christianity amongst the Yoruba to develop at its own pace in matters such as abandoning holy objects from traditional religious practice.

In 1853, a mission station at Ibadan was established, and in 1854 the CMS launched a second major mission along the Niger, in which Crowther again took part. In 1857 he followed this up with further exploration of openings for missionary work amongst the Nupe and Hausa peoples. For nearly fifty years the vast Niger territories were served by a steady flow of lay and ordained missionaries mainly from Sierra Leone, a mission to Africa by Africans.

In 1851, Crowther travelled to England again, and this impressive and well educated black clergyman made a profound impression on the Queen and Prince Albert, and government ministers. In 1864 this former slave boy was ordained in Canterbury Cathedral as the first black African bishop of the Anglican communion. It was a step of huge significance for world Christianity, and, to Henry Venn, appeared the dawning of his vision of a self-governing African church, and the 'euthanasia of missions':

'The effect of this appointment upon the whole of the native ministry throughout our Missions has been remarkable. It has given them a lively demonstration of the truth that a native Church is not to be kept too long in a state of dependence, but that the mother Church will commit the superintendence to a native Bishop as soon as the native church is ripe for such a measure. By this a great impulse has been given to native ministers to cultivate a manly independence of mind, and to recognise the responsibilities of their position.'[28]

Yet it is likely that there were other motivations behind the consecration. Coming at the time from falling donations and numbers of volunteers to the CMS it had great publicity value. It also demonstrated the commitment of

---

28   H. Venn, quoted in J. Cox, 'Religion and Imperial Power in Nineteenth-Century Britain', in ed. R.J. Helmstadter, *Freedom and Religion in the Nineteenth Century*, Stanford, Stanford University Press, 1997, 368.

Henry Venn on the 'Euthanasia of Missions'

'The object of the Church Missionary Society's missions, viewed in their ecclesiastical aspect, is the development of Native Churches, with a view to their ultimate settlement upon a self-supporting, self-governing, and self-extending system. When this settlement has been effected, the Mission will have attained its *euthanasia*, and the Missionary and all Missionary agency can be transferred to the regions beyond.'[1]

1   H. Venn, 'The Native Pastorate and Organization of Native Churches', 1851, in M.A.C. Warren (ed), *To Apply the Gospel*, Grand Rapids, Michigan, Eerdmans, 1971, 28.

---

the CMS to an Episcopal church order, in the face of the competing challenge of Anglo-Catholic missions. That Crowther lacked the unqualified support of European missionaries in West Africa is clear. Nor did the appointment of Crowther truly fulfil the ideals of Henry Venn for a native episcopate, for although a Yoruba, he was made bishop of an area east of the Niger, the language of which he did not speak, in effect a foreign bishop. Nonetheless, Crowther established courteous and friendly relations with local Muslim rulers, developing an African Christian approach to Islam. He avoided anything that appeared openly controversial, or which might arouse hostility or suspicion. Questions about Christianity were answered only with direct quotations from the Bible, and he tried to build on areas of common ground between elements in the Qur'an, and biblical passages.[29] His approach to engagement with Islam was not continued after his death in 1891.

Sadly, by that date, the hope of an African church led by Africans, which had brightened with his consecration had faded. Henry Venn's death in 1873 deprived Crowther of a powerful ally. Irregularities in the behaviour of his assistants were uncovered, which were viewed with intolerance by European missionaries who arrived in the 1880s. Moulded by enthusiasm for Keswick holiness teachings, they set exacting standards for not only missionary candidates, but also African converts.[30] They quickly grew frustrated by Crowther's unwillingness to take action until complaints were proved. Adopting a purist approach to mission, they rejected the gradualism of Simeon, Venn and Crowther. Baptism, it was felt, was offered too readily, and genuine conversions were too few. The newer breed of missionaries adopted the native dress of other Hausa religious teachers, and argued that preferment should be solely on the basis of qualification and personal merit. Whilst this appeared a highly principled stand, it effectively

29   Details of the encounters are found in S. Crowther, *Experiences with Heathens and Mahomedans in West Africa*, London, SPCK, 1892.

30   Porter, *Religion Versus Empire?*, 251–256.

discriminated against Africans who enjoyed fewer opportunities for training. Crowther, then over eighty, was sidelined, and died a broken man. From his death in 1891 until 1951 there was no further African diocesan bishop, although a few African assistant bishops were appointed and served well. The self-governing principle of Venn faded. Some, influenced by the growing racist ideology of the time, claimed that Crowther was a weak bishop, and that 'the African race' lacked the capacity to rule. Crowther's treatment remains a controversial subject.[31]

Genuinely self-supporting, self-governing, and self-propagating churches were only achievable when missionaries left entirely, or when the indigenous church had sufficient size and resources to be free of missionary control. This occurred with some success in the Niger Delta under Crowther's son Archdeacon Dandeson Crowther. Here churches operated within the Anglican communion, but away from the control of the CMS. By the end of the nineteenth century they were self-propagating, and for a while self-supporting, until its rapid growth made it financially dependent again, but in the late nineteenth century such examples were rare. The failure to establish an indigenous leadership for the West African church fed into the development of African instituted churches, and eventually African nationalism.[32]

Buxton's scheme encouraged other missionaries to direct their attentions to West Africa, including the Methodist Thomas Freeman, who moved from Sierra Leone to continue his work in what is now Nigeria. In 1843, a party of Baptist missionaries, with 42 volunteers from Jamaica, helped establish a small Baptist church amongst the indigenous peoples of the Cameroons at Fernando Po, despite illness and the discouragement of the majority of the party returning home. Church of Scotland missionaries began work in Calabar in 1846. The Basel Mission had begun work in the Gold Coast, now Ghana, in 1828. After twelve years of almost fruitless work in a country ravaged by the slave trade, eight missionaries had died. The surviving worker, Andreas Riis persevered, and was eventually supported by other missionary arrivals. A key component of their work was, as Buxton had argued, agricultural development. Cocoa was found to grow well, and by 1900 the country was the leading producer in the world. In 1884 large parts of the Cameroons were ceded to German sovereignty, which brought significant Lutheran involvement. The work of German and American Baptist missionaries ensured that the Baptists were to become one of the largest Protestant communities in the Cameroons.[33]

---

31 For an African view see E.A. Ayandele, *The Missionary Impact on Modern Nigeria: 1842–1914*, London, Longmans, 1966; S. Neill, *History of Christian Missions*, 377 gives the traditional view.

32 Walls, 'Legacy of Crowther', 163–64. On the influence of African Independent churches see J.B. Webster, *The African Churches among the Yoruba*, Oxford, Clarendon Press, 1964.

33 Stanley, *History of the BMS*, 106–117.

DAVID LIVINGSTONE

Buxton's dream for the end of slavery in Africa through Christianity and commerce was to live on in the work of a young medical student present at the meeting of Buxton's society in 1840. David Livingstone (1813–73) was to devote himself to the extinction of the slave trade, and placing Africa at the heart of the Christian and humanitarian conscience. Livingstone argued, as had Buxton, that evangelical urgency to promote the gospel should go hand in hand with humanitarian concern for the oppressed, and that British power should be used to intervene on the part of those who were the victims of the slave trade.

Livingstone's working life began in a textile mill in Blantyre, Scotland at the age of ten. Like William Carey, although of humble origins, he possessed a sharp mind. In the evenings, and in spare moments during his work in the mill, he studied hard. Reared in a devout evangelical home, with grandparents who spoke only Gaelic, he attended the Independent chapel in Hamilton, and was converted as a teenager. As many another Scottish lad-o'-pairts, Livingstone was able to advance himself far beyond his original status in life through education, studying theology and medicine. He joined the London Missionary Society in 1840. His plan to serve in China was thwarted by the Opium Wars, and he turned his attention instead to Africa, where he arrived in 1841. Here he worked with Robert Moffat (1795–1883), another Scottish missionary sent out by the LMS—they accounted for 200 out of the first 1,300 candidates.[34] Moffat had arrived in South Africa in 1815 with little education and no formal theological training. In 1819 he moved north from the Cape Colony to Kuruman where he spent the rest of his life working amongst the Bechuana in what is now Botswana. He became a figurehead for missions in Africa, a much respected leader and diplomat, although it was 1829 before he baptised his first converts, and the work of translating the Bible into Tswana was not completed until 1857. Although operating in patriarchial fashion and placing little store on African traditions, Moffat demonstrated what could be achieved through Christianity and civilization when Africans were free.

During his two and a half years at Kuruman, Livingstone married the Moffat's eldest daughter Mary. Driven by Christian zeal, Livingstone was not a team worker, and found it hard to relate to those who could not operate at his pace. He was unable to settle to Moffat's painstaking approach, and instead embarked on a peripatetic life intended to prepare the way for evangelism in regions beyond current missionary influence. He reached Lake Ngami in 1849, and the Zambezi River in 1851. The following year Livingstone controversially decided to leave his wife and children in Scotland, believing the risks of such exploratory trips for them were too great. There Mary lived an increasingly unhappy life,

---

34 A. Walls, 'The Scottish Missionary Diaspora' in *The Cross-Cultural Process in Christian History*, 260.

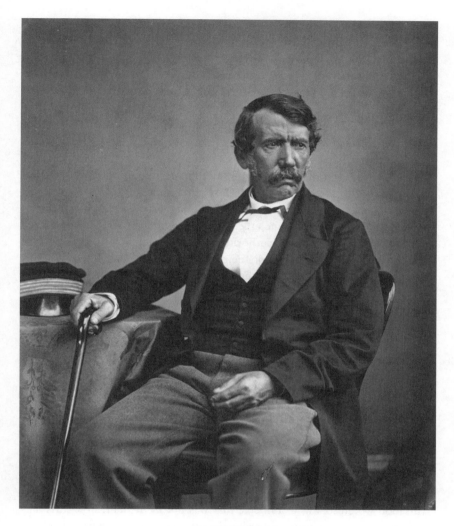

David Livingstone

struggling to bring up their children in a land foreign to her. Livingstone was acutely aware of their sufferings, but considered them a sacrifice necessary for a higher purpose. His letters home to his children are filled with tender longing that they might embrace a personal faith in Jesus Christ.

More than anyone else in the nineteenth century, Livingstone opened up inland Africa for the Christian gospel. He embarked on a series of missionary journeys, the first of which took him to Angola and the West Coast of Africa, and then, refusing to desert his African bearers, to Quilimane on the East Coast. He won respect and affection for his compassionate treatment of Africans. He became convinced that the only way for Africa to be transformed and the slave trade ended was through the gospel, and that this would be best accomplished by Africans. He returned to London in 1856 as a hero, heralded by the Royal Geographical Society for one of the great voyages of exploration. The following year he published his *Missionary Travels and Researches in South Africa*, which highlighted the persistence of the Central African slave trade, and had a powerful effect on generating interest in mission work in Africa. Livingstone was convinced that missionaries should be as determined to reach the heart of Africa as the slave trader was.

Livingstone's pioneering missionary exploration was not entirely to the taste of the LMS, from whom he ceased to receive financial support in 1857: his later journeys were sponsored by the British Government and the Royal Geographical Society. His second journey centred on Mozambique, an account of which was published in 1865. Here he encountered the activities of Arab slave traders, against whom the Portuguese authorities took little action. His famous print 'Gang of captives met at Mbame's on their way to Tette,' and an image of a captive unable to keep up with the caravan being executed, presented abolitionists with new and powerful motivation to continue their campaign. Livingstone's voice was not alone, with protests from German missionaries on the Gold Coast in the 1850s, Scottish missionaries in Malawi in the 1870s, and French missionaries in Tanzania, Uganda and Zaire in the 1870s. Livingstone began to believe that the Bible and the plough needed further assistance—a secure context which could only be achieved with the intervention of governments.[35]

However, except for a short period during 1857, Livingstone was not an advocate of white rule in Africa to accomplish this purpose, nor of widespread white settlement.[36] He shared Buxton's Enlightenment confidence in the power of civilisation, coupled with an overarching emphasis on the centrality and the power of Christianity, and a creative partnership with commerce. The priority remained Christianisation: 'I appreciate the effects of commerce much, but those of Christianity much more.'[37] If the love of Christ entered the heart, civilisation would follow. Commerce that was not in the hands of Christians would be worse than nothing, as he believed the Arab slave traders proved.

This approach was powerfully promoted in his writings and speaking tours. In 1857, Livingstone declared in a speech at Cambridge University that he was returning to Africa to 'make an open path for commerce and Christianity'. Speaking of the work he had begun, he announced, 'I LEAVE IT WITH YOU'.[38]

---

35   Manning, 157–59.

36   A. Ross, *David Livingstone: Mission and Empire*, London, Hambleton and London, Chatto and Windus, 2002, 242.

37   I. Schapera (ed) *Livingstone's Missionary Correspondence 1841–1856*, London, Chatto and Windus, 1961, 310.

38   D. Livingstone, *Cambridge Lectures*, ed. W. Monk, London, 1858, 24.

The parallels between Buxton's Niger Expedition, and Livingstone's ideas for government sponsored solutions for the Zambezi region are strong. Cotton cultivation was promoted as an alternative source of income to slave trading, and to reduce the dependence of the British cotton industry on the slave produced cotton of the southern United States.

The conviction of an alliance between Christianity and commerce as the answer to Africa's problems was widely shared. Bishop Samuel Wilberforce, speaking in 1860, stated—'There is little hope of promoting commerce in Africa, unless Christianity is planted in it; and ... there is very little ground for hoping that Christianity will be able to make its proper way unless we can establish a lawful commerce in the country.'[39]

Livingstone's understanding of the nature of mission was all-encompassing:

'My views of what is missionary duty are not so contracted as those whose ideal is a dumpy sort of man with a Bible under his arm. I have laboured in bricks and mortar, at the forge and at the carpenter's bench, as well as in preaching and in medical practice....I am serving Christ when shooting a buffalo for my men, or taking an astronomical observation, or writing to one of His children who forget.'[40]

Although direct fruit from Livingstone's pioneering work is hard to measure, the indirect results were of enormous significance. His work inspired the establishment of an LMS mission station at Kololo in 1858, and the prestigious Anglican Universities' Mission to Central Africa started in 1859. Charles Frederick Mackenzie was consecrated bishop for the diocese in Central Africa to be created by the mission, the first in a hoped-for chain of episcopates stretching from Cape Town to Cairo. His appointment symbolised how Anglo-Catholic Anglicans had embraced overseas mission in a major way. The mission sought to use the Zambezi River to reach the highlands of the Shire, where Livingstone had promised living conditions suitable for Europeans, and a ready response to the Gospel. Led on the field by Mackenzie, it united the flexibility of the voluntary missions movement, with ideas of community, and strong Episcopal oversight.

The enthusiasm of Livingstone for the Zambezi Mission paralleled that of Buxton for the Niger Expedition, and both ended in failure, at least in the short term. Livingstone accompanied the party which set off up the Zambezi in high hopes in 1862. En route they liberated a train of captive slaves, who became the nucleus of the community they were to form, but then things began to disastrously fall apart. Within a year, Mackenzie was dead, and three other

39 S. Wilberforce, Speech at Leeds, 25 May 1860, in S. Wilberforce, *Speeches on Missions,* ed. H. Rowley, London, 1874, 212–213, quoted in Porter, *Religion Versus Empire?,* 96.

40 Quoted in W.G. Blaikie, *The Personal Life of David Livingstone,* London, John Murray, 1880, 216.

missionaries soon followed him to the grave. The party became embroiled in local political conflicts, and it quickly became clear that Livingstone had gained only a superficial understanding of the area. To his dismay, the mission retreated to Zanzibar, where between 1864 and 1868 it regrouped, and formed a more successful base. Here the slave market was closed, and on its site a church was erected, later to become a Cathedral. From Zanzibar Christianity was to be extended far into East Africa.

By 1864 Livingstone's star had fallen. It was twenty years before the mission along the Zambezi was resumed, and although he secured another government consulate and further sponsorship from the Royal Geographical Society, Livingstone passed largely from the public eye. In November 1871 he was famously 'found' by a reporter from the *New York Herald*, Henry Morton Stanley in Ujiji. Stanley symbolised all that Livingstone was not, the well-equipped explorer leading the way for those who would by force parcel up what was left of Africa into European colonies. Nonetheless, Livingstone saw Stanley's journalism as a way of publicising the East coast slave trade that was so damaging to Africa.[41]

Livingstone's latter years were spent wandering amongst African villages, a haggard, bearded man, often hungry and ill, continuing his ministry of exposing the evils of slavery, opening doors through which missionaries could follow, and speaking of a 'Redeemer who was his Master.'[42] He died as he knelt by his bedside on 29 April 1873 in the village of Chief Chitambo, in modern Zambia. His faithful followers Susi and Chuma, buried his heart in the village where he died, but then oversaw an epic journey in which his African bearers lovingly carried his body and belongings 1,500 miles back to the coast. The final resting place for this Scottish nonconformist missionary, who began working life as a boy in a cotton mill, was to be amongst the rulers and heroes of the British state in Westminster Abbey, London.[43]

The famous dictum of Livingstone was 'I view the end of the geographical feat as the beginning of the missionary enterprise.' His steady advocacy of the cause of central Africa inspired others to complete the work of exploration, or engage in Christian mission. In expeditions in 1875 and 1877, Stanley followed the Congo River to its source. In 1878 missionaries from the Livingstone Inland Mission began work along its course, followed by the Baptist Missionary Society. Although after the 1860s, confidence in the providential alliance between Christianity, commerce and civilisation was shaken, Livingstone's vision remained influential. The Lovedale Institution, in South Africa, started by the Glasgow Missionary Society in 1841, continued to offer elementary education,

41 A. Ross, *Livingstone*, 222–230.
42 Ross, *Livingstone*, 197.
43 Ross, *Livingstone*, 234–38.

David Livingstone: Exploration, Christianity and Civilisation

'I view the end of the geographical feat as the beginning of the missionary enterprise. I take the latter term in its most extended signification and include every effort for the amelioration of our race; the promotion of all those means by which God in his providence is working and bringing all his dealings with man to a glorious consummation.'[1]

---

1   D. Livingstone, *Missionary Travels and Researches in South Africa*, London, 1857, 673–74.

---

training for school masters, catechists and mission agents, and artisan and agricultural skills.[44] Other Scottish Presbyterians embraced Livingstone's vision, developing missionary work in Blantyre, and Livingstonia, in modern Malawi. Stanley later worked with King Leopold II of Belgium in forming the International African Association, with the purpose of exploration, trade, and anti-slavery activity. Between 1880 and 1900 large scale slave trading within Africa was ended largely by the activity of European colonial powers, but this was also testimony to Buxton and Livingstone's enduring legacy, and the continued condemnation of the practice of slavery by missionaries.

In East Africa, missionary progress was slow. The LMS reached Madagascar in 1818, led by David Jones, winning the favour of the king Radama, who allowed the promotion of Christianity. In 1831, the first group of twenty-eight converts were baptized. However, under Radama's successor, persecution of Christians followed, with possibly some 200 killed, and others scattered to live in the forests. When the persecutions ended in 1861 it was found that despite persecution the church had increased some four-fold, the scattered Christians having sustained their faith through reading the New Testament in Malagassy. After being forced out of Ethiopia, the CMS missionary Johann Ludwig Krapf (1810–81) established a mission station at Mombasa in Kenya in 1844. Within two months his wife and only child had died, but Krapf battled on for a further thirty years. After two years he was joined by Johannes Rebmann. Their activity was confined mainly to the coast, where people were deeply traumatized by the operations of Arab slave traders. Although seeing limited success, they laid foundations upon which a strong Anglican church in East Africa was built. Their travels inland led to the 'discoveries' of Mount Kenya and Mount Kilimanjaro, although their accurate reports of snow on the tops of these mountains close to the equator were dismissed by unbelieving scientists in Europe, who believed it was the sun shining on limestone rock formations!

---

44   See R.H.W. Shepherd, *Lovedale in South Africa: The Story of a Century 1841–1941*, Lovedale, Lovedale Press, 1941.

MISSIONS TO THE MIDDLE EAST

Mid-nineteenth century Christian missionary effort to strongly Islamic areas, especially the Middle East, was of a significantly smaller scale than to other regions, and levels of response were low. There was generally limited understanding of Islam and little study of Arabic in the West.[45] However, Karl Gottlieb Pfander (1803–65), who had previously worked amongst Muslims in the Russian Empire before he joined the CMS in 1840, made an important contribution. His *Mizan-ul-Haqq* (*The Balance of Truth*) was to become a standard missionary apologetic work used amongst Muslims. In 1831, the ABCFM established missionary work in Turkey: most who responded were adherents of the Eastern Churches, especially Armenians, and a new evangelical denomination for them was formed in 1846, which received legal recognition in 1850. A CMS mission to Egypt lasted from 1818 to 1862, with limited success; United Presbyterians from the USA arrived in 1854, and saw response from a number of Coptic Christians.

Anglican pioneers from the London Society for Promoting Christianity among the Jews reached Jerusalem in 1820. In 1842 a joint bishopric of Jerusalem was founded by British and Prussian authorities, as a way of extending Christian influence in Palestine, and protecting Protestant Christians, just as Russian and French authorities protected Orthodox and Roman Catholic Christians. The arrangement lasted until 1886, when it became a purely Anglican bishopric. The joint bishopric was deeply controversial, shaped by the pre-millennial theology of its proponents, including Lord Shaftesbury, who attributed eschatological significance to conversions amongst the Jews. [The Church of Scotland dispatched a commission of enquiry about possible mission to Palestine in 1839, although the focus of this endeavour eventually became the Jews of Central Europe.]

PROGRESS IN MISSIONS IN THE SOUTH PACIFIC

In the South Pacific the LMS was particularly active, building on earlier pioneering endeavours, with significant success. In 1830, John Williams left 18 Tahitian teachers on Samoa, and within a generation most of the population had embraced Christianity. Within nine years of his baptism in 1830, a leading chief, Taufaahau, had declared himself king of the Tonga group of islands, and introduced a Christian law code. The first Methodist missionaries arrived on Fiji in 1835, but saw only limited fruit from their work until a revival in 1845 brought numerous conversions. Eventually the chief, Thakombau, a leading opponent of Christianity, was converted, and in 1854 baptised. By 1868, from a population of some 120,000 people, around 106,000 islanders were reported

---

45 The emerging understanding of, and commitment in terms of mission to, Islamic areas is discussed in A. Walls, 'Africa as the Theatre of Christian Engagement with Islam in the Nineteenth Century', *Journal of Religion in Africa* 29 (No. 2, 1999), 155–74.

to be attending Christian worship, and over 20,000 were church members or communicants.

The early pioneering work of the CMS in New Zealand also yielded steady results. The declaration of British sovereignty in 1840 brought large-scale white settlement, although there was significant hostility towards the Maori community. Nonetheless, Christianity spread rapidly, and by 1854 it was reported that 99% of Maoris had professed Christianity. George Selwyn (1809–78), who became Anglican bishop of New Zealand in 1841,[46] also promoted wider missionary work. In 1860 John Coleridge Patteson (1827–71) was consecrated the first bishop of Melanesia. Patteson's murder by islanders on Nukapu in 1871, in revenge for five islanders killed by white traders, made a deep impression, and awakened deeper interest in the South Pacific.

Missionary work could be dangerous and unpredictable. John Gibson Paton (1824–1907), a Scottish missionary from the Reformed Presbyterian Church,[47] was sent to Tanna in the New Hebrides (now Vanuatu) in 1858. He lived for four years under constant threat of death from the suspicious islanders, his first wife and child died, and he saw no obvious fruit from his work. He withdrew in 1866 and worked for the next fifteen years on the small island of Aniwa, during which time most of the population converted to Christianity.[48]

THE OPENING OF THE FAR EAST

As in Africa, the middle decades of the nineteenth century saw foundations laid for future work in the Far East, but Japan remained a far-from-fertile context for the promotion of Christianity. The first Roman Catholic priest to enter Japan in the modern era arrived in Tokyo in 1858, and others moved to Hakodate and Nagasaki. To their amazement, in Nagasaki they found a community of some 20,000 Roman Catholic believers, whose origins lay in seventeenth century missionary endeavours. They had survived as secret believers despite the terrible persecution endured when Japan was a closed country, and developed their own informal leadership structures. Only around half were willing to place themselves under the authority of the French Roman Catholic missionaries, who proved critical of their attempts to contextualise Roman Catholicism. Nonetheless, Christianity remained illegal in Japan, and after news of these Roman Catholic believers filtered out to the authorities between 1869 and 1873 some 4,000 were arrested and ordered to recant. Those who refused were transported to remote areas, where harsh treatment led to

---

46   Neill, *Christian Mission*, 255–56.

47   I.J. Shaw, 'John Paton and Urban Mission in Nineteenth-Century Glasgow', *Records of Scottish Church History Society*, Vol. XXXV, 2005.

48   On Paton see James Paton (ed), *John G. Paton, DD, Missionary to the New Hebrides: An Autobiography*, 2 volumes, London, 1889.

a number of deaths. The first Episcopal convert in Japan was reported in 1866, and in 1872 nine men were baptised by missionaries from the Reformed Church, and formed into the Kirisuto Ko Kwai, the Church of Christ.

In 1867 the last of the Shogûns, protectors of the emperor, resigned, and the Meiji era began. Devotion to the emperor intensified, together with a deep patriotic feeling for Japan. Although the anti-Christian edicts were rescinded in 1873, it was 1889 before Japanese subjects were granted freedom of religion, 'within the limits not prejudicial to peace and order, and not antagonistic to their duties as subjects,'[49] and Christianity only progressed slowly.

KOREA

The long genesis of Roman Catholicism in Korea began in 1777 when a group of Korean scholars began to study Matteo Ricci's (1552–1610) treatises in Chinese. One was sent to Peking to enquire further into the faith, where he was baptized with the name Peter. On his return a locally organised and propagated form of Roman Catholicism began to take root in Korean soil. When a Chinese priest, James Ti-Yu, was sent to work with them, he found a community of 4,000 Korean Roman Catholics. Roman Catholicism attracted opposition from Confucians and practitioners of traditional religion for being seen to resist the cult of the ancestors. It was also considered a possible focal point for rebellion, and was therefore rendered illegal. Ti-Yu was executed in 1801, and many martyrdoms followed, including three European priests who reached Korea in 1836 and 1837 but were executed after just three years. Nonetheless, the Roman Catholic Church in Korea continued to grow secretly: by 1866 there were reckoned to be 25,000 Christians. Further politically motivated persecutions in the mid-1860s saw two bishops, seven priests, and around 8,000 Korean Roman Catholics killed, a tragedy from which Korean Roman Catholicism never fully recovered.

The pioneer Protestant missionary to Korea was the Welsh Congregationalist Robert Thomas (1839–1866). In 1865 he spent several months on the west coast learning the language, exploring possibilities for a mission, and distributing Chinese Bibles. He returned in 1866 on an American ship seeking opportunities for trade in the forbidden country. Ignoring warnings from the authorities, tragedy struck after the vessel ran aground, and the crew of twenty-three killed. The most widely accepted account of Thomas's death is that he struggled ashore, where he died at the hands of a soldier to whom he was offering a Chinese Bible. He became the first Protestant martyr in Korea. It was twenty years before Protestants returned. When Samuel Moffett, a pioneering missionary in Pyengyang (Pyongyang) started a catechumen's class in 1892, one of the candidates was a man who had received a Chinese New Testament from Thomas.[50]

---

49   Neill, *History of Christian Missions*, 277.
50   S.J. Moffett, *History of Christianity in Asia, Vol. II, 1500–1900*, Maryknoll, Orbis, 2005, 530.

China

The vast population of China was closed to missionary endeavour for significant parts of the nineteenth century. Robert Morrison (1782–1834) reached Canton in 1807, and after 1809 he worked as an official translator for the East India Company in their trade with China. He laid foundations for future work with his translation into Chinese of the New Testament (1813), the Old Testament (1819), and a Chinese dictionary. He baptised a small number of converts, the first in 1814. One of them, Liang Fah, became the first Chinese person to be ordained to Protestant ministry. Morrison believed that work amongst Chinese living outside the country would open doors to China itself. He encouraged the establishment of colleges in Malacca and Macao, offering studies in Asian languages, English, and science, which Morrison hoped would prompt enquiry into Christian revelation. The beginnings were slow, but between 1818 and 1833 forty students completed the course and fifteen were baptized.

The tea trade gradually opened China up to the world, although by the 1830s it was in good part financed by trade in opium. After 1839, naval power secured further Western trading opportunities through the morally questionable 'Opium War.' The subsequent 1842 Treaty of Nanking allowed foreigners to live in five Treaty Ports around the coast, and Hong Kong to pass into British sovereignty. Despite opposing the aggression, missionaries saw the treaty as a Providential opportunity to open up a country of 300 million people to Christianity. The first eighteen years after 1842 saw over two hundred British, European and American missionaries reach the treaty ports, asserting religious freedom for themselves and their converts. Their tacit acceptance of the fruits of military aggression did little to enhance the reputation of Christianity in Chinese eyes in the periods of political instability that were to shake the country into the twentieth century.

Dr Karl Gützlaff (1803–51) proved a zealous if somewhat eccentric pioneer of mission in Thailand and China. In his book *China Opened* he urged European missionary societies to embrace the Treaty of Nanking as an opportunity for the propagation of the gospel that could not be missed. His inspiring vision to reach all eighteen provinces of China by mobilising as many Chinese evangelists as possible collapsed when most of those he entrusted with the task proved not to have been converted at all, but to be fraudsters and opium addicts. Undaunted, Gützlaff formed the Chinese Evangelization Society, although it lacked a secure financial basis, and by 1859 was unable to pay its agents regularly.[51] In 1865, there was still no mission work in eleven out of eighteen Chinese provinces, and in the other seven it had advanced little beyond the coast.

William Chalmers Burns (1815–68) had in 1839 been instrumental in bringing revival to parishes in Kilsyth and Dundee in Scotland, but he was strongly

---

51 On Gützlaff see H. Schlyter, *Karl Gützlaff als Missionar in China*, Lund-Copenhagen, Gleerup, 1946.

impelled to preach the gospel where it had not been previously heard. He arrived in China in 1847, and proved a fine Chinese scholar, producing a translation of *Pilgrim's Progress*. Burns made several illegal missionary journeys inland, seeing some success in his work. These visits were to inspire another notable pioneer, James Hudson Taylor (1832–1905), who arrived in China in 1854, aged just twenty-one, to work with Gützlaff's Chinese Evangelization Society. He accompanied Burns on some journeys to the interior of China. Although he resigned from Gützlaff's society in 1859, he still referred to him as the 'grandfather of the China Inland Mission.' In 1855, Hudson Taylor took the radical step of shaving his head apart from a pigtail, and adopting the wearing of Chinese clothes, believing that Western culture was a liability, not an asset, to missionary work. The step shocked the Western community in Shanghai, as did his decision to live by faith for his needful supplies.

Deeply burdened that there were just ninety-one Protestant missionaries for China's 300 million people, in 1865 Hudson Taylor founded the China Inland Mission, which was to become, for a time, the largest mission in the world. The CIM was open to candidates from any denomination provided they could sign its strongly conservative doctrinal declaration. The mission welcomed single women, and those with a rugged pioneering spirit but who lacked educational attainments. Some of them became notable scholars and experts in Chinese. The mission was directed not from London but the mission field, China. The mobility, simplicity, and devotion of CIM workers who lived and associated with Chinese in their widespread evangelism to unreached inland areas, challenged other missionaries, although their work was viewed by some as risky and superficial. Despite many difficulties, by 1882 the mission had visited all the provinces, and located missionaries in fifteen out of eighteen of them.

Nineteenth-century China remained far from stable, increasingly beset by political division. The Taiping rebellion from 1850 to 1864 arose out of the visionary experiences of its founder, Hong Xiuquan, who claimed to have met his true family—God, the Virgin Mary, and his elder brother Jesus, and to have been given a prophetic mission to redeem China. Hong formed his followers into an army which stormed Nanking in 1853, controlled much of central China, and sought the overthrow of Manchu domination. The rebellion cost hundreds of thousands of lives, before it was brutally crushed by the Manchus. The syncretistic practices of the rebels included some learned through contact with Christian missionaries. The missionaries who had contact with the Taiping rebels generally concluded that religion was being used as a cloak by which to win influence and favour from Western powers.[52] Some believed that the Taiping movement opened China up to Christian influence. It certainly

---

52   On the Taiping rebellion see J.K. Fairbank, *China: A New History*, Cambridge, Mass., Harvard University Press, 1992, 206–212.

suggested a weakening of the dominant hold of Confucianism on the Chinese mind. Further treaties between European powers and China in 1859 granted permission for travel into the interior, guaranteed the toleration of Christianity, protection for missionaries, and in theory for Chinese Christians.

South East Asia

In South-East Asia, Christianity made slow progress in lands dominated by Buddhism and Islam. Congregationalist missionaries entered Thailand in 1831, but withdrew eighteen years later, during which time no Thai convert had been baptised. Baptists arrived in 1833, and Presbyterians in 1840, but struggled in the face of official hostility to foreigners, and it was 1859 before the Presbyterians baptized their first Thai convert, Nai Chune. Mission work in Borneo advanced more rapidly in the hands of Anglican missionaries after 1847. In Indonesia, Dutch rule allowed for ministry to Dutch settlers, but preaching to the large Muslim population was discountenanced, for fear of provoking hostility, although the attitude was less rigorous when it came to animistic peoples. Nonetheless, through the work of independent Christian pioneers who settled in Java after 1810, some communities were founded of converts from Islam. In 1849, the missionary J.E. Jellesma established a centre at Modjowarno: using lay evangelists, the East Javanese Church grew rapidly, seeing significant numbers of converts from Islam. The Baptist work in Burma pioneered by Adoniram Judson saw greatest advance amongst non-Buddhist tribes. Anglican efforts in Burma involved significant educational effort, and a bishop for Rangoon was consecrated in 1877.

India

In 1843, fifty years after Carey had arrived in India, Baptist Missionary Society churches in the vast sub-continent had just 1,449 members, 454 of whom were in Calcutta, 465 in North India, and 530 in Ceylon (Sri Lanka). The contrast with the 2,141 Baptists found on the small island of the Bahamas in the Caribbean is stark.[53] Christian missions were making only limited progress amongst the dominant Hindu population. The caste system meant that converts were subject to significant social and economic ostracism: few were prepared to pay the high social price of conversion.

The Scotsman Alexander Duff (1806–78) proved highly influential upon missionary approaches in India. His thinking was moulded by the Calvinistic heritage of the Scottish Reformation, the evangelicalism of Thomas Chalmers, and the Scottish Common Sense Philosophy of the Moderate Party which argued that divine Providence worked through rational argument and the dynamics of economic and social progress. His post-enlightenment educational

---

53 Stanley, *BMS*, 141–141.

Alexander Duff

philosophy proposed that Christianity should be promoted within a framework of education, the model followed in mission to the Scottish Highlands. Duff believed that to assist Hindu audiences in understanding biblical revelation and the Christian world-view there was a need to engender in the Indian mind a spirit of Western rational enquiry and intellectual renewal. Simple open air bazaar preaching, would not work in the Indian context. As the early Christian apostles had preached in Greco-Roman societies already prepared by 'civilisation' for the gospel, so such a seed-bed needed to be created in India.

In 1830, Duff opened a school in Calcutta, with the help of the Hindu reformer Ram Mohun Roy, offering the children of higher castes a high quality Western Christian education in English. By targeting education at the higher castes, Duff believed that converts would occupy strategic roles in Indian society, and their influence would percolate down to the lower castes. Educationally, the project was a success, with enrolment averaging 800 over ten years.

Similar institutes were established in Bombay (1832), Madras (1837) and Nagpur (1844). Duff's influence ensured that English remained the dominant educational medium, although some feared that training the human mind was being placed before training in divine knowledge. The Calcutta School produced only around 50 converts, and they were often ostracised by their own families, or accompanied by threats to close a school down, or create civil disturbance. Many were more interested in self-advancement through education than in the Christian principles behind it. Nonetheless, such converts as there were came from prominent families, and a number went on serve as ministers or Christian lay leaders. Duff also proved an eloquent promoter of mission, inspiring many to volunteer, or financial contribution. The first chair of missiology at the Free Church of Scotland's New College, in Edinburgh was established as a result of his encouragement of the scientific study of missions.[54]

The appropriateness of the educational strategy appeared confirmed when government grants for schools in India were made available after 1854, which many missions felt compelled to accept, especially after they were made available to Hindu and Islamic schools. Yet, such grants were already being fiercely debated by churches in Britain, and some missionaries echoed the doubts of Rufus Anderson as to the priority given to high-level education. Although of use in training future ministers, education was only an indirect evangelistic means. In a utilitarian age, as statistical evidence for the limited returns from the large expenditure mounted, confidence in the strategy flagged. After the Indian Mutiny of 1857 the heavy educational emphasis fell into disfavour. British and American evangelicals attracted to the immediacy of Finney's revivalism, preferred to emphasise evangelistic activism. Greater prominence was given to indigenous workers preaching in the vernacular. Those marginalised by caste or tribal background, illness, poverty, or social deviancy, responded in greater numbers to the work of the missionaries, than those provided with high-level education. Some mission leaders feared Christianity would be overwhelmed by poor and uneducated Christians.[55]

Although the amount of missionary endeavour in India was increasing, there were in 1851 still only 339 ordained missionaries working with 19 societies, in

---

54 I.D. Maxwell, 'Civilisation or Christianity? The Scottish Debate on Mission Methods, 1750–1835', in B. Stanley, ed., *Christian Missions and the Enlightenment*, 136–140.

55 Porter, *Religion Versus Empire?*, 165.

a country of over 150 million people. Of the 91,000 Indian Christians, 51,300 of them were in the Tinnevelly area and South Travancore, with only 40,000 spread across the rest of India's vast expanse. There were few Indian pastors, and income from local churches was insufficient for their support. One hundred years after Carey's arrival in India, a self-governing, self-supporting church looked a distant prospect.

Yet, a real, and often unrecognised, work had begun amongst India's tribal groups. American Baptist missionary work in the Telegu area was on the point of closure when contact with a local man Yerraguntla Periah, converted through CMS missionaries, revealed a large number who had come to the Christian faith through his work. Soon thousands joined them, with 8,691 adults baptised in six months in 1878 alone: in 1882 there were 20,865 Telegu church members. The Lutheran Johann Evangelista Gossner (1773–1858) founded the Gossner Mission in Bihar in 1839, which saw 900 converts in its first eighteen years. By the 1960s the Gossner Evangelical Lutheran Church, numbered over 200,000 members, testimony to the legacy of Gossner and his successor Johann Detloff Prochnow.[56]

Missionary work amongst the Santāls, led by the Norwegian Lars Olsen Skrefsrud (1840–1910) in the years after 1867 produced a church of some 15,000 adherents by 1910. In the fifty years after Welsh Calvinistic Methodists started work in the Khasi hills of Assam in 1841, some 10,000 came to the Christian faith. Mission fields close to India were also being opened up. The LMS began work in Ceylon (Sri Lanka) in 1804, joined by the Baptists in 1812, the Methodists in 1814, and the ABCFM in 1817, although all found limited response from the Buddhist population of the island.

The cause of mission on the Indian sub-continent was severely rocked by the Indian Mutiny of 1857, sparked by the fears of Sepoy regiments that they would be forcibly converted to Christianity. Thirty-eight men, women and children from the missionary community were killed. So too were many Indian Christians, victim to hostility directed towards things associated with the West. The vigorous military response of the British government to the Mutiny further served to create negative sentiment towards the work of Christian missions in India. Many sermons preached on 7 October 1857, the day of national humiliation held after the Mutiny, called on God to aid the British forces in India: the effective suppression of the rebellion was viewed as an outworking of divine providence.[57] Yet some Christians saw the Mutiny as divine judgement for the failings of British rule in India, and for their indifference towards mission. If peace was to be maintained in the future, it was believed that Christianity needed to be spread more widely. The British government responded to the

56   A.F. Walls, 'The Eighteenth-Century Protestant Missionary Awakening in Its European Context', in B. Stanley (ed), *Christian Missions and the Enlightenment*, Eerdmans, Grand Rapids, 2001, 43.

57   B. Stanley, 'Christian Responses to the Indian Mutiny of 1857', in W.J.Sheils (ed) *The Church and War, Studies in Church History, Vol. 20*, Oxford, Blackwell, 1983, 281–82.

crisis with increased public works and commercial development, such as the extension of the railway system, whilst some Indians turned their thoughts towards nationalism. Queen Victoria issued a careful proclamation in 1858: 'Firmly relying ourselves on the truth of Christianity and acknowledging the solace of religion, we disclaim alike the right and desire to impose our convictions on any of our subjects'.[58]

ROMAN CATHOLIC MISSIONS

European Roman Catholic overseas mission, which had led the way in the sixteenth and seventeenth centuries, was significantly weakened by the dissolution of the Jesuit order in 1773, and then the French Revolution, which left only around 300 serving Roman Catholic missionaries across the world.[59] The tide turned after 1814, when Pius VII re-established the Jesuit order. A range of new orders were established in the nineteenth century, with a strong mission interest, such as the Marists (1817), and the White Fathers, formed in 1868 for missionary work in Algeria. With Roman Catholic missionary activity no longer able to rely on the patronage of kings and rulers, the support of the laity took on a more significant role.

Pope Gregory XVI (1831–46) proved to be a key figure in promoting Roman Catholic mission activities. He created bishoprics and prefectures in missionary areas, including a vicariate-apostolic for the Cape of Good Hope in 1837, for the West African coast north of Angola in 1842, Egypt in 1844, and for Central Africa in 1846. Jesuit priests reached the Upper Nile in 1847. By the middle of the century, a centralised and well-controlled Roman Catholic effort was under way to reach the whole of Africa.[60] There were sixteen vicariates in India by 1869, and over twenty bishops by the 1880s, although none were Indians. As with Protestantism, education played a significant part in Roman Catholic mission work in India, and in this the Jesuits took a leading role, although only small numbers passed through the colleges into the priesthood.

Roman Catholic missionaries continued their work in China, sometimes in secret, in the face of tumultuous political changes, and periods of persecution. At least four were killed between 1814 and 1840. The treaties of the middle decades of the century allowed Roman Catholic missions greater access to the eighteen provinces, and the main religious orders and societies entered the country, together with a large number of sisterhoods. The government of Napoleon III used French Roman Catholic priests as a way of extending its influence, allowing it to be portrayed as the protector of Roman Catholicism

---

58   A.T. Embree 'Christianity and the State in Victorian India: Confrontation and Collaboration', in R.W. Davies and R.J. Helmstadter (eds), *Religion and Irreligion in Victorian Society: Essays in Honour of R.K. Webb*, London, Routledge, 1992, 151.

59   Neill, *Christian Missions*, 334

60   A. Hastings, *The Church in Africa 1450–1950*, Oxford, Clarendon, 1994, 249.

throughout the world. This gave Roman Catholic missionaries a measure of political influence in China, which assisted them with the protection of their converts. The link between imperialism and the promotion of Roman Catholicism meant that some embraced its teachings with mixed motives.

MOTIVATIONS TO MISSION

The progression of Christian mission in the middle decades of the nineteenth century suggests elements of both continuity and discontinuity with earlier decades. The enlightenment legacy remained important: reason was deemed vital in assisting people to accept the claims of biblical revelation, making education central to missions endeavour, although the cultural values imparted alongside it brought an association with Western cultural imperialism. Yet, although some sought a balanced partnership between spiritual, social and economic change, the continued expansion of Christianity cannot solely be explained in terms of the Enlightenment. Others believed Christianity could transform societies without laying a foundation of rational knowledge through western education. Those impatient of the slow work of civilising mission urged the primacy of preaching. Generally the marriage of Christianity with commerce was looking suspect.

What was meant by 'civilisation' was unclear. To some it was the adoption of Western building styles, with doors particularly on bedrooms, and Western dress—an emphasis reinforced by middle-class religious public opinion in Britain. Robert Moffat believed: 'It would seem a strange anomaly, to see a Christian professor lying at full length on the ground covered with filth and dirt, and in a state of comparative nudity, talking about Christian diligence, circumspection, purification, and white robes! The Gospel teaches that all things should be done decently and in order.'[61] Missionary families could also be significant forces in imposing cultural values. Maggie Paton, serving with her husband John on Aniwa refused to play the harmonium to commence a Sunday service when a tribesman dressed in nothing more than war paint was present.[62] Other missionaries deplored the way Western dress could become a symbol of prestige and social advancement, and urged their followers to wear indigenous clothing, rather than Western, and set a personal example. Rufus Anderson complained of how mission work had simply produced individuals 'foreign in their manners, foreign in their habits, foreign in their sympathies.'[63] The emphasis on civilisation meant that some people declared themselves Christians for other reasons than simply a change of personal religious

---

61 R. Moffat, *Missionary Labours and Scenes in Southern Africa*, 11th edn, New York, 1852, 332, quoted in J. Cox, 'Religion and Imperial Power', p. 354.

62 M. Paton, *Letters and Sketches*, 132.

63 Quoted in Hutchinson, *Errand to the World*, 80–82.

convictions. As evidence accumulated from the mission field, strategy became empiricist and pragmatic, allowing for a plurality of approaches, appropriate to different contexts.[64]

Missionaries convinced that the Lordship of Christ over the world required the toppling of idols tended to identify false religion with darkness and degradation of peoples, with idolatry seen as the greatest of crimes against God. However, condemnation of idolatry could easily become denunciation of non-Western cultures as heathen and primitive that sounded almost racist. Early Baptists in India had translated some works of Hindu literature, although mainly to understand how the Hindu mind worked, and allowed early converts to retain their original names, even if of Hindu deities. This acceptance of aspects of wider culture became harder to maintain when the Christian civilisation of Western Europe or North America was assumed to be a model of Christian society. The success of missionary models such as Sierra Leone, where an educated African middle class was created, typified by Samuel Crowther, bolstered such confidence. Yet voices were calling for a need to move off mission station verandas and to live amongst local communities. Links between Western missionary endeavour and nineteenth-century colonialism are much debated (see ch. 13) but between the 1830s and 1850s it has been concluded that there is no evidence that 'the bible naturally either followed or preceded the flag.'[65]

The growing awareness of the size of the missionary task deepened the recognition of the need to train and utilise indigenous catechists, teachers, evangelists, and pastors. By the 1860s the key pioneering work in many areas had been done, scripture translation had borne fruit, but because the number of converts remained small, the self-governing, self-supporting, and self-propagating churches envisaged by Henry Venn rarely appeared. Instead, a dependency culture was created within mission churches, and reluctance by missionaries to empower local leaderships with responsibility.

Developments within Western Christianity continued to shape mission in the middle decades of the nineteenth century. Religious revivals increased the emphasis on activism in extending Christianity, bringing an increased flow of volunteers for overseas missionary service, and deepened interest in personal holiness and consecration. Until the 1880s, an optimistic postmillennialism generally prevailed: even if immediate fruit was limited, confidence remained that where one sowed, one day another would reap.

Sections of the Christian church previously suspicious were drawn into the missions movement. The early pan-evangelical vision of missions gave way to denominationalism, which could prove a severe problem. Rather than simply planting churches where there had previously been none, mission became

---

64 Stanley, 'Christian Missions and the Enlightenment', 194–197.
65 Porter, *Religion Versus Empire?*, 162; see also Stanley, *Bible and Flag*.

an exercise in planting outposts of denominations such as Presbyterianism, Lutheranism, or Anglicanism. Competition and even animosity on the mission field presented a mixed message. The development of indigenous, independent, churches, quite separate from the European intellectual culture, was part of the reaction against this.

A prime motivation toward mission remained the profound theological conviction of the 'lostness' of those who did not embrace the Christian message. In a missionary sermon in London in January 1843 Robert Moffat challenged his hearers over the 'teeming millions...moving onward every day like some vast funeral procession; onward and downward, sadly and slowly, but certainly to the regions of woe... All idolaters, we are told, have their portion in the lake which burneth with fire and brimstone.'[66] Mission leaders reflected deeply, and often sensitively on the subject. Livingstone comforted himself before the appalling prospect with the knowledge that the 'Judge of all the earth will do right.' Henry Venn was sure that the heathen who died without ever hearing the offer of the gospel would not be punished with the same punishment as those who rejected it.[67] By the 1880s, amongst some denominations, such theology was being questioned, leading Hudson Taylor in 1884 to insert a clause in the CIM's basis of faith requiring assent to the doctrine of the everlasting punishment of the lost.[68] Missionaries driven by this urgency of saving souls were less influenced by political and imperial considerations than those who embraced temporal understandings of the kingdom of God, for whom spreading the benefits of Western civilization was important.

The sense that Divine Providence lay behind the provision of extensive overseas territories, sometimes unsought, to European nations, provoked assumptions that they had been commissioned by God to bring the gospel to such parts of the world. This concept of sacred trust to use influence beneficently was particularly strong in Britain, and was echoed in America in the 1880s and 1890s, even when the manner of acquisition appeared morally dubious.

A shift in the holistic dimension of missiological thinking was taking place in the later nineteenth century. Whilst the triumvirate of Christianity, civilisation, and commerce had predominated in areas afflicted by slavery, the development of a medical missionary strategy added another dimension. From as early as the eighteenth century medical doctors had worked with the Tranquebar mission. The American John Scudder began medical work in Ceylon in 1819, and Peter Parker in China in 1835. The Edinburgh Medical Missionary Society was founded in 1841 to assist with the preparation of medical workers for the mission

66   J. Campbell (ed), *The Farewell Services of Robert Moffat in Edinburgh, Manchester, and London*, London, 1843, 109, quoted in Stanley, *Bible and Flag*, 65.

67   D. Livingstone, *Missionary Travels and Researches in South Africa*, London, 1857, 90; W.R. Shenk, *Henry Venn—Missionary Statesman*, New York, 1983, 27.

68   Stanley, *Bible and Flag*, 67.

field, and also to offer medical support for the poorest in the city. Before long it was supporting work in China, India, and Syria. The Baptist mission started in Orissa, India in 1822, included significant social concern, particularly running orphanages in the Kond hills for children rescued from child sacrifice rituals.[69]

Despite missionary mortality remaining high, and many projects coming to nothing, a steady flow of recruits continued. Accounts of the dedication of missionaries suffering hardship and discomfort, and sometimes violent opposition, or fatal tropical disease, served to increase the resolve of others to volunteer. In 1850 Allen Gardiner, a former Commander in the British Navy, landed on Tierra del Fuego, one of the remotest spots imaginable, to commence a mission amongst the Patagonians. The failure of the ship carrying their provisions for the winter to arrive condemned Gardiner and his six companions to a tragic death from starvation. They died strong in their faith, as Gardiner recorded in his diary—'Poor and weak as we are, our boat is a very Bethel to our souls for we feel and know that God is here. Asleep or awake, I am, beyond the power of expression, happy'.[70] Their sacrifice was widely reported. Twenty-two years later the first group of Tierra del Fuegans was baptised. Even Charles Darwin applauded the efforts of the South American Missionary Society, the work of which extended to Chile, Paraguay, Argentina, and Brazil. Others questioned the cost not only of missionary's lives, but also of their wives and children. The redoubtable Maggie Paton rebuffed the doubters:

'Fools...may chatter against missionaries marrying, and shake their heads about the distractions of a family. We who are in the thick of the work, and know all sides to the question, feel overwhelmingly thankful that God has given us these children... Our Bairns are little Missionaries, every one. They have called forth in the Natives a softened feeling towards us, and in us towards the Natives and their Children.... The life of the Christian Home is the best treatise on Christianity—a daily object-lesson which all can understand'.[71]

The desire to simply propagate imperial or Euro-centric values is insufficient explanation for this phenomenon. Some were probably too ready to embrace martyrdom; others too reliant on European administrators and soldiers. Yet for most the desire to spend and be spent, to endure sacrifice of self and loved ones, even unto death, sprang ultimately from the profoundest religious convictions as to the truth of the message of Jesus Christ, and from compassion for those who lived and died without hearing and embracing it.

---

69   Stanley, *BMS*, 162–172.

70   A. Gardiner, 'Diary', quoted in Neill, *Christian Mission*, 271.

71   M. Paton, *Letters and Sketches from the New Hebrides*, reprinted Harrisonburgh, Sprinkle, 2003, 108–109.

D. Bosch, *Transforming Mission: Paradigm Shifts in Theology of Mission*, Maryknoll, NY, Orbis, 1991.

A. Hastings, *The Church in Africa, 1450–1950*, Oxford, Clarendon, 1994.

W.R. Hutchison, *Errand to the World: American Protestant Thought and Foreign Missions,* Chicago, University of Chicago Press, 1987.

S.H. Moffett, *A History of Christianity in Asia, Vol. II, 1500–1900*, Maryknoll, Orbis, 2005.

S. Neill, *History of Christian Missions*, Harmondsworth, Penguin, 1986.

A. Porter, *Religion Versus Empire? British Protestant Missionaries and Overseas Expansion, 1700–1914*, Manchester, Manchester University Press, 2004.

A. Ross, *David Livingstone: Mission and Empire*, London, Hambleton and London, 2002.

W. Shenk, *Henry Venn, Missionary Statesman*, Maryknoll, New York, 1983.

B. Stanley, *History of Baptist Missionary Society 1792–1992*, Edinburgh, T&T Clark, 1992.

B. Stanley (ed), *Christian Missions and the Enlightenment*, Grand Rapids, Eerdmans, 2001.

B. Sundkler and C. Steed, *A History of the Church in Africa*, Cambridge, CUP, 2000.

A. Walls, *The Missionary Movement in Christian History: Studies in the Transmission of Faith*, Maryknoll, Orbis, 1996.

A. Walls, *The Cross-Cultural Process in Christian History*, Maryknoll, New York, Orbis, 2002.

10

Religious Responses to Revolutions in Science

Revolutions in the realm of theology in the nineteenth century were matched by equally profound changes in the field of natural philosophy, or science, as it became known. This was nothing new: from Copernicus, to Galileo, to Newton, scientific advance had consistently challenged inherited explanations of the cosmos, raising questions with profound theological implications. The difference in the nineteenth century was that the questions of scientists became part of a polemic against theistic world-views. Science increasingly presented itself as an all-encompassing, explanation of cosmic reality, the authority of which could be only challenged on the basis of alternative scientific proof.

Theology had reigned as the Queen of Sciences during the Middle Ages, attracting the cream of intellects, but in the midst of the intense theological debate of the Reformation era, major advances in scientific fields, such as astronomy, were to take place. General revelation in the natural world was placed alongside special revelation in scripture. The study of nature demonstrated not only the existence but also the attributes of God, it was to think God's thoughts after him, and demonstrate the wise design of creation. Nonetheless, well before the nineteenth century the seeds for a discontinuity between a natural and a religious world-view had been sown. René Descartes (1596–1650) had proposed a fundamental division between matter, which could be felt and measured, and thought, or 'spirit'- the world of consciousness. This so-called 'Cartesian dualism' pointed towards a breakup of the prevailing comprehensive world-view, between physically measurable, scientific matters, and the theological and spiritual realm, and ultimately between faith and reason.

Natural theologians in the seventeenth and eighteenth centuries believed that the universe obeyed laws that were comprehensible not only to God, but also to the human mind. Vital to this was the growing understanding of the phenomenon of universal gravitation. Its discoverer, Isaac Newton (1642–1727), a farmer's son who went on to become a Fellow of Trinity College, Cambridge, pioneered advances in mathematics and physics, although he attributed his achievements to the work of his predecessors, believing that he had seen further because he stood on giant's shoulders. The implications of what Newton saw were profound indeed: in the face of new scientific understandings, what place had magic and superstition, or Christian understandings of miracles, or even faith? Yet Isaac Newton remained a devout, if somewhat unorthodox Christian. To him, the rotation of the planets and their satellites in the same direction pointed to their divine Author: 'For it became who created them to set them in order. And if he did so, it is unphilosophical to seek for any other Origin of the World, or to pretend that it might arise out of Chaos by the mere laws of Nature...'.[1]

The argument that evidence of design in the cosmos demonstrated the existence and attributes of God remained the backbone of natural theology until the nineteenth century. In his *Essay on Population* (1798) Thomas Malthus argued that Providential laws governed human nature and the natural world, rewarding Christian virtue, and setting boundary lines which humans should not contravene. In *Natural Theology* (1802) William Paley argued that the intricacy and complexity of the natural world spoke of design, and therefore a Designer. It was possible to argue from this to a Creator God, and to God's dealings with mankind in Jesus Christ. Creation displayed the wisdom, goodness, justice, benevolence and goodness of God.

Nonetheless, well before Darwin, natural theologians were moving away from the idea of regular interventions by God in the natural world. To Newton, God did not show his glory by regularly and actively intervening in his creation, but by creating and sustaining natural processes. As William Whewell argued in his 1834 Bridgewater Treatise, *Astronomy and General Physics Considered,* 'events are brought about not by insulated interpositions of Divine power, exerted in each particular case, but by the establishment of general laws.'[2] Charles Darwin, schooled in the tradition of English natural theology, made use of this quotation in 1859. It was to readers in this tradition that his famous writings were particularly addressed.[3] The inherent goodness of the system being described also began to be questioned. In his 1850 poem, *In Memoriam*,

1   I. Newton, *Opticks...*, London, 1730, 4th edn, 376.

2   W. Whewell, *Astronomy and General Physics Considered with Reference to Natural Theology*, London, William Pickering, 1834, 356.

3   The debt of Darwin to natural theology is discussed in J. H. Brooke, 'The Relations Between Darwin's Science and his Religion', in *Darwinism and Divinity: Essays on Evolution and Religious Belief*, ed J. Durant, Oxford, Blackwell, 1985, 40–75; and J.R. Moore, *The Post-Darwinian Controversies*, Cambridge, CUP, 1979.

The Argument from Design of Natural Theologians

'Now, when the multitude of animals is considered, the number of parts in each, their figure and fitness, the faculties depending on them, the variety of species, the complexity of structure, the success, in so many cases, and felicity of the result, we can never reflect, without the profoundest adoration, upon the character of that Being from whom all these things have proceeded; we cannot help observing what an exertion of benevolence creation was; of a benevolence so minute in its care, how vast in its comprehension.

When we appeal to the parts and faculties of the animals, and to the limbs and senses of animals in particular, we state, I conceive, the proper medium for the proof of the conclusion we wish to establish'.[1]

1   W. Paley, *Natural Theology*, London, 1802, 252–53

---

the poet Alfred Lord Tennyson, subject to many religious doubts, spoke of 'Nature red in tooth and claw'. Conceptions of a bleaker, less explicable, world than that of the natural theologians began to emerge.

THE ADVANCE OF GEOLOGY

The idea of permanency and wise design in the world began to be questioned in the late eighteenth century and early nineteenth century as geologists and palaeontologists started to discover indications of a process of change in the surface of the earth. Some understood this to be evidence of a series of creation periods, separated by profound geological upheavals; these were related to the six days of Genesis, but they were no longer to be read as literal days. Others suggested that geological evidence pointed to a process of continuous change, which was still in operation. James Hutton's *Theory of the Earth*, published in 1795, proposed that the earth had existed for an extremely long period.

The origination and early history of the earth, as set out in the Biblical chronology, was falling under debate. In his *Evidence and Authority of the Christian Revelation* (1817), the Scottish evangelical Thomas Chalmers noted the way the Old Testament account of human origins was being dismissed by religious sceptics on the basis of geological 'speculations,' and they were quickly progressing to question the whole Bible. Chalmers offered a range of solutions to the difficulties raised by geological findings, although he did not commit himself to one in particular. He believed that God could have 'transformed the heavens and earth from previously existing materials,' and that there could have been an interval of 'many ages' between what was performed 'at the beginning,' and the creative work set out in Genesis chapter 1, verse 2, which ascribes acts to specific days. To Chalmers, the biblical genealogies fixed the antiquity of humanity, but not necessarily the age of the earth. To him, the historical evidence of God's creation remained, 'in all the obstinacy of experimental and well-attested facts', which any 'enlightened' reader, who was at all 'candid or philosophical' should allow to stand.[4]

Geologists and palaeontologists such as Georges Cuvier and William Smith began to propose that it would take millions of years to achieve the present geological form of the world. Discoveries revealed that now extinct plants and animals, such as dinosaurs, once populated the earth. In his *Principles of Geology*, the first volume of which was published in 1831, Charles Lyell explained the history of the earth by proposing vast periods of time over which uplift, and then subsequent erosion by wind and water, had taken effect. Some geologists spoke of regular, continuous progress, rather than a series of catastrophes and creations which required miraculous intervention.

Geological advance was forcing some orthodox Christians to concessions. Adam Sedgwick (1785–1873), Woodwardian Professor of Geology at Cambridge, and an early mentor to Charles Darwin, was firmly convinced of the revelation of God the Creator in the natural world, and the fuller revelation of God in the gospel of the Lord Jesus Christ,[5] yet in 1831 he argued that the geological evidence did not support the Biblical account of Noah's Flood. Geologists claimed that the fossil evidence suggested that simpler plants and animals were found in the earliest rock strata, and more recent strata contained fossils that more closely resembled present species. At first, this was not viewed as evidence of evolution. The fossils in the Cambrian strata were considered evidence of an act of special creation, whereas rocks dated before this period appeared free of fossils. The transitions between the strata appeared abrupt, which was interpreted as a series of creations and extinctions. Harmony with the biblical account of Creation was sought by suggesting that the Book of Genesis only described the final creation of plants and animals, and did not allude to earlier creations because they had no relationship to the spiritual needs of humans.

Hugh Miller (1802–1856), a stonemason from Cromarty, North-East Scotland, became an avid collector of the rocks and fossils which abounded in his local area, and developed into a remarkable, self-taught, geological and fossil expert. By the 1830s he was corresponding with leading geologists and scientists. Writing few academic papers, he publicised most of his discoveries in newspaper columns, or through lectures. It was some time after he had begun to study geology that Miller underwent an evangelical conversion experience. The striking examples of geological processes, rock types and fossils he discovered

---

4   T. Chalmers, *The Evidence and Authority of the Christian Revelation*, 5th edn, Edinburgh, William Blackwood, 1817, 202–205.

5   Sedgwick's Memorial Tablet in Dent Church, Yorkshire, outlines his twin emphasis on God's revelation in Creation and Jesus Christ.

in his local area led the hardworking stonemason to profound wonder at the handiwork of the divine Artisan.

In 1839, Miller became the editor of the weekly religious newspaper, *The Witness*, and continued to write about geology from a thoroughly theistic viewpoint, moulded by his evangelical Calvinism. His 1849 work on geology bore the title *The Footprints of the Creator*, and *The Testimony of the Rocks* (1856) was subtitled 'Geology in its Bearings on the two Theologies, Natural and Revealed.' Miller remained convinced that the Bible was pledged by its Divine Author to no falsehood, lamenting how theologians had often pledged it 'to false science'. He advocated special creation, writing powerfully against the emerging evolutionary teaching of his day, but his account of creation was a modified one. He argued that a longer time-frame than the biblical genealogies allowed was required to explain geological processes, and the formation of coastal features such as caves, and the raised beaches on which the waves of the sea had once broken. Miller proposed that the days of the Genesis creation account were, 'great periods, not natural days,' which he sought to identify with vast geological periods. The creatures mentioned on each day of the biblical account were illustrative of the types of what was created in each of those periods. Then 'God the Creator, who wrought during six periods, rested during the seventh period,' which to Miller was that of Redemption. He argued against the evolution of new species after Creation—'we have no evidence whatever that he recommenced his work of creation,—as, on the contrary, man seems to be the last formed of creatures.'[6]

Miller spoke of progressive creation rather than progressive development and evolution: 'The march of Nature is an onward and ascending march: the stages are slow, but the tread is stately; and to Him who has commanded, and who overlooks it, a thousand years are as but a single day, and a single day as a thousand years.'[7] His Calvinistic theology did not inhibit Miller's ability to rejoice in the beauty of what he observed, or his reverence for the God of nature. Geology became to Miller an apologetic tool. Through witnessing the appearance of new and more complex life forms in each great epoch as recorded in the fossil record, he believed it was possible to observe the miracle of creation, behind which lay a creative Agent.

This approach left some significant questions. Why would an omnipotent and omniscient God keep on intervening at the end of each day / epoch, and allow previously created species to be set aside? To Miller, God's way in creation, as with his permission of suffering, were all matters of profound mystery. Each

6   H. Miller, *The Testimony of the Rocks: Or, Geology in its Bearing on the Two Theologies, Natural and Revealed*, Edinburgh, Thomas Constable, 1857, reprinted Thoemmes Press, 2002, 130–32, 153.

7   H. Miller, *The Old Red Sandstone; or, New Walks in an Old Field*, Edinburgh, W.P. Nimmo, (1841), 22nd edition, 1879, 279.

created being represented in the geological record had simply come and fulfilled its created purpose, and when it was completed it had gone.[8] Attempts to reduce these mysteries to theories and law were impossible—'all nature rises up against us in our presumptuous rebellion.'[9]

The eminent naturalist Philip Gosse (1810–88), a member of the Plymouth Brethren, retained a belief in a six-day creation, and a world only a few thousand years old. In his work *Omphalos* (1857) he attempted to reconcile the Genesis account with the findings of geology. Gosse suggested that there was a pre-Creation world which had been formed into the present one, with fully evolved, and sometimes extinct species, which explained the presence of fossils. The world itself had been created 'as though' it had been in existence for thousands of years. Just as Adam was created an adult, so creation had been produced mature. Even the trees in the Garden of Eden, if cut down, would have had rings which showed growth.[10] Others sought the best of both worlds. In 1839, the Congregationalist John Pye Smith (1774–1851) set out his view that the Genesis account only referred to a sequence of creation events in Western Asia, not to the longer process of geological change elsewhere on the planet, which could be seen as a series of separate original creations in different, but distinct, epochs. However, Pye Smith maintained that humanity had descended from a single human pair.[11]

To Miller and Gosse, the questions posed by geology related to the issue of final authority. Did this lie with the geological account of the world's formation, or with the Biblical account? To them scripture remained the ultimate authority, and they strove to reconcile science with the Scripture account. For Moses Stuart (1780–1852), professor at Andover Seminary, Massachusetts, because Christ had affirmed the Pentateuch to be of divine origin, to question it was to doubt not only scriptural authority, but also that of Christ. Stuart did concede, however, that the Bible was not a training manual for scientists, and that the findings of modern geology were compatible with Genesis.[12]

Sir Daniel Wilson (1816–92), the Episcopalian Professor at University College, Toronto, went a step further and sought to distinguish between different types of authority within the Bible. In 1855, Wilson argued that the creation story was incidental to the central thrust of the Bible, that Genesis was not designed for the aid of the geologist, and that scripture did not set out a system of science.

8   Miller, *The Testimony of the Rocks*, 245, 237.

9   H. Miller, *Footprints of the Creator, or the Asterolepis of Stromness*, (1849), 12th edn, Edinburgh, W.P. Nimmo, 1870, 277–78.

10   P.H. Gosse, *Omphalos: An Attempt to Untie the Geological Knot*, London, John Van Voorst, 1857.

11   J. Pye Smith, *On the Relation Between the Holy Scriptures and Some Parts of Geological Science*, London, 1839.

12   M. Stuart, *Critical History and Defence of the Old Testament Canon* (1845), London, 1849.

By the 1860s, although not a full Darwininan, and still believing in a common origin for humanity, Wilson conceded that humans could have originated from an advanced ape.[13]

The professor of geometry at Oxford University, Baden Powell (1796–1860), father of the founder of the Boy Scout movement, went considerably further and contended that Genesis was irreconcilable with the evidence of geology. Where the word of God was incompatible with the evidence from the works of God, the Word should give way. He suggested that Genesis might contain ideas borrowed from other ancient sources, and be parable rather than history. He saw science as a revelation of God, and an aid to theology. Well before Darwin published his views, Baden Powell argued that some form of evolution was the only scientific answer to the problem of creation. By 1859 he was writing that Nature followed the distinct laws of God, and that humans had evolved by these natural laws.[14]

CHARLES DARWIN (1809–1882)

On 24 November 1859 a book was published that shook not only the scientific world, but also the theological one. It continues to do so today. Darwin effectively presented an alternative Book of Genesis, based on the authority not of biblical revelation, but of scientific theory. The first edition of Darwin's *On the Origin of Species* sold out on the day of publication, and a second was ready by January 1860. During the lifetime of its author, the book went through six editions, and by 1895 had sold 47,000 copies.

Charles Darwin was both the son and grandson of highly successful medical doctors who had amassed fortunes through their work, and astute marriages to wealthy women. His mother belonged to the Wedgwood pottery manufacturing family. Although reared in a family with strong Unitarian sympathies, and with a freethinking father and grandfather, Charles was baptised into the Anglican Church, and schooled at Shrewsbury School under a future Anglican bishop. His academic career was not distinguished. He studied medicine at Edinburgh University, but left after two years without taking a degree. At Edinburgh he met Dr Robert Grant, a leading zoologist, who helped rekindle his childhood love for the subject. Grant was also an early evolutionist, following the ideas of the French naturalist Jean Baptiste Lamarck (1744–1829). Darwin and Grant attended the Plinian Society at the university, where radical and materialist philosophical ideas freely circulated, and scientific matters were debated.

---

13   D. Wilson, 'The Unity of the Human Race', *Canadian Journal 3, (1855)*, 230, and *Prehistoric Man: researches into the Origin of Civilisation in the Old and New World*, Cambridge, 1862, cited in C. Kidd, *The Forging of Races: Race and Scripture in the Protestant Atlantic World, 1600–2000*, Cambridge, CUP, 2006, 132–33.

14   O. Chadwick, *Victorian Church*. Vol. I, London, A&C Black, 1966, 551–55.

After giving up medicine at Edinburgh, Darwin was pragmatically encouraged by his freethinking father to study at Cambridge with a view to entering the Anglican ministry. This was an occupation with a guaranteed income, respectability, and leisure time to indulge his interest in natural history. Cambridge was then a stronghold of conservative politics, and theological orthodoxy. John Henslow, professor of botany, and Adam Sedgwick, professor of geology, taught that society was kept in order by God's will, as was the natural world. At Cambridge, Darwin again studied with little enthusiasm or diligence. Nonetheless he possessed sufficient ability to be ranked tenth amongst the non-honours students. Darwin remained willing to accept the truth of Christianity, and affirm the Creed, but the exposure to radical ideas begun in Edinburgh continued in Cambridge. His brother became an open anti-Church freethinker, and admirer of German philosophy.

At this crucial moment, facing the question of how prepared he was to take holy orders, find a parish, and settle into the clergyman's life, an attractive alternative was suddenly presented to Darwin. Via Professor Henslow he received an offer to sail as a naturalist and captain's companion on the H.M.S. *Beagle* to investigate and map the South of America. The ship was captained by Robert FitzRoy, an evangelical Christian, who was to formulate very different conclusions on the basis of the natural evidence they were to encounter. The expedition on the *Beagle* lasted from 1831 to 1836, a journey which saw Darwin travel round the world, be dreadfully ill, and come close to shipwreck and death in a terrific storm off South America. He returned with copious observations, specimens, and profound thoughts as to the geological and biological evidence he had witnessed. The years after his return were spent wrestling with the deep questions it had raised—were species permanent and immutable, and what was their origin? Darwin's name was made with the publication of the account of his voyage on the Beagle, but he was unhappy that in the final volume FitzRoy put forward his alternative evangelical reading of the evidence, that the fossils found in the Andes were not the product of vast ages of geological change and development, but of a catastrophic flood such as that recorded in Genesis.

Darwin's fame as a naturalist spread rapidly on his return. Although he set foot in an England where a Reforming Whig government was breaking down traditional walls of monopoly interest and privilege, this was not the time for sudden and dramatic public departures from scientific and theological orthodoxy. Despite his internal mental revolution, he spent the first years back in England carefully building his scientific reputation amongst his early encouragers, such as Charles Lyell. He was elected to the governing Council of the Geological Society, and won the friendship and patronage of leading scientific minds. As his scientific views became more radical, he was aware of the harm that could be done to his hard earned reputation and status in society if they became prematurely known, nor had he a wish to offend friends who were sincerely religious. To him a world progressing by created 'natural laws' reflected more accurately the ways of a Creator, than a world in which He had to interfere regularly. In 1842 he began in his notes to refer to the process of 'natural selection.' The struggle for existence was one of pain, cruelty and death, in which nature selected the best-adapted, and progress resulted. Darwin discerned in the natural world an outworking of Hegel's dialectic of thesis and antithesis, which at this stage he saw as evidence of the power of the Omniscient Creator.

In 1839, Charles Darwin married his first cousin, Emma Wedgwood, and four years later they left London to live in a former parsonage in Downe, Kent. Here he enjoyed the life of a gentleman of modest means, generously supported by income from his father and the money Emma brought to the marriage. Emma was from a Unitarian family which had turned to Anglicanism as their wealth and status increased. Her faith was simple, but strong. Charles was open to Emma about his growing religious uncertainties, which she found deeply troubling, provoking in her 'melancholy thoughts'. She urged him to read Jesus' farewell discourse to his disciples in John's gospel, with its admonition to love, but also its warnings 'If a man abide not in me, he is cast forth as a branch that is withered; and men gather then cast them into the fire where they are burned' (John 15:6). Emma consoled herself that although Charles doubted, he did not disbelieve. She continued in her faith, and her reading of the Bible, but religious differences remained a cause of heartache in their marriage, especially in Charles' frequent illnesses, when she worried over his eternal fate.

Nonetheless, Emma proved a devoted wife and nurse. The cause of his frequent headaches, insomnia, shivering, faintness and vomiting, was never truly ascertained, but the inner turmoil over his scientific views, his eroding religious views, the threat to his status in society, and his concern for Emma, were undoubtedly contributory factors. Darwin's scientific scepticism taught him never to believe anything until it was proved. To Emma this militated against religious belief, which concerned matters beyond that sort of proof, and even beyond comprehension. When he privately shared some of his views on evolution to friends, he said it was like 'confessing to a murder.' News of the death of his unbelieving father in 1848 made him so physically ill he was unable to attend the funeral.

It was the death of his beloved eldest daughter, Anne, in 1851, when she was only ten that proved the most profound, and insurmountable, shock to Darwin's faith. She had been periodically unwell throughout her life, and had never fully recovered from a severe attack of scarlet fever two years previously. Darwin believed that Anne suffered from his own hereditary weakness of chronic digestive problems. He viewed her as an almost perfect child, who suffered with uncomplaining patience. His own suffering, and that of Anne and others, drove him from the idea of a beneficent God. He interpreted suffering as part of the process of natural selection and survival, rather than there being any intelligent Being involved in it. He found little comfort in Emma's faith, or from belief in an afterlife, believing that eternal punishment was immoral. At the time of Anne's death Darwin was reading the freethinking Unitarian Francis Newman, who argued that human immortality could not be proved from the Bible. Newman's spiritual autobiography, *Phases of Faith*, especially confirmed Darwin in his doubts. Faced by his daughter's death, Darwin's physical and emotional state tottered. He could not bring himself to attend the funeral, and never visited her grave. Emma's belief in eternal punishment also faded over the years, and she hoped that her increasingly unbelieving husband might one day share eternity with her.

At Downe House, Darwin was a pillar of the community. He became a magistrate, and his children were christened at the parish church, which they attended with their mother. His sons were tutored by Anglican clergymen. Darwin attended church only occasionally, but he gave generously for church repairs, and supported the clergymen in their parochial charities for which he served as treasurer.

THE THEORY OF EVOLUTION

Darwin was not the first person to propose that change in species of plants and animals had taken place over a long period of time. In the late eighteenth century Darwin's own grandfather, Erasmus, had written an account of evolution, and in 1809 Lamarck had speculated that biological species were mutable, and proposed an atheistic evolutionary scheme. By the time Darwin wrote his *Origin of Species*, at least twenty others had considered aspects of evolution, and such ideas had become fairly widely known. In 1823 William Wilberforce, the anti-slave trade campaigner, was appalled to find in Long's *History of Jamaica* an ugly racist strain with its laborious comparisons of the black race with the baboon species. Long declared, distastefully, that he did not think 'an oran outang husband would be a dishonour to a Hottentot female'.[15] Evolutionary ideas of human origination also circulated amongst radical socialists. An agent of the Manchester City Mission in 1841 recorded the following interchange with a disciple of Robert Owen:

> 'There is no God, did you see him?
> 'Then, how did you come here?'
> 'By others.'
> 'But how did the first parents come?'
> 'By some other race of animals such as baboons or monkeys.'[16]

15 Long, quoted in W. Wilberforce, *An Appeal to the Religion, Justice and Humanity of the Inhabitants of the British Empire, in Behalf of the Negro Slaves in the West Indies*, London, J. Hatchard and Son, 1823.

16 *Report of the Manchester and Salford Town Mission*, Manchester, 1841.

Thomas Malthus's essay *On the Principle of Population*, which Darwin read in 1838, observed that, in general, living organisms produced many more offspring than can be expected to survive to maturity. To Darwin, this raised the question—which offspring survived, and why? He concluded that favourable variations, such as advantages in gaining food or escaping predators, would be preserved, and unfavourable ones destroyed. This 'descent with modification' was seen in the breeding of desirable characteristics in domestic animals.

Discoveries in the 1820s of the remains of humans who had co-existed with now extinct species of animals, such as mammoths, led to questioning of the recent origin of humanity, and proposals of earlier datings. The lack of evidence of transitional fossils in the rock strata held many geologists back from evolutionary thinking. They considered that some form of special creative activity was needed to effect major transitions, such as from gills to lungs. In *Vestiges of the Natural History of Creation*, published in 1844, Robert Chambers argued that a natural law of development governed the history of life, which explained the emergence of physical, mental and moral qualities. This materialist explanation was challenged by natural theologians who believed it challenged the basis of Christian morality and Christian mission. The mistakes made by Chambers in the biological information in the book, and his flawed scientific method, were quickly exposed by other naturalists, but Darwin took further the idea of constant development, from inferior types to superior. He had abandoned the certainty that species were immutable.

Although Darwin's contribution was not new, or unique, it was his work that attracted popular notice, combining close scientific observation with accessible style. Later geological finds appeared to close some of the gaps between fossil forms in the strata, but the presence of sudden transitions, and the origin of major groups, was to remain a matter of disagreement among palaeontologists. True to his own theory, Darwin's progression to his theory of origins was gradual and evolutionary. Although unconvinced by the godless evolutionary ideas of Lamarck, in the 1830s he began privately to work out his own scheme of evolution by divinely-ordained natural laws. He patiently accumulated evidence which was expressed most clearly in his later works, *The Descent of Man* (1871), and *The Expression of Emotions in Man and Animals* (1872).

Independently of Darwin, the naturalist Alfred Russel Wallace (1823–1913) had come to similar conclusions, and the two had been in correspondence. In 1858 Wallace sent Darwin his essay *On the Tendency of Varieties to Depart Indefinitely from the Original Type*, in which the principles of natural selection were explained, suggesting that if he thought it worthwhile it should be sent to Charles Lyell. This placed Darwin in a predicament, for he had long delayed publishing the results of his own painstaking studies. Eventually, a joint paper from Wallace and Darwin was read at the Linnean Society in July 1858, and then published in the journal of the society. Darwin gave up a learned multi-volume work on natural selection, which he had been writing since 1856, and instead produced a shorter book, *On the Origin of Species*, which focussed on evolution.

Wallace was a self-educated scientist. As a young man he was greatly influenced by hearing lectures in the 'Hall of Science' on Tottenham Court Road, and through reading the works on popular socialism of Robert Owen, which had an anti-religious tone. Wallace became a religious sceptic, especially after reading David Strauss's *Life of Jesus*. He rejected orthodox religion as 'degrading and hideous,' believing that the 'only true and wholly beneficial religion' was that which 'inculcated the service of humanity, and whose only dogma was the brotherhood of man.'[17] Between 1848 and 1852 he tried to make his living by collecting natural history specimens from the Amazon River, but his return voyage ended in disastrous shipwreck, with almost all of his valuable collection lost. Wallace's theory of natural selection, similarly inspired by reading Thomas Malthus, concluded that 'in every generation the inferior would inevitably be killed off and the superior would remain—that is, the fittest would survive.'[18]

Darwin's *Origin of Species* begins with his voyage on the Beagle, where he believed his observations relating to organic life, and geological forms, shed light on that 'mystery of mysteries', the origin of species. His overarching thought, and his rejection of special creation, was set out in his original introduction—'the view which most naturalists until recently entertained, and which I formerly entertained—namely, that each species has been independently created—is erroneous'. He now declared himself convinced that 'species are not immutable', that those belonging to 'what are called the same genera are lineal descendents of some other and generally extinct species'. Some had previously considered variation within species possible, but only within limits, but Darwin now argued that descent with modification could result in the appearance of new species. He was also convinced that 'Natural Selection has been the most important, but not exclusive, means of modification'.[19]

Although the idea of change and development in the universe had been proposed by geologists and palaeontologists, Darwin now argued for the existence of a mechanism of change in the organic world which eliminated the presence of wise design in the formation of species. This modification had taken place over a long period: 'This has been effected chiefly through the natural selection of numerous successive, slight, favourable variations', which, together with adaptation to external conditions, 'seem to us in our ignorance to arise spontaneously'. Darwin was aware of some of the problems his theory

17   A.R. Wallace, *My Life: A Record of Events*, 2 vols, London, Chapman and Hall, 1905, vol. 1, 88–89.

18   Wallace, *My Life*, Vol I, 361–62.

19   C. Darwin, *On the Origin of Species by Means of Natural Selection, or the Preservation of Favoured Races in the Struggle for Life*, London, John Murray, 1859, [facsimile reprint, 1967], Introduction to First Edition.

raised, especially the issue of the transitional phase. Although there were gradations in the form of the eye, how could an eye evolve, when only a fully functional eye is of any use? His only solution was to propose gradual change over 'incomprehensibly vast' periods of time.[20]

THE THEOLOGICAL IMPLICATIONS OF DARWIN'S VIEWS

To Darwin, once he had discovered natural selection, Paley's argument for the existence and goodness of God based on order and design in nature failed. Instead he saw a struggle of competition. The apparent cruelty and wastefulness of Nature cried out against belief in Providence: 'What a book a Devil's chaplain might write on the clumsy, wasteful, low and horridly cruel works of nature!... My God, how I long for my stomach's sake to wash my hands of it—for at least one long spell'.[21]

The implications of Darwin's views were profound. He was proposing an alternative to the biblical account of the beginnings of mankind, aware of the enormity of the scientific and theological questions he was raising. Although he did not explicitly state it until the publication of *The Descent of Man* in 1871, Darwin was proposing that humans were no different from other animals, and that even the apparent uniqueness of humanity could be explained by natural selection. If the Genesis account was wrong, and humans were simply evolved animals, the reality of man's spiritual nature was in doubt. And as animals, what moral responsibility did humans possess?

Until the 1840s Darwin had spoken of an omniscient Creator, who ruled by means of divine laws. Although rejecting the argument by design, he nonetheless retained a great reverence for the laws of nature. In the *Origin*, Darwin publicly remained theistic, with a strong sense of wonder over what he described. The struggle for life brought forth, 'the most exalted object which we are capable of conceiving, namely the production of higher animals.' He saw grandeur in the fact that life, which had been 'originally breathed into a few forms or into one,' brought forth from so simple a beginning, 'endless forms most beautiful and most wonderful that have been, and are being, evolved.'[22] Darwin was too sensitive to Christian friends and relations to present an openly non-theistic case in 1859.[23]

The conflict within Darwin created by the theological implications of his scientific views deepened, especially over the issue of suffering. In July 1860, he wrote to Asa Gray in America:

20   C. Darwin, *The Origin of Species*, 6th edn, London, John Murray, 1872, Conclusion.

21   *The Correspondence of Charles Darwin 1858–59*, Vol 7, Cambridge, CUP, 1991, 121–122.

22   C. Darwin, *On the Origin of Species by Means of Natural Selection, or the Preservation of Favoured Races in the Struggle for Life*, London, John Murray, 1859, [facsimile reprint, 1967], 484–90.

23   *Correspondence of Darwin*, Vol 7, 507–11.

'An innocent and good man stands under tree and is killed by flash of lightning. Do you believe that God *designedly* killed this man? Many or most persons do believe this; I can't and don't ... Yet, as I said before, I cannot persuade myself that electricity acts, that the tree grows, that man aspires to loftiest conceptions all from blind, brute force.'

He signed himself, 'Your *muddled* and affectionate friend'.[24]

Charles Darwin—Loss of Faith in the Bible

I had gradually come, by this time, to see that the Old Testament from its manifestly false history of the world and from its attributing to God the feelings of a revengeful tyrant, was no more to be trusted than the sacred books of the Hindoos, or the beliefs of any barbarian... that the more we know of the fixed laws of nature the more incredible do miracles become, —that the men at that time were ignorant and credulous to a degree almost incomprehensible to us .... This disbelief crept over me at a very slow rate, but was at last complete... and have never since doubted even for a single second that my conclusion was correct.[1]

1 *Autobiography of Charles Darwin 1809–1882*, ed. N. Barlow, New York, Harcourt Brace, 1959, 85–86.

Darwin was losing the struggle to maintain any form of personal faith, although it is unclear whether loss of faith preceded, or followed, loss of belief in the divine role in biological activity. His belief in the divine origin, and authenticity, of the Bible, had fallen away as he developed his views on natural selection and evolution in the late 1830s. Doubts over the historical accuracy of the Old Testament fed into his doubts about the biblical account of creation. Yet, in the conclusion of the *Origin*, Darwin still maintained that his work did not necessarily undermine religious feelings:

I see no reason why the views given in this volume should shock the religious feelings of anyone... A celebrated author and divine has written to me that he has "gradually learned to see that it is just as noble a conception of the Deity to believe that He created a few original forms capable of self-development into other and needful forms, as to believe that He required a fresh act of creation to supply the voids caused by the action of His laws."[25]

---

24 Charles Darwin, letter to Asa Gray, 3 July, 1860, in *The Correspondence of Charles Darwin, 1860*, Vol 8, Cambridge, CUP, 1993, 273–74.

25 *Origin of Species*, Chapter 15, Conclusion, 216.

In the *Origin* words such as 'creation', 'creature', and 'created', appear over 100 times, and the word 'Creator' is used seven times, although such words are usually found in the context of rejection of the views of supporters of special creation.[26] The word 'God' appears just once, in rejection of the view that God created fossils. The word 'Evolution' never appears. Theistic language recurs:

> 'To my mind it accords better with what we know of the laws imposed on matter by the Creator, that the production and extinction of the past and present inhabitants of the world should have been due to secondary causes.... There is grandeur in this view of life, with its several powers having been originally breathed by the Creator into a few forms, or even one.'[27]

At this stage, to Darwin, the impossibility of conceiving that such an amazing universe occurred by chance remained one of the chief arguments for God's existence. The implication that humanity descended from lower life forms, notably apes, was there, but not explicitly stated. Even Alfred Wallace argued that the development of human kind was a separate case requiring special treatment.

Charles Darwin—Natural Selection Destroys the Argument by Design

'The old argument of design in nature, as given by Paley, which formerly seemed to me so conclusive, fails now that the law of natural selection has been discovered. We can no longer argue that, for instance, the beautiful hinge of a bivalve shell must have been made by an intelligent being, like the hinge of a door by man. There seems to be no more design in the variability of organic beings, and in the action of natural selection, than in the course which the wind blows'.[1]

1   *Autobiography of Charles Darwin*, ed. N. Barlow, London, Collins, 1958, 87.

In 1871, the *Descent of Man* appeared, although with the help of Darwin's daughter, it was pruned of its most anti-religious parts. Here he explicitly argued that humanity was not a work of special creation fashioned in the image of God, nor fallen from perfection in Eden, but instead had risen from lower life forms, the chance product of natural variation and selection. Man, 'the wonder and glory of the Universe' had descended from monkeys over a long period of time. To Darwin this conclusion was inescapable—'unless we wilfully close our eyes, we may, with our present knowledge, approximately recognize

---

26   See P.H. Barrett, D.J. Weinshank, and T.T. Gottleber, *A Concordance to Darwin's Origin of Species*, Ithaca, Cornell University Press, 1981.

27   *Origin of Species*, conclusion.

our patronage; nor need we feel ashamed of it.'[28] The most important difference between humans and animals was the moral sense, or conscience, but this too was a product of the evolutionary development of intellectual powers and social instincts.[29] From this moral sense arose a sense of the divine: 'The idea of a universal and beneficent Creator of the universe does not seem to arise in the mind of man until he has been elevated by long-continued culture'. Yet, even here Darwin refused to reject all religious forms of origination, speaking of 'that grand sequence of events, which our minds refuse to accept as the result of blind chance.'[30]

Wallace was reluctant to see natural selection as the sole explanation for human moral, spiritual and intellectual capacities, even among 'savages', and suggested some other agency lay behind them. In later life he searched for intelligence, or intelligences, in the unseen universe of 'Spirit' in an attempt to explain human intellectual and moral faculties. This led him to explore hypnotism, or mesmerism as it was called, and then spiritualism. He investigated table-tapping, spirit messages, and forms of spirit communication. This alarmed Darwin, and disgusted friends like T.H. Huxley who dismissed them as 'twaddle'. On the basis of his belief that the 'spirits' communicated with humans, he argued for morality and social justice, deeply troubled by those who used the natural selection theory to justify ruthless competition in commercial and industrial life.[31]

EARLY RESPONSES TO DARWIN

Reaction to Darwin's *Origin* in Britain was varied. There is no doubt that Darwin had strategic friendships in high places, which were carefully cultivated. T.H. Huxley, Darwin's great supporter in later years, declared, 'How extremely stupid not to have thought of that!' The political radicals loved it. The Unitarian Harriet Martineau argued that it overturned both revealed and Natural Religion. Adam Sedgwick at Cambridge wrote to his former protégé of how he read parts of the book 'with absolute sorrow, because I find them utterly false and grievously mischievous'. He warned that replacing design with natural selection was a step towards atheism, and would inflict on humanity 'a damage that might brutalize it,' because it broke the link between the material world and the moral order—an issue Darwin himself struggled over. He went on to

---

28   C. Darwin, *The Descent of Man and Selection in Relation to Sex*, 2 vols, London, John Murray, 1871, Vol. 2., 528.

29   Darwin, *Descent of Man* Vol 1, London, John Murray, 1871, 70–73, 106.

30   *Descent of Man*, Vol 2, 395–36.

31   On Wallace's thinking as to the origin of the spiritual nature see H. Clements, *Alfred Russel Wallace: Biologist and Social Reformer*, London, Hutchinson, 1983, 110–127.

warn Darwin, that 'on one condition only… we shall meet in heaven'—if they accepted God's revelation in nature and the Bible.[32]

Other Anglicans were far more positive, paving the way towards a widespread assimilation of Darwin's views into Protestant theology. Charles Kingsley, argued that the creation by God of 'primal forms capable of self-development' left him with 'just as noble a conception of Deity,' as if God had regularly intervened by special acts to create new life-forms.[33] The biblical scholar F.J.A. Hort wrote to B.F. Westcott in March 1860, 'Have you read Darwin?… In spite of difficulties, I am inclined to think it unanswerable.'[34] Even the Tractarian Dean Church did not believe that Darwin's theory was 'incompatible with ideas of a higher and spiritual order.'[35] Moderate clergymen tended to hold their counsel, waiting to see if the new scientific ideas would prove well-founded.

Those with a disinclination to believe in the literal inspiration of the Bible were most ready to embrace Darwin's views. In *Essays and Reviews*, which appeared three months after the *Origin*, Frederick Temple, then Headmaster of Rugby School, wrote 'If geology proves to us that we must not interpret the first chapters of Genesis literally… the results should still be welcome.'[36] Baden Powell believed that the *Origin* would bring about a revolution of opinion in favour of the 'grand principle of the self-evolving powers of nature.' *Essays and Reviews* itself proved highly controversial, being denounced in a letter in *The Times* signed by the Archbishop of Canterbury and twenty-two bishops. However, the major focus of opposition to *Essays and Reviews* was to its authors' acceptance of the fruits of biblical criticism.[37]

While Darwin sought to steer clear of the religious controversies his works created, an alliance between pro-Darwin scientists and liberal churchmen was being forged. Leslie Stephen observed in his 1873 essay, *Darwinism and Divinity*, 'Darwinists are not necessarily hoofed and horned monsters, but are occasionally of pacific habits, and may even be detected in the habit of going to church.'[38] Yet, for Stephen it was the reading of Darwin that brought the final loss of faith, as doubt grew into agnosticism.

By the 1870s and 1880s the weight of scientific opinion was on Darwin's side, and many theologians followed. Twenty-five years on from the *Essays and*

32 Darwin, *Corespondence*, Vol. 7, 390, 399.

33 F. Darwin (ed), *The Life and Letters of Charles Darwin*, Vol 2, London, John Murray, 1887, 287–88.

34 F.A. Hort, *The Life and Letters of F.J.A. Hort*, vol. 1, London, Macmillan, 1896, 414.

35 M.C. Church, *The Life and Letters of Dean Church*, London, Macmillan, 1895, 153.

36 F. Temple, 'The Education of the World', in *Essays and Reviews*, London, Longman, Green, Longman, Roberts, 1861, 47.

37 O. Chadwick, *Victorian Church*, Vol II, London, A&C Black, 1970, 75–83.

38 L. Stephen, 'Darwinism and Divinity', in *Essays on Freethinking and Plainspeaking*, London, Longmans, Green, and Co, 1873, 59.

Reviews storm, in his 1884 Bampton lectures, Frederick Temple openly endorsed theistic evolution, which he believed strengthened the arguments of natural theology—'He did not make things... but He made them make themselves.' To Temple, evolution was a continuing process by which the pain and imperfections of the natural world were being diminished. However, he suggested an early difference of origin between humans and animals, believing it quite possible that the 'spiritual faculty' came about as the result of a 'direct creative act.'[39] Temple's ready assimilation of Darwin into Christian cosmology was typical of liberal Protestant scholars in the late nineteenth and early twentieth century, and did not disbar him from becoming Archbishop of Canterbury. By the end of the century, evolution was a doctrine at least permissible and even respectable amongst theologians, clergy, and the laity of the established church.

It was not only those open to a liberal version of Protestantism who embraced what Darwin had to say, voices close to evangelicalism were also attracted. The Scottish Free Churchman, Henry Drummond (1851–97), studied in Edinburgh and Tübingen, before working with D.L. Moody in his evangelistic campaigns in Scotland in the 1870s and again in the 1880s: evangelism was the passion of his life. He became Professor of Natural Science at the Glasgow Free Church College, and in his works *Natural Law in the Spiritual World* (1883), and *The Ascent of Man* (1884) he offered an optimistic view of the moral, social and spiritual development of the world, using Darwinian language. He pointed to the struggle for life, but also to the Christian development in the social, moral, and spiritual realm in the late nineteenth century, which was 'as real an evolutionary movement as any that preceded it'. The struggle for the life of others was overtaking the struggle for life itself.[40] Some were shocked, and a motion that the contents of *The Ascent of Man* be examined by a special committee was put to the Free Church Assembly, but was not carried.

The response from many evangelicals to the challenge of Darwin's thinking was of strong opposition. The redoubtable Baptist preacher C.H. Spurgeon warned that if the theory was accepted, 'in theology, its influence would be deadly; and this is all I care about.' He declared, 'I have read a good deal on the subject, and have never yet seen a fact, or the tail of a fact, which indicated the rise of one species of animal from another... I believe it to be a monstrous error in philosophy, which will be a theme for ridicule before another twenty years.'[41]

Before the publication of Darwin's *Origin of Species*, most American Protestants saw natural history as the basis for a defence of the Christian world-view, and willingly reconciled any minor anomalies. Darwin's work was

---

39   F. Temple, *The Relations Between Religion and Science*, London, Macmillan, 1884, 115–118, 176, 186.

40   H. Drummond, *The Ascent of Man*, 6th edn, London, Hodder and Stoughton, 1897, 443

41   C.H. Spurgeon, Letter of 1887, in *Autobiography*, Volume IV, London, 1893, 133-34.

initially attacked as an attempt by unbelievers to present a naturalistic world-view. Nonetheless, by 1875 the majority of the scientific camp had embraced the evolutionary position, and arguments focussed on the theological implications of the theory. The Presbyterian Asa Gray, Professor of Natural History at Harvard, proved a strong supporter and encourager of Darwin, and was comfortable reconciling Darwinism with belief in the existence of God. He played down the theological implications of Darwin's thesis, believing that the *Origin* maintained a theistic view, and created no new problems for believers. Although Gray moved away from an understanding of design in nature, he continued to believe that there was purpose. Many Protestant theologians felt that they had no alternative but to accept the theory and the arguments of science, and followed Gray's acceptance that evolution was reconcilable with Christianity. Their response was to accommodate Christian theology to suit the theory. For some this required only small adjustments, for others the only way to stop intelligent men and women from turning from Christianity was to heavily reconstruct theology within a contemporary, evolutionary framework. They were convinced that evolution showed that God operated, and made himself known, throughout his creation by a process of gradual, continuous, and progressive change.

The American Congregationalist minister, Henry Ward Beecher (1813–87), contended for a reconciliation between Darwinism and theism. To Beecher, God had revealed himself in the geological record as well as in the Biblical revelation: a Father-God should be substituted for a frowning God.[42] The Christian evolutionist Lyman Abbott (1835–1922) typified the widespread accommodation to evolution. In his 'New Theology', God was depicted in evolutionary fashion: 'all nature and all life is one great theophany;... there are not occasional interventions in the order of life which bear witness to the presence of God, but life itself is a perpetual witness to His presence'. He rejected the doctrine of the Fall and redemption as inconsistent with evolution, arguing that mankind had progressed from a lower to a higher spiritual condition, and human history as the story of the slow and steady victory of Christian love, freedom, and democracy.[43]

Abbott typified those who believed that the conflict between Darwinism and the church was over. With the advance of Modernism as a theological movement in the years after 1900, theology was rendered compatible with the advances of science. Religion, politics and science were drawn together to promote an agenda of social reform, which was seen as part of the evolutionary progress in nature and humanity towards the Kingdom of God. Such confidence

---

42   See H.W. Beecher, *Evolution and Religion*, New York, Howard and Hulbert, 1885, 128.

43   L. Abbott, *The Theology of an Evolutionist*, London, 1897, 9–10, 73; L. Abbott, *The Evolution of Christianity*, London, 1892, 66, 258.

was to receive a bitter blow during the horrors of the First World War, and drew forth a strong reaction in the twentieth century from Karl Barth's neo-orthodoxy, and from fundamentalism. To some, the modernist capacity to reconcile Christianity with an evolutionary humanism, produced little more than a secular, humanistic religion. Even Darwin's great defender, T.H. Huxley, was astonished at the apparent elasticity in the ways Christians could interpret the Bible—'There must be some position from which the reconcilers of science and Genesis will not retreat'.[44] Yet by 1900, with church attendance in America increasing, some proclaimed the accommodation to the world of science had successfully prevented the masses from abandoning the faith.

Others were convinced that the attempt to admit evolution into Christian thinking was theologically profoundly dangerous. It appeared to produce a theology that was changeable, and lacking in the foundational certainties necessary in changing times. They feared that Christianity had been reduced to the values it proclaimed, rather than its truths. A small, but distinguished, group of religious thinkers argued that the theory of evolution could not be embraced without abandoning doctrines that were essential to Christianity, especially the claim that the Scriptures were reliable as an infallible source of truth. The theory of organic evolution was to them a secular theory, the product of fallible human science. Their understanding of biblical authority led them to hold firmly to the doctrine of special creation, and to reject a theory that clearly seemed to contradict scriptural revelation. To make Christian theology conform to the dictates of the contemporary world, no matter how advanced the scientific argument, would be to adulterate the gospel. Darwinian science was a profound threat to not only the doctrine of Creation, and Scripture, but also to understandings of God's Providence, and to the Biblical scheme of morality. As Miller and Gosse had claimed in the earlier geology controversy, the debate was ultimately not between scientists and theologians, but between people who embraced fundamentally divergent views as to the source of truth and knowledge.[45]

Matthew Maury, founder of the science of oceanography, argued in 1855 that:

'the Author of the great volume which nature spreads out before us.... is also the Author of the book which Revelation holds up to us; and though the two works are entirely different, their records are equally true; and when they bear upon the same point... it is as impossible that they should contradict each other as it is that either should contradict itself.[46]

44   T.H. Huxley, *Essays on Some Controverted Questions*, London, 1894, 89.

45   See J. H. Roberts, *Darwinism and the Divine in America: Protestant Intellectuals and Organic Evolution, 1859–1900*, Madison, University of Wisconsin Press, 1988, esp. pp. ix–xvi; 233–242.

46   M. Maury to 'My Dear Sir', January 22, 1855, in Maury Collection, Division of Manuscripts, Library of Congress, Washington D.C, quoted in J.C. Greene, *Darwin and the Modern World View*, Louisiana State University Press, Baton Rouge, 1961, 13.

Any conflict lay with the 'blindness and weakness' of the interpreter, who had misinterpreted either the science, or the Bible.

The biblical account of the origination of humanity from a single pair was defended not simply from a desire to affirm Biblical authority, but also as crucial to the whole Christian system. To Donald Macdonald of the Free Church of Scotland, the atonement was the 'cardinal doctrine of Christianity', and rested 'on the assumption that all men are descended from the first Adam, and involved in his guilt.' Salvation was procured for them by Jesus Christ, the second Adam. The consequence was stark: if there were tribes not descended from Adam, how could they participate in the blessings of the gospel? In 1877 the leading Canadian intellectual, Sir William Dawson, declared that if the Biblical account of human creation was surrendered, it would render 'the Bible history worthless', reduce humanity to 'isolation of race from race', destroy 'the brotherhood of man' and the Christian message of the atonement, 'which proclaims that "as in Christ all dies, so in Christ shall all be made alive."'[47]

The Roman Catholic Church, in response to Darwin, affirmed its belief in the inspiration and authority of the Bible. In 1895, a book on evolution by the Roman Catholic priest Eduard Leroy was condemned by the Holy Office, and another by the American Roman Catholic, John Zahm withdrawn from circulation. A Pontifical Biblical Commission established in 1902 instructed Roman Catholic scholars to maintain 'substantial authenticity' and 'Mosaic integrity', and argued that whatever the authors of scripture asserted, should be believed to be asserted by the Holy Spirit. The idea that the Apostles could have expressed erroneous ideas whilst under the inspiration of the Holy Spirit was rejected. Scriptural authority and church tradition were to be the bedrock of the defence against the advances of Modernity.[48]

One of the most robust responses to Darwin came from the Presbyterian Charles Hodge (1797–1878), Professor of Theology at Princeton Theological Seminary. Hodge would not countenance a separation of science and theology, and therefore deemed Darwinism incompatible with Christianity. In *What is Darwinism?* (1874), Hodge asserted that 'the denial of design in nature is virtually the denial of God,' answering his own question definitively, 'What is Darwinism? It is atheism'.[49] He pointed out many gaps in Darwin's argument, and that his theory was unprovable. He declared the 'incredibility' of the idea that all living things sprung originally from 'the same primordial germ.'[50] Hodge did not accept Archbishop Usher's dating of the world to some four thousand years

---

47   D. MacDonald, *Creation and Fall*, Edinburgh, 1856, 373; J.W. Dawson, *The Origin of the World According to Revelation and Science*, London, 1877, 263, both quoted in Kidd, *The Forging of Races*, 127–129.

48   J.C. Greene, *Darwin and the Modern World View*. Louisiana State University Press, Baton Rouge, 1961, 16–17.

49   C. Hodge, *What is Darwinism?*, New York, Scribner, Armstrong, 1874, 173, 177.

50   C. Hodge, *What is Darwinism?*, 143, 144–45;

Charles Hodge—Natural Selection Leads to Atheism

'the conclusion of the whole matter is that the denial of design in nature is virtually the denial of God. Mr Darwin's theory does not deny all design in nature, therefore his theory is virtually atheistical; his theory, not he himself. He believes in a Creator. But when that Creator, millions on millions of ages ago, did something—called matter and living germ into existence,—and then abandoned the universe to itself to be controlled by chance and necessity, without any purpose on his part as to the result or any intervention of guidance, then He is virtually consigned, so far as we are concerned to non-existence... Mr Darwin's admirers adopt and laud his theory, for the special reason that it banishes God from the world'.[1]

1   C. Hodge, *What is Darwinism?*, 158.

---

before Christ, thinking it likely that the names in the genealogies represented more than one generation. It was possible that the world was eight to ten thousand years old.[51] Hodge was open to a form of theistic evolution following on from an act of special creation, accepting the possibility of development of species as long as it was under divine control. But he still insisted that each species was, 'not derived, evolved, or developed from pre-existing species... if at any time since the original creation new species have appeared on the earth, they owe their existence to the immediate intervention of God.'[52]

Hodge's ultimate concern was that natural selection robbed God of his role in creation, with atheism as the inevitable result, although he did not believe Darwin had reached that conclusion personally. He found it impossible to believe that the eye was not the result of design, although Hodge did not argue, as the natural theologians did, from design to God. Instead, starting with the foundational principle that God existed, it followed that things would be designed. Even evolutionary theism was little better than atheism—describing a God who did nothing to control the course of nature, or the events of history. Hodge was sure that Biblical teaching never conflicted with true scientific fact, and where discrepancies appeared, presuming the interpretation of the Bible was correct, there was ultimately something wrong with the science. Darwin's views threatened not just the doctrine of Biblical inspiration, but also, if the Creation and the Fall were not based on fact, the great doctrines of sin and redemption. If humans were little more than close cousins to the apes, how could Christian morality be sustained? The work of Hodge and others kept the debate alive into the twentieth century, and it continued through the

51   C. Hodge, *Systematic Theology*, Vol II, New York, 1872, 40–47.
52   Hodge, *Systematic Theology*, Vol. II, 26.

Fundamentalist-Modernist debates of the following decades, culminating in the famous Scopes trial of 1925.[53]

THE HUXLEY-WILBERFORCE DEBATE

On 30 June 1860, the year after the publication of the *Origin of Species*, a legendary encounter took place at a meeting of the British Association for the Advancement of Science between the arch-defender of Darwin, T.H. Huxley (1825–1895), and the Bishop of Oxford, Samuel Wilberforce (1805–73). 'Soapy Sam', as the son of William Wilberforce was affectionately known, had been invited to respond to a paper by Professor John Draper of New York, on the subject of Darwin and Social Progress. The meeting drew an audience of some 700, although Darwin, who shrank from open debate, was not present. There are few recorded eye-witness accounts of what did, or did not, happen,[54] but the traditional version is that Wilberforce sought to belittle and deride the Darwinian view, and mockingly asked whether it was 'through his grandfather or his grandmother' that he had been descended from a monkey. What may have been intended as a jest to lighten a very lengthy debate, misfired. Huxley reportedly rebuked Wilberforce, asserting he was not ashamed to have a monkey for a relative. There are different versions of what he then went on to say, and Huxley's speech was not audible to all. Some thought Huxley said that he would rather be descended from an ape than a bishop. Others remembered him as saying that he would be ashamed to be related to a man who used great gifts and influence to plunge into 'scientific questions with which he has no real acquaintance, only to obscure them by an aimless rhetoric... and skilled appeals to religious prejudice.'[55]

The historical reality behind the interchange is complicated—and the 'legendary account' was actually written forty years after the event. To Huxley's supporters his riposte was the classic put down, but to others his words used towards a senior bishop were just plain rude. Whatever the exact detail, Huxley robustly defended the author of the *Origin*, although he believed that Darwin's views needed no defence. Huxley, who invented the word 'agnostic,' was convinced that nothing could be said with intellectual integrity except what was

53   John T. Scopes was a Tennessee teacher charged with teaching evolution contrary to state law. Despite the robust defence of Scopes by the leading criminal lawyer, Clarence Darrow, Scopes was found guilty and fined $100. The trial was believed to have done much to discredit fundamentalism.

54   The debate is discussed, with slightly different assessments as to the outcome in J.R. Lucas, 'Wilberforce and Huxley: A Legendary Encounter', *Historical Journal*, 22, 1979, 313–30; and A. Desmond and J.E. Moore, *Darwin*, London, Michael Joseph, 1991, 492–499.

55   Letter from J.R. Green, an undergraduate at Oxford to the geologist Boyd Hawkins, in L. Huxley, 'The Great Debate', in *Life and Letters of Thomas Henry Huxley*, New York, Appleton and Co, 1901, Vol. I, 192–204. This extract is found in *Charles Darwin: Interviews and Recollections*, ed. H. Orel, London, Macmillan, 2000, 176.

Samuel Wilberforce

conclusively proved by the scientific evidence. He was determined to show that religious men no longer had the right to hold scientific men to account. Science was not an alternative truth to religion, it was 'the' truth which no amount of religious argument could alter.

Yet Wilberforce was no ignorant and unthinking cleric. He was a capable scientist with a first class degree in mathematics who had successfully challenged Robert Chambers' *Vestiges* in 1847, and had published a review of Darwin's *Origin of Species* in the *Quarterly Review*. Most of the naturalists at the Oxford meeting supported his position. Wilberforce argued that the facts did not support the theory of evolution: a hypothesis had wrongly been raised to the status of causal theory. To the bishop, the absence in the geological record of signs of one species developing into another disproved Darwin. Although Darwin acknowledged this, he believed it was the product of the imperfect geological record. Wilberforce also quoted archaeological evidence that showed animal, plant, and human forms of today were clearly identifiable with those existing over thousands of years previously, suggesting their unalterable character. Although there were selective pressures, they did not cause a change of species, and hybrids over time tended to revert to type: 'rock-pigeons were what rock pigeons had always been'. Biologically, hybridisation only produced sterility. Wilberforce also hinted at the racist implications of Darwin's views— did they mean that some parts of the human species were at a lower level of evolutionary development?[56]

Darwin acknowledged that Wilberforce's contribution to the *Quarterly Review* was 'uncommonly clever', exposing some of the weak points in his argument. It seems likely that Wilberforce was helped by Rev. Richard Owen, a leading anatomist, who had coined the phrase 'dinosaur', and had for a long time been a friend and supporter of Darwin. As a theologian, Wilberforce was appalled at Darwin's suggestion that human ancestry derived from the apes. Darwin's theory directly conflicted with the word of God as to the spiritual and moral condition of mankind: 'Man's derived supremacy over the earth; man's power of articulate speech; man's gift of reason; man's free will and responsibility; man's fall and man's redemption; the incarnation of the Eternal Son; the indwelling of the Eternal Spirit,—all are equally and utterly irreconcilable with the degrading notion of the brute origin of him who was created in the image of God, and redeemed by the Eternal Son assuming to himself his nature'.[57] In the famous debate Wilberforce was supported from the floor by none other than Robert FitzRoy, captain of the *Beagle*. FitzRoy, now an admiral, held up a Bible and implored the audience to believe God rather than man on such matters. In the ensuing commotion he was shouted down.

Each side went away thinking they had scored the decisive blow. Many simply considered it an entertaining score draw. Whatever the outcome, the debate was indicative of the considerable difficulty the church would have in circumscribing the articulate and confident opinions of the growing, and influential, scientific community. If Wilberforce won the debate on the day by eloquence and humour, Huxley won the war. Science was developing its own assertive apologetic, and in the hands of Huxley and others, it took on a strongly anti-religious dimension. Over the next twenty years, the Darwinians became the majority party. The days of the amateur, often clerical, scientist were passing,

---

56   *The Quarterly Review*, CVIII, July 1860, 225–264.

57   S. Wilberforce, Review of Darwin's *"Origin of Species"*, *Quarterly Review* 108, 1860, 258.

a generation of professional scientists was emerging. Science was breaking free of ecclesiological and theological constraints, and valued its new-found intellectual autonomy. The legend of Huxley's encounter with Wilberforce served this purpose well.[58]

Huxley's relish in championing Darwin's views was such that he was known as 'Darwin's bulldog'.[59] Like Darwin, he suffered from frequent illness—stomach ailments, headaches, and depression. He trained as a doctor, and in 1846 he took a naval post as assistant surgeon on the voyage of HMS Rattlesnake to study the waters of North-east Australia. The lectures he delivered, based on his observations and experiments during the four-year voyage made his name in scientific circles. He became lecturer in Natural History at the Royal School of Mines, and later Professor at the Royal College of Science. In coining the term 'agnostic', Huxley did not explicitly deny the existence of God, but asserted that he did not know as a fact whether there was such a thing as personal immortality. He had no problem with people reading the Bible, believing it superior to the work of other sects, ancient or modern. He rejected outright infidelity, finding in scenery and music a beauty that hinted at an Author. Nevertheless, to Huxley the standard of truth was always science, and religion could not be scientifically verified. He argued that throughout the history of science, the forces of faith had fought a losing battle in attempts to repress the advance of the human intellect: 'Extinguished theologians lie about the cradle of every science.'[60]

As Roman Catholics and evangelicals had done, Huxley saw the key issue was authority, especially biblical authority. At the heart of his attack on Christian theology lay an assault on the inspiration of the Bible. When this obstacle was removed, he believed that the authority of scientific method and discovery, drawing on the disciplines of geology, palaeontology, biology and anthropology, would stand unchallenged. By 1893, he was surprised how easy the victory had been. Huxley observed that in place of 'plenary inspiration', theologians had been reduced to proposing an 'inspiration with limited liability,' the limit being susceptible of 'indefinite fluctuation in correspondence with the demands of scientific criticism'. This was the easiest resort for theologians, but to Huxley's eyes, it was 'likely to end in disaster'.[61]

To Huxley, retaining adherence to a theological creed in the face of the advance of scientific method was committing intellectual suicide. The

---

58   A thorough analysis of the historical sources, and reasons for the promulgation of various versions, is found in J.R. Lucas, 'Wilberforce and Huxley: A Legendary Encounter', *Historical Journal*, 22, 2, 1979, 313–30.

59   On Huxley see M.A. di Gregario, *T.H. Huxley's Place in Natural Science*, New Haven, Yale, 1984; J.V. Jenson, *Thomas Henry Huxley: Communicating For Science*, Newark, University of Delaware Press, 1991.

·60   T.H. Huxley, *Collected Essays 1893–94*, Vol, 2., London, MacMillan, 52.

61   T.H. Huxley, *Science and Hebrew Tradition: Essays*, New York, Appleton, 1910, vii.

alternative scientific creed could control disease and famine, and render people more humane and civilised. In 1871 he declared himself, to the German biologist Anton Dohrn an apostle for science, a missionary whose role was to 'convert the Christian Heathen of these islands to the true faith.'[62]

DARWIN'S LATER RELIGIOUS VIEWS—CONVERSION TO CHRISTIANITY?

Darwin's own religious life underwent a process of fluctuating change. Religious belief, or lack of it, was to him a private matter. As he wrote, 'what my own views may be is a question of no consequence to any one but myself.'[63] Reared in a sceptical home, amongst Unitarians who had converted to Anglicanism, then training for the Anglican priesthood but never taking a parish, and choosing a wife who had embraced simple evangelical views, the contradictions are apparent. At crucial moments he was aware that it would cost him much if he revealed what he really thought. He kept his religious journey, and doubts, to himself. Darwin suggested he was forty before he gave up Christianity,[64] although he retained its respectable veneer as a polite country gentleman. Although he propounded the theory of evolution, with its profound religious implications, and with fame and fortune secure, he still waited ten years after the term 'agnostic' was coined before he identified himself with it. Rather than being an outright unbeliever, it was rather that he found it difficult with the human mind to conclude the reality of Divine existence.

Open alliances with atheists were avoided by Darwin, troubled by the hurt he might cause to the religious feelings of his wife. Yet he read the evolutionary arguments for a humanistic religion in the American Free Religious Association's tabloid *The Index*, and declared: 'I admire them from my inmost heart and agree to almost every word.'[65] In his autobiography, started in 1876, and completed late in his life, but designed only for the private use of the family, he declared he could no longer see how anyone 'wished Christianity to be true.' If the language of the New Testament were correct, many in his family, including his father, brother, and best friends, would be everlastingly lost. This was, to Darwin, 'a damnable doctrine.' He remained comfortable in his agnosticism: 'I feel no remorse from having committed any great sin. I believe I have acted rightly in steadily following and devoting my life to science.'[66]

Darwin saw that if his writings were seen as an overt attack on religious

62   Letter to the German biologist Anton Dohrn, 7 July, 1871, *Life and Letters of Thomas Henry Huxley*, New York, Appleton, 1916, Vol. 1, 389.

63   F. Darwin (ed), *The Life and Letters of Charles Darwin*, 3rd edn, Vol. I, London, John Murray, 1887, 304.

64   Moore and Desmond, *Darwin*, 656–58.

65   Moore, *Darwin Legend*, 44.

66   In Moore, *Legend*, 46, Moore and Desmond, *Darwin*, 636.

world-views, his thesis would have less credibility. With a deep respect for social order, he feared the harm that the amorality and atheism of many secularists and militant freethinkers might do to society. When his friend, the eminent geologist Charles Lyell died almost blind, absorbed in troubled questionings about an after-life, Darwin could offer no answers from his respectable agnosticism.[67] Yet, as he himself approached the end of life, Darwin affirmed he was not 'in the least afraid to die.'[68] His wish was to be buried unobtrusively in the parish churchyard, but his influential friends, including, rather incongruously, the agnostic Huxley, pressurised clergymen to have him buried in Westminster Abbey amongst the illustrious dead of the nation, a few feet from Isaac Newton. In his funeral sermon, Dean Farrar demonstrated how Darwin's views had been accepted as normative within the Christian canon: 'I read in every line the healthy, noble, well-balanced wonder of a spirit profoundly reverent, kindled into the deepest admiration for the works of God.'[69] A Christian burial service in Westminster Abbey appeared an act of reconciliation between faith and science.

Even though knowledge of his true religious views began to creep out after his death, when the *Life and Letters* of Darwin appeared in 1886, it was carefully edited by the family to present a modest, hesitant agnostic who gradually gave up Christianity. In spite of this, as early as the 1880s the so-called 'Darwin Legend' that he converted to Christianity on his death bed began to circulate, and came to public prominence in 1915, based on a report of a visit to Darwin by Lady Elizabeth Hope just before he died.[70]

Darwin had approved the request of James Fegan, a member of the Plymouth Brethren, to hold evangelistic meetings in the temperance meeting-room Darwin had set up in the village of Downe. A number in the village were converted, including a notorious local drunkard. Two members of the Darwin's domestic staff attended and subsequently became members of the local church. On one occasion Fegan and a group of orphan boys visited Darwin's home, and sang a few hymns on the lawn before the Darwin family and their servants, for which they were rewarded with sixpence each. During Fegan's absence, Lady Elizabeth Hope, who also held evangelistic and temperance meetings in Kent, supplied his place, and claimed to have called on Darwin six months before he died. She reported she found him reading the Epistle to the Hebrews, which he

---

67   Moore and Desmond, *Darwin*, 612.

68   Moore, *Legend*, 52, quoting F. Darwin, *Life and Letters*, 3: 358.

69   F. Darwin, (ed) *The Life and Letters of Charles Darwin*, Vol. III., London, John Murray, 1887, Appendix I.

70   The 'Legend,' and the evidence behind it, is fully explored by J. Moore, a leading expert on Darwin, in *The Darwin Legend*, Grand Rapids, Baker Books, 1994. Moore provides relevant supporting documents. The full account of Lady Hope's visit first appeared in written form in the American Baptist Magazine the *Watchman-Examiner* in August 1915, as reported by Lady Hope to Professor A.T. Robertson of Southern Baptist Theological Seminary, Louisville at the Northfield Conference that month. She had apparently shared the story with friends in London before 1907.

said he loved. Lady Hope claimed he asked her to preach about Jesus Christ in his summerhouse to his servants and neighbouring tenants, and to sing some hymns, and he would listen from his open window. The family apparently were against this, and the service was never held.

The story raises a number of questions, but even Lady Hope did not recount an evangelical conversion of Darwin, only hinted that his views on Christianity had mellowed late in life. Darwin was certainly willing to make donations to the South American Missionary Society's work amongst the Fuegan people he had visited on the Beagle, but this may simply have been from a desire to improve their social condition. The account of Darwin reading the Bible goes against the evidence of his family as to his rejection of Christianity at the end of his life. They were with him at his deathbed, and reported his last words. Some in the family, particularly his wife Emma, would have rejoiced in a change of heart by Darwin, but they recorded none. Elizabeth Hope did not report her visit until thirty years later, after she had fallen into some discredit and bankruptcy. The account provoked angry reaction and denials from the Darwin family, who were careful over the image of their father after his death, and did not want his name to be used to support the evangelical cause. The sons of Darwin all died as evolutionists and freethinkers. The evangelist James Fegan, who knew the Darwins well, rejected the conversion story as 'an illustration of the recklessness with which the Protestant Controversialists seek to support any cause they are advocating.'[71]

Nonetheless, the account, often highly embellished, widely circulated in North America in the years after 1915, particularly in the 1920s in the thick of the campaign against the spread of Darwinian teaching in North America. However, William Jennings Bryan, the leading fundamentalist campaigner, refused to make use of the story, convinced instead that Darwin's faith had been destroyed by his teaching of evolution.

THE WIDER INFLUENCE OF DARWINISM

Darwin's teaching on natural selection undercut a key basis for social morality, the ethical implications of which were profoundly troubling to Darwin. Would any one 'trust in the convictions of a monkey's mind, if there are any convictions in such a mind?'[72] Darwin's views on the development of human morality were influenced by his experience of the Fuegians on the Beagle expedition—a people, naked, bedaubed with paint, 'living like wild animals on what they could catch.' He could as readily accept he was descended from a monkey or a baboon, as

71   Letter of J.W.C. Fegan to S.J. Pratt, 22 May 1925, The rejection of the story was also made in a letter to John Kensit, of the Protestant Truth Society that same month. The letters are in Moore, Legend, 154–163.

72   Letter of Charles Darwin to William Graham, July 3, 1881, in Life and Letters of Charles Darwin, ed. F. Darwin, Vol I, London, John Murray, 1887, 285.

those who delighted to torture their enemies, practiced infanticide without remorse, readily eliminated the weak in mind or body, and were haunted by superstition. Nonetheless, he was left with a difficulty in accommodating high social values such as obedience, courage, sympathy, and mutual aid, into his scheme. He noted that amongst the Fuegans, those who survived commonly exhibited a vigorous state of health: 'We civilised men, on the other hand, do our utmost to check the process of elimination; we build asylums for the imbecile, the maimed, and the sick; we institute poor laws; and our medical men exert their utmost skill to save the life of every one to the last moment.' Allowing the weak members of society to propagate their kind created an evolutionary difficulty: 'No one who has attended to the breeding of domestic animals will doubt that this must be highly injurious to the race of man.'[73] He was caught in a tension between his humanitarian praise for compassion towards the disabled and the poor, rejoicing in the prospect of a future in which these higher moral instincts would be fixed by inheritance, and fears that these might ultimately prove harmful.[74] Alfred Wallace, co-founder with Darwin of natural selection, was clearer that evolution was favourable to the advance of civilisation and morality, whereby the competitive and antagonistic instinct should be changed into one of co-operation and co-ordination for the good of all.[75]

It was not long before Darwin's views were taken further. His son Leonard became first president of the Eugenics Society, devoted to breeding a 'better' people. Leonard called for 'racial deterioration' to be prevented through legal and tax incentives, arguing that the poor, and the least fit socially and physically, should be deterred from reproducing. However, those in honourable and well-paid jobs should be allowed to have four children, to enhance the upward march of evolution.[76] The English philosopher Herbert Spencer (1820–1903), who coined the phrase 'the survival of the fittest,' argued that in society, as in nature, competition between individuals and races provided the impetus to social, material, and moral progress. Spencer was propounding social evolution as early as 1850, but after Darwin's views were published in 1859, he united biological and social theory, observing 'a continuous over-running of the less powerful or less adapted by the more powerful or more adapted societies ... and, occasionally, an extermination of inferior varieties.'[77] From Spencer's views came Social Darwinism, which helped intellectually to underpin imperialism. Although Spencer argued that ingenuity and co-operation would replace the

73   C. Darwin, *The Descent of Man*, 133–34.

74   Darwin, *Descent of Man*, 125.

75   H. Clements, *Alfred Russel Wallace: Biologist and Social Reformer*, London, Hutchinson, 1983, See Chapters 16 and 17, 163–194

76   Leonard Darwin, *What is Eugenics?*, 7, 68, 75, quoted in Moore, *Darwin Legend*, 103.

77   H. Spencer, *The Principles of Sociology*, New York, Appleton, 1877, 108.

use of force in the struggle for existence, this emphasis was all-too-quickly ignored, and the expansion of societies claiming cultural, and racial superiority, backed by military strength, appeared to receive justification. Social Darwinism, coupled with eugenic thinking, was later used to justify the domination, or removal, of racial groups which were claimed to be less pure, developed or desirable. This fatal combination of ideologies underlay the rise of Nazism in twentieth-century Germany.

Many across Europe and America seized on Darwin's scientific writings as confirming their religious scepticism. In Germany his views were strongly endorsed by the growing body of freethinkers, including the zoologist Ernst Haeckel, and the renowned physician Ludwig Büchner. After reading Darwin, Karl Marx claimed him as an ally from the world of science, 'this is the book which contains the basis in natural history for our view'.[78] Marx used the Hegelian dialectic method, to describe society in terms of evolutionary progress through conflict, from antiquity to feudalism, from feudalism to capitalism, and then to a classless society. When Darwin was sent a copy of Das Kapital, he carefully avoided endorsing it, confessing that he knew little of the German language and political economy.[79]

The consonance between Darwinism and aspects of wider social thought helps explain its ready acceptance. Utilitarianism proposed decision making and laws on the basis of the greatest good of the greatest number whilst Darwin spoke of the natural processes of survival and extinction for the dominant and fittest groups. Laissez-faire economics argued that economic processes function best with little external interference—the same principle underlay natural selection. Hegel's dialectic understanding of progress through struggle was common ground. In Germany, theologians argued that if the Bible was to be examined, it should only be done by scientific methodology. The progressive, optimistic, implications of Darwin were readily embraced, yet the challenge to Christianity from Darwinism was profound. By the twentieth century, Darwin's 'theory' of evolution was as firmly established as Newton's 'law' of gravity. The rise of Darwinian science coincided with the decline of faith in Western Europe. Although unknown to many church-goers, the ideas of Darwin were widely debated amongst the intelligentsia. For some, adjustments to their theistic world-view were simple, for others the fundamental irreconcilability of matters of science and faith remained. Had the ultimate source of authority now become science?

---

78   In R.L. Meek (ed), *Marx and Engels on Malthus*, New York, 1954, 171.
79   Desmond and Moore, *Darwin*, 601–602.

Further Reading

T. Chalmers, *The Evidence and Authority of the Christian Revelation*, 5th edn, Edinburgh, William Blackwood, 1817.

C. Darwin, *Origin of Species*, Introduction by R.E. Leakey, London, Faber and Faber, 1979.

C. Darwin, *The Descent of Man and Selection in Relation to Sex*, 2 vols, London, John Murray, 1871.

A. Desmond and J. Moore, *Darwin*, London, Michael Joseph, 1991.

J. Durant, *Darwinism and Divinity: Essays on Evolution and Religious Belief*, Oxford, Blackwell, 1985.

C. Hodge, *What is Darwinism?*, New York, Scribner, Armstrong, 1874.

J.R. Lucas, 'Wilberforce and Huxley: A Legendary Encounter', *Historical Journal*, 22, 2, 1979, 313–30.

H. Miller, *The Testimony of the Rocks: Or, Geology in its Bearing on the Two Theologies, Natural and Revealed*, Edinburgh, Thomas Constable, 1857, reprinted Thoemmes Press, 2002.

J. Moore, *The Darwin Legend*, Grand Rapids, Baker, 1994.

H. Orel (ed), *Charles Darwin: Interviews and Recollections*, London, Macmillan, 2000.

J.H. Roberts, *Darwinism and the Divine in America*, Madison, WI, University of Wisconsin Press, 1988.

J. Moore, *The Post-Darwinian Controversies*, Cambridge, CUP, 1979.

B.M.G. Reardon, *Religious Thought in the Victorian Age: A Survey from Coleridge to Gore*, London, Longman, 1995.

M. Shortland, (ed) *Hugh Miller and the Controversies of Victorian Science*, Oxford, Clarendon, 1996.

R.M. Young, 'The Impact of Darwin on Conventional Thought', in A. Symondson (ed), *The Victorian Crisis of Faith*, London, SPCK 1970.

11

Revolutions in American Religion and Society: the Shadow of Civil War

Christianity was a highly pervasive feature of the dynamically changing nineteenth-century American society, helping to mould its national cultural values, yet it was competed over and divisive territory. The freedom which Americans enjoyed to practice the religion of their choice did not bring greater tolerance, but a diversity of approaches to the interpretation of Christian teaching and models of Christian practice. The first Amendment deregulated religion, but made no attempt to establish what 'the' religious truth was, and as the nineteenth-century progressed, a multiplicity of claims about it were unleashed. A free market in religious opinion followed, with religion hawked across the land like any other product in the years before the American Civil War.[1] Many had their own vision of what godly America would look like, with little prospect that those visions would be united through compromise or consensus.[2] Over the big issues confronting America, such as the role of women in society, or slavery, the churches had much to say, but it was often delivered by means of diametrically opposing arguments, usually based on varying interpretations of the Bible.

The Changing American Society and Economy

By 1861, the population of the United States had reached 31 million, a rise from 8.4 million in 1815. It was to reach 99.1 million in 1914. New York's population

---

1   R. Laurence Moore, *Selling God: American Religion in the Market Place of Culture*, New York, Oxford University Press, 1994.

2   On this see R. Carwardine, *Evangelicals and Politics in Antebellum America*, New Haven, Connecticut, Yale University Press, 1993.

reached one million, and Philadelphia half a million: by 1860, nine American cities had populations of over 100,000 people. There was a significant geographical shift of population away from the eastern seaboard, as millions sought out the opportunities of the vast new Western territories. In 1800 less than 500,000 people lived West of the Appalachians, by 1860 this was 15 million.[3] The populations of Mid-West towns mushroomed—Cincinnati had 25,000 residents in 1830, and 161,000 in 1860. Chicago was just a trading post in 1830, a town of 5,000 in 1840, and a burgeoning city of 109,000 twenty years later.

The American industrial revolution was well underway by the middle decades of the nineteenth century, characterised by technological innovation beginning with the textile mills in New England. A transport revolution accompanied that in industry: with steam shipping facilitating the movement of vast supplies of agricultural products and manufactured goods on America's vast internal lakes, navigable rivers, and coastal waters. By 1860, along the Mississippi valley alone there were over a thousand paddle-steamers. Nonetheless, for much of the mid-nineteenth century, roads into the vast interior of the States remained hopelessly inadequate. When in 1834 the English Independent minister Andrew Reed visited America, he endured a journey across Ohio in a coach advertised as 'splendid', which took 28 hours to cover 110 miles, often on roads up to the axle-trees in mud.[4] Railways brought greater transport benefits. By 1860 over 50,000 miles of track had been laid, with all the major cities East of St Louis connected.

America was a land of opportunity, its population boosted by huge inflows of immigrants from Europe. One and a half million Irish migrants arrived between 1840 and 1860, often in great poverty, in the wake of the Irish Potato famine. By the 1850s, 280,000 immigrants were arriving each year. In 1860, of the American population, one in eight was not native born. Over a million Germans chose the new opportunities of America, and 35,000 Chinese arrived, mainly to California. America had become, in the words of Walt Whitman, 'not merely a nation but a teeming of nations'. Yet immigrants arrived in the middle of the century to a society that was unsure of itself, displayed in hostile attitudes towards newcomers, and growing nativist sentiment. The poorest and least educated placed great strains on the housing system and social provision of the previously ethnically and culturally homogenous New England area. Arrivals in the later decades were able to enter a more settled scene, often assisted by family and friends who had already become established.

American Gross National Product more than doubled between 1800 and 1860. For those with jobs and willing to work long hours, wages could be

3   S. Thernstrom, *A History of the American People: Volume 1: to 1877*, Orlando, Florida, Harcourt Brace Jovanovich, 1989. 236.

4   A. Reed, *Narrative of a Visit to the American Churches*, Vol. I, London, Jackson and Walford, 1835, 141–144.

good. However, industrial employment was far from secure, with serious trade depressions in 1837, and 1857. Whether industrialisation and urbanisation brought an actual increase in standards of living, as opposed to simply an increase in income levels, is as much debated in America as in Britain. Certainly working and living conditions could be poor, with a lack of sanitation and clean water, a burgeoning crime problem, and overcrowded housing. The poorest immigrants, or those without skills, gravitated into the slum ghettos of the cities, where housing was cheapest, but of the most inferior quality.

The drive to expand America Westwards into land between the Appalachians and the Mississippi was into territory already the possession of 125,000 Native Americans. In the war of Independence, Americans had courted the Native Americans as allies, but growing ethnocentric thinking saw their presence as increasingly something to be feared. By the 1820s, Thomas Jefferson's policy of assimilation was waning, despite the efforts of missionaries and federal agents. Andrew Jackson, elected President in 1828, believed that treaties with Indians were 'an absurdity not to be reconciled to the principles of our government'.[5] The Removal Bill of 1830 uprooted tribes east of the Mississippi, and resettled them in territory in the west. In theory, the removals were voluntary, backed by provisions and cash incentives, but those who refused to relocate were rounded up by the Army. Some 90,000 were forced westward along the 'trail of tears' towards barren reservations. Few white Americans seriously objected to the policy: some even arguing that it would assist the advance of Native Americans towards a civilised Christian society. In reality, the opposite was true. In Georgia, the Cherokee under the leadership of figures such as Elias Boudinot (1802–39) had been working hard to build a Christian republic, when in the 1830s they found themselves being forced to move West.

The 'frontier' itself was also progressively moving westwards throughout the nineteenth century, assisted by the settling of the border with Canada at the 49th parallel in 1844. Decisive victories against the Native American Indians, and then the development of railways, the Federal postal service in 1863, and the introduction of barbed wire after 1874, made the life of frontiersmen more straightforward. Repeating the pattern of the earliest arrivals in New England, settlers continued to see themselves as chosen by God for a specific task. In 1845, the Democratic newspaper editor John O'Sullivan declared it the 'manifest destiny' of Americans to possess the rest of the continent beyond the Mississippi River, which had been handed by Providence to Americans. Yet, few found that their dreams for a new life were realised; agricultural conditions were little better, communities were unstable and often violent, beset by frequent scarcity

5   James Monroe, Message to Congress, 25 January 1825; and Letter from Andrew Jackson to James Monroe, 1817, both quoted in E.H. Spicer, *A Short History of the Indians of the United States*, New York, D. Van Nostrand, 1969, 228–229.

and the sense of isolation from the East. Nonetheless, the sense of a God-given opportunity, coupled with the religious revivalism of the early nineteenth century, ensured that life in the 'wild-West' was not entirely godless.

America was not only expanding to the West. In December 1845 Florida joined the Union. Between 1845 and 1853, through a mixture of warfare, treaty, and purchase, Texas, New Mexico, and California all became part of the United States. Although the accession of these new states accentuated the slavery issue, America became a truly continental nation. The discovery of gold deposits in California inspired a rush of prospectors into the area: the population soared from 14,000 in 1848 to 100,000 the following year, and doubled again by 1850 when it became America's thirty-first state.

New England's economic and demographic strength bolstered its intellectual and reforming leadership. This was the heartland of movements against slavery, for peace, temperance, the rights of women, and for improvements in education. Between the 1830s and the 1860s, the so called 'American Renaissance' saw a great flowering of literary and cultural endeavour, with New England at its centre. Nathaniel Hawthorne, Walt Whitman, Emily Dickinson, and Ralph Waldo Emerson helped shape a distinctly American national culture, separate from that of Europe, informed by optimistic readings of American history and democracy. Their work was indicative of increasing intellectual independence from patterns inherited from Puritanism, evangelicalism, and even the liberal and humanist approach of Unitarianism. This was reflected in Transcendentalism—an understanding that the essence of meaning in the world 'transcended' dogma and human institutions, coming instead through the intuitive faculties of humans. Yet, for all the aspiration towards cultural independence, the influence of European Romanticism, of Wordsworth, Coleridge and Goethe, was unmistakeable.[6]

CHANGES IN RELIGIOUS LIFE IN ANTE-BELLUM AMERICA

Visitors to mid-nineteenth century America were struck by how religious a nation it was. Alexis de Tocqueville observed in the 1830s how 'the spirit of religion and the spirit of freedom... united intimately with one another: they reigned together on the same soil'.[7] Despite being struck by the roughness and uncouthness of the way of life the further West he travelled in the United States in 1834, the English Congregationalist Andrew Reed was impressed by the

---

6   The developing intellectual and cultural scene in America is explored in C. Davidson, *Revolution and the Word*, New York, Oxford University Press, 1986.

7   A. de Tocqueville, *Democracy in America*, ed. and trans. by H.C. Mansfield and D. Winthrop, Chicago, Chicago University Press, 2000, 282, quoted in M. Noll, '"Christian America" and "Christian Canada"', *Cambridge History of Christianity: World Christianities, c. 1815–1914*, ed. H. McLeod, Cambridge, CUP, 2006, 364.

remarkable level of religious activity. Cincinnati, with a population of 30,000, had 21 churches; all 90 families resident in Granville, Ohio, attended church. He attributed much religious strength to the adaptability of American Christianity, bringing 'life and virtue', and its particular theological emphases: 'the spirit of regeneration animates it; and evangelical truth is more familiar to it.'[8]

Studies suggest that the religious adherence of the population, which had grown rapidly in the years after Independence, from 17% in 1776 to 34% in 1850, had then levelled off until 1870, before reaching 45% in 1890, and 53% in 1916.[9] In terms of church attendance and giving to religious institutions, the United States became the most Christian nation in the world. The Second Great Awakening fed Arminian elements into Calvinist theology, coupled with an optimistic postmillennial theology, and calls for disinterested action in moral reform. Methodism was the largest denominational body in mid-nineteenth century America, with, 20,000 churches and 1.7 million members in 1861; the Baptists were second with over 11,000 churches in the mid-1840s. There were some 1,500 Congregationalist churches and 2,000 Episcopal churches in the mid-1840s. The Presbyterians adapted more successfully to the new American order in the nineteenth century than they had in the immediate aftermath of Independence: their 2,000 churches of 1830, had risen to some 6,400 by 1860. Other evangelicals sought to order themselves on simple Bible-based lines, free of inherited traditions and creeds. By 1860 there were 2,100 Disciples of Christ churches. Waves of Protestant migrants, such as the Lutherans and Mennonites, added their own denominational traditions to the rich mix.

Although church and state were separated, America still displayed the distinctive cultural values of a Christian society. The Sabbath was often strictly observed, churches ploughed vast efforts into Sunday Schools, and social projects. By 1830, the American Bible Society was distributing over 300,000 copies or portions of the Bible annually. The voluntary agency was the primary channel for endeavours towards moral improvement, temperance, Sabbath observance, and education. Whilst engagement in wider political life remained suspect, being open to abuse and corruption, Christians saw the potential for mass political action to achieve their wider purposes, especially in the sabbatarian and temperance causes. The Republican party capitalised on the energy of evangelical Protestantism with greatest success. In the South, evangelicals tended towards a defence of the existing social order.[10]

---

8   A. Reed and J. Matheson, *Narrative of a Visit to the American Churches*, Vol. I. London, Jackson and Walford, 1835, Vol. I, 165–168; Vol. II, 275, 280.

9   R. Finke and R. Stark, *The Churching of America, 1776–1990*, New Brunswick, NJ, Rutgers University Press, 16.

10   R. Carwardine, *Evangelicals and Politics in Antebellum America*, New Haven, Yale University Press, 1993, 320–323.

An economic crisis in 1857 brought a crash in stockmarkets, and unemployment soared above 10%. Prayer meetings started in New York soon grew to number thousands, and before long a revival movement had spread across the United States, and into parts of Western Europe.[11] The ethical code of revivalism infused the values of temperance into evangelical Protestantism. The renunciation of not just ardent spirits, but of all alcohol, was seen as the sign of a truly converted person. Average consumption of alcohol fell by 56% in the 1830s, and a further 42% between 1840 and 1845.[12] Temperance gradually extended its remit from individual moral persuasion, into the use of legislative means to prohibit the sale of alcohol. In 1851, Maine became a 'dry' state, and votes in other states were hotly contested.

Roman Catholicism was faced with significant challenges in adapting to post-Independence American culture. It slowly moved from being a missionary outpost, semi-independent of European jurisdiction, with a significant role for the laity, towards increased dependence upon the papacy. Vast waves of migration from Europe transformed the Roman Catholic community, which numbered only around 0.3 million in 1830. In 1860 there were some 2,550 Roman Catholic Churches, with a Roman Catholic population of around 3 million— some 10% of the population. By 1910 Roman Catholicism claimed over 12 million communicants, compared to 22 million amongst Protestants.[13] The Roman Catholic Church eventually became the largest single denomination in the United States. In 1900, around 50% of America's Roman Catholic population was Irish. Of over 5 million German migrants, some 30 percent were also Roman Catholics. Between the 1880s and 1920 around four million Italians also crossed the Atlantic, together with large numbers of Poles. Under severe social and economic pressures, many Roman Catholic immigrants clung tenaciously to conservative religious and cultural values, in a denomination far from comfortable in the republican, denominationally pluralistic, United States.[14]

Nonetheless, tension between Roman Catholics and Protestants remained a recurring aspect of the American religious scene, accentuated by Roman Catholic resistance to the non-sectarian religious education offered in public schools, focussed around commonly agreed moral principles. The Roman Catholic leadership offered instead their own independent schools and social relief provisions: in 1910 there were over 300 Roman Catholic hospitals, and 52,000 orphans were being cared for. The establishment of female Roman

11   See R. Carwardine, *Transatlantic revivalism: popular evangelicalism in Britain and America, 1790–1865*, Westport, Conn., Greenwood Press, 1978.

12   Thernstrom, *History of the American People*, I, 262.

13   J.P. Dolan, *The American Catholic Experience: A History from Colonial Times to the Present*, Notre Dame, University of Notre Dame Press, 1992, 158–220, 255.

14   Dolan, *American Catholic Experience*, 127–157.

Catholic religious orders in the United States after 1809, such as the Sisters of Charity founded in Baltimore by Elizabeth Ann Seton (1776–1821) gave women opportunities to take a role in providing education. Their schools became well known high quality educational provision—by 1900 there were over 3,800 parochial schools, and 663 girls' academies, mainly run by nuns.[15] These did much to consolidate and extend religious practice in the Roman Catholic community, but produced a closely knit, tightly controlled religious sub-culture, in many ways separate from wider society.

Antipathy between Roman Catholic and Protestant communities spilled over into violence, leaving thirteen dead in Philadephia in 1844, and anti-Roman Catholicism was a persistent theme in Protestant rhetoric. In 1833, the Native American Association was established to oppose the influence of Roman Catholic migration, attracting to their membership white professional men, skilled workers, and farmers, who feared their way of life was threatened, and advocated nativist policies. Such suspicion fuelled defensive attitudes amongst Roman Catholics. In 1863, Irish mobs protested against the draft to fight in the Civil War. Fearful that they would lose their jobs to emancipated slaves, they rampaged through New York lynching a number of black Americans. The mayhem cost over one hundred lives.

Revolutions in the Role of Women in Society

Throughout the nineteenth century, average family size in America began to fall. In 1800, women on average bore 7 children during their lifetime. By 1860 this was down to 5.2, with evidence of deliberate attempts to limit family size, largely through later marriage and restraint. Women began to seek greater control of their lives, and seek wider access to opportunities for social engagement. Theology that stressed the importance of human choice in effecting spiritual change, fed into decision making to effect social change. Yet, most women accepted the notion of separate spheres, theirs being the domestic and social one, maintaining the emotional, moral, and often religious well-being of the family.[16]

The church and its associated meetings provided a social avenue which contributed towards a new sense of female collective and public activity.[17] Selling Bibles, distributing tracts, raising funds for benevolent and missionary purposes, and providing the bulk of the workforce in the 50,000 Sunday Schools that had

---

15   S.H Lindley, *'You Have Stepped Out of Your Place': A History of Women and Religion in America*, Louisville, Kentucky, Westminster John Knox Press, 1996, 217–220.

16   M. Westerkamp, *Women and Religion in Early America, 1600–1850*, 135.

17   The significant role played by women in antebellum reform movements is discussed in L. Ginzberg, *Women and the Work of Benevolence, Morality, Politics and Class in the Nineteenth-Century United States*, New Haven, Yale, 1990; B.L. Epstein, *The Politics of Domesticity: Women, Evangelism and Temperance in Nineteenth-Century America*, Middletown, Wesleyan University Press, 1981; J.W. James (ed), *Women in American Religion*, Philadelphia, University of Pennsylvania Press, 1982.

sprung up by the 1820s, gave women significant influence, if not control over, aspects of religious practice. Here women gained rich opportunities for social organisation and leadership, bolstering their demands for equal educational opportunities, access to the professions, and eventually the right to vote.

Much endeavour was invested in helping those with a lifestyle very different from that of middle-class women, especially those who were poor and living in the squalor of the industrial city, such as immigrant women, prostitutes, and those affected by alcohol abuse. The New York Female Moral Reform Society was founded in 1834 to reduce sexual immorality, and indecent behaviour and speech: by the 1840s moral reform was a national movement. The temperance cause, the largest of the voluntary reform movements, was part of female protest against the domestic violence, poverty, and desertion inflicted on women and children by alcohol-abusing husbands and fathers: over half the membership of temperance societies was female. Campaigns for Sabbath observance, and the closure of taverns on Sundays, were also pro-women and pro-family, through keeping men away from alcohol and at home with their wives and children. Such campaigns reinforced to campaigners a sense of their powerlessness in a male dominated society, and fed into discussion of the need to assert women's rights. Evangelical teaching, republican ideals, and an increasing social sensitivity to cruelty and violence, were all contributory factors.[18] They may have lacked formal political rights, but both black and white American women had a very significant role to play in reforming American society.[19]

The campaign against slavery also helped to politicise women, and undermine separate spheres thinking. It combined social, political, and religious elements, as women asserted their God-given right to protest publicly against the evils of slavery, but their activity in public speaking could prove as controversial as that of the cause they spoke in, especially when they spoke to mixed audiences. Although evangelical religious societies gave women some opportunities for engagement, those who had gained experience in speaking in African-American churches, or with the Quakers, took a foremost role, as did the Unitarians. The Quaker Grimké sisters advocated both abolitionism and the right of women to speak out in the cause. By 1837 there were over 1,000 American anti-slavery societies, 77 being for women only.

18 On women and social concern see L. D. Ginzberg, *Women and the Work of Benevolence: Morality, Politics, and Class in the Nineteenth Century United States*, New Haven, Yale University Press, 1990; C. Stansell, *City of Women: Sex and Class in New York 1789–1860*, Urbana, University of Illinois Press, 1987. The role of women in the temperance movement is the subject of Ruth Bordin's, *Women and Temperance: The Quest for Power and Liberty, 1873–1900*, New Brunswick, N.J., Rutgers University Press, 1990.

19 On American reforming movements see R. G. Walters, *American Reformers, 1815–1860*, New York, Hill and Wang, 1978; S. Mintz, *Moralists and modernizers : America's pre-Civil War reformers*, Baltimore, Johns Hopkins University Press, 1995.

The Rights of Women: July 1848.

Resolved, that all laws which prevent women from occupying such a station in society as her conscience shall dictate, or which place her in a position inferior to that of man, are contrary to the great precept of nature, and therefore of no force or authority...

Resolved, that woman has too long rested satisfied in the circumscribed limits which corrupt customs and a perverted application of the Scriptures have marked out for her, and that it is time she should move in the enlarged sphere which her great Creator has assigned her...'[1]

1   Declaration of Sentiments in 'Report of the Women's Rights Convention', Seneca Falls, N.Y., July 19–20, 1848 quoted in T.K. Wayne, *Women's Roles in Nineteenth-Century America*, Westport, Conn., Greenwood Press, 2007.

The abolitionist movement split after 1840, over the right of women to participate and speak on equal terms. Elizabeth Cady Stanton (1815–1902) had been reared in a strict Presbyterian home, and experienced powerful religious impressions through the preaching of Charles Finney, but she came to reject evangelicalism because it placed conversion before any other social agenda. Stanton's husband worked for the abolitionist movement. She and Lucretia Mott saw a continuity between the cause of the slave and of the rights of women: 'For while the man is born to do whatever he can, for the woman and the Negro there is no such privilege.'[20] Frustrated at the unequal treatment of women in the anti-slavery movement, in 1848 they arranged a convention at Seneca Falls, New York, to discuss the social, civil, and religious condition of women. It was attended by some 300 men and women, a significant number of whom were Quakers. Using the Declaration of Independence's assertion that all, men and women, are 'endowed by the creator with certain inalienable rights,' the convention agreed a declaration calling for women to have 'immediate admission to all the rights and privileges which belong to them as citizens of the United States.' An aspect of their protest was the 'subordinate' position afforded to women in the churches, particularly the way they were denied access to higher levels of religious education, and opportunities in professional ministry.[21] By the 1850s, the women's rights cause had emerged as a separate movement

20   E.C. Stanton, quoted in S.J. Kleinberg, *Women in the United States, 1830–1945*, Basingstoke, Macmillan, 1999, 89,

21   E.C. Stanton, *A History of Woman Suffrage*, 2 vols, Rochester, N.Y., Fowler and Wells, 1889, Vol. I., 70–71; 'Seneca Falls Declaration of Sentiments and Resolutions', in eds. E.C. Dubois and L. Dumenil, *Through Women's Eyes: An American History with Documents*, 3rd edn, Bedford, St Martin's, 2005, A18–A21.

from abolitionism, although similar methods of tract distribution, petitioning, platform speeches, sermons, and appeals to the press, were employed.

The campaign was joined in 1851 by Susan Anthony (1820–1906), of Quaker background, experienced in the temperance, moral reform, and anti-slavery movements, and one of the most powerful advocates of the rights of women. Sojourner Truth (1797–1883), born as the slave-girl Isabella, received her freedom in 1828, and after a conversion experience she began to travel as a preacher. A tall powerful woman, with a deep voice capable of holding large audiences, she powerfully condemned the dual oppression of women through racism and the denial of their right to vote. The leading black male abolitionist, Frederick Douglass (1818–1895), was also a strong supporter of the rights of women.

The Civil War disrupted the momentum of the women's rights campaign, but when it was over, the divisions between it and abolitionism appeared clearer than ever. To many, the demand for the vote superseded other moral causes. Stanton's urging of the rights of women, but denial of them to black Americans, had racist overtones. In 1869, Wyoming became the first state to grant the right to vote to women, and Utah, Colorado, and Idaho followed before the end of the century. Women had to wait until the ratification of the 19th Amendment of the US constitution in 1920 before they were granted the vote in presidential elections.[22]

Stanton and other feminists eventually pushed their critique of the church's restrictions on the role of women into criticisms of Christianity itself. With others she published the *Woman's Bible*, a commentary on a selection of Bible passages, asserting that the roots of the social inequality, subordination and oppression of women lay within the Old and New Testaments. It was a highly controversial book, and served to alienate Stanton from many Christian women, as did her claim in the late 1850s that marriage was not a divine institution, but a human creation. The *Woman's Bible* was censured at the 1896 convention of the National American Woman Suffrage Association, and women's rights found only moderate support from theological liberals and advocates of the social gospel.[23]

Through the middle decades of the nineteenth century, a system of public

---

22   On the movement for women's rights see E. Flexner, *Century of Struggle: The Women's Rights Movement in the United States*, Harvard, Belknap, 1975; C. Bolt, *The Women's Movements in the United States and Britain from the 1790s to the 1920s*, New York, Harvester Wheatsheaf, 1993. The role of women in benevolence and social reform activities is explored in L.D. Ginzberg, *Women and the Work of Benevolence: Morality, Politics and Class in the Nineteenth Century United States*, New Haven, Conn., Yale University Press, 1990. On links between women's rights and anti-slavery, see J.F. Yellin, *Women and Sisters: The Anti-Slavery Feminists in American Culture*, New Haven, Conn., Yale University Press, 1989. The participation of black women in the women's rights campaign is explored in R. Terborg-Penn, *African-American Women in the Struggle for the Vote, 1850–1920*, Bloomington, Indiana University Press, 1998.

23   E.C. Stanton, et al, *The Woman's Bible, Part I*, 1895, *Part II*, 1898, New York, European Publishing C, 1895, 1898.

schools was developed which included children whose parents were too poor to pay. Religious instruction became an important, though much discussed aspect of public educational provision, in which Sunday Schools continued to play a vital role. Female education also proved controversial, promoted by some on the grounds of social and religious utility, as one writer asserted: 'The best security which a people can have for whatever is elevated in intellect, morals, manners, courage, enterprise, benevolence or patriotism in the rising generation, next to the general diffusion of Christianity, is in the thorough cultivation of the *female mind*.'[24] Female literacy in New England reached 100% in 1840.

By 1870 over half of the 200,000, teachers in the USA were women, although the figure was much smaller in the South, and they received less than half the pay of their male counterparts. After the Civil War, the education of African-Americans was a central component of Reconstruction, and 9,000 teachers, of whom some 4,000 were women, were sent to the South. Some 600,000 African Americans were enrolled in schools by 1870. With fifteen colleges where black women could train as teachers, teaching offered significant employment opportunities for educated black women, despite the continuing intimidation and violence they faced.[25]

By the 1830s opportunities for women in higher education were emerging. Co-educational classes started at Oberlin College in 1833, with over 300 female graduates having emerged with bachelor's degrees by 1860. There were all-women universities in the North by the 1870s and 1880s, and women began to take degrees from previously all-male universities. In the face of great opposition, they also began to gain admission to the legal and medical professions. Elizabeth Blackwell became the first female graduate of the all-male Geneva Medical College, in New York in 1849, and in 1864 Rebecca Lee Crumpler graduated from the New England Female Medical College to become the first black woman to qualify as a medical doctor. By 1900, she had been joined by over 100 others, one third of whom had graduated from Howard University Medical School.[26]

24   New Bernian, 'Female Education', in *Weekly Raleigh Register and North Carolina Gazette*, 16 Feb. 1848, in D.A. Copeland, *The Antebellum Era: Primary Documents on Events from 1820–1860*, Westport, Conn, Greenwood, 2003, 75.

25   N.F. Cott (ed), *No Small Courage: A History of Women in the United States*, New York, Oxford University Press, 2000, 195, 301; C. Clinton and C. Lunardini (eds), *The Columbia Guide to American Women in the Nineteenth Century*, New York, Columbia University Press, 2000, 44; T. Dublin, *Transforming Women's Work: New England Lives in the Industrial Revolution*, Ithaca, N.Y, Cornell University Press, 1994, 205–207; G. Collins, *America's Women: 400 Years of Dolls, Drudges, Helpmates, and Heroines*, New York, HarperCollins, 2003, 107–110.

26   On women in the medical profession see R.J. Ruth (ed), *'Send us a Lady Physician: Women Doctors in America, 1835–1920*, New York, Norton, 1985.

WOMEN PREACHERS

In the mid-nineteenth century women began to play an increasingly public role in religious affairs.[27] Harriet Livermore was the first woman to preach a sermon before the United States Congress in 1827. At least sixty women have been identified as publicly preaching between 1820 and 1845, although most were from sectarian groupings, rather than mainstream denominations.[28] Most women who believed that they had a call to the ministry tended to opt for missionary service. In its first fifty years the American Board of Commissioners for Foreign Missions sent out 1250 workers as preachers, pastors, catechists, doctors and teachers, of whom 691 were women. Many others conducted active ministries as wives of mission workers. The Society of Friends had a long-established pattern of allowing women a public speaking role, making them the natural leaders in projects of moral reform, such as abolition of slavery. Phoebe Palmer became a widely known speaker and promoter of holiness teaching.[29] African-American churches in the African-Methodist tradition tended to lead the way in the acceptance of women as preachers. Belief that the commission to preach came directly from the Holy Spirit effectively by-passed the rules of human authorities, and proved an authentication that transcended racial divides.[30]

Antoinette Brown was the first woman to graduate from divinity school in 1850, becoming the first woman ordained as a minister of a Congregational church in 1853. Anna Howard Shaw became the first female ordained Methodist minister in 1880, although this was revoked four years later. By 1888, some twenty women were serving as ministers of churches in the United States, including Baptists and Unitarians, with a further 350 Quaker women preachers, and some 500 female evangelists. The African Methodist Episcopal Zion Church granted women a vote in their churches in 1876, and began ordaining black women as deacons in 1895, and elders in 1898, the first black denomination to do so. In the African Methodist Episcopal Church, women were licensed to preach in 1884, but did not have access to ordination until 1948. Women were also prominent in new religious movements formed in the middle decades of the century. Ellen Gould White (1827–1915) was a founder, and early leader, of the Seventh Day Adventist church, started in 1863. Christian Science was founded in 1879 by Mary Baker

---

27 Collier-Thomas, *Daughters of Thunder*, 18–22; E. B. Higginbotham, *Righteous Discontent: The Women's Movement in the Black Baptist Church, 1880–1920*, Cambridge, MA, Harvard University Press, 1993.

28 C. A. Brekus, 'Let Your Women Keep Silent in the Churches': Female Religion and Evangelical Religion in America 1740–1845, Yale University PhD dissertation, 1993, 1–4, appendix 407–12, quoted in Westerkamp, *Women and Religion*, 142–43.

29 On Phoebe Palmer see chapter 15.

30 W.L. Andrews (ed), *Sisters of the Spirit: Three Black Women's Autobiographies of the Nineteenth Century*, Bloomington, Indiana University Press, 1986; B. Collier-Thomas, *Daughters of Thunder: Black Women Preachers and Their Sermons, 1850–1979*, San Francisco, Jossey-Bass, 1998, 1–100.

Eddy (1821–1910), promoting teaching which presented God as both male and female, and the role of Eve as a spiritual model for women (see ch. 15).

CHURCHES AND THE SLAVERY ISSUE

Although the slave trade between America and the wider world had ended in 1808, the continued ownership of slaves in the middle decades of the nineteenth century, in an advanced country such as the United States, was a shock to outside eyes. Andrew Reed declared, 'The deepest oppression of man, where the rights of man are professedly most honoured! No, this cannot continue. Slavery and liberty cannot exist together; either slavery must die, or liberty must die.'[31] The framers the United States Constitution in 1787 had compromised on the issue in order to maintain the fragile Union. 'Life, liberty and pursuit of happiness,' was proudly proclaimed, whilst being denied to millions on the basis of their skin colour. The policies of individual states varied. In 1775, Rhode Island was the first to outlaw slavery, followed by six others by 1804. Anti-slavery sentiment was boosted by the Second Great Awakening, which added moral impulsion to reform movements, including abolition. However, hope that a genuine lead would be taken by the churches in the antislavery movement faded when it was suppressed in churches in the South. Even in the North, African Americans found themselves marginalised.

In 1800, just under half of the American population lived in the southern states, the source of much wealth, and political power. The Presidency was held by men from the South in forty out of the first forty-eight years of the new nation's existence. Yet the wealth of the South was firmly rooted in the practice of enslaving and exploiting African Americans, which left the area increasingly isolated from the other states and Europe. Power in the South was in the firm grip of an educated planter elite, who dealt with slaves in oppressive or paternalist fashion, and who fiercely defended their interests. In the North, vast waves of immigration from Europe proved that cheap labour could be found without needing to resort to slavery.

Industry was far less developed in the South than in other parts of the United States—in 1860 the region had just 30% of the nation's railroads, and 15% of the nation's factories. Although Richmond, Virginia, had major iron foundries, some making use of slaves, and some cotton mills, Southern capital was focussed on investment in slave-operated agriculture. Cotton production soared from just 3,000 bales in 1810, to 732,000 in 1830, and almost 5 million in 1860, valued at $249 million, accounting eventually for 60% of the value of all exports. Over 90% of cotton was grown by slaves, who were a vital component of American economic prosperity.

31 A. Reed and J. Matheson, *Narrative of the Visit to the American Churches*, London: Jackson and Walford, 1835, Vol. II, 268–9.

By 1860 the population of the cotton states had reached 5 million. Although there were 400,000 slave owners, 850,000 white southerners owned no slaves at all. The white population in the South was increasingly dwarfed by the number of enslaved African-Americans, totalling 1 million in 1800 and 4 million in 1860. Growing demand for slave labour led to thousands of slaves in states such as Maryland and Virginia being literally 'sold down the river,' the Mississippi. They were relocated through auctions and forced marches, sometimes chained together, to slave estates further South.[32]

Slaves had few rights: they were unable to marry freely, own property, or travel without a pass. They could not file law suits or testify against masters in court, making their legal protection almost impossible. Nonetheless, although slaves were undoubtedly oppressed, with women in particular facing physical and sexual abuse, the life-expectancy of a southern slave of 36 years old in 1850 was little different from the 40 years of white Americans. Generally slave masters realised that over-working and under-feeding slaves was no way to treat an economic asset, and some slaves performed vital economic functions as skilled craftsmen. Yet it was a system that depended on actual or threatened physical coercion, reinforced by the perpetuation of ignorance: illiterate slaves were believed to be less rebellious.[33] In 1861, the numbers of school-age children enrolled in education in the South were less than half the levels found in other parts of the country. It was a legacy of educational deficit bequeathed to future generations.[34] So too was the prevalent culture of violence. In the South the homicide rate was over four times higher than in the Northeast of the United States. With scant chance of success, most slaves discounted the notion of improving their lot by violent means. Instead, around a thousand slaves a year escaped during the 1840s and 1850s, helped by the Underground Railroad, a system organised by black and white abolitionists, to facilitate their hazardous passage to northern states or to Canada.

By 1860, there were also 500,000 free African-Americans, around half of them living in the southern states, mostly working as tenant farmers or labourers. In the northern states a few free African-Americans reached professional and middle class status, but most lived the life of second-class citizens, with limited economic opportunity, and significant local hostility, and in places they had

32 Thernstrom, *History of the American People*, 275. On US slavery see P. Kolchin, *American Slavery, 1619–1877*, London, Penguin, 1993.

33 The experience of black and white women in the South is discussed in E. Fox-Genovese, *Within the Plantation System: Black and White Women in the Old South*, Chapel Hill, University of North Carolina Press, 1988; D.F. Gilpin, *Mothers of Invention: Women of the Slaveholding South in the American Civil War*, Chapel Hill, University of North Carolina Press, 1996.

34 Slave culture in the South is explored in E. Genovese, *Roll, Jordan, Roll: The World the Slaves Made*, New York, Pantheon, 1974; L. Levine, *Black Culture and Black Consciousness*, New York, Oxford University Press, 1977; J. Boles, *Black Southerners, 1619–1869*, Lexington, University Press of Kentucky, 1983.

restricted access to the law and were subject to stringent Black penal codes. They were denied equal access to education, hospitals, theatres, churches—even in death they were treated as inferiors in cemeteries. Some were even kidnapped by white traders who sold them back into slavery in the South.

AFRICAN-AMERICAN CHRISTIANITY

The Second Great Awakening had left the South 90% Protestant, of whom 90% were Baptists or Methodists. By 1850, there were some 87,000 black Methodists, and 150,000 black Baptists. Methodism had attempted to oppose slave-holding amongst its members in the South, but pressure from the planters forced a retreat. Although Christianity was readily embraced by African-Americans, its denominational form, structure, and theology was dominated by the dictates of white Christian culture. Sometimes slaves were denied permission to join African-American churches, their masters insisting they worshipped under their watchful eyes. Away from that gaze, an informal folk Christianity emerged, experiential and non-intellectual, a product of indigenous African-American slave culture. It was spontaneous and exuberant, marked by the singing of spirituals, impromptu religious meetings, and prayer meetings. In traditional African societies, women had played a significant religious role, and they came to occupy important positions within African-American Christianity.[35]

The inconsistencies of white Southern Christianity were palpable. Most slaves attended the same churches as their masters, heard the same sermons, sang the same songs, were even baptised in the same water, but sat in segregated seating. Some masters required attendance, and punished those absent. Most white preachers concentrated upon the spiritual needs of their hearers, but by stressing the virtues of obedience and submission to earthly authorities, enforced social control. Slaves were given little scope to take the biblical themes of spiritual redemption and liberation literally, and scriptural justifications for the practice of slavery were emphasised. Thomas Affleck instructed the overseers of his slaves that 'an hour devoted every morning to their moral and religious instruction would prove a great aid to you in bringing about a better state of things amongst the Negroes…The effect upon their general good behaviour, their cleanliness and good conduct on the Sabbath is such alone as to recommend it to the Planter and Overseer'.[36] Even black preachers often felt constrained to preach messages that did not give offence to white masters, although some were skilled in the use of terminology with double meanings, which slaves could understand. Black preachers also became significant community leaders.

35   N.I. Painter, *Sojourner Truth: A Life, A Symbol*, New York, Norton, 1995. See also S.J. Yee, *Black Women Abolitionists: A Study in Activism 1828–90*, Knoxville, University of Tennessee Press, 1992.

36   Thomas Affleck, quoted in W.E. Montgomery, *The African-American Church in the South, 1865–1900*, Baton Rouge, Louisiana State University Press, 1993, 31; or Genovese, *Roll, Jordan, Roll*, 186–92.

In the North, African-Americans formed significant communities, in which churches, schools, and benevolent agencies were established. The discrimination they encountered in racially mixed congregations led many African-Americans to exercise self-determination by forming their own churches, which became the centre of black community. Black religious leaders helped establish schemes for community self-defence, and became leading spokesmen for abolition. Frederick Douglass (1817–1895), born of a black Maryland slave mother and white father, had escaped to the North when a young man, and became the leading African-American abolitionist. He was an eloquent spokesman for immediate abolition, rather than gradual and compensated emancipation.[37]

Black churches proved a vital link in the Underground Railroad for escaping slaves on their journey to freedom. However, in the South, churches run by free blacks sometimes consciously separated themselves from slave churches, or barred slaves from membership. Conscious that their free status depended on the sanction of white Southerners, they disassociated themselves from anything that might destabilise their social position. Here the expression of Christianity was very different from the indigenous folk expression of slave Christianity.[38] Andrew Reed attended a black church in Lexington, Virginia, in 1834, heard a fine sermon from a black preacher, heartfelt singing of an Isaac Watts hymn, and judged the worship and level of spirituality superior to what he had observed at white services.[39]

In the 1830s, as the abolitionist campaign in the North strengthened, some argued that extensive promotion of Christianity amongst the slaves in the South would preserve unity and order in the region. These arguments fell under suspicion after 1831 when Nat Turner, a respected African-American Baptist preacher from Virginia, was impelled by religious visions he had received to believe that African-American liberation was at hand, and would come about through apocalyptic violence. In the uprising he led, fifty-five whites were killed, and slaves liberated from their plantations, before Turner and around fifty associates were captured, and most of them hanged. Around a hundred African-Americans were killed in reprisals. Although a rare event, it left white planters fearful of any sign of discontent, and more reluctant to grant freedom to slaves.[40] The teaching of slaves to read and write became illegal in many Southern states, as did the free association of slaves at meetings of religious revival. Turner's response was unusual. Most slaves drew dignity, patience and courage from their Christian faith, bringing meaning to their lives in the face of oppression.

---

37 On the work of this leading African-American abolitionist see W. McFeely, *Frederick Douglass*, New York, Norton, 1991.

38 Montgomery, *African-American Church*, 10–37.

39 Reed, *Narrative of American Visit*, Vol. I, 216–222.

40 Turner's revolt is explored in H. Tragle (ed) *Southampton Slave Revolt of 1831*, Amherst, University of Massachusetts Press, 1971.

THE ABOLITION MOVEMENT

In 1816 the American Colonization Society was founded to promote the freeing of slaves by their masters in return for compensation, and to assist with their return to Africa. Based on the British colony of Sierra Leone, Liberia was established in West Africa for the reception of former American slaves. Most free African-Americans opposed the colonization solution, preferring to fight for their constitutional rights, as did the American Anti-Slavery Society. The abolitionist William Lloyd Garrison declared the policy of the American Colonization Society a 'conspiracy against human rights'.[41]

Garrison was the most famous abolitionist of the antebellum era, beginning his Boston-based newspaper the *Liberator* in 1831. For his views, Garrison encountered verbal and physical opposition, with southern states offering rewards for his arrest, or of those who distributed his paper. Although opposing slave rebellions, he rejected moderation: 'Tell a man whose house is on fire to give a moderate alarm... but urge me not to use moderation in a cause like the present.' Garrison exposed the racism of those who denied black slaves were created in the image of God.[42] His voice was joined not only by Quakers and Unitarians, but also by many from traditional evangelical backgrounds. Arthur and Lewis Tappan promoted their views from New York in the *Journal of Commerce*. Even John Brown was from a Congregational family steeped in the theology of Jonathan Edwards. The South's own small, but persistent, abolitionist movement should also not be ignored, typified by the work of the Congregationalist John Fee, of Kentucky, until his expulsion from the state in 1859.[43] Conservative theology was not inimical to radical abolitionist sentiment.

In Britain abolition had become a hallmark of evangelicalism, the evidence of a moral consciousness that abhorred sin. In America, although abolitionists used evangelical style tactics akin to revivalism, with outdoor meetings, testimony, oratory, and dramatic appeals to sign anti-slavery petitions, evangelicalism was not united on the abolition cause. Charles Finney strongly supported abolition, but was unhappy with students who gravitated to the abolition cause rather than to the Christian ministry. The schism that would plunge the United States into war was prefigured by divisions within churches on the issue. In 1844–45 the Baptist mission agency split over complaints that slave-holding missionaries had been appointed. From the schism grew the Southern Baptist Convention, which became the largest Protestant denomination in the early

41   L. Sanneh, *Abolitionists Abroad: American Blacks and the Making of Modern West Africa*, Cambridge, MA, Harvard University Press, 1999; *Liberator*, Boston, 23 April 1831, 34, quoted in Copeland, *Antebellum Era*, 34.

42   W. L. Garrison in the *Liberator*, 1 Jan. 1831; 17 Nov. 1837 quoted in Copeland, *Antebellum Era*, 112, 114.

43   Fee's campaign is discussed in V.B. Howard, *The Evangelical War Against Slavery and Caste*. Selinsgrove, Susquehanna University Press, 1996.

twentieth century. Methodists divided in the same year over whether bishops could hold slaves. If Christian denominations were to dissolve into disunion over the issue, there was little prospect that wider society would fare better. At the time when Christianity exerted its strongest ever influence over the nation, it signally failed to provide the moral leadership to resolve social conflicts, and became instead a contributory factor in them.

Formed in 1833, the American Anti-Slavery Society adopted a moderate stance of moral suasion, attracting some 250,000 members by the end of that decade. In 1835 it produced over a million pieces of abolitionist literature. Congress received petitions with nearly half a million signatures between 1835 and 1838, more than half of them from women. Female abolitionist networks were highly significant in raising funds, producing literature, organizing speaking engagements, teaching free African-American children and helping with the Underground Railroad.

INCREASING TENSION WITHIN THE UNION

The compromise effected amongst the states at Independence on the slave-holding issue, continued in the first half of the nineteenth century. When the Mississippi had been the Western border of the United States, slavery was permitted in states south of the Ohio River and the Mason-Dixon line. In 1812 Louisiana entered the Union as a slave-holding state. The application in 1819 for admission by the slave-holding state of Missouri, west of the Mississippi, but north of the Ohio River, polarised abolitionist and pro-slavery sentiment, and threatened the balance between slave and free states. The balance of power within the Union was only maintained when Missouri was admitted simultaneously with Maine, a free state in which African-Americans had the vote. The right of self-determination by individual states on the slavery issue remained in conflict with the concept of the Union. The Southern sense of cultural distinctiveness, and institutional separation, increased. Southern voices no longer apologised for slavery as a necessary evil, arguing that there was little difference between black slaves in the south and wage-slaves in the north.

Growing tension over the issue of slavery is reflected in a series of landmark events. The Amistad case decided the fate of a ship-load of African slaves who in 1839 had escaped from their Spanish captors, and arrived off the American coast. Their defence against deportation back to slavery in the Spanish Caribbean was led by John Quincy Adams, formerly the sixth President of the United States. In a landmark decision in 1841 they were liberated by the Supreme Court for return to Africa. Adams, a devoted Christian, recorded in his diary the opposition he had faced:

'The world, the flesh, and all the devils in hell are arrayed against any man who now in this North American Union shall dare to join the standard of Almighty God to

---

The Defense of Slavery as an Institution

'slave labour, in an economical point of view, is far superior to free negro labour;... if an immediate emancipation of negroes were to take place, the whole southern country would be visited with an immediate general famine... the slave is not only *economically* but *morally* unfit for freedom... idleness and consequent want are, of themselves, sufficient to generate a catalogue of vices of the most mischievous and destructive character... liberate slaves, and every year you would hear of insurrections and plots, and every day would perhaps record a murder... Look to the slaveholding population of our country, and you every where find them characterized by noble and elevated sentiments, by humane and virtuous feelings... the slaves of a good master are his warmest, most constant, and most devoted friends; they have been accustomed to look up to him as their supporter, director and defender'. [1]

1   T. Drew, *The Virtues of Slavery, The Impossibility of Emancipation*, 1831. in, S.M. Gillon and C.D. Matson, *The American Experiment: A History of the United States, Vol. I, to 1877*, Boston, Houghton Mifflin, 2002, 482–83.

---

put down the African slave-trade... Yet my conscience presses me on; let me but die upon the breach'.[44]

The publication of Harriet Beecher Stowe's (1811–1896) novel *Uncle Tom's Cabin*, strengthened the emotional commitment of abolitionists to the cause: by 1861, American sales exceeded one million copies. It was the first popular novel to focus on the lives of African Americans, depicting the humanity of slaves, and the inhumanity to which they were subjected. The subtitle of the book encapsulated its message: Tom was 'The man who was a thing'. The Christlike Tom, dies to save others and refuses opportunity of escape.

The 1850s became a pivotal decade. The Fugitive Slave Act, passed in 1850, required federal officials to help planters seeking to return runaway slaves. The law was controversially made retrospective, leaving slaves who had escaped to freedom many years before, facing arrest and return: those assisting fugitives could be fined $1,000 and jailed. The Fugitive Act cast all African-Americans, whether slave or free, under suspicion, strengthening public sentiment against slavery in the North, and convictions that southern planters had too much power. Then, in 1857, the Supreme Court ruled that Dred Scott, a Missouri slave who had lived in the slave-free states of Illinois and Wisconsin for several years

44   A. Nevins (ed) *Diary of John Quincy Adams (1794–1845)*, New York, Charles Scribner's Sons, 1951, 519. On the Amistad case see H. Jones, *Mutiny on the Amistad*, Oxford, Oxford University Press, 1987; I.F. Osagie, *The 'Amistad' Revolt*, Athens, University of Georgia Press, 2000.

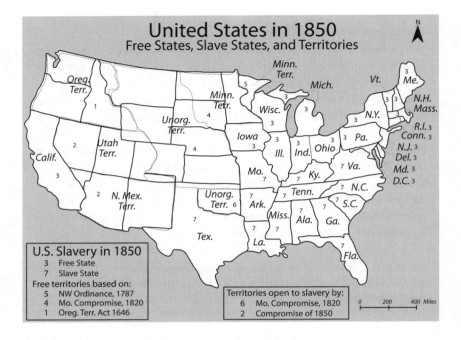

United States in 1850
Free States, Slave States, and Territories

U.S. Slavery in 1850
3 Free State
7 Slave State
Free territories based on:
5 NW Ordinance, 1787
4 Mo. Compromise, 1820
1 Oreg. Terr. Act 1646

Territories open to slavery by:
6 Mo. Compromise, 1820
2 Compromise of 1850

0   200   400 Miles

before returning to his home state, had no constitutional rights, because he was not a citizen. A slave who lived in a free state was not thereby made free. Slaves were not persons, but property, and as such could be legally owned in all parts of the United States. The verdict delighted Southern slave-owning opinion, but now potentially opened the whole of the United States to slavery, and raised questions over the status of the 250,000 free African-Americans.[45]

One active abolitionist, who had played a significant role in the Underground Railroad, was John Brown (1800–1859). Unsuccessful as a farmer, cattleman, and land speculator, he relocated to Kansas with his sons, believing he was called by God to lead a 'holy war' against those seeking to extend slavery into the area. In 1854, the decision as to whether Kansas and Nebraska would be slave-free or not had been vested in the outcome of a local popular vote. After a rigged election in 1855, when many proslavery votes had been illegally cast and supporters of anti-slavery intimidated from voting, Kansas descended into bitter conflict. By the end of 1856, nearly 200 people had been brutally killed, and $2 million in property destroyed. Finally, after further free and fair elections, Kansas was eventually admitted to the Union as a slave free-state in 1861.

In October 1859, Brown, who had engaged in violent anti-slavery responses to the atrocities committed by pro-slavery supporters, decided to seize the

45 An assessment of the case is given in D. Fehrenbacher's, *Slavery, Law and Politics: The Dred Scott Case in Historical Perspective*, New York, Oxford University Press, 1981; and *The Dred Scott Case: Its Significance in American Law and Politics*, New York, Oxford University Press, 1978.

moment, and assist the southern slaves in rising up to claim their freedom. In a daring raid he captured the federal arsenal at Harper's Ferry, Virginia, and waited for the Southern slaves to join him and claim their freedom. 'God's angry man' was captured in the ensuing battle, during which seventeen people were killed, including two of his sons. He was charged with treason and executed. Brown claimed that he acted on behalf of God's 'despised poor', which was 'no wrong, but right', and that America's guilt for the sin of slavery would not be purged without the shedding of blood. His death provoked vast mourning parades in the North.[46] William Lloyd Garrison heralded Brown as 'one of the bravest and noblest of those who have fallen martyrs to a great idea'.[47]

The new Republican party, whilst opposing slavery in the new territories, kept its distance from Brown's work. In the summer of 1860, the Methodist abolitionist Anthony Bewley was lynched by a Texas mob, further inflaming religious and political communities in the north. Southern planters deepened their resolve to resist attempts at abolition.

ABRAHAM LINCOLN

Born in 1809, Abraham Lincoln combined legal work with a rising career in politics, and by 1846 he had won a congressional seat as a Whig candidate. In Illinois in the 1850s he helped draw together the remnants of the Whig party, with others, including disillusioned Democrats, into support for the new Republican party. Its focus was on tariffs to protect the American economy, and land grants to railways, as much as on opposition to slavery. In 1858, Lincoln declared compromise over the issue of slavery no longer possible: 'this country cannot endure permanently half slave and half free'. Unless slavery were set on 'the course of ultimate extinction,' advocates of the 'slavocracy' would push it forward until it was lawful in 'all the states, old as well as new'. He argued for gradual abolition over decades, with compensation, for slaveholders.[48] Lincoln believed that all, black or white, were created equal, and that all had the right claimed in the Declaration of Independence, to 'life, liberty, and the pursuit of happiness,' and to 'eat the bread, without leave of anybody else, which his own hand earns.' However, there were limits to what he attempted:

I have no purpose to introduce political and social equality between the white and the black races. There is a physical difference between the two, which in my judgement will probably forever forbid their living together upon the footing of perfect equality,

---

46   *Herald*, New York, 3 Nov 1859, quoted in Copeland, *Antebellum Era*, 399. John Brown's complex character is explored in a series of scholarly essays edited by Paul Finkelman, *His Soul Goes Marching On: Responses to John Brown and the Harper's Ferry Raid*, Charlottesville, University Press of Virginia, 1995.

47   W.L. Garrison, in the *Liberator*, 7 Sept. 1860, quoted in Copeland, *Antebellum Era*. 403.

48   S. Thernstrom, *History of the American People*, 363–64.

Abraham Lincoln

and inasmuch as it becomes a necessity that there must be a difference, I…am in favour of the race to which I belong having the superior position.[49]

When Lincoln was chosen as the Republican candidate for the US Presidency, he faced a Democratic party, divided on the slavery issue, which fielded two

---

49   A. Lincoln, Speech in debate with the Democrat Stephen Douglas in Ottawa, Illinois, Saturday August 21, 1858, in S.M. Gillon and C.D. Matson, *The American Experiment: A History of the United States*, Houghton Mifflin, Boston, Mass., 2002, 560. See also R. Johannsen, *The Lincoln-Douglas Debates of 1858*, Oxford, Oxford University Press, 2008.

candidates. This contributed to his victory in the 1860 election, although he had very little voter support in the South. To many Southerners, Lincoln's commitment to the 'ultimate extinction' of slavery was intolerable. Although a moderate on the issue, when determined action was needed he did not shirk the challenge.

THE CIVIL WAR

In December 1860, South Carolina voted to withdraw from the Union. Six other states followed suit, and in February 1861 formed a rival nation, the Confederate States of America. Four more joined the Confederacy after the outbreak of hostilities. To Lincoln, allowing those who did not agree with the democratic will of the majority to leave was in fact anarchy, and endless disputes and further secessions would follow. In his inaugural address of 4 March 1861, Lincoln was cautious and pacific: 'We are not enemies but friends. We must not be enemies. Though passion may have strained, it must not break our bonds of affection.'[50] Peace talks failed, and the 'bonds of affection' were ripped apart on 12 April, 1861, as confederate guns opened fire on the federal outpost of Fort Sumter, in Charleston Harbour.[51] It was four years before they fell silent.

The American Civil War was a far from equal contest, with 22 million people in the Union states, compared to 9 million people in the Confederate states, of whom 3.5 million were slaves. Yet the Union forces needed to subdue an area nearly the size of Western Europe. The troops of the South fought bravely and determinedly, skilfully led by leaders such as General Lee, who capitalised on the caution and indecisiveness of Northern generals. The Civil War cost 600,000 lives: one in every four soldiers died.

The Civil War was initially an attempt to stop the spread of slavery, rather than a campaign for outright abolition, but the slow progress achieved in the early stage of the war, with vast casualties, radicalised opinion in the North. Lincoln's Emancipation Proclamation took effect on 1 January 1863, declaring slaves 'henceforth forever free,' although he carefully limited the proclamation to slave-holding states taking part in the Confederate rebellion. Nonetheless, the proclamation gave the Northern troops a clear moral purpose: Frederick Douglass heralded it, 'this righteous decree.' Only in that year did the Union troops begin to score significant victories, notably at Gettysburg in July 1863, after which Lincoln made his famous address: 'That this nation, under God, shall have a new birth of freedom—and that government of the people, by the people,

---

50   S. Thernstrom, *A History of the American People*, 373.

51   A thorough overview of America immediately before, and in the early years, of the Civil War is given in K. Stampp's two books, *America in 1857: A Nation on the Brink*, New York, Oxford University Press, 1990; and also *And the War Came: The North and the Secession Crisis, 1860–61*, New York, Greenwood Press, 1980.

for the people, shall not perish from the earth.' He asserted the proposition that 'all men are created equal.'[52] Northern troops under Generals Grant and Sherman won a series of decisive battles, before General Lee surrendered the Confederate army on 9th April 1865, with Richmond, Virginia in ruins.[53] The Union had been upheld, but at appalling cost. Five days later President Lincoln, who had been re-elected in 1864, was assassinated in Washington. It was left for others to work out what 'Freedom' in the re-unified nation would look like.

THE CHURCHES, SLAVERY AND THE CIVIL WAR

On the threshold of the American Civil War, America was the world's most actively Christian nation, which might have suggested that the war would be unlikely. Yet the participants invested the conflict with religious meaning. Soldiers on both sides believed they were in Christian armies, and that God was on their side: those closest to God would win the victory. Both sides called days of thanksgiving, or days of fasting, as their campaigns scored successes or failures. Religious revivals were reported amongst troops of both the North and the South; Bible studies were well attended, religious tracts and books widely read. As General Sherman's army marched through Georgia the band struck up the Old Hundredth, and soon 5,000 men were singing 'Praise God from Whom all Blessings flow'. Slaves themselves held firmly to the belief that God would hear their cries, and grant deliverance from oppression. Even suffering was read in a redemptive way, as Harriet Beecher Stowe explained: 'Ours sons must die, their sons must die. We give ours freely; they die to redeem the very brothers that slay them; they give their blood in expiation of this great sin.'[54]

Both sides used images of faithful Christian soldiers in the war to promote a 'muscular' version of Christianity. Robert E. Lee was presented in the South as saintlike, in comparison to the Northern soldiers. General Thomas 'Stonewall' Jackson, another Southern general, was widely known in both the North and the South as a Presbyterian deacon, and Sunday School Superintendent, who was concerned for the spiritual state of his soldiers, and encouraged revivals amongst them. Caught in the 'friendly fire' of his own troops, his death was a deep blow to the Confederate side.[55] After all the blood spilled and devastation reeked, America strangely emerged an even more Christian nation after the Civil War than before.

---

52 Quoted in Gillon and Matson, *The American Experiment: A History of the United States*, 564.

53 The events of the Civil War are explored in B. Simpson, *America's Civil War*, New York, St Martin's, 1996, and A.C. Guelzo, *The Crisis of the American Republic: A History of the Civil War and Reconstruction Era*, 1995.

54 H. Beecher Stowe, quoted in L.P. Masur (ed), *The Real War Will Never Get in the Books: Selections from Writers During the Civil War*, New York, Oxford University Press, 1993, 245.

55 D.W. Stowell, 'Stonewall Jackson and the Providence of God', in eds. R. Miller, H. Stout, C. Wilson, *Religion and the American Civil War*, Oxford, OUP, 187-207.

Although the Civil War was a product of economic, political, and cultural factors, it also involved a conflict over matters of biblical interpretation.[56] The Second Great Awakening, with its opportunities for lay preaching and exhortation, extension of education, and widespread availability of Bibles and Christian literature, helped to democratise the hermeneutical task. In Britain evangelicals had resolved the issues raised for biblical interpretation by slavery in favour of the abolitionist position. However, Americans encountered significant difficulty in separating their cultural understandings on issues of race from Scriptural understandings. America's 'iconic book', became contested territory.

Many in the South argued that because slavery was present in the Bible, acceptance of the practice was a matter of faithful obedience to Scripture, even though no other body of Protestants in the English-speaking world shared that conclusion. Defence of slavery was linked with defence of Biblical authority. George Fitzhugh put it bluntly: 'if white slavery be morally wrong, be a violation of individual rights, the Bible cannot be true'.[57] To J.H. Hopkins, Bishop of Vermont, an assault on the institution of slavery was an assault on the authority of the Bible itself. Hopkins argued that enslaved Africans were from the cursed lineage of Ham, given over to heathen idolatry.[58] Others argued that passages in the Old and New Testament represented the permanent inequality of the races, and argued that African-American slaves were supported by a system of cradle to grave benevolence. To James De Bow, 'Divine Providence, for His own high and inscrutable purposes, has rescued more than three millions of human beings from the hardships of a savage state, and placed them in a condition of greater comfort than any other labouring class in the world'.[59] Slavery, it was argued, was the best means for civilising slaves, and raising their status.[60]

John Henry Thornwell, the leading Presbyterian theologian of the South was in no doubt that 'the relation betwixt the slave and his master is not inconsistent with the word of God...We cherish the institution not from avarice, but from

---

56 The clearest treatment of this is found in Mark Noll's, 'The Bible and Slavery' in R.M. Miller, H.S. Stout, and C.R Wilson. (eds), *Religion and the American Civil War*, New York, Oxford University Press, 1998, 43–73. The discussion below largely follows Noll's argument. See also M. Snay, *Gospel of Disunion: Religion and Separatism in the Antebellum South*, Cambridge, CUP, 1993.

57 G. Fitzhugh, *Cannibals all!, or Slaves Without Masters*, ed. C. Vann Woodward, Cambridge, Mass., 1960, 199–200, quoted in C. Kidd, *Forging of Races*, 142.

58 M. Stuart, *A Critical History and Defence of the Old Testament Canon* (1845), London, 1849; J. H. Hopkins, *A Scriptural, Ecclesiastical and Historical View of Slavery*, New York, 1864.

59 J. De Bow, *De Bow's Review*, New Orleans, July 1855, in Copeland, *Antebellum Era*, 119–120.

60 The defence of slavery by the Southern planters is set out in L. Tise, *Proslavery: A History of the Defence of Slavery in America, 1701–1840*, Athens, University of Georgia Press, 1987; D.G. Faust (ed), *The Ideology of Slavery: Proslavery Thought in the Antebellum South, 1830–1860*, Baton Rouge, University of Louisiana Press, 1981.

principle'.[61] Attacking the literal reading of Biblical texts about slavery ranked alongside attacks on the geological accuracy of Moses' creation account.[62] He argued that the church should not interfere in social or political matters, and that the Bible contained no explicit command to emancipate slaves. Such arguments shocked likeminded evangelical Presbyterians outside the South. According to the magazine of the United Presbyterian Church in Scotland, such thinking was: 'the foulest and most revolting that has ever been enunciated since our blessed Redeemer hung upon the cross of shame, and bore away the sins of the world. Sympathy with the Southern States! We have as much sympathy with them as with a gang of robbers or a crew of pirates!'[63] American Presbyterians in the North and South were willing to kill each other over the issue.

Reading scripture through the lens of prevalent cultural and social values in the South created inconsistencies that defenders of slavery did not readily appreciate, or at least acknowledge. It is little surprise that mission from slave-holding whites to those they were subjugating, enjoyed limited success.

The linking of a defence of slavery with defence of the authority of the Bible placed Northern abolitionists in a difficult position. Some responded by arguing that, because the Bible contained some sanction for slavery, it should not be used as the key text in the debate. Others attempted to draw a distinction between the letter of the Bible, which might appear to sanction slavery, and its spirit, which was plainly against it, but for this they were accused of theological liberalism. Abolitionists argued that the condition of slaves in the American South was far different from the institution of slavery described in the Old Testament. They stressed that Scripture contained the principles by which slavery was to be ended: the theme of liberation, both spiritual and physical, was a strong Biblical image, especially in the New Testament. They argued that the Bible represented the progressive revelation of the will of God, from a permission of slavery in the Old Testament, to the radical spiritual principles that would undermine it in the New. It was also claimed that the argument basing support for the continuance of slavery on its presence in the Old Testament, would also allow polygamy, or the dietary and purity laws of the Old Testament, to continue.

Although the Northern Congregationalist, Henry Ward Beecher, declared 'I should like no better amusement than to answer the sermons of men who attempt to establish the right of slavery out of the Bible,'[64] others were pushed

61   J.H. Thornwell, 'Our National Sins', in *Fast Day Sermons: or the Pulpit on the State of the Country*, New York, 1861, 44. Discussion of the attempt to justify the holding of slaves is found in S.R. Haynes, *Noah's Curse: The Biblical Justification of American Slavery*, Oxford, OUP, 2002.

62   Thornwell, 'Our National Sins', 50.

63   'The Civil War in America, and Our Present Difficulty', *United Presbyterian Magazine*, new series, 6, Jan 1862, 2, quoted in Noll, *America's God*, 401.

64   H.W. Beecher, 'Peace Be Still', in *Fast Day Sermons*, 289.

onto the defensive by the Southern approach, struggling to decide whether slavery was a sin in itself, or whether it was a permissible institution that needed to be regulated properly to avoid it becoming an evil. The leading Presbyterian theologian in the North, Charles Hodge recognised that on both sides the debate was less about scripture, and 'more or less subject to the controlling influence of public opinion, and of the life of the community to which they belong'.[65] Hodge's views became clearer over time, but in 1871 he declared his long-standing conviction that 'slaveholding is in itself a crime, is anti-scriptural and subversive of the Word of God'. Hodge argued that only legitimate slavery was found in the Bible, and that it was so hedged with ameliorations that, when pursued to their logical conclusions, would bring slavery inevitably to an end. Texts about slavery needed to be read in the fuller context of the rest of scripture. The claim in 1861 by Benjamin Palmer, first moderator of the Southern Presbyterian Church, that the South had a divine assignment to perpetuate slavery was to Hodge, a 'monstrous perversion'. Hodge argued, against Thornwell, that Reformed theology contained a moral obligation to encourage or critique social and political issues. He called for emancipation 'by the silent and holy influence of the gospel, securing the elevation of the slaves to the stature and character of freemen', although he doubted whether even free African Americans should be given the vote. Nonetheless he warned in 1857, 'If the South deliberately keep these millions in this state of degradation, they must prepare themselves for the natural consequences, whatever they may be.'[66] He wondered whether war on slaveholders was a Christ-like thing to do, for it would be against other Christians, albeit those engaged in a sinful practice, but he accepted that war, appalling as it was, might be the means to a higher end— the destruction of slavery.[67]

African-American Christians were also strong proponents of a biblical literalism, reading scripture through their own experience, the narrative theology of their own Spirituals, dreams and prophecies, to see the Bible as a book of dramatic narratives, with the Exodus story as key. African Americans held firmly to the promises of Biblical texts such as Acts 17, 26: God 'made of one blood all nations of men for to dwell on the face of the earth'. To Frederick Douglass, the use of the Bible to defend slavery involved taking scripture

65   C. Hodge, 'The General Assembly', *Princeton Review* 37, July 1865: 506, quoted in Noll, *America's God*, 403.

66   C. Hodge, 'Slavery', *Biblical Repertory and Princeton Review: The Index Volume from 1825–1868*, Philadephia, Peter Walker, 1871, 15; C. Hodge, 'Slavery', *Princeton Review* 7 (1835), reprinted in C. Hodge, *Essays and Reviews*, New York, 1857, 573–611, quoted in Noll, 'The Bible and Slavery', 60.

67   On Hodge and slavery see J.W. Stewart, *Mediating the Center: Charles Hodge on American Science, Language, Literature and Politics*, Princeton, Princeton UP, 1995, 71–87; and J.W. Stewart, 'Introducing Charles Hodge to Postmoderns', in J.W. Stewart and J.H. Moorhead (eds), *Charles Hodge Revisited: A Critical Appraisal of His Life and Work*, Grand Rapids, Eerdmans, 2002, 33.

passages out of context. In this 'noble, Christian missionary institution', why were whips, chains, thumbscrews and fetters necessary?[68] The Roman Catholic Church supported the anti-slavery cause in the North, although heavy losses of Irish soldiers at the front, economic hardships, and hostility to the draft which seemed targeted at the poorest Irish sections of society, reduced the rate of Roman Catholic recruitment as the war progressed.[69]

Those who interpreted the Bible in a pacifist way were left with severe dilemmas. If nothing was done, slaves would remain in bondage, so most Quakers decided to fight on the Union side.[70] Abraham Lincoln articulated the greatest paradox of all. Both armies believed God was on their side, but 'God cannot be *for* and *against* the same thing at the same time. In the present civil war it is quite possible that God's purpose is something different from the purpose of either party.'[71] In his Second Inaugural in 1865, Lincoln noted how the 'prayers of both could not be answered, that neither has been answered fully.' No one side could unequivocally identify itself with God's purposes: 'The Almighty has His own purposes'. He offered a nuanced interpretation matched by few American theologians of the day, urging 'malice toward none; charity for all', and to 'bind up the nation's wounds... to do all we can to achieve and cherish a just, and lasting peace'. All needed to be entrusted to God 'whose ways were not always known but were always just.'[72] Lincoln's ability to so interpret events may have reflected his own distance from mainstream American Christianity. He placed a strong emphasis on Providence, and his speeches were redolent with Biblical overtones and images. He had no time for those who scoffed at religion, but he joined no church and read little theology.[73] When people said that God was on the side of the Union, he preferred to say that he hoped the Union was on God's side.[74]

68   F. Douglass, 'Ought American Slavery to be Perpetuated,' in *Douglass' Monthly*, Jan 1859, 5, quoted in Noll, 'The Bible and Slavery,' 54.

69   On Catholic approaches see R.M. Miller, 'Catholic Religion, Irish Ethnicity, and the Civil War', in eds. Miller, Stout, Wilson, *Religion and American Civil War*, 261–298.

70   P. Brock, *Pacifism in the United States: From the Colonial Era to the First World War*, Princeton, Princeton University Press, 1968, 717–723.

71   A. Lincoln, 'Meditation on the Divine Will,' in ed. R.P. Basler, *The Collected Works of Abraham Lincoln*, 9 vols., New Brunswick, New Jersey, 1953, Vol. 5, 403–04. See also W.J. Wolf, *The Religion of Abraham Lincoln*, New York, Doubleday, 1963, 147–48.

72   A. Lincoln, 'Second Inaugural Address', 4 March 1865, in M.P. Johnson, *Abraham Lincoln, Slavery, and the Civil War*, Boston, Bedford/St Martin's, 2001, 321, see also R.C. White, *Lincoln's Greatest Speech: The Second Inaugural*, New York, Simon and Schuster, 2002.

73   Noll, *America's God*. pp. 426, 436. On Lincoln's religion see A.C. Guelzo, *Abraham Lincoln: Redeemer President*, Grand Rapids, Eerdmans, 1999.

74   On Lincoln's faith see W.J. Wolf, *The Almost Chosen People. A study of the religion of Abraham Lincoln* New York, Doubleday, 1959; K. Thompson, ed., *Essays on Lincoln's Faith and Politics*, Lathan, University Press of America, 1983.

Lincoln: The Perplexity of Moral Purpose in the Civil War

Both read the same Bible, and pray to the same God; and each invokes His aid against the other. It may seem strange that men should dare to ask a just God's assistance in wringing their bread from the sweat of other men's faces; but let us judge not that we be not judged. The prayers of both could not be answered; that of neither has been answered fully...If we shall suppose that American Slavery is one of those offences which, in the providence of God, must needs come, but which, having continued through His appointed time, He now wills to remove, and that He gives to both North and South, this terrible war, as the woe due to those by whom the offence came, shall we discern therein any departure from those divine attributes which the believers in a Living God always subscribe to Him? Fondly do we hope—fervently do we pray—that this mighty scourge of war may speedily pass away...With malice toward none; with charity for all; let us strive to finish the work we are in; to bind up the nation's wounds; to care for him who shall have borne the battle, and for his widow and orphan—to do all which may achieve and cherish a just and lasting peace, among ourselves, and with all nations.[1]

1   A. Lincoln, 'The Second Inaugural Address', March 4, 1865 in ed. M.P. Johnson, *Abraham Lincoln, Slavery, and the Civil War*, Boston, Bedford/St Martin's, 2001, 321.

When in 1865 the Union flag was raised once more at Fort Sumter, where it had all begun, Christians in the North were convinced of God's miraculous overruling to end slavery. Despite the North's military unpreparedness, and Lincoln's inexperience, something that human action alone could not have achieved, had been accomplished. Charles Hodge declared it 'one of the most momentous events in the history of the world. That it was the design of God to bring about this event cannot be doubted'.[75] The South remained convinced that infidel and rationalistic voices had prevailed over a Bible-honouring society; suffering and defeat could be part of God's purposes.[76] Both North and South had produced a synthesis of cultural and religious values that shaped interpretation of the Bible, and the conflict itself, and which was hard to break free after the conflict ended.[77] The emphasis by Christian thinkers after the war on the need not just to believe the gospel, but to 'do' it, was to feed into the Social Gospel movement (see ch. 14).[78]

---

75   C. Hodge, 'President Lincoln', *Biblical Repertory and Princeton Review*, 37, July 1865, 439–40, quoted in Noll, *America's God*, 433–434.

76   J. Adger, 'Northern and Southern Views of the Province of the Church', *Southern Presbyterian Review*, March 1866, 410, in Noll, *America's God*, 434.

77   M. Noll, *America's God*, 436–38.

78   P.S. Paludan, 'Religion and the American Civil War', in ed. R.M. Miller, H.S. Stout, C.R. Reagan, *Religion and the American Civil War*, New York, Oxford University Press, 1998, 34–35.

THE POST CIVIL-WAR PERIOD

The Civil War might have been over, but the battle for civil rights for African Americans had not been won. Deeply ingrained racist attitudes, even in the North, were not easily overcome: some states began to pass laws forbidding black Americans from renting land, and limiting the type of jobs they could undertake. In response, Republicans in the Congress pushed through the Fourteenth Amendment which extended citizenship to black Americans, and forbade states from depriving citizens of 'life, liberty, or property without due process of law,' and from denying any person 'equal protection of the laws'. The Fifteenth Amendment, passed after the Congressional elections of 1868, declared that the right to vote could not be denied to a citizen on account of 'race, colour, or previous condition of servitude'. It did not, however, prevent the series of property qualifications, poll taxes, tests of literacy, and other laws that were used to restrict the access of black Americans to their voting rights. Between 1868 and 1870 some 700,000 new black voters were added to the electoral rolls, but widespread intimidation, including hundreds of murders of black voters on the way to the polls by white supremacist groups, including the Ku Klux Klan, drastically reduced the number of those who participated in elections.

The glorious hope of Horace Bushnell that, through the sacrifices of the war, America had atoned for its sin, attaining a unity 'where God's cherubim stand guard over grudges and hates and remembered jealousies, and the sense of nationality becomes even a kind of religion,'[79] was sadly misplaced. Although white planters had lost their slaves, they retained the land, and through the system of sharecropping maintained control over former slave labour. By 1885 nearly 75% of black southerners were working as sharecroppers, allowed to farm parts of former plantations by landlords who provided land, tools and seed, in return for half the crops grown, and sometimes more. A dependent, and often heavily indebted existence, followed. As American Presidents turned their attention to the needs of poor whites, Black Americans were left economically and politically second-class citizens.

Southern Christians, although chastened by defeat in war, did not easily surrender their views as to the racial superiority of white Americans, or the rightfulness of their cause. Robert L. Dabney, a notable Presbyterian theologian, served as 'Stonewall' Jackson's chief of staff. On the General's death Dabney declared, 'while man is mortal, the cause is immortal.'[80] In 1867 Dabney was still opposing the ordination of African Americans, and racial intermarriage,

---

79   H. Busnell, 'Our Obligations to the Dead', in *Building Eras in Religion*, New York, 1881, 329, quoted in Noll, *America's God*, 423.

80   R.L. Dabney, *True Courage: A Discourse Commemorative of Lieut. General Thomas J. Jackson*, Richmond, Virginia, 1863, 23.

albeit on the basis of the 'righteous, rational *instinct* of pious minds,' rather than explicit scripture verses.[81]

The freedoms granted to African Americans brought opportunity to choose where to worship. Many found that the racially mixed congregations they had previously been forced to attend appeared too reminiscent of relations under their former slave way of life, and formed autonomous black churches. In 1860, the Methodist Episcopal Church, South, had a black membership of 270,766, but by 1866 it had dropped to just 78,782, most transferring to black-led churches. Between 1860 and 1896, the African Methodist Episcopal Church grew from 20,000 members to 450,000; the AME Zion grew from 4,600 to 350,000, most of the growth taking place in the South. The largest number of black Christians was found in the Baptist churches, which grew from 150,000 in 1850, to 500,000 in 1870, and over 2 million by 1905.[82]

The ageing black abolitionist, Frederick Douglass, declared in 1883 that white church goers had not yet 'conquered this feeling of colour madness'. The message of white missionaries to the South remained suffused with the cultural attitudes of the northern middle classes, denominational rivalries, and racial attitudes. Segregated seating remained a feature of some mixed race churches, making integration a difficult option. Black preachers sent by the Baptists, AME churches, and AME Zion churches, received a far more positive reception. The policy of separate identity was pursued with significant success. African-American churches owned property worth $56.6 million in 1906, with at least nineteen separate black denominations at the start of the twentieth century.[83] Yet, exercising freedom of choice over where to worship was not without considerable risk. Many black churches were attacked or burned down by white vigilante groups, and a number of black preachers, were attacked or killed.[84] Black ministers like Booker T. Washington preached a message of self-reliance, hard-work, and frugality, patiently accepting racial discrimination and political disenfranchisement. In contrast Henry M. Turner who was to rise to the rank of bishop in the AME church, for a short period held a seat in the Georgia legislature, and called for an immediate and complete end to racial discrimination. Frustrated in his efforts, he then called for emigration back to Africa, away from the oppressions of America.[85] Black denominations also readily embraced the missionary task, starting congregations in the Caribbean,

81   R.L. Dabney, 'Ecclesiastical Equality of Negroes', in *Discussions: Evangelical and Theological*, (1890), London, Banner of Truth, 1967, Vol. 2, 207.

82   Lincoln and Mamiya, *Black Church*, 25–63.

83   Montgomery, *African-American Church*, 342–43; C.E. Lincoln and L.H. Mamiya, *The Black Church in the African American Experience*, Durham, Duke University Press, 1990, 21–46.

84   Montgomery, *African-American Church*, 36–57.

85   Montgomery, *African American Church*, 337–340.

and sending missionaries to Liberia and South Africa, establishing strong religious networks between the United States and these areas.

At the beginning of the twentieth century African-American Christianity, with its legacy of slavery and racial discrimination, remained significantly isolated from the mainstream of American social and religious life. Yet significant changes were underway. The low level of literacy amongst slaves was being reversed, reaching some 70% of the African American population by 1900, with increased numbers of skilled workers, and shopkeepers. Businessmen, and professionals were part of an emerging urban black middle class. Black clergymen were held in high esteem by their congregations, and often left their mark with major building projects.[86] The strength and influence of the black churches of America makes it no surprise that when the civil rights movement emerged forcibly in the 1950s, its driving force was the African-American churches and their leaders.

Stability and wealth brought church order and practice that mirrored that in the white Congregational, Presbyterian, and Episcopal churches, well-suited to the black middle class, but less so to poor and less well-educated African-Americans. The importance of experiential religion with realised sanctification, was lost in more ordered church life, or through demands for social transformation, as promoted by the Social Gospel movement. The rise of the black holiness movement was one aspect of the reaction to such trends, with its emotional appeal, its demands for radical renunciation of the pleasures of the world, and emphasis on the power and authority of the Bible which was to be literally interpreted (see ch. 15).

CONCLUSIONS

America's cultural and social life before and immediately after the Civil War derived significant strength from Christianity. Much impetus was channelled through the major voluntary agencies that did much to reform society, yet the divisions that afflicted the wider Christian community also beset these voluntary bodies. Temperance societies disagreed over whether to seek the total prohibition of alcohol; abolitionists divided over whether to advocate immediate abolition, or facilitating opportunities to return to Africa. Others argued that the campaign for the rights of women was more important. Churches in the South found it hard to escape the social and cultural values of their context that would have been required if they were to stand out against slavery. Divisions on matters of policy and especially biblical interpretation, meant that the numerical strength of Christianity never truly achieved its transformative political and social potential in nineteenth-century America.

---

86 Montgomery, *African-American Church in the South*, 333–36.

FURTHER READING

D.A. Copeland, *The Antebellum Era: Primary Documents on Events from 1820–1860*, Westport, Conn., Greenwood, 2003.

J.P. Dolan, *The American Catholic Experience: A History from the Colonial Times to the Present*, Notre Dame, University of Notre Dame Press, 1992.

S.M. Gillon and C.D. Matson, *The American Experiment, A History of the United States: Volume I: to 1877*, Boston, Houghton Mifflin Company, 2002.

A.C. Guelzo, *Abraham Lincoln: Redeemer President*, Grand Rapids, Eerdmans, 1999.

D.G. Hart and H. Stout (eds), *New Directions in American Religious History*, New York, Oxford University Press, 1997.

S.J. Kleinberg, *Women in the United States, 1830–1945*, Basingstoke, Macmillan, 1999.

R.M. Miller, H.S. Stout, and C.R Wilson. (eds), *Religion and the American Civil War*, New York, Oxford University Press, 1998.

W.E. Montgomery, *Under their Own Vine and Fig Tree: The African-American Church in the South 1865–1900*, Baton Rouge, Louisiana State University Press, 1993.

C. Stout, *The New Heavens and New Earth: Political Religion in America*, New York, Harper and Row, 1974.

S. Thernstrom, *A History of the American People, Volume 1: to 1877*, Orlando, Florida, Harcourt Brace Jovanovich, 1989.

T.K. Wayne, *Women's Roles in Nineteenth Century America*, Westport, Conn., Greenwood Press, 2007.

M.J. Westerkamp, *Women and Religion in Early America 1600–1850*, London, Routledge, 1999.

12

CHRISTIANITY AND EMERGING NATIONAL IDENTITIES

In pre-industrial societies, religion had been used by rulers as a way of legitimating their authority, creating close connections between Christianity and national identities. Religion was also associated in stable agrarian societies with the maintenance of traditional values and a sense of common national social and cultural identity. Although Napoleon ensured that the pope was present when he was crowned emperor, in modern urban and industrial societies the connection between crown and mitre was expected to decrease, making such strategies unnecessary. Many religious leaders felt that the role of religion in national life was diminishing. Therefore, the persistence of religion in the policies of increasingly modern and democratic nineteenth century states appears surprising. Religious forms continued to remain significant in civic life, even in the wake of social, urban, industrial and political revolutions.

The need to maintain religious symbols and language in the aftermath of political revolutions was notable, even if the results were deliberately vague, as in the new-born United States of America. Ongoing religious influence was witnessed in battles over the control of education, the development of political parties with strong religious identities, and the maintenance of norms of behaviour controlled by strong religious components. The reasons for this persistence are varied. One factor was a widespread revival in religious life that occurred in the first half of the nineteenth century, a revival which affected groups as theologically diverse as evangelicals and Roman Catholics. Another was the way that religious institutions remained firmly embedded in social structures. In rural areas, the clergy often formed part of local elites that had much influence on the process of social change, or resistance to it. The existence of confessional pluralism required serious national engagement over ways to find a *modus operandi*. Whilst rural Swiss cantons remained predominantly Roman Catholic, urban ones were Protestant; Southern Germany and the Western Rhineland was predominantly Roman Catholic, North and East Germany was mainly Protestant. The eventual political dominance of Prussia brought the dominance of Protestantism within the German state (see Chapter 6). Although the unsuccessful *Kulturkampf* was a break with the nineteenth-century trend of toleration and acceptance, it was part of a wider pattern developing towards the end of the century, and was matched by increasingly intolerant attitudes towards the Jews in Europe.

The Reformation left four distinctive religious areas in Europe. A predominantly Roman Catholic area covered the Italian States, Spain, France, Austria, and Belgium. In the North, Scandinavia was predominantly Protestant; to the East was an area of Orthodox domination—Russia, Greece, and the Balkans; in a series of other countries the religious complexion was mixed—Germany, the Netherlands, Switzerland, and Britain. In Roman Catholic, and predominantly Protestant areas, the close ties between the political and religious structures meant that political opposition also implied opposition to the church. Where there was no strong Free-church movement into which dissatisfaction could be channelled, anticlericalism could become strong. Where there were Free churches, or where Pietist or revival movements were influential, popular anticlericalism was less pervasive. This was also the case where strong national causes were closely allied to a particular religious identity, as with Roman Catholicism in Ireland or Poland.

In countries that had been defeated, and left devastated, by the relentless march of Napoleon's armies across Europe, political maps were redrawn, but also there was the growth of a deeper sense of identity between individuals and the state. Nationalism was given a decisive boost. Whilst the French rejoiced in the achievements of their revolutionary armies, Russians, Spaniards, Prussians, and the British, prided themselves on their eventual resistance of them. As political nationalism deepened, so did civic nationalism, as the rights central to the French Revolution were extended to the individual citizens of nations. Yet, often being a 'nation' had less to do with political boundaries. In Germany it involved sharing a common culture, language, and race, the *Volk*. In Greece, Hellenistic culture became a unifying force.

Within a generation of Napoleon's defeat in 1815, the clash between national and ethnic identity was to come to the fore in Central Europe and the Balkans. The Austro-Hungarian Habsburg empire encapsulated German-speaking Austrians, Italians, Poles, Hungarians, Czechs, and Slovenes. The Turkish Empire included a variety of ethnic groups—Serbs, Croats, Bulgarians, Romanians,

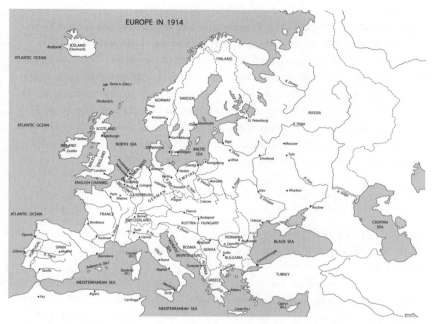

Montenegrins, and Greeks, all increasingly insistent on their independence. The Russian Empire saw similar challenges from Poles, Finns, and Ukrainians in the West, and others in the East, although Polish claims to autonomy were decisively defeated by the Russian army in 1831. The competing claims of Russia and France over parts of the Middle East precipitated the Crimean War of 1855. In the Russian and Turkish empires, nationalism served to break up empires, but in Germany and Italy it helped to create them. Whether in the ending of former empires, or in establishing cohesive entities from piecemeal political arrangements, Christianity played a significant role. Sometimes national identity was so strong that Christian leaders were unable to maintain a critical distance from wider developments, into which they were inexorably drawn.

GREECE AND THE BALKANS

The growing influence of a Western educated intelligentsia was significant for nationalist protest movements, which became more prominent and effective throughout the Ottoman Empire in the early nineteenth century. Although in 1815 Serbia, Bosnia, Romania, Bulgaria, Montenegro, Albania and Greece remained nominally under Turkish control, it was a complex and volatile situation, in which religion was an important component. The presence of the 12 million Greek Orthodox Christians within the Ottoman Empire was tolerated, but they were subjected to severe reprisals whenever Turkish rule was threatened. Russia, desirous to control access to the Black Sea through the

---

GREEK INDEPENDENCE: The Proclamation of Independence Issued by the Greek National Assembly which met at Epidaurus 27 January 1822
'We, descendants of the wise and noble peoples of the Hellas... find it no longer possible to suffer without cowardice and self-contempt the cruel yoke of the Ottoman power which has weighed on us for more than four centuries... The war which we are carrying on against the Turk... is not aimed at any single part of the Greek people; it is a national war, a holy war, a war the object of which is to reconquer the rights of individual liberty, of property, and honour—rights which the civilised peoples of Europe, our neighbours, enjoy today...'[1]

1   Source J.H. Robinson, *Readings in European History*, London, Ginn, 519–20.

Dardanelles, claimed the right to protect Orthodox Christians throughout the Ottoman Empire. Britain and Austria, on the other hand, saw the Ottoman Empire as a counterpoise to Russian influence.

In Turkish-controlled Greece, a growing interest in Greek culture and literature, and its classical past, deepened the sense of Greek identity. Added to this was growing interest in revolutionary ideas from France, spurring hopes of ending Ottoman rule. Much of this interest was of a secular nature, and was opposed by the clergy, who sought to censor secular and atheistic literature from the West. Yet, this was more than simply Orthodox opposition to the Enlightenment, and the capacity of Orthodoxy to accommodate its church, pastoral, and educational approach to the post-Enlightenment context is increasingly recognised.[1] From 1800 onwards, Orthodoxy also needed to come to terms with nationalism, as Balkan peoples resisted Ottoman rule, and new nations emerged.

In Greece, fighting broke out in 1821. Although Greek Independence was proclaimed the following year, the conflict was to last until 1831. The efforts of the ruthless but efficient Turkish general, Ibrahim Pasha to crush the revolt saw some 35,000 Greek and Turkish Christians killed, with others persecuted severely.[2] In 1828, Russia declared war on Turkey, granted autonomy to Serbia, and occupied Moldavia and what is now Romania. Greek Independence was recognised in 1830, and Otto of Bavaria was crowned its first king in 1833.

The immediate reaction of the Ecumenical Patriarch of Constantinople, Gregory V, to the Greek Revolution of 1821 was to condemn it. Nonetheless, he was hanged for treason by the Turkish authorities on Easter Sunday in 1821.

---

1   P.M. Kitromilides, *The Legacy of the French Revolution: Orthodoxy and Nationalism*, in *The Cambridge History of Christianity: Vol 5, Eastern Christianity*, ed. M. Angold, Cambridge, CUP, 2006.

2   Barrett, *World Christian Encyclopaedia*, 28–29.

His execution, followed by those of other senior prelates across the Ottoman Empire, with others dying in prison, afforded the nationalist cause a host of martyrs, ironically from those who had initially opposed it. These deaths linked the philosophy and values of orthodoxy to nationalism. A by-product of the conflict was a loosening of ecclesiastical control from Constantinople, empowering local clergy. Many local priests joined the fighting, and some assumed important roles in the military leadership. Bishops who survived the Turkish repression came to endorse Greek nationalism, whilst maintaining deep respect for the orthodox faith and order. The 1827 'Political Constitution of Greece' asserted the freedom of religion and worship, before stating that the religion of the 'Eastern Orthodox Church of Christ is the religion of the state.' The spiritual authority of the patriarchate of Constantinople remained, and in 1830, Konstantios I sent his blessings to the new Greek state.

After centuries of existence under a sometimes hostile Ottoman regime, the church in Greece was now the object of respect and positive support from the civil authorities. Financial assistance was offered, and measures to ease ecclesiastical regulation were passed intended to place Orthodox values at the heart of the new Greece. Although the state showed it believed in the Orthodox Church, and the Church assented to nationalism, it was gradually drawn under the influence of the civil authorities, and in danger of being used by the state. Ioannis Kapodistrias, the first Greek head of state, was a devout Orthodox believer, with the religious and moral health of the nation dear to his heart. However, questions were raised over how a free and autonomous church could remain under the authority of a Patriarch in Constantinople who was a vassal of the Ottoman Turks.

After the accession of Greece's first king, Otto of Bavaria (1833–62), the Orthodox Church in Greece was declared in 1833 independent of that in Constantinople. Otto, a Roman Catholic, was head of the new autocephalous Greek Orthodox Church, with its governance placed in the hands of crown-appointed clerical officials. It was a highly political solution, designed to boost national independence, and bolster royal power. Greece found itself with the type of church-state relationship associated with Scandinavia, or German Protestant states. The Orthodox church was placed under pressure to accept the new situation, monasteries were forfeited to the crown, and bishops restricted. Eventually the bishops gave their assent, but there was widespread opposition from monks. This assent led the Patriarchate in Constantinople to consider the Greek Church schismatic, and it was seventeen years before the patriarchate agreed procedures to formally grant autocephaly to the church of Greece.

The eventual autonomy of the Greek Orthodox Church created a model for the Orthodox Church to transform itself into a series of national churches. However, this created the danger that in return for national recognition, orthodox churches could be drawn by states into their own nationalist agendas, in which the claims of the nation overrode all other claims. The patriarchate in Constantinople remained firm in its insistence that unilateral declarations of independence were not permitted, but were to be negotiated.[3]

In Serbia, revolts against Turkish rule after 1804 led to the country being virtually independent by 1830. When Serbia applied for autonomy from Constantinople the process was far more straightforward than it had been for Greece. Autocephaly was granted in 1879, the year after Serbia was recognised as a fully independent kingdom by the major powers. The church effectively became a department of the state, and in 1903 orthodoxy was recognised as the state religion.

The creation of Romania out of the principalities of Wallachia and Moldavia in 1859, was followed in 1865 by a bill proclaiming the independence of the Church of Romania. As with Greece, protests from the Patriarchate led to a controversy that lasted twenty years. Autocephaly was only granted in 1885, four years after the recognition of Romania as an independent kingdom in 1881. After 1918, the Orthodox Church was the dominant religion of Romania, although the state kept the church under close supervision, with significant involvement in the appointment of bishops. The state remained willing to offer favours to the Roman Catholic and Uniate churches, a cause of significant concern to the Orthodox Church.

The struggle for Bulgarian ecclesiastical independence was even more difficult, and complex, preceding national independence. Although the Ottoman Empire granted the Bulgarian church autonomous church administration in 1870, it came without the approval of the patriarchate. A synod at Constantinople defrocked the Bulgarian bishops for claiming ecclesiastical autonomy before political autonomy had been granted, and in 1872 excommunicated the Bulgarian Church. Yet moves for ecclesiastical independence spurred moves for political independence, and Bulgaria became an autonomous principality in 1878 with a high level of democracy, and Orthodoxy was declared the religion of the state. Although Bulgaria became an independent kingdom in 1908, the rift with the Patriarchate was only healed in 1945, and until then the church remained outside the communion of the Orthodox churches. However, Orthodoxy and nationalism had become closely intertwined in the Balkan struggles for power and territory.

In the wake of the Crimean War, when Britain, France, and Turkey sought to restrict Russian control over the Black Sea and Balkans, and destroyed the Russian naval base in Sebastopol, religious equality was promised by the Sultan

---

3   See C.A. Frazee, *The Orthodox Church and Independent Greece, 1821–51*, Cambridge, Cambridge University Press, 1968.

to all subjects in the Ottoman Empire. Yet this did not permanently secure the position of Christians in the Balkan region. Further episodes of severe persecution in Bulgaria and Bosnia in 1875–78 culminated in the massacres of Armenian Christians by the Turks. In 1896 some 200,000 were killed, followed by the appalling genocide of 1914–15 in which somewhere between 1.1 and 1.8 million Armenians were killed out of a total population of 2.5 million.[4]

RUSSIA

Russia was another nation in which one religious form dominated, and where the involvement of the state in the affairs of the church was very significant.[5] The Russian Orthodox Church had claimed autocephaly in 1448, although this was not granted by the Patriarch of Constantinople until 1589, when Russia was granted its first Patriarch. In the eighteenth century, under Peter the Great, attempts were made to subordinate the church to the state. The 1721 constitution of the church abolished the office of Patriarch in the Russian Orthodox Church, and made the Tsar the head of the church. Archbishops and Metropolitans of Moscow continued to be appointed, but the governance of the church was placed in the hands of a Holy Synod, which operated under a lay chief procurator, appointed by the Tsar. By the nineteenth century the chief procurator was the *de facto* ruler of the church. Although the church enjoyed extensive privileges as the established religion of the empire, its activities were significantly controlled, and it was increasingly subject to the machinations of court politics with bishops nominated and moved for political reasons.

The Russian Orthodox Church could not escape the influence of enlightenment ideas of toleration, and individual conscience. In 1773 the Empress Catherine II issued an Edict of Religious Toleration, which allowed liberty to confessions other than the Orthodox Church. Clergy became increasingly aware of Western traditions: the reading of Pietist literature, brought a renewed emphasis on Bible reading, prayer, and activities of social concern such as prison visiting.

As with Germany and Italy, the role of Napoleon in a deepening sense of national identity in Russia was significant. By the time his army of 500,000 men had reached the gates of Moscow in 1812, it had been depleted to half its size, despite only one major battle having been fought. Russian nationalism was

---

4   On the Balkan situation see W. Simpson and M. Jones, *Europe, 1783–1914*, London, Routledge, 2000; P.W. Schroeder, *The Transformation of European Politics 1763–1848*, Oxford University Press, 1994; A. Macphie, *The Eastern Question*, London, Longman, 1996.

5   On the churches in Russia see K. Parry (ed), *The Blackwell Companion to Eastern Christianity*, Oxford, Blackwell, 2007; S. Dixon, 'The Russian Orthodox Church 1721–1917', in M. Angold (ed) *The Cambridge History of Christianity: Vol 5, Eastern Christianity*, Cambridge, CUP, 2006; G.A. Hosking (ed), *Church, Nation and State in Russia and Ukraine*, Macmillan, Basingstoke, 1991.

stirred by the French intrusion. The Russian policy of frequent skirmishing attacks, and the depths of the Russian winter, forced Napoleon into humiliating retreat. Under Tsar Alexander I (1801–25), Russian church and society opened itself to liberalisation. In 1813 the Russian Bible Society was founded, with the New Testament translated into Modern Russian by 1819. A full translation of the Bible was not completed until 1876, and distributed by the British Society, but a translation officially approved by the Orthodox Church only appeared in 1882. Some foreign missionaries were allowed to work amongst the non-Christian peoples of the Russian Empire.

Under Alexander's successor, Nicholas I (1825–55), reform, which was already waning, gave way to reaction; openness to the West was abandoned. The reign of Nicholas saw a regeneration in Orthodoxy, through a newly assertive Russian Orthodox Church. Increasing Westernisation was countered by attempts to return the church to its historic roots, emphasising it as a distinctly Russian entity. Foreign learning was rejected—the Bible Society was closed in 1822. When it re-opened in 1831 it was restricted to work with the non-Russian peoples of the Russian Empire. In 1820, the Jesuits were forbidden to operate in Russia, and British missions in Siberia placed under close scrutiny, before most were closed in the 1830s. The Russian church was not to be one amongst many others, but the dominant church, with disunity and heterodoxy discountenanced. It also sought to be an expansive church. Major attempts were made to promote Russian orthodoxy in the Russian empire, an important aspect of which was the task of translating the Bible into local languages. Much endeavour was also devoted to translating Greek documents into Russian.

Innokenti Veniaminov (1797–1879) engaged in missionary labours for forty-four years, including work on the remote Aleutian Islands. He founded the Orthodox Missionary Society, which continued its work until 1917. Veniaminov eventually became an archbishop, overseeing a vast territory from the Aleutians to Kamschatka and Yakutsk, even travelling to the far north of Siberia to visit Christians. In 1867, now an old man, he became Metropolitan of Moscow. By 1899, the Russian Church had twenty missions inside the Russian empire, and foreign missions in Alaska (part of the Russian Empire until 1864), Korea, China, Japan and Persia.

The Orthodox mission to Japan was started in 1861, by Ivan Kasatkin. By 1882 there were 7,611 baptized Christians, which had increased to 34,782 in 1914, with thirty-five Japanese priests and one hundred and six catechists. The Orthodox Church in Japan survived the upheavals of the war between Russia and Japan in 1904–05, but the Russian revolution of 1917 cut off support from its base, and it slipped into decline.

In the work of mission within Russia, policies of earlier centuries were repeated, with state sponsored conversion campaigns against the Old Believers,[6] Lutherans, and Muslims. Orthodoxy was the only church granted the right of proselytism. In 1839, the Uniate Church of the Old Believers was reunited with Orthodoxy through a state policy of proselytism. From 1843 onwards, Jews were targeted, and over half the 50,000 Jewish recruits to the army were baptised. Seventy-four thousand Latvians and Estonians were encouraged into Orthodoxy between 1845 and 1847. From 1845 onwards, significant attempts were made to teach Christianity to the Muslim children of the Volga and Urals in their own language. Some conversions were forced, or came after significant inducements were offered. When a purge of Muslims was rumoured in 1856, over half a million left for the Ottoman empire. However, civil unrest brought a weakening of the policy, and many converts returned to their previous adherence.

The 1848 revolutions in Europe left Tsar Nicholas I untouched, but when Russia was drawn into war with Turkey over the right to protect Orthodox Christians who lived in the Ottoman Empire, she found herself also in conflict with France and Britain. Humiliating defeat in the resulting Crimean War left the Russian army looking hopelessly outdated, and the nation out of touch with progress in Western Europe. The zeal for reform returned under Alexander II (1855–81), whose policies resembled those of the Gorbachev's *perestroika* (reform) and *glasnost* (openness) in the late twentieth century. Alexander was determined to move Russia out of the medieval past, and drew up legislation to emancipate the 23 million serfs, who made up 31% of the population. Serfs were treated as the property of their master, who controlled most aspects of their lives, forced to work for him, or pay feudal dues. The upheaval was as great as the emancipation of the slaves in the United States in the 1860s, and it was achieved without a Civil War, and without the deep theological debates that had polarised Christian opinion on the subject: the Orthodox Church had little to say against serfdom.

In the second half of the nineteenth century, Russia looked to be integrating into the Western world. A Russian religious renaissance saw a period of spiritual renewal within Orthodoxy, with theologians and writers rediscovering the treasures of the church's own heritage and liturgy. Resistance to conversion

---

6   Attempts to reform the Russian Orthodox Church in the 17th Century, with the adoption of Greek liturgical practices, provoked a number of priests from Moscow parishes to split from the Russian Church. Although greatly persecuted they continued as effectively an underground church, becoming more noticeably present, and consequently viewed as a threat by the Orthodox Church in the nineteenth century. In 2005, Old Believers groups still numbered over 2 million communicants. M. Burgess, *The Eastern Orthodox Churches: Concise Histories with Chronological Checklists of their Primates*, Jefferson, N. Carolina, McFarland and Co, 2005, 218.

campaigns forced church leaders to emphasise mission within Russia, based on an intellectual defence of orthodoxy, and pastoral methods. Deepening pastoral awareness fed into calls from the clergy for social and political reform. When demands for church reform were rejected by the state authorities, reforming clergy were pushed into public disputes which became highly politicised.[7] The religious renaissance was accompanied by the writings of social prophets who probed the issues of the day, and proposed spiritual solutions to secular problems. In his great novels, *War and Peace* (1869) and *Anna Karenina* (1877), Leo Tolstoy expansively explored aspects of deep moral and spiritual crisis. In other works he sought to set out the spiritual truths of the Gospels in a simple style accessible to ordinary people. Tolstoy chose to adopt the simple lifestyle of a peasant, repudiating state structures, and arguing for non-violence. Although immensely popular both home and abroad, Tolstoy found himself excommunicated by the Russian Orthodox Church in 1901 for his criticisms of orthodoxy.

Similarly affected by the Russian religious renaissance was Fyodor Dostoevsky (1821–81). Imprisoned between 1850 and 1854 for involvement in revolutionary socialist circles, he passed through a religious crisis and converted to the Russian Orthodox Church, with a deep personal commitment to its spirituality. His novels, such as *Crime and Punishment* (1866), and *The Brothers Karamazov* (1880) explored the issues of sin, redemption, and personal responsibility for actions. Dostoyevsky looked to times of 'universal harmony' which would transcend the tragedy of mankind.

For all his reforms, Tsar Alexander II faced a number of assassination attempts before his death. His end was particularly tragic. After some of his Cossack guards were killed in a failed attempt to assassinate him, he stepped from his coach to comfort the dying, and was killed by a second suicide bomber. His son, Alexander III (1881–94) followed a more repressive autocratic policy, emphasising Russian nationality, of which orthodoxy was a key component. Between 1880 and 1905, the Russian Orthodox Church was kept under stricter bureaucratic control, and demands for a reforming synod were held back. The church was not prospering. Although the number of churches had increased from 31,333 in 1840, to 40,205 in 1890, despite rising population, the number of Orthodox clergy had fallen from 116,728 clergy, to 96,892.

In Alexander's policy of 'Russification', the official language of the empire was declared to be Russian, and minorities such as the 7.9 million Poles, 1.2 million Armenians, and 22.4 million Ukrainians were subject to severe administrative and religious control. To be Russian was to belong to the Russian Orthodox Church. The five million Jews in the Russian Empire also faced severe official economic and social restrictions, and accompanied 'pogroms', waves of persecution inspired by Russian nationalists who blamed Jews for the

---

7   Dixon, 'Russian Orthodox Church', 330–347.

assassination of Alexander II. In fear, thousands emigrated, heading for Western Europe and the United States. Others joined revolutionary protest groups.

The last Tsar, Nicholas II (1894–1917) adopted reform when it was forced on him, but too late to save the Romanov dynasty. By then the Tsar was head of a Russian empire of different languages, ethnic groups, and religions. Being Russian became more about being a part of the empire, than simply being Orthodox. Partial reform, which was then halted, contributed to the pent-up resentment unleashed in the revolution of 1917. Russian society became increasingly polarised, with revolutionaries looking to extreme programmes, coupled with Marxism and atheism.

Some clerics sided with trade unionists in the revolutionary turmoil of 1905. Other church leaders argued bitterly amongst themselves. Some demanded reform in the Orthodox Church, loosening its bonds to the state, accompanied by religious liberalisation, and freedom for non-Orthodox believers. Others demanded that the full liturgical order be retained. A need to reform the Orthodox Church was recognised,

In April 1905, the Tsar, under growing political pressure, issued an edict of toleration, granting Russians personal choice in matters of faith, an unprecedented step. Orthodox theologians, who had claimed Patristic authority for state intervention to protect their church, struggled to respond to this new environment of religious pluralism. Growing numbers of the intelligentsia were inclining towards atheism and positivism, and anti-clerical sentiment increased. Religious toleration allowed many to leave Orthodoxy. Many thousands amongst the Tartars, and other tribal groups, returned to Islam and paganism: the policy of forced Christianisation had produced only superficial results. By 1907, one third of the Orthodox population of the diocese of Kholm had converted to Roman Catholicism.

In the freer social and political atmosphere, significant numbers of Russians rejected the liturgical constraints of Orthodoxy for the freer system of evangelical Protestantism. Although proselytising Orthodox believers was forbidden, by the 1860s Bible colporteurs carrying religious books and Bibles, which they read from and sold, were travelling through the Russian countryside, albeit they were constantly fearful of arrest. In the Ukraine, German Mennonite and Lutheran colonists held weekly hours (*Stunde*) of Bible study. When some of their workers and neighbours professed conversion, and organised their own small churches, these *Stundists* sought to remain within the Orthodox Church. Opposition from priests pushed them away from orthodoxy, and influenced by German Baptists and Mennonites, in the late 1860s a number accepted believers baptism. An attempt to form a Russia Baptist Union was made as early as 1884. The visit in 1874 of an English nobleman, Lord Radstock, to St Petersburg lay behind another evangelical stream in Russia, the *Pashkovites*. Radstock had been converted during the Crimean War, and joined the Plymouth Brethren.

His evangelistic Bible Studies followed by prayer and discussion, were attended by a number of aristocrats, leading to a number of prominent conversions, including Princess Lieven, and Colonel Pashkov. The latter became the leader of a brethren-style movement known as Pashkovism. The numbers of converts being won by the Russian evangelical groups brought repressive measures encouraged by Orthodox leaders. Most evangelical leaders had faced periods of imprisonment or exile before the revolution in 1917, buildings were confiscated, and sometimes children removed from their parents. The activities of the *Stundists* were made illegal by the Ministry of Internal Affairs in 1894.

The liberal measures of 1905 brought an upsurge in Evangelical Protestantism. The Baptist preacher, William Fetler, attracted regular congregations of 2,000 in St Petersburg, and reported 'a great reaping and gathering season.'[8] By 1905 there were in Russia, 86,538 Baptists, and 20,804 other Evangelical Christians: the saying 'Every Baptist a missionary', had indeed been true. The period of liberalisation did not last long, and by 1910 religious meetings outside registered buildings needed police permission, evangelization and the instruction of children was forbidden, and policemen were required to attend every prayer meeting.

The Bolshevik Revolution of 1917 was not the watershed for churches that might be expected in the light of later events. Indeed, for the churches it initially brought relief. The Orthodox Church was able to elect its first Patriarch since 1721. Non-orthodox churches were boosted by a decree that every citizen could profess any religion, or none, and previous restrictive laws were lifted, a situation evangelicals quickly took advantage of. By 1929 there were 500,000 baptized evangelicals, with some 4 million adherents, but after 1929 persecution began to rapidly whittle away numbers. Russian Christians increasingly faced the issue of how to relate to a totalitarian society in which religion played no part in conceptions of national identity, and atheism was officially promoted.

ITALY

In Italy, another historic centre of Christianity, the nineteenth-century *Risorgimento* was to bring a major clash between Italian nationalism and the Roman Catholic Church. It culminated both in the creation of a united Italian kingdom, and also a Roman Catholic Counter-*Risorgimento* which sought to oppose the forces of revolution. The end of the Napoleonic wars in 1815, left Italy a series of small states, with a form of unity derived from the overarching control of the Austrian Habsburg Empire, and also by their shared Roman

---

8 On Evangelicalism in Russia see R.S. Latimer, *With Christ in Russia*, London, Hodder and Stoughton, 1910, 26, 31; Simon Dixon, 'Russian Orthodox Church', in *Cambridge History of Christianity: World Christianities c. 1815–1914*; H. Brandenburg, *The Meek and the Mighty: The Emergence of the Evangelical Movement in Russia*, Mowbrays, London, 1974; W. Sawatsky, *Soviet Evangelicals Since World War II*, Scottdale, Herald Press, 1981.

Cavour's Appeal To The Pope To Renounce His Temporal Power, 1861

'One thing remains to be done: convince the pontiff that the Church can be independent even by losing her temporal power... Holy Father, the temporal power is no longer a guarantee of independence for you. Renounce it, and we will give you the freedom for which you have been asking all great catholic powers in vain for three centuries... We are ready to proclaim in Italy this great principle: A free church in a free state... freedom should permeate the entire religious and civil society. We want economic freedom, administrative freedom, full and absolute freedom of conscience... that the principle of freedom be applied to the relations between church and state.'[1]

1 *Discoursi parlamentari del Conte Camillo di Cavour*, Rome, 1872, Vol. XI, 346–48, quoted in S.Z. Ehler, (ed), *Church and State through the Centuries*, London, Burns and Oates, 1954, pp. 346-48.

Catholicism. Attempts to overturn Austrian rule in the 1820s and 1830s, and especially through the revolutions of 1848, were unsuccessful. The tendency of the papacy, in an attempt to ensure social and religious stability, to endorse Austrian policy left it identified as the opponent of nationalism, and fuelled smouldering discontent in the Papal States. When Pius IX turned from the path of liberal reform in 1848, anticlerical sentiment amongst liberals and patriots deepened, with the papacy blamed for the failure of reforming movements. Popular opinion began to shift decisively against the combination of spiritual and temporal power vested in the papacy.

The accession in 1849 of Victor Emmanuel II (1820–78) to the throne of Piedmont, in the North of Italy, brought to the fore a figure sympathetic to Italian reunification, and willing to face down the hostility of the papacy in the cause. The achievement of a united Italy in 1870 owed much to his influence, along with the vision of the prophet of unification, Giuseppe Mazzini (1805–72); the courageous and shrewd military tactics of Giuseppe Garibaldi (1807–82); and the political acumen of Count Camillo Cavour (1810–60), Prime Minister of Piedmont from 1852. Cavour distrusted the mob, and retained a place for a Roman Catholicism in the free state he hoped for. French troops helped those from Piedmont end Austrian control of Northern Italy in 1859. Bourbon-controlled southern Italy, from Sicily to Naples, fell to Garibaldi's forces the same year. The first Italian parliament met in Turin in March 1861, although at the time 17 million of the country's population of 23 million were illiterate, and only 2% actually had the right to vote.

By 1867 only Rome, the last of the Papal States, was not part of the united Italy. Its status was preserved by French troops which remained until 1870 when, in the aftermath of France's defeat in the Franco-Prussian War, they were removed. The Pope refused to abandon Rome without a show of resistance, but after a brief assault the city fell. In October 1870 Rome was incorporated into Italy after an overwhelming vote by its citizens to do so. Although the Pope was promised inviolability, and offered financial compensation, Pius retreated into the Vatican, seeing himself as a prisoner, condemning the 'sacrilegious' seizure, and pronouncing the excommunication of those behind the invasion. He forbade Roman Catholics from taking part in Italian elections and political life, refusing to recognise the new Italian state. The Italian government sought to restore relationships in 1871, with a promise of diplomatic immunity for the Pope, and a revenue sum to compensate for the loss of the Papal States.

The claim of the Pope to oversee the instruction, direction, and governance of the Christian world, fundamentally clashed with liberal demands for popular sovereignty, and nationalist demands for control to be vested in the hands of the state. It took until 1929 for the Roman Catholic Church to be reconciled to the Italian state. The political unity achieved between 1859 and 1870 was no panacea for the problems Italy faced, with low levels of industrial development and economic activity. The New World seemed far more attractive—in the 1890s, 300,000 people per year emigrated from Italy; after 1900 this rose to 500,000.[9]

IRELAND

Another predominantly Roman Catholic area in which national identity was formed in the midst of nineteenth-century conflict was Ireland. Despite comprising 80% of the population, Roman Catholics faced significant social and political discrimination. Until the 1870s, the Established church of Ireland was in fact the episcopalian Church of Ireland, the denomination of just 11.9% of the population in 1861. A further 8% of Ireland's population was Presbyterian, but 96% of them lived in the northern counties of Ulster. A failed Irish rising in 1798 precipitated the formal union of the Parliaments in Westminster and Dublin in 1801. Irish nationalist hopes were channelled into non-armed forms, in which Roman Catholicism held a key place.[10] The British government was

9   On Italy see D. Beales, *Italy and the Risorgimento*, London, Longman, 1982; S.M. Di Scala, *Italy from Revolution to Republic: 1700 to the Present Day*, Oxford, Westview Press, 1995; F. Coppa, 'Italy, the Church and the Risorgimento', in *Cambridge History of Christianity: World Christianities c. 1815–1914*, 233–249.

10   On Roman Catholicism and Ireland see S. J . Connolly, *Religion and Society in Nineteenth-Century Ireland*, Dundalk, Dunalgan Press, 1985; D. Keenan, *The Catholic Church in Nineteenth-Century Ireland*, Dublin, Gill and Macmillan, 1983; P. Corish, *The Irish Catholic Experience: A Historical Survey*, Dublin, Gill and Macmillan, 1985; S. Gilley, 'Catholicism in Ireland', in H. McLeod and W. Usterf, *The Decline of Christendom in Western Europe, 1750–2000*, Cambridge, CUP, 2003, 99–111. On Protestant responses to Roman Catholicism see D. Bowen, *The Protestant Crusade in Ireland 1800–1870*. Dublin, Gill and Macmillan, 1978.

unable to exercise a veto over the appointment of Roman Catholic bishops, and controversially found itself until the 1870s subsidizing the Maynooth Seminary, where Roman Catholic priests were trained, in an attempt to assuage Roman Catholic opinion.

A crucial role was played by the Irish Roman Catholic layman, Daniel O'Connell (1775–1847), whose politics were popular, constitutional, democratic and non-violent. He succeeded in creating a sympathetic alliance with Irish priests. O'Connell also worked closely with Protestant Irish nationalists, and resisted papal intervention in Irish politics: his sentiments were 'our religion from Rome, our politics from home.' Nonetheless, by the time of his death Irish nationalism and Roman Catholicism seemed almost inseparable. Roman Catholicism maintained the support of the laity through its endorsement of Irish language and culture, sport, and the rights of tenant farmers.

Famine in the 1840s proved a watershed in Irish social and religious history, affecting the poorest in society. Over one million Irish died, and millions more migrated, precipitating a decline in population from over 8 million in 1841, to less than 4.5 million in 1921. It occurred when Roman Catholicism, although numerically dominant, was not in itself strong: Irish Roman Catholic society was associated with low levels of education, and high levels of alcohol abuse. Church attendance was somewhere between 20 and 40% in rural areas before 1840, although a further 20% did not attend because of illness, age, or through duties of caring for little children. Roman Catholicism revived later in the nineteenth century, when attendance reached 70% in the towns, and up to 90% in the early twentieth century: regular church-attendance became characteristic of the Irish Roman Catholic poor. Such was the size of the Irish Diaspora that Irish Roman Catholicism exercised an influence far greater than the number of Roman Catholics based in Ireland. Seventy Irish-born bishops, and a further one hundred and fifty of Irish descent, are thought to have attended the First Vatican Council in 1869–70.

Under the watchful gaze of Paul Cullen, who became Ireland's first Cardinal, priests were subjected to more rigorous training, stricter discipline, with an increased emphasis on mission and retreats, and discouragements of overt involvement in politics. Cullen was a moderniser in his concern to assist poor Roman Catholics, to promote popular education, and emphasise the equality of Roman Catholics before God, but his theological opinions remained conservative, and his inclinations anti-Protestant. Ultramontane Roman Catholicism, with strong devotional adherence to the Virgin Mary, and the Saints, richly decorated shrine churches and worship that involved all the senses, all had a part in winning post-Famine Irish Roman Catholics back to the mass, although the devotional 'revolution' of post-1850 Ireland may in fact have started before 1850. Ireland was to witness the highest level of church attendance amongst Roman Catholics in the world. It also attracted the fervent opposition from Protestants, who believed Irish Roman Catholicism was more Roman than Rome itself. Ironically, both sides of the sectarian divide held remarkably similar 'Victorian' social and moral values, typified by regular Sunday observance in 'Sunday clothes' and temperance crusades.

Irish Roman Catholic renewal was also in part a response to the so-called 'Second Reformation' which began in the 1820s, but reached its peak in the famine years of the 1840s. In this Protestant Evangelicals in the Church of Ireland sought the evangelisation of poverty-stricken Roman Catholics, in part through programmes of social concern, including offering free soup, and education to poor Roman Catholic children. Although conversions were reported, the Second Reformation was not a widespread success. Revivals in Ulster in 1859 touched Protestant communities profoundly, but Ireland remained predominantly Roman Catholic.

Irish Roman Catholicism retained a distinctive folk element. The claims from a range of witnesses that the Virgin Mary had appeared with St Joseph, St John the Evangelist, and the Lamb of God on the wall of the chapel in Knock, County Mayo, in 1879 had a distinctly anti-modern element. However, their accounts were publicised in a distinctly modern way. The apparition was read as a sign of blessing on Roman Catholic Ireland, whereas the appearances at Lourdes were seen as a condemnation of unbelieving France.

The established Church of Ireland was subject to controversial reform by the British government in the 1830s, which preserved its status until disestablishment in 1871. It was a final acceptance of the minority position of Anglicanism. Nonetheless, the wounds of long and bitter historical, political, ecclesiological, and theological conflict deepened into sectarianism. Although a number of Irish Anglicans in the South chose to support Independence, in the North Anglicans and Presbyterians developed a strong Protestant counter-culture in the face of the predominant Roman Catholic one, expressed through bodies such as the Orange order. Large-scale Roman Catholic migration into industrial areas, such as Belfast, increased the potential for conflict: by 1861, 34% of the city's population was Roman Catholic.

The lead in calls for Irish Home rule from the 1870s was taken by Charles Stewart Parnell (1846–1891), a Protestant landowner, although his fall from grace was a severe blow to the cause, after an adulterous affair became public. The failure of the British Prime Minister, W.E. Gladstone, to secure Home Rule legislation in the 1880s split the British Liberal party, and bred deep frustrations. In 1912, faced with the growing likelihood that Home Rule would be granted, some 500,000 Ulster Protestants, a quarter of the province's population, signed the Covenant. They pledged themselves to not recognise a Home Rule parliament, and to use all means necessary to defeat it.

While Civil War loomed in the North, it broke out in the South in the depths of the First World War with the 1916 Easter Rising, an attempt to violently overturn British rule. The deaths of the protagonists were seen by many Roman Catholics as Christian martyrdom. The independent Ireland that did emerge in 1921 was popularly understood to be a Roman Catholic nation. Although formally religiously neutral, the Roman Catholic Church was granted a 'special position' in the Irish constitution, with other religious denominations recognised and protected, even though they comprised only 7% of the population. But it was not a united Ireland, with six counties in the north, forming Northern Ireland, remaining under British rule, leaving a legacy of sectarian division between Roman Catholic and Protestant, in which the position of each side was strongly shaped by opposing religious identities.

SCANDINAVIA

In Sweden, Norway, Denmark and Finland, the religious form that had emerged from the sixteenth century was of territorial churches with a Lutheran confession, in which Church and state were closely connected. Religious belief and church practice formed an important part of state legislation. Although Lutheranism was the only religious form allowed in the Nordic region, different countries had their own liturgies, hymns and forms of church order. During the nineteenth century, under political pressures and revivalist tendencies, Lutheran territorial churches gradually developed into national churches, operating in states in which the principles of religious freedom and religious pluralism were accepted.[11]

In 1808, Finland separated from Sweden to become an autonomous Grand Duchy, in which Lutheranism was maintained. It was 1917–18 before Finland became an independent nation-state, but Lutheranism remained the majority church. Between 1814 and 1905, Norway and Sweden were united under one monarchy, with each country keeping its own ecclesiastical structure. The loss of Schleswig-Holstein to Germany after war in 1864, reduced Denmark to a small nation-state. Despite this gradual fragmentation of the region into independent nation states, the growing sense of threat from Russia and Germany brought a deeper sense of Scandinavian identity. The common bond of Lutheranism proved a unifying cultural and social force. In the new state constitutions that emerged, Lutheranism supplied the recognised confession of faith. Its tradition of worship and liturgy in vernacular languages enhanced their importance and development. Attendance at a church school became

---

11 On religion and national identity in Scandinavia see I. Brohed (ed), *Church and People in Britain and Scandinavia*, Bromley, Chartwell-Bratt, 1996; L.S. Hunter (ed), *Scandinavian Churches*, London, Faber and Faber, 1965; D. Thorkildsen, 'Scandinavia: Lutheranism and National Identity', in *Cambridge History of Christianity: World Christianities, c.1815–1914.*

compulsory in eighteenth-century Norway and Denmark. In Sweden and Finland, the religious education of children was vested in the household, but ministers conducted regular visitation to test knowledge of religious teaching. In the nineteenth century, however, the control of the Lutheran church over education weakened, and religion became just one important subject among others in the curriculum.

A significant feature of the Nordic church experience in the nineteenth century was revivalism, which had strong inter-Nordic and international links. Building on both Pietism and Moravianism in the early eighteenth century, it frequently had a domestic basis, but was given dramatic impetus by dynamic revivalists. It proved a modernising, democratising force, aiding social mobility, presenting opportunities for lay leadership, and feeding into liberal political movements, and eventually to modern religious pluralism. The revival movement in Norway led by Hans Nielsen Hauge (1771–1824) was absorbed into the Norwegian Lutheran church, bringing some of its vigour into the National Church, and a stress on preaching for awakening and moral change. In Sweden, religious revivalism was lay dominated, and seen by church and state authorities as a form of social rebellion, promoting increased separation between the established church and religious revivalism. Whilst for some revived faith brought an emphasis on community, in the thinking of the Danish philosopher and theologian, Søren Kierkegaard (1813–55) authentic faith should be less about institutional Christianity, and more about individuality, subjectivity and authenticity.

In 1845 the connection between being Norwegian and being Lutheran was broken when religious Dissenters were given freedom to practice their faith. Religious faith was recognised as a voluntary and personal matter, allowing Dissent to co-exist with the state church in the later nineteenth century. Legislation which made baptism, confirmation, and participation in communion compulsory had been abolished by 1920. After 1860 it was possible for Swedish citizens to leave the Church of Sweden, but religious dissent was not possible in Finland until 1889, and full religious freedom came only in 1922.

CANADA

When, in 1867, the 'Dominion' of Canada was formed, its title derived from Psalm 72 v 8: 'he shall have dominion also from sea to sea:' Canada was to be spoken of as 'His dominion'. The role of Christianity in the formation of national identity was to be more overt than with its neighbour, the United States. Confederation was viewed as a way of further Christianizing the nation. Canada had fought hard to preserve its independence from the United States, through resistance to incorporation in 1812, and to armed attempts to create republican systems in Upper Canada and Quebec, patterned on that in the United States. Loyalty to Britain remained the political preference. Although geographical similarities between the United States and Canada were marked, with sparsely populated vast open territories, with great extremes of climate, the experience of churches tended to diverge.

The first major Christian presence in Canada had been Roman Catholicism, and it was only in the nineteenth Century that Protestant numbers came to equal those of Roman Catholics. From then on a careful compromise policy was exercised, balancing Protestant and Roman Catholic, French-speaking and English-speaking interests. There was a tendency for Canadian Christians to retain a closer link with European churches, especially those from England, Scotland, Ireland and France, than was the case in America.

The growth of religious life in Canada was steady, without the major phases of expansion experienced in the USA, although the arrival in the 1780s of a wave of settlers from America, who had fought on the defeated British side in the war of Independence, significantly boosted numbers attending churches. So too did the 'New Light' ministry of Henry Alline (1748–84), which brought Awakening in Nova Scotia. Thomas McCulloch (1776–1843) went on to help shape Nova Scotia's 'evangelical creed'.

In 1791, the Constitutional Act created an established status for the Roman Catholic Church in Lower Canada, and Roman Catholic support for the British in the war of 1812 all-but ended attempts to turn Quebec into a Protestant province. By 1819 there were two Roman Catholic dioceses in Lower Canada, Quebec and Montreal, each with some 200,000 Roman Catholics. Most schools and hospitals were run by religious orders. Increased demands by professionals and businessmen for a republican political system were resisted, and an armed rebellion put down in 1837. With a steady supply of priests, and an encouragement of Roman Catholic literary life amongst intellectuals, a strongly Roman Catholic society in Lower Canada emerged.

In Upper Canada, immigration from the United States was a major feature. In the 1791 Constitution Act, public land was set aside for the support of Protestant ministers (the Clergy reserves). After the war of 1812, attempts to create an Anglican establishment as the foundation of Christian civilisation in Upper Canada were strongly promoted, creating conflict with Dissenters, especially Methodists, who were increasing rapidly in numbers. Antagonism gradually mellowed into co-operation, as Anglicans, Methodists, and Presbyterians began to work together to promote a non-establishment Christendom by means of education and influence on the government. By 1867 there was a strong sense of Protestant cultural identity in English-speaking Canada. In 1900, around half of Toronto's population was in church each Sunday, and in smaller towns and villages attendance was even higher. Although high, these levels did not match those found in Quebec, where attendance at mass reached 90%. When in 1896, Wilfrid Laurier became Canada's first Roman Catholic prime minister, he helped secure a compromise whereby public money was given to fund the schools of the minority Protestant community in Quebec, and in turn public support was offered to Roman Catholic schools in Protestant provinces, a situation very different to that in the United States.

The challenges of science, biblical criticism, and social Christianity were faced without the level of controversy created in the United States, with most Protestants settling on a form of moderate evangelicalism, which stressed regeneration and personal morality. In 1906 a Lord's Day Act was passed to maintain observance of Sunday, and to protect the rights of workers. Interest in the Social Gospel was to develop in the mid-twentieth century.[12] Ultramontane Roman Catholicism resisted socialism, but encouraged a communal approach to public life.

The challenges of maintaining competing denominational systems in sparsely populated areas brought a growing interest in Protestant union, on the basis of a broadly evangelical theology. The thinking of Nathanael Burwash (1839–1910), a leading Methodist theologian and educator, was important to these developments, which led ultimately to the creation of the United Church of Canada in 1925.

LATIN AMERICA

Forces akin to those in revolutionary America and France were channelled into independence movements in Latin America during the nineteenth-century. Political instability characterised Spain and Portugal between 1820 and 1850 as they oscillated between absolutist monarchy, revolution, military intervention, and the instalment of liberal regimes. In 1820, after revolution in Spain, the king was forced for a short period to renounce absolutist rule, and accept a liberal constitution. Such sentiment was quickly exported to the Latin American colonies, despite stern resistance from governments in Madrid and Lisbon, desirous to maintain empire. The remarkable solider-statesman, Simón Bolívar (1783–1830) helped lead successful revolutionary campaigns in Venezuela (1817, with independence finally secured in 1821), Colombia (1819), Equador (1822), and Peru (1824). The independence of Upper Peru was proclaimed in 1825, and named Bolivia in Bolívar's honour.

The traditional stance of the Roman Catholic Church was of loyalty to monarchy and rejection of revolution, and this was reflected in the initial reaction from the papacy to the beginnings of revolution in Spanish America, and from bishops who owed their appointments to the crown. The reaction of others, however, was quite different. Some went so far as to finance, arm, and encourage anti-revolutionary forces. A number of priests served as chaplains in armies of revolution, and others became active in the rebel ranks. Political enthusiasm mingled with religion to produce deep devotion to the sacred cause of liberty. Priests like Miguel Hidalgo

12 On the Social Gospel see chapter 14.

played a key role in the fight for independence in Mexico. Although liberal anti-clericalism and traditionalist Roman Catholicism were to later clash, in Spanish speaking areas bishops came to see that Independence movements were often conservative, and supported them. In the 1830s the pope began to recognise the legitimacy of the new Latin American republics, and the post-colonial churches began to look directly to Rome for leadership and authority, rather than indirect authority that came via Spain.

One revolutionary desire was to remove the religious element from public life. However, the legal existence of the Roman Catholic religion was not threatened, even by radicals, who recognised its significant role in the Hispanic inheritance, and valued its social cohesive influence, its capacity to bring continuity in the moral realm. The exception was Bolívar's 1826 constitution for Bolivia which did not recognise the church. Nonetheless, the assembly in Bolivia ignored his opinions, and set up a state church. Bolívar himself came to recognise the expediency of bringing the clergy within the machinery of the state.[13]

The colonial past bequeathed to the church wealth and revenue, yet there were great inequalities, and priests in rural parishes could be extremely poor. In some areas they were considered to be of low moral and educational standard, criticised for living with women, and appropriating the funds of the parish for their own use. Bishops also had great difficulties in supplying sufficient clergy—in Bolivia in 1850 there were 50% fewer priests than in 1800. Mexico did better, with attempts to improve clergy education, and the number of priests increasing from 3,463 in 1826 to 4,533 in 1910, although population was also rising.

In the years of transition, the Roman Catholic Church sought to retain its position of influence and privilege in the face of attempts by new regimes to control the institutions of the church. The issue of patronage in the appointment of clergy was to occasion great controversy. Patronage was claimed by the Mexican state in 1821; Chile assumed it in 1818, Argentina in 1819, Bolivia in 1826, Uruguay, Venezuela and Ecuador in 1830. During the period of monarchy in Brazil (1822–89) strong control of the church was retained, with bishops nominated, and tithes collected by the government. After the fall of the monarchy, the church was able to control its own affairs, founding new seminaries, and ensuring the training of more clergy.

Another source of conflict came over the growing liberal sentiment amongst politicians and the developing ultramontane tendencies amongst the higher

13   E.R. Norman, *Christianity in the Southern Hemisphere: The Churches in Latin America and South Africa*, Oxford, Clarendon Press, 1981, 1–24. See also J. Lynch, 'Latin America: The Church and National Independence', in *Cambridge History of Christianity: World Christianities*, 395–411; E. Dussel (ed), *The Church in Latin America 1492–1992*, Tunbridge Wells, Burns and Oates, 1992; L. Bethell (ed), *The Cambridge History of Latin America, Vol. III, From Independence to c. 1870*, Cambridge, CUP, 1985, and *The Cambridge History of Latin America, vol. IV, c. 1870–1930*, Cambridge, CUP, 1986.

clergy. Those creating liberal and secular states in Latin America demanded reductions in the influence of the church, freedom of conscience, and removal of discrimination based on religious profession. State control was sought over areas previously monopolised by the church, such as the registration of births, marriages and deaths. Civil Marriage was granted in Uruguay in 1837, in Chile in 1884, and Argentina in 1888. This decisively weakened the social control of the church, as did the secularization of cemeteries—starting in Mexico in 1856. Tithes were abolished in Argentina in 1822, Chile in 1825, Mexico in 1833, and Venezuela in 1834. In Argentina, between 1830 and 1860 the Roman Catholic Church adopted a pattern of compromise with the ruling dictatorship, winning protection but conceding to the government control of the appointment of bishops. The 1853 constitution granted funding to the Roman Catholic Church as the religion of the state, but only after 1860 did the Roman Catholic Church in Argentina begin to move forward positively, expanding the numbers of parishes, and seeing growth in religious orders, with significant involvement in education, and social welfare.

Despite such endeavours, the Roman Catholic Church in nineteenth-century Latin America was not noted for its active social conscience. In Brazil the Roman Catholic Church owned slaves, and was not enthusiastic about abolition. An attempt in 1888 to win the support of the pope for the Brazilian abolition campaign was unsuccessful. Amongst the rural and urban poor of Latin America, Roman Catholicism saw a strong conservative emphasis on the veneration of the Virgin Mary, but also in popular expression there often remained elements of ancient folk practice and magic. This owed much to the fragility of life, with disease, starvation, and natural disasters regular occurrences, but in Mexico and Guatemala, where there were large Indian populations, the borders between official and folk religion became almost indistinguishable.[14] The role of Roman Catholicism in national and popular culture could not simply be defined by patterns of attendance, belief or practice. Even where adherence to the Roman Catholic faith was strong, the moral laxity of many Latin American Roman Catholics struck observers from Rome, with cases of drunkenness, sex outside marriage, and gambling reported. Many priests kept concubines, a practice accepted by the local populace.

Religious toleration was another area of significant disagreement between the new liberal governments and Roman Catholic authorities, who associated it with secularisation. The Constitution of 1830 in Uruguay fully granted religious toleration, and there was a limited measure in Brazil in 1824. In Chile, an alliance between Protestantism and liberal political sentiment was forged, and a reduction in church control of education followed, with the state expanding its school and university provision. The teaching of Roman Catholicism

14   Norman, *Christianity in the Southern Hemisphere*, 48–62.

remained compulsory in Costa Rica and Columbia, after 1886, but in Brazil it was only permitted outside normal school hours after 1891. Religious teaching was completely prohibited in Cuba after 1899.

The growth of Protestantism in Latin America was very slow in the face of the dominant Spanish-Portuguese Roman Catholic culture, and it tended to be linked to the presence of foreign nationals. Its adoption could form part of a protest by elements of the educated middle classes against the dominant cultural values of Latin American society. Other adherents were found amongst migrant communities who often remained inward looking, such as the Welsh Methodists of Patagonia. Membership never amounted to more than a few thousand in each country, largely from historic denominations—Lutherans, Presbyterians, Methodists, Baptists and Episcopalians. Most missionary endeavour tended to originate in the United States, and for some it was part of extending American cultural values, or the respectability ethos of hard-work and thrift. Occasionally, religious movements among the indigenous population broke out which were beyond the capacity of the missionary community to handle, such as the outbreak of weeping, dancing, tongue-speaking and visions amongst the Methodists of Valparaíso in 1909, repeated not long afterwards in Santiago. These isolated outbursts pointed ahead to the huge spread of Pentecostalism in Latin America in the later twentieth century, especially amongst the socially marginalised urban poor. Latin American Pentecostalism was to become part of a rejection of ordered institutional Christianity, in favour of egalitarian, spontaneous forms, semi-independent from traditional European forms.[15]

The disestablishment of religion was accomplished in 1890 in Brazil, in 1919 in Uruguay, and 1925 in Chile. Disestablishment in Columbia (1853), Mexico (1859), and Guatemala (1879) was far more contentious, and occasioned great hostility. Elsewhere, structural links between Church and State were maintained, and anti-clerical sentiment strongly resisted. Where the church was weaker, such as in Venezuela, its privileges eroded more readily. Such was the strength of Roman Catholicism that, even after disestablishment, governments sought to retain a strong control over churches. Mexico's Constitution of 1857 gave its federal government the right to intervene in matters of worship and ecclesiastical form. Roman Catholic Churches needed to develop strategies for surviving in a context of toleration and religious pluralism. A tendency to look to Rome for resources and direction followed, and from Europe came priests and members of religious orders to assist ongoing mission amongst the nominally catholic population. Nonetheless, the later nineteenth century saw large numbers leaving the Roman Catholic Churches in Latin America. Some, from the professional realms of society, chose to do so for intellectual reasons,

15   Norman, *Christianity in the Southern Hemisphere*, 62–70.

for others it was lack of access to churches and priests. Some parishes in La Paz numbered 18,000 people, making attendance very difficult.

It has been argued that the Latin American church in the nineteenth century passed, at varying speeds, from the 'Christendom' model, where Roman Catholicism and political society were closely identified, to independence when the 'political' church in the later nineteenth century saw alliances forged with conservative political interests to resist liberalising tendencies. Finally, the 'ghetto' church developed, with withdrawal from an increasingly secular society into the twentieth century.[16] By 1914, across Latin America, despite Christianity retaining a strong part in national life and culture, churches found themselves increasingly unable to rely on the protection of the state or law.

THE JEWISH EXPERIENCE OF NATIONAL IDENTITY

The nineteenth century brought developments which were to prove of great significance to the Jews. Between the destruction of the Second Temple in Jerusalem and the establishment of the state of Israel in 1948 they existed as a Diaspora, a people with a distinct and cohesive religious and cultural identity, but without a fixed political or territorial centre. In medieval and early modern Europe they faced regular persecution, frequently forced to live in ghettos. Jewish identity was more than simply a religious one: scholars moved freely between various communities of the Diaspora, and social welfare arrangements internal to the community strengthened inter-community connections, as did ties forged by economic activity.

In European society, the Jews remained a small, but significant, minority—in 1850 around 0.3% of the French population was Jewish, 0.2% in England, and 1% in Germany, but there were significant local variations—in Frankfurt the percentage was 8%. The nineteenth century brought vastly different experiences for these communities. Jewish populations came eventually to benefit from the social liberalisation which brought a gradual removal of legal and political discrimination against religious minorities, and growing opportunities to actively function within the wider societies where they resided. Figuratively, and sometimes literally, ghetto walls came down. Jews had increased opportunities to choose where they would reside, work, and worship. The reduced application of religious tests for participation in social life allowed Jews to embrace widespread economic, social, and political opportunities, and eventually to take up citizenship in European nation-states. It also allowed them to express their Jewish identity in non-religious ways, to be Jewish independently of Judaism and religious sentiment: a loyal Jew could also be a loyal citizen. The need to fashion a dual identity, both as Jews and as citizens of their country of

---

16 I. Vallier, *Catholicism, Social Control, and Modernization in Latin America*, Englewood Cliffs, N.J., Prentice-Hall, 1970, 7.

Jewish Emancipation in Britain: The Jewish Relief Act

Where it shall appear to either House of Parliament that a Person professing the Jewish Religion, otherwise entitled to sit and vote in such House, is prevented from so sitting and voting by his conscientious Objection to take the Oath…which by an Act passed or to be passed in the present Session of Parliament has been or may be substituted for the Oaths of Allegiance, Supremacy, and Abjuration in the Form therein required, such House…may omit the Words "and I make this Declaration upon the true Faith of a Christian," and so long as such Resolution shall continue in force the said Oath, when taken and subscribed by any Person professing the Jewish Religion to entitle him to sit and vote in that House of Parliament, may be modified accordingly…as far as respects the Title to sit and vote in such House, have the same Force and Effect as the taking and subscribing by other Persons of the said Oath in the Form required by the said Act.[1]

1   An Act to provide for the Relief of Her Majesty's Subjects professing the Jewish Religion. *(1858, July 23. 21 & 22 Victoria, c. 49.)*

---

residence became acute and replaced the need to choose between a religious and a national identity. This created the ultimate dilemma for the Jewish and other faith communities in wartime when they were commanded to fight, and kill, their co-religionists living in other countries.

The legal Emancipation of the Jews in nineteenth century Europe proceeded slowly, and at varying paces in different countries, but had been achieved in most of Western Europe by 1900. The Jewish religion was recognised by Napoleon Bonaparte's Concordat with the Pope in 1801, and after 1831 rabbis received payment from the state alongside Roman Catholic priests and Lutheran pastors. In England, Jewish emancipation came in 1858. It took until 1875 before it was completed across Germany. Before emancipation, full integration required conversion to Christianity, and even after the granting of civil liberties, it remained the way to complete acceptance, although from many who converted, Christianity received only nominal adherence.[17] Alongside emancipation came the significant right to practice openly and freely their own religion, Judaism. Nonetheless, the degree to which traditional beliefs and practices could be retained, whilst integrating into European society, was to prove a difficult issue.

For some nations, adapting to the religious pluralism created by the acceptance in their midst of a section of their population very different in religion, culture, dress and appearance, was difficult. From some, there was an expectation that granting Jews political emancipation would quickly bring assimilation or

17   On assimilation and community strengthening see J. Frankel and S.J. Zipperstein, *Assimilation and Continuity: The Jews in Nineteenth Century Europe*, Cambridge, CUP, 1992.

conversion. For all too many, despite the advance of liberal values, the presence remained of an ugly and pervasive undercurrent of anti-semitism. Jews in many areas found themselves facing widespread and severe persecution.

National governments in Europe continued to retain significant influence over their populations. A Prussian law of 1847 required every Jew to be a member of a local congregation, a policy designed to restrict religious reform. In 1876, this policy was reversed as Jews were allowed to withdraw from Jewish organisations without ceasing to be Jews—the same law held true for Roman Catholics. In France in 1831, Judaism became a religion subsidised by the state, with government financing synagogue building, and paying the salaries of rabbis, a situation which continued until 1905, and bringing considerable state influence over Jewish religious life.

The pressures of the liberal, and increasingly secular agenda told heavily on some groups of European Jews. In France, Jews tended to sacrifice religious practice in favour of assimilation which allowed them to embrace social, political and business opportunities. Difficult choices were needed over education, which was vital for access to the professions or positions of influence. Jewish families had little option but to send their children to public schools, which held classes on Saturdays, so separating their children from attendance at religious worship. It was hard to be a fully practising religious Jew and enjoy the full fruits of civic equality in modern society. In England, where the toleration of Christian dissent was more firmly rooted, Jews appealed for genuine cultural pluralism, that allowed them to be fully participating members of society, without having to choose to compromise elements of the full and free practice of their religious faith.

During the nineteenth century there was, amongst Jews, an increased variety of understandings and expressions of what the beliefs, and demands, of Judaism actually were. Judaism was not immune from the secularising pressures that were to affect Christian denominations in the nineteenth century: freedom to practice religion included freedom to choose not to practice religion.[18] Some adopted secular Judaism, which freed individuals from both external social restrictions, but also the internal restrictions of the faith community. Whilst many men withdrew from public attendance at synagogue worship, a factor influencing some of the reform movements, domestic observance of Jewish customs remained strong, and was especially perpetuated by Jewish women. The cult of domesticity and increased feminization of piety, strong in Christian

---

18 On Jewish responses to the liberal social and political context see J. Frankel and S.J. Zipperstein, eds. *Assimilation and Community: The Jews in Nineteenth-Century Europe*, Cambridge, CUP, 1992; D. Cesarani, ed., *The Making of Modern Anglo-Jewry*, Oxford, Blackwell, 1990; P.C. Albert, *The Modernization of French Jewry: Consistory and Community in the Nineteenth Century*, Hanover, NH, 1977; D.C. Itzkowitz, 'The Jews of Europe and the Limits of Religious Freedom', in ed. R.J. Helmstadter, *Freedom and Religion in the Nineteenth Century*, 151–171.

communities, was also a feature of middle-class Jewish homes. This focus on domestic religious observance reduced the tensions between open religious observance and the expression of emancipated citizenship by integration into wider society.

As Jews engaged with wider cultural and social circles, the conservative rabbinate of the eighteenth century gradually lost its influence, and expressions of a modernising ideology began to be noticed, demonstrating significant borrowing from non-Jewish thinking.[19] The Jewish Enlightenment, or *Haskalah*, led to an openness to wider intellectual trends amongst its followers the *Maskilim*. They sought to modify religious practice in ways that would make it easier for Jews to participate in the modern world, as well as making the faith more accessible to nineteenth-century minds. This produced not only reform movements, but also a conservative, Orthodox, defence.[20]

The first expression of the Jewish *Haskalah* was found in Berlin, where there was encouragement for Jews to embrace engagement with wider society and intellectual trends. Although full abandonment of Judaism was never advocated, nor uncritical acceptance of non-Jewish bourgeois values, it was an approach posing significant challenges for Jewish identity. A key figure in the eighteenth-century *Haskalah* was Moses Mendelssohn, although he was more a reformer of Jewish life rather than a reformer of Judaism.[21]

The *Maskilim* sought to reject what they considered outmoded or superstitious, adjusting religious practices, such as liturgy, dress, and burial customs, in ways that might conform with wider society. This included preaching in the vernacular, singing assisted by choirs or organs, and more ordered forms of prayer. The clothes Jews wore in the social sphere were modernised and westernised. Concern as to the outward appearance of synagogues led to building and restoration projects.

Interest in reviving Hebrew as a way of reviving wider Jewish culture led initially to increased publication of literature in the language. Jewish journalism served a growing body of journals and newspapers from France to Russia, with the beginning of titles such as the *Allgemeine Zeitung des Judentums* in Germany, and the *Jewish Chronicle* in London. Some were in Hebrew, others in the local vernacular, and proved a channel of expression for politicised sections of the

19   On Jewish modernity see J. Katz (ed), *Toward Modernity: The European Jewish Model*, New Brunswick, Transaction Books, 1987.

20   The Reform movement is discussed in M.A. Meyer, *Response to Modernity: History of the Reform Movement in Judaism*, Oxford, OUP, 1988—the Mendelssohn reference is on p. 13. See also J. Katz, *Out of the Ghetto: The Social Background of the Jewish Emancipation 1770–1880*, Cambridge, Mass., Harvard University Press, 1973; J. Katz, *The Role of Religion in Modern Jewish History*, Cambridge, Mass., Harvard University Press, 1975.

21   On Mendelssohn see A. Altman, *Moses Mendelssohn: A Biographical Study*, London; Routledge and Kegan Paul, 1973.

Jewish community. Through networks of foreign correspondents they shared news of Jewish communities across the world, and helped to establish a climate of popular Jewish opinion. A wide variety of literary studies in Hebrew and Yiddish (especially in Eastern Europe) appeared, together with other languages, which covered many aspects of Judaism, especially on the Jewish religion and history. Russia, in particular, produced a number of fine writers from within the Jewish community. A rapidly increasing readership, and a growing international Jewish consciousness saw Jews in the West of Europe avidly reading what was produced by Eastern European Jews. Martin Buber introduced Chassidic tales into the German-Jewish context. Renewal in Jewish cultural life fed desires for a renewal of Jewish spiritual life.

The need for Jews to express their identity politically was also a feature of their nineteenth century experience. Much activity was focussed upon campaigns for greater equality, and against anti-Semitic discrimination. In 1828, the Board of Deputies of British Jews was established in London to further political emancipation, and to represent Jewish interests in wider society. In this role it exercised considerable influence over the Jewish community itself—government permission to solemnise marriages was only granted to those which had the approval of the Board of Deputies. Its general adherence to Orthodox Judaism helped restrict the spread of reform movements in Britain. In France the *Alliance Israélite Universelle* was a forum for national and international political activities, but also engaged in social welfare and educational programmes. Both bodies comprised wealthy, influential, and culturally well-integrated Jews.[22]

Despite its limited overall effects, in the West the *Haskalah* did leave a strong legacy through increased educational opportunities for Jews, for Jewish scholarship, and in the movement for synagogue reform and vernacular sermons. The major reforming impetus in Germany was over by the 1870s, but in the United States more far-reaching liturgical changes were attempted in the 1890s. As with Christianity, efforts at reform proved divisive. Even the Reform movement in mid-nineteenth century Germany was divided between radical reformers, moderate reformers, and the Neo-orthodox. They remained distinct from the conservative traditionalists, the Old Orthodox. For the Orthodox, the defence of traditional teaching and life was more important than winning liberty of conscience. By the second half of the century accommodation between the two groups was becoming unlikely. The orthodox understanding was reformulated in even more conservative ways, bringing not only defence of even the smallest dimension of religious practice, but also traditional cultural practice, into the essence of Judaism.[23]

22   See J. Frankel, *Prophecy and Politics: Socialism, Nationalism and the Russian Jews 1862–1917*, Cambridge, CUP, 1981.

23   See S.M. Lowenstein, *The Berlin Jewish Community: Enlightenment, Family and Crisis, 1770–1830*, Oxford, OUP, 1994.

The *Haskalah* in the East, although sharing common features with that in the West, was eventually to move in a different direction, bringing an emphasis on Hebrew, and the rich cultural legacy of Judaism itself.[24] It too faced stern resistance from the rabbinic authorities, especially in the 1830s and 1840s when enlightened Jews sought to co-operate with the Tsarist government and move Judaism into the modern era. By the end of the century, thoughts were turning towards Jewish nationalism, and also socialism. In Russia, owing to the country's different social system, Jewish political movements took on different forms to elsewhere. In 1897 the *Bund*, the General Jewish Labour Union in Russia and Poland was formed, which was to become the most powerful Socialist Party in Russia, uniting Jewish and Socialist thinking. In the same year, the first Zionist congress was convened, and bases for the movement for a Jewish national homeland soon formed in most major centres.

Whilst in Western Europe upward social mobility saw middle-class Jews adopting the values of bourgeois society, in Eastern Europe Jews continued to endure deep discrimination, and restrictions on their movements, such as the 'Pale of Settlement' in areas under Russian domination. Restricted to small-scale trading, and the harsh working conditions of the clothing trade, severe poverty was common. Hopes of benefiting from liberalising, modernising Western progress in Eastern Europe suffered a severe blow with the Russian pogroms of 1881—84. These were upsurges of violent persecution against Jews, some spontaneous, others more organised. Those from 1903 to 1905 left thousands of Jews dead or injured. Young Jews were radicalised by poverty, overpopulation, and anti-Semitic persecution.

In the West, anti-Semitism never really went away. The case of the Jewish army Captain, Alfred Dreyfuss, who was falsely convicted of treason, saw the unleashing of rabidly anti-Semitic sentiment in France. The championing of the case against Dreyfuss by influential Roman Catholic voices backfired against the church and fuelled deep anticlerical sentiment. Political anti-Semitism remained a significant vote winner in Austria, and parts of Germany.

The widely different experiences of Jews in East and Western Europe in the nineteenth century fuelled a sense of social and cultural alienation between them, contributing to a declining sense of unity within the wider Jewish community. Even the experience of Jews within the 'Pale' could vary significantly.[25] The term Judaism itself was falling under considerable strain. By the end of the century it was increasingly difficult to identify the set of beliefs by which it was possible to define what it was to be a Jew. Jews wrestled with the fundamental issue

---

24   The Eastern European response to *Haskalah* is explored in I. Etkedes, *The Eastern European Jewish Enlightenment*, Jerusalem, 1993.

25   S. Volkov, 'The Jewish Project of Modernity: Diverse or Unitary?', in H. Kaelble (ed), *The European Way: European Societies During the Nineteenth and Twentieth Centuries*, New York, Berghahn, 2004, 226–252.

of whether they simply possessed an ethnic and religious identity, or whether they should look beyond being a Diaspora community and return to being a gathered national community. Debates about Jewish cultural identity were overtaken in the twentieth century by the more profound question of how to survive. Jewish socialism in Russia was decimated by the advance of the Soviet state; Nazism and the holocaust threatened the very existence of German and East European Jewish communities, whether Orthodox or Reformed. For many, the only hope lay in the Zionist vision of creating a distinctly Jewish state, Israel.

CONCLUSIONS

Religion continued to be a stubbornly persistent influence on national life during the nineteenth century. Where there was an accepted link between church and state, membership rates remained high, but as the century wore on, such membership also tended to be highly nominal, with high rates of unbelief especially in European cities. When religion played a part in establishing, or maintaining, national unity, criticism of the church was reduced. The desires of governments to enforce conservative social values in the wake of revolutionary change assisted the widespread revival of religious life experienced of the first half of the nineteenth century. So too did the growth of sectarian religious expression amongst the lower and middle classes, seeking a form of religious expression more conducive to their independent minded and aspirational cultural values. The capacity of Roman Catholicism to embrace, and endorse expressions of popular religious devotion, and to recruit priests from lower social strata, gave it significant impetus. Whilst resisting the increase of State powers on it, the Roman Catholic structure itself grew more centralised, hierarchical, and bureaucratic.

As the century progressed, churches responded to suggestions of declining influence through conducting strong internal, or home, mission. (see chapter 14) Although political unification in Germany and Italy brought great expansion in the power of the nineteenth-century state, religion was still considered to play a remarkably significant role in state formation and maintenance, as seen in the *Kulturkampf* in Germany, the constitutions of new nations in Latin America, and the 'Dominion' title adopted by Canada. However, by the start of the twentieth century this was changing. Anticlerical and secular thought brought the link between religion and national identity under increasing question in some nations. For some governments, Disestablishment, the separation between church and state, was not enough, and they were instead intent in creating secular states. Before long some of these were even openly atheistic.

FURTHER READING

M. Angold (ed) *The Cambridge History of Christianity: Vol 5, Eastern Christianity*, Cambridge, CUP, 2006.

L. Bethell (ed), *The Cambridge History of Latin America, Vol. III, From Independence to c. 1870*, Cambridge, CUP, 1985.

L. Bethell (ed) *The Cambridge History of Latin America, vol. IV, c. 1870–1930*, Cambridge, CUP, 1986.

J. Frankel and S.J. Zipperstein, *Assimilation and Continuity: The Jews in Nineteenth Century Europe*, Cambridge, CUP, 1992.

D.C. Itzkowitz, 'The Jews of Europe and the Limits of Religious Freedom', in ed. R.J. Helmstadter, *Freedom and Religion in the Nineteenth Century*, Stanford, Stanford University Press, 1997.

D. Keenan, *The Catholic Church in Nineteenth-Century Ireland*, Dublin, Gill and Macmillan, 1983.

K. Parry (ed), *The Blackwell Companion to Eastern Christianity*, Oxford, Blackwell, 2007.

W. Simpson and M. Jones, eds., *Europe, 1783–1914*, London, Routledge, 2000.

B. Stanley and S. Gilley, *Cambridge History of Christianity: World Christianities c. 1815–1914*, Cambridge, Cambridge University Press, 2006.

13

MISSIONS IN THE AGE OF IMPERIALISM

'When the missionaries came to Africa they had the Bible and we had the land. They said "Let us pray". We closed our eyes. When we opened them we had the Bible and they had the land.'[1]

The much quoted saying of Jomo Kenyatta, father of twentieth-century Kenyan independence, encapsulates the negative perceptions of many as to the relationship between missions and imperialism. The statement is both evocative and provocative, highlighting the need for some evaluation of the vexed relationship between missions and imperialism in the late nineteenth century, which is the focus of this chapter, together with an assessment of the achievements of Christian cross-cultural work up to 1914. The remarkable global, and in time organic, growth of the Christian church from the late nineteenth century onwards, increasingly the result of the activities of indigenous believers, seems to defy the widely accepted narrative that missions were one part of a cruel imperial policy, shot through with convictions as to Western cultural superiority, and drive for material wealth.

By the end of the nineteenth century the visionary hopes of early nineteenth century pioneers for truly global missionary endeavour were beginning to be fulfilled, although the making of a world Christian church was still in its early stages. The years after 1880 certainly saw an increased pace of activity. The Church Missionary Society recruited just 721 candidates between 1800 and 1880; but in the next twenty years, 921 joined its ranks. The CMS missionary

---

1 J. Kenyatta, quoted in P. Jenkins, *The Next Christendom: The Coming of Global Christianity*, Oxford, Oxford University Press, 2002, 40.

force almost doubled from 630 in 1890, to 1,238 in 1900.[2] The early decades of the twentieth century also saw a significant upturn in missionary interest in the United States.

The explanations for this deepening concern are varied, and even conflicting. A range of religious, social, political and ideological factors were at work, although the relative significance of each is open to debate. That the high point of missionary recruitment coincided with the age of High Imperialism suggests that the two phenomena were connected, but the evidence for a positive relationship between the two is less clear than might at first appear.

IMPERIALISM AND COLONIALISM

The terms imperialism and colonialism have been subject to a variety of definitions, usually negative, sometimes used as equivalent and interchangeable terms, although they are to be differentiated. The essence of imperialism is the control of another country or people by an alien national or racial group, and is generally censured as inherently exploitative. It involves a conflict of cultures, but the conflict is not an equal one. One aspect of imperialism was colonization— the settlement of alien communities in other territories. Colonialism is another aspect of imperialism, a process by which an imperial power imposes its control, and takes legal sovereignty, of a territory without a process of widespread settlement, although colonization can be part of this process, such as in Kenya or Zimbabwe.[3] Imperialism can also take the form of wielding political influence without either formal political rule or human settlement.

Understandings and perceptions of imperialism were not fixed, and developed during the nineteenth century itself. In the wake of the French Revolution, imperialism was usually viewed in negative terms, as associated with despotic rule and forms of national expansion. In the middle of the century it was associated either with attempts by Britain to use overseas possessions to enhance power and prestige in the world, or with the aggressive militarism and extension of French power by the Emperor Napoleon III who ruled from 1852 to 1870. Later in the century the belief grew that imperialism could be a positive phenomenon, based on principles of morality, civilization, and colonial self-governance, and the 1880s saw a significant burst of imperial activity, with the so-called 'scramble for Africa'.[4] In 1895, Lord Rosebery, future British Liberal Prime Minister described Liberal Imperialism as 'maintenance of the Empire... the opening of new areas for our surplus population... the suppression of the

---

2   G. Hewitt, *The Problems of Success: A History of the Church Missionary Society 1910–1942*, Vol. 1, London, SCM, 1971, xiv-xv.

3   On these definions see B. Stanley, *Bible and the Flag*, 34–35; D.K. Fieldhouse, *Colonialism, 1870–1945: An Introduction*, London, Wiedenfeld and Nicolson, 1981, 4–6.

4   Stanley, *Bible and the Flag*, 35–36.

slave trade...the development of missionary enterprise, and ...the development of our commerce.'[5] National self-interest and philanthropic idealism, a sense of responsibility and trusteeship for areas under imperial control, deepened by a century of missionary activity and thinking, mixed incongruously with theories of Anglo-Saxon racial superiority, turned Imperialism into High Imperialism. In his famous poem of 1899, laden as it is with imperialist images of racial superiority, Rudyard Kipling expressed this sense of duty and moral obligation to take up the 'white man's burden,' to guard, civilise and improve the condition of the 'dark peoples of the world'. Lenin's *Imperialism: The Highest Stage of Capitalism* (1916) was a decisive riposte to High Imperial thinking, depicting it as the outworking of selfish economic and financial interests striving for world markets, which had precipitated the First World War.

Imperial expansion was haphazard, far from well planned, sometimes unwanted, driven at times by a series of crises within internal power structures, which provoked an aggressive response from insecure European nations beset by their own national power politics. It seems unlikely that there was much, if any, net economic gain to imperial powers from imperialism. Territories were annexed not on a profit-and-loss economic basis, but to protect existing interests. At times this helped them to move from pre-colonial subsistence modes, in which slavery could play an important role, towards modernization.

Entering the modern capitalist world and permitting citizens to engage in international economic activities, brought a threat to centuries old ideological systems. In the later decades of the nineteenth century some previously closed countries, particularly in the Far East, opened themselves up to trade with all the cultural risks that entailed. In Africa, the promise of raw materials, precious stones, and metals, led to economic and political manoeuvring to gain access to exploit such resources. Boundaries were often decided by Europeans that bore little relationship to traditional tribal settlement patterns, sometimes grouping together bitter enemies. The political history of many of these 'nations' has inevitably remained troubled ever since.

The decline of the Ottoman Empire allowed European powers to extend their influence, but in some places political weakness brought a return to a more rigorous form of Islam. The early nineteenth-century leader of the Fulani, wandering Muslim herdsmen from Senegal who moved across much of West Africa, was Shehu Usuman dan Fodio. He called for jihad against Muslims who refused to enforce *sharia* law. Jihad helped the Fulani to reform Islam in the less committed tribes, and to extend it to practitioners of African religions. In East Africa, Arab traders dealing in slaves and ivory took Islam with them as they travelled. In places it looked as if Africa might become predominantly Muslim.

---

5   Quoted in R. Koebner and H.D. Schmidt, *Imperialism: The Story and Significance of a Political Word 1840–1960*, Cambridge, CUP, 1964, 194.

Rudyard Kipling—'The White Man's Burden' (1899)

'Take up the White Man's burden—
Send forth the best ye breed—
Go bind your sons to exile
To serve your captives' need;
To wait in heavy harness,
On fluttered folk and wild—
Your new-caught, sullen peoples,
Half-devil and half-child....

Take up the White Man's burden—
And reap his old reward:
The blame of those ye better,
The hate of those ye guard—
The cry of hosts ye humour
(Ah, slowly!) toward the light:—
"Why brought ye us from bondage,
Our loved Egyptian night?"

Take up the White Man's burden—
Have done with childish days—
The lightly proffered laurel,
The easy, ungrudged praise.
Comes now, to search your manhood
Through all the thankless years,
Cold, edged with dear-bought wisdom,
The judgement of your peers!'[1]

1 *Rudyard Kipling's Verse 1885–1926*, London, Hodder and Stoughton, 1927, 320–321).

These advances placed the ancient Christian church in Ethiopia under severe pressure, and the attempts by Ethiopian rulers forcibly to convert Muslims to Christianity brought only superficial conformity.

The received wisdom that missionaries travelled to less developed parts of the world with the Bible in one hand and flag and gun in the other, or at least were the handmaiden of colonial exploitation, remains stubbornly persistent. The anthropologists Jean and John Comaroff described missionaries in early nineteenth century South Africa as 'agent, scribe, and moral alibi' for colonizers.[6]

6 J. and J. Comaroff, *Of Revelation and Revolution: Christianity, Colonialism and Consciousness in South Africa*, 2 vols, Chicago, University of Chicago Press, 1991, Vol. I, 8.

This negative account of missions advance is often held alongside relativist and pluralist views that all religions, or none, are of equal value, and that any attempt to encourage, or impose, a set of religious values where another already exists is arrogant and unnecessary. Of all religious systems, the one portrayed as filled with Western prejudices and inhibitions is Christianity. In the eyes of Marxist-Leninist critics, Christian missionaries were agents of Western capitalism and imperialism. In pre-independence India, missionaries were similarly considered closely associated with imperialism.[7] Black theologians have argued that trader, settler, and missionary worked together as the agents of the colonial powers for the subjugation of black people and the territorial expansions of imperialist powers.[8] In Latin America, Liberation theology developed out of bitter opposition to European colonialism in a region where the Roman Catholic Church had been identified with the colonial landowning elite. For their perceived complicity in colonial and capitalist oppression, Christian missionaries were accused of proclaiming a theology that destroyed local cultural values and resources. In the post-colonial period, particularly in the 1960s and 1970s, church leaders from the ecumenical movement and the two-thirds world continued to articulate the view that colonialism represented paternalism and exploitation. This brought calls for a suspension of sending missionaries to allow younger churches to break free from bondage to the West.[9]

Some missiologists from the West have accepted these accusations, condemning cultural imperialism, and the refusal of missionaries to grant autonomy to the churches they had founded.[10] Certainly, not all missionary personnel shared the enlightened Carey's thinking about the value of indigenous culture, the capacities of indigenous leadership, or Henry Venn's vision of self-sustaining, self governing, and self propagating churches. Many seemed unable to escape the influence of developing theories of racial superiority and inferiority.

The determined efforts of late nineteenth-century overseas missionaries stand in contrast to the declining in belief and practice increasingly evident within European Christianity. It looked as if the parent plant was attempting to send out offshoots to ensure its survival. This raises questions as to whether mission was the product of a recognition that the battle at home was being lost, and other, easier targets, for Christianisation were needed. Conversely, was Christianity readily embraced in the majority world because it was one aspect of the wider acceptance of modernity?

---

7   Stanley, *Bible and Flag*, 11–15, 38–39.

8   N. Pityana, 'What is Black Consciousness', in B. Moore (ed), *Black Theology: The South African Voice*, London, C. Hurst & Co, 1973, 59, quoted in Stanley, *Bible and Flag*, 11.

9   Stanley, *Bible and Flag*, 26–27.

10   D.M. Paton, *Christian Missions and the Judgement of God*, London, SCM, 1953, 25; see also K.M. Panikkar, *Asia and Western Dominance: A Survey of the Vasco Da Gama Epoch of Asian History 1498–1945*, London, Allen and Unwin, 1959, 293.

Yet the connection between growing Christianisation and imperialism is far more complex than simple explanations suggest. Indeed, it was not the wealthy, or politically powerful, who embraced the Christian message in significant numbers. Instead it was amongst the poor, the socially marginalised, and powerless, that Christianity achieved its most positive reception, especially young people and women. Most embraced the faith through the ministry of an indigenous convert, maybe a catechist, teacher, or evangelist, rather than from a European.[11] And the simplest, and all-too-easily dismissed, explanation for acceptance was that the message met the needs of the hearer, and that they believed that it was true. Philip Jenkins has pointed out the curious twist to Kenyatta's negative view of missions, for it is the African convert, not the European, who ends up holding the Bible. The tenacity with which the new converts clung to their new found faith is also remarkable. From very small numbers in the 1870s, and despite great initial persecutions, some 75% of Ugandans were thought to be Christians by the end of the twentieth century. Similar instances of growth despite early persecution were found in China and Korea.[12]

CHANGING MISSIONARY RECRUITMENT AND STRATEGY

The changing late-nineteenth-century social and political context, of which imperialism was a part, helped shape the form Christian missions took. Notable was the substantial growth in the missionary contingent of the United States, a nation without the colonial ambitions of late-nineteenth-century European powers. American churches had been more inward-looking in the mid-nineteenth century, but by 1890 there were 2,716 American missionaries, and 4,159 in 1900. Two hundred missionary societies, and nearly two-hundred thousand people, attended the vast New York Ecumenical Missionary Conference of 1900, opened by the President, William McKinley.[13]

Denominational mission societies became increasingly self-conscious, encouraging missionaries to found churches in the image of their parent bodies, to do mission 'our way'. National characteristic could also shape approaches to mission. American Methodist missions have been characterised as 'entrepreneurial and pragmatic, opportunistic and optimistic, flexible and adaptable.' American missions often reflected Finney's spiritual-pragmatic ethos, confident that with appropriate levels of energy, money, sacrifice, efficiency, and perseverance, results would follow.[14] Some Europeans complained this led to hastiness and superficiality, preoccupation with numbers, and over-emphasis

---

11 B. Sundkler and C. Steed, *A History of the Church in Africa*, Cambridge, CUP, 2000, 88–89.

12 Jenkins, *Next Christendom*, 44.

13 G.H. Anderson, 'American Protestants in Pursuit of Mission: 1886–1986', *International Bulletin of Missionary Research*, Vol. 12, 98–102; Bosch, *Transforming Mission*, 301–302.

14 Hempton, *Methodism: Empire of the Spirit*, 168.

on English as a means of education. In contrast, the European approach, notably by German missionaries, was steady and patient, emphasising the attainment and use of indigenous languages.[15]

Another very significant reason for late nineteenth-century missionary expansion was increased willingness to accept single women as missionary candidates. Missionary wives had long taken on duties on the field alongside their family roles, especially in the realm of education, with a recognition that some responsibilities could only be properly undertaken by women. This led to calls for women missionaries to be sent out to undertake specific ministries, such as teaching girls and other women. By 1900, there were 1,200 single American women missionaries serving on the field, supported by 41 different women's agencies at home. Some came with their own professional qualifications. There was also increased investment in the training of indigenous women, with 40 schools training Bible women in China in 1902, and a further 30 in India.[16] In 1887, the Anglican CMS opened its doors to single women missionary candidates, and between 1895 and 1904, sent out 391 male missionaries, and 425 females.[17] By 1910, fifty-five per cent of all missionary personnel were women.

The work of pioneering women helped change perceptions. The indomitable Charlotte Diggs "Lottie" Moon (1840–1912), standing just four feet and three inches tall, left her work as a teacher in Georgia in 1873 for China, where she operated against the wishes of her field director, and engaged in evangelism. In this she saw significant success at P'ing-tu. The many converts won through her ministry were gathered into churches, but as a female Southern Baptist missionary she was not permitted to lead these, and so trained indigenous pastors for the work. Within 20 years, the Chinese pastor at P'ing-tu had baptized over 1,000 converts. Lottie Moon also sought to raise the profile of overseas mission in her denomination. With only thirty-five male Southern Baptist missionaries in China compared to 500 ministers in Virginia alone, there was work to be done. She was a person of profound compassion, which led to her premature death. When famine struck, she could not bear to keep food for herself when starving children came to her door. She died in 1912 from illness brought on by malnutrition. Yet the impact of her work did not end there.

---

15   Hutchison, *Errand to the World*, 131–133.

16   On the role of women in overseas mission from America see P.R. Hill, *The World Their Household: The American Women's Foreign Missionary Movement and Cultural Transformation 1870–1930*, Ann Arbor, University of Michigan Press, 1985; D. Robert, *American Women in Mission: A Social History of their Thought and Practice*, Macon, Ga, Mercer University Press, 1996; R.A. Tucker, 'Women in Mission: Reaching Sisters in Heathen Darkness', in Carpenter and Shenk, *Earthen Vessels*, 251–280.

17   The role of Women in British Protestant Missions between 1865 and 1910 is explored in R.A. Semple, *Missionary Women: Gender, Professionalism, and the Victorian Idea of Christian Mission*, Rochester NY, Boydell, 2003.

In 1888 she initiated a Christmas offering, to raise funds amongst Southern Baptist women for missionary work in China. After 1918, it became the Lottie Moon Christmas offering: in 1992 it raised $80 million.[18]

Another notable female missionary pioneer was Mary Slessor (1848–1916), brought up in circumstances of great poverty and unhappiness created by her father's alcoholism. She worked for a number of years as a mill-weaver in Dundee, and sought to improve her own education, gaining vital experience in the slums as a Sunday School teacher. She was accepted by the United Presbyterian Church to work with the Calabar Mission, in modern Nigeria, where she arrived in 1876. With spirit and capabilities to match Lottie Moon, she was sent in 1888 to work on her own in Okoyong, a troubled area with significant economic and social difficulties. Here she stood resolutely against witchcraft, alcohol abuse, and the killing of twins, promoting education and practical skills training for girls. She became highly skilled in local languages, and was held in such respect that the most powerful chiefs made her the arbiter of their disputes. Such was her status locally, that when British rule was introduced in 1898, she was appointed Vice-Consul, probably the first British woman magistrate in the empire.

Mary Slessor was less of an evangelist, and more the creator of a framework in which Christianity could flourish. She constantly urged the expansion of mission into new fields, and in 1905 began a work in Okot Obong. Her work ensured that the Ibo were more extensively Christianised than tribes in other parts of Nigeria. She combined rugged individualism with great seriousness, tenderness with individualism, good humour and practicality, but she was a controversial character, defying much of missionary convention. Although single, she adopted a number of abandoned or orphaned African children. Her work and example did much to promote the cause of mission in West Africa, and to introduce women to opportunities for service in the mission field. Despite such notable examples, women missionaries remained theologically and institutionally less influential than their numerical presence might have suggested.

The late nineteenth-century also saw an increasing number of university-trained men being recruited by missionary societies. There was also a reduced expectation that missionaries should be ordained. In 1852 non-ordained missionaries accounted for 52% of the Protestant missionary force, by 1901 it was 70%, and they were predominantly women. The rising importance of medical work brought increased openings for lay missionaries, especially single women. The American doctor Clara Swain began medical missionary work in India in 1870. Although considering herself primarily an evangelist, by 1880 she was treating 7,000 patients a year. Fanny Butler arrived in India in 1880, and from her small dispensary grew a modern well-equipped hospital. Although such work was not new, the size, scope, and general acceptance of medical

18   See C. B. Allen, *The New Lottie Moon Story*, Nashville, Broadman Press, 1980.

missions was. The formation of the London Medical Missionary Association in 1878 was an indication that missions were taking medical work increasingly seriously. In 1880 the LMS had six medical missionaries; by 1905 there were 45, out of a total missionary force of 277.

The understanding of the role of medical work in missionary strategy also developed. From initially being seen as preparatory work, removing barriers to the reception of the gospel, it came instead to be seen as 'applied Christianity', no longer sub-ordinate to evangelism.[19] In China, where anti-foreign feeling was strong, medical work reduced resistance to traditional missionary efforts, especially with the growing effectiveness of treatments. Where there were significant missionary hospitals, overall direction was often handed to the medical superintendent, reinforcing the strategic role of medical work, which began to be ranked alongside educational work in its significance.

The increased popularity of interdenominational faith missions was a further significant component in the extension of missionary interest. As early as 1824, Edward Irving had urged the London Missionary Society to base its missionary practice on the simplicity of faith of the apostles, careless 'of all earthly rewards'.[20] Highly influential in the development of 'faith' principles was George Müller, whose brother-in-law, Anthony Norris Groves, worked between 1829 and 1852 as an independent missionary in Baghdad, and then near Madras, simply relying on the irregular voluntary contributions of friends from home.

Hudson Taylor drew heavily on Müller's principles in the foundation of the CIM. His firm conviction was that God's work, done in God's way, would not lack God's supplies. In America, other conservative missionary leaders endorsed similar principles, reacting against the large and inflexible bureaucratic structures that mission agencies had become, and the rising tide of liberal theology. They preferred premillennial theology, stressing the urgency of mission in the light of the imminent return of Christ. Matthew 24:14 became an important text, linking the end time to the completion of the missionary task. The watchword, 'the evangelization of the world in this generation,' was embraced because of its eschatological significance, with the belief that missionary effort could hasten the coming of the day of the Lord, which would not take place until every nation had an opportunity to respond to the Christian message. Many hoped this would occur before 1900. Such thinking influenced Grattan Guinness's Regions Beyond Missionary Union, the Christian and Missionary Alliance of A.B. Simpson, and the Evangelical Alliance Mission of Frederik Franson. The personal magnetism of inspirational founders and promoters of faith missions was important in their success, as

19   Porter, *Religion Versus Empire?*, 311–312.

20   E. Irving, *For Missionaries After the Apostolical School: A Series of Orations*, London, 1825, xxvi, 119.

James Hudson Taylor— A Million a month

'And the gospel must be preached to these people in a very short time, for they are passing away. Every day, every day; oh, how they sweep over! ... There is a great Niagara of souls passing into the dark in China. Every day, every week, every month they are passing away—a million a month in China are dying without God. And what a wonderful difference there is in dying with God as a Saviour, and dying without God'[1]

1 J. Hudson Taylor, quoted in M.W. Moorhead (ed), *The Student Missionary Enterprise; the Second International Convention of the Student Volunteer Movement, 1894*, Boston, T.O. Metcalf, 1894, 48.

---

were the informal theological and personal networks associated with Müller and Hudson Taylor. For them, convictions as to the fate of the lost remained a primary motivation to mission, and the Great Commission of Jesus Christ to his disciples, particularly as recorded in Matthew 28:18–20, was used to impel Christians with a sense of duty to mission. At the Mount Hermon student conference of 1886, William Ashmore challenged those present to 'Show, if you can, why you should not obey the last command of Jesus Christ.'[21] The holiness emphasis was also a feature of the Student Volunteer Movement formed in the United States in 1886, followed by the Student Volunteer Missionary Union in 1892. These attracted both postmillennialists and premillennialists.

The rise of the faith missions created a need for the training and education of lay personnel. The emphasis on the Bible as the core of missiological training underpinned the training institution which became the Moody Bible Institute, and the Boston Training School, founded by A.J. Gordon, which, through later merger, became the Gordon-Conwell Seminary. By the early twentieth century there were fifty pre-millennial training schools preparing workers for mission. Even the Scofield Reference Bible, the bedrock of premillennial personal devotions, was designed as a theological reference work for missionaries who would have no access to theological libraries.[22]

The annual Keswick convention held in Britain from 1875 onwards became a major recruiting ground for missions, calling participants to entire consecration to Christ. The visits of D.L. Moody to Britain in 1873–75 and the 1880s also deepened interest in evangelism and mission in revivalist and holiness circles. Universities proved a fruitful source of missionary recruits, and here Moody's ministry helped attract volunteers imbued with the public school, 'muscular Christian' emphasis on the value not only of learning, but also of leadership,

21 Bosch, *Transforming Mission*, 341.
22 D. Robert, 'The Crisis of Missions', in *Errand to the World*, 29–45.

James Hudson Taylor

duty, discipline, godliness, sacrifice, and athleticism. Notable recruits included the 'Cambridge Seven', who went to serve with the China Inland Mission in 1885. They were Cambridge University students from privileged backgrounds, some of whom had demonstrated sporting prowess: C.T. Studd was an England cricketer. They proved a powerful inspiration, illustrating the influence of the new missiological trends by joining the interdenominational CIM, rather than the denominational CMS as might have been expected.[23] Studd went

23 On the Cambridge Seven see A.T. Polhill-Turner, *A Story Re-Told: 'The Cambridge Seven'*, London, Morgan and Scott, 1902.

on in 1912 to found the 'Heart of Africa Mission,' which later became the Worldwide Evangelization Crusade. D.E. Hoste (1861–1946) became Hudson Taylor's successor as CIM Director, and W.W. Cassels (1858–1925) became in 1895 the first Anglican bishop in Western China. The willingness of the CIM to accept single women also boosted recruitment: as early as the 1880s they represented 45% of candidates. Often assigned to work in pairs, they were given opportunities to work independently of resident male oversight.

Priorities in mission work continued to be debated. By the 1880s, assumptions as to the value of both commerce and Christianity as handmaidens of the gospel were questioned. So too was Alexander Duff's emphasis on high-level education, especially in English, as the cornerstone of missionary work, because of the limited numbers of converts produced. In India it was the lower castes and tribal groups who responded most readily, not the higher castes as Duff hoped. Missionaries holding pre-millennial theology saw their task as to save the greatest number of 'heathen' from the degenerating world in as short a time as possible. Their immediate, individualist, and other-worldly theology, often pessimistic in tone, could prove anti-imperialist. Evangelism, holiness, and defence of Christian orthodoxy, were given priority over educational or medical projects—not that the benefits of these were entirely rejected.[24]

Some postmillennialists, drawing on the thinking of Albrecht Ritschl and F.D. Maurice, stressed the kingdom of God as more of a present ethical reality than a future eschatological event. This brought an inclination to downplay its eternal dimensions, including the return of Christ. The Fatherhood of God and the brotherhood of mankind became dominant motifs, with a more optimistic view of the spiritual state of the heathen, and the potential of non-Christian religion. In mission this meant a less explicit emphasis on individual conversion, and more on the steady inculcation of Christian Western civilisation to create systems and structures informed by Christian values. Education, spreading the benefits of Western technology and medicine, and projects of social relief, took increased prominence. At times what was advocated looked like a form of liberal imperialism. Justification for the transformational mission agenda of the 'social gospel' was claimed in the words of Jesus—'I have come that they may have life and have it abundantly' (John 10:10).[25]

In 1902, James Dennis's *Christian Missions and Social Progress*, based on extensive questionnaires and reports from missionaries, emphasised the civilising achievements of missions. Dennis reported that where missions

24 On Missions and Eschatology see H. Peskett, 'Missions and Eschatology', in ed. K.E. Brower and M.W. Elliott, *The Reader Must Understand: Eschatology in the Bible and Theology*, Leicester, Apollos, 1997.

25 L. Newbigin, *The Open Secret: Sketches for a Missionary Theology*, Grand Rapids, Eerdmans, 1978, 103.

had been established there had been a reduction in adultery, alcohol abuse, infanticide, polygamy and cannibalism, and increased industry and respect for women. He reported agricultural progress, schemes of famine relief, and medical advance. Even missionaries with a conservative perspective were bringing social progress,[26] although they interpreted this as the product of gospel advance, not the cause. Henry Frost, North American Director of the CIM argued that whilst 'Christianity civilises, it is never true that civilisation Christianizes.'[27]

All too often missionaries found it impossible to separate Christian influences from wider post-enlightenment socio-economic and socio-political influences. Those who championed the merits of Western scientific and rational approaches, as if they were part of the gospel itself, underplayed the challenge to the materialist world-view of the West inherent in Christianity itself. The model of civilisation striven for looked like conformity to the cultural norms of the European and American middle classes. By the end of the century, some missionaries were actively discouraging Africans from adopting European dress, for fear of creating European Africans with a nominal Christianity, devoid of true spiritual life. Others came to recognise a kinship between rural cultures in missionary areas, and biblical times.

As the extent of Christian missionary activity increased, it brought increased contact with other religious expressions. Traditional religions often came in as many different forms as tribal groups, demonstrating a deep respect for animals, plants, and the environment, and an awareness of the spirit world and the importance of ancestry, that Western minds found hard to appreciate. In his writings, James Dennis could not avoid making demeaning references to non-Western cultures. Debates continued as to whether enculturation into the ways of European civilisation was an essential pre-requisite for promoting the Christian gospel. Christian missionaries were often surprised by the vigour and adaptability of practitioners of other religions, who were quite prepared to imitate their methods of education and dissemination of religious literature. In China, Yang Wen-hui (1837–1911), who for a while associated with Christian missionaries, learned English and took interest in the development of science, then printed and distributed the Buddhist canon, which he gave to monasteries. For his work he has been called the 'father of modern Chinese Buddhism'. In India, some Hindus claimed Jesus as another incarnation of what is best in other religions, and used elements of his teaching, as means by which Hinduism could be reformed.

26   J.S. Dennis, *Christian Missions and Social Progress*, 3 vols, New York, Fleming H. Revell, 1897–1906.

27   H. Frost, in *The Fundamentals*, Vol 12, Chicago, Testimony Publishing Co., 1915, 86.

THE EXPANSION OF WORLD CHRISTIANITY IN THE IMPERIAL AGE

India

In 1858, the direct control of the British government in India replaced that of the East India Company. The official policy was of non-interference in religious matters, although government representatives disagreed on how this was to be interpreted. Heavy investment in the provision of education by Christian missions, some of which accepted government grants, meant that Christians, although only a small proportion of India's population and often drawn from the lower classes, became one of the best educated groups of society. Foundations were laid for the significant Indian Christian middle class of the twentieth century.

However, Hindu and Muslim leaders began to see Christian schools, which were attended in large numbers by non-Christians, as undermining their religious position. In the 1870s, movements for the purification of Hinduism developed, which were also strongly anti-Christian and anti-Western, made attempts to re-convert to Hinduism those who had converted to Christianity. Meanwhile, others called for a mutual recognition of the spiritual traditions of East and West, with understanding and respect replacing proselytism. Some believed that the best way to spread Christian influence was to permeate Hindu culture with Christian values.

These developments coincided with a fall off in the number of Indians converting to Christianity late in the century. In the 1880s and 1890s Baptist and Methodist sources criticised missions for creating 'hothouses' of subsidized Christians, who were at best dependent on missionaries, and at worst exploiting them. Calls followed for less education, more evangelism, and for approaches that reduced the dependency of converts.[28] The need for indigenous leadership was becoming apparent to all, except, ironically, some of the missionaries themselves. Imad-ud-din, was a leading Islamic scholar converted to Christianity in 1866 after a long spiritual search. He became a noted preacher, and writer, and was awarded a Doctor of Divinity degree by the Archbishop of Canterbury in 1884. 'Pandita' Ramābai, (1858–1922) the daughter of a Brahman scholar, became a leading teacher of Sanskrit, and embraced Christianity in the 1880s after the death of her husband. She became famed for her care for Hindu widows, and famine victims, and her institution at Mukti ('deliverance') cared for hundreds of girls, many of whom came to Christian faith.[29] The man who became the first Anglican Indian bishop, Vedanayakam Samuel Azariah (1874–1945) was raised in a low-caste Christian family. He worked with the YMCA between 1895 and 1909, and founded two indigenous missionary societies, before in 1909 beginning work amongst the outcasts of

---

28   Porter, *Religion Versus Empire?*, 276.
29   Neill, *Christian Missions*, 304–05.

the Dornkal region. A man of outstanding abilities, Azariah was ordained into the Anglican Church that year, and three years later he became the first native-born assistant Anglican bishop in India. His consecration, despite opposition from both missionaries and Indian Christians, reflected the growing capacity of indigenous Indian Christians. However, it was not until 1930 that he was ordained as a full diocesan bishop.[30]

Alexander Duff's influential educational work was continued by William Miller (1838–1923). In 1863 he became principal of a struggling school, and over the next forty years used Duff's principles to develop it into the nucleus of Madras Christian College, and affiliated it to the University of Madras. Miller argued that missions had been reduced to targeting tribal groups, and outcasts, and that an individualistic approach to mission would not work with Hindus. The college was designed to create the conditions in which Christianity could grow in a Hindu setting, awakening moral responsibility and awareness of the spiritual world necessary for later evangelical conversion.[31] It was, however, work amongst the tribal groups that continued to see most success in the late nineteenth century, with indigenous Christians playing a vital role. In the Telegu area alone, in thirty years one million people joined the Church. Amongst the Chuhras in the Siālkot district of the Punjāb the evangelist Ditt, a disabled hide seller, saw most of the community brought into the Christian faith by 1914.[32]

The connection between Christianity and imperialism in India is a complex one. Certainly Christian campaigns to end the practise of sati (widow burning), and attempts to undermine the caste system, in the name of Christian compassion were not the acts of those complicit in imperialist oppression. Together with campaigns against the exploitation of Indian peasants by European planters or Indian landlords, they sowed political ideals of the rights and equality of all Indian citizens that were to be of significance in the movement for independence which India achieved in 1947.[33]

By 1900 the Christian population of India had reached 2,735,000, a significant increase on the 820,000 of 1800. Roman Catholics made up the largest proportion, more than doubling during the century, from 0.8 million in 1800, to around 1.9 million. The rate of increase in the Protestant population was more rapid, but from a much smaller base of around 20,000 in 1800. Between 1850 and 1901, the Indian Protestant community increased tenfold, although

---

30   On Azariah see S.B. Harper, *In the Shadow of the Mahatma: Bishop V.S. Azariah and the Travails of Christianity in British India*, Grand Rapids, Eerdmans, 2000.

31   A. Walls, 'The Scottish Missionary Diaspora', in *Cross Cultural Process in Christian History*, 267–269.

32   Neill, *Christian Missions*, 309.

33   G.A. Oddie, *Social Protest in India: British Protestant Missionaries and Social Reforms 1850–1900*, New Delhi, Manohar, 1979, 245–251.

it should be remembered that the population of India had also increased, from around 150 million to 255 million. For all its expansion, Christians still numbered only a little above 1% of the population.[34]

China

Although the number of Protestant missionaries in China had increased from just one in 1807, to eighty-one in 1858, in 1860 there were still only 351 Protestant church members in the treaty ports. Roman Catholic missionaries were operating far more extensively: priests and converts were to be found in all of China's eighteen provinces in 1858. However, the work of James Hudson Taylor and Timothy Richard illustrates how missions thinking and practice was changing and developing.

The China Inland Mission, founded in 1865, flourished despite the predictions of those who expected its rapid demise. Indeed, in 1887 alone the CIM brought one hundred and two new missionaries to China. Although convinced of the merits of believer's baptism, Hudson Taylor downplayed ecclesiological differences on such issues in the light of the urgency of the missionary task, allowing pioneers to establish churches according to their own background, be they Presbyterian, Episcopal, Methodist, or Baptist.[35] By 1900, over a quarter of the 2,785 Protestant missionaries in China were connected to this non-denominational society, which emphasised the centrality of preaching and prayer in the mission task. The CIM asked for volunteers to go to the mission field without explicit financial guarantees, but in dependence on God to supply.[36]

Hudson Taylor combined conservative theology with a radical missionary strategy that was open-minded, and flexible.[37] The policy of extensive itinerancy was designed to subvert official Chinese restrictions on missionary activity amongst the mass of the populace. The CIM was also quick to bring indigenous colleagues into leadership positions in the mission—by 1880 there were more Chinese workers in the mission than foreign workers. The best known of these was Xi Shongmo (c. 1830–1896), a Chinese scholar who had fallen prey to opium addiction before his conversion to Christianity. Pastor Hsi, as he became

34   D. Barrett (ed), *World Christian Encyclopaedia*, New York, Oxford University Press, 2001, Vol. 1, 360. By 2000 the Christian community including adherents was reckoned at 62 million, or 6.2% of the population, of whom 40 million were Protestants.

35   A.J. Broomhall, *Hudson Taylor and China's Open Century, Vol. 7: It is Not Death to Die*, London, Hodder and Stoughton, 1989, 156.

36   Hudson Taylor's strategy is discussed in D.W. Bacon, *From Faith to Faith: The Influence of Hudson Taylor on the Faith Missions Movement*, Singapore, OMF, 1984.

37   Hudson Taylor and the CIM are thoroughly covered in the seven volumes of A.J. Broomhall's *Hudson Taylor and China's Open Century*, London, Hodder and Stoughton, 1981–1989.

known, went on to establish rehabilitation refuges for opium addicts, and he became superintendent of a wide area of the mission.[38]

Timothy Richard, a Welshman, was to prove a key figure in the work of the Baptist Missionary Society in China. After his arrival in 1870, he served in the Shandong and Shanxi provinces. Richard became a proponent of missionary practice which at times stood in contrast to the approach of the CIM. Using the instruction of Jesus to his disciples in Matthew 10:11, 'enquire who is worthy,' he argued that mission efforts should be aimed primarily at those seeking after religious truth and those with the power to mould public opinion. He came to believe that missionaries should promote Christianity in ways adapted to Chinese culture, and that the Chinese themselves should be the main missionary force.

Richard pushed mission into new avenues when a devastating famine was experienced in northern China in 1876–79, which cost some nine-and-a-half million lives. Richard used the catastrophe to call people to repentance and turn to God, but he also disseminated news of the devastation in wealthy areas of China and overseas. With David Hill, of the English Wesleyan mission, he became a leading agent in distributing relief funds. For some, the first contact they had with Christians was through their role in disaster relief, and such compassionate activity won the gratitude of many Chinese towards the mission. It proved a decisive moment in developing missionary consciousness, making emergency relief an ongoing feature of overseas mission concern, undertaken as compassionate service, not simply to pave the way for evangelism. Mission was about being and doing, as well as preaching.

Much of Richard's later missionary career was spent promoting, alongside Christian thinking, economic modernization, and Western technological advance in fields such as meteorology, designed to help in the event of a further famine. Wider knowledge was disseminated through publishing, and promoting Western-style university education. Richard hoped that Christian professors would permeate Chinese culture, particularly the rising intellectual class, with Christian ideals. American missionaries strongly embraced the challenge of developing university-level Christian institutions. The first was St John's College opened by Episcopalians in Shanghai, which had 13 students in 1880. Others in Nanjing, Guangzhou, and near Beijing, followed in the next two decades, run by Methodists, and American Presbyterians and Congregationalists. The interdenominational University of Peking was incorporated in 1890. In 1905, Shandong Christian University was founded by Baptist and Presbyterian missionaries. As in India, the strategy was problematic.

---

38   On Pastor Hsi see Mrs H. Taylor, *Pastor Hsi: Confucian Scholar and Christian*, London, OMF, 1972, and A. Austin, *China's Millions: The China Inland Mission and Late Quing Society, 1832–1905*, Grand Rapids and Cambridge, Eerdmans, 2007.

Many educated in schools and colleges accepted Christian baptism, but failed to integrate themselves into worshipping congregations, being more interested in the practical, ethical, and social dimensions of the Christian faith than its spiritual dimensions.

Richard also stood at the forefront of developing missiological understandings of other religions and cultures, especially the need for dialogue that involved giving, but also receiving and learning. In 1911 he wrote, 'There was a time when every religion considered itself true and every other religion false... the time is now come to say that there shall be only *One* religion in the future, and that one will contain what is truest and best in all past religions which reveal the Divine in them'.[39] Richard believed that in some of the Buddhist sects in China there were ideas which were God's preparatory work for future Christian evangelism, and his attempts to express Christianity in a form more acceptable to the Confucian mind were also controversial, and saw him accused of syncretism.

Failures in mission were, to Richard, not failures of the gospel, but of Western theology, which was in need of revision. At a time when growing theological liberalism amongst Baptists in Britain was being challenged by C.H. Spurgeon during the Down Grade Controversy, Richard's downplay of personal conversion, traditional understandings of sin, limited reference to the atonement, and absence of clear Christological reference in some of his published works, raised considerable suspicions of incipient liberalism amongst his colleagues, and caused the China Inland Mission to withdraw from association with him.[40]

The American Presbyterian John Nevius served as a missionary in China for more than forty years, with over twenty spent at Chefoo in Shandong Province.[41] He regularly visited Richard on his evangelistic tours into Shanxi, and was impressed by the mission stations he operated. Nevius's missionary strategy, which echoed themes from Henry Venn and Rufus Anderson, as well as Richard, was set out in his *Methods of Mission Work*, published in 1886.[42] Although he recognised the need to meet physical needs through acts of kindness, Nevius argued that the 'primary and ultimate work' of the missionary was 'of preaching the Gospel', using 'every possible mode of presenting Christian truth,' especially

39   T. Richard, *The New Testament of Higher Buddhism*, Edinburgh, T&T Clark, 1910, 142.

40   Stanley, *BMS*, 175–190. See also A. Walls, 'The Multiple Conversions of Timothy Richard: A Paradigm of Missionary Experience', in *Cross Cultural Process in Christian History*, 236–258.

41   On Nevius see H.S. Nevius, *The Life of John Livingston Nevius*, New York, Fleming H. Revell, 1895; E.N. Hunt Jnr, 'John Livingston Nevius 1829–1893', in *Mission Legacies: Biographical Studies of Leaders of the Modern Missionary Movement*, ed. G. H. Anderson, et al, Maryknoll, NY, Orbis, 1995, 190–197.

42   J. L. Nevius, *Methods of Mission Work*, Shanghai, Presbyterian Press, was later republished as J.L. Nevius, *The Planting and Development of Missionary Churches*, 3rd edition, New York, Student Volunteer Movement for Foreign Missions, 1899.

The Nevius Method of Mission

'Christianity has been introduced into the world as a plant which will thrive best confronting and contending with all the forces of its environment; not as a feeble exotic plant which can only live when nursed and sheltered...'

'Not giving pecuniary employment to new converts will probably retard our work for a time, at least so far as numbers of adherents is concerned, but it will promote work in the end...

'It is our principal aim that each man, woman, and child shall be both a learner from some one more advanced, and a teacher of some one less advanced... In this way much time is saved, the gifts of all are utilized and developed, and the station as an organized whole grows in knowledge, strength, and efficiency.' [1]

1   J.L. Nevius, *The Planting and Development of Missionary Churches*, 3rd edition, New York, 1899, rep. 1958, 26, 32.

---

widespread itinerant preaching.[43] Nevius stressed that converts should support themselves by their own labours rather than becoming paid agents dependent upon missionary support. The emphasis on Bible study and training was strong—each individual Christian was to learn from someone more qualified and then teach another. Those employed as full-time workers should be the best qualified whom the church could support financially, and church buildings paid for from the giving of local Christians. In all, a culture of dependence on missionary personnel and finance was to be avoided from the outset, lessening the pain of transition when missionaries were withdrawn. In 1890, Nevius visited Presbyterian missionaries in Korea, teaching his methods, which proved deeply influential there, although they were less positively received by his colleagues in China.[44] His work was also used in the classes of those preparing for missionary service with the Student Volunteer Movement.

The years between 1895 and 1927 saw China progressively throw off the ancient imperial yoke, and move towards becoming a modern nation state. Yet, ravaged by periodic famine, and periods of social unrest, China remained dangerously unstable. As political reform advanced in the 1890s, so did opportunities for mission, especially in the aftermath of the national humiliation in defeat in the Sino-Japanese war which weakened the forces of conservatism. Then in 1898 the Empress Dowager seized control in Beijing, executed some reforming leaders

43   J.L. Nevius, *China and the Chinese*, Philadelphia, Presbyterian Board of Publication, 1882, 346–7, 367, 369.

44   On the Nevius method in Korea see C.A. Clark, *The Korean Church and the Nevius Method* (1930), repr. Seoul, Christian Literature Society, 1937; R.E. Shearer, *Wildfire: Church Growth in Korea*, Grand Rapids, Mich., Eerdmans, 1966.

and began to re-assert traditional values. An anti-foreign mood left missionaries subject to periodic attack. China descended into chaos in 1899 and 1900, with the Boxer Rising, an extremist group who practiced occult rites including gestures like those used in boxing. Their hostility to the ruling dynasty was also channelled furiously against foreign communities, including missionaries, believed to be agents of Western powers. The bloodshed was horrific. Although amongst Roman Catholic missionary personnel, perhaps only five bishops, thirty-one European priests, and nine sisters, were killed, the wider Chinese Roman Catholic community suffered greatly, losing 20–30,000 members The Russian Orthodox Mission to China lost around 3,500 members. One hundred and thirty-five adult Protestant missionaries were killed, together with fifty-three of their children, and some 2,000 national converts. The CIM, whose policy was to refuse to call for the assistance of consuls to defend their interests, lost 88 missionaries. Many national Christians only survived by publicly renouncing their Christianity, although most were later restored to their communities.

Order was only restored by the intervention of Western powers, and the perpetrators of the atrocities were brutally punished. Compensation was ordered for the loss of lives and property, but most Protestant societies, including the CIM, declined it. Those who accepted were viewed as benefiting from Western military conquest, and the humiliation of China by Western powers. China became more open to Christianity especially after rebellion against the Ch'ing (Manchu) dynasty in 1911–12, and the establishment of the Chinese Republic, some of whose leaders had enjoyed missionary education. The heyday of missionary efforts in China followed, and an era of rapid expansion for Christianity.

Protestant mission to China attracted huge investments of time, money and energy. When in 1877 the first General Missionary Council was held by Protestant missions in China, 473 missionaries were reported. Despite political instability, rebellion, and loss of missionary lives, the number of Protestant missionaries and their wives in China had by 1914 reached 5,462, four times the numbers of 1890. The previous British missionary dominance was gradually being superseded. In 1905, 45% of Protestant missionaries were British and 35% were American: by 1922 the respective figures were 18% and 51%. The membership of the Protestant community in China grew from 13,035 in 1876, to 112,800 in 1899, and by 1914, over 252,000: when adherents were added it was over half-a-million people.[45]

---

45   K.S. Latourette, *A History of the Expansion of Christianity: Vol. 6, The Great Century in Northern Africa and Asia 1800–1914* (1944), reprinted Exeter, Paternoster, 1971, 337–38; Moffett, *Christianity in Asia*, 469, 473–74.; D. Barrett, ed., *World Christian Encylopaedia*, New York, Oxford University Press, 1982, 231. By the year 2000, despite the forced withdrawal of Christian missionaries in 1949, the professing Christian population of China was reckoned to be nearly 80 million, or 7.1% of the total population, with 71 million Protestants. The Chinese government estimate for the time was 25 million Christians, whilst others suggest 50 million as a realistic estimate.

The long-standing Roman Catholic presence in China gave it a strong base, as did the growth of its indigenous clergy. In 1870 the number of Chinese Roman Catholics was estimated to be 383,000, with 639 missionary priests and 369 Chinese priests. By 1901 the figure was 720,000 baptized Roman Catholics, and despite the tragedies of the Boxer rebellion, over 1.4 million in 1912, with 2,255 priests, of whom 834 were Chinese.[46] Nonetheless, the Christian community still numbered less than one percent of the 472 million population.

Japan

Protestant missionaries had entered Japan in 1859, but only during the 1880s did they begin to see any significant success in their labours. By 1882 the Protestant community included 451 missionaries and 25,514 members in 1888. Mission work in Japan suffered from much duplication. Episcopalian missionaries from America, Britain and Canada worked without consultation in overlapping projects before Edward Bickersteth (1850–97), an Anglican bishop in Japan, in 1887 drew Episcopal work together into the Holy Catholic Church of Japan. In 1877 the United Church of Christ in Japan was formed, linking the work of three Presbyterian missions.

Roman Catholicism was able to build on the large number of secret believers discovered by its missionaries on their arrival in Japan after 1858. With Japanese Roman Catholics numbering 44,500 in 1891, Pope Leo XIII constituted a Roman Catholic hierarchy for the country. The first Japanese priest was ordained in 1883, and by 1910 there were thirty-three, with a Roman Catholic community of some 63,000. There was generally a growing conviction that Japanese churches should be organised on a Japanese basis, with an indigenous leadership quickly installed. Japanese Christian leaders included the Bible teacher Kanzo Uchimura (1861–1931), whose bible lectures could attract a thousand hearers in Tokyo, although Uchimura steadfastly resisted the idea of the formation of a Church by his hearers.

A sign of the progress of Christianity in Japan was its invitation, together with representatives of Shinto and Buddhism, to the Three Religions Conference held in 1912. Christianity, thus publicly recognized, committed itself with the other religions, to promoting national morality, improving public discipline, and maintaining the honour of the Imperial Household. This created a dilemma for many Christians who were fearful of the impositions that Japanese nationalism might make on them.

Korea

Korea remained a largely 'closed' country until the 1880s, with the small numbers of indigenous Christians, mainly Roman Catholics, subject to rigorous

---

46 Latourette, *Great Century in Northern Africa and Asia 1800–1914*, 293, quoting French Roman Catholic missionary sources.

persecution. The work of Horace Allen (1858–1932), an American missionary doctor who obtained a position as the medical officer of the American legation, proved highly significant. Allen opened the door to Protestant missions after he rose to the rank of American ambassador to Korea, and physician to the royal court. The attitude of Korea to the West formally changed in 1882 with the signing of a treaty with the United States of America. Modernization projects led by American companies followed, bringing a Western hospital, and railways and waterworks. The first Protestant converts came about through contacts with missionaries across the border in China. The first was reported in 1876, and two years later, Suh Sang-Yun, a trader whose business took him into China, was converted. The small group of believers he gathered together in his home in 1883 became the cradle of Korean Protestantism. Methodist and Presbyterian missionaries arrived in 1885. The following year, the first converts from Protestant missionary endeavour were baptised. By 1894 some 236 were reported, with Methodists and Presbyterians leading the way. Thereafter the growth of the Korean church became prodigious.

The long cherished model of an independent, self-supporting, self-propagating national church was core to Protestant missionary strategy in Korea from the earliest years. Although when John Nevius visited in 1890 there were only around 300 Protestant adherents, and no ordained Korean Presbyterian pastors, he urged the practice of these principles from the very beginning. The strong indigenous leadership which emerged preserved the Korean church from missionary domination, and sustained it in times of opposition. Academic and theological training at a higher level was established. The Presbyterian system came to predominate in Korean Christianity, and the Presbyterian theological seminary of Korea produced its first seven graduates in 1907.

Revival in 1907 brought fresh life and growth to the church, with a renewed commitment to evangelism. So successful was Protestant mission in Korea, that the tiny Protestant community of 265 in 1890, had by 1910 risen to 167,352. The number of Roman Catholics had increased from 17,577 to 73,517.[47] When in 1910 Korea was annexed to Japan, Protestant churches fell under Japanese suspicions, and a large number of arrests followed in 1911, which substantially slowed the growth of the church. Nonetheless, the hostile soil in which Robert Thomas had shed his blood in 1866 (see chapter 9) had, within fifty years, produced a remarkable harvest.[48]

47 Moffett, *Christianity in Asia*, 531–545.

48 D.B. Barrett, ed., *World Christian Encyclopaedia*, 2nd edn, New York, Oxford University Press, 2001, 662. By the turn of the third millennium, Protestants numbered some 35% of Korea's population, and Roman Catholics around 8%.

MISSIONS IN THE FAR EAST

Periods of persecution against Roman Catholics in Indo-China presented France with pretext for military intervention in the 1860s, and eventually occupation in 1885 after 115 priests were killed. Under French protection Roman Catholicism grew substantially, with a large Roman Catholic population in the area by the mid-twentieth century, but between 1900 and 1914 only a few Protestant missionaries were able to enter Laos, Vietnam and Cambodia.

As with Korea, it was American Protestant missionaries who had a vital role in opening to Christianity the country of Siam, which was to change its name to Thailand, 'the land of the free.' They were allowed to offer education to members of the royal court in the 1840s, and again in the 1860s under the modernising rule of the Buddhist king Mongkut, and his son Chulalongkorn, who reigned from 1868–1910. Their influence was seen in the edicts of religious toleration proclaimed in 1870 and 1872. However, Thai national identity was deeply shaped by Buddhism, the national religion, with the nation's reforming king also acting as a reformer of Buddhism. American Presbyterians worked for eighteen years before in the late 1850s they saw a Siamese convert. Only with great effort was he able to persuade the missionaries that his conversion was genuine. Roman Catholic priests, who had worked periodically in Siam since 1567, were expelled from the country in 1779, but a treaty of 1856 with France allowed foreign priests to travel freely, and build schools and hospitals. The Roman Catholic community in Siam grew steadily, from 2,300 Roman Catholics in 1800, to 24,600 in 1896. The first Thai priest was ordained in 1880.

Although in 1912 there were 36,000 Thai Christians, they still numbered less than 1% of the population, and most were Chinese rather than Thai by origin. The total Protestant community in the country numbered only 5,000. Medical work proved an effective means of mission to the Thai: the first mission hospital opened in 1882, and attracted support from the king. A network of mission schools was started in 1852: by 1900, Presbyterian missions were running 29 schools, but only 24 small churches existed. Progress was little helped by the failure to produce a complete Bible in the Thai language until 1893, and by a confrontational approach to Buddhism. In 1894, sixty-six years after the first Presbyterian missionary reached Siam, there was only one ordained Thai minister. The growth of Christianity continued to be slow into the twentieth century.[49]

In 1898, the Americans overturned Spanish rule in the Philippines, ending the Roman Catholic monopoly of missionary work in the islands, although Roman Catholicism continued to predominate. The failure of the Roman

---

49   For further details see Moffett, *Christianity in Asia*, 531–545. Barrett, *World Christian Encyclopaedia*, 2001, 734 notes that in the year 2000 there were an estimated 1.4 million Christians in Thailand, of whom 1.18 million were Protestants, just 2.2% of the 61.4 million population.

Catholic Church to promote a Filipino priesthood and appoint Filipino bishops had produced resentment, out of which the Philippine Independent Church was formed. By the end of the nineteenth century it attracted some 7% of the population. American Presbyterian missionaries arrived in 1899, and Baptists in 1900, followed by workers from most major denominations.

The leading players in the establishment of Christianity in Indonesia were missionaries from Holland, the colonial power, and also from Germany. Mission work was accomplished at significant cost. In 1834, two American missionaries, Samuel Munson and Henry Lyman attempted to reach the Batak peoples, but were killed and eaten by cannibals. In 1859, missionaries from the Rhenish Missionary Society were forced out of Borneo after an uprising, and settled on Sumatra in 1861. In 1862 they were joined by the indomitable missionary pioneer Ludwig Ingwer Nommensen (1834–1918), from Schleswig-Holstein. Work amongst the Batak people was started. By 1866 there were only fifty-two Christians, but the conversion of some notable chiefs changed the context. In 1876, there were 2,056 Christians, and, through a genuine 'people's movement' numbers reached 103,525 in 1911. The original intention had been to form a Lutheran church, but by 1881 Nommensen's influence had helped to create a genuinely Batak church, retaining aspects of Batak law and culture that did not conflict with Christianity. Batak pastors were eventually ordained into equal status with the missionaries. Dutch missionaries were much slower to ordain local pastors.

THE PACIFIC REGION

In 1870, LMS missionaries arrived on the south coast of New Guinea, a deeply mountainous and conflict ridden area, in which over 500 distinct languages were spoken, and cannibalism remained. Anglicans arrived in the north in 1891, and by 1898 had built their first cathedral. Methodist missionaries began working on the islands to the east of New Guinea.

The LMS missionary James Chalmers arrived in New Guinea in 1877. Son of a Scottish stonemason, Chalmers was to New Guinea what Livingstone was to Africa. In his pioneering work he sought to win the confidence of indigenous peoples, and saw significant success amongst a number of tribes. After nearly 25 years of successful work in New Guinea, Chalmers and Oliver Tomkins were killed and eaten by a group of local cannibals.[50] Their deaths served to spur renewed and increasingly successful attempts at mission amongst unreached tribes.

Dutch missionaries from the Utrecht Missionary Union arrived in Western New Guinea (Irian Jaya) 1861, but after twenty-five years of work there were only twenty believers, with more missionary deaths than converts. A policy of

---

50 On Chalmers see R. Lovett, *James Chalmers: His Autobiography and Letters*, London, Religious Tract Society, 1902.

seeking tribal conversion was adopted, with native evangelists labouring for many years to instruct a tribal group in Christianity. The result was a Lutheran church which numbered some 200,000 in the 1960s.

With much of the South Pacific occupied by Protestant missionaries, Roman Catholics sought fresh fields in which to operate. However, in islands such as Tahiti, Tonga, and the tiny Gilbert and Ellice Islands, attempts were made to enter areas where Protestant work was well established. With the support of the French authorities they were successful in Tahiti, but not in Tonga. In order to avoid denominational rivalry in Papua New Guinea, under Australian control after 1894, Roman Catholic missionaries were assigned a section of the southern coast as base for their operations.

MISSIONS TO AFRICA

The death of David Livingstone in 1873 brought renewed focus on the Zambezi region, and his unfulfilled vision of introducing commerce and Christianity into the heart of Africa to thwart the continuing slave trade. After attending Livingstone's funeral in 1874, James Stewart, Principal of the Free Church of Scotland's institution at Lovedale in South Africa, called for the creation of a memorial to Livingstone, a great centre 'of commerce, civilisation and Christianity' in the Zambezi region, to teach 'the truths of the gospel and the arts of civilised life.'[51] The Church of Scotland began work at Blantyre (Malawi), and the Livingstonia Mission was founded by the Free Church in 1875, initially based at Cape Maclear, before it eventually moved to Livingstonia in 1881. By 1909 it had established eight mission stations, with schools, medical work, and industrial and agricultural training designed to counteract the influence of slavery. Livingstonia and Blantyre, eventually led by Robert Laws and David Scott, became distinguished humanitarian champions of African interests. The Nyasaland protectorate was established by the British government in 1895 after pressure from the missions to deal with social instability caused by crime, and Arab chiefs whose power and wealth owed much to the slave trade. Events in central Africa showed that missions could have a vested interest in the extension of empire, but their championing of African rights sowed also seeds for twentieth-century African nationalism.[52]

Leopold II, King of the Belgians, annexed the Congo in 1885, and declared it the Congo Free State. His action opened the door for ruthlessness and

51   J. Wells, *Stewart of Lovedale: The Life of James Stewart*, London, Hodder and Stoughton, 1909, 125–26.

52   On missionary work, churches and politics in Livingstonia see J. McCracken, *Politics and Christianity in Malawi 1875–1940: The Impact of the Livingstonia Mission in the Northern Province*, 2nd edition, Blantyre, African Books, 2000; B. Pachai (ed), *Livingstone Man of Africa: Memorial Essays 1873–1973*, London, Longman, 1973; J. Johnston, *Robert Laws of Livingstonia*, London, Pickering and Inglis, 1935.

exploitation, but also for free trade and Christian civilization. The Belgian government assumed control in 1908. In 1884, English Baptists began mission stations at 100 mile intervals along the Congo River, followed by American missionaries in lower reaches of the river. The mission stations were rapidly populated by freed slave children, outcasts from tribes, and young men desiring education and advancement. This brought quick numerical success for the missionaries, but with it a failure to penetrate African tribal life and culture more widely. In 1893 there were only seventy-nine Africans in the Congo Baptist churches, although numbers reached 492 in 1900. Baptist missionaries played an important role in opposing policies of forced labour and heavy taxation adopted by colonial authorities in response to the culture of lawlessness.[53] The American Presbyterian Mission at Luebo was more numerically successful. Church membership was 3,000 in 1904, and had more than doubled to 7,000 in 1914. Congo was one of Roman Catholicism's major mission fields, with the encouragement of Leopold, who preferred Belgian missionaries to French. By 1910 there were some 50,000 baptized Roman Catholics, with 191 priests, none of whom were Congolese.

In the south of Africa, mission was assisted by the friendliness of local chieftains, such as Moshesh, paramount chief amongst the Basutos. By 1872 there were over 2,000 communicants, and many more believers, in his region, with Moshesh having announced he was a Christian in 1868. In order to resist the encroachments of the Boers, Basutoland became a British protectorate. Khama Boikano of the Bamangwato in Bechuanaland (Botswana) also became a Christian before in 1872 he succeeded to his father's chieftainship. As a Christian chieftan, over the next fifty years he fiercely resisted the presence of alcohol amongst his people. In 1885, much of Bechuanaland became a British protectorate, but Cecil Rhodes' attempts to include his territory in the British South Africa Company were resisted successfully after Khama visited Queen Victoria to plead his case. Khama skilfully furthered the interests of his own tribe, whilst capably retaining his Christian integrity.

The imperial expansion of the later nineteenth century brought growing European empires into collision with Islam, then enjoying a period of revival and expansion in North Africa, and Sudan. Islam had taken a hold in Uganda, through the presence of Arab settlers, before Christian missionary work began in 1875. CMS missionaries reached Kampala in 1877, and were received by the young King Mutesa, and French Roman Catholic missionaries arrived two years later. After the death of Mutesa, the royal court was divided into Protestant, Roman Catholic, and Muslim religious parties. The region descended into civil war after 1884 when Mutesa was succeeded by his volatile eighteen year old son, Mwanga. The newly arrived Bishop James Hannington was speared to death

53   Manning, *Slavery and African Life*, 163–64.

together with most of his party on the orders of Mwanga in 1885, and repression of Christians was severe—some two hundred converts were slaughtered. The difficulties deepened in 1888 when Mwanga was deposed by his brother, Kabaka, a Muslim, who attempted to create an Islamic state.

Civil war was ended by the establishment of a British protectorate in 1894, in part influenced by missionary voices seeking to guarantee a Christian presence in the country, although the need to keep the headwaters of the Nile out of French or German control was undoubtedly significant.[54] Here imperialism worked to the advantage of Christian mission, and Uganda was peacefully carved up into Protestant and Roman Catholic areas, which served as a buffer against Islamic expansion. By 1896 Anglicans had 6,905 baptized members, and over 50,000 inquirers. Although the Baganda became great evangelists to neighbouring tribes, European missionaries resisted the vision of a Native Anglican Church mooted by Bishop Alfred Tucker (1849–1914), who served in Uganda from 1893–1911: it was only partially fulfilled by 1914.

Early mission endeavours in the mid-nineteenth century Kenya (see ch. 9) were built on by Anglican, United Methodist, and Presbyterian missionaries. They were later joined by agencies including the Salvation Army, and the Africa Inland Mission. The historic Christian church of Ethiopia, with its unique blend of ancient Coptic and Judaic elements, had continued undisturbed through much of the nineteenth century. Although Italian influence was to culminate in invasion of Ethiopia in 1935, Roman Catholic hopes of assimilating the Ethiopian Church were unfulfilled.

Areas of East Africa previously under the influence of the sultanate of Zanzibar were claimed by European powers, but this did not suddenly open doors for mission. Colonial powers believed that the maintenance of Islamic influence and the control of Christian expansion in Muslim areas was the best way to accomplish social and political stability, creating tension between Christian missions and colonial authorities. The idea of a race with Islam for Africa developed, with attempts to occupy areas before Muslims arrived. At the Cairo missions conference of 1906, W.R.S Miller of Northern Nigeria complained that the British government were allowing Muslim missionaries unrestricted access in the Plateau area, where they claimed people had long experienced harsh treatment and slavery at the hands of Muslim rulers.[55] There was also disappointment that the high hopes that Christianity and commerce would raise the moral and economic tone of West Africa remained unfulfilled.

54 The Bugandan political situation is explored in M. Wright, *Buganda in the Heroic Age*, London, Oxford University Press, 1971; H.B. Hansen, *Mission, Church and State in a Colonial Setting: Uganda 1890–1925*, London, Heinemann Educational, 1984.

55 A. Walls, 'Africa as the Theatre of Christian Engagement with Islam in the Nineteenth Century', *Journal of Religion in Africa* 29 (No. 2, 1999), 171–72.

ROMAN CATHOLICISM IN AFRICA

Cardinal Lavigerie (1825–92) was the dominant figure in Roman Catholic missions in North and Central Africa. He was appointed Archbishop of Carthage by the pope, and primate of Africa. By conviction, a missionary, Lavigerie hoped to turn Algeria into a Christian country, and a base for the extension of Christianity across North Africa. In 1868, he founded the White Fathers as a body of secular priests, with lay brothers in a community. They were bound together by an oath for life to work in African missions in obedience to their superiors. Any attempts at direct preaching met with strong resistance from Muslims, so they concentrated on practical demonstrations of Christianity. When a devastating epidemic of cholera and typhus struck Algiers, it left 1,800 orphaned children. Lavigerie organised care and support for them, obtained permission to bring them up as Christians, and settled them in Christian villages. Lavigerie worked hard to fight against slavery, which continued its pervasive hold in North Africa.

Lavigerie believed strongly that French expansion in Africa was opening doors for Roman Catholic missionaries. He was quite willing to work where there was already a Christian presence, such as Uganda, which became one of the strongest mission fields for Roman Catholicism, whilst neglecting other areas with no Christian presence. Lavigerie encouraged the extension of Roman Catholicism into Tanganyika (Tanzania), Nyasaland (Malawi) and Kenya in the late 1880s and 1890s. In Angola and Mozambique the colonial influence of Portugal left the Roman Catholic Church in a position of privilege.

The death rate amongst Roman Catholic missionaries in West Africa was as high as that amongst Protestant missionaries, with few surviving above three years. Nonetheless, fresh recruits were always readily at hand, and a significant Roman Catholic presence was built up in Nigeria, and in the Cameroons where after 1900 the Roman Catholic missionary presence was four times the size of the Protestant one. The creation of an African priesthood was beset by many problems, including paternalist European attitudes similar to those found amongst Protestant communities. Even in 1923 there were just 66 African priests in tropical Africa, excluding Ethiopia and Madagascar.

THE MIDDLE EAST

Early in the nineteenth century Henry Martyn had been able to engage in open dialogue with Muslim scholars, but by late century penalties against both missionaries and their converts in some Islamic areas had become severe, and converts were few. Optimism for an increased Christian presence in the Middle East, typified by the creation of the Jerusalem bishopric in 1841, waned. Hopes turned to some form of renewal within the tolerated Orthodox churches as the means by which Christianity would advance. Mission inspired by enthusiasm for holiness and premillennial thinking brought renewed engagement with Islam, furthered by the eventual decline of the Ottoman Empire.

The Irish Anglican missionary Robert Bruce spent two years in Iran, learning Persian and the teachings of Islam. In 1871, at the end of his stay nine Muslims requested baptism, but progress was slow and the Anglican mission never strong. It was 1961 before the first Persian bishop of the church was consecrated. A tiny mission to Arabia began in 1891, but over the next fifty years reported just five converts. After the British assumed control of Egypt, Anglican missionaries sought to work in co-operation with the Coptic church, and to engage with Islam through debate and explanation of Christian truth. Protestant missionary work in North Africa began as early as 1829, but the formation of the North Africa Mission in 1882 helped facilitate endeavours in Morocco, Tunis, Algeria and Libya. Amongst workers with the Algiers Mission Band was the artist Lilias Trotter.

SOUTH AMERICA

Roman Catholicism remained the dominant religious form in Central and South America in the nineteenth century, and by 1914 there were hardly more than 500,000 Protestants across the whole of this area. The Anglican South American Missionary Society focussed its efforts on Indian peoples in Chile and Paraguay who had not been reached by Roman Catholicism. Americans led the way in Protestant missionary endeavours. The American Congregationalist Robert Kelley settled in Rio de Janeiro in 1855, Presbyterians followed in 1859, American Methodists in 1876, and American Episcopalians in 1889. Foundations were being laid for the phenomenal growth of Protestantism in the twentieth century, especially in the form of Pentecostalism.

IMPERIALISM AND MISSIONS: CAUSE AND EFFECT?

The last quarter of the nineteenth century was without doubt when the framework for Christianity to become a truly world religion was established. It was also a period of significant imperial advance, a very mixed phenomenon, undertaken with a great variety of motives. Connections between the two are indisputable. Missionaries often concentrated on the territories over which their government ruled: when the French Cardinal Lavigerie (1825–1892) sent out his 'White Fathers' to Africa, he urged them to remember that they were working for France as well as the Kingdom of God.[56]

However, studies have shown that the relationship between missionary activity and the promotion of colonial involvement is far more complex than the sometimes ideologically-driven negative assessments have suggested.[57] The

---

56   S. Neill, *History of Christian Missions*, 349.

57   Stanley, *Bible and Flag*, 29.

need for protection for missionaries, missions' property and interests, adherents and converts, meant that the stability brought by the development of empire was a useful expedient to missions in volatile areas. This brought a danger that missionaries, in debt to colonial authorities for the protection and subsidies they brought, might collude with them, and not protest when human rights were infringed.

Missionary partnership with colonial authorities was seen in attempts to bring religious and social change through education, and agricultural and industrial development. The humanitarian agenda of missionaries, and Christian public opinion at home, ensured that the sense of responsibility over what had been entrusted to imperial authorities remained high on the agenda. Some advocates of mission argued that wise exercise of imperial authority could atone for a nation's sins, such as involvement in the slave trade, and be a force for righteousness.[58] Although playing a significant role in the colonial process, there was no unequivocal commitment by missionaries to imperialism, and proving a straightforward causal link between them and imperialism and capitalist exploitation has proved extremely difficult.[59]

The involvement of mission societies in conferences at which imperial policy was shaped illustrates this. At the Conference on Colonial Questions held in Berlin in 1885, large parts of Africa were effectively carved up amongst the European powers. In his invitation Bismarck noted the responsibility of nations to encourage missions and 'other enterprises which are likely to be of service in spreading useful knowledge'. For some this meant a strong Christian engagement, but the presence of Turkey at the conference meant that a far less clear articulation was possible.[60]

The significant work of missionaries who devoted themselves to the study of indigenous languages, to preaching the Christian message and convincing individuals of their inherent worth in the sight of God, and thereby empowering and developing the self-understanding of often marginalised people, should not be forgotten. Nor should the occasions when missionaries did call colonial authorities to account over human rights abuses. Missionaries continued their steady campaign against the continued existence of slavery in late nineteenth-century Africa, reinforced by decisions at the Berlin Conference of European colonial rulers. An international agreement for the abolition of the slave trade was signed in 1890, although a policy of gradualism was adopted, and in Congo it was ten years before the slave trade ended.[61]

58   D. Bebbington, 'Atonement, Sin, and Empire, 1880–1914', in A. Porter, ed., *The Imperial Horizons of British Protestant Missions*, Grand Rapids, Eerdmans, 2003, 26, 28.

59   Stanley, *Bible and Flag*, 38–53.

60   Porter, *Religion Versus Empire?*, 278–279.

61   Manning, *Slavery and African Life*, 159–62.

As the nineteenth century progressed, colonised nations began to be judged increasingly according to levels of civilisation of the West, and also according to the criterion of race, with Western racial characteristics deemed superior to those of other races. Mixed motives of genuine piety, patriotism, together with undertones of racial superiority, began to shape missions policy. Ecclesiastical imperialists argued that nation, church, mission and empire should be closely linked. The ambiguous relationship between Christian missions and imperial aspirations is amply demonstrated in the case of Germany, but parallels could be found elsewhere. Before the 1880s, Pietist influence had made German missionaries less concerned with the identity of the societies for whom they worked, and more with the desire to serve wherever the opportunities lay— many opting for the Anglican CMS. The Berlin Conference brought a decisive change. Some voices in the German missionary community called for colonial expansion both as an outlet for surplus population, and as a way of protecting the work of established missionary endeavour. Friedrich Fabri (1824–1891), director of the Rhenish Missionary Society from 1857–1884, despite opposition from others in the German missionary community, argued that the stability of colonial rule would bring great benefits to missionary endeavour. In turn, well-run missionary work would benefit both mission and the fatherland. Although German imperial expansion was not extensive, the sense of white racial superiority gathering momentum in Germany was repeated on the mission field. In places two Lutheran churches were founded, one for white settlers, the other for black converts, demonstrating little social or theological understanding of the concept of equality.[62]

As the missionary movement shifted from being the work of radicals on the margins into the mainstream of Christianity, the influence of the social and political thinking that lay behind late-nineteenth-century imperialism proved hard to resist. The value to governments of missionaries who settled in territories, understood local languages, and had a beneficially controlling influence over native people compatible with policies of civilisation, was increasingly appreciated. Working for the kingdom of God, and the interests of empire, no longer seemed incompatible. Mary Slessor, deeply respected where she worked, appeared the obvious candidate for consular office in her area, and it seemed equally obvious to her that she could combine the role with missionary service.

However, any simple correlation between the rise of overseas mission and the high age of Imperialism fails in the case of the United States. By 1910 the American missionary force had replaced that of Britain as the largest in the world: the sixteen missionary societies of the 1860s had in 1900 become 90. Yet this growth was not caused, or matched, by the rush for physical empire

62 Bosch, *Transforming Mission*, 307–312.

found in Europe, despite the annexation of the Philippines in 1898. Americans were keen to extend relationships into areas where fruitful opportunities for promoting trade existed, as in the cases of Japan and Korea, and this could open opportunities for missionary enterprise. American missionary thinkers thought instead in terms of 'spiritual imperialism.' Convinced that America had been providentially inspired to seek its own liberty, they saw themselves as promoters of religious and spiritual liberty.

Early in the nineteenth century Georg Hegel presented the course of world history as a progression from childhood, represented by China, India, and Greece, to adulthood, represented by modern Western Europe: 'Europe is the absolute end of history, just as Asia is the beginning.' Hegel was convinced that Western civilisation was indisputably superior to any other.[63] As such ideas became widespread, they inevitably permeated missiological thinking. Christianity was believed to lie behind the cultural progress and success of the West. Western Christian culture, by means of educational, scientific, and economic advance was seen as key to the social advance and civilisation of other parts of the world. When missionaries stressed the value of the benefits of Western civilisation, the susceptibility of missionaries to political influence, and the charge of Western cultural imperialism increased. Despite the endeavours of Timothy Richard and others to increase understanding of non-Western cultures, late nineteenth-century promoters of mission, still stressed the depravities, immoralities and superstitions of those to whom they ministered in order to emphasise the needfulness of their work. Particular attention was given to cases that most offended late-nineteenth century sensibilities—polygamy, human sacrifice, witchcraft, corruption and bribery.[64]

Many mission practitioners seemed unaware of their own ethno-centrism as they propagated their own values of morality, respectability, and individualism. Although Roman Catholic missionaries allowed a measure of 'accommodation' to local cultures, and Protestant missionaries allowed an element of indigenization, the limits of such were dictated by the standards of Western middle-class paternalistic benevolence. Western clothes, Western customs, Western forms of music and worship were promoted as the 'Christian way' in many missionary contexts.

CONCLUSIONS

The historic strength of Christianity in Western Europe, coupled with enlightenment convictions as to the superiority of European culture, created

---

63   G.W.F. Hegel, *Lectures on the Philosophy of World History*, transl. H.B. Nisbet, Cambridge, CUP, 1975, 197.

64   E.g. J. Dennis, *Christian Missions and Social Progress: A Sociological Study of Foreign Missions*, 3 vols, Edinburgh, Oliphant, Anderson and Ferrier, 1897, 1899, 1906.

a conviction of the 'manifest destiny' of Western nations to extend the gospel throughout the world. This sentiment corresponded with the heyday of colonialism between 1850 and 1914.[65] Attempts were made to distinguish between wise imperialism, which allowed opportunities for the spread of the word of God, and late nineteenth-century deviations. As the campaigning Congregationalist journalist W.T. Stead put it, 'What Antichrist is to Jesus of Nazareth, jingoism is to true Imperialism'.[66] There was a need to gladly bear the 'white man's *burden*'.

There were a variety of imperialisms, expressed in different contexts and by different imperial powers. In some areas, imperial domination brought the betterment of the people affected. In others, where imperial aggression was simply a product of commercial and strategic military considerations, areas benefited little. Whilst the high age of imperialism did coincide with the highest numbers of British missionary recruits, when missionary recruitment fell-away in post-1918 Britain, enthusiasm for empire continued unabated into the 1920s. Many missionaries were left caught between seeing imperialism as a providential way of reshaping the world, and remaining neutral so as not to compromise their message.

In the late nineteenth century, the visionary thinking of Venn, for self-governing, self-supporting, self-propagating, churches was not entirely forgotten, but was often set to one side as not yet attainable. Paternalist attitudes fuelled distrust in the capacity of the leaders of the younger churches for self-governance. The poverty of the churches formed did little to encourage this process of entrustment with independency.

The 'watchword' of missions in the early twentieth century was to be 'the evangelisation of the world in this generation,' a phrase redolent of the optimistic self-confidence of Western missions. (See final chapter) By 1900 there were over 520 million Christians from a world population of 1.6 billion, but of these 368 million were to be found in Europe, and just under 60 million in North America. The evidence upon which to base the claim that the world could be evangelised within a generation was shaky: some 54% of the world's population was still 'unevangelized'.[67] Protestant missionary efforts had produced just 1.5 million converts by 1900, although this had risen to between 2 and 3 million by 1910. In the major mission fields the younger churches still represented less than 1% of population. But the machinery by which hopes of world evangelization could be fulfilled was being put into place. In 1902 there were 558 American

65   Neill, *History of Christian Missions*, 322–396.

66   W.T. Stead, *The Best or the Worst of Empires: Which?*, London, 1906, quoted in Bebbington, 'Atonement', 30.

67   'Global Table 5: Status of Global Mission, Presence and Activities, AD 1800–2025', *International Bulletin of Missionary Research*, Vol 31, no. 1, (Jan 2000), 32.

and European missionary societies, with 7319 mission stations, 14,364 mission churches, 20,458 schools, 379 hospitals, 452 Bible translations, 94 colleges and universities. With a missionary labour force in that year of 18,682 missionaries, with 79,396 indigenous workers, the annual world missionary budget had reached $21 million.[68] Yet, the claim of K.S. Latourette that the nineteenth century was 'the great century' of missionary expansion needs to be set in wider perspective. The 1902 figures for missionary endeavour are dwarfed by those from 2000, when there were 420,000 foreign missionaries from all denominations worldwide.[69]

68   J.S. Dennis, *Centennial Survey of Foreign Missions*, New Tork, Fleming H. Revell, 1902, 263, in Hutchison, *Errand to the World*, 100.

69   K.S. Latourette, *A History of the Expansion of Christianity, Vol. 4, The Great Century*, (1941), repr. Exeter, Paternoster, 1971; 'Status of global mission, presence and activities, AD 1800–2025,' *International Bulletin of Missionary Research*, Vol. 31, no. 1 (Jan 2000), 32—figure for foreign missionaries (aliens).

FURTHER READING

D.W. Bacon, *From Faith to Faith: The Influence of Hudson Taylor on the Faith Missions Movement*, Sevenoaks, OMF, 1984.

D. Bosch, *Transforming Mission: Paradigm Shifts in Theology of Mission*, Maryknoll, NY, Orbis, 1991.

S. Gilley and B. Stanley, (eds) *Cambridge History of Christianity, Volume 8: World Christianities, c. 1815–c. 1914*, Cambridge, Cambridge University Press, 2006.

A. Hastings, *The Church in Africa, 1450–1960*, Oxford, Clarendon Press, 1994.

W.R. Hutchinson, *Errand to the World: American Protestant Thought and Foreign Missions*, Chicago, Chicago University Press, 1987.

S.H. Moffett, *A History of Christianity in Asia, Vol. II, 1500–1900*, Maryknoll, Orbis, 2005.

S. Neill, *History of Christian Missions*, Harmondsworth, Penguin, 1986.

J.L. Nevius, *The Planting and Development of Missionary Churches*, 3rd edition, New York, 1899, repr 1974, Phillipsburg, NJ, Presbyterian and Reformed.

A. Porter, *Religion Versus Empire? British Protestant Missionaries and Overseas Expansion, 1700–1914*, Manchester, Manchester University Press, 2004.

A. Porter (ed), *The Oxford History of the British Empire*, Vol. 3, *The Nineteenth Century*, Oxford, Oxford University Press, 1999.

B. Stanley, *The Bible and the Flag: Protestant Missions and British Imperialism in the Nineteenth and Twentieth Centuries*, Leicester, Apollos, 1990.

B. Sundkler and C. Steed, *A History of the Church in Africa*, Cambridge, CUP, 2000.

14

MISSION AT THE HEART OF EMPIRES: CRISIS IN LATE NINETEENTH-CENTURY CITIES

When in 1883 the English Congregationalist, Andrew Mearns, produced a small pamphlet about social and religious conditions in the city at the heart of the British Empire, he evocatively called it, *The Bitter Cry of Outcast London*. Describing the 'rookeries,' Mearns deliberately evoked the anti-slave-trade campaign, describing thousands 'crowded together amidst horrors which call to mind... the middle passage of a slave ship... courts reeking with malodorous gases arising from accumuations of sewerage and refuse scattered in all directions... dark and filthy passages swarm with vermin.'[1] The tone of the *Bitter Cry* demonstrated how the revival of religious life experienced across evangelical, Roman Catholic, and Anglo-Catholic traditions in the first half of the nineteenth century, had given way to preoccupation with social questions. In association with significant economic depression and unemployment, the late nineteenth century represented a watershed in European and North American religious life. It became starkly apparent that, as well as vast mission fields in Africa, Asia, and South America, there were also at the very heart of the Christian empires that had conquered those lands, vast numbers who never attended church, or who had little or no awareness of the content of the Christian message. William Booth, founder of the Salvation Army, titled his 1890 scheme for urban restoration *In Darkest England, and the Way Out*. Slum ministry was an extension of the nineteenth-century missionary movement.

1   A. Mearns, *The Bitter Cry of Outcast London*, London, James Clarke and Co, 1883, 4.

How the Other Half Lives, written also in 1890 by the journalist and photographer, Jacob Riis, shocked middle-class readers with images of poverty-stricken children living in New York's tenement slums. Riis described them as nurseries of disease, pauperism, crime, and moral decay, throwing up: 'a scum of fifty thousand human wrecks to the island asylums and workhouses year by year; that turned out in the last eight years a round half million beggars to prey upon our charities... they touch the family life with deadly moral contagion'.[2] So too in Germany, Wilhelm Riehl, lamented, 'Europe is becoming sick as a result of the monstrosity of its big cities'.[3] Mounting statistical evidence, and the views of social observers, and Christians who laboured in the urban heartlands of Britain, mainland Europe, and North America, combined to create the impression that physical decay was being matched by moral and religious decline.

To some, declining church attendance in Western Europe is convincing proof of the theory of secularisation—that the more modern, and scientifically advanced a nation becomes, the less inclined people are to resort to supernatural explanations of life and nature. Yet, the evidence and its significance has been much debated, and it reveals considerable variation not only between Europe and North America, but also within countries. Indeed, the relationship between church attendance and personal religious belief has historically proved a complex one: since the nineteenth century many have maintained patterns of belief without formally belonging to a church or religious organisation.

A vast amount of creative endeavour was ploughed into attempts to remedy the perceived crisis. For some, the solution was more of what had been done before, albeit in a more modern and efficient way. For others new ways of engaging in urban mission were required. The 'social gospel' emerged out of the theological reformulation some proposed, shaped by liberal theology, and the modernist agenda, an attempt to find an appropriate contextual urban expression of the Christian message.

Secularisation

At the end of the Civil War the American abolitionist and reformer Wendell Phillips predicted 'our cities will strain our institutions as slavery never did'.[4] Urban sociologists such as Lewis Wirth were to argue in the twentieth

---

2   J. Riis, *How the Other Half Lives*, 1890, Introduction, quoted in G. Clarke, ed, *The American City: Literary Sources and Documents, Vol. II, America as an Urban Culture*, Mountfield, Helms Information, 1997, 66.

3   W.H. Riehl, *Die Naturgeschichte des Volkes als Grundlage einer deutschen Social-Politic*, 4 vols, Stuttgart, Cotta, Vol. 1., 1854, 75, quoted in A. Lees, *Cities, Sin, and Social Reform in Imperial Germany*, Ann Arbor, University of Michigan Press, 2002, p25.

4   Wendell Phillips, quoted in J. Strong, *The Twentieth Century City*, New York, Baker and Taylor, 1898, 101–102.

century that urban life had created a different set of social relationships to rural life, and that this was part of the process of cultural modernity. These included the recognition and toleration of widespread diversity; increasingly impersonal social relations; the application of rationality to the processes of everyday existence; and secularization of tradition.[5] Religious organisations were required to respond to the profound challenges of this new social nexus. The relationship between urban growth, church attendance, and patterns of religious belief, raises significant questions about whether religious adherence is environmentally sensitive. Does the experience of the nineteenth-century Western urban church set a pattern which other societies will follow when they reach a similar stage of urban development? Did the coincidence of urban growth with rising class conflict mean that class-riven societies produced class-riven churches?

Secularisation has been seen as the process whereby the ways of interpreting reality are emancipated from assumptions of dependence on the supernatural—in Europe, the Christian God. Questioning or rejection of 'religious' assumptions, values, practises or institutions, as science, rationality, and bureaucracy advance, is read as an aspect of secularisation.[6] Max Weber called the way the modern world increasingly explained the previously inexplicable through natural science, medicine, and social science, *Entzauberung*, often translated 'disenchantment'. Rationalisation and disenchantment were both the process of secularisation, and the result of the process. Science replaced religion as the source of knowledge about the world, professional and governmental agencies took over roles once held by clergy, religious pluralism created relativism in religious values, and moral absolutes were no longer binding. The religious viewpoint became only one of many competing claims to authority. Declining church attendance, and separation of the church from the state, are seen as evidence of secularisation.

However, the simple equation between the spread of modernity and secularisation is not as straightforward as once assumed.[7] Growing attention

---

5   L. Wirth, 'Urbanism as a Way of Life', *American Journal of Sociology*, 44, July 1938, 1–24.

6   A. Gilbert, *The Making of Post-Christian Britain: A History of the Secularization of Modern Society*, Longman, Harlow, 1980, 5–9.

7   For examples see R. Stark and W.S. Bainbridge, *The Future of Religion: Secularization, Revival and Cult Formation*, Berkeley, CA, University of California Press, 1985; R. Finke and R. Stark, *The Churching of America*, New Brunswick, NJ, Rutgers University Press, 1992; R. Finke, 'An Unsecular America' in S. Bruce (ed), *Religion and Modernization: Sociologists and Historians Debate the Secularization Thesis*, Oxford, Clarendon, 1992, 145–169; D. Martin, *A General Theory of Secularisation*, Oxford, Blackwell, 1978; and *On Secularisation: Towards a Revised General Theory*, Aldershot, Ashgate, 2005. The secularisation theory is restated by S. Bruce, *Religion in the Modern World: From Cathedrals to Cults*, Oxford, OUP, 1996; Peter Berger has drawn back from earlier support for secularisation—see 'Secularisation in Retreat', *National Interest*, 46 (Winter) 1996–97: 3–12.

has been paid to popular religion, exploring belief patterns and their expression, both formal and informal, and the important role played by women in the religious life of nineteenth-century communities.[8] Evidence from the time of Britain's rapid industrialisation and urbanisation between the 1830s and 1880s, suggests there was no decline in formal church attendance, and that religion remained a very significant part of the culture and values of the working class. Indeed, the steepest decline in religious attendance seems to have not occurred until the 1960s, when industry was also beginning to decline.[9] Church membership in America, was only 17% in the 1770s, 34% in 1850 after the great advances of American revivalism, but in the late-twentieth century, the great 'secular' age, was above 60%. Projecting these figures forward, Rodney Stark argues, 'the vision of a religionless future is but illusion'.[10] The experience of the church in the twentieth century under communist rule in the Eastern Bloc and in modern China, has led to a significant questioning of the traditional secularisation thesis, and pointed to many different secularisation stories and outcomes in different countries. Although it has been argued that there is a strong *prima facie* case for thinking that West European societies underwent a 'significant degree of secularisation in the nineteenth century', it is now recogised that the term should be used in a broad and flexible way.[11]

THE NATURE OF URBAN GROWTH

Between 1800 and 1900 the population of Europe almost doubled, from 146 million to 295 million, and became increasingly urban. In Britain town dwellers outnumbered those in rural areas by 1851, in Germany by 1891, although not until 1931 in France. Between 1800 and 1890, the percentage of the population living in towns of over 10,000 inhabitants grew steadily from 4% to 28% in the USA, and from 21% to 62% in Britain. Although the USA had no cities of more than 100,000 people in 1800, by 1890 twenty-eight exceeded that size.

The population of Britain, doubled between 1851 and 1911, to reach 40.8 million. Much of this growth was absorbed into cities. London rose from nearly 2.4 million inhabitants in 1850, to 7.2 million in 1910. The 'Great Wen' spread inexorably—by 1891, 25% of London's population was suburban. No other British city could compare for size, although after 1900 Manchester reached 714,000 and Glasgow 784,000. Living conditions were often harsh. Bad diet,

8   See L. Davidoff and C. Hall, *Family Fortunes: Men and Women of the English Middle Class, 1780–1850*, London, Routledge, 2002; and essays by T. Kselman, and S.C. Williams in H. McLeod, *European Religion in the Age of Great Cities, 1830–1930*, London, Routledge, 1995.

9   See C. Brown, *The Death of Christian Britain*, London, Routledge, 2000.

10   Stark and Bainbridge, *The Future of Religion*, 1; see also R. Finke and R. Stark, *The Churching of America, 1776–2005*, Piscataway, N.J., Rutgers University Press, 2005.

11   H. McLeod, *Secularisation in Western Europe, 1848–1914*, Basingstoke, Macmillan, 2000, 12–16, quotation p. 12.

polluted drinking water, poor ventilation, and limited understanding of hygiene, proved a deadly combination. The most dangerous period of life was infancy. In 1899, some 163 out of every 1,000 children died before their first birthday; in Liverpool it was 218.9 per 1000 in the 1870s.[12]

The population of France grew from from 26.9 million in 1800, to 41 million in 1911, slower than in Britain, but nonetheless significant. The capital city again dominated. Paris had half a million residents in 1800, one million by 1850, and 2.8 million in 1911. Lyons and Marseilles were by then above half a million in population, and twelve cities were over 100,000 by 1890. With large-scale migration into Paris, and natural population growth peaking, urban congestion became inevitable. Land values, rents, and building heights went ever upwards. By 1900 around 50% of Parisiens were living in inadequate or overcrowded dwellings. Cholera epidemics continued until 1884, no surprise when 20% of Paris's drinking water came from the Seine, a river then renowned for its stench. Baron Haussmann's scheme of urban improvement greatly increased the number of sewers, and helped bring clean water to the city on vast aqueducts, but more prosaic domestic sewerage schemes had to wait until after 1894. Behind the fine facades and sweeping boulevards, slums remained. Paris was also spreading—between 1861 and 1896 the population of Paris grew by 50%, but that of its wider area, the Département de la Seine, rose by 203%.[13]

Germany's population also grew relentlessly, from 36.8 million in 1858, to 67 million in 1914, despite large scale overseas emigration. Germans were also migrating within the country, especially to industrial towns and cities. In 1800, just two German cities, Berlin and Hamburg, had populations above 100,000, with Berlin the largest at 172,000. Fifty years later, Berlin had reached 450,000, and just over 2 million in 1910. Over half-a-million Berliners lived in the city's suburbs. Hamburg's population at the time stood at 1.1 million. Munich, Cologne, Leipzig and Dresden's were all above 500,000. Such rapid, unplanned growth, meant that the poor urban living and sanitary conditions, with concomitant outbreaks of disease, experienced in Britain were repeated in Germany. In 1875, 20% of Berlin's residents lived at a population density of five persons per room.[14]

Population growth in America increased by 56.4% in the 1880s, and by nearly a third between 1890 and 1910, to reach over 84 million. The fastest levels of growth were in major urban areas, driven by immigration, particularly from

12   F. Crouzet, *A History of the European Economy, 1000–2000*, London, University Press of Virginia, 2001, 19–30.

13   P. Mathias and M.M. Postan (eds), *Cambridge Economic History*, Vol. VII, Part II, Cambridge, CUP, 1978, 244–247, 488–89; C.G. Pooley, ed, *Housing Strategies in Europe, 1880–1930*, Leicester, Leicester University Press, 1992, 227; J.M. Merriman, ed, *French Cities in the Nineteeth Century*, Hutchinson, London, 1982, 221.

14   C. Pooley, ed, *Housing Strategies in Europe, 1880–1930*, Leicester University Press, Leicester, 1992, p.241; Mathias and Postan, *Cambridge Economic History*, VII, 442–44

Europe. Between 1880 and 1899, some 8.5 million migrants arrived, and 10 million between 1905 and 1914, with 1.1 million in 1906 alone. They tended to converge on urban areas: in 1890, around 40% of Chicago's population, and 35% of Boston's, had been born outside the country, compared with a national average of 10%. A further 194,000 African-Americans also migrated from the south to the north, driven out by discrimination and violence, and attracted by economic opportunities.[15]

With a population of 800,000 in 1860, New York, Manhattan and the Bronx, doubled in size between 1870 and 1900. However, the scope of the city was far greater: Greater New York contained 3.4 million residents in 1898, second only to London as a world city. Land was scarce, and expensive. Manufacturing was centred around the dense concentrations of immigrant workers, many of them Roman Catholics or Jews. 2.3 million of the 3.4 million population were housed in tenements. In the Lower East Side, population densities reached 1,700 per acre. Elsewhere, Chicago's population rocketed from 109,000 in 1860, more than doubling in each succeeding decade to above 1 million in 1890, and 2.7 million in 1920; Philadelphia's grew from 565,000 in 1860 to 1.8 million in 1920.[16]

NINETEENTH CENTURY CHURCH ATTENDANCE
A complex array of evidence suggests that in late-nineteenth-century Europe, urban growth took place at the same time as declining active religious observance. Although Germany was over 80% Protestant, in 1869 only 3% of members of Protestant churches in Berlin actually attended services on a Sunday. Despite evidence of an upturn in religious practice in the 1880s, by 1913 attendance was down to 1%. Although Roman Catholics were more regular in church attendance, less than 5% of the whole population of Berlin were in church on a Sunday. There was great diversity across the city: the wealthy Western areas, where attendance was deeply rooted in patterns of social respectability, saw higher levels of church going. In the industrial suburbs, where poverty was significant, regular church attendance was at its lowest. Communion attendance in 1890 was 23.1% amongst the wealthy, but only 9.5% amongst the poorest. Wider religious observance was higher than church attendance, but far from universal. 89% of babies born to Protestant parents were baptised in 1910, 72% amongst Roman Catholics. 81% of burials of Roman Catholics were conducted by a priest, and 62% of Protestant burials in the presence of a pastor. 56% of Protestant marriages were in a church, and 49% of Roman Catholic

---

15   M. Bradbury and H. Temperley, *American Studies*, London, Longman, 1998, 132.

16   R.A. Mohl, *Urban America in the Industrial Age, 1860–1920*, Arlington Heights, Harlan Davidson, 1985, 13–17.

marriages. Around 5% of Berlin's population was Jewish, although before 1914 many converted to Protestantism to avoid social discrimination.[17]

A variety of causes for this declining pattern of religious observance were discerned. Berlin had long suffered from a shortage of church buildings; indeed between 1739 and 1835 no new Protestant parish churches had been constructed. Across the whole of Prussia, the number of church buildings only increased from 16,412 in 1816 to 17,854 in 1867. In 1890 some working-class parishes in the north of the city had 60,000 residents; Holy Cross parish had 128,000. There were 9,593 Berlin Protestants for every clergyman, and 26.5 Protestants for every church seat available. Berlin was an extreme case, but low levels of clergy provision were reported across Europe—in Paris there was only one Roman Catholic priest for every 5,760 residents in the peripheral *arrondissements* in 1906. Many believed this was significant in the church losing touch with the working classes in the late-nineteenth-century European city.[18]

Religious life was marked by increased religious pluralism in Berlin. Whilst some turned from the state religion to outright unbelief, others looked to the Free churches for the means to express their religious sentiments. The Apostolic churches, grew from just over 1,100 members in 1881, to 10,000 in 1910, and Baptists, Methodists, the Salvation Army, were also present. Dismissed by some as 'sects', they held to a strict moral code, and offered a strong sense of community, something which working and lower middle class adherents felt lacking in the state churches. The religious characteristics of Berlin were repeated in cities like Hanover. Although around 25% of the population attended communion in 1900, and over 90% of weddings were celebrated with a religious service, church attendance was only 5% in 1870, and despite climbing to 6.4% in 1895, it was down to 4% in 1909. German urban culture was characterised by a popular, if latent, form of piety, particularly expressed at times of personal or national crisis—illness, tragedy, epidemic, or war. Although Berlin's churches were crowded at major religious festivals, and 95% of the population were still affiliated to either the Protestant, Roman Catholic, or Jewish communities in 1914,[19] on a weekly basis, the level pattern of church attendance remained low. Whether Berlin conclusively proves the case that late nineteenth century modernity brought secularisation and religious decline is debateable, as evidence from other cities shows.

Although the city of Paris was notorious for high levels of religious

17   H. McLeod, *Piety and Poverty: Working Class Religion in Berlin, London, and New York, 1870–1914*, New York, Holmes and Meier, 1996; pp. 10–20; McLeod, *European Religion*, 12–15.

18   McLeod, *Piety and Poverty*, 1–8.

19   McLeod, *Piety and Poverty*, 17–19; McLeod, *European Religion*, 90–113; McLeod, *Religion and the People of Western Europe*, Oxford, OUP, 1981, 81–83.

indifference and unbelief, church attendance in the early twentieth century was still 15%, far higher than in Berlin.[20] Although the lowest levels of religious attendance were most apparent in urban areas, as in other parts of Europe, it seems that urban dwellers were replicating rural patterns. Attendance at Easter communion varied greatly. 72.5% participated in Metz, whereas just 4.9% of men and 24.1% of women participated in Limoges. Although in Paris the number of children being baptised fell from 89.2% to 58.6% between 1865 and 1908, and the percentage of marriages that included a religious service fell from 84% to 57.3% between 1875 and 1908, in a city reputed for indifference and unbelief the majority were still opting for Roman Catholic rites of passage. The major difficulty for the Roman Catholic Church was keeping pace with the physical expansion of Paris. The eastern working-class quarter of Belleville grew in size from 96,147 in 1861 to 216,620 in 1911, but throughout that period was served by only three parishes. Between 1861 and 1914, the number of Parisiens per priest increased from 3,056 to 4,790. There was also a great disparity of religious practice within the city. In the seventh *arrondissement*, an aristocratic area, 45.9% of the population took communion at Easter, and almost 90% chose a religious ceremony for their funeral, whereas only 5.8% attended communion in the twentieth *arrondissement*, and only 10.7% had a religious funeral. Even within classes there was diversity—the upper middle class were noted for their religious adherence, the lower middle class for being strongly anti-clerical.[21]

Evidence grew that working-class Parisien men were rejecting Roman Catholicism. For this, a variety of causes were proposed: for some the close association between Roman Catholicism and the higher social orders was a cause of resentment. Yet, even where many were disillusioned with, or indifferent to, its teachings and official practice, most retained a notional adherence to it through the rites of passage, although the movement for civil burial after the 1860s proved a major challenge. For others, socialism and nationalism were a form of religion, and spiritism and the occult also proved attractive. At times, dividing lines were unclear—the folk belief of many Parisians mixed Roman Catholic and occult elements. Nonetheless, rather than atheism triumphing in Paris, belief patterns were adapted and changed to suit personal circumstances.

In Britain complaints as to the low state of religious life in urban areas had existed since the eighteenth century. The 1851 Religious Census offers significant insight into religious behaviour at the time, although the reliability of the statistics produced has been justifiably questioned. Church seats were available for 57% of the 17,927,609 population, although in places for less than 20%.

---

20 A significant study of religious experience especially in Paris in the period 1870–1914 is T. Kselman, 'The Varieties of Religious Expereince in Urban France', in H. McLeod, ed., *European Religion in the Age of Great Cities*, 165–190. What follows is largely based on Kselman's study.

21 McLeod, *European Religion*, 26–31.

10,896,066 church attendances were counted on census Sunday, although these were spread across several services during the day, and some attended more than once. After allowances were made for those who were unwell, required to work on a Sunday, or who were looking after children, it was estimated that 12,549,326 (70%) of the population could have attended that Sunday in 1851, but only 7,261,032 did so. This meant that 5,288,294 of those able to attend at least one service 'neglected altogether to do so'. With only between 35% and 50% of the population in church, the majority were elsewhere on a Sunday. There were great regional variations, with attendance as high as 71.4% in some rural areas, 49.7% in towns with a population of over 10,000, but just 34.7% in industrial Manchester. Whether this was a high point compared to earlier in the century is unclear.[22]

Explanations of the evidence have been varied. Horace Mann, who compiled the statistics and the accompanying report, was sure that it was the labouring poor, in the most crowded parts of the cities, who were least likely to attend church. This he attributed to 'inert indifference', rather than overt infidelity. Non-attendees were 'unconscious secularists... engrossed by the demands, the trials, or pleasures of the passing hour, and ignorant or careless of a future.'[23] A strong correlation has been observed between levels of attendance in cities and in the rural areas from which many had migrated. Although church attendance in Manchester was under 35%, in Cumbria, a county from which many urban migrants came, it was just 37.3%. A similar census conducted in Scotland suggested overall church attendance was slightly higher than in England, although there were more multiple attendances.

Further local surveys undertaken between 1851 and 1881, decades of rapid population growth, suggest church attendance was around 38%. Churches were just about holding their own in percentage terms, and seeing numerical increase in attendance and membership. Nonetheless, the real number of those not attending church was also increasing. The late 1880s appear the tipping point, after which the trend is a gentle decline. The *Daily News* religious census conducted in London in 1902–03 reported around one million of Londoners attending worship services, only 22% of the population, or 19% allowing for multiple attendances. There were great variations, from 6% in the poor East End area of Bethnal Green, to 43% in leafy Blackheath. Other religious groups reported similar experiences. In 1903 synagogue attendance in London was reckoned to be just 25% of the Jewish population on the first day of Passover.

22 K.S. Inglis, 'Patterns of Religious Worship in 1851', *Journal of Ecclesiastical History*, 11, 1960; N.F. Pickering, 'The 1851 Census a Useless Experiment?', *Journal of Sociology*, Vol 18, No. 4, 1967; H. Mann, *Census of Great Britain, 1851: Religious Worship, England and Wales. Report and Tables*, London, Eyre and Spottiswode, 1853, p.cxxxix—cli.

23 H. Mann, *Census*, p.clviii 2, 39.

The evidence of oral historians studying the period from the late 1870s to 1914 yields somewhat higher figures, with 40% of working class mothers reported as attending church in industrial areas, and between 20 and 40% of men. These figures reached 50% in Wales and Scotland.[24]

One of the difficulties in discerning an inevitable link between the development of modern urban and industrial societies, and a loss of religious faith in the late nineteenth century, is the experience of the churches in the American city. Here there was a much higher level of working-class religious participation than seems evident in European cities. Whilst a close relationship between urbanisation and secularisation could be claimed on the basis of evidence from the migrant Jews of Eastern Europe, or German Lutheran migrants to America, the situation was different amongst Roman Catholics. The American population grew by 33.6% between 1890 and 1906, but church membership increased by 60% across America, and by 87% in the cities. The most notable growth was experienced by the Roman Catholic Church, which grew by 93.5% overall, and 101.8% in the 117 largest urban areas. Protestant membership grew by 44.8% nationally, and 71.7% in urban areas. By 1906, the number of Americans who were members of a church was 39%, and in cities the figure was 46%. Despite fears to the contrary, church adherence responded positively to the American urban environment, as religious organisations reacted with innovation and flexibility to the new challenges.[25]

The extent of religious diversity, with a wide variety of faith expressions, especially among Protestants, was a notable product of migration. Competition between the Protestant and Roman Catholic traditions served to consolidate their relative identities. New York was a case in point: in 1870, 45% of its population had been born in other countries. By 1914, Roman Catholics (Irish, Italian, and German), Lutherans and Jews made up 75% of the population: most of them were working-class, with the majority maintaining a religious profession. The place of religion within urban migrant communities varied. For some, the new cultural context was a place in which patterns and traditions from the past were to be upheld and change resisted, for others adaptation was positively embraced. The flourishing black Baptist, Methodist, Holiness and Pentecostal churches often served as a way of celebrating black identity.[26]

24 O. Chadwick, *Victorian Church*, Vol 2, London, A & C. Black, 1970, 225–227, quoting *Daily News* religious census 1881 and *British Weekly* religious census 1886; H. McLeod, 'New Perspectives on Victorian Working-Class Religion: The Oral Evidence', *Oral History Journal*, 14 (1986): pp. 31–49.

25 Bureau of the Census statistics, cited in K.J. Christiano, *Religious Diversity and Social Change: American Cities, 1890–1906*, Cambridge, Cambridge University Press, 1987, 20–21.

26 Christiano, *Religious Diversity and Social* Change, 117–155; McLeod, *Piety and Poverty*, 49–54; B.E. Carroll, *The Routledge Historical Atlas of Religion in America*, New York, Routledge, 2000, 120–123; R.M. Miller and T.D. Marzik, eds., *Immigrants and Religion in Urban America*, Philadelphia, Temple University Press, 1977.

Size of Town	Population	Anglican attenders	% of total population	Non-Anglican Attenders	% of overall population	Total Number of attenders	% of overall population
London	2,362,236	338,617	14.3%	260,472	11.1%	599,089	25.4%
Towns over 100,000 population (8 towns)	1,268,507	143,808	11.3%	201,757	15.9%	345,565	27.2%
Towns 50,000–100,000 (17 towns)	1,105,421	154,155	13.9%	236,513	21.4%	390,668	35.3%
Towns 20,000 – 50,000 (34 towns)	1,033,964	197,555	19.1%	210,897	20.4%	408,452	39.5%
All Towns over 20,000	5,770,128	834,135	14.5%	909,639	15.7%	1,743,774	30.2%
All places under 20,000	12,156,681	2,694,232	22.2%	2,826,038	23.2%	5,520,270	45.4%
England and Wales Total	17,927,609	3,528,367	19.7%	3,735,677	20.2%	7,264,044	40.5%

Source: Census of England and Wales: Religious Worship 1851, Tables, pp. clxxvii-clxxix; ccxcvii-ccxcviii.

The total number of attenders was calculated by counting two-thirds of total attendances to account for multiple attendances.

At the beginning of the twentieth century, Manhattan church attendance was 38.6% of the population, 49.6% amongst Roman Catholics, far greater than in European cities. Church membership was even higher: 59.4% overall, and 81.6% amongst Roman Catholics. The highest levels of religious adherence were recorded amongst the 34,400 Baptists, of whom 79.1% were church members, and 79% attended church.[27] All this suggests a high level of working-class religious practice: over half of the 22% of New York's population of 'Irish' stock were employed in semi-skilled or unskilled occupations, and 91% of them identified themselves as Roman Catholics.

The German immigrant community of New York was less inclined to religious practice. Of some 250,000 German Roman Catholics in 1901, only about 69,300 were members of Roman Catholic parishes. In Manhattan, Lutherans recorded the lowest levels of membership at 13.1%, and attendance of just 5.2%. This replicated the low attendance patterns of the fatherland. Choirs, clubs and lodges often met on a Sunday in competition with church services.[28] Nonetheless, many thousands retained a Lutheran connection, expressed through participation in rites of passage—weddings, funerals, baptisms, and attendance at occasional services.

Eastern-European-born Jews constituted another significant section of New York's immigrant population. By 1915, a quarter of the city's population was Jewish. They settled at first in Manhattan, working in the garment industry, then spread into Brooklyn, Harlem, and the Bronx. They appeared a highly visible and thriving community, building some large, prestigious synagogues, although many congregations met in rented premises and were too small to pay a rabbi. The percentage of Jews claiming affiliation to a synagogue was lower than that for Roman Catholic or Protestant church membership—only 26% in Eastern Brooklyn. Many younger American-born Jews preferred to identify themselves as American, rather than through their Jewish roots. Interest in socialism and secularism, strong in the Russian Jewish community, was also reflected amongst New York Jews. Yet, a strong sense of Jewish identity remained, even if religious practice was declining. A distinctively American form of Judaism emerged, shaped by the different sub-cultures of immigrant communities, and characterised by pluralism of expression, including Orthodox, Reform, and Conservative forms.[29]

Working Class Religious Life
The attitude of the urban working class to religion in the nineteenth century has proved of particular interest to historians. Friedrich Engels' observation

27 *New York Times*, 24 November 1902.

28 H. McLeod, *Piety and Poverty*, 62–66.

29 On Jewish migration and settlement in New York see I. Howe, *World of our Fathers*, New York, New York University Press, 2005; McLeod, *Piety and Poverty*, 74–79.

in 1844 that 'the workers are not religious and do not attend church,'[30] appears to confirm the viewpoint of those who claim an unmistakable link between urbanisation and secularisation, with the growing influence of working-class consciousness and organisation turning people away from formal religious expression. The fragmented nature of nineteenth-century urban society, with its local subcultures, and slum areas in which there was minimal social control, is also believed to have rendered the supervision of morals, belief, or religious practice, difficult. Yet, patterns of religious attendance remained surprisingly robust. The capacity of churches to adapt to social change, develop new missionary and pastoral strategies and institutions, was notable. For all their diversity, and tension, nineteenth-century cities displayed a significant functional pluralism.

Local studies of individual churches from across a range of denominations, have revealed strong levels of working-class church membership and adherence. As they were the largest segment of the population, this is unsurprising. In Glasgow, between 72% and 87% of church members were working class, and this was above 90% in some Manchester congregations.[31] Church attendance amongst the working-class Irish immigrant population of both England and Scotland also remained high. In Wales, most nonconformist chapels remained solidly working class in membership, strongly influencing cultural life in the Welsh valleys. The evidence suggests that the British working class generally continued to hold religion as a significant element of its values until the early twentieth century, when religious alienation amongst working men began to become more strongly present.[32]

One notable feature was the greater propensity towards religious adherence by women than men, with often two female members of each congregation for every male. Churches and chapels were considered a culturally acceptable environment for social engagement for women, whereas church attendance was not generally associated with images of masculinity. In Paris, women tended to be upholders of domestic piety, especially among the middle classes. Walls were adorned with cruifixes, in the corners of rooms stood statues of the Virgin Mary, prayers were offered at mealtimes and at the start and end of each day. In Britain, Roman Catholic Churches appeared to have some success in retaining the adherence of working men, in part through the provision of Roman Catholic Social Clubs.[33]

---

30   F. Engels, *Condition of the Working Class in England, 1844*, repr. Oxford, Blackwell, 1958, 125.

31   C.D. Field, 'The Social Structure of English Methodism', *British Journal of Sociology*, XXVIII, 1977; P. Hillis, 'Presbyterianism and Social Class in Nineteenth Century Glasgow, a Study of Nine Churches', *Journal of Ecclesiastical History*, XXXII, 1981; I.J. Shaw, *High Calvinists in Action*, Oxford, OUP, 2002, 121–24.

32   See E.T. Davies, *Religion in the Industrial Revolution in South Wales*, Cardiff, University of Wales Press, 1965.

33   H. McLeod (ed), *European Religion*, 23–31.

Whilst studies in the mid-twentieth century emphasised the long-standing weakness of the churches in urbanised and industrialised areas, the inadequacy of attendance statistics as an accurate measurement of religious attitudes has been increasingly recognised. The presence of a 'diffusive,' popular Christianity, identified by Horace Mann in 1851, with its acceptance of a range of recognisably Christian beliefs, and a general commitment to a Christian ethic, proved remarkably persistent throughout the centuries, and across European cities.[34] It was in good part the result of the ongoing efforts of churches. A pattern of 'believing without belonging' was established, which became more pronounced in the later decades of the nineteenth century.[35]

The causes of declining levels of religious attendance were much debated. An increased focus was placed on the impact of environment. When Andrew Mearns described the 'rookeries' of London in *The Bitter Cry*, he questioned how moral probity, let alone religious practice, could be maintained in such conditions. In Glasgow, Donald Macleod highlighted the 'suggestive' coincidence that 120,000 people in the city did not attend church, at a time when 126,000 lived in overcrowded accommodation. It was wrong, he believed, to shower urban residents with religious tracts whilst 'leaving them to swelter in dens, and under conditions where Christian life is so difficult, if not impossible.'[36] Poverty was believed to be a significant barrier to church attendance when combined issues such as the cult of respectability, which expected decent Sunday clothes to be worn to church, or the practice of pew renting, necessitating a significant and regular outlay to secure a sitting in most churches. Although some 9,113 out of 11,155 churches in England had by 1890 no rented pews, the damage had been done. Despite comprising the major component of many urban congregations, the working classes were heavily under-represented in the leadership of most churches, which contributed to the impression that they were class-ridden institutions.

Unbelief spread at a different pace in different nineteenth-century contexts. From the 1790s onwards, Paris saw the emergence of distinctive groups of unbelievers, a trend furthered by secular and anti-clerical government policies later in the century. In English cities a small but vociferous body of working-class and lower-middle-class adherents professed unbelief, joined after 1880 by middle-class unbelievers who styled themselves 'agnostics'. In Berlin, religious

34   E.R. Wickham, *Church and People in an Industrial City*, London, Lutterworth Press, 1957, 11. See J. Cox, *The English Churches in a Secular Society: Lambeth 1870–1930*, Oxford, OUP, 1982; S. Williams, 'Urban Popular Religion and the Rites of Passage', in H. McLeod (ed), *European Religion*.

35   The phrase is from G. Davie, *Religion in Britain Since 1945: Believing Without Belonging*, Oxford, Blackwell, 1994.

36   Mearns, *Bitter Cry*, 4; D. Macleod, *Non-churchgoing and the Housing of the Poor: Speech Delivered in the [Church of Scotland] General Assembly, 30 May 1888… in Support of Overture on Non-churchgoing by the Presbytery of Glasgow*, Edinburgh, W. Blackwood and Sons, 1888, 8–18.

scepticism had taken root among the upper middle class by the 1860s and 1870s, with the Social Democrats vocal in their rejection of organised religion. Those of aristocratic rank were noted for their piety, as were the lower middle class.[37]

Church Responses to Urban Need

Although many continued the urgent and activist patterns of earlier in the century, the deepening sense of alarm at the social and political consequences of filthy environment, inadequate sanitation, unemployment, and poor diet, created a growing conviction that solutions were beyond the limited resources of churches. The sustainability of many projects was further weakened as many affluent church members moved towards the suburbs.

The need for wider social reform in American cities remained a deep challenge. In 1890, Andrew White, President of Cornell University declared, 'the city governments of the United States are the worst in Christendom—the most expensive, the most inefficient, and the most corrupt.' The role of churches and voluntary agencies was to remain crucial in urban areas, but responses were on the whole limited, piecemeal, and inefficient, with charitable provision favoured above national intervention.[38] In 1890 it was estimated that New York spent $8 million dollars on public and private charity. Moral reform was targeted at the drinking saloon, the brothel, and the gambling den. The moral indignation of temperance reformers, which led ultimately to prohibition, overlapped with indignation against corrupt bosses. By 1908, half of Chicago was 'dry,' and the campaign culminated in 1918 with the Eighteenth Amendment, outlawing the manufacture, sale, and use of alcoholic beverages. Rev. Charles Parkhurst's determined stance against saloons and brothels in New York led in 1892, to the formation of a City Vigilance League, to raise moral standards in government, police, and society. By the 1890s, calls for moral regeneration and purity reform had become a mass movement, with scores of local vigilance and law-and-order societies, and social purity alliances. In 1895, the American Purity Alliance was formed, followed by the National Vigilance Society in 1911. Lotteries, gambling, pornography, horse-racing, Sunday sport, and vaudeville shows, were among the targets for the opposition of the campaigners. The same concerns troubled Ludwig Weber, a Berlin pastor, who feared the adolescent portion of the city's population was sinking into a mire of immorality, prostitution, and alcohol abuse. In 1889 he helped establish the General Conference of German Morality Leagues, which attracted to its fold city missions, missions for the rehabilitation of prisoners, and rescue homes for 'fallen' women.[39]

---

37 McLeod, *European Religion*, 26–31.

38 A.D. White, 'The Government of American Cities', *Forum Magazine*, quoted in Mohl, *Urban America*, 114–115, 147–59

39 Mohl, *Urban America*, 128–133; Lees, *Sin and Social Reform in Germany*, 84–88.

New churches continued to be built apace. In Birmingham, England, the number of Anglican churches doubled between 1851 and 1891. Yet for all the impressive endeavour, church accommodation failed to keep pace with population growth. In Berlin, despite the efforts of both Protestant and Roman Catholics, significant deficiencies remained in the 1890s, although the church tax ensured that the parishes that existed were on the whole well-staffed, with several pastors, assistants, and nurses.[40]

Attempts were made by both Protestants and Roman Catholics to maintain contact with the working classes by engaging in social work, running clubs for men, workers, young women and men, and sporting clubs. Some of these also served to create alternative sub-cultures to shield their adherents from alternative world-views. Many parishes provided poor funds, others offered bread rolls and coffee to the homeless. In the 1880s and 1890s, the Nazareth parish in Berlin engaged in a determined parochial strategy to reach working people by 'love in word and deed'. It ran a wide range of benevolent institutions, from parish nurses to a children's hospital, a children's home, and an institution offering work to the unemployed.[41]

The efforts of town and city missions remained as urgent as ever. It was claimed that between 1869 and 1884, the London City Mission's agents had brought 115,412 people to worship services, sent 173,000 children to school, 'reclaimed' 14,446 women, and visited 52,467 death beds.[42] The late-nineteenth-century Bishop of Liverpool, J.C.Ryle, advocated additional clergy, Scripture Readers, and lay visitation, as the solution to the religious needs of the urban poor of Liverpool.[43] Yet early-century enthusiasm for parish visiting ebbed away, as the supply of volunteers waned. The social observer Charles Booth noted the high esteem in which city missioners were held, but apart from them he believed 'good visitors are rare... the unpopularity of the church is partly due to the right claimed of visiting anywhere...the people bear it with great fortitude'.[44]

By 1900, deaconesses were at work in every parish in Hanover, funded by the churches, the city, and even local factory owners. They visited, taught nursery school children, and cared for the sick. Clubs and societies to supplement regular parish services and bible studies were established, with parish evenings of entertainment being held, and brass bands started. Other churches utilised

40   H. Macleod, *Piety and Poverty*, 19–20.

41   H. Neubauer, *Geschchte der Nazarethgemeinde 1835–1925*, Berlin, 1926, 28–33, quoted in McLeod, *Piety and Poverty*, 20–21, 51.

42   J. M. Weylland, *These 50 Years, the Jubilee Volume of the London City Mission*, London, S.W. Partridge & Co., 1884, p18.

43   J.C. Ryle, *First Charge to the Clergy of Liverpool*, Liverpool, W. Hunt & Co., 1881, p7.

44   Charles Booth, *London Labour and the London Poor, Third Series, Religious Influences*, London, Macmillan & Co., 36, 290.

parish helpers, who were laymen with two or three years of training. The *Die Berliner Stadtmission* (Berlin City Mission) employed evangelists from the working classes to break down social and cultural barriers between the urban poor and the churches, and to channel the efforts of lay Christians into charitable activities. The mission won the active support of evangelical parishes, but as with city missions in Britain, found poorer adherents more comfortable with meeting in rooms and halls than in respectable parish churches, where they felt socially ostracised by their lack of education and suitable clothes. The Evangelical Association, a city mission patterned on that in Berlin was founded in Hanover in 1865. Urban missionary work was combined with charitable activities, and lectures of an apologetic nature. Middle-class female volunteers were the principal agents.[45] The Inner Mission, started in the 1840s by Johann Hinrich Wichern, attracted the participation of large numbers of Lutheran clergy. It was a church-supported programme of evangelization and charitable activity, in which social and moral reform were key components, offered as a counter-balance to social unrest, and the threat of communism. Through it a large network of diaconal social service organisations was established in evangelical churches.[46] Yet, strategies based on extensive social care provision were fraught with difficulties. They were expensive, and heavily dependent on gifts from wealthy members, which placed those running the schemes, including pastors, in their debt. Some recipients of charity objected to the strong religious component that often accompanied the practical support offered.

The condition of children remained a significant concern in the nineteenth-century city. The superintendent of the Glasgow police reported thousands of street children who had no names, 'only nicknames like dogs.'[47] Many were orphans, or abandoned by their parents, and formed into gangs of juvenile 'artful dodgers,' living by means of begging or petty crime. By running day schools, ragged schools, Sunday schools, and schemes to redeem the leisure hours of young people, huge investments continued to be made in attempting to win their adherence to Christianity, or at least stem the widespread losses to the churches after children entered teenage years. The Boys Brigade was founded in Glasgow in 1883, using a system of drill, military style uniform, and discipline, alongside regular Bible studies and church parades. In the late-nineteenth century context of imperialism, it proved immediately popular,

45   H. Otte, '"More Churches—More Churchgoers": The Lutheran Church in Hanover Between 1850 and 1914', in McLeod, *European Religion*, 99–102, 107; 'Die Berliner Stadtmission', in K. Elm and H.-D. Loock (eds), *Seelsorge und Diakonie in Berlin*, Berlin, 1990, 455ff, cited in McLeod, *Piety and Poverty*, 12–16.

46   Lees, *Cities, Sin and Social Reform in Germany*, 80.

47   E. Chadwick, *Report on the Sanitary Condition of the Labouring Population of Great Britain*, 1842. Edited with an introduction by M. W. Flinn, Edinburgh, Edinburgh University Press, 1965, 198.

and by 1900 there were 75,000 members world-wide.[48] From this also grew the Boy Scouting movement, founded by Robert Baden-Powell. Within seven years of the first 'Scouting' camp being held on Brownsea Island in 1907, there were 150,000 boy scouts. The Girl Guides followed in 1909, intended to make 'girls better mothers and guides to the next generation.'[49] The Young People's Society of Christian Endeavour was started by the Reverend Francis E. Clark at Williston Congregational Church in Portland, Maine in 1881. By 1911 it was an interdenominational movement with over 2.7 million American members, and a further 1.2 million in Canadian and overseas chapters. The pledge of Christian Endeavour members was to apply religion, through some concrete service, to society, through missions, charities and social programmes.

Attempts to Christianise the leisure time of young people lay behind the work of the YMCA, founded in 1844. In 1910, membership stood at a quarter of a million young people, in over 196 city associations. The provision of sporting facilities, such as gymnasia, proved an increasingly important dimension of their work. Elsewhere churches ran cycling clubs, rowing clubs, and Sunday School cricket leagues, in an attempt to convey an attractive, manly version of 'muscular Christianity.' A number of British professional soccer teams, such as Everton, and Glasgow Celtic, owed their origins to these efforts of local churches.

Christian activism was expressed on a wider canvas than that of the individual church and parish. Civic pride fused with religiously motivated humanitarian concern in the 'civic gospel' movement. In Birmingham it took the form of sweeping re-organisation of the functions and finance of local government. Headed by Joseph Chamberlain, of Unitarian background, in 1873 the Liberals swept to power in the city. Inspired by influential nonconformist ministers such as George Dawson and R.W. Dale, Christians were urged to engage in society as Councillors, as Guardians of the Poor, and on School Boards and hospital committees. Holding such office was deemed to be operating as a minister of God. Local gas and water companies were purchased by the council, to be run for the benefit of the community, and profits used to fund civic improvements. Slums were demolished, art galleries, libraries, and parks provided, and the centre of Birmingham redeveloped.[50]

Glasgow's 'Civic Gospel,' in the third quarter of the nineteenth century, had a distinctly evangelical flavour, combining voluntary agencies for the spiritual and moral improvement of the populace, with local legislative solutions to urban problems. Responses to long-standing social issues included the introduction

48   On the Boys Brigade see J. Springhall, *Sure and Steadfast: a History of the Boys' Brigade, 1883–1983*, London, Collins, 1983.

49   See K. Heasman, *Evangelicals in Action*, London, Geoffrey Bles, 1962, 95–112.

50   See D. Judd, *Radical Joe: A Life of Joseph Chamberlain*, Cardiff, Cardiff University Press, 1993; A. Briggs, *A History of Birmingham 1865–1938*, Oxford University Press, London, 1952.

of strict alcohol licenses to reduce the incidence of drunkenness, improvements in sewerage disposal, and policies to demolish slums. When middle-class ratepayers rebelled at the mounting cost of constructing the vast Loch Katrine reservoir to ensure clean water for the city, the Free Church minister Rev Robert Buchanan declared in a special sermon: 'filth is a great enemy and hindrance to godliness. To live in it, is almost inevitably to lose that self-respect which lies at the bottom of all moral and social progress.'[51] By the end of the century the civic gospel ethos was being superseded by municipal socialism, but the importance of the alliance between churches and local councils was still recognised. As one housing commission reported in 1891: 'it is essentially the function of the Christian church to organise such agencies and to bring to bear such influences as shall move the poor to live decent and clean lives in the decent and clean houses provided for them.'[52]

Others sought to exercise Christian influence on a national arena. Adolf Stoecker, (1835–1909), who had worked in the Inner Mission in Germany, was appointed court preacher at Berlin Cathedral in 1874. Endeavours in evangelism, through the city mission, and investment in social concern projects, were combined with an attempt to radically challenge Liberalism and Social Democracy. In 1878, Stoecker founded the Christian Social Workers party, loyal to Germany and the Kaiser. The party had little impact in the 1878 election, but Stoecker was elected to the Reichstag in 1881 as a Conservative. He remained an influential but controversial figure, combining conservative theology, with a 'Tory-radical' policy of improvments in living and working conditions, and rejection of laissez-faire economics. He argued that social distress in big cities brought moral decline, revolutionary agitation, and alienation from Christianity. Many Protestant parishes in Berlin followed Stoecker's emphasis on social welfare, theological conservatism, patriotism, and hostility to Social Democracy, which he believed cut Germans adrift from Christianity. However, some in the working class were alienated by these emphases.[53]

The impression grew that the hold of churches on the inner-urban populace was slipping away. The poorer the area, the greater the problem appeared to be. Although there was hostility, or the promotion of alternative religious viewpoints, the main issue was apathy. As one observer lamented in 1904: 'if the works done in South London today... had been done in Sodom and Gomorrah,

---

51 See C Brown, '"To be Aglow with civic ardours': the 'Godly Commonwealth' in Glasgow 1843–1914." *Records of the Scottish Church History Society* 26, (1996): 177–178.

52 *Report of the Commission on the Housing of the Poor in Relation to their Social Condition*, Glasgow, 1891, quoted in ed. R.J.Morris and R. Rodger, *The Victorian City: A Reader in British Urban History 1820–1914*, London, Longman, 1993, 73.

53 H. McLeod, *Piety and Poverty*, 22–23; McLeod, ed., *European Religion*, 12–13. On Germany in this period, see also chapter 6.

they would have repented in sackcloth and ashes.' South London responded instead with polite indifference.[54] Religious organisations continued to attempt innovative and flexible strategies designed to break down walls of indifference. Some were practical, others involved major theological reconstruction, but all were motivated by the belief that Christian engagement was crucial to resolving urban need, as typified by the following examples.

THE SETTLEMENT MOVEMENT

Canon Samuel Barnett (1844–1913), an educated, well-connected Anglican clergyman, chose in 1871 to decline the richly-endowed parishes open to him, and work instead in St Jude's parish, in Whitechapel, East London. For the next twenty-two years he served in what was considered the poorest parish in London. Broad-church in his theology, Barnett had no outstanding gifts as a preacher or pastoral visitor, but proved an innovator in urban mission. In 1869, he had founded the Charity Organisation Society, designed to improve connections between charities, and counter the dependency culture of individuals who made multiple claims to different charities. In Whitechapel he used his powers to ensure that poor relief was distributed to the most needy, and have the worst of slum property demolished. In 1885 he promoted the Artisans' Dwellings Act, to assist with the construction of new homes. Barnett inspired Octavia Hill's 'ethical investment' project, in which she purchased an area of the worst slum property in London. Convinced that the root of the housing problem was behavioural, Hill rented her properties in paternalistic fashion, establishing a co-operative relationship with her tenants, offering incentives for the maintenance of premises, and for sending children to school. Hill's housing experiment significantly influenced the subsequent housing policy of many local authorities.[55]

Aware of the limited impact one clerical individual could have on a crowded urban parish, Barnett called on the higher orders of society to influence the East End of London for good, and drew around himself a group of educated and likeminded individuals. In 1883, Toynbee Hall was opened in Whitechapel, designed to look like an Oxford college in the heart of the East End. It was designed as a 'bridge between the Two Nations,' occupied by a 'resident lay gentry.' They supported Barnett in the parish, and largely through educational work amongst working men, diffused knowledge, truth, and love to the lower classes. Barnett sought to awaken a sense of civic and social duty amongst young Oxford undergraduates, who were invited to visit St Jude's, and at the end of their courses to live in community in Whitechapel, whilst working elsewhere

---

54   C.E.F. Masterman, 'The Religious Life of London', quoted in Chadwick, *Victorian Church*, II, 238.

55   On Octavia Hill see G. Darley, *Octavia Hill*, London, Constable, 1990. Her thinking is set out in *Homes of the London Poor*, London, Macmillan, 1875.

Samuel Barnett on the Settlement Movement, 1884

'The poor need more than food: they need knowledge, the character, the happiness which is the gift of God to this age... The settlement would be common ground for all classes... At the weekly receptions of all sorts and conditions of men the settlers would mingle freely in the crowd. ... University men, barristers, Government clerks, curates, medical students, or business men... The one uniting bond would be the common purpose... to do something to improve the condition of the people... poverty in its large sense, including poverty in the knowledge of God and man—is largely due to the division of classes. A University Settlement does provide a remedy which goes deeper than that provided by popular philanthropy'. [1]

1   S.A. Barnett, 'The Universities and the Poor', *Nineteenth Century*, 15, (Feb. 1884), 255–61.

---

in London. They were the future leaders of society, destined for careers in the civil service, parliament, as wealth creators, or in the church. Their presence was intended to have a socially leavening effect, inculcating moral and social values, and reducing class tension, but the process was two-way, and the young leaders learned as much as the urban masses they cared for.

Barnett served as Warden of Toynbee Hall from 1884–96. Parish entertainments of an 'improving' nature were arranged, and Oxford dons invited to lecture to parishioners. Barnett was convinced of the improving power of not only Christianity and education, but also high culture. His wealthy friends were persuaded to mount an exhibition of works of art in Whitechapel. Alongside this was a library, creating an environment in which all could enjoy rational recreation.

The impact locally may have been limited, but nationally it was far greater. Toynbee Hall spawned a number of imitators, including the Anglo-Catholic Oxford House; the Congregationalist Browning Settlement; and the Wesleyan Bermondsey Settlement. By 1913, there were 27 settlements in London, 12 elsewhere in England and 5 in Scotland. Students from universities and public schools developed a deepening sense of the responsibility of the higher orders to disseminate education and civilising influence to those below them. The novelist H.G. Wells dismissed the settlement movement as 'benevolent picnicking,'[56] but Toynbee Hall was visited by members of the government, who came to see for themselves the condition of the poor, and solutions to urban problems. William Beveridge, architect of the British Welfare state in 1945, was a later warden of Toynbee Hall, and Clement Attlee, British Labour Prime Minister after 1945, was a one-time resident.

In Germany, Walter Classen (1874–1954), influenced by Barnett's attempts to

56   Quoted in M.B. Reckitt, *Faith and Society*, London, Longmans, 1932, 98 footnote.

Samuel Barnett

overcome poverty in its fullest sense, including poverty of the knowledge of God, established the Hamburg Volksheim. Despite having a thorough theological education, Classen chose to support the daily lives of urban dwellers through social work in Hamburg, rather than pastoral ministry, as a way of combating the threat of Social Democracy. Classen deplored the physical deprivations of city dwellers, ranging from abusive fathers to treeless streets. Modelled on Toynbee Hall, the Volksheim sought to cultivate 'fellowship with the poor' through personal contact between the educated middle class and the workers, and creating a sense of community. It offered free legal advice, a reading room, continuing education classes, and lectures on literary, scientific, philosophical and theological subjects, attended by over 3,500 people in 1905–06. There were Sunday concerts, visits to art exhibitions, clubs for gymnastics, hiking and rowing. By 1914 over 2,500 children attended various organisations it ran. Meetings ended with an epilogue, or an uplifting story. Although extensively admired, the Volksheim was not widely copied across Germany.[57]

In the 1880s, Settlement Houses began to appear in the slum areas of many American cities, with over 100 founded by 1900. Often staffed by women, they sought to understand and engage sympathetically with the urban masses. Some took a strong role in opposing environmental problems such as slum housing, or in moral purity crusades against drink, gambling, and prostitution. Those in the National Federation of Settlements were non-religious, but many others had a religious affiliation, running Bible study classes, Sunday schools, recreational and educational programmes. Settlements tended to be paternalistic in their approach, seeking conciliation and a promotion of American values, in which sobriety, church attendance, and Sunday School ranked high. Jane Addams, who in 1889 opened Hull House in Chicago, was increasingly convinced that the poor were victims of the economic system, and economic as well as social and environmental reform, was required.[58]

D.L Moody and Urban Revivalism

To Dwight Lyman Moody (1837–1899), the proper response to the secularising challenges of late-nineteenth century society was holding crusades for religious revival, by which the evangelization of thousands might be effected. Moody innovatively refined and deployed the revivalism of Charles Finney in efficient, highly organised, urban fashion.[59] This domesticated version of Bible-only revivalist religion proved highly popular on both sides of the Atlantic. Initially embarking on a career as a shoe salesman, after an evangelical conversion Moody became active in Sunday School teaching, and the Chicago YMCA. Such was his success that shoe selling was set aside, and the undenominational

---

57 Lees, *Sin and Social Reform in Germany*, 256–286.

58 On the settlement movement in the United States see M. Carson, *Settlement Folk: The Evolution of Social Welfare Ideology in the American Settlement Movement, 1883–1930*, Chicago, University of Chicago Press, 1990.

59 On revivalism see R. Carwardine, *Trans-Atlantic Revivalism: Popular Evangelicalism in Britain and America, 1790–1865*, Westport, Conn., Greenwood, 1978; J. Kent, *Holding the Fort: Studies in Victorian Revivalism*, London, Epworth, 1978; W.G. McCloughlin, *Modern Revivalism: Charles Finney to Billy Graham*, New York, Ronald Press, 1959.

D. L. Moody

Illinois St Church was established for his converts. Never ordained, and with limited educational attainment, Moody became an effective preacher, delivering sermons in a homely, practical way, liberally dosed with anecdotes, concluding with a direct, often emotional, appeal for decision to believe the gospel. Dressed in non-clerical garb, and amply proportioned, he looked to all-the-world like a successful grocer. His simple revivalist message, and avoidance of theological intricacies and debate, was designed to create as few barriers to the gospel as possible, and secure widespread co-operation from church leaders. Beyond the call to conversion, the theology that interested him revolved around two poles—the imminent premillennial return of Christ, and the need for personal holiness. His philosophy in gospel preaching was simple: 'God has given me a lifeboat and said "Moody, save all you can"'.[60]

60   On Moody see W.R. Moody, *The Life of Dwight L. Moody*, London, Morgan and Scott, 1900; J.F. Findlay, *Dwight L. Moody: American Evangelist, 1837–1899*, Chicago, University of Chicago Press, 1969; L. Dorsett, *A Passion for Souls: The Life of D.L. Moody*, Chicago, Moody Press, 1997.

His counterpart in a well-crafted revivalist team was Ira D. Sankey (1840–1908), a former revenue clerk, possessed of a ready facility to compose, or adapt, simple gospel solos with catchy choruses, which he played on the harmonium. Sankey's singing of the gospel deepened emotional receptiveness towards Moody's message, and sealed it home after the preaching was over. Sung with affecting pathos, his solos about lost sheep, or prodigals returning, produced an affecting climax to the proceedings. Even the Scots were won over to Sankey's solos and his 'kist o' whistles.'

Moody scored notable success with his tour of major cities in Britain from 1873–75. After a faltering start, the campaigns were characterised by extensive advertising, large interdenominational organising committees, with wealthy lay backers. It was estimated that 2.5 million people heard him on his first visit to Britain, although many were repeat hearers. He expressed a particular concern to reach the poorest in society, especially on his return campaigns in the 1880s and 1890s, but it appears that those on the fringes of the subculture of church and chapel life were those who responded most readily. Moody's focus was predominantly urban, although his impact was far wider. His message appealed to residents of West End mansions, and impoverished East Side slums. He broke down denominational barriers, and attracted widespread, but not universal, support.

Moody turned revivalism from a mass of locally based initiatives into a vast, well co-ordinated, ecclesiastical organisation. His campaigns in the United States became remarkably successful. In the late 1870s, he packed the 5,000 seat Brooklyn Rink for a month, a 10,000 seat arena in Pennsylvania, and the New York Hippodrome were filled with 14,000 per night for ten weeks. The package remained the same—homely, old time religion, delivered in rapid conversational style, replete with emotionally-charged gospel hymns. When he died in 1899, it was estimated Moody had addressed 100 million people, and

---

Moody and Sankey Preaching in New York, 1876

'certainly Moody possesses little rhetorical power, less culture, and no learning; yet his unusual earnestness and simplicity keep all hearers enchained. The impression is left that there is some truth behind the man, greater than he… It cannot be said either, apart from the public features of the meetings, that there is much that is exciting or sensational in them. There is, indeed, preparation and organisation. Mr Sankey's use of recitative and lively airs… are very attractive and effective for his objects… The entire absence of controversial and denominational elements in this meeting is a suggestion to our clergymen which will be heeded.'[1]

1   Editorial *New York Times* February, 1876 quoted in W.R. Moody, *D.L. Moody*, New York, Fleming H. Revell, 1900, 266.

---

personally prayed with 750,000 sinners. Yet, for all the effort and expense, and large crowds attracted, Moody's revivalism failed to substantially re-orientate the religious viewpoint of the working class.

Moody's primary base was Chicago, a city characterised by many pathologies of rapid industrial–urban growth, with significant social unrest, strikes, and housing problems. Of these issues, Moody was well aware, but his solution was not social reconstruction, but personal regeneration. Nonetheless, he still promoted projects for the relief of individual needs. He delivered relief parcels to troops during the American Civil War. By 1886 there were some five hundred boys and girls, from orphaned or impoverished backgrounds, at the schools he established in Northfield, Massachusetts. Advocacy of the temperance cause, a frequent dimension of his campaigns, was also a manifestation of his social concern. The Women's Christian Temperance Union, led by Frances Willard (1839–98), a Methodist teacher who worked closely with Moody, conducted successful campaigns to reduce the manufacture and consumption of alcohol. Temperance campaigners sought to protect poor women and children from the added pressure upon meagre incomes imposed by alcohol abuse.

One aspect of Moody's legacy was the Bible Institute for Home and Foreign Mission, started in Chicago in 1889. It was designed to train lay evangelists especially for the task of both overseas and home mission, with an urban emphasis. Moody also had a significant impact on overseas mission through his inspiration of the Student Volunteer Movement, launched in 1888. The agenda of revivalism, whether in the hands of Moody, or later preachers such as Billy Sunday, was not to challenge or redress the fundamental economic and social issues of his day. There remained a sense that an aggressive stance on social issues could prove a barrier to the gospel. Although there was a high level of racial integration in Moody's Northfield schools, his protests at preaching to racially segregated congregations in the South came to nothing, and he continued with the meetings. The evangelistic task, in the light of the imminent return of Christ, was considered paramount.

ROMAN CATHOLIC URBAN MISSION

One of the most successful ventures in urban mission was the endeavour in the second-half of the nineteenth century to win back lapsed Roman Catholics to the mass. In part it was a response to the determined proselytism of Protestant missionaries in urban areas, and involved a conscious replication of a number of Protestant approaches. A significant proportion of Roman Catholic urban populations were of immigrant origin. In early nineteeth-century Britain, the small and fairly well-assimilated Roman Catholic community did not always welcome the waves of Roman Catholic migrants from Ireland, spurred by poverty and lack of economic opportunity, which culminated in the disastrous

Irish potato famine of the 1840s. In cities such as Manchester, Liverpool, and Glasgow they settled in the poorest areas, and in the cheapest, and worst, housing. The experience of Roman Catholic migrants from Southern Europe into American cities later in the century was similar. They took the lowest paid, and least popular forms of work. Those who arrived in the midst of trade depression faced a sectarian backlash, accompanied by accusations that they were taking the jobs of local workers. Anti-Catholicism became a major feature of many nineteenth-century urban societies. Up to half of the migrants were believed to have lapsed from the mass and confession, although this may have been a repetition of previous low attendance patterns in Ireland.

The mission to reclaim the lapsed to the mass initially involved investment in personnel rather than new buildings. Existing buildings were used to capacity, with multiple services held on Saturday evenings and throughout Sundays. Priests from Ireland were recruited, with a ministry closely adapted culturally to the migrants. They were willing to live in the heart of the poorest areas, were readily at hand to administer the sacraments when called for. They readily drew on techniques employed by Protestants: Passionist and Rosminian missionaries conducted revivalist meetings, dressed in flamboyant vestments, preaching with drama and intense emotional appeal, culminating in a large procession through the parish and a celebration of the mass. Response was focussed upon restoration to the confessional, or rededication by renewal of baptismal vows.[61]

Such religious means were accompanied by a social-conscience agenda, such as the role of Cardinal Manning in resolving the London dock strike in the 1880s. Social provisions developed in association with Roman Catholic Churches included the 'Society of St Vincent de Paul,' temperance societies, and Irish societies. Investment in the provision of education for Roman Catholic children was also key, through the extensive provision of voluntary schools both before and after the interference of the state in education in 1870. Although such provisions tended to isolate Roman Catholics from the rest of society, they strengthened internal community bonds and religious loyalty. The ability of a predominantly poor, urban, community to mobilise resources for schools, hospitals, monastic houses, and other charitable institutions, was notable.

By maintaining the strong connection between Irish identity and the Roman Catholic faith, and securing the active involvement of the laity themselves, priests did much to reverse the leakage of their members, and retain the sympathies of the working classes, especially working-class men. In New York, Roman Catholics benefitted greatly from the strength of the Irish sub-culture. With a cathedral, churches, free parochial schools, hospitals, orphanages, homes for the elderly and homeless, clubs and societies and a range of social welfare

61   On Roman Catholic revivalism see Kent, *Holding the Fort.*

agencies, social provision was extensive, and prevented resort to Protestant alternatives. The Roman Catholic Church operated as a powerful social and religious institution, which lay at the heart of an alternative culture, and which enhanced support for the Democratic Party.[62]

Alongside its strong cultural appeal, a work of transformation and adaptation to the modern, and predominantly urban, context was conducted by American Roman Catholicism, under the leadership of Cardinal Gibbons. The Archbishop of St Paul, John Ireland, promoted responsible trade unions, believing it impossible to speak to workers of spiritual duties until their material conditions were improved. A careful balance was struck between the support of labour in its grievances, and maintenance of social order and law. Leo XIII's encyclical *Rerum Novarum* (1891) was appealed to, supporting 'class collaboration' instead of class conflict: 'capital needed labour, and labour needed capital'.

In Paris, church charities supported working-class women in childbirth, offered day care to the children of working mothers, recreation for teenage girls, and libraries. The Ligue Patriotique des Françaises was founded in Paris in 1902. By 1910 it had, amongst its other endeavours, founded 124 libraries and 121 recreational societies, with 600,000 members in 1914. Through these provisions, members of the middle and upper classes sought to inculcate Roman Catholic values amongst the working classes. Religious orders, with membership increasing from 12,300 in 1808, to 135,000 in 1878, were responsible for a significant amount of social care in French cities, through their work as teachers and nurses. Although the secularization of schools during the 1880s reduced their influence, as did their expulsion from the Paris hospitals, 12,887 nuns were still working as nurses in 1912, whilst others ran homes for the elderly, those with mental illness, and rescue homes for prostitutes.[63] In an increasingly secular political and social context, Roman Catholicism remained an important dimension of late nineteenth-century French urban life.

WILLIAM AND CATHERINE BOOTH—HOLINESS REVIVALISM AS URBAN MISSION
Urban revivalism was expressed in a different form through the work of William Booth (1829–1912) and his wife Catherine (1829–1890). They coupled a revivalist emphasis on conversion with holiness teaching, and over time, an active social concern. William Booth left the Wesleyan Methodists in 1855, and joined the Methodist New Connexion, where he enjoyed remarkable success as a preacher; in 1861 he took the decision to operate independently. Booth began tent meetings on an old Quaker burial ground in the East End of London,

---

62 H. McLeod, *Piety and Poverty*, 56–62.

63 See O. Sarti, *The Ligue Patriotique des Françaises—A Feminine Response to the Secularization of Society*, New York, Garland, 1992; and R. Gibson, *A Social History of French Catholicism, 1789–1914*, London, Routledge, 1989.

> **William Booth—'In Darkest England'**
> 'As there is a darkest Africa is there not also a darkest England?... May we not find a parallel at our own doors, and discover within a stone's throw of our cathedrals and palaces… tragedies as awful, ruin as complete, or ravishments as horrible, as if we were in Central Africa; … Fever is almost as chronic there as on the Equator. Every year thousands of children are killed off by what is called defects of our sanitary system…Drunkenness and all manner of uncleanness, moral and physical, abound… A population sodden with drink, steeped in vice, eaten up by every social and physical malady, these are the denizens of Darkest England.'[1]
>
> 1   W. Booth, *In Darkest England and the Way Out*, London, Salvation Army, 1890, 9–15.

aided only by 'God, the Holy Ghost, and an open Bible.'[64] Booth believed that the urban poor could never be reached from within the churches and chapels: it was necessary to take the gospel to hired halls and into the open air. On what were often rowdy streets, he used a brass band to attract a crowd, accompany rousing singing, and 'blow down the opposition.' Women preachers, dramatic advertising, military-style uniforms and titles, were all aspects of Booth's antidote to clericalism. By the late 1870s the work had become the 'Salvation Army,' Booth became General Superintendent, then simply 'the General.' The Salvation Army's revivalist-holiness meetings could be intense, dramatic and emotional, with people shouting, jumping, swooning, and laying sacrifices, such as pipes, tobacco, and brooches, on the altar as testimony to their renunciation of the world. Opposition was swiftly stirred, from police concerned over social order, the Established Church complaining of the 'vulgarisation of religion', and the rabble-like 'Skeleton Army' who delighted in disrupting the proceedings. Nonetheless, the Salvation Army grew remarkably—the *British Weekly* census of 1887 recorded 53,591 in attendance at its meetings in London.

The particular concern of the Booths was the 'submerged tenth,' the poorest classes who appeared impervious to the outreach endeavours of churches. In the year of Catherine's death, 1890, William published *In Darkest England and the Way Out*, a comprehensive programme of his scheme of 'social salvation.'[65] Booth rejected criticisms that this implied an abandonment of holiness revivalism and its emphasis on individual salvation. The relief of temporal

64   On Booth and the Salvation Army see H. Begbie, *The Life of William Booth*, 2 vols, London, Macmillan, 1920; P.J. Walker, *Pulling the Devil's Kingdom Down: The Salvation Army in Victorian Britain*, Berkeley, University of California Press, 2001; N.H. Murdoch, *The Origins of the Salvation Army*, Knoxville, University of Tennessee Press, 1994.

65   R. Sandall, *The History of the Salvation Army*, 1947– 55, Vol 3, p63– 74 refer to it as 'The General's Change of Mind'.

misery would make it 'easy where it is now difficult, and possible where it is now all but impossible, for men and women to find their way to the Cross of our Lord Jesus Christ'.[66] He believed that Moody's lifeboat needed to be equipped with the means for social support as part of the first stage of rescue.

Twenty years of slum mission work left Booth believing that urban conditions rendered many so vulnerable that their choice was stark—'starve or sin'.[67] He appealed on behalf of those on the verge of the abyss, the homeless, the unemployed, criminals and their children 'cursed from birth with hereditary weakness of body and hereditary faults of character'. Meeting social need was connected to meeting spiritual need. Without an accompanying personal inner change, experience taught him: 'you may clothe the drunkard, fill his purse with gold, establish him in a well furnished home, and in three or six or twelve months he will once more be on the Embankment, haunted by delirium tremens, dirty, squalid, and ragged'. Booth proposed a comprehensive rescue scheme revolving around three 'colonies'. The 'city colony,' supplied the immediate needs of the destitute and daily 'moral and religious influences,' the 'farm colony,' offered industrial or agricultural training and moral and religious rehabilitation—the salvation pathway led ultimately away from the city. A final 'overseas colony,' in South Africa, Canada, or Western Australia was projected. Smaller, less ambitious projects included labour bureaux, and 'slum sisters' who lived in the midst of the poor, visiting the sick, caring for children, and preaching to the outcasts of society'. Newly discharged prisoners were assisted by the Prison Gate Brigade, and fallen women supported in rescue homes.[68]

There was never enough money to fully implement the far-reaching £1 million scheme, but social concern was established as a key component in reaching Darkest England. By the time of Booth's death, the Salvation Army's basic shelters were crowded each night, genuine converts were reported, and a farm colony in Essex operated. The publication of *In Darkest England* in 1890 was certainly not the radical departure some have proposed: by 1886 the Salvation Army was already actively working with destitute men, prostitutes, discharged prisoners, and deserted wives. In 1888 the first depot providing food and shelter was opened. Catherine Booth's influence appears a significant influence, together with a desire to give full expression to the socially active ministry of women officers.[69] In good part through the prodigious efforts of the Booth's numerous children, the Salvation Army had become an international

---

66   W. Booth, *In Darkest England and the Way out,* London, Salvation Army, 1890, 3–4.

67   Booth, *Darkest England,* 13.

68   Booth, *Darkest England,* 66, 86, 92, 111, 159.

69   On this see A. Higginbotham, 'Respectable Sinners: Salvation Army Rescue Work with Unmarried Mothers 1884–1914, *Journal of Social History,* Vol. 36, No. 3, 2003, 216–231.

movement.[70] It also provoked other similar organisations, such as the Anglican Church Army, founded by Wilson Carlile in 1882. Yet Salvation Army officers were on the whole not reclaimed alcoholics, but lower middle class Christians seeking an active outlet for their Christianity. For many, a sojourn in a shelter was a temporary haven at times of crisis, before old ways were resorted to. If the 'submerged tenth' was reached by the Salvation Army, it did not demonstrate a lasting propensity to change its religious or social attitudes.

WALTER RAUSCHENBUSCH (1861–1918)

In the late nineteenth century some proponents of urban mission drew strongly on theological liberalism's emphasis on the ethical component of the Christian gospel. Reform, not just of the individual, but of wider society, was believed possible. In America this was connected to an optimistic postmillennial belief that the kingdom of God was achievable. The proponents of the Social Gospel sought to draw attention to the moral crises of industrial-urban society, and in a forward-looking, if idealistic way, adapt the Christian gospel to modernity. They challenged the middle class tendency to associate upholding religious orthodoxy with maintaining the social status quo, typified by the handsomely paid Henry Ward Beecher's response to the millions rendered unemployed in the trade depression of 1873: 'I do not say that a dollar a day is enough to support... a man and five children if a man would insist on smoking and drinking beer... the man who cannot live on bread and water is not fit to live.'[71]

The ruthless nature of economic competition, and the apparent heartlessness of economic monopolies, greatly troubled Walter Rauschenbusch (1861–1918), who, along with Washington Gladden (1836–1918), has been called the 'Father of the Social Gospel in America.' Born in Rochester, New York, of German immigrant parents, Rauschenbusch was raised in an atmosphere of conservative Baptist piety. He graduated from the University of Rochester in 1884, and Rochester Theological Seminary in 1886, where questions were raised about his orthodoxy, especially over his views of the Old Testament. He accepted the pastorate of the small Second German Baptist Church in New York City, on the edge of the notorious 'Hell's Kitchen' slum, where he worked from 1886 to 1897. Here the classic pathologies of urban deprivation—poverty, poor housing, malnutrition, disease, ignorance and crime—were at their worst. Urban pastoral work proved harrowing: faced with an endless procession of funerals he questioned, 'Why did the children have to die?' The streets were filled with men who were 'out of work, out of clothes, out of shoes, and out

---

70 On the Salvation Army in the United States see D. Winston, *Red Hot and Righteous, The Urban Religion of the Salvation Army*, Cambridge, Mass., Harvard, 2000.

71 Quoted in H. Wish, 'Urbanism and the Church', in R.A. Mohl and N. Betten. *Urban America in Historical Perspective*, New York, Weybright and Talley, 1970.

of hope'.[72] Life in the immigrant German communities of New York was particularly harsh. His ministry coincided with a period of trade depression, at its deepest in 1893. From 1882–86 wage cuts of 20–30% were experienced, and unemployment reached 2 million. The 1890s saw 14,000 strikes supported by 3.7 million workers. Fears rose of widespread social disorder and collapse.

Although his initial emphasis was upon evangelism, Rauschenbusch became convinced that individual conversion and individualistic philanthropy was an ineffective response to poverty, ill health, and economic insecurity, which were rooted in the capitalist system. Christianity was losing its way: 'The larger our cities grow, the less hold does religion seem to have over the multitude of men and the general life'.[73] As he sought for a new expression of Christianity he turned to the writings of liberal theologians such as Bushnell, Ritschl, and Adolf Harnack. Although friends warned him he was substituting social work for religious work, his emphasis in preaching switched to Christ the man, the unique religious personality, who initiated the Kingdom of God. He concluded that theology should not come from outside, but from context, especially from contact with human suffering, and the need to change human lives. The result was set out in *Christianizing the Social Order* (1912), and a *Theology for the Social Gospel* (1917). Concepts of biblical inerrancy and substitutionary atonement were rejected, as was pre-millennial theology, which Rauschenbusch believed silenced the social conscience by focussing on the imminent return of Christ.

Rauschenbusch argued that a salvation 'confined to the soul and its personal interests was an imperfect and only partially effective salvation.' Instead of historic creedal formulations, it was to be expressed in communitarian terms of moral or social progression: 'Salvation is the voluntary socializing of the soul.' So too with the character of God: 'A theological God who has no interest in the conquest of injustice and fraternity is not a Christian God... Its God must join the social movement'.[74] The unifying principle of Rauschenbusch's theology became the 'kingdom of God.' Christ's work was the 'social redemption of the entire life of the human race on earth;' the social ideal of primitive Christianity was seeing 'a divine social order established on earth'. The Kingdom of God made 'love to God and love to man the sole outlet for the energy of religion', it dealt 'not only with the immortal souls of men, but with their bodies, their nourishment, their homes, their cleanliness, and it makes those who serve these fundamental needs of life, veritable ministers of God.' The concept of the reign of God on the earth unified Rauschenbusch's thought about salvation, teaching

---

72   C.H. Hopkins, *The Rise of the Social Gospel in American Protestantism, 1865–1915,* 1940, repr. New York, AMS, 1982, 216.

73   W. Rauschenbusch, 'The Stake of the Church in the Social Movement', *American Journal of Sociology,* 3, July 1897, 29–30.

74   W. Rauschenbusch, *A Theology for the Social Gospel,* New York: Macmillan, 1917, 49, 178, 95, 99.

Walter Rauschenbusch: The Social Gospel

'The industrial and commercial life today is dominated by principles antagonistic to the fundamental principles of Christianity … if our time and strength were not used up either in getting a bare living or in amassing unusable wealth… then there might be a chance to live such a life of gentleness and brotherly kindness and tranquillity of heart as Jesus desired for men. It may be that the co-operative Commonwealth would give us the first chance in history to live a really Christian life without retiring from the world…'[1]

1   W. Rauschenbusch, *Christianity and the Social Crisis*, New York, Macmillan, 1907, 339–42.

---

the young, the pastoral care of the poor and the frail, the study of the Bible, church union, political reform, the reorganisation of the industrial system, and international peace.[75] The Kingdom of God was to be found in the church, in the family, in the industrial organization of society, and in the state: it 'realizes itself through them all'.[76] Although Rauschenbusch made religion and ethics inseparable, highlighting poverty and oppression, he had surprisingly little to say about race.

In *Christianity and the Social Crisis* (1907) Rauschenbusch railed against 'materialism' and 'mammon', the oligarchies and monopoly powers of industry: 'Man is treated as a *thing*, to produce more things… Our commercialism has tainted our sense of the fundamental human verities and values. We measure our national prosperity by pig-iron and steel instead of by the welfare of the people.' The wealth of a nation rested instead in 'the way men live justly with one another and humbly with their God'. Social institutions, professions and oligarchies, 'superpersonal forces', and 'composite personalities' needed to be converted, redeemed and brought under the law of Christ,[77] so that co-operation would triumph over competition, fraternity above coercion, and public good above private gain.[78]

The influence of Rauschenbusch was considerable. With other ministers, he formed the nondenominational Brotherhood of the Kingdom movement. Concern to create a united voice on social issues of the day led in 1908 to the foundation of the Federal Council of Churches. Figures such as Theodore Roosevelt and Woodrow Wilson consulted him. Washington Gladden joined him in demanding reforms such as a minimum wage, old age pensions, income

---

75   W. Rauschenbusch, *Christianizing the Social Order*, New York, Macmillan, 1912, 67, 69; 96–102; 93.

76   W. Rauschenbusch, *A Theology for the Social Gospel*, New York: Macmillan, 1917, 144–45.

77   W. Rauschenbusch, *Christianity and the Social Crisis*, 1907, repr. New York, Harper and Row, 1964, 369–72.

78   W. Rauschenbusch, *A Theology for the Social Gospel*, Nashville, Abingdon, 1945, 226.

and inheritance tax, housing reform, and government ownership of the railways, and key industries such as coal-mining. In the Roman Catholic Church, Father John A. Ryan similarly urged labour reform and social justice legislation.

CONCLUSION

The development of modern urban contexts was viewed in negative light in an array of late-nineteenth-century settings, inspiring fears of unbridled sexuality, moral degeneration, inborn criminality, and political collapse. Religion and philanthrophy worked together to produce effective responses. Although much activity was shaped by the pragmatic consideration of what worked locally, churches and Christian charities were able to draw on a wide international discourse. Across America, Germany, France and Britain a close nexus of ideas emerged, meaning that urban mission practiced by a wide range of religious bodies had many common points.

The pace of religious decline varied. It was most marked in Germany in the later nineteenth century, but in France, after the disastrous years of the late eighteenth century, the situation stabilised. Church attendance in the United States proved highly resilient to the advances of modernity, even in the urban environment, and may have been positively enhanced by it. Although evidence of a downturn in religious adherence became noticeable in Britain after 1880, attendance at church-related activities remained a significant part of urban life, especially for women. For a large body of others, a form of religious faith was retained in which a Christian identity was claimed, certain elements of belief and practice were accepted, but regular church attendance not deemed essential. People who may have outwardly appeared indifferent maintained resilient folk belief systems, which appeared at crisis moments in life, often by a resort to the church's 'rites of passage'. Middle class urban identity continued to be strongly shaped by church-going up until 1914, despite widening exposure to the findings of modern science.

There is no single cause for the changing pattern of religious life in the late-nineteenth and early-twentieth-century city. Until recently, the theory of progressive secularization linked to modernization, was the most widely held explanation of European religious decline. Others have argued that the issue is not modernity, but the advent of religious toleration and competition, whereby religious practice shifted from being a requirement of the state to a matter of personal choice. Class conflict compounded discomfort with worshipping with those of different social backgrounds, especially when it was in an Established Church. For some, resort to nonconformity, or even the formation of Labour Churches was a solution. For others, Socialism was an attractive alternative religion.

In Europe, the later decades of the nineteenth century saw a range of forces coalesce which made a decline in church attendance more likely. Liberal theology, despite its appeal to the modern mind, challenged and destabilised the simple certainties of the faith for many. The non-work related time of urban residents became increasingly contested space. Increased leisure activities offered an alternative means of emotional stimulus, especially the attractions of professional sport and entertainment. Church, charitable, and private efforts to address social and moral issues were gradually succeeded by local authority and government intervention in education, housing, sanitation, social relief and health provision, although their efforts often built on the pattern first set by the churches. The German state led the way in public social policy, followed by France and then Britain. Between 1880 and 1911, life expectancy at birth in Germany increased by a third, and the death rate fell by one half. Social insurance schemes helped secure the moral and physical health of the German empire.[79] In the wider social arena, churches began to look marginalised.

There was a diversity of experiences in different cities. Berlin's large parishes, absence of clergy, anti-clericalism and opposition to religion amongst the working classes seem untypical, although such patterns were seen in Paris to a lesser degree. The capacity of a state church to alienate a significant section of society was seen in Germany. In North America, the lack of a connection between church and state removed one potent source of anticlerical feeling and religious alienation, as did the more fluid class structure, and presence of ethnic ties which brought a greater tendency to religious commitment. Despite the overall trends, churches continued to determinedly engage with the urban context, although it was becoming clear that in Europe theirs was not a heroic advance, but a determined rearguard defence.

FURTHER READING

H. Barnett, *Canon Barnett: His Life, Work and Friends*, London, John Murray, 1919.

S. Barnett, *The Ideal City*, (1893–94) in H. Meller (ed), *The Ideal City*, Leicester, Leicester University Press, 1979.

W. Booth, *In Darkest England and the Way Out*, London, Salvation Army, 1890.

C. H. Evans, *The Kingdom is Always Coming: A Life of Walter Rauschenbusch*, Grand Rapids, Eerdmans, 2004.

B.J. Evenson, *God's Man for the Gilded Age: D.L. Moody and the Rise of Modern Mass Evangelism*, New York, Oxford University Press, 2003.

J.V. Hickey, *Urban Catholics. Urban Catholicism in England and Wales from 1829 to the Present Day*, London, Geoffrey Chapman, 1967.

H. McLeod, *Piety and Poverty: Working Class Religion in Berlin, London, and New York, 1870–1914*, New York, Holmes and Meier, 1996.

H. McLeod, *European Religion in the Age of Great Cities, 1830–1930*, London, Routledge, 1995.

D. Winston, *Red Hot and Righteous: The Urban Religion of the Salvation Army*, Cambridge, Mass, Harvard UP, 2000.

15

OLD DEFENCES, NEW EXPRESSIONS: NINETEENTH-CENTURY AMERICAN CHRISTIAN THOUGHT AND EXPRESSION

The capacity of American Christianity to accommodate itself to the dynamic social, intellectual and political context of America between the Revolution and the Civil War, undoubtedly contributed to its success. American preachers and theologians, with highly mobilised churches, and endeavours towards moral and social reform, helped forge a Christian culture that was predominantly Protestant and evangelical, although widespread immigration made the Roman Catholic religious presence increasingly notable. The process of adaptation was two-way, with real potential for prevalent social and cultural forms to shape the way in which individuals gave expression to their understanding of the Christian message. The Civil War exposed that tendency, and contributed to the break down of the synthesis of Christian theology and American ideology.[1] The middle and later decades of the nineteenth century saw an erosion of the dominance of postmillennialism, with strife, dissension, war, famine, and slavery slowly disappearing as the gospel inexorably progressed. This had much to do with the profound tragedies of the Civil War, which undermined the optimism of American evangelicalism, prompting increasing numbers to embrace the urgency and pessimism of premillenialism. Those who moved in a liberal direction in their theology inclined to a diluted postmillennialism.

Without the controlling force for social structure offered by the presence of a religious establishment, the nation that considered itself the providentially-appointed agent for the promotion of 'freedom' and liberty became a fertile context for a multiplicity of fresh expressions in religious thought and practice.

---

1 M. Noll, *America's God: From Jonathan Edwards to Abraham Lincoln*, Oxford, OUP, 2002, 443–445.

Other religious movements deviated radically from orthodox Christian doctrine. Such capacity for fresh expression was not only true of new fringe religious movements, some touched the heart of mainstream denominations and theological colleges, provoking divisive doctrinal disputes and heresy trials. The struggles of conservative evangelicals to defend the orthodoxy of doctrinal formularies such as the *Westminster Confession* were matched by those of Roman Catholics to uphold the conservative social and theological line of the papacy, and strong ultramontane devotional tendencies in the developing republican, individualistic, and democratic American context.

Protestantism in America was represented in all its multiform variety, from erudite and articulate Presbyterians and Congregationalists, to sectarian groups that coalesced around a charismatic leader who had little theological training. The nineteenth century brought an increased emphasis on individualized forms of expression, greater focus on spiritual inwardness and individual action, which appeared better adapted to the modernizing, rational and market-oriented society. The result was a shift in emphasis from the transcendence of God to the immanence of a relational God. God's revelation was equated more closely to Scripture, and theology became less deferential towards creeds and historical formulations, the laity less inclined to simply receive the insights of intellectual authorities. By 1860, there emerged an influential blend of evangelical Protestantism, republican political ideology, and common sense moral reasoning.[2] Yet, for all the adaptability and a capacity for new expression, striking limitations remained, notably the failure to provide adequate responses to racism, or urban deprivation.

A significant growth in opportunities for theological training was a major feature of nineteenth-century American Christianity. By 1860 there were at least fifty seminaries, designed to turn college graduates into men fit for the Christian ministry. One quarter were Presbyterian, with Princeton, New Jersey, being the notable leader. Although Protestant evangelicalism, whether in Calvinistic or Methodist form, remained the most influential religious force, settler groups, such as the Dutch Reformed, the Lutheran, the Mennonites, and the Moravians, were less sure where they fitted in the spectrum. Even the peace-loving Quakers were divided, between the evangelical 'Gurneyites', and the rationalistic 'Hicksites.' The growing challenge of liberal theology gave an edge to theological debate, as did the rise of premillennial thinking.

THE ATTRACTION OF NEW RELIGIOUS MOVEMENTS
Freedom of religious expression also brought freedom to deviate from inherited patterns of belief and practice. For all the liberties of the New World, a notable group viewed American society as irredeemable. Radical alternative models, led

2 Noll, *America's God*, 3–17.

by visionary individuals, proved attractive, especially to those disillusioned with existing churches. A utopian religious community existed at New Harmony, Indiana, between 1814 and 1825, attracted by Adventist interpretations of contemporary events, visions of cosmic harmony, and the ideal of living out the pattern of the early church set out in Acts 2 and 4. After they moved to Pennsylvania, the British socialist Robert Owen used the site to create a secular community of free-thought, community education, co-operation and the sharing of private property. It attracted eight hundred residents, but survived only a few years, ending far from harmoniously. The community of 'Bible Communists' formed by John Humphrey Noyes (1811–1886) at Oneida, New York, was even more radical. Operating between 1848 and 1881, they shared not only property, but a 'complex marriage' system, which transcended both monogamy and polygamy, with children raised communally. Five offshoot communities were founded before Noyes left the United States for Canada in 1876.

During the economic volatility of the 1840s, apocalyptic speculation intensified. William Miller (1782–1849), a New England Baptist preacher, predicted that the Second Coming of Christ would take place on October 22, 1843, based upon a reading of Daniel 8:14. Miller was typical of popular revivalist figures possessed of limited training who developed large followings on the basis of leadership ability, advertising, and powers of persuasion. Thousands prepared for the coming apocalypse by selling their goods, bidding farewell to their loved ones, and preparing for the millennial reign of Christ. Major newspapers reported the fevered expectations. The 'Great Disappointment' followed when the Second Coming failed to materialise. Miller hastily re-calculated the date of the end-times to the following year, but when this also passed uneventfully the movement fell apart. Some abandoned any profession of Christianity, some turned to Spiritism.

One group of Miller's followers adopted the Adventist teaching of Ellen G. White (1827–1915). She argued that Christ had in fact entered the heavenly sanctuary in 1843 as a prelude to his return to earth to establish the New Jerusalem and cleanse the earthly sanctuary. Her followers taught that the Jewish Sabbath had never been abrogated, and should be observed on the seventh day of the week, rather than the Christian Sunday. Having spent most of her life struggling with poor health, Ellen White became convinced that illness was caused by violation of one of nature's laws. From 1863 onwards she promoted a diet of fruit, vegetables, grains, and nuts, and abstinence from tea, coffee, meat, butter, eggs and cheese, which, she argued, caused disease and unhealthy sexual desires. The healing properties of water were also promoted. Despite her early ill-health, Ellen White lived until the age of eighty-seven, and at her death left 136,000 disciples, hundreds of treatment rooms and thirty-three sanatoriums. Her followers included members of the Kellogg family, who made their fortune from making breakfast cereals, developed as a healthy vegetarian option.

Other religious movements emphasised the freedom Americans could enjoy by escaping the traditional confines of organised, creedal, religious systems, and by rejecting traditional doctrines such as the Trinity and the deity of Christ. They offered an alternative, or supplemental, source of authority and tradition to that of the Bible, and gathered round an authoritative figurehead, presenting their own religious teachings as the only way of salvation.

The most successful of the new religious groups native to America that emerged in this period was founded by Joseph Smith (1805–44). It drew on the Adventist and millennial speculations of the time, although elements of continuity with freemasonry, with which Smith and some of his followers had acquaintance, have been suggested.[3] In 1827, Smith claimed to have discovered a set of golden tablets written in hieroglyphic text which had been buried by descendants of two lost tribes of Israel, which travelled to the New World around 600 BC, until a true prophet should find them. He translated them, and in 1830 published his findings as the *Book of Mormon*. With five others he organised his Church of Jesus Christ of Latter-Day Saints, based on this book, the Bible, and other teachings revealed through Smith, including expectations of a Second Coming of Christ to preside over an American Zion in the West. This linking of the New World with the ancient biblical world offered both historical roots and an American identity to the movement. Smith's followers became known as Mormons, and despite the rejection of a number of orthodox Christian doctrines, drew a significant following from those tired of the mainline Christian denominations. Mormonism promoted revelations from heaven, miracles, apostolic gifts, visions, speaking in tongues and prophecy. It portrayed a deity who, according to the *Book of Mormon,* declared 'I am a God of Miracles.'

Living largely in closed community, the Mormons embraced well-organised and extensive proselytizing activity, and a commitment to good works. Mormonism was in many ways a movement of young people: by 1845, there were 1,900 young lay preachers, many of artisan status. They were sent out, not with sophisticated arguments, but with a capacity for convincing people of the value of the movement by their sincerity. Freedom of thought was restricted, and absolute loyalty to Joseph Smith and his teaching was required. The hostility from neighbouring communities that the movement aroused forced Smith's followers into a peripatetic existence, driven from New York, to Ohio, then Missouri. Between 1839 and 1844 the Mormons settled in Nauvoo, Illinois, and here Smith declared he had received a revelation supporting the restoration of Old Testament patriarchal polygamy, although this did not become formal

---

3   J.L. Brooke, *The Refiner's Fire: The Making of Mormon Cosmology 1644–1844*, Cambridge, Cambridge University Press, 1994, 94–104; D.J. Buerger, *The Mysteries of Godliness: A History of Mormon Temple Worship*, San Francisco, Smith Research Associates, 1994, 40.

Joseph Smith—his First Vision, 1820

'I saw two personages, whose brightness and glory defy all description, standing above me in the air. One of them spoke unto me, calling me by name, and said—pointing to the other—'THIS IS MY BELOVED SON, HEAR HIM'.... I asked the personages who stood above me in the light, which of all the sects was right—and which I should join. I was answered that I must join none of them, for they were all wrong, and the personage who addressed me said that all their creeds were an abomination in His sight'.[1]

---

1   B.H. Roberts (ed), *History of the Church of Jesus Christ of Latter-Day Saints*, Salt Lake City; Deseret Book Co, 2nd edn, revised, 1962, Vol 1, 4–6, in Gaustad, Religion in America, Vol. 1, 350–52.

---

doctrine until 1852. The Mormon leadership also believed that slavery was a divine institution.

By 1844, there were some 26,000 Mormons, and a militia established, with Smith as general: he even ran that year for the presidency of the United States. However, growing local opposition led to Smith and his brother being arrested and charged with polygamy. If the American government was to place no constraints on absolute religious liberty, popular mass reaction would. On June 22, 1844, an enraged mob attacked the jail, killing the two prisoners. Nonetheless, the cultural and physical space of the United States allowed the Mormons to survive beyond the reach of law or angry mob. Smith's most loyal supporter, Brigham Young (1801–77), born of a family of Methodist lay preachers led the largest group of Mormons to the arid Great Salt Lake Basin, Utah. Here, through the imposition of an authoritarian structure and rigorous discipline, a fragmented and volatile apocalyptic sect was turned into a highly successful religious community. The population of Utah was just 11,380 in 1850, but by the time of Brigham Young's death in 1877 it was 115,000, including many Mormon converts who migrated from Britain and Scandinavia. Under intense pressure from the federal government, the practice of polygamy was formally abandoned in 1890.[4]

The sense of religious upheaval and dissatisfaction with traditional Christian teaching in the years after the Civil War created a climate in which further new radical religious movements flourished. In 1866, the highly sensitive and intensely religious Mary Baker Eddy (1821–1910) set forth her views on the Divine Science of healing, describing sickness, disease, evil and sin, as errors of the mortal mind. The movement claimed to be a return to a more primitive form of Christianity, with a renewed emphasis on healing, combined with a form of

---

4   D.J. Davies, *Introduction to Mormonism*, Cambridge, Cambridge University Press, 2003, 1–33. See also Brooke, *Refiner's Fire.*

positive thinking. It was also a strong reaction against the Congregationalism of her upbringing, her own ill health, and troubled personal life. Mary Baker Eddy's first husband died, she divorced a second, and her third died after a few years of marriage. She suffered from chronic spinal pain, and after failing to benefit from the 'healing' properties of mesmerism and spiritualism, she developed her own faith healing approach. In 1875 she set out her teaching in *Science and Health According to the Scriptures*, which she claimed had been dictated by God. The Church of Christ, Scientist, was established in Massachusetts in 1879, before moving the headquarters to Boston in 1892. In 1906 the Mother Church in Boston claimed 40,000 members, with 25,000 reported elsewhere. The *Christian Science Monitor* was founded in 1908, which combined lectures on the faith, with quality journalism, especially reporting on foreign affairs.

The teachings of Charles Taze Russell (1852–1916) similarly grew out of dissatisfaction with traditional Christian teaching, but was more influenced by revivalism and premillennial Adventist speculation than Christian Science had been. In 1870 Russell started a Bible class in Pittsburgh, and made initial predictions that the Second Coming of Christ would occur in 1874, subsequently revised to 1914. Russell, an able and imaginative communicator in both oral and written form, promoted his ideas through well-attended lectures, tracts and magazines, and through his multi-volume *Studies in the Scriptures* (1886–1904) which was widely read and established the core of his followers' teachings. In 1884 the Zion's Watch Tower Tract Society was established. Alongside its strict ethical teachings, the movement significantly turned away from traditional orthodoxy. Russell rejected the Trinity as 'a false, unbiblical doctrine' originated by Satan. He believed that the son of god was the first creature made by Jehovah, who may be called 'a god', but not God.[5] The title Jehovah's Witnesses was not adopted until 1931 under the leadership of Joseph Rutherford, who took over from Russell in 1917.

AMERICAN THEOLOGY IN THE MAINSTREAM DENOMINATIONS

The Modification of Calvinism

For Methodists, doctrinal formulation played a secondary role to the missionary task. They operated within the practical and theological system established by John Wesley, continued by his able American lieutenants, Francis Asbury and later Nathan Bangs (1778–1862). Methodist theology centred on the free availability of Christian salvation, which was to be offered to all, and evidenced in holiness—the experience of Christian perfection was a real possibility in this life. Methodists came to different interpretations from Calvinists on issues such

---

5   On Russell, see D. Horowitz, *Charles Taze Russell: An Early American and Christian Scientist*, New York, Philosophical Libary, 1986.

as the scope of Christ's atonement, and the capacity of all, through prevenient grace, to choose Christ and a holy life. In the middle decades of the nineteenth century, Methodism began increasingly to endorse and promote the Christian republican vision, embracing conceptions of freedom, virtue and responsibility in public action. This reflected an 'intellectual Americanization' of Methodist theology, closely attuned to the American context as the movement became more middle class. This trend had parallels amongst Calvinists who embraced 'New School' theology.[6] As the Calvinistic hegemony, prevailing from the Puritan period, was challenged by the growing strength of Methodism in the nineteenth century, American theology was drawn in an increasingly Arminian direction, with greater stress on the capacity of humans to contribute both to personal salvation, and in efforts towards holiness. Calvinists and Methodists helped shape, and were also shaped by, the growing republican emphasis on trusting in the personal capacities of citizens, and common-sense philosophy that valued human ethical insights.

Early in the nineteenth century, Unitarianism was perceived to be the biggest threat to the Calvinistic tradition, with its stress on the benevolence of God, human potential, and the application of the test of reason to what was to be accepted in the scriptures. In 1808 the Andover Seminary was founded after a Unitarian was appointed as professor of theology at Harvard. Designed for those who had already completed an arts-based course of study, the seminary taught biblical, systematic, historical and practical theology. Princeton Theological Seminary followed in 1812, reflecting the growing confidence and theological energy of Presbyterianism. By the 1830s, similar institutions had been started by the Baptists, Lutherans, and Episcopalians. In 1860 there were over fifty schools for the graduate education of ministers, although only two were Methodist and four were Baptist. As seminary professors sought to further their own theological education, growing numbers spent time in Europe where they were exposed to wider theological currents.[7]

Between 1795 and 1817, under the Presidency of Jonathan Edwards' grandson Timothy Dwight, Yale maintained a moderate version of the Edwards tradition. One of Dwight's students, Asahel Nettleton (1783–1844), devoted his ministry to the promotion of revival, finding that preaching the doctrines of total depravity, election, reprobation, and the sovereignty of God were no barrier to the popularity and success of his work.[8] However, when Nathaniel William Taylor (1786–1858), another of Dwight's students, became professor of Theology at Yale in 1822, he argued that the best defence against Unitarianism would be to develop

---

6 M. Noll, *America's God*, 330–345, 354.

7 On the extension of seminary education see G.T. Miller, *Piety and Intellect: The Aims and Purposes of Ante-Bellum Theological Education,* Atlanta, Scholars Press, 1990.

8 B. Tyler, *Memoir of the Life and Character of Asahel Nettleton*, Hartford, Robins and Smith, 1844.

a 'Modified Calvinism,' which accorded a greater place to the human will, and less emphasis on divine sovereignty. This would make Calvinism relevant in the increasingly affluent republican context. Taylor offered a measure of intellectual freedom in the interpretation of Christian truth: Calvinist teaching on human depravity was re-expressed as Man's 'free choice of some object rather than God as his chief good… His sin is his own… his guilt is all his own.'[9] Such views were readily embraced by many revivalists. In the era of President Andrew Jackson, when the freedom and the power of individuals were watchwords, such teaching also struck a popular note. Nonetheless, Old School Calvinists, especially at Princeton Theological Seminary, were convinced that this was part of a creeping liberalism.

When, in 1832, Lyman Beecher became founding president and theology professor at Lane Theological Seminary, Cincinnati, he promoted similar views to Taylor. He also sought to counter the lawlessness of the American frontier by urging moral reform, opposition to slavery, and advocacy of temperance. Beecher was accused in a heresy trial of abandoning Reformed orthodoxy, and opening the door to Unitarianism, but was acquitted by his presbytery and synod. 'New School' Presbyterianism was more open to the Plan of Union with the Congregational Church which began in 1801, as well as to decentralised church government and authority, and co-operative ventures with other evangelicals.[10] By 1822, six Presbyterian seminaries were associated with the New School, and a further six with the Old School. Allowing liberty of conscience in doctrinal matters also eased the path for those inclined to move in a liberal direction.

At the New Lebanon Conference, New York, in July 1827, the place of Charles Finney's revivalist practice within Presbyterianism was debated. Finney's robustly popular theology controversially disregarded much in the Westminster Confession. All at the conference agreed in their longing for true revival, and genuine religious experience, as opposed to unholy manifestations, but there were divisions over whether Finney's revivalism was the genuine article. To Nettleton, it gave too much place to natural human capacity, whereas Lyman Beecher simply believed that Finney was using the wrong measures. Finney depicted individuals as moral agents, with powers which God required them to exercise: 'The thing to be done is that which cannot be done for him. It is something *he must do*, or it will never be done.'[11] To Finney's opponents, this

---

9   N. W. Taylor, *Concio and Cerlum: A Sermon Delivered in the Chapel of Yale College, September 10, 1828*, New Haven, Hezekiah Howe, 1828, 5–38, quoted in Hardman, *American Christianity*, 140.

10   On Taylor see S.E. Mead, *Nathaniel William Taylor (1786–1858): A Connecticut Liberal*, Chicago, University of Chicago Press, 1942; and on Beecher see S.C. Henry, *Unvanquished Puritan: A Portrait of Lyman Beecher*, Grand Rapids, Eerdmans, 1973.

11   C. Finney, *Lectures on Revivals of Religion*, (ed. W.G. McLoughlin), Cambridge, Mass., Belknap Press, 1960, 342.

was Pelagianism, making conversion an act of the individual. To Old School Presbyterians, especially in the South, Finney's emphasis on striving in the theological and social spheres replaced dependence on God with an idolatrous reliance on self. Their call for a concentration on spiritual issues contributed to a lack of action on slavery. Nonetheless, Nettleton's revival preaching within the traditional Calvinist framework generally lost out to the popularity of anti-Calvinist revivalism.

'New School' Presbyterians, such as Albert Barnes (1789–1870) downplayed Presbyterian distinctives in co-operative ventures with other evangelicals. Barnes studied at Princeton, and his second pastorate was at the historic First Presbyterian Church in Philadelphia. Barnes took a broader view of the atonement than most Calvinists, denied the imputation of Adam's sin to humanity, and argued that Christ's death created the conditions for all to be saved. He believed that humans had a power within their own natural resources to choose God, although the Holy Spirit was also instrumental in the work of conversion. In 1830, Barnes was charged with doctrinal error by his Presbytery for holding these views, but was acquitted by the General Assembly.[12]

In 1838 Old School Presbyterians acted decisively against the New School's growing lack of clarity on doctrinal issues by ending the cooperative Plan of Union with the Congregationalists. This removed from the denomination 28 presbyteries, 509 ministers, and 60,000 communicants, to which the Plan of Union had substantially contributed. In response, the New School formed its own Assembly, precipitating a rift that lasted in the North to 1869. Presbyterians were no longer able to agree upon a common interpretation of scripture and the Westminster Confession.

The Rise of Theological Liberalism

Protestant liberalism presented itself throughout the period as a third way between radical unbelief, and the confines of traditional Protestant orthodoxy. Liberal theologians attempted to interpret Christianity from the perspective of modern knowledge and ethical values, without resting upon external authority sources such as the Bible. Traditional views were considered malleable in the light of modern thought, especially advances in the natural and social sciences. Theological adaptation was deemed necessary if Christianity was to counteract atheistic rationalism, and present a coherent and relevant social and ethical view for life in modern society. With its roots in Enlightenment methods of critical scholarship, and eighteenth-century Continental rationalism, liberalism was strengthened by romanticism, pietism, and absolute idealism. The influence of Schleiermacher's endeavour to connect theology with contemporary culture, science and politics, arguing that religion both creates and is created by the

12   Noll, *America's God*, 300–306.

culture in which it operates was clear. Religion was to be a civilising and socialising force.

In the years after the Napoleonic wars a steady stream travelled from the United States to Germany to study. However, most American liberal scholars were prevented from direct access to German scholarship by the language barrier. The result was a broader version of Christian liberalism, to a great degree a product of the pulpit, and influenced by earlier American theological traditions.[13] Liberal theology stressed the immanence of God and the human life of Christ. It was optimistic as to human nature, discerning a universal religious sentiment found amongst different religions, and emphasising good works before Christian profession or confession. It argued that the Bible should not be interpreted literally. By the late nineteenth century, liberalism was becoming widespread in Congregational, Episcopal, Methodist, Baptist and Presbyterian circles, although it was stronger in the North than the South, where, fresh from waves of revival, orthodoxy was less questioned.

American Unitarianism had proved a seed bed in which many early liberal theological ideas were tested and developed well before liberal thinking became a major force in Europe. William Ellery Channing (1780–1840) was the leading proponent of Unitarianism, the intellectual influence of which far exceeded its small numerical strength. Channing argued that the work of the preacher was to purge theology of its corrupting tendency to be dry or scholastic, and keep it abreast of contemporary intellectual developments.

Ralph Waldo Emerson (1803–1882) attended divinity school at Harvard when it was inclined towards Unitarianism. He worked for three years as a minister in Boston before embarking on life as a lecturer, essay writer and poet. Emerson and the Transcendentalists rejected external authority, stressed divine love, and emphasised how imagination, insight and instinct made up the religious intuition, by which the soul is linked to God. Once this is realised, the soul can achieve union with God, breaking free from the materialistic layers of life. The reality of God lay within, which he called the benevolent God-principle, 'The Over-Soul.' Emerson spoke of 'self-reliance', confidence in the powers of individual vision, with no place in his system for evil or sin, and therefore no need for salvation or a Saviour. He came close to pantheism, and his views were even rejected by Unitarians, although Transcendentalism played a significant role in promoting the study of world religions.

Some Congregationalists and Presbyterians, exposed to Unitarianism and liberalism, moved in radical directions. Theodore Parker (1810–60),

13 D.E. Miller, *The Case for Liberal Christianity*, San Francisco, Harper and Row, 1981; G. Dorrien, *The Making of American Liberal Theology: Imagining Progressive Religion, 1805–1900*, Louisville, Westminster John Knox, 2001, xix-xxi.

a Congregationalist minister who knew German liberal scholarship, denied biblical authority and the deity of Christ in 1841, before moving into the transcendental belief that Christianity rested on universal truths which came by intuition and transcended revelation. To Parker, religion became in essence morality, leading him into active campaigns for prison reform, temperance and the abolition of slavery.

Horace Bushnell (1802–1876), has been seen as the father of American theological liberalism, with a lasting influence on both the Social Gospel movement in the late nineteenth century, and modernism in the twentieth. His significance parallels that of F.D. Maurice in England, and displays the pervasiveness of romanticism through his reading of Coleridge and Schleiermacher. For much of his life Bushnell was an isolated figure, beset by doubts and sensitivities, and disaffected with the Congregational Church of his youth. After an unhappy period of study at Yale, he tried teaching, journalism and the law, before in 1833 he became minister of North Church, Hartford, where he remained for the next twenty-five years.

Bushnell was influenced by Nathaniel Taylor's more optimistic and benevolent view of God and his willingness to question inherited doctrinal patterns. However, he believed that Taylor remained too near the rigid certainties of the Calvinism he had rejected as a young man. Bushnell also took Greek and Hebrew courses from Josiah Willard Gibbs (1790–1861), who had closely followed developments in German linguistic and biblical scholarship, and helped pioneer their use in America. Gibbs argued that critical speculation as to the historical origins of the Bible was compatible with Christian orthodoxy. Bushnell was impressed with what Gibbs had to say about words and their meanings, and the place of language in conveying religious truth.

Bushnell distinguished between literal words, such as the names for physical things, and figurative words, which derive from human thought and spirit. Although these convey an image of something, they are never able to communicate exact thought from one mind to another, and there will always be an element of misunderstanding. Therefore, theological words would always be inexact, never able to convey the precise truth intended, meaning there would always be theological disagreements.

In *God in Christ* (1849) Bushnell argued that the Bible was to be read not as a collection of propositions, but as 'inspirations and poetic forms of life; requiring also, divine inbreathings and exaltations to us, that we may ascend into their meaning.'[14] It was impossible to be dogmatic in theological matters because it was necessary to use 'analogies, signs, shadows, so to speak, of

---

14   Bushnell, 'Preliminary Dissertation on the Nature of Language as related to Thought and Spirit', in *God in Christ*, 3rd edn, Hartford, Edwin Hunt, 1852, 46–70, 90.

the formless mysteries above us and within us.'[15] Just as poets express the inexpressible through paradox and contradiction, so too the truths of the Incarnation and the Trinity are expressed in seemingly contradictory and paradoxical language. Creeds therefore, although they had a value, should be read as poetical not literal. Doctrine needed to be held 'in a certain spirit of accommodation,' revised and restated to find a bridge between traditional faith and the contemporary world, whilst seeking to guard against unbelief. The key thing to Bushnell was not logic or reason, but 'right sensibility,' knowledge of God and Christian truth from the heart: 'What is loftiest and most transcendent in the character of God, his purity, goodness, beauty and gentleness, can never be sufficiently apprehended by mere intellect, or by any other power than a heart configured by these divine qualities.'[16] The teachings of Jesus Christ were, to Bushnell, utterances of truth, rather than arguments about truth: 'truth is that which shines in its own evidence, that which *finds* us… and thus enters into us.'[17]

Bushnell saw few conversions in his church, and opposed Finney's revivalism as too individualistic. In *Discourses on Christian Nurture* (1847) Bushnell developed the view that nurture and steady growth within a Christian family was a better way to God than through a datable, dramatic and emotionally charged conversion. In bringing up children there was a need at first to inculcate religious feeling, rather than doctrine: 'to bathe the child in their own feeling of love to God and dependence on him, and contrition for wrong before him… to make what is good, happy and attractive; what is wrong, odious and hateful… as the understanding advances… opening upon it gradually the more difficult views of Christian doctrine and experience.'[18] Children reared in the household of faith might never know a time when they were not Christians. Opponents claimed Bushnell was undercutting the grace of God and the work of the Holy Spirit in conversion, replacing them with education. Nonetheless, the idea of Christian 'nurture' became very important in American churches, and patterns of Christian education in churches began to change.

In February 1848 Bushnell reported experiencing a mystical experience of Christ, after which his preaching became more incarnational, a 'simple outspeaking' of his experience. Religion was not to be a matter of duty based on morality; God's purpose through the incarnation was to form a 'divine

---

15   H. Bushnell, *God in Christ: Three Discourses, Delivered at New Haven, Cambridge, and Andover, with a Preliminary Dissertation on Language*, Hartford, Edwin Hunt, 1849, 77.

16   Bushnell, *God in Christ*, 301, 302.

17   Bushnell, *God in Christ*, 93, 74–75.

18   Bushnell, *Views of Christian Nurture, and of Subjects Adjacent Thereto*, Hartford, Edwin Hunt, 1847, 36–37.

Bushnell—The Way of Christ

'all formulas of doctrine should be held in a certain spirit of accommodation... For when they are subjected to the deepest chemistry of thought, that which descends to the point of relationship between the form of truth and its interior formless nature, they become, thereupon, so elastic and run so freely into each other, that one seldom need have any difficulty in accepting as many as are offered'. [1]

1   H. Bushnell, *God in Christ,* 3rd edn., Hartford, 1852, 82.

---

life' in the believer, 'a Christ in the image of your soul.'[19] Bushnell also argued that religion and science needed to respect each other, because nature and the supernatural were all one system of God. The Bible was both to convert the world, but also to be converted to the world. Yet, he was sceptical about Darwin's theories, believing that they could not be proven, although he was more willing to accept developments in geology.

In the thinking of Bushnell, significant attention was given to moral reform, believing that America had a redemptive purpose in the world, but that the nation's character was being undermined by slavery, unbelief, materialism and Roman Catholicism. Although he opposed slavery, he did not join the abolitionist movement, and could not break free from prevalent assumptions that black people were culturally inferior to white. His works also contain significant anti-semitic remarks, and whilst he believed that female education was of value as a way of cultivating virtue, giving women the right to vote went 'against nature'.[20]

The views of Bushnell initially met with widespread rejection, from Unitarians to conservative Calvinists. Bushnell was subjected to severe pressure from other Congregational Churches and threatened with trial for heresy. In 1852 his own church withdrew from the local Consociation to protect him. To Charles Hodge, Bushnell's views on the nature of language, and the impossibility of communicating objective religious truth, were a major threat to Biblical authority. Although Hodge conceded that language was at times imprecise, this did not mean that authors could no longer be trusted, or that God only revealed himself to the imagination and feelings rather than to human reason: 'The Bible is not, a cunningly devised fable... The revelations of God are addressed to the

---

19   H. Bushnell, 'Christ the Form of the Soul', sermon preached at Hartford, Feb. 1848, in H. Bushnell, *The Spirit in Man, Sermons and Selections,* New York, Charles Scribner Sons, 1903, 59–60, in Dorrien, *American Liberal Theology,* 141–42.

20   Dorrien, *American Liberal Theology,* 110–133.

whole soul, to the reason, to the imagination, to the heart and to the conscience. But unless they are addressed to reason, they are as powerless as a phantasm'.[21]

Bushnell, retired in 1859, and devoted his last years to writing *The Vicarious Sacrifice*,[22] in which he rejected the idea of the atonement as sin-bearing, and saw it as a symbol of God's fellow-suffering love. Only a suffering God can relate to suffering beings, and save them. Bushnell emphasised the subjective dimension of the human response to Christ's work, by which individuals are reconciled to God and respond with repentance and changed lives. He inclined to a hope of universal salvation, but conceded that scripture did not teach this.

Bushnell's critical orthodoxy pushed liberalism into the denominational mainstream, and established a framework for American theological liberalism. His approach heralded a shift in theological method from reason to the heart. His views became most influential during the 1880s and 1890s with the rise of the Social Gospel in the North, and as liberal theologians moved substitutionary atonement from the centre-stage of Christianity. His later followers disregarded his doubts over Darwinism, and the radical Biblical criticism of David Strauss, and stressed Bushnell's emphasis on the teaching and moral character of Jesus.[23] His works became standard reading at many seminaries including Yale and Andover. American liberalism believed it was achieving a convergence of Christianity, evolutionary thinking, and biblical criticism, to produce a modern theistic world-view that was an alternative to the scientific.

One figure particularly influenced by Bushnell was Henry Ward Beecher (1813–1887), who during his ministry moved away from the modified Calvinism of his father Lyman Beecher, into evangelical liberalism. From 1847 he exercised a powerful preaching ministry at Plymouth Church, Brooklyn Heights, attracting congregations of over 2,500. At a time when Americans were becoming less willing to respond to the perplexities and challenges of life by simple submission to the sovereign will of God or the authority of the Bible, Beecher purveyed a modernized, popular form of Protestantism, attractive to middle class Americans, promoted through his journalism, lecturing and preaching. As a preacher he rejected doctrinal exactitude, emphasising the need for conversion, and a warm, personal religion. He followed Bushnell in rooting religious experience in the imagination and feeling. Beecher explained that his theology was framed by pragmatic and personal considerations, 'I gradually formed a theology by practise—by trying it on, and the things that really did

---

21   C. Hodge, 'Bushnell's Discourses', *The Biblical Repertory and Princeton Review*, 21, (1849): 269 in J.W. Stewart and J.H. Moorhead (eds), *Charles Hodge Revisited: A Critical Appraisal of His Life and Work*, Grand Rapids, Eerdmans, 2002, 24.

22   H. Bushnell, *The Vicarious Sacrifice, Grounded in Principles of Universal Obligation*, New York, Charles Scribner and Co., 1866.

23   Dorrien, *American Liberal Theology*, xviii.

Church Attendance By Religious Grouping
in the United States 1860-1906

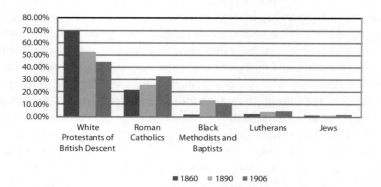

Source, M. Noll, *America's God: From Jonathan Edwards to Abraham Lincoln*, Oxford, Oxford University Press, 2002, Table 13.1.

God's work in the hearts of men I set down as good theology, and the things that did not, whether they were true or not, they were not true to me'.[24] He was a strong advocate of temperance, political reform, the abolition of poverty and disease, and women's rights in the 1860s, which few other Protestant leaders were willing to embrace. Influenced by his sister, Harriet Beecher Stowe, he took up the anti-slavery cause in the 1850s, and during the Civil War Beecher argued that slavery was a greater sin than war, giving his religious blessing to the army of the North. In *Evolution and Religion* (1885) Beecher ridiculed theologians and churchmen who rejected advances in geology and biology, urging a theological accommodation with Darwinism, and accepting evolutionary theory.[25] Beecher found himself engulfed in accusations of adultery during the 1870s, charges which he rebutted, although his reputation was badly tarnished.

Princeton and the defence of Calvinism
Princeton Seminary was the largest and most influential centre of training for the Christian ministry in America in the nineteenth century, educating 6,386 students between 1812 and 1920, some of whom were to go on to hold notable ministerial positions. In its first hundred years, Princeton graduates included

---

24 H.W. Beecher, Lecture to Congregational Association 1882, quoted in ed. R.A. Mohl and N. Betten, *Urban America in Historical Perspective*, New York, Weybright and Talley, 1970, 212–13.

25 Dorrien, *American Liberal Theology*, 178–213. The Beecher family is explored in M. Rugoff, *The Beechers: An American Family in the Nineteenth Century*, New York, Harper and Row, 1981. On Henry Ward Beecher see C.E. Clark, Jr, *Henry Ward Beecher: Spokesman for a Middle Class America*, Urbana, Ill., University of Illinois Press, 1978.

56 moderators of Presbyterian denominations, and five Episcopal bishops. Here scholars promoted a Presbyterianism pinned squarely to the Westminster Confessions and Catechisms, resistant to Finneyite revivalism, emotionalism, rationalism, and liberalising trends. Archibald Alexander (1772–1851), the first Professor and Principal, established a theological framework for the seminary which lasted a century, combining thoroughgoing Presbyterian orthodoxy with devotion to the Bible, and interest in traditional revival and genuine Christian experience. Princeton was to be a bastion against the New Divinity, and incipient infidelity.[26] One of Alexander's most able students was Charles Hodge (1797–1878), who also studied at the universities of Halle and Berlin in Germany between 1826 and 1828. Here Hodge attended lectures by Schleiermacher, and learned the importance of rigorous intellectual effort required from theologians if the pressures from rationalism and romanticism were to be resisted. When he returned to lecture at Princeton, Hodge sought to counter the intellectual flow of nineteenth-century German critical theology, rejecting Hegel's thinking as implicitly pantheistic, and Strauss's *Das Leben Jesu* as decisively flawed. Hodge wrote extensively in the *Biblical Repertory and Princeton Review*, of which he was the editor for over forty years. By the 1840s he was one of the major figures in American theological and ecclesiological circles.

Hodge's theological centre was the Bible: 'it is written' had more attraction for him than Romanticism, the rationalism of Kant, the experiential mysticism of Schleiermacher, or Emerson's Transcendentalism. He preferred structure to ambiguity. Rather than adapting the content of theology to suit the modern context, Hodge was determined to integrate science, theology, politics and ethics with Calvinist piety. The traditional Calvinistic orthodoxy of the Westminster Confession was to be both preserved and made relevant to modern commercial, democratic and intellectual society. In 1872, Hodge proudly claimed 'I am not afraid to say that a new idea never originated in this Seminary,'[27] but this did not imply evidence of intellectual weakness, or lack of creativity in theological effort.

God's revelation of himself was, to Hodge, rooted in the Bible, which it was the duty of the theologian to study, as the scientist studied nature: principles were to be derived from facts, not forced on them. True science and theology were both based on the grounds of scientific induction. The theologian was to collect facts, and show their internal relation, their harmony and consistency. Charles Hodge argued that although there were external evidences as to the truth and authority of scripture, the internal evidence was compelling, but this

---

26 On Alexander see J.W. Alexander, *The Life of Archibald Alexander*, New York, Charles Scribner, 1854; L.A. Loetscher, *Facing the Enlightenment and Pietism: Archibald Alexander and the Founding of Princeton Theological Seminary*, Westport, Conn., Greenwood, 1983.

27 A.A. Hodge, *The Life of Charles Hodge*, London, T. Nelson and Sons, 1881, 521.

Charles Hodge—the Nature of Biblical Revelation

'The Bible is to the theologian what nature is to the man of science. It is his store-house of facts; and his method of ascertaining what the Bible teaches, is the same as that which the natural philosopher adopts to ascertain what nature teaches... The duty of the Christian theologian is to ascertain, collect, and combine all the facts which God has revealed concerning himself and our relation to Him. These facts are all in the Bible... the Theologian [is] to be guided by the same rules as the Man of Science.'[1]

1 Charles Hodge, *Systematic Theology,* 3 vols, London, Edinburgh, 1871, I: 10–11.

---

could not be appreciated until the heart was right with God. The Bible itself 'speaks in his name, it assumes his authority. How can these claims be false and yet the Bible so holy... in the correspondence between all its statements respecting God, man, redemption, and a future state, and all our judgements, reasonable apprehensions, and personal experience?'[28] Scripture, therefore, was the product of the infallible intellect of God, 'he is its author... he says whatever the Bible says... everything which the Bible affirms to be true is true.' God used the writers as his organs of communication; the Holy Spirit oversaw the exact words which are recorded in Scripture.[29] This was even the case with scientific matters, as Hodge explained when discussing geology: 'As the Bible is of God, it is certain that there can be no conflict between the teachings of the Scriptures and the facts of science'. Differences that existed were either capable of harmonisation, or proved to be false.[30]

In interpreting the Bible, Hodge appealed to the Common Sense argument. 'It is a monstrous evil to make the Bible contradict the common sense and common consciousness of men. This is to make God contradict himself'.[31] His forceful Calvinism was also shot through with spiritual ardour and warmth.[32] Thorough

28   C. Hodge, *The Way of Life,* London, Religious Tract Society, 1841, republished Banner of Truth Trust, London, 1959, 24, 16.

29   C. Hodge, 'Inspiration', *Biblical Repertory and Princeton Review,* XXIX, October 1857, 661–63. See also Hodge's *Systematic Theology, vol.* I, 151–188.

30   C. Hodge, *Systematic Theology,* London and Edinburgh, 1871–73, Vol I, 573–74; M. Noll, *The Princeton Theology 1812–1921, Scripture, Science and Theological Method from Archibald Alexander to Benjamin Breckinridge Warfield,* Grand Rapids, Baker, 1983, 25–27.

31   Hodge, *Commentary on the Epistle to the Romans,* [1886], revised ed., Grand Rapids, 1947, 151, quoted in Noll, *America's God,* 318.

32   Hodge's biography is set out in his son, A.A. Hodge's *The Life of Charles Hodge,* London, T. Nelson and Sons, 1881; his life and work is assessed in J.W. Stewart and J.H. Moorhead (eds), *Charles Hodge Revisited: A Critical Appraisal of His Life and Work,* Grand Rapids, Eerdmans, 2002.

Charles Hodge

biblical scholarship, needed to be matched by obedient lifestyle—'Beware a strong head and a cold heart'.[33] Hodge's *Systematic Theology*, which appeared between 1872 and 1873, was to prove a bulwark of conservative Presbyterian theological education, his thinking moulding nineteenth-century American Calvinism, influencing both friends and opponents. He was succeeded by his son, Archibald Alexander Hodge (1823–1886), who as Professor of Didactic and Polemic Theology continued to express his father's views, including those on

33 C. Hodge, *Princeton Sermons: Outlines of Discourses, Doctrinal and Practical*, London, Banner of Truth, 1958, xvi.

4

the inspiration and authority of scripture as the foundation of Christian truth and faith, clearly and concisely. He supported Biblical inerrancy, arguing that the original autographs of scripture were without error, although they no longer existed. Nonetheless, scripture as the church now had it, contained only very minor blemishes.

Benjamin Breckinridge Warfield (1851–1921), who succeeded to A.A. Hodge's Professorship, maintained the traditional views of Princeton into the early twentieth century, when the tide of theological opinion was turning against them. Warfield studied under Charles Hodge, and for a short period in Leipzig, before spending thirty-three years at Princeton Seminary as the redoubtable defender of Calvinist orthodoxy and scriptural inerrancy. His wide-ranging writings show he was well-versed in the fields of science.[34] Between 1892 and 1910 Warfield's ideas influenced attempts to assert belief in scriptural inerrancy as vital for membership of the Presbyterian Church. Warfield was to bring this teaching to its fullest expression, arguing that because all scripture was inspired by God, it by nature could not contain errors. If errors in the Bible were proved, its authority would be completely lost.[35] He opposed those who believed they could uphold the religious truth of the Bible whilst subjecting its pages to rigorous historical criticism: discerning a core of religious truth in a book filled with errors and inaccuracies was impossible to Warfield. The means and the message conveyed had to be in conformity. Warfield took the battle to the modernists. Instead of restating Christian belief in terms of modern thought, he called for modern thought to be stated in terms of Christian belief.[36] Nonetheless, Warfield was prepared to accept that evolution could be accommodated into the Biblical faith, seeing theistic evolution as a way of understanding biblical cosmology, although he rejected explaining the world solely in terms of scientific criterion.

The last of the great defenders of the Princeton Tradition was J. Gresham Machen (1881–1937), who studied under Warfield, and taught New Testament at the seminary from 1906 to 1929. When in that year the seminary underwent a Liberal realignment at the hands of those who believed that Princeton Theology was no longer viable in the light of modern theological and scientific

34   F.L. Patton, 'Benjamin Breckinridge Warfield—A Memorial Address', *Princeton Theological Review*, 19 July 1921, 369–391.

35   A.A. Hodge, *Outlines of Theology*, 1860, reprinted Banner of Truth, 1972, 66; B.B. Warfield, *The Inspiration and Authority of the Bible*, Philadelphia, Presbyterian and Reformed, 1948. Criticisms of Warfield's approach are found in E. Sandeen, *The Roots of Fundamentalism: British and American Millenarianism 1800–1930*, Chicago, University of Chicago Press, 1970, who argued that Warfield raised Scripture to an unhealthy position above historical critical enquiry. John D. Woodbridge, *Biblical Authority: A Critique of the Rogers / McKim Proposal*, Grand Rapids, Zondervan, 1982 argued that teaching on the inerrancy of scripture is to be found throughout the history of the church.

36   B.B. Warfield, *Critical Reviews*, Oxford, Oxford University Press, 1932, 322.

advance, a number of professors left. Machen became a principal founder of Westminster Theological Seminary.[37]

The attempt of the Hodges, Warfield, and Machen to defend Confessional orthodoxy and high views of scripture inspiration using informed scholarship, whilst avoiding pietistic anti-intellectualism, occurred as the tectonic plates of theology were shifting. It was the Presbyterian dimension of a wider conservative defence of confessional orthodoxy, yet the growing influence of historical critical study and science later in the century was to create significant difficulties for the appeal to Common-Sense Philosophy. Hodge's *Systematic Theology* appeared in the 1870s, not long after the attempts of German Lutherans such as E.W. Hengstenberg (1802–69) to restore their church to confessionalism, and to promote the verbal inspiration of scripture in the face of rationalist and subjectivist interpretations. The same decade saw Tridentine orthodoxy reasserted at the first Vatican Council.

Liberals and Conservatives in Conflict

The Princeton approach encountered significant resistance from some American Presbyterians. Deep fault lines emerged between those convinced that the Bible remained the divinely preserved and authoritative Word of God, and those who argued that the Scriptures should be read and interpreted no differently from other ancient religious texts. The result was a series of high profile cases in which conservatives attempted to resist the challenges to orthodoxy. In 1874, the Presbyterian David Swing (1830–1894) was charged with heresy for denying substantial elements of the Westminster Confession of Faith. Swing was a popular preacher, addressing weekly congregations of several thousand, and his books sold well. He argued that all religious expression, in scripture, doctrine, or creed, was formulated within a culture, and needed to be understood in terms of that culture. Therefore the Bible contained religious expressions produced by the context in which it was written, and which were not always absolutely valid and needed to be set on one side. He considered creedal formulations, 'a certain assemblage of words', even less reliable. Christianity was a way of living, rather than a doctrinal system. Swing's trial received widespread coverage in the religious press. The Chicago Presbytery supported Swing by 48 votes to 13, unwilling to convict him because of the imprecise nature of Swing's language, and a growing disinclination to press for absolute confessional orthodoxy. Swing eventually left the Presbyterian Church to start an independent cause, which met in a music hall, and was attended by several thousand each week, testimony to the appeal of his version of modern theology.

Charles Briggs (1841–1913) studied in Berlin before, in 1874, he began teaching at Union Theological Seminary, where he worked for nearly forty years. Briggs

---

37   See N.B. Stonehouse, *J.G. Machen, A Biographical Memoir*, Grand Rapids, Eerdmans, 1954.

sought to combine the fruits of biblical higher criticism with theological reflection. He argued that scripture was infallible in matters of faith and practice, but not in all details of history or science. Scripture contained the Word, but was not itself the Word. Briggs believed he was still being true to evangelical doctrine when he claimed that the internal, spiritual sense of scripture was fully inspired, but not its external words, and that Christianity would not fall if the biblical miracles were explained in naturalistic terms. Over time Briggs trod the path of liberalism more firmly. In 1893 he was found guilty of heresy, and removed from the Presbyterian ministry, but in 1900 he was ordained into the Episcopal Church, continuing to work at Union Seminary. In 1892, Union Theological Seminary separated itself from the official jurisdiction of the Presbyterian Church, and became an independent interdenominational seminary strongly identified with the liberal and modern agenda. By the 1890s, Yale Divinity School had also moved in a liberal direction, as had Andover, originally founded as a bastion of orthodoxy in the face of Unitarianism. They were followed in the twentieth century by Boston University, which had Methodist roots, and the University of Chicago Divinity School, founded by Chicago Baptists.[38] Nonetheless, despite the steady liberalisation of Presbyterianism in its essential hold on the Westminster Confession, attempts to modify its confessional basis between 1874 and 1903 were rejected. The Confession might not have been deemed entirely right, but no reasonable alternative was deemed satisfactory.

These trends also became evident in New England Congregationalism after 1875. Much influenced by Bushnell, the Congregationalist Washington Gladden (1836–1918) was strongly liberal in his theology: in the early 1870s he spoke of doctrines such as that of original sin as 'outmoded' and 'immoral.' Gladden saw an organic link between religion and politics, arguing that social justice could be achieved by applying Christian principles and methods to resolving social problems. He served on the Columbus City Council, believing that the work of God's kingdom involved regenerating both individuals and society: commerce, industry, learning, laws, and amusement were all to be claimed for Christ, in fulfilment of the prayer 'Thy Kingdom Come.'[39] In his *Working People and their Employers* (1876), Gladden called for fairness to employees. His principles caused him to reject a gift to a Congregational organisation from the oil magnate John D. Rockefeller, because he considered it tainted money. The idea of the interpenetration of religion and culture, the sacred

---

38   Dorrien, *American Liberal Theology*, 337–370. On Briggs see M.S. Massa, *Charles Augustus Briggs and the Crisis of Historical Criticism*, Minneapolis, Fortress, 1990. Briggs's views are set out in C.A. Briggs, *Biblical Study: Its Principles, Methods, and History*, 2nd edn, New York, Charles Scribner's Sons, 1883.

39   See J.H. Dorn, *Washington Gladden: Prophet of the Social Gospel*, Columbus, Ohio; Ohio State University, 1967.

and the secular, became strong in the American context, particularly with its emphasis on Progress. Proponents were convinced that they were building the kingdom of God, and that America was truly being Christianised. By the end of the nineteenth century an increasing number of American liberals became convinced that economic inequality was the core theological issue. Walter Rauschenbusch (1861–1918) was to become the foremost theologian of this Social Gospel. [See Chapter 14]

Between 1830 and 1930 some 10,000 Americans studied in Germany, half of them at the University of Berlin. The peak decade was the 1890s, when 2,000 made the journey, 1,300 of them to Berlin. The attraction of Ritschl's ethical idealism, together with respect for Bushnell and social gospel thinking, saw Liberal theology making decisive advances in American academic circles in the early twentieth century. In 1908, thirty-three American Protestant denominations founded the Federal Council of Churches. Modernist Protestant thinkers entertained high ecumenical hopes for reunion with Roman Catholicism, also experiencing its own modern impulses. Signs of progress appeared to abound—democracy, education, science all suggested that the world was advancing by means of modern culture. Liberal theologians believed they had freed American Christianity from the confines of Scriptural and confessional orthodoxy. By 1914 American liberalism was claiming the status of academic orthodoxy, and in 1920 at least a third of American Protestant ministers identified with its theological approach, together with more than half of the religious journals and publishing houses, and many key figures in denominational hierarchies.[40] Yet, as the depth of the social crisis in urban and industrial society became clear, accentuated by the horrors of the First World War, optimistic assumptions as to human nature and progress began to erode. Some wondered whether, if the liberalising process were pursued, American Christianity would survive in a historically recognisable form.

American Roman Catholicism
The division found in nineteenth-century Protestantism between liberal and conservative was replicated, although to a lesser degree, amongst Roman Catholics. Liberal Roman Catholics sought more freedom of association with Protestants, to make greater use of public schooling, and concede more authority to the state. They sought an American form of Roman Catholicism which was progressive and sympathetic to elements of modern thought, compared to European ultra-montane Roman Catholicism. In the 'Americanist' controversy of the late 1890s, the degree to which American Roman Catholics could accommodate themselves to the modern American agenda, both social

---

40   W.R. Hutchison, *The Modernist Impulse in American Protestantism*, Cambridge, Mass., Harvard University Press, 1976, 3–4.

and theological was debated. When John Zahm, professor of Physics and Chemistry at the University of Notre Dame, Indiana, published *Evolution and Dogma* in 1896, arguing in favour of theistic evolution, he found himself under censure from the Vatican, and in 1898 he was forced to withdraw his book from circulation. The following year, Pope Leo XIII's encyclical *Testem Benevolentiae*, (1899) condemned as 'Americanism' attempts by theological modernists to mould doctrine to suit liberal, individualist culture. The errors spelled out by Pope Pius X in 1907, included the promotion of biblical criticism and accommodation to modern science: modernism was the synthesis of all heresies. His encyclical, *Pascendi Dominici Gregis*, proposed establishing a 'council of vigilance' in each diocese to watch for modernist errors, and suspected books were removed from seminary libraries. Fear of being charged with heresy brought an emphasis on safe conservative theology. Although American bishops were divided on the issue, the influence of the papacy over the church grew, and the spirit of independency, long cherished in American Roman Catholicism, waned.[41] A prevalent Roman Catholic social conservatism, together with devotion rooted in private religious practice, militated against widespread campaigns for social justice, although the support of local priests for striking Roman Catholics became a notable feature of the strikes against the monopolies in coal and steel between 1890 and 1910. Systems of social ethics did begin to be formulated, culminating in the 1919 Bishops' Programme of Social Reconstruction, which advocated minimum wage legislation, public housing, insurance for sickness, old age and unemployment, and control of monopolies. Enthusiasm for social reconstruction was not maintained through the 1920s.

THE GROWTH OF PREMILLENNIALISM

As theological liberalism gained ground in progressive circles, dispensational premillennialism was also growing in popularity in some conservative evangelical circles. Dispensationalism had emerged amongst the Plymouth Brethren in England and Ireland in the 1830s, and spread to North America in the 1850s, its key proponent being John Nelson Darby (1800–1882). Its very literal reading of parts of scripture contrasted sharply to liberal approaches, but also differed from those of traditional orthodox biblical and historical scholarship. From both sides it attracted concerted opposition. The premillennial scheme interpreted biblical history in terms of a series of eras, or dispensations, usually given as seven. The age of the church, lasting from Pentecost to the return of Christ, would end in judgement and the establishment of the millennial reign of Christ, with an earthly kingdom in Jerusalem. As the conviction grew after the Civil War that churches and Christian culture were in decline, and that

---

41   Dolan, *American Catholic Experience*, 294–320.

theological liberalism was sowing the seeds of apostasy, interest in biblical prophecy intensified, such signs being read as a precursor of the return of Christ.

The developing premillennial movement, which attracted significant Presbyterian interest, was strengthened through gatherings such as the Niagara Bible Conference, which started in 1875. Most of the conference leaders accepted Darby's dispensationalist interpretation of the Bible, especially D.L. Moody. His theological approach, along with that of his close associates R.A Torrey (1856–1928), A.C. Dixon (1854–1925), and A.J. Gordon (1836–1895), also shaped wider evangelism and missionary activity: in the light of the apparently imminent return of Christ, evangelism and holy living were the things most needful. Dispensationalism also became rooted in the emerging Bible institutes, such as the Moody Bible Institute (1886), and the Bible Institute of Los Angeles (1907). The most influential formulation of the scheme was the Scofield Reference Bible (1909), with annotations on the text provided by the lawyer turned minister C.I. Scofield (1843–1921). In these circles, serious engagement with advancing theological liberalism was not encouraged. In 1899, D.L. Moody proposed to one scholar that there be a moratorium for ten years on discussion of theological liberalism at his annual Northfield Conference: 'just let us get on with the practical work of the Kingdom.'[42]

TOWARDS FUNDAMENTALISM

At the time when Roman Catholicism was denouncing Modernism as flagrant heresy which the faithful should avoid at all cost, it was also being subject to robust critique from conservative evangelicals and dispensationalist leaders. Named after a series of pamphlets published between 1910 and 1915 called *The Fundamentals: a Testimony to the Truth* (1910–15), Fundamentalism has become a blanket term to embrace many reactions to modernism. Although it was not coined until 1920, it is generally associated with dispensational premillennialists. The rise of this type of Fundamentalism represented a move away from the Princeton-style Conservative synthesis of convictions as to the supreme authority of the Bible with the belief that thorough understanding of developments in modern European theology and scientific thinking was vital if Modernism was to be exposed as not only different to Biblical Christianity, but as antithetical to it. Therefore, there is a need to draw a distinction between those committed to finding intellectual grounds for the defence of the fundamentals of orthodoxy, and the Fundamentalism which ventured little from simple assertions of Biblical authority, an inward-looking holiness piety, militant opposition to modern culture, and pessimism about human

---

42   George Adam Smith quoted in H. Drummond, *Dwight L. Moody: Impressions and Facts*, New York, McClure, Phillips and Company, 1900. p. 30.

progress.[43] It has been argued that it was only at the World's Conference on Christian Fundamentals in 1919 that millenarians became fundamentalists, and the movement took on the assertiveness that was to characterise its campaigns of the 1920s against Modernism in major denominations and the teaching of biological evolution in schools.[44]

The *Fundamentals* pamphlets were written by a range of anti-modernist scholars, including significant non-dispensationalists from Princeton, designed to promote foundational orthodoxies. They stressed the historicity of the virgin birth of Christ, the resurrection, the literal and imminent Second Coming, substitutionary atonement for sin through the sacrificial death of Christ, and the inerrancy of the Bible. The specific challenges of modernism were addressed. G.F. Wright's volume on evolution argued that 'by no stretch of legitimate reasoning can Darwinism be made to exclude design'.[45] Although North American Fundamentalism is usually seen as the antithesis of the social gospel movement, one of the pamphlets called 'The Church and Socialism', stressed 'A true gospel of grace is inseparable from a gospel of good works... These social teachings of the gospel need a new emphasis today by those who accept the whole gospel, and should not be left to be interpreted and applied by those alone who deny essential Christianity.'[46] However, later Fundamentalists in North America did not see things in the same way, and the process of retreat from the social concern agenda in the USA has been termed 'The Great Reversal'.[47] The term 'Social Gospel' became synonymous with theological liberalism and anti-evangelicalism, a distraction from the 'main thing', which was urgent evangelism. If society was to be changed, it would come through individual conversions: conversion changed people, and changed people would change society.

As theological pressures grew, attempts were made by denominations to outline a small body of fundamental doctrine which would sum up orthodox Christian belief. In 1910, the Presbyterian General Assembly sought to challenge the growing Liberal-Modernist agenda by setting out a five-point declaration of essential beliefs. These were the inerrancy of Scripture; the Virgin Birth

43   See G.M. Marsden, *Fundamentalism and American Culture: The Shaping of Twentieth-Century Evangelicalism 1870–1925*, New York, Oxford University Press, 1980; W.R. Hutchinson, *The Modernist Impulse in American Protestantism*, Cambridge, Harvard University Press, 1976.

44   E.R. Sandeen, *The Roots of Fundamentalism: British and American Millenarianism 1800–1930*, Chicago, University of Chicago Press, 1970, 160 argues for a distinction between the fundamentalist movement and the fundamentalist controversy, believing that it was at the 1919 World's Conference on Christian Fundamentals, that millenarians became fundamentalists.

45   G.F. Marsden, 'The Passing of Evolution', in *The Fundamentals: A Testimony to the Truth*, 12 vols, Chicago: Testimony Publishing Company, 1910–1915, Vol. VIII, 19.

46   C.R. Erdman, 'The Church and Socialism'. *The Fundamentals*, Vol. xii, 1911.

47   D. Moberg, *The Great Reversal, Evangelism Versus Social Concern*, London, Scripture Union, 1973.

of Christ; the substitutionary atonement of Christ; the bodily resurrection of Christ; the historical authenticity of biblical miracles. These became the 'five points' of Fundamentalism in the 1920s, although the premillennial return of Christ replaced the authenticity of miracles, which was already covered by the statement on inerrancy. Through this means, significant elements of Princeton theology came to be affirmed by a wide range of bodies, including Baptists, dispensationalists and millenarian groups.

Holiness Teaching and Pentecostalism
Christian perfection had been a strong feature of Wesleyan Methodism, since John Wesley identified a second and distinct experience subsequent to justification, and different to progressive sanctification. Aspects of holiness teaching also became part of the revivalist agenda. Charles Finney believed that the 'baptism or sealing of the Holy Spirit subdues the power of desires, and strengthens and conforms the will... making the whole being an offering to God'.[48] Such a second, decisive experience after conversion would allow the Christian life to be lived at a higher level, with greater victory over sin. Holiness teaching gained ground in an American evangelical scene seeking new impetus, conscious that the fire of the Second Great Awakening had burned low. In the core themes of revivalism, ruin, redemption and regeneration, ruin became increasingly identified with drink, Sabbath breaking, gambling and sexual immorality.

Although it gained a significant following amongst America's wealthy and educated classes, the holiness movement in North America was far from the middle class, white, Anglican phenomenon it became in England in the 1870s, where the Keswick Convention, first held in 1875, was a focus for the new spirituality. Both Methodist and more Reformed strands of the holiness movement had transatlantic dimensions. James Hudson Taylor of the China Inland Mission promoted both holiness and premillennialism in his speaking engagements on both sides of the Atlantic, including Moody's Northfield Conference. The holiness movement countered the emphases in Liberal theology on outward ethical conduct, gradual change through natural human capacities, and the merits of advancing civilization, with a realized experience of holiness through the direct intervention of God. Holiness thinking was influenced by Romanticism, but also the linking of spiritual progress to moments of crisis betrayed echoes of Hegelian and evolutionary thought. The emphasis upon a present and felt holiness also owed something to the shift in theological thinking away from the atonement and towards the incarnation.

From the 1830s onwards, women played a significant role in the 'Holiness' movement. Notable was Phoebe Palmer (1807–74) reared in a devout Methodist home. She lamented that hers had not been the paradigm conversion experience

---

48   C. Finney, *Power from on High*. Reprinted, London, Victory Press, 1944, 42.

Phoebe Palmer—Experience of 'Holiness' Blessing

'Between the hours of eight and nine—while pleading at the throne of grace for a present fulfilment of the exceeding great and precious promises;... and making an entire surrender of body, soul, and spirit;... I received the assurance that God the Father, through the atoning Lamb, accepted the sacrifice; my heart was emptied of self, and cleansed of all idols, from all filthiness of the flesh and spirit, and I realized that I dwelt in God, and felt that he had become the portion of my soul, my ALL IN ALL.' [1]

---

1   P. Palmer, *The Way of Holiness* (1843), London, 1845, 95–96.

---

of conviction of sin, despair, deliverance, and felt assurance, and suffered the trauma of the death of three children in infancy, one in a fire. This deepened her sense of spiritual emptiness, before she found the assurance she lacked, an ability to rest on the promises of God, and a freedom to sacrifice all and live only for God. This experience she shared with others at prayer meetings in her home. In 1840 she started a Tuesday meeting 'for the Promotion of Holiness' in New York, which became very popular, and was attended by both men and women, clerical and lay.[49] As her reputation grew, Phoebe Palmer accepted speaking engagements across the United States, and then in Britain where she undertook a major speaking tour between 1859 and 1864. This helped root her teachings in British Methodism and then the Salvation Army, through her influence on William and Catherine Booth. The Salvation Army demonstrated that holiness was not simply an inward and experiential phenomenon, but could have a significant practical outcome.

Phoebe Palmer's writings proved immensely popular. *The Way of Holiness* (1843) went through three editions in its first year of publication,[50] and her monthly publication the *Guide to Christian Perfection* was widely read. She spoke of the need for 'entire consecration'—the total surrender of the self to God, by which believers placed their all 'upon the altar', and made public testimony to the fulfilment of biblical promises, as part of a simple, literal, Biblicist faith. This second blessing was identified with the baptism of the Holy Spirit. The readiness with which phrases such as 'entire consecration', 'heart purity', and 'the way of holiness' passed into devotional vocabulary and hymnology reflects the influence of the movement. To some it was a restoration of the validity and power of the lay reading of scripture which had characterised early Methodism, at a time when others were consumed by the quest to be intellectually relevant.

49   On Phoebe Palmer see C.E. White, *The Beauty of Holiness: Phoebe Palmer as Theologian, Revivalist, Feminist and Humanitarian*, Grand Rapids, Eerdmans, 1986.

50   See T.C. Odin (ed), *Phoebe Palmer: Selected Writings*, New York, Paulist Press, 1988.

Phoebe Palmer's argument was uncomplicated. If people relied more simply, and firmly, on the Bible, rather than the opinions of men, they would be more happy and more useful. Her work probably made her the most influential Christian woman of the nineteenth century. It was based on a sense of special anointing, without ordination or formal sanction. She argued that it was the duty of women to preach if they had gifts to do so—the ordination of Christ and the empowerment of the Spirit was of most importance, although such ministry did not necessarily mean claiming authority over men.[51]

Prayer meetings for revival influenced by the holiness movement began in a number of cities in 1857. When the stock market crashed, destroying many businesses, the intensity of prayer deepened. Within six months, 10,000 people were gathering each day for prayer in New York. Churches were filled, then theatres. It was an orderly trans-denominational movement, which spread rapidly, with a strong role for the laity, and emphasis on prayer. Estimates of the numbers converted in the revival range from 500,000 to 1 million.[52]

By 1886 there were some 200 meetings for the promotion of holiness, involving not only Methodists, but also Presbyterians, Congregationalists and Baptists. Within Methodism, official opposition grew, through fears that holiness had become a church within the church. Some became convinced that holiness was only achievable through separation from denominations. Between 1880 and 1905, some 100,000 left Methodism for a proliferation of new holiness groupings, attracting both black and white members, many from the rural poor and urban working class. Their services were characterised by emotional worship, faith healing, and premillennial theology. In 1881, Daniel Sidney Warner left Methodism with a group of followers to found the Church of God. Phineas F. Bresee (1838–1916) formed a congregation in Los Angeles in 1895, from which the Church of the Nazarene developed. The global reach of the holiness movement was impressive. Religious revival along the West African coast was reported in 1876–78, and again in 1885, characterised by a stress upon holiness and preparedness for the Second Coming of Christ.[53] The Welsh revival of 1904–05 was similarly marked by holiness influences. [see chapter 16]

The birth of Pentecostalism
The oppressive grip of slavery upon American society, and the continuing

51 P. Palmer, *Tongues of Fire on the Daughters of the Lord*, in M. Westerkamp, *Women and Religion in Early America 1600–1850: The Puritan and Evangelical Traditions*, New York, Routledge, 1999, 153.

52 J.E. Orr, *The Second Evangelical Awakening in America*, London, Marshall Morgan and Scott, 1952, 31–33. See also T.L. Smith, *Revivalism and Social Reform: American Protestantism on the Eve of the Civil War*, New York, Abingdon, 1957.

53 A. Porter, *Religion Versus Empire? British Protestant Missionaries and Overseas Expansion, 1700–1914*, Manchester, Manchester University Press, 2004 pp. 244–45.

prevalence of racist attitudes towards the black population, made religion a powerful source of other-worldly consolation. The radical message of the black church also offered a subversive means of expression and protest. To poor African-Americans, with little prospect of success in the material world, the holiness movement offered an immediate means of experiencing and expressing the fruits of the gospel. It preserved the freedom, spontaneity, and vitality of revival-style religious life which had brought significant conversions in earlier decades, and allowed for expression of elements of African-American folk religion. A number of holiness groups developed strongly in urban areas with significant black populations.[54]

In Pentecostalism a range of forces coalesced, amongst which holiness was prominent. So too was a restorationist emphasis that the experience of baptism in the Holy Spirit, and renewed stress on holiness and physical healing, were all part of a restoration of the New Testament miracles that would precede the return of Christ. An important figure was William Seymour, born amidst poverty and racial discrimination in Centreville, Louisiana, in 1870. Initially working as a hotel waiter, he became a Methodist, and then joined an interracial group called the Evening Light Saints, who advocated entire sanctification, healing by the power of God, interracial worship, and granting permission to women to preach. Seymour came under the influence of Charles Fox Parham (1873–1929), who had founded the Bethel Bible College in Topeka, Kansas, in 1900. Parham argued that the definitive sign of a person having been baptised in the Holy Spirit was speaking in tongues, as at the day of Pentecost. Agnes Ozman was the first to report experiencing glossalalia after Parham had laid hands on her, and prayed that she would receive the power of the Spirit. By January 1901 he and half his students reported experiencing this phenomenon. Glossolalia was not new to America, having been noted in the Shaker movement of Mother Ann Lee, and amongst the early Mormons. Incidents were also reported in the West of Scotland in 1830, and the following year at the Scotch Presbyterian Church in London where Edward Irving was the minister.[55] However, from obscure beginnings in Kansas and Los Angeles, this new wave of Pentecostal expression was to become a movement of global significance by the end of the century. [see chapter 16]

By 1905 Parham had started an 'Apostolic Faith' movement, and a Bible School in Houston, Texas, which William Seymour attended. When Seymour moved to Los Angeles he began working with a Black Holiness Church, but the view that speaking in tongues was the sign of baptism in the Spirit was not widely accepted and he was asked to leave. He resorted to holding prayer

54   On black holiness churches see V. Synan, *The Holiness-Pentecostal Tradition : Charismatic Movements in the Twentieth Century*, Eerdmans, Grand Rapids, 1997.

55   C.G. Flegg, *Gathered Under Apostles: A Study of the Catholic Apostolic Church*, Oxford, OUP, 1992.

meetings in homes, and at one in Bonnie Brae Street in April 1906 a number of people reported experiencing the Baptism in the Spirit. Seymour started the Apostolic Faith Gospel Mission, and hired an old Methodist church at 312 Azusa Street, where he preached to a mixed congregation of blacks and whites. The Pentecostal revival that began here was characterised by tongue speaking, prophesying, and exuberant worship, including shouting and jumping. It attracted African Americans, white Americans, Mexicans and Asians, and created a local sensation, emphasising the three requirements of conversion, holiness or sanctification, and baptism in the Holy Spirit. Seymour's teaching offered spiritual fulfilment and power to the oppressed and voiceless poor. It was significant in being a movement largely begun by a black minister, which channelled the enthusiastic religious practice of African-American churches into a mixed-race body, although white Americans later withdrew from it. Azusa Street became the principal centre of the more radical dimension of the holiness tradition. Many international visitors were attracted, seeking ecstatic worship experiences, physical healing, and the gift of tongues, and returned home to promote these happenings in their own churches. By the end of 1906, there were nine Pentecostal churches in Los Angeles.

Pentecostalism emerged as a radical, primitivist, experiential, alternative to the advance of scientific Darwinism, liberalism, and the Social Gospel movement; it was also, in part, a religious response to racism. Its radical experiential basis suggests dissatisfaction with established evangelical denominations, and its primitivist sentiment a debt to romanticism. However, although American Pentecostalism held significant appeal for the socially disinherited, it has been shown that Pentecostals were representative of a broader cross-section of society, including manual workers and a few professionals.[56] Whilst liberal theology placed religious feeling above religious authority, in Pentecostalism feeling was stressed alongside supernaturalism, dramatic signs of the Spirit's transforming power, and a conservative approach to orthodox Christian doctrine. There was often a strong premillennial emphasis, and a conviction that the reappearance of the charismata was closely linked to the imminent second coming of Christ. Pentecostals also argued that the atonement of Christ provided both physical and spiritual healing in the present. The 'full gospel' was fourfold—personal conversion, baptism in the Holy Spirit accompanied by speaking in tongues, physical healing by faith, and the expectation of the imminent return of the Lord. Full and equal recognition was offered to the spiritual gifts exercised by women: Lucy Farrow and Neely Terry served as pioneering women ministers

---

56   R.M. Anderson, *Vision of the Disinherited: the making of American Pentecostalism*, Oxford, OUP, 1979; G. Wacker, *Heaven Below: Early Pentecostals and American Culture*, Cambridge, Mass, Harvard University Press, 2001.

alongside Seymour at Azusa Street, although women were generally restricted to more conventional roles.

In its early manifestations, Pentecostalism was subject to bitter opposition from other churches, including holiness churches. Adherents were dismissed as 'holy rollers' for their uninhibited expression of raw religious emotion in what appeared chaotic and deafening meetings. The movement was also subject to early divisions. The largely African-American Church of God in Christ, which was to become the world's largest Black Pentecostal Church, emerged from the holiness movement under the leadership of Charles Harrison Mason (1866–1961), the son of former slaves. Its leaders adopted Pentecostal emphases after attending Azusa Street in 1907, but others left to form the non-Pentecostal Church of Christ (Holiness), USA. By 1916 there were some 30,000 African-American adherents of such holiness and Pentecostal churches, far smaller in number than the predominant Baptist and Methodist churches, and with distinct differences of practice.[57]

The racial egalitarianism of the early meetings gradually succumbed to prevalent racial views, especially in the South. In 1907, Parham withdrew from association with Azusa Street, and in the following year the white members withdrew. The Assemblies of God was formed in 1914, which included white pastors ordained by Mason: it was to become the largest white Pentecostal denomination. It rejected aspects of practice found at Azusa Street, including the role of women as ordained pastors, elders, or bishops,[58] and reduced the three stage experience of early Pentecostalism—conversion, sanctification, and baptism in the Spirit, to conversion and Baptism in the Spirit, marked by speaking in tongues.

CONCLUSION

Nineteenth-century American Christianity was diverse and complex, vibrant yet divided, capable of being intellectually challenging yet also of uncritical credulity and superficiality. Whilst profound debates as to forms of doctrinal expression were being played out, a growing emphasis on the place of felt religion was manifest in both liberal churches, and in the evangelical holiness and Pentecostal movements. Though much divided, Christianity remained a strongly shaping force of American culture. Gospel songs, such as Joseph Scriven's 'What a Friend we have in Jesus', or the compositions of blind

---

57   On early Pentecostalism see Wacker, *Heaven Below*; I. MacRobert, *The Black Roots and White Racism of Early Pentecostalism in the USA*, Basingstoke, Macmillan, 1988; H. Baer, *The Black Spiritual Movement: A Religious Response to Racism*, Knoxville, University of Tennessee Press, 1984, 3–42.

58   C.E. Lincoln and L.H. Mamiya, *The Black church in the African American experience*, Durham, Duke University Press, 1990, 80–84.

hymn-writer Fanny J. Crosby (1820–1915) became iconic, a profound support to the personal piety of many. Their simple theology, largely innocent of the complexities swirling around the American churches, retained a capacity to mould patterns of spirituality that exceeded weightier theological writings.

In many ways, American Christianity reflected the American experience: personal freedom and individualism were predominant. But if authority was not to be placed in ancient church order or hierarchies, it could be vested in an individual's interpretation of Scripture, as the multiplicity of new religious movements showed. Entrepreneurial skill, and achievement measured numerically, still appeared of more importance than theological exactitude. The voluntary mode of action was preferred to that of the state. By the early twentieth century, the trajectory of theology in mainstream denominations was moving in a liberal direction, but conservative evangelical and Roman Catholic traditions were not giving up without a fight. Sometimes this was from an intellectual basis, although increasingly fundamentalists sought to do this without resort to technical theological apparatus.

FURTHER READING

J.W. Brown, *The Rise of Biblical Criticism in America, 1800–1870: The New England Scholars*, Middletown, Conn., Wesleyan University Press, 1969.

D. Copeland, *The Antebellum era : Primary Documents on Events from 1820 to 1860*, Westport, Conn., Greenwood, 2003.

D.J. Davies, *Introduction to Mormonism*, Cambridge, Cambridge University Press, 2003.

J.P. Dolan, *The American Catholic Experience : a Social History from Colonial times to the Present*, Garden City, New York, Doubleday, 1985.

G. Dorrien, *The Making of American Liberal Theology: Imagining Progressive Religion, 1805–1900*, Louisville, Westminster John Knox, 2001.

K. J. Hardman, *Issues in American Christianity: Primary Sources With Introductions*, Grand Rapids, Michigan, Baker, 1993.

W.R. Hutchison, *The Modernist Impulse in American Protestantism*, Cambridge, Mass., Harvard University Press, 1976.

G.M. Marsden, *Fundamentalism and American Culture: The Shaping of Twentieth-Century Evangelicalism 1870–1925*, New York, Oxford University Press, 1980.

M. Noll, *America's God: From Jonathan Edwards to Abraham Lincoln*, Oxford, Oxford University Press, 2002.

J.W. Stewart and J.H. Moorhead (eds), *Charles Hodge Revisited: A Critical Appraisal of His Life and Work*, Grand Rapids, Eerdmans, 2002.

G. Wacker, *Heaven Below: Early Pentecostals and American Culture*, Cambridge, Mass, Harvard University Press, 2001.

16

CONCLUSION: THE DAWN OF THE WORLD CHURCH

The 'long' nineteenth century opened with William Carey convinced that for the gospel 'a glorious door is opened and is likely to be opened wider and wider.'[1] It closed as a fundamental shift in religious geography not only in the West, but across the world, was beginning to take place, although it took the rest of the twentieth century for it to be fully realised. Small and emerging religious movements had, over the course of a century, become global religious phenomena. Wesley's followers emerged from the tiny but zealous group in the 1730s to become by 1900 a vast body of some 30 million people spread across six continents. In 1750, perhaps 22% of the world population of 1.6 billion was Christian. Eighty-five percent of Christians were white, and the scriptures were available in 60 languages. By 1900, this had increased to 34.4% Christian (still 81.1% white), and it is estimated that 51.3% of the world had been evangelized in some way. The Bible, or parts of it, was available in 537 languages. One estimate suggests that as the twentieth century opened, there were around 266 million Roman Catholics, 134 million Protestants, and 115 million Orthodox worldwide.[2]

There is no doubt that the legacy for world Christianity of the years covered by *Churches, Revolutions and Empires* was very great. Many of the issues that challenge and shape the churches of the twenty-first century were already operative and influential in the late nineteenth century. In the period 1789–1914, Christianity faced some of the most profound challenges since the time of the

---

1 W. Carey, *Enquiry*, Section 5, 'The Duty of Christians in General.'

2 Barrett, *World Christian Encyclopaedia*, 27–29. Cf the figures in the *Atlas of Global Christianity*, (Edinburgh, Edinburgh University Press, 2010) which use self-description as the basis for Christian affiliation, rather than membership.

apostles. In the wake of the Enlightenment and the Industrial Revolution, the transformation of social, political, economic, and religious contexts made revolution a dominant theme. By the beginning of the twentieth century, monarchies had been toppled, the powers of others severely constrained, and inherited systems of order transformed. Europe and North America saw the rising social and political dominance of the middle classes with their bourgeois values.

The revolutionary issues with which Christianity had wrestled produced major internal tensions. As post-enlightenment philosophy impacted theological expression, it provoked the profound reconstruction of theological liberalism, and in turn defences of Christian orthodoxy, and eventually Fundamentalism. In science, Charles Darwin had, in the eyes of many interpreters, effectively written a new book of Genesis, with an alternative account of cosmic and human origins. This posed fundamental questions about Biblical authority, and of the relationship between faith and science. Christians wrestled over the role they should take in politics, with the formation of political parties with Christian identities in some countries, but conscious avoidance of this in others. Christianity continued to be a profoundly shaping force in matters of national identity. The capacity of Christianity to adapt in diverse ways to these changes, as well as the growth of the world church, made it possible to speak of World 'Christianities' by the beginning of the twentieth century. Nonetheless, by the end of the nineteenth century, churches in the cities of Western Europe were not thriving, although generally North America followed a different trajectory. With over 50% of the world population in the 21st Century urban, this pattern of the engagement of Christianity with the urban world has great significance for religious history.

A number of issues, which were to be of particular significance for twentieth century Christianity, are the focus of this final chapter. They reflect how the activities and beliefs of the complex of institutions which make up Christianity, were, and continue to be, shaped by the social and cultural context in which they have operated. Belief and practice had been interwoven with most aspects of life in the late eighteenth century, and continued to be so during the most of the nineteenth century, even if of declining significance in Europe. The increasing recognition of the rights that should be afforded to women was a major issue for both churches and society to resolve, as was the rise of ideologies such as Marxism, which offered an alternative non-religious social structure, and the emergence of Freudian psychoanalysis which sought to interpret human experience in a non-religious way. Internal pressures within Christianity led some along paths of ecumenicity and church union, yet the rise of Christianity as a world religion gave increased scope for diversity of Christian expression. It also highlighted the need for it to be understood as a belief system alongside those sincerely held by millions of adherents of other religions. Over all these trends, shadows continued to loom—the ugly legacies of racist thinking and practice, and the drive for imperial dominance by world powers, making the prospect of international conflict of devastating proportions all-the-more likely.

CHALLENGES FOR CHRISTIANITY IN THE WEST

The multiform challenges Christianity faced in the nineteenth century bore witness to how hard it would need to work to sustain itself in the face of the economic, political, and demographic changes of the twentieth century. Attempts to radically deconstruct the Christian consensus of the West were to become more sustained, and indeed successful. One major challenge would come after the 1917 Bolshevik revolution in Russia, when a once strongly Christian state adopted a non-theistic ideology, which it sought to promote globally. Communism was to become a powerful vehicle for anti-colonial and nationalist protest.

Another nineteenth-century legacy to impact the Western mind in the twentieth, was that of modern psychoanalysis. Working on the case of 'Anna O', who suffered from severe hysteria, Sigmund Freud found that helping her to talk about unpleasant events that had occurred in her youth alleviated her symptoms. The 'talking cure' became a key dimension of the work of mental health professionals. In his work *The Interpretation of Dreams* (1900) he rooted dreams and fantasies in early sexual experiences. Freud believed he could explain the inner dimensions of the human condition in a scientific way. His approach was strongly deterministic and mechanistic: present experience was deeply conditioned by the past. The explanation of reality offered by psychoanalysis made it a rival cosmology to traditional religion. The key social function of traditional religion was, to Freud, to repress antisocial tendencies, such as unrestrained sexual impulses. He argued that when humans were only a little above the apes, sons fought their fathers to be the dominant males in society and to possess his females. Religion was part of overcoming this social structure. Freud argued in *Totem and Tabu* (1911–13) that the beginnings of religion, morality and social life were to be found in the Oedipus complex. This alternative range of explanations and solutions for problems in human experience offered by psychoanalysis displaced the need to call upon an external deity to explain life. In a world in which long held religious certainties were collapsing beyond recognition, it proved an attractive counter-ideology.[3]

The rising recognition of social and political rights for women was also to significantly challenge churches in the West. Until the twentieth century, women experienced an inferior legal and social status, with limited rights over property, and the custody of children. Opportunities for their social advancement and

---

3 There are many biographies of Freud including L. Breger, *Freud : Darkness in the Midst of Vision*, New York and Chichester, John Wiley, 2000.

education developed slowly. In 1878 women were allowed to take degrees at London University, but progression towards their political emancipation was slow. In 1893 women in New Zealand were given the vote, followed by Finland in 1907 and Norway in 1913. In America they had to wait until the ratification of the 19th Amendment of the US constitution in 1920 before they could vote in presidential elections. In Britain, the campaign of the suffragettes to secure the vote for women ranged from demonstrations and mass marches, to destruction of property, and acts of self-sacrifice through the hunger strike of prisoners. Increased employment opportunities for women during the First World War served to enhance their cause. Women were given the vote in Germany and the United Kingdom in 1918, although in the latter it was 1928 before the Equal Franchise Act gave the vote to men and women over the age of 21. Women in France had to wait until 1944. In the extension of women's rights, the role of the church is debateable. Churches tended to support a patriarchal view of marriage and society, which did not favour the extension of the rights of women. However through voluntary activities run by churches in social concern and welfare, they were afforded significant opportunities for leadership, social engagement, and self-expression, which paved the way for future employment opportunities. Emmeline and Christabel Pankhurst, leaders of the campaign for female suffrage in Britain, also held strong Christian convictions.[4] Debates about the role of women in positions of church leadership were to become of increased prominence in the later twentieth century, challenging existing church structures, and patterns of inter-church union.

The need to express the Christian faith in ways relevant to the modern mind remained a pressing issue for churches. The Modernist endeavour towards doctrinal revision in Europe and North America continued, but not without challenge. The Congregationalist R.J. Campbell's radical work, *The New Theology* (1907) was a notable example, but by 1915 it was out of circulation, and the author had turned to Anglicanism. The 1912 collection of Anglican modernist essays, *Foundations*, edited by B.H. Streeter encountered opposition from Anglo-Catholic conservatives, and even the liberal-inclined Bishop of Oxford, Charles Gore.

Some evangelicals sought to bridge the gap between their conservative theology and those seeking the liberty offered by Modernism. Henry Drummond (1851–1897), a Scottish writer, and gifted preacher active in D.L. Moody's campaigns, argued in *The New Evangelicalism* (1899) for a 'A Gospel for the Age': the gospel was not bad in itself, it was a 'bad fit'. He argued that too often a 'God to be feared,' was preached, there was not 'humanity enough' in presentations of Jesus Christ, and preaching on salvation focussed too much on life after

---

4   T. Larsen, *Christabel Pankhurst: Fundamentalism and Feminism in Coalition*, Woodbridge, Boydell, 2002.

death. He rejected propositional preaching—the aim was 'not to prove things, but to make men see things'.[5] Yet, some have suggested that this approach was counterproductive, and that the alienation of many from the church owed much to the modification of the Christian message, communicated by preachers trained in the shadow of Darwin and German biblical criticism.[6] The Anglo-Catholic, E.B. Pusey, stressed the value of the stark realities of the traditional Christian message, 'the Day of Judgment will alone reveal how many millions will love Him for ever, who would never have loved Him, unless the fear of Hell had first scared them to seek Him, and so to know Him and to love Him.'[7]

The need to defend orthodoxy galvanised some. In England, C.H. Spurgeon's attempt to challenge the growing influence of theological liberalism through the 'Downgrade' controversy of the 1880s attracted a number of supporters, although few were willing to follow his church out of the Baptist Union, which he deemed compromised by concessions to theological liberals. Spurgeon declared of the modern theological agenda—'A new religion has been initiated, which is no more Christianity than chalk is cheese; and this religion, being destitute of moral honesty, palms itself off as the old faith with slight improvements.'[8] What was to some appropriate adaptation to contemporary times, was to others reducing Christianity to simply becoming a reflection of wider society. Pope Pius X's decrees *Lamentabili*, and the encyclical *Pascendi*, prompted a more effective purge of modernists. In America, *The Fundamentals* (1910–1915) attempted to draw a line in the sand over which conservative evangelicals should not step. By the 1920s the predominant characteristics of the Fundamentalist sub-culture had become strong Protestantism, determined resistance to theological Modernism, and militant opposition to aspects of secularization and modern culture. Interest in revivalism, and adherence to premillennial theology also featured highly, as did holiness influences. Premillennial thinking became preoccupied with the intricacies of various schemes about the future, which tended to divert attention from the wider call of mission.[9]

One product of theological change was a desire to make less of doctrinal and ecclesiastical distinctions. The nineteenth century, shaped by the enlightenment's encouragement of independence of thought and self-expression, with growing democratic pressures, had been notable for the range of divisions between, and amongst, denominations. As the twentieth century dawned, there were those

---

5 H. Drummond, *The New Evangelism and Other Essays*, London, 1899, 4–10.

6 M. Watts, 'Why did the English stop going to church?', *Dr Williams Library Forty-Ninth Lecture*, London, 1995.

7 E.B. Pusey, *The Church of England a Portion of Christ's One Holy Catholic Church, and a Means of Restoring Visible Unity. An Eirenicon*, New York, D. Appleton and Company, 1866, 18.

8 C.H. Spurgeon, 'Another Word Concerning the Downgrade', *Sword and Trowel*, August, 1887.

9 Bebbington, *Evangelicalism in Modern Britain*, 190.

who were determined to put the paths of separation over often minor issues behind them. In 1902, William Patrick (1852–1911) proposed union between Presbyterians and Methodists, in Canada, and Congregationalists joined the discussions. The Basis of Union was accepted by Congregationalists in 1910, and Methodists in 1911, and in 1925 two-thirds of Presbyterians also voted to enter the United Church of Canada. 1900 saw the union of two of the largest Presbyterian denominations in Scotland, the Free Church and the United Presbyterian Church, to form the United Free Church. This paved the way for reunion of the major Presbyterian bodies into the Church of Scotland in 1929. The early twentieth century was also to see increasingly united work between missionaries from traditional denominations, and movements towards Protestant church unity in China and India.

Whilst some sought union in altered structures that would break down doctrinal and ecclesiological barriers, others found themselves drawn towards radical, experiential forms of Christianity. From these they derived a considerable sense of togetherness with others who shared the same emphases. The Welsh Revival of 1904–05 appears the last of the great nineteenth-century revivals, not to be repeated in the West in the twentieth century. Crossing many Protestant denominational boundaries it spread through Wales, where some 100,000 professed conversion, and into other parts of Britain, with related revivals reported as far afield as Los Angeles, India and Korea. At the heart of events was a young candidate for the ministry Evan Roberts (1878–1951), although only a small percentage of all the converts came to faith at meetings in which he was present. Before the revival Roberts underwent a profound second-blessing experience which he identified as the Baptism of the Holy Spirit, and which brought a distinct holiness emphasis to the revival.[10] This he continued to promote after the revival was over, along with an associate, Jessie Penn-Lewis.[11] He urged people to a four point plan—to put away unconfessed sin, to put away things doubtful, to do what the Spirit prompts towards complete obedience, and to publicly confess Christ as Saviour. Roberts would on occasion urge his congregations to pray one after the other 'send the Holy Spirit now, for Jesus Christ's sake'. Such occasions were often characterised by weeping, and loud singing. Some shouted, others spoke of visions, there were faintings and bodily convulsions.[12] Some were of the opinion that the

---

10   On the debate about the links between the revival and the holiness see E. Evans, *The Welsh Revival of 1904*, Bridgend, Evangelical Movement of Wales, 1969, 52–54, 168–69.

11   E. Roberts and J. Penn-Lewis, *War on the Saints*, Leicester, 1916, 2nd edn., 284–95.

12   Evans, *Welsh Revival*, 84, 89; see also P.B. Jones, *Rent Heavens: The Revival of 1904*, London, Pioneer Missions, 54, and P.B. Jones, *Voices from the Welsh Revival, 1904–05*, Bridgend, Evangelical Press of Wales, 1995.

expectation of the dramatic left people unwilling to listen to preaching.[13] Certainly, preaching was a less prominent feature of this revival than of others, and many converts proved open to the growing influence of liberal theology. Public witness and evangelism were a noted part of the revival—with inter-church marches stopping outside public houses to sing hymns, and preach short sermons. Personal evangelism at coal mines, iron foundries, and work yards became common place. Along with the large number of conversions, the holiness emphasis was accompanied by a significant reduction in reported crime in local communities it affected: convictions for drunkenness between 1903 and 1906 were reported as having dropped by 48% in the County of Glamorgan, and rates of illegitimate birth by 40%.[14]

The Welsh Revival created a context which assisted the spread of Pentecostalism in Britain. George Jeffreys, was converted in the revival, and in 1915 founded the Elim Evangelistic Band, out of which in 1926 the Elim Four Square Alliance of British Churches (later the Elim Pentecostal Church) was founded. Other British Pentecostal churches gathered together as the Assemblies of God in 1924, in which Donald Gee, another figure from the Welsh revival, played an important role. The Apostolic Church was a smaller Pentecostal group, emphasising the ongoing nature of the offices of prophet and apostle, led by Daniel Powell Williams after he believed he had a call to apostleship in 1913.

The spread of Pentecostalism, especially from Asuza Street, Los Angeles (see chapter 15), was rapid not only in Britain, but also globally. Pentecostal experiences were reported in Norway in 1907, and then Sweden, through the work of a Methodist minister, T.B. Barratt who reported receiving the baptism in the Spirit in America. Pentecostals were present in Germany, and Italy, Chile, and Brazil before 1910. By 1908 there were thirty-two centres in Britain where Pentecostal gifts were exercised. A.A. Boddy (1854–1930), an Anglican vicar from the North-East of England, seen as the Father of British Pentecostalism, was influenced by Barratt, and promoted Pentecostal experiences in All Saints' Church, Sunderland, where people were introduced to the Baptism in the Spirit and speaking in tongues. Boddy's attempts to promote Pentecostalism at the Keswick convention were unsuccessful, although he organised a series of influential conventions in Sunderland between 1908 and 1914. Another Anglican, Cecil Polhill, one of the 'Cambridge Seven' who had served as a missionary with the China Inland Mission in Tibet, organised meetings in London for those seeking Baptism in the Spirit and Healing. Boddy believed that Pentecostalism should be a movement within established churches, which would melt away

---

13   Evans, *Welsh Revival*, 101.

14   J.V. Morgan, *Welsh Religious Revival 1904–05*, London, Chapman and Hall, 1909, 247.

denominational boundaries, but Pentecostals tended to form independent churches, which then linked together into denominational structures.[15]

WORLD MISSION AND EDINBURGH 1910

The connections between the growing trend towards Protestant ecumenical thought and the missionary impulse of the nineteenth century are notable. The interaction of missionaries at conferences, and the 'comity' arrangements to prevent overlap and uneconomic duplication of resources, all served to foster the spirit of co-operation. As early as 1806 William Carey had proposed that a conference be held at the Cape of Good Hope of Christians of all denominations, from all quarters of the world. He believed that 'we could understand one another better, and more entirely enter into one another's views by two hours conversation than by two or three years epistolary correspondence.'[16] In the late nineteenth century, Carey's vision began to be fulfilled as missionary conferences were held in Liverpool (1860), London (1878 and 1888), and New York (1900) which was attended by 2,500 delegates. The pioneering Kikuyu conference held in Kenya in June 1913, brought together Scottish Presbyterians, Anglicans, and other missions, and sought to create a united Protestant front against both Islam and Roman Catholicism. It produced proposals for common baptismal procedures and inter-communion, which some saw as a portent for the future of the world church, although these were sternly rejected by Anglo-Catholics, provoking divisions amongst Anglicans.[17]

The conference that most fully worked out Carey's vision was held at Edinburgh in 1910. It was designed as an opportunity for up to date, scientific reflection upon the state of mission in the early twentieth century, the promotion of Christian co-operation and the ecumenical consolidation of mission in the face of rivalries between denominations and growing colonial power. However, the gathering was not truly ecumenical, with no representatives from the Roman Catholic or Orthodox Churches, but was instead Protestant, broadly evangelical, with a significant Anglo-Catholic grouping.[18] Although entitled the World Missionary Conference, it did not truly reflect the global Christian community. Of 1215 official delegates, 509 were British, 491 came from North America, 169 from continental Europe, and 27 from the white colonies of

---

15   W.J. Hollenweger, *The Pentecostals*, London, SCM, 1972; 29–175. On Pentecostalism in Britain see W.K. Kay, *Pentecostals in Britain*, Carlisle, Paternoster, 2000; D. Gee, *The Pentecostal Movement*, Luton, Assemblies of God, 1949.

16   Quoted in M. Kuriakose, *History of Christianity in India*, Madras, 1982, 82.

17   Frank Weston, Anglo-Catholic bishop of Zanzibar saw the associations of the Evangelical bishops of Mombasa and Uganda with nonconformists as heretical—see H.M. Smith, *Frank, Bishop of Zanzibar: The Life of Frank Weston*, London, 1926, 145–170.

18   When the Lausanne Conference on World Evangelization was called in 1974, the 2,700 delegates included over half from the two-thirds world, and representatives from over 151 countries.

South Africa and Australasia. In fact, only 19 delegates came from the non-Western world, 18 of whom were from Asia. Only one indigenous black African Christian was in attendance, Mark Hayford from Ghana.[19] Even the dominant British and North American contingent was not entirely representative—of 120 American mission boards, only 35 sent representatives, mainly from the largest organisations. Just 207 official delegates were women, and their presence was little reflected in the programme or the speakers.

Much of the planning for the conference was in the hands of its secretary J.H. Oldham. The chairman was John Mott (1865–1955), an American Methodist layman, who had never served as a missionary. The conference opened with greetings being read out from King George V, the former US President Theodore Roosevelt, and the Imperial German Colonial Office. Reports given at Edinburgh showed that Christianity had gained a footing in all parts of the world although Tibet, Afghanistan and Nepal remained closed, and some remote regions had not been reached or access was restricted by colonial powers. Christian missions had experienced a measure of success from China to Tierra del Fuego, with converts from every race, and every major world religion reported. The increasing maturity of the younger churches was reported, producing a ready supply of Christian nationals, and leaders whose ability was steadily being recognised. Humanitarian concern was now an acknowledged part of the missionary agenda; protests against prostitution, child marriage, opium trafficking, and in favour of temperance, were being lodged. Delegates were even willing to criticise aspects of colonial policy.

There was an element of confidence, even triumphalism, about the successes of mission. In his opening address the Anglican Archbishop Randall Davidson declared 'it may well be that "there are some standing here tonight who shall not taste of death till they see,"—here on earth, in a way we know not now,—"the Kingdom of God come with power"'.[20] Nonetheless, the conference showed the capacity of Christianity to be shaped by both missionary and indigenous Christians adaptations to local contexts, and break inherited moulds. There were signs of a recognition that simply regurgitating theological formulations from the West would not help local Christians find an expression of Christianity that was authentically their own. Christianity was becoming a world religion.[21]

Whether the World Missionary Conference at Edinburgh was a landmark, or a watershed, in mission history is debateable. It was significant in terms

19   B. Stanley, *The World Missionary Conference, Edinburgh 1910*, Grand Rapids, Eerdmans, 2009, 8–13.

20   *World Missionary Conference*, 1910, Vol. ix, Edinburgh and London, Oliphant, Anderson and Ferrier, n.d., 150.

21   See R. Rouse and S. Neill (eds) *A History of the Ecumenical Movement 1517–1948*, London, 1954; Stanley, *Edinburgh 1910*, 160.

The 'World Church'—Edinburgh 1910

'the Church on which we report presents itself no longer as an inspiring or distant ideal, nor even as a tender plant or a young child, appealing to our compassion and nurturing care. We see it now an actual Church in being, strongly rooted, and fruitful in many lands. The child has, in many places, reached, and in others is fast reaching, maturity; and is now both fitted and willing, perhaps in a few cases too eager, to take upon itself its full burden of responsibility and service'[1]

---

1 World Missionary *Conference Reports of Commission II*, Edinburgh and London, Oliphant, Anderson and Ferrier, 1910, quoted in Stanley, *Edinburgh 1910*, 133..

---

of future ecumenical endeavours, although close study of the debates rather than the official publications, has brought some reassessment of the degree of unity and ecumenicity in the proceedings themselves.[22] From the conference emerged a desire to remove duplication, and promote co-operation in order to fulfil the potential of missions, with hopes that the unity expressed on the mission field would be expressed in the home circles. A conference in Calcutta in 1914 included calls for a heavier focus on Indian leadership of local churches. Attempts were made to set boundaries of operation, and the establishment of National Councils of Churches in places like China, Nigeria, Zambia, and Swaziland. From Edinburgh came not only the International Missionary Council formed in 1921, but there were also some connections with the 1925 Universal Conference on Life and Work, and the 1927 World Conference on Faith and Order. These two organizations merged in 1948 to create the World Council of Churches.[23]

With a world-wide British Empire, growing French and German empires, and the United States emerging as a vast economic power, the potential for Christian influence across the world was as never before. Yet, not far below the surface were tensions experienced by partners in mission operating in imperial contexts, over whether to be good citizens loyal to the Western powers, or whether to operate in truly independent or ecumenical fashion. The First World War undermined the sense of international missionary solidarity. The Treaty of Versailles even allowed German mission property to be appropriated by the allied forces.[24] The growing theological division in the 1920s within

---

22   See B. Stanley, Church, State, and the Hierarchy of "Civilization": The Making of the "Missions and Governments" Report at the World Missionary Conference, Edinburgh 1910, in Porter, *Imperial Horizons*, 58–84.

23   See R. Rouse and S. Neill (eds) *A History of the Ecumenical Movement 1517–1948*, London, 1954.

24   Hutchison, *Errand to the World*, 133–136.

Protestantism into conservative and liberal groupings further fractured the informal inter-denominationalism of the nineteenth century.

Protestant evangelicals had stressed the need to look beyond the promotion of denominational structures in the higher task of promoting the gospel, as Melvill Horne, who had spent a year in Sierra Leone put it in 1794, 'It is not Calvinism... not Arminianism... It is not the hierarchy of the Church of England; it is not the principles of Protestant Dissenters, that [the missionary] has in view to propagate. His object is to serve the Church Universal.'[25] Although the London Missionary Society had not succeeded in remaining interdenominational much into the early nineteenth century, international faith missions proved more successful in later decades, accommodating evangelicals with very different ecclesiological views. The North American Student Volunteer Movement, and its British arm, the Student Volunteer Missionary Union, operated on this basis, and other pan-evangelical bodies, such as the YMCA, showed a growing interest in mission, spreading their work world-wide. Faith missions, with their internal inter-denominationalism, were less interested in wider ecumenical developments, their attentions absorbed by the urgent task of global evangelisation.

THE WATCHWORD

The origin of the watchword of late nineteenth and early twentieth century missions, the 'evangelisation of the world in this generation' may lie with a speech of A.T. Pierson, an American Presbyterian. Invited by D.L. Moody to speak at the Mount Hermon Conference in 1886, Pierson had declared his conviction that because of political and technological changes, the world could be evangelised by 1900. He issued the rallying cry, 'all should go, and go to all.' If one in twenty Protestants volunteered for the mission field, he believed that the world would be evangelised in twenty years.[26] From that conference came one hundred student volunteers for mission—by 1910 there were 5,000.[27] The watchword helped to enlarge the vision, and purpose of many, to add to zeal, prayer and self-sacrifice, to increase the sense of momentum in world religions. What was meant by the motto was debated. To some it was contact with those who had never heard the gospel, to others, genuine conversion.

One body upon which the watchword was notably influential was the Student Volunteer Movement, launched at Moody's Northfield Conference in

25   M. Horne, *Letters on Missions: Addressed to the Protestant Ministers of the British Churches*, Bristol, 1794, 11, quoted in Porter, *Religion Versus Empire?*, 49.

26   The role of Royal and Robert Wilder is discussed in H. Peskett, 'Missions and Eschatology', in ed. K.E. Brower and M.W. Elliott, *The Reader Must Understand: Eschatology in the Bible and Theology*, Leicester, Apollos, 1997, 313.

27   D.L. Robert, 'The Origin of the Student Volunteer Movement Watchword; The Evangelisation of the World in this Generation', *International Bulletin of Missionary Research*, 10, (Oct. 1986), 146–149.

> ## John Mott—The Evangelisation of the World in this Generation
> 'The value of medical, educational, literary, and all other forms of missionary activity, is measured by the extent to which they prepare the way for the Gospel message, promote its acceptance, manifest its spirit and benefits, multiply points of contact with human souls and increase the number and efficiency of those who preach Christ... In some parts of the world, more people have been led to accept Christ through educational effort than through any other agency... [medical work is] one of the most powerful, effective, and directly evangelistic agencies which the church possesses... the proclamation of the Gospel by the living voice [remained the most significant voice...] ... the baptism of converts... their organisation into churches [are]... means to the mighty and inspiring object of enthroning Christ in individual life, in family life, in social life, in national life, in international relations, in every relation of mankind'. [1]
>
> 1 J. Mott, *The Evangelization of the World in this Generation*, New York, Student Volunteer Movement, 1905, 11–16.

1888, at which Hudson Taylor was a speaker. It built on the appeal of Moody's revivalism amongst students, and the strength of support for the YMCA and YWCA. Its impact on missions societies from the CIM through to the CMS was strong—some 506 missionaries sent out by the CMS between 1892 and 1898 were influenced by the Student Volunteer Movement.[28] Its characteristics reflected the late nineteenth century conservative religious context—pre-millennial, non-denominational, ecumenist, and open to the laity. In 1894 the World Student Federation was formed, as a global umbrella movement for the national expressions of the SVM.

In 1900, John Mott surveyed the achievements of mission in his book, *The Evangelisation of the World in this Generation*, and cast his gaze forward to what was possible with advances in the modern world, particularly those in transport, science, medicine, and publication. He observed the growing impact of 77,000 indigenous evangelists, pastors, and teachers. Mott followed others in re-interpreting the 'watchword' to mean that each generation should evangelise itself, by presenting Christianity to each individual in the world, in each generation. Before 1914, conservative missiologists still entertained an optimistic anthropology, convinced that problems would be solvable with the application of advanced thinking from the West, but growing numbers feared that the 'watchword' implied a superficial presentation of the gospel without a continuing work of discipling converts. By 1921 the term was largely disregarded.

28 E. Stock, *History of the Church Missionary Society*, Vol. 3, 689–90.

THE ACHIEVEMENTS OF CHRISTIAN MISSION

Much criticism has been levelled at missionaries for their destruction of indigenous cultures, and the introduction of the worst of Western lifestyle— from the imposition of the wearing of Western clothes, to Western literature and perpetuating the divisions of the Western church. Undoubtedly, grievous mistakes were made. Whilst few overtly advocated imperial policies, many served indirectly as effective empire-builders. But in terms of finance, personnel, and direct influence, the influence of missionaries was as nothing compared to the activities of western traders who often treated indigenous peoples with great cruelty, and a barrier to their exploitative activities. Indeed, it could be argued that the activities of Western missionaries ensured the survival of some tribes who might otherwise have been wiped out, by championing their cause and cultures in the face of imperial threat. Although it was capable of being used as a means of social control, the emphasis on education by missionaries was a significant social provision, offered the socially marginalised a vital means of self-improvement. By the early twentieth century provision had been extended to include higher education, with the creation of explicitly Christian universities in Hong Kong, China, and Beirut, areas where Christianity was not the dominant religion. Medical work had become an intrinsic part of mission activity, with settled centres developing significant dispensaries and hospital facilities. The act of translating the scriptures into local languages, involving detailed study of dialect, idioms, and culture, producing grammars, primers and dictionaries where none had previously existed, helped ensure the preservation of vernacular languages and cultures which would otherwise have become extinct. This often took place before other Western influences permeated cultures, ensuring they were preserved in language before Western influence became too strong.

World Christianity as it developed was therefore more than simply the creation of the missionary movement, but also the product of the interaction between the work of missions and local expressions of the faith. This was a factor in the development of indigenous movements for political self-expression, which delegates to Edinburgh 1910 began to feel troubled about. The capacity of indigenous people to take from missionaries what they wanted, and to leave the rest, should not be underestimated. Education might be more readily accepted than the religious message that accompanied it. The sense that groups of individuals who considered themselves a people should have the right to a national identity and self-governance, which had drawn together nations such as Germany and Italy in the nineteenth centuries, also began to appear in Asia and Africa as a by-product of colonial rule. Many of the future leaders of such nationalist movements were a product of missionary education. Missionaries may have created a dependency culture amongst their adherents, but were also themselves highly dependent upon indigenous peoples who worked as household assistants, or translators, catechists, teachers, or preachers. Seeking local equivalents for biblical words and concepts provided a means by which local cultures could shape the form the Christian message would take. Women were given opportunities often denied to them in traditional societies— the majority of baptisms resulting from early mission work in Africa were of women. Missions offered refuges for escaped male and female slaves, or from unwanted arranged marriages. Conversion was more than a simple surrender to white dominance: most conversions were in fact the product of the work of indigenous evangelists.[29] Indeed only when Christian growth was able to develop from indigenous bases was it able to become a truly global movement, something genuinely achieved in the twentieth century.

The connection between the global expansion of Christianity, and the expansion of Western political influence was a complex one. American missionary thinkers, some of whom were less affected by the taint of the imperial scramble that had engulfed Europe in the late nineteenth century, could view mission as an act of disinterested benevolence, or national altruism. Yet their endeavours were often undertaken in parallel with the extension of the economic and strategic interests of the USA (particularly in the Far East), and a promotion of middle-class American cultural, scientific, and social values.

The 1884–85 Berlin Conferences urged a physical presence in areas claimed by imperial powers, and offered opportunities for missionary advance. Colonial ambitions, deep spirituality, and a sense of compassion for, and responsibility towards, indigenous people, created a mix of motivations. Missionaries could support imperial intrusion whilst arguing with colonial authorities over education and the morality of government policy, or protest when they offered benefits to Islam, especially in Africa. White settlers often lived in social and physical isolation from local peoples. Barriers to the promotion of social justice, such as premillennial eschatology, strongly individualistic understandings of conversion, and recurring racist distrust of non-whites remained.

The primary intent of missions in 1914 remained to Christianise, and claims of a simple, direct and causal, relationship between Christianity and imperialism have been rightfully subjected to serious re-evaluation by scholars.[30] Imperialism was the product of many factors, political, economic, social, military, intellectual, and theological. Imperial power came not simply from the barrel of gun, but through trade, technology, and literature. Christian responses varied: some, such as the faith missions, consciously sought to distance themselves from colonial influences, and as easily acted as agents of anti-imperialism, as of

---

29 Porter, *Religion Versus Empire?*, 316–320.

30 Porter, *Religion Versus Empire?*, 330.

imperial values.[31] The missionary dimension of the 'high imperial age' proved as likely to subvert imperial structures, as to reinforce them.[32]

By the early twentieth century, the expansion of Christianity in places was becoming rapid. People movements were noted amongst the Baganda in Uganda. In the Telegu country, north of Madras, India, in thirty years a million lower caste 'dalits' entered the churches, rendering redundant the patriarchal leadership patterns that had worked for a limited number of dependent converts. Yet an indigenous leadership was very slow to emerge. In 1914 the Roman Catholic Church had no non-European bishops, except the four appointed for the ancient Church of the Thomas Christians between 1887 and 1896. Across the whole of Africa there were still only a small number of native priests before 1920.[33]

The achievement of Roman Catholic missionaries in the nineteenth century was prodigious, compared to their low ebb in 1800. Although Protestants had often a head start of up to fifty years in some areas, Roman Catholic missions advanced rapidly, supported by the overseas ambitions of Roman Catholic nations especially the French. With a ready supply of recruits, and a flexible approach to baptism, they came to rival and outnumber Protestants in many areas. By 1914 there were seven million baptized Roman Catholics in Africa, with a further million under catechetical instruction. Close association with governmental imperial ambitions brought tensions, and mixed motives, with competition with Protestants in Christianised areas, whilst other fields were left neglected. Hostility between Roman Catholic and Protestant missionaries could be intense. The dependence of Roman Catholic missionary areas on the practical and spiritual leadership of white Roman Catholics remained absolute up until 1914.

In 1800, around one per cent of Protestant Christians lived outside Europe and North America; by 1900 that was 10%. There were few examples of large-scale conversion by that date, although the picture was starting to change in India and Africa. The axis of the Christian world was beginning to shift from the northern to the southern hemispheres. If the nineteenth century was the great century of Christian missions, the great century of worldwide Christian

---

31   A. Porter, 'Church History, History of Christianity, Religious History: Some Reflections on British Missionary Enterprise Since the Late Eighteenth Century', *Church History*, Sept. 2002, Vol. 71, no. 3, 563–565.

32   See A. Porter, 'Religion, Missionary Enthusiasm, and Empire,' in ed. A. Porter, *The Oxford History of the British Empire*, Vol. 3, *The Nineteenth Century*, Oxford, 1999, 222–246; N. Etherington, 'Missions and Empire' in ed. R. Winks, *The Oxford History of the British Empire*, Vol. 4, *Historiography*, Oxford, 1999, 303–314; See R. Elphick and R. Davenport (eds), *Christianity in South Africa: A Political, Social and Cultural History*, Oxford, James Currey, 1997.

33   Sundkler and Steed, *Church in Africa*, 627.

growth was to be the twentieth century: by the end of the twentieth century, 60% of Christians lived in Africa, Asia, and South America. Christianity's remarkable transcontinental appeal cannot be explained simply in terms of the work of imperial conquerors.

Indigenous Christianity

Colonial rule by European powers was to have significant impact not only on the endeavours of missionaries, but also on the efforts of indigenous Christians to express Christianity in the very late nineteenth and early twentieth centuries. Despite the sacrificial labours of the missionary community, progress in the extension of Christianity through their work was extremely slow. The most prescient missionaries saw what was happening, that indigenous Christian evangelists, teachers and catechists were in a few years able to accomplish more than well-trained missionaries over many decades. Some mission converts, with a strong passion for evangelism, and high standards of piety, created boundaries between themselves and their own cultures and tribes people: mixed political agendas and tendencies towards attitudes of racial superiority also acted as a drag factor. The failure of converts to rise to higher positions in churches, together with continuing racist attitudes, began to breed significant tension, frustration and resentment, creating a sense of estrangement amongst indigenous Christians. However, the majority of converts stayed with the mission church, which in Central and South America, was the Roman Catholic Church.

From the 1880s onwards in Africa a significant number of African Independent churches emerged, which were willing to accommodate elements of African traditional religions, especially their consciousness of the spirit-world. Their leaders often began to preach independently as a result of what they believed was some special revelation from God, dream or vision. In the churches they created, visions and charismatic gifts took a prominent place. The vigorous growth of Pentecostalism in South America and elsewhere was a similar product of indigenisation. Such separation from mission churches appeared radical and dangerous to European missionaries, who feared concessions to local culture rendered them too closely associated with traditional religion.

In 1892, Mangena Mkone left Wesleyan Methodism to form the Ethiopian Church in Pretoria, South Africa. Its title, drawn from Psalm 68, 'Let Ethiopia hasten to stretch her hands out to God,' emphasised distance from the white denomination. It was a reminder that African Christianity long pre-dated the modern missionary movement, opening up the possibility of a pan-African Christian identity. Other churches called themselves 'Native', or 'African'.[34]

---

34   P. Jenkins, *The Next Christendom: The Coming of Global Christianity*, Oxford, OUP, 2002, 52 [note 33].

The work of a Liberian preacher from the Grebo ethnic group, William Wadé Harris (c. 1865–1929), was one striking example. Harris had been fostered between the ages of twelve and eighteen by a Methodist pastor, and wrote and spoke Grebo and English fluently. He was converted around 1881 or 1882, was baptised and began a preaching ministry. He was confirmed in 1888, at the age of twenty-three, by the bishop of the Episcopal Church in Liberia, and between 1892 and 1908 he worked as a school teacher and Bible teacher with the Episcopal Church. Harris came into contact with a variety of theological and ideological traditions which were affecting the region, including nationalist thinkers, and the American Charles Taze Russell's Watch-Tower movement.

Harris joined other Grebo and Kru indigenous peoples in sharply opposing the small group of African-American settlers who had come to Liberia in the years after 1822, and who monopolised political and economic power, and supported rebellion against them. Although this drew some support from White American missionaries, Harris was jailed for his calls for the Kru and Grebo region to be made a British Protectorate. According to his later account of events, in jail in 1910, he was awakened one night by a visitation from the angel Gabriel. He was told he was in heaven, and that he would be anointed by God a prophet like Daniel. He then experienced a triune anointing by God, with the spirit descending upon his head like a jet of water. His instructions included giving up Western-style clothes, and shunning the use of fetishes. Thus called, he embarked on the ministry of a prophet, announcing as he went, 'I am a prophet. I am Harris, Harris the prophet of God'.[35]

After his release, Harris preached in Liberia with little effect, but in 1913 he began a series of dynamic evangelistic journeys across West Africa. Clad in striking white robe and turban (symbol of a transformed, pure and separate life), he walked barefoot, carrying a six-foot bamboo cross, and a small bowl for baptising converts in the name of the Father, the Son and the Holy Spirit. The Bible (the English Authorized Version) was his constant resort, the source of answers to the issues he encountered. Harris majored on the New Testament, but made much use of Exodus, Daniel and Ezekiel. He also carried John Bunyan's *Pilgrim's Progress*, a work also shaped by prison experience. He described himself as 'Elijah', 'the carpet on which Christ wipes his feet', and the 'Carrier of Christ, the horse of Christ'. He humbly called himself a 'Kru-boy', willing to take passage on any passing ship, and travel in his missionary cause. He preached in a booming voice in Pidgin English, which was widely spoken along the coast,

---

35   On Harris see D.A. Shank, *Prophet Harris, the 'Black Elijah' of West Africa*, Brill, Leiden, 1994; G.M.Haliburton, *The Prophet Harris: A Study of an African Prophet and his Mass-Movement in the Ivory Coast and the Gold Coast 1913–1915*, London, Longman, 1971; S.S. Walker, *The Religious Revolution in the Ivory Coast: The Prophet Harris and the Harrist Church*, Chapel Hill, N. Carolina UP, 1983.

The Teachings of Wadé Harris as practised by his followers in 1916

Love God and thank Him on all occasions.

Love your neighbour and do him no harm.

Love your wives and do not treat them like captives.

Respect the wives of others.

Do not bear false witness.

Do not steal.

Do not be jealous of your neighbour.

Instead of coveting your neighbour's possessions, work to earn them for yourself.

Consider suicide an accident and pity the one who cut short his days: bury him decently.

Abortion is a crime punished by God.

If your wife dies, offer gifts to those who bring their condolences, but do not shave your head.

Rest on Sunday.

While polygamy is not forbidden, monogamy is recommended.[1]

---

1   R. Grivot, 'Le Cercle de Lahou (Côte D'Ivoire)', *Bulletin de l'Institut Français d'Afrique Noire*, iv, Jan-Oct, 1942, quoted in G.M Haliburton, *The Prophet Harris*, London, Longman, 1971.

---

or through local interpreters. His message was largely orthodox Christianity, stressing the need to love one another, and to obey the Ten Commandments. The emphasis on the power of Christ over the spirits was strong. He offered baptism to the repentant, without the long period of catechetical preparation required by missionary churches. In seventeen months he preached to some 200,000 people in the Ivory Coast and Ghana, claiming some 100,000 converts whom he baptised. Accounts circulated of dramatic encounters with traditional religious leaders, of hidden fetishes burned by mysterious fire, and of occasions when so many sought baptism that he utilised sudden downpours of rain instead, pronouncing blessing in the name of the Father, Son and Holy Spirit.[36]

Aware of the power of witchcraft over the African mind in a way European missionaries were not, Harris called Africans to radical renunciation of the occult, spirits and cult-figures or fetishes of traditional African religions. These he believed were possessed of spiritual force, and should be destroyed by burning. Stories circulated of sudden death befalling those who had been baptised after falsely claiming to have destroyed their fetishes. His emphasis on spiritual healing was particularly significant in areas where epidemic disease was

---

36   E. Isichei, *A History of Christianity in Africa*, London, SPCK, 1995, p285f; Sundkler, *Church in Africa*, 196–201.

prevalent. God's power was more than sufficient, but required strict obedience. God's judgement could bring death or illness to the disobedient, and fire from heaven could descend at once. He emphasised strict observance of the Sabbath, and prohibition of adultery, but in other areas, his message was less clear. He did not condemn polygamy, but believed it in need of reform. He travelled in the company of several 'wives' who participated in his missionary work, at least one of whom bore him a child. A number of Harrist churches were also formed, such as the Église Harriste. In the churches he founded he placed twelve apostles, usually educated Africans who were employed by Europeans, and who significantly influenced the movement. These churches also featured traditional music and dance, liturgical vestments, and self-supporting preachers chosen by local congregations. However, many of his followers joined mainstream denominations, including Roman Catholicism, but Harris's preference was that they joined the Methodists.[37]

In 1915, with Europe engulfed in war, the French colonial administration expelled Harris from the Ivory Coast, fearful of his past reputation. He returned to Liberia, where he continued to preach, and made several trips to Sierra Leone, but without the success of his early journeys. He died in poverty in Liberia in 1929. Harris's proved the most successful of all missions to West Africa: the speed and scale of his success shocked missionaries who had struggled with little fruit over many years, and as a result of his work they found the numbers attracted to their churches significantly boosted. However, the determination by missionary bodies such as the Wesleyan Methodists, to strictly enforce monogamy were met with stiff resistance by Africans who had been inspired to radical religious change by an African.

The work of Harris prefigured the twentieth-century advance of Christianity in Africa and other continents through locally-led indigenous movements free from traditional ecclesiastical structures, attracting the poor and marginalised, led by often untrained but zealous male and female preachers and prophets. Harris's work had parallels in that of Garrick Sokari Braide in the Niger Delta between 1912 and 1916, before his imprisonment in 1916 and his death in 1918. 'Zionist' churches, with an emphasis on faith healing and speaking in tongues, were operating in southern Africa in the 1890s. Traditional aspects of African religion, such as exorcism, ecstatic dance, the prophet-healer figure, and rites of purification and initiation, stood alongside Biblical and Christ-centred forms of Christianity. The South African Zion Christian Church (ZCC) was one of the most successful, established in 1910 by Engenas Barnabas Lekganyane. A number of these churches followed the customs of particular peoples, such as the Zulus, and operated as ethnically-based churches, mixing pilgrimages and ritual taboos and with liturgical calendars intertwined with

37   Jenkins, *Next Christendom*, 49, references 26 and 27.

traditional seasonal patterns. By the 1920s the Zion movement had reached Swaziland, Basutoland and Zimbabwe.[38] The Bamalaki in Uganda broke away from missionary Christianity in 1914, offering instant baptism, without a long period of catechetical preparation. They argued that dependence on missionary medicine was as bad as consulting traditional diviners and mediums, because sickness was caused by evil spirits or witchcraft.

The impact of these hugely varied African independent churches was strong: it was possible to be both Christian and truly African. Opportunities emerged for liturgical innovation, contextual forms of evangelisation, experiments with ecclesiastical structures, and dialogue with practitioners of traditional religions. They gave opportunities for women to hold prominent leadership positions. Polygamists were often allowed to retain their wives on conversion, along with traditional customs related to birth, marriage and death. Mission churches generally considered them as syncretistic, product of a superficial understanding of the gospel, yet they were extremely popular, fully rooted in the African context, and a distinctively African expression of Christianity. Their religious expression appeared more consistent than that of many adherents of missionary Christianity who attended a mission church on a Sunday, but consulted mediums and diviners through the week.

The radical separation of indigenous forms of Christianity from its colonial bearers was demonstrated not just in religious form, but also in movements for political independence. John Chilembwe (c. 1871–1915) was mentored by Joseph Booth of the Zambezi Industrial Mission, who took him from the position of cook, to send him to a black college in West Virginia, from whence he returned to found the Providence Industrial Mission at Chiradzu. His withdrawal from association with whites troubled the authorities, and in 1915 he launched an armed revolt against British rule in Nyasaland (Malawi), mixing elements of nationalism, social justice, and Christian teaching. Chilembwe's revolt, and the six others in Africa between 1906 and 1927, deepened white concerns about African Independent churches.[39]

Independent church movements such as those in Africa, represented both the success and failure of missionary endeavour. They also showed the capacity of Christianity to indigenise in areas where previously it was unheard of. The result was a multi-form variety of expressions in local cultures, some of which were radically different from dominant Western expressions. Indeed, instead of the theological liberalism that appeared set to dominate in the West after 1914, by the year 2000 the churches of the non-Western World would often be characterised by 'a much greater respect for the authority of scripture,

38   Jenkins, *Next Christendom*, 52–53, fn 35.
39   Jenkins, *Next Christendom*, 49, fn 28.

especially in matters of morality; a willingness to accept the Bible as an inspired text and…a special interest in the supernatural elements of scripture.'[40]

CHRISTIANITY AND WORLD RELIGIONS

The increasing presence of Christianity as a global phenomenon increased scope for its comparison with other world religions, which was to be of great significance for the twentieth century global political and religious scene. Christianity grew in size and influence at a time when Buddhism and Islam were also growing in self-confidence, and displaying an increasingly expansive mind-set. Marxism was also to prove a significant threat, even outside Europe. The revived strength and confidence of Hinduism fed into the creation of the Indian National Congress, formed in 1885, and interest in Indian self-governance. Missionaries were particularly alert to the rising influence of Islam in the East and in parts of Africa, with the Islamic approach to women, its allowance of slavery, and policy of aggressive expansion, subject to much criticism. In areas under British colonial control, missionaries felt that authorities were being too sensitive to Muslim feelings in an attempt to avoid confrontation.

The growing evidence of the existence of a world religious economy, together with changing attitudes towards other faiths, is demonstrated by the calling in 1893 of the World's Parliament of Religions, held in conjunction with the World's Fair in Chicago. Nineteenth-century missionaries were confident of the superiority of Christianity above other religions, a view closely intertwined with the conviction that Western culture was superior to that of other cultures. Nonetheless, from the 1870s onwards, a more positive attitude towards world religions can be discerned: some missionaries sought to move from direct confrontation towards engagement and debate, with a willingness to see aspects of religious truth in religions such as Islam.

As early as 1845, the English theologian F.D. Maurice, who had begun to question the doctrine of eternal punishment, argued in *The Religions of the World in the Relations to Christianity*, that all religions contained truth and goodness, although he was still sure that the ultimate answer was to be found in Christ.[41] In India, missionaries strove to present Christianity in less confrontational ways towards Hinduism. Some were prepared to accept elements of revelation within Hinduism, with Christianity as the fulfilment of what lay partially revealed elsewhere. Although the religious and ethical superiority of Christianity continued to be asserted, Christ was portrayed by some less as a focal point of doctrine, and more as a teacher of ethical idealism and social justice to whom the devotion of all was due.[42] In China, Timothy Richard similarly sought to find

---

40   P. Jenkins, *The New Faces of Christianity*, Oxford, OUP, 2006, 4.

41   G. Rowell, *Hell and the Victorians*, Oxford, OUP, 1974, 79–89; 190–192.

42   Stanley, *Bible and Flag*, 164–165.

areas of common ground with Buddhism and Confucianism, and to express the Christian faith in terms accessible to the Chinese mind and context.[43] The study of comparative religion, coupled with growing convictions as to the absolute goodness of humanity, and widespread interest in the embryonic science of anthropology, brought growing convictions that value systems were relative. By 1890, Liberal theologians were proposing that major world religions such as Hinduism, Buddhism, Confucianism, and Islam offered some form of saving knowledge of God, although they still maintained that religion was most truly demonstrated in Jesus Christ. Christianity may have been a superior religion, but it was not an exclusive one.

At the World's Parliament of Religions, Christians mixed freely with leaders of other religions. To Christian liberal theologians, this was an exercise in mission: that all participants recited the Lord's Prayer each day was seen as a progressive sign. The organiser of the event, the Presbyterian J.H. Barrows, believed that the Parliament would herald the world-wide triumph of liberal, Protestant American Christianity. He believed that other religions contained beauty, truth, and goodness, but he was sure that Christianity was the fulfilment of other religions, rather than their destruction, and would one day become the world religion. It was up to Christianity, in a field of free contest, to prove itself the superior religion. By no means all participants agreed. The Hindu, Swami Vivekanda, believed it 'an impossible hope' that religious unity would come about through the triumph of one religion over others.[44]

Liberal theologians departed from the World's Parliament of Religions making calls for fairer treatment of other faiths, an end to blaming them for all the ills of non-Western cultures, and to attributing every success of the West to Christian influence. There was a marked willingness to listen to and learn from other perspectives: other religions, especially those from Asia, were held in higher regard.[45] The Parliament reflected the transformation in thinking about missions being led by liberal theologians. The post-millennial hope of an end-time golden age of the gospel, was being reshaped into expectations of a golden age of social change, with an emphasis on the ethical implications of salvation and the brotherhood of humanity. Through civilising and social projects, a broadly Christian environment would be created, increasing the likelihood of accepting Christian principles. Influenced by Horace Bushnell's views on Christian nurture, less emphasis was placed on decision as a way of entering the Christian life, and more on a gradual absorption of Christianity. Doctrinal certitude was seen as less important because religious language was

---

43   See Chapter 13 above.

44   J.H. Barrows, *The World's Parliament of Religions*, 2 vols, Chicago, Parliament Publishing, 1893, 171.

45   Bosch, *Transforming Mission*, 313–325.

symbolic rather than absolute, especially on issues such as eternal punishment, which was widely rejected by liberal theologians.[46] By the 1880s liberal thinkers were speculating on whether the unreached millions who had never heard the gospel would have a posthumous chance to hear and embrace it.[47]

Such speculations on the religious merit in other faiths, and the eternal fate of practitioners of other religions was, to conservative thinkers, sowing seeds of apathy and paralysis in mission. The premillennialist, A.T. Pierson, editor of the *Missionary Review of the World* between 1887 and 1911, condemned the World's Parliament of Religion as 'the Devil's master-piece of strategy to keep the hosts of God within the walls of luxurious indolence, when they should be moving outward against the citadels of superstition and idolatry.' It was, to Pierson, an instance of when 'God's elect flirted with the daughters of the enemies of the Lord.'[48] D.L. Moody simply ignored the Parliament, and used the World's Fair as an opportunity to present the gospel to attendees. For six months he hired the auditorium, together with theatres, halls, and tents, from which big-name evangelistic preachers proclaimed and sang 'the old Gospel [in] the power of the Holy Ghost.'[49] Conservative advocates of mission steadfastly maintained that the uniqueness of Christ, and the conviction of the eternal condemnation of the lost, were powerful motives to mission. In 1894 Hudson Taylor presented to the Student Volunteer Movement the stark vision of 'A great Niagara of souls passing into the dark in China, every day, every week, every month…A million a month in China, they are dying without God.'[50] The emphasis on mission at the Keswick convention in England remained strong, with many devoting themselves to service as missionaries after attending meetings there.[51]

Nonetheless, the war of 1914 was to weaken the confidence of Western minds as to the superiority of their civilisation above 'primitive' cultures they encountered, and made it less attractive to those to whom it was being disseminated. Some began to search for more authentic, and attractive, indigenous cultures. The weakening of European economies during and after the war tended to reduce European missionary endeavour, with the American missionary force moving to the fore. With reduced resources for colonial government, European powers adopted a form of indirect rule which ceded much authority to local rulers,

---

46   G. Wacker, 'Second Thoughts on the Great Commission: Liberal Protestants and Foreign Missions 1890–1940', in Shenk, *Earthen Vessels*, 281–300.

47   Hutchison, *Errand to the World*, 103–105.

48   A.T. Pierson, 'The World's Parliament of Religions: A Review', in *Missionary Review of the World*, 17, 1894, 882, 893–4; and A.T. Pierson, *The Crisis of Missions*, New York, Robert Carter and Brothers, 1886, 294.

49   Dorsett, *Moody*, 391.

50   P.A. Varg, 'Motives in Protestant Missions, 1890–1917', *Church History* 23 (1954): 71.

51   T. Yates, *Christian Mission in the Twentieth Century*, Cambridge, CUP, 1996, 23.

a number of whom were Muslims. This helped to keep the peace, but served to advance Islam.

THE STUBBORN PERSISTENCE OF RACIST TENDENCIES

Slavery, and the hard-won battle to end it, left a troubling legacy into the twentieth century. The Americas had been physically transformed by the labours of black slaves, but the attitudes instilled by years of slave-trading and slave holding, left deeply ingrained racist thinking and practices of racial discrimination in both America and Europe. By the late nineteenth century, the issue of race, and racial classification, had become a significant theme in Western intellectual discourse. Justification for this was claimed by the 'scientific evidence' of biology, ethnography, anthropology, and even the pseudo-science of phrenology. Imperial pre-eminence, where it existed, was believed to be a product of racial and cultural superiority of white above black. Yet, whilst Christianity was expanding into becoming a truly global religion, the same intellectual sources were also steadily undermining the Christian hegemony of Western thought. Evolutionary biology and biblical criticism challenged the previous Christian apologetic basis, and conceptions of biblical authority.

One crucial issue arising from the evolutionary approach to matters of Creation, was how to account for racial differences. Those who argued for monogenesis, that humans sprang from a single pair of parents, Adam and Eve, explained these differences in terms of the influence of climate, environment, and local social patterns. If farmers could, through interbreeding, produce wholly white or wholly black cows, surely the same would be true of humans post-Creation. However, evolutionary thinking strengthened the arguments of those who proposed polygenesis: differences had arisen either because of a series of separate divine creative acts for different races, or because they had developed from lower animal life in different ways in different regions, whether by divine overruling or not. The implications were profound. Polygenesis had been proposed as early as Voltaire and the freethinking Deists in eighteenth century Britain, and speculation as to multiple human origins increased with the discoveries of aboriginal peoples in the New World. Its leading proponent in mid-nineteenth century America was the Swiss-born geologist and naturalist Louis Agassiz, who, whilst still accepting the reality of Adam and Eve, proposed multiple originations for different races not described in Genesis.[52] Similarly, in their *Types of Mankind*, J. Nott and G. Gliddon argued that the Genesis account of creation described the origin of those who were white, with the creation of other races not being specifically recorded. Others suggested a racial division had taken place after the Flood, between the descendants of Shem (the Jews), Japheth (white peoples), and Ham (non-white peoples). One risk of polygenesis,

---

52   Kidd, *Forging of Races*, 88–92; 140–42.

when set alongside evolutionary biology, was to see one race as superior to others: this featured heavily in the justification of the continuation of slavery in ante-bellum America.[53] Social anthropology, influenced by social Darwinism, also proposed certain peoples as being at a lesser level of evolutionary development. By the late nineteenth century Aryan thinkers were proposing that the Nordic / Saxon races were the most advanced on the evolutionary scale: cultural superiority was believed to reflect racial superiority.

Nonetheless, the depth and virulence with which racist ideology exploded at the end of the nineteenth century was surprising. It led to the physical segregation of blacks from whites, and the removal of black people from positions of influence. In 1865, a revolt of black ex-slaves demanding equal access to the land and the legal system in Jamaica was crushed by the British governor, the Jamaican legislature was dissolved, the West Indian population disenfranchised, and crown colony government imposed. In the 1880s black teachers and administrators found themselves removed from office. In Africa, Portuguese administrators restricted the access of black people to leadership positions; racial segregation was enforced on the grounds of 'health' by French administrators in the 1890s, and in South Africa the labour force in the diamond and gold mines was segregated. In the United States, despite the emancipation of the slaves, ways of maintaining control over them, and access to their labour, without resort to overt physical force were developed by their former owners. Limited educational opportunities, poverty, and ongoing racial discrimination ensured America's black population were hugely disadvantaged in a white-dominated society. In the 1890s the 'Jim Crow' laws brought segregation of housing, schooling, and public facilities.

Slavery and then racism condemned black people to exist as an underpaid and overworked labour force. The social and economic patterns of African life were severely damaged by slavery, shaping and defining the continent's needs in the twentieth century. Although slavery was curtailed, it gave way to the use of coerced labour by colonial governments to recruit porters who carried burdens for long distances, mended roads, or worked on other construction projects, for minimal or no reward. Colonial labour systems also increased migratory patterns, requiring men to travel great distances to work in mines, or projects such as railway construction.

Missionary journals of the late nineteenth century still recorded accounts of domestic slavery, cannibalism, witchcraft, and the burial alive of slaves and widows of deceased persons, evidence to some of innate savagery, to others, of satanic influence upon those they ministered to. Such accounts, together

---

53   J. Nott and G. Gliddon, *Types of Mankind*, 4th edition, Philadelphia, 1854, 555–59; S. D. Baldwin, *Dominion, or the Unity and Trinity of the Human Race*, Nashville, Tennessee, 1858 in Kidd, *Forging of Races*, 144–45.

with evidence of dishonesty, bribery and corruption, often created a sense of distrust amongst missionaries of those they came to serve. Racist distrust was far greater amongst the wider body of white European settlers, whose ability to undermine by their behaviour much of the work of the missionaries was bitterly lamented. 'Scientific racism' began to make its presence felt in some areas of colonial administration. The explorer Richard Burton was openly racist in his views of Africans, and critical of the humanitarian values of missionaries, dismissing Samuel Crowther with the ugliest of racist language.[54]

Some of the fiercest resistance to racial tendencies came from Christian missionaries who insisted that the grace of God was freely available to all in the world; that Christ's atoning death and resurrection was for peoples of all races; and that all races were capable of responding to the gospel. Many missionaries retained confidence that indigenous peoples, freed from oppression and ignorance, could equal the achievements of the European mind. Their willingness to treat black Christians as brothers in Christ appalled white colonists, as did their willingness to train non-whites for ordination, and place them in positions of leadership. Settlers resisted the widespread educational endeavours, and undiscriminating medical support offered to local peoples by the missionaries.

Although theories of racial superiority and inferiority were rejected by pioneers such as David Livingstone,[55] and most missionaries were not conscious imperialists, such ideology began to permeate culture so thoroughly that missionaries were not immune from its influence. As mission organisations became increasingly institutionalised in the West, they became more imbued with Western racist attitudes which showed limited respect for indigenous cultures and the capacity of local converts for religious leadership. The vision for self-governance, articulated by Henry Venn, was not lost, but the anticipated time-scale for the devolution of power was greatly lengthened. The slow progress of many regions in terms of educational and technological advance and social change, and the negative assessments of social anthropologists, left some doubting the capacity of such peoples to advance. So too did the frequency of major rebellions in which countless lives were lost—whether the Indian Mutiny, or the Boxer Rebellion in China. Questions were raised as to whether the Christian hope, and indeed confidence, in the power of the gospel to raise certain races, had been misplaced. However, these unpalatable theories had an unexpectedly positive side. Belief in racial pre-eminence brought a sense of obligation to weaker and less favoured societies to civilise and convert them to

---

54   Cox, 'Religion and Imperial Power', 368 cites a particularly distasteful example from Burton's *Wanderings in West Africa*, New York, 1991, 207.

55   Ross, *Livingstone*, 216–217.

Crowther with African Clergy

Christianity. Missionaries also called colonial governments to account over the imperial trusteeship they exercised.

Missions stations were run in increasingly paternal fashion, and patronising attitudes demonstrated, with demeaning references made to 'African character and habits.' Some doubted whether indigenous Christians possessed the financial, administrative, ethical, and even spiritual capacities to act as leaders in significant positions. The 1880s and 1890s saw an increased presence of ethnocentric or racially conscious missionaries, highly critical of the faults of indigenous leaders, and judging them by uncompromising standards framed by Western thinking. This was the case in West Africa where Samuel Ajayi Crowther, the Anglican bishop since 1875, found himself isolated and shorn of much of his power by young white English missionaries influenced by Keswick holiness teaching.[56] There were those such as David Scott in Nyasaland, and Bishop Alfred Tucker in Uganda, who fought to defend traditional egalitarianism, believing in the capacity of Africans to equal what Europeans could do,[57] yet, after Crowther, the CMS appointed only white bishops in Africa until the middle of the twentieth century.

Such attitudes encouraged support for 'Ethiopian' churches, which had wholly African leadership. They looked back to the golden age of early African Christianity, and forward to the days when a truly indigenous African church would be formed, despite the barriers of Islam, traditional religion, and

---

56   Porter, *Religion Versus Empire?*, 282–289.

57   A. Ross, 'Christian Missions and Mid-Nineteenth-Century Change in Attitudes to Race: The African Experience', in Porter, *Imperial Horizons*, 85–105.

James Johnson

European racist attitudes. The belief also remained that only Africans could truly evangelise Africa, and a church free of European domination could be built. It reflected a growing consciousness that Africans existed as a distinct race. One promoter of Ethiopianism was the extremely able African, James Johnson (1836–1917), educated at Fourah Bay, Sierra Leone, as Crowther had been. After working as a schoolteacher he was ordained a priest in 1866. Johnson promoted a missionary vision for the African church, calling it back to the days of African spiritual leaders such as Tertullian, Cyprian, and Augustine. 'Holy' Johnson was a fervent evangelical, committed to securing rights to education for Africans, and the development of a self-sufficient church. Although willing to support separatists, he remained loyal to the Anglican Church himself. Yet, for all his clear abilities he only reached the rank of Assistant Bishop, serving under Crowther's white successor.[58] As native African Churches spurred by ongoing racist attitudes increasingly began to break away from mission-founded churches to seek a truly African form of Christianity, foundations were also laid for modern forms of African nationalism. Whether the Christianity exported by the Western church had been transformed into something entirely different by its non-Western recipients, reacting to the presence and strategy of missionaries, is debated. However, elements of continuity with European patterns remained.[59]

World Christianity to be Authentic For Local Needs

'We advocate no new Gospel, and our chief concern is with the permanent and fundamental elements of theology. These are neither oriental nor occidental, but in order to build up the Church on these lasting foundations Christian theology must be written afresh for every fresh race to whom it comes, so that it may justify itself to all as the abiding wisdom that cometh from above... and not be misrepresented as if it were no more than a precipitation from the antiquated text-books of the West.'[1]

1 World Missionary *Conference Reports of Commission II*, Edinburgh and London, Oliphant, Anderson and Ferrier, 1910, quoted in Stanley, *Edinburgh 1910*, 160.

---

58   On James Johnson, see E.A. Ayandele, *Holy Johnson: Pioneer of African Nationalism, 1836–1917*, London, Frank Cass, 1970. Ethiopianism is discussed in O. Kalu, 'Ethiopianism and the Roots of Modern African Christianity', in S. Gilley and B. Stanley, eds, *Cambridge History of Christianity: World Christianities, c. 1815–c. 1914*, Cambridge, CUP, 2006, 576–592.

59   J. Cox, *The British Missionary Enterprise Since 1700*, London, Routledge, 2008, 20–21.

THE SHADOW OF WAR

Observers of Christianity in the early years of the twentieth century had a strong sense that they were living at a turning point in the history of Christianity. Missionaries, buoyed by the optimism of the Edinburgh conference, expected further breakthroughs. Protestant and Roman Catholic modernist theologians confidently articulated new theologies for the modern age. With steamships circling the oceans of the globe, and railway lines reducing travel times across continents, and with rapid European colonial expansion, opportunities for church advance seemed unprecedented. Yet in the previous European heartlands of Christendom, strongly shaped by their Established churches, the dominance of Christianity was waning. The rise of nonconformity and evangelicalism in Britain had weakened denominational boundaries, and secularism and anticlericalism had become well rooted in continental Europe and parts of Latin America. In Italy the wealth and privileges of the Roman Catholic Church had been greatly eroded. Church attendance in Germany was low. In Argentina, Brazil and Chile, state subsidy of the Roman Catholic Church had ended, and in France in 1905–07 the separation of state and church was effected. European Christendom was passing.

Late nineteenth-century nationalist sentiment produced a united Germany, and a united Italy, each with imperialist ambitions, competing with those of France, Turkey, Austria and Britain. The claims of the nation state began to be viewed above any other loyalties. In 1914, the Archbishop of Canterbury, Randall Davidson, wrote a letter to the chief court chaplain of the German Kaiser in which he expressed his anxiety over the world political situation, declaring 'war between two great Christian nations of kindred race and sympathies is, or ought to be, unthinkable in the twentieth century of the Gospel of the Prince of Peace.'[60] The 'unthinkable' happened. War could have broken out any time between 1904 and 1914. That the flash-point was the Balkans is no surprise; here Christianity most notably rubbed shoulders with Islam, and was the site of serious tensions which remained into the late twentieth century, as events were to prove. Nationalists in the Balkan states shared a common desire to be free of Turkish rule. The Pan-Slavism between Russia and Balkan states, united by ties of language and Orthodox religion, proved a powerful combination. Other European peoples desired independence from Austrian rule. War between Italy and Turkey in 1912 was joined by Russia, and a Balkan League of Serbia, Bulgaria, Montenegro, and Greece. Within a month all of Turkey's European territories had been captured, but the Balkan League could not agree on the division of the spoils. Further war ensued, in which Germany offered support to Turkey, in order to gain access to the Black Sea, thus alarming Russia.

---

60   G.K.A. Bell, *Randall Davidson: Archbishop of Canterbury*, 2nd edn, London, Oxford University Press 1938, 732–33.

In June 1914, Archduke Ferdinand, heir to the Austro-Hungarian Empire, chose to visit Sarajevo and inspect the imperial troops based there. He fatefully chose 28th June, Serbian national day. He was felled by the assassin's bullet of Gabriel Princip, a twenty-year old Serbian student. Whether the Serbian government was involved or not is unclear, but the walls of sense caved in, and Europe descended into war. Austria declared war on Serbia; Russia mobilised in support of Serbia, and so Germany declared war on Russia, and then France. When Belgium was invaded by German troops on their way to France, Britain was drawn in. Political parties and churches overwhelmingly, and uncritically, endorsed the war. The German Kaiser Wilhelm II called Germans to fight as a Christian nation, 'humble before God, but with the joy of battle in the face of the enemy, we trust in the Almighty to strengthen our defence and guide us to good issue.'[61] Strangely, governments, chaplains and clergymen on both sides were saying the same things. Christianity was enlisted both on the side of bellicose rhetoric, and to provide comfort and consolation to the victims of war. Technology as much as ideology caused such mass destruction, and technological failure was a part of the reason why the killing was not ended sooner. The madness lasted for four years, leaving more than 8.5 million soldiers dead, let alone civilian casualties. Although the First World War was the culmination of processes which started much earlier, it dealt a profound blow to liberal social, political and religious optimism. The world looked a very different place after 1914. The concept of European Christendom was probably buried amongst the war dead in the fields of Flanders and Northern France. To find the axis of Christianity it would be increasingly necessary to look, as the twentieth century wore on, towards the churches of the Global South.

61　Speech in Reichstag 4 August 1914, in A.J. Steinhoff, 'Christianity and the Creation of Germany', *World Christianities c. 1815–1914*, 300.

FURTHER READING

D. Bosch, *Transforming Mission: Paradigm Shifts in Theology of Mission*, Maryknoll, NY, Orbis, 1991.

J. Cox, *The British Missionary Enterprise Since 1700*, London, Routledge, 2008.

S. Gilley and B. Stanley, (eds) *Cambridge History of Christianity, Volume 8: World Christianities, c. 1815–c. 1914*, Cambridge, Cambridge University Press, 2006.

W.R. Hutchinson, *Errand to the World: American Protestant Thought and Foreign Missions*, Chicago, Chicago University Press, 1987.

P. Jenkins, *The Next Christendom: The Coming of Global Christianity*, Oxford, OUP, 2002.

C. Kidd, *The Forging of Races: Race and Scripture in the Protestant Atlantic World, 1600–2000*, Cambridge, CUP, 2006.

S.H. Moffett, *A History of Christianity in Asia, Vol. II, 1500–1900*, Maryknoll, Orbis, 2005.

A. Porter, *Religion Versus Empire? British Protestant Missionaries and Overseas Expansion, 1700–1914*, Manchester, Manchester University Press, 2004.

A.Porter (ed), *The Oxford History of the British Empire*, Vol. 3, *The Nineteenth Century*, Oxford, 1999.

L.O. Sanneh, *West African Christianity: the Religious Impact*, London, Allen & Unwin, 1983.

D.A. Shank, *Prophet Harris, the 'Black Elijah' of West Africa*, Brill, Leiden, 1994.

B. Stanley, *The World Missionary Conference, Edinburgh 1910*, Grand Rapids, Eerdmans, 2009.

G. Wacker, *Heaven Below: Early Pentecostals and American Culture*, Cambridge, Mass., Harvard, 2001.

Subject Index

A

*A Practical View of the Prevailing
  Religious System* (book) 77-8

Abbott, Lyman 323

Abeokuta.. 281

Abolition Act (1807).................................... 148

Absolute Spirit 181, 186, 189

Act of Union (1801) 70, 72

Adams, John Quincy 354-5

Addams, Jane 461

Additional Curates Society 209

Affleck, Thomas 351

Africa 20-1, 131-5, 137-8,
  .... 160-2, 277-9, 524-8

African Baptist Missionary Society 20

African Civilisation Society 280

African Methodist Episcopal
  Church (US) 17-19, 348, 367

African-American Christians (US) 16-22,
  .... 351-2, 363, 367-8, 503-5

agnosticism 327, 330-2

Alarm to the Converted (book) 26

alcohol law reform (US) 29-30, 342, 464

Alexander, Archibald 490

Alexander I, Tsar 378

Alexander II, Tsar 379-81

Alexander III, Tsar 380

Alleine, Joseph 26

Allen, Horace 424

Allen, Richard 17-19

Allen, William 224

*Allgemeine Zeitung des
  Judentums* (newspaper) 397

Alliance Israélite Universelle (France)
 398

Alline, Henry 389

Alton Locke (novel) 266

American Anti-Slavery Society 353-4

American Baptist Missionary Board 118

American Bible Society 31

American Board for Foreign Missions 9,
  ....118-19, 348

American Colonization Society 353

American Free Religious Association 331

American Purity Alliance 453

'American Renaissance' 340

American Society for the Promotion
  of Temperance 30

American Women's Suffrage Association
 346

'Americanism' 496-7

Anderson, Rufus 275-6, 300

Andover Seminary (1808) 481

Anglican Church Army 469

Anglican National Society 215

Anglican Society for Propagation
  of the Gospel in Foreign Parts 97

Anglicanism
  and anti-slavery movement 154
  and British politics 223
  and Christian mission 110-14
  and Darwinism 321
  and Disestablishment movement 213
  and Industrial Revolution (Britain)
  .... 71-8, 91, 203
  in Ireland 386
  and liberalism 234

and Oxford Movement 253-64

preaching of 211

Anna Karenina (novel) 380

Anthony, Susan 346

anti-Semitism 372, 398-9

anti-slavery movement

and Christian mission 126, 152-60,

....277-8, 284-6

and Christianity 145-8, 151-7, 161, 349-54

and enforcement of abolition 148-9

and mechanisms of slavery 134-5

and mortality rates 136

in pre-Civil War USA 354-9

and Quakers 16, 86, 141, 145,

.....................................147, 344-6, 364

roots of 139-43

successes of 144-5, 148

and US Civil War 359-65

and women 344-6

Anti-Slavery Society 151, 156, 157

Antoinette, Queen Marie 42, 48

architecture (church) 261

Arnold, Thomas 74, 260

Articles of Confederation (US) 4

Artisans' Dwellings Act (1885) 458

Asbury, Francis 12-13, 14, 23, 114

Ashmore, William 412

Assemblies of God 505, 515

'Astronomy and General Physics

Considered' (essay) 306

atheism 320, 325-6, 331-2

Australia 113-14

Austria 49

Awakening (France) 58

Azariah, Vedanayakam Samuel 416-17

B

Baden-Powell, Robert 456

Bahrdt, Karl Friedrich 174

Balkans 376-7, 538

Baptist Missionary Society 99, 100-8,

....277, 295, 419

Baptist Triennial Convention 119

Baptists

and anti-slavery movement 153-4,

....155-6, 157-8

in Britain 86-7

and Christian mission 409-10,

....419-20, 428

preaching of 212-13

in USA 15, 20, 23

Barnardo, Thomas 219-20

Barnes, Albert 483

Barnett, Canon Samuel 458-61

Barratt, T.B. 515

Barrows, J.H. 530

Barth, Karl 175, 180

Basel Mission (Switzerland) 110, 283

Bastille (France) 43, 63, 68

Baur, Ferdinand Christian 186-7

Beagle (H.M.S.) 312, 316, 329, 333

Beattie, James 139-40

Bebbington, David 213, 216

Beecher, Henry Ward 323, 362, 469,

....488-9

Beecher, Lyman 9, 26, 28, 482, 488

Belgium 244

Bell, Andrew 215

Bellamy, Joseph 7

Bentham, Jeremy 234-5

Berlin Conference on Colonial

Questions (1885) 432-3

Berlin Missionary Society 110

Beveridge, William 459

Bewley, Anthony 357

Bible

as 'America's Iconic Book' 31

and Christian mission 123-4,

....411-12

and creation account 308-11,

...............................317-20, 324-5, 532

as God's revelation 490-1

as historical truth 187, 188

claimed to be mythical symbolism
...............183-4, 186, 485-6, 487-8

rejection of 8, 37

and slavery 145-6, 361-4

and social reform 264-5

translations of 105-6, 110-11,

....120-1, 509

'Bible Communists' 477

Bible Institute for Home and

Foreign Mission 464

Bickersteth, Edward 423

Bill of Rights (US) 9-10

Bingham, Rev. Hiram 118

Bismarck, Otto Von 169-70, 432

Blackwell, Antoinette Brown 29

Blackwell, Elizabeth 347

Board of Deputies of British Jews 398

Boardman, George 122

Boddy, A.A. 515

Boers 117, 428

Bogue, David 108

Boikano, Khama 428

Bolivia 390-1

Bolívar, Simón 390-1

Bonaparte, Napoleon 53-60, 166-7,

....372, 377-8

Book of Mormon 478

Boone, Daniel 22

Booth, Catherine 466-9

Booth, Charles 216, 454

Booth, Joseph 528

Booth, William 439, 466-9

Bosch, David 123

Boston Training School 412

Boudinot, Elias 339

Bourne, Hugh 83-4

Boxer Rising (China) 422, 534

Boy Scouting movement 456

Boys Brigade 455-6

Braide, Garrick Sokari 527

Brainerd, David 97

Bridges, G.W. 152

Brienne, Loménie de 38

Briggs, Charles 494-5

Bright, John 217

Britain

and Act of Union (1801) 70, 72, 85

anti-slavery movement in 140-5,

.... 155-8

Christian involvement

in politics 221-8

church attendance in 202-3, 442,

.................446-7, 449, 451-2, 454, 472

education in 214-18

expansionism of 125-6

and French Revolution 63-4

and German theological revolution 193

Industrial Revolution see Industrial

Revolution (Britain)

Jewish Emancipation in 395

middle classes of 199

philanthropic institutions 213-14

population growth 69, 89-90,

....................................198, 199, 442-3

poverty in 199-201

reform movement in 70, 71, 92,

.... 228-30

Religious Censuses in 202-3,

....446-7, 449

revolution potential in 64-8

and slave trade 135, 138, 151

social deprivation in 198-202,

..........................204-8, 213-14, 218-19

and spread of liberalism 249-67

unemployment in 199

urbanisation of 68-9, 197-201,

....228, 442

and US War of Independence 1-3

voluntary bodies in 88-91

British and Foreign Bible Society 82, 88, 110

British and Foreign School Society 214

British Association for the Advancement

of Science 327

British East India Company 99, 110, 113, 416

Brotherhood of the Kingdom movement ... 471

Brown, Antoinette 348

Brown, David 110

Brown, John 353, 356-7

Bruce, Robert 431

Bryan, Andrew 17

Bryan, William Jennings 333

Buchanan, Claudius 110

Buchanan, Rev Robert 457

Buddhism 425

Bulgaria 376

Bull, Parson G.S. 221

Bunting, Jabez 83, 157, 250

Burke, Edmund 63

Burma 119-22, 295

Burns, William Chalmers 293-4

Burton, Richard 534

Burwash, Nathanael 390

Bushnell, Horace 366, 485-8

Butler, Fanny 410-11

Buxton, Thomas Fowell 134-5, 151, 157,

.... 224-5, 278-80, 283-4, 286-7

C

Calcutta School 297

Calvin, John 177

Calvinism

    in Britain 87, 212

    and Christian mission 108

    and evangelism 100-1

    in USA 480-3, 489-94

Cambridge Camden Society 261

Campbell, R.J. 512

Canada 5-6, 388-90

Cane Ridge Meeting 24, 25

cannibalism 109, 415, 426, 533

canonic institution 55

Carey, Dorothy 102, 104

Carey, Lott 20

Carey, William 87, 95-7, 100-8, 119,

.... 127-9, 407, 509, 516

Carlile, Wilson 469

Carlyle, Thomas 201

'Cartesian dualism' 305

Cassels, W.W. 414

caste system (India) 104, 297, 417

Catherine II, Empress of Russia 377

Catholic Apostolic Church 210

Catholicism

    in Britain 84-5, 203-4, 223

    in Canada 389-90

    in China 422-3

    and Christian mission 96-7, 100,

    .... 123, 299-300, 422-5, 430, 523

    and Darwinism 325

    and French Revolution 36-42,

    ....45-50, 52, 54-60

    in Germany 167-70, 180

    and Irish nationalism 384-7

    and Italian nationalism 382-4

    in Latin America 390-4

    and liberalism 240-9, 267-8

    and urban mission 464-6

    and urbanisation 446, 448, 450

    in USA 5, 6, 342-3, 476, 496-7

Cavour, Count Camillo 383

Chalmers, James 426

Chalmers, Thomas 116, 124, 204-8,

    .... 209-10, 228, 307-8

Chamberlain, Joseph 456

Chambers, Robert 315

Channing, William Ellery 9, 484

Chapels Act (1834) 251

Charity Organisation Society 458

Charles X, King of France 40

Charles, Thomas 82

Chartist movement (Britain) 265-6

Chauncy, Charles 9

Chilembwe, John 528

China 293-5, 409-11, 415, 418-23, 529-30

China Inland Mission (CIM) 411, 413-15,

    .... 418-19, 421, 500

China Opened (book) 293

Chinese Evangelization Society 293-4

Christian Instruction Society 209

Christian mission

achievements of 521-9

and 'civilisation' 300-1, 315,
.... 333, 434

and Anglicanism 110-14

and anti-slavery movement 126,
.... 152-60, 277-8, 284-6

and Catholicism 96-7, 100, 123,
.... 299-300, 422-5, 430

and Church of Scotland 115-16

and colonialism 404-8, 432-3, 524

and David Livingstone 284-9

development of theory 273-6

and Edinburgh Missionary Conference
.... 516-19

and Enlightenment 300

expansion of 96, 122-8, 416-24

Far Eastern 291-2, 425-6

and imperialism 271-2, 403-4,
.... 431-5, 518, 522

and Methodism 114-15, 272

Middle Eastern 290, 430-1

motivation to 300-3

and Niger Expedition 160, 278-83

and Presbyterianism 115-16, 410

and racial superiority 533-5

recruitment and strategy 408-15

and Reformation 96-100

rejection of 95, 107

and South Africa 116-18, 129

South-East Asia 295

South Pacific 290-1, 426-7

and USA 114-15, 118-22, 272,
.........................275-6, 408-12, 433-4

and Western culture 434-5

see also urban mission

Christian Missions and Social
Progress (book) 414-15

Christian Science movement 348, 480

Christian Social Union (CSU) 267

Christian Social Workers Party (Germany)
....457

Christian Socialism 264-7

Christianity

and anti-slavery movement 145-8,
.... 151-7, 161, 349-54

and British politics 221-8

challenges to 509-16

and education 88-91, 214-16

and evolution 314-24

expansion of 95-6, 522-4, 529

and First World War 538-9

and French de-Christianisation 49-52

and geology 307-11

and German theology 172-91

and growth of science 305-7

and liberalism 483-9, 494-6, 530-1

and liberty 33

and Marxism 238-9

and morality 77-8, 92, 172-3

and motivation to mission 300-3

and national identity 371-3, 400

philosophical criticism of 182-3

and population growth 442-4

rejection of 37-8

and revivalism 24-9

and secularisation 440-50

and slavery 14, 16-22

and social reform 228-30, 470-2

transplanted to North America 2, 5

and US Civil War 360-5

and Western cultural imperialism
.... 434-5, 521

and world religions 529-32

Christianity and the Social Crisis (book)
.... 471

Christianizing the Social Order (book) 470

Church Missionary Society (CMS) ...99, 111-13,
.........................128-9, 273-5, 277, 281-3

Church of England Children's Society 219

Church of England Total
Abstinence Society 225

Church of Jesus Christ of Latter-Day Saints
.... 478-9
Church of Scotland 78-80, 115-16,
.... 147, 204, 211, 251-3, 325, 427
Church Pastoral Aid Society 209
Church Penitentiary Association 227
Church, R.W. 255
circuit system (Methodist) 14-15
City Vigilance League (New York) 453
Civil Constitution of the Clergy (France)
.... 45-9
civil rights 233-4, 366-8
Civil War (US) 359-65, 475
'civilisation' 300-1, 315, 333, 434
Clapham Sect 76, 85, 110-12, 143-5, 161, 254
Clark, Reverend Francis E. 456
Clarkson, Thomas 135, 141
Classen, Walter 459-61
Close, Francis 211
Clowes, William 84
Coal Mines Regulation Act (1842) 222
Coke, Thomas 23, 114-15, 127, 153
Colenso, Bishop John 193-4, 272
Coleridge, Samuel Taylor 210
colonialism 404-8, 428, 432, 524
Committee of Public Safety (France) 50
Communism 236-9, 249, 442, 511
Communist Manifesto 238-9
Concordat (1801) 55-6, 395
Concordat (1813) 58-9
Congo 427-8
Congregational Union (Britain) 87
Congregationalists 484-8, 495-6, 514
Constitutional Act (1791) 389
Consulate rule (France) 53-60
Contribution to the Critique of Hegel's
    Philosophy of Right (book) 238
Contributions to Old
    Testament Introduction (book) 190
Cook, Captain James 102, 126
Copernican Revolution 173
Corn Laws (Britain) 223

Cornwallis, Lord 1
Corporation Act (1828) 86, 154, 222
cotton industry 138, 161, 287
Cowper, William 75
Cranfield, Thomas 218
Crime and Punishment (novel) 380
Crimean War 373, 376, 379
Critique of Pure Reason (book) 173
Cromwell, James 115
Crosby, Fanny J. 506
Crowther, Samuel Ajayi 279-83, 535
Crumpler, Rebecca Lee 347
Cullen, Paul 385
curés (French parish priests) 39, 42
Cuvier, Georges 308

D

d'Alembert, Jean Le Rond 38
Dabney, Robert L. 366-7
Daily News (newspaper) 447
Dale, David 228
Darby, John Nelson 497-8
Darwin, Charles
    and Christian mission 303
    death of 332-3
    formation of theories 181, 311-14
    and morality 333-4
    religious life of 331-3
    responses to 320-31
    and theory of evolution 314-20, 510
    wider influence of 333-5
Darwinism and Divinity (essay) 321
Das Kapital (book) 335
Davidson, Randall 517
Dawson, Sir William 325
De Bow, James 361
de Tocqueville, Alexis 340
de-Christianisation (France) 49-52
Declaration of Independence (US) 4, 6, 140
Declaration of the Rights of Man
    and the Citizen (1789) 43-4, 48, 140
Deed of Declaration (1784) 250

Defoe, Daniel 197

deism 6-7

Demerara Rising (1823) 154-5

Denmark 387-8

Dennis, James 414-15

denominational pluralism (US) 5

Descartes, René 305

Destitute Children's Dinner Society........ 218

DeWette, Wilhelm 190

Dickens, Charles 201-2, 235

Diderot, Denis 38

dinosaurs 308, 329

Directory rule (France) 52-3

Discourses on Christian Nurture (book) 486

Disestablishment movement (Britain)

....213, 234

Dispensationalism (US) 498

Divine Providence 295, 298, 302, 361

Dohrn, Anton 331

Dostoevsky, Fyodor 380

Douglass, Frederick 346, 352, 359,

....363-4, 367

Dow, Lorenzo 84

Down, Dr John 227

'Downgrade Controversy' 212, 420, 513

Dreyfuss, Alfred 399

Drummond, Henry 322, 512-13

Duff, Alexander 116, 295-7, 414, 417

Dutch East India Company 98

Dwight, Timothy 7, 9, 26, 481

E

Easter Rising (Ireland) 387

Eclectic Society 111

Eddy, Mary Baker 348-9, 479-80

Edict of Nantes (1598) 41

Edict of Religious Toleration (1773) 377

Edinburgh Medical Journal 226

Edinburgh Medical Mission 213-14,

....302-3

Edinburgh Missionary Conference

(1910) 516-19

Edinburgh Missionary Society 106

education 88-91, 214-18, 347, 414

Education Act (1870) 216

education reform (US) 30

Edwards junior, Jonathan 7

Edwards, Jonathan 2, 7, 9, 74, 127-8

Eliot, George 186

Eliot, John 97

Emancipation Proclamation (1863) 359

Emerson, Ralph Waldo 484

Encyclopédie (Encyclopaedia) 38

Engels, Friedrich 186, 201, 236-9, 450-1

England in 1815 (book) 64

English Dissenting Movement 86, 91, 154,

.... 156, 234, 253

Enlightenment

and Christian mission 122-5, 300

and France 36-8, 47, 166

and Germany 166, 168, 170-2,

.... 179-80

and liberalism 234

and reformist movements 79

and slavery 139-40

Enquiry into the Obligations

of Christians (book) 101-2, 128

Entzauberung ('disenchantment') 441

Equal Franchise Act (1928) 12

equality 236-40

Equiano, Olaudah 142, 278

Erasmus 314

Essay on Population 306

Essay on the Development of

Christian Doctrine 262

Essay on the Principle of Population 70

Essays and Reviews (book) 321-2

Estates-General (France) 42-5, 48

Ethiopia 524

Eugenics Society 334

Evangelical Association (Germany) 455

Evangelical Party (Scotland) 79, 251

Evangelical Revival 64-5, 74, 79-82,

.... 86-7, 98, 126-8, 141-2

'Evangelisation of the world'...............519-20

evangelism

  and Calvinism 100-1

  during Industrial Revolution(Britain)

 74-80

  and slavery 21-2

  and social stability 64-7

  and Tractarianism 263

  see also Christian mission

Evidence and Authority of the Christian

  Revelation (book) 307-8

evolution 532

Evolution and Dogma (book) 497

Evolution and Religion (book) 489

evolution, theory of 314-24, 333-4, 489

F

Fabri, Friedrich 433

Factory Bill (1843) 223

faith 189

Far East missions 291-2, 425-6

Fee, John 353

Fegan, James 332, 333

Female Aid Society 226-7

Female Moral Reform Society (US) 31

Ferdinand, Archduke Franz 539

Feuerbach, Ludwig 187-8, 238

Finland 387-8

Finney, Charles 26-9, 353, 461, 482-3

First Amendment (of US Constitution)

  ....9-11, 337

First Vatican Council 247

First World War 518, 531, 538-9

Fitzhugh, George 361

FitzRoy, Robert 312, 329

Fletcher, John 16-17

Fodio, Shehu Usuman dan 405

Forge Valley (US) 3

Fort Sumter (US) 359, 365

Foundations (essays) 512

Foundling Hospital (Britain) 219

Fourah Bay Institution 113

Fox, Charles 143-4

France

  anti-Semitism in 399

  anti-slavery movement in 140

  church attendance in 445-6, 451-2

  Constitution of 44

  Consulate rule of 53-60

  de-Christianisation of 49-52

  Directory rule of 52-3

  empire of 55

  and Enlightenment 36-8, 47, 166

  and Estates-General 42-5, 48

  and German theological revolution 193

  and Indo-China 425

  nationalism in 372

  population growth in 443

  pre-revolutionary 35-42

  spread of liberalism in 240-4

  support for US War of Independence

  .... 1, 3, 35

  war with Austria 49

Francke, August 98

Franco-Prussian war (1870) 169

Franklin, Benjamin 4, 6

Frederick William II, King 166, 167, 174

free trade 233, 234, 253

Freemasonry 38, 478

French Revolution

  Britain's view of 63-4

  causes of 35-6

  effects on the church 45-9

  and Germany 165-7

  legacy of 60-1

  and spread of liberalism 233

  start of 43-5

  and War of Independence (US) 1, 33, 35

French-Indian War (1754-63) 1, 2

Freud, Sigmund 188, 511

Friedrich Wilhelm III, King 176, 179

Frost, Henry 415

Froude, Richard Hurrell 157, 257

Fry, Elizabeth 151, 225

Fuegans 333-4

Fugitive Slave Act (1850) 355

Fulani 405

Fuller, Andrew 100

Fundamentalism (US) 498-505, 513

G

Gale, George 26

Gallican church (France) 39-41, 45, 48-9, 57

Gardiner, Allen 303

Garibaldi, Giuseppe 383

Garretson, Freeborn 13, 19, 115

Garrison, William Lloyd 353, 357

geist ('spirit') 171

General Conference of German
      Morality Leagues 453

General Missionary Council (China) 422

Geological Society 312

geology 307-11, 321, 489

George, David 16, 149

Germany

    and Christian mission 433

    church attendance in 166, 168,

    ....192-3, 444-5, 454-5

    and Enlightenment 166, 168,

    .... 170-2, 179-80

    formation of empire 168-9

    and French Revolution 165-7

    Jewish communities in 398, 399-400

    and moral reform 453

    and Napoleon Bonaparte 166-7

    nationalism in 166-7, 372

    population growth in 443

    reform movement in 167-8

    and Social Democracy 192

    and theological reconstruction ... 172-93,

    .... 244, 490

    urbanisation of 167

Gibbs, Josiah Willard 485

Girl Guides movement 456

Gladden, Washington 469, 471-2, 495-6

Gladstone, W.E. 254, 263, 386

Glasgow 197, 204-11, 225, 452, 455

Glasgow City Mission 208

Glasgow Missionary Society 106, 116, 288-9

glasnost (openness) 379

Gloucester Journal (newspaper) 88

God

    consciousness of 178

    as creator 6, 305-11, 317-20, 326

    existence of 173-4, 305-6

    and faith 189

    judgement of 527

    kingdom of 189-90, 470-1

    and liberty 47

    as love 37

    obedience to 65

    Providence of 324

    purposes of 364-5

    rejection of 171

    relationship with 172, 177

    revelation of 490-1

    and revival 28

    and scientific proof 305-6

    and soul 484, 487-8

    sovereignty of 7, 75

    as 'Spirit' 181-2

    and suffering 488

    truth of 179

    union with 189

God in Christ (book) 485-6

Goethe, Johann Wolfgang von 171

Gold Coast (Africa) 97, 283

Gordon Riots (1780) 84

Gordon, A.J. 412

Gordon-Conwell Seminary 412

Gore, Charles 263

Gosse, Philip 310

Graf, Karl Heinrich 190

Grant, Charles 110

Grant, Dr Robert 311

Gray, Asa 317-18, 323

'Great Awakening' (US) 2, 16

'Great Reversal' 499

Greece 372-6

Greek Orthodox Church 375-6

Gregory XVI, Pope 242, 299

Grimké, Angelina 31

Grimké, Sara 31

Groves, Anthony Norris 411

Grunow, Eleonore 76

Guide to Christian Perfection (weekly
 publication) 501

Guthrie, Thomas 210-11, 218

Gützlaff, Dr Karl 293-4

H

Hackney Phalanx (reform movement)
 .... 73-4, 254

Haiti 140

Haldane, James 79-80, 116

Haldane, Robert 79-80, 116

Halévy, Elie 64-8

Hall, Robert 64

Halle 98, 99, 128

Hamburg Volksheim 460-1

Hampden, R.D. 260

Hampden-Sydney College (US) 25-6

Hannington, Bishop James 428-9

Hard Times (novel) 201-2, 235

Harms, Claus 191

Harris, Howell 74

Harris, William Wadé 525-6

Harrop, John 198-9

Haskalah ('Jewish Enlightenment') 397-9

Hasseltine, Ann 119, 121

Hatch, Nathan 23-4

Hauge, Hans Nielsen 388

Haussmann, Baron 443

Hawker, Robert 63

Hayford, Mark 517

Headlam, Stuart 267

Hegel, Georg 180-3, 238, 335, 434, 490

Hengstenberg, E.W. 191, 494

Henslow, John 312

Hernnhut 98-9, 128

Hidalgo, Miguel 390-1

High Church (Britain) 73

High Imperialism 405

Hill, David 419

Hill, Octavia 458

Hinduism 113, 301, 415-16, 529-30

History of Israel (book) 190

History of Jamaica (book) 314

Hodge, Archibald Alexander 492-3

Hodge, Charles 234, 325-6, 363,
 ....487-8, 490-2, 494

Holiness Revivalism 466-9

'Holiness' movement (US) 500-2

Home Rule (Ireland) 386

Hook, William Farquhar 211

Hope, Lady Elizabeth 332-3

Hopkins, J.H. 361

Hopkins, Samuel 7, 16

Horne, Melvill 519

Hort, F.J.A. 321

Hoste, D.E. 414

housing reform (Britain) 227-8

How the Other Half Lives (book) 440

Hudson Taylor, James 294, 302,
 ....411-13, 418, 500, 520, 531

Hume, David 8, 139, 173

Huntingdon, Countess of 82

Hutcheson, Francis 6

Hutton, James 307

Huxley, T.H. 320, 324, 327-30, 332

I

Ibadan 281

Ibrahim Pasha 374

Imad-ud-din 416

imperialism
 and Christian mission 271-2,
 .... 403-4, 431-5, 518, 522
 and colonialism 404-8, 428, 432
 and Darwinism 334-5

*Imperialism: The Highest Stage of
 Capitalism* (book) 405

In Darkest England and the Way Out (book) 467-8

In Memoriam (poem) 306-7

India .... 98-9, 102, 104-8, 110-14, ... 119, 295-9, 407, 416-18, 529

'Indian Missions' (article) 107

Indian Mutiny (1857) 297, 298

Indian National Congress 529

indigenous Christianity 524-9

Industrial Revolution (Britain)

    and Catholicism 84-5, 203-4

    and Church of England 71-8, 203-4

    and Church of Scotland 78-80

    and Jewish Community 87-8

    and Methodism 80-4, 203

    perceptions of 201-2

    progress of 68-70

    religious life during 70-1, 85-7, 202-4

    and slavery 138

    and urbanisation 197-201, 228

    and voluntary bodies 88-91

    and working conditions ....198-9, ...221-2, 224

Inner Mission (Germany) 455, 457

Institutes of the Christian Religion (book) 177

International Missionary Council 518

Ireland 70, 72, 85, 384-7, 464-5

Ireland, John 466

Irving, Edward 210, 411, 503

Islam 405-6, 416, 428-31

Israel 394

Italy 245-9, 382-4

J

Jackson, Andrew 339, 482

Jackson, General Thomas 'Stonewall' ....360, ...366

Jamaica 153-5, 157-8, 277

Jamaican rebellion (1831) 158

James, John Angell 211-12

Jansen, Cornelius 40

Jansenism 40-1

Japan 291-2, 423

Jefferson, Thomas 6, 10, 33

Jeffreys, George 515

Jehovah's Witnesses 480

Jesuits 96-7, 100, 299

Jesus Christ

    death of 182

    devotion to 175

    divinity of 37, 174, 189

    and eternal truths 184-5

    humanity of 86

    kingdom of 265

    as Messiah 183-4

    role of 9

    Second Coming of .... 127, 477, 478, ... 480, 504

    and truth 178-9, 181, 187, 486

Jewish Chronicle (newspaper) 397

Jewish Relief Act (1858) 395

Jihad 405

John Draper 327

Johnson, James 536-7

Johnson, Richard 113

Jones, Griffith 88

Judaism 42, 48, 58, 87-8, 394-400

Judson, Adoniram 119-22, 295

K

Kampala 428

Kant, Immanuel 43, 172-4

Kasatkin, Ivan 378

Keble, John 255-7, 260, 262

Kenya 403, 404, 429

Kenyatta, Jomo 403, 408

Keswick Convention 500, 531

Kierkegaard, Søren 388

Kilham, Alexander 82-3, 250

Kingdom of Christ (book) 265

Kingsley, Charles 227-8, 264, 266, 321

Kipling, Rudyard....................................405-6

Knibb, William 155-6, 158-9

Ko Tha Byn 122

Korea 292, 423-4

Krummacher, Friedrich 191

Ku Klux Klan (US) 366

Kulturkampf ('struggle for civilisation')
.... 169-70, 248, 372

L

L'Avenir (newspaper) 241-2

La Vie de Jésus (book) 193

Lacordaire, Henri 241, 242

Lamarck, Jean Baptiste 311, 314

Lamennais, Félicité de 241-2

Lancaster, Joseph 214

Latin America 390-4, 407

Latourette, K.S. 436

Laurier, Wilfrid 389-90

Lavigerie, Cardinal 430, 431

Laws, Robert 427

Lazarus 184

Lectures on Revival (book) 28

Lee, General Robert E. 359-60

Lee, Mother Ann 9, 503

Leeds Mercury (newspaper) 222

Legislative Assembly (France) 48

Lekganyane, Engenas Barnabas 527

Lenin 405

Leo XIII, Pope 249, 423, 466, 497

Leopold II, King 427-8

Leroy, Eduard 325

Liang Fah 293

liberalism

    and Catholicism 240-9, 267-8

    and Christianity 483-9, 494-6, 530-1

    and Methodism 250-1

    and Oxford Movement 253-64

    and Protestantism 249-50

    and Scotland 251-3

    spread of 233-4

    and Utilitarianism 235-6

Liberator (newspaper) 353

Liberia 525-7

Lincoln, Abraham 357-9, 364-5

Linnean Society 315

Livermore, Harriet 348

Livingstone, David 284-9, 302, 427, 534

Livingstonia Mission 427

'Locality Principle' 206-7

Locke, John 37

London Bible and Domestic
    Female Mission 214

London City Mission 208-9, 218

London Medical Missionary Association
....411

London Missionary Society 99, 108-10,
.... 116-17, 126, 411, 519

London Moonlight Mission 227

London Society for Promoting
    Christianity among the Jews 290

Lord's Day Act (1906) 390

Lord's Day Observance Society (Britain) 224

Louis XV, King 36

Louis XVI, King 38-9, 42-5, 48-9

Louis XVIII, King 240

Lourdes 247

Ludlow, J.M. 266

Luther, Martin 167

Lutheran church 167-8, 174, 179,
....191-2, 387-8

Lux Mundi (collection of essays) 263

Lyell, Charles 308, 312, 332

Lyman, Henry 426

M

Macaulay, Zachary 143, 149

Macdonald, Donald 325

Machen, J. Gresham 493-4

Mackenzie, Charles Frederick 287

Maclaren, Alexander 212

MacLeod, Norman 211

Malaya 98

Malthus, Rev. Thomas 70, 306,
.... 315, 316

Manchester 201, 215

Mann, Horace 447, 452

Manning, Cardinal 465

Maret, Anne 41

Marine Society (Britain) 219

Marsden, Samuel 113-14

Marshman, Joshua 104, 106

Martineau, Harriet 320

Martiniana, Cardinal 54-5

Marty, Martin 31

Martyn, Henry 110-11, 430

Marx, Karl 183, 188, 191, 236-9, 267, 335

Marxism 238-9, 265-6, 529

Mary (the Virgin Mary)........................ 247-8

Maskilim 397

Mathew, Father Theobald 225

Maurice, Frederick Denison 264-7, 485, 529

Maury, Matthew 324

Maynooth Seminary (Ireland) 223

Mazzini, Giuseppe 383

McCallum, Duncan 115

McCheyne, Robert Murray 210

McCulloch, Thomas 389

McKinley, William 408

McNeile, Hugh 211

Mearns, Andrew 439, 452

Melvill, Henry 211

Mendelssohn, Moses 397

mental illness 227

Methodism

    and anti-slavery movement 153

    and Calvinism 480-1

    and Christian mission 114-15, 272

    and Industrial Revolution 64-7,

    ....80-4, 203

    and liberalism 250-1

    in USA 12-15, 16-19, 23

Methodist Missionary Society 272

Methods of Mission Work (book) 420

Mexico 390-1, 392, 393

Miall, Edward 213

Middle East 290, 430-1

'Middle Passage' (slave trade) 135-7, 439

Mildert, William van 73

Mildmay Medical Mission 213

military technology 125

Mill, John Stuart 235

Miller, Hugh 308-10

Miller, William......................................417, 477

Mirabeau 43, 45

Missionary Travels and Researches
    in South Africa (book) 286, 289

missions *see* Christian mission

Mizan-ul-Haqq (book) 290

Mkone, Mangena 524

Moderate Party (Scotland) 79

modernism 323-4, 441, 445,
    ....472, 498-9, 512-13

Moffat, Robert 284, 300, 302

Moffett, Samuel 292

Montalembert, Charles 241

Montesquieu 140

Moody, D. L. 322, 412, 461-4,
    .... 498, 519-20, 531

Moon, Charlotte Diggs 'Lottie' 409-10

morality 6-7, 40, 51, 77-8, 92,
    .... 172-3, 333-4

Moravianism 71, 98-9, 175

Morley, Samuel 213

Mormonism 478-9

Morrison, Robert 293

Morse, Rev. Jedidiah 33

Mott, John 517, 520

Mott, Lucretia 345

Mow Cop Camp Meeting 83-4

Müller, George 219-20, 411

Municipal Reform Act (1835) 223, 253

Munson, Samuel 426

Murray, John 9

N

Napoleon III, Emperor 404

Napoleon, Louis 242-3

Nasmith, David 208

'National Apostasy' (sermon) 255

National Assembly (France) 43, 45-7

National Children's Home (Britain) 219

National Convention (1794) 140

National Federation of Settlements 461

National Guard (France) 43, 45

national identity 371-3, 400

National Reform Association (US) 8,
.... 10, 32

National Society (Britain) 73

National Temperance League 225

Native American Association 343

Native Americans 22-3, 97, 339

Natural Law in the Spiritual
    World (book) 322

natural selection 315-19, 321,
.... 325-6, 333-5

Natural Theology (book) 306-7

Nazism 335

Neale, J.M. 261

Netherlands Missionary Society 117

Nettleton, Asahel 9, 26, 28, 481-2

Nevius, John 420-1

New Divinity (US) 26

New Guinea 426

New Lebanon Conference .... (1827) 482

New Poor Law (Britain) 200

New York Female Moral Reform Society
....344

New York Herald (newspaper) 288

New Zealand 291

Newman, Francis 313

Newman, John Henry 211, 234,
.... 240, 246-8, 257-64

Newton, Isaac 37, 306, 335

Newton, John 75, 147

Niagara Bible Conference 498

Nicholas I, Tsar 378-9

Nicholas II, Tsar 381

Nicholas V, Pope 132

Nietzsche, Friedrich 192

Niger Expedition 160, 278-83, 287

Noll, Mark 4

Nommensen, Ludwig Ingwer 426

Norway 387-8

Noyes, John Humphrey 477

Ntiskana 117

O

O'Connell, Daniel 244, 385

O'Kelly, James 13

O'Sullivan, John 339

Oastler, Richard 222

Oberlin College (US) 29, 30

Obscene Publications Act (1857) 224

Oldham, J.H. 517

Omphalos (book) 310

On Religion: Speeches Addressed to
    Its Cultured Despisers (book) 176-7

On the Origin of Species (book) 311, 314,
.... 316-23, 327-8

On the Principle of Population (essay) 315

On the Slavery and Commerce of
    the Human Species (essay) 141

On the Tendency of Varieties to Depart
    Indefinitely from the Original Type (essay)
.... 315

'Opium War' 293

Organic Articles (1802) 57

Orphan Working School (Britain) 219

orphanages (Britain) 219-21

Orthodox Missionary Society 378

Otto, King of Bavaria 375

Ottoman Empire 373-4, 376-7

'Over-Soul' 484

Owen, Rev. Richard 329

Owen, Robert 228, 236, 316, 477

Oxford Movement (Britain) 74, 253-64

Ozman, Agnes 503

P

P'ing-tu 409

Paine, Thomas 8, 33, 140

Pal, Krishna 104

'Pale of Settlement' 399

Paley, William 74, 306-7, 317, 319

Palmer, Benjamin 363

Palmer, Phoebe 348, 500-2

Pankhurst, Christabel 512

Pankhurst, Emmeline 512

papal infallibility 247-8

Parham, Charles Fox 503

Parker, Joseph 212

Parker, Theodore 484-5

Parkhurst, Rev. Charles 453

Parnell, Charles Stewart 386

Pashkovism (Russia) 381-2

Paton, Maggie 300, 303

Patrick, William 514

Patteson, John Coleridge 291

Peel, Robert 225

Pennefather, William 213

Penn-Lewis, Jessie 514

Pentecostalism 502-5, 515-16

Perceval, Spencer 76

perestroika (reform) 379

Periah, Yerraguntla 298

Pfander, Karl Gottlieb 290

philanthropic institutions (Britain) 213-14

Philip, John 117-18

Phillips, Wendell 440

'philosophes' 38, 40, 41, 61

Pierson, A.T. 519, 531

Pietism 98, 172, 433

Pilgrim's Progress (book) 217, 294, 525

'Pious Clause' 113-14

Pitt, William 143-4

Pius VI, Pope 48

Pius VII, Pope 54-6, 58-9, 299

Pius VIII, Pope 240

Pius IX, Pope 234, 245-9, 263, 383-4

Pius X, Pope 497, 513

Plinian Society (Edinburgh University) 311

pogroms (Russia) 380-1, 399

Polhill, Cecil 515

Political Constitution of Greece (1827) ... 375

Politics for the People (series of tracts) 266

polygenesis 532-3

Poor Law (Britain) 69-70, 200, 219

Pounds, John 218

Powell, Baden.......................................311, 321

preaching (Britain) 209-14

Premillennialism (US) 497-8, 513

Presbyterianism

    and Calvinism 482-3

    and Christian mission 115-16,

        ....410, 420-1, 424-5

    and Darwinism 325-6

    and Industrial Revolution 78-80,

        .... 86, 204

    and liberalism 251-3

    and slavery (US) 361-3

    in USA 7-8, 490, 494-5

Primitive Methodists 250

Princeton Theological Seminary 234,

    ....481-2, 489-94

Princip, Gabriel 539

Principles of Geology (book).....................308

prison reform (Britain) 224-5

prostitution 226-7

Protestantism

    in Britain 85-7, 223

    in Canada 389-90

    and Darwinism 322-3

    in France 41, 48, 51, 57-8

    in Germany 167-70, 180

    in Ireland 385-7

    in Latin America 393

    and liberalism 249-50

    missionary work

        see Christian mission

    in Russia 381-2

    in USA 342-3, 476

Public Worship Regulation Act (1875) ... 260

Pugin, Augustus Welby 261

Puritanism 2, 7

Pusey, Edward Bouverie 259, 263, 513

Q

Quakers 16, 31, 86-7, 141, 145,
.... 147, 203, 344-6, 364
Quaque, Philip 97
Quarterly Review (journal) 328-9

R

'racial deterioration' 334
racial discrimination 17, 19, 131,
.... 139-40, 152, 162, 433
'racial superiority' 433, 532-7
Radstock, Lord 381-2
Ragged Schools (Britain) 218
Raikes, Robert 88-9
Ramābai, 'Pandita' 416
Rauschenbusch, Walter 469-72, 496
Reed, Andrew 212, 219, 227, 338,
.... 340-1, 349, 352
Reform Act (1832) 70, 159, 161, 223
Reformation 96-100, 305, 372
refractory churches (France) 47, 49
Reid, Thomas 6
religious liberty 5, 10-11, 44, 154
Religious Tract Society (Britain) 88
Removal Bill (1830) 339
Renan, Joseph Ernest 193
Republicanism (US) 11, 357
revivalism (US) 24-9, 225, 342, 461,
.... 463, 466, 482-3
Rhenish Missionary Society 433
Ricci, Matteo 292
Richard, Timothy 418-20, 434, 529-30
Riehl, Wilhelm 440
Riis, Jacob 440
Risorgimento (Italy) 382
Ritschl, Albrecht 188-90
Roberts, Evan 514
Robespierre, Maximilien 51
'Rocket' (Stephenson's) 69
Roman Catholic Emancipation Act (1829)
.... 85

Roman Catholic Relief Act (1778) 84
Roman Catholicism see Catholicism
Romania 376
Romanticism 171-2, 173
Rosebery, Lord 404-5
Rothschild, Nathan 87-8
Rousseau, Jean Jacques 37-8, 54, 140
Rowland, Daniel 74, 82
Roy, Ram Mohun 297
Royal Geographical Society 286, 288
RSPCA (Royal Society for the Prevention
of Cruelty to Animals) 224
Russell, Charles Taze 480
Russia 377-82, 399
Russian Bible Society 378
Russian Orthodox Church 377-8, 380-2
Russian revolution 378, 382
Rutherford, Joseph 480
Ryder, Henry 111
Ryland, J.C. 102
Ryle, J.C. 211

S

Sabbath observance 32, 76, 224,
.... 341, 344, 527
Sadler, Michael 221
Salt, Titus 228
Salvation Army 439, 467-9
Samoa 109, 290
Sandwich Islands (Hawaii) 118
Sankey, Ira D. 463
Sanscoulottes (French urban movement) 43
sati (widow burning) 417
Scandinavia 387-8
Schlegel, Friedrich 168
Schleiermacher, Friedrich 175-80,
.... 191, 483-4
Schön, Friedrich 280
School Boards (Britain) 216
Schwartz, Friedrich 99
science
and geology 307-11

growth of 305-7

and proof 313, 330

and secularisation 440-1

and theory of evolution 314-20

as ultimate authority 335

Science and Health According to the Scriptures (book) 480

'scientific racism' 534

Scottish Common Sense Philosophy ......6-7, ...140, 295, 494

Scotland 78-80, 106-7, 204-8, 251-3

Scott, David 427

Scott, Dred 355-6

'scramble for Africa' 404

Scripture Readers Association 209

Second Great Awakening (US) ....20, 23-9, ...341-2, 349, 351, 361, 500

'Second Reformation' 386

'Second Terror' (France) 52

secularisation 440-52, 472-3

Sedgwick, Adam 308, 312, 320-1

self-consciousness 187-8

Selwyn, George 291

Serampore Trio (India) 104-6, 119

Serbia 376

Seton, Elizabeth Ann 343

Settlement Movement 458-61

Seventh Day Adventists 348, 477-8

Seymour, William 503-4

Shaftesbury, Lord ....197, 215, 218, ...221-2, 224, 227-8, 290

Shaker movement (US) 9, 503

Sharia law 405

Sharp, Granville 149

Sharpe, Sam 157-8

Sherman, General 360

Shrewsbury, John 155

Siam 425

Sidmouth, Lord 67

Sierra Leone ....112-13, 115, 149-50, ...274, 278-80

Simeon, Charles...........................75-6, 110, 111

Sino-Japanese war 421

slavery

abolitionist movement

see anti-slavery movement

in the Americas 136-7

and Christianity 14, 16-22

development of 131-2

emancipation from 150-60

and Enlightenment 139-40

extent of 132-4

and Industrial Revolution 138

'justifications' for 139, 146, 147-8

mechanisms of 134-6

mortality rates 135-6

and racial discrimination .... 17, 19, ...131, 139-40, 152, 162

and religious liberty 154

trade routes 132

and US Constitution 140

Slessor, Mary 410, 433

Smith, Adam 70, 139, 215

Smith, John 155

Smith, John Pye 310

Smith, Joseph 478-9

Smith, Sydney 106, 107

Smith, William 308

Social Darwinism 334-5

Social Gospel movement ....469-71, 485, ...488, 496, 499

Socialism 236-9, 249, 264-7

Society for Promoting Christian Knowledge 97

Society for the Propagation of the Gospel at Home (Scotland) 80

Soubirous, Bernadette 247

South Africa 116-18, 129, 428

South African Missionary Society 117

South American Missionary Society 303, 431

South Pacific missions 290-1, 426-7

South-East Asia mission 295

Southern Baptist Convention 353

Southey, Thomas 64

Spencer, Herbert 334

Spurgeon, C.H. 212, 219, 322, 420, 513

Sri Lanka 98

St Bartholomew's Day massacre (France) 41

Stanley, Henry Morton 288-9

Stanton, Elizabeth Cady 29, 345-6

Stark, Rodney 442

state churches 234, 243

Stead, W.T. 435

Stephen, James 143

Stephen, Leslie 321

Stephenson, George 69

Stephenson, Thomas Bowman 219

Stewart, James 427

Stiles, Ezra.. 3-4

Stoecker, Adolf 169, 457

Stowe, Harriet Beecher 355, 489

Strauss, David F. 183-6, 236, 316, 488

Streeter, B.H. 512

Stuart, Moses 310

Studd, C.T. 413-14

Student Volunteer Missionary Union 412

Student Volunteer Movement 412,
.... 464, 519, 531

Stundists (Ukraine) 381-2

suffragette movement 512

Sunday School Union (Britain) 88

Sunday Schools 88-91, 206, 216-17,
....343-4, 347

Sunday, Billy 464

Supreme Being (cult of the) 51

Swain, Clara...410

Sweden 387-8

Swiney, Sam 155

Swing, David 494

Syllabus of Errors (Papal) 246

Symmes, William 8

System of Doctrine Contained in Divine
Revelation (book) 7

Systematic Theology (book) 491-2, 494

T

Tahiti 109, 427

Taylor, Nathaniel 9, 481, 485

Taylor, William 272

Temperance movement 225-6, 342, 464

Temple, Frederick 321-2

Tennyson, Alfred Lord...............................307

'Terror' (France) 50-1

Test Act (1828) 86, 154, 222

Thackeray, William 202

The Age of Reason (book) 8

The Ascent of Man (book) 322

The Bitter Cry of Outcast London (pamphlet)
....439, 452

The British Churches in Relation to the
British People (book) 213

The Brothers Karamazov (novel) 380

The Christian and Civic Economy of
Large Towns (book) 206-7

The Christian Faith (book) 176-9

The Condition of the Working Class
in England (book) 236-8

The Descent of Man (book) 315, 317, 319

The Evangelisation of the World in this
Generation (book) 520

The Expression of Emotions in Man
and Animals (book) 315

The Footprints of the Creator (book) 309

The Interpretation of Dreams (book) 511

The Life of Jesus Critically Examined (book)
.....................................183-4, 236, 316

The Life of Jesus for the People (book) 185-6

The New Evangelicalism (book) 512-13

The New Theology (book) 512

The Pentateuch and Book of Joshua
Critically Examined (book) 194

The Religions of the World in the
Relations to Christianity (book) 529

The Rights of Man (book) 8

The Testimony of the Rocks (book) 309

The Vicarious Sacrifice (book) 488

The Way of Holiness (book) 501

'*The White Man's Burden*' (poem) 405-6

The Witness (newspaper) 309

Theological Liberalism (US) 483-9, 497-8

Theology for the Social Gospel (book)

.... 470

'theophilanthropy' 52-3

Theory of the Earth (book) 307

Tholuck, Friedrich 191

Thomas, John 102, 104

Thomas, Robert 292, 424

Thompson, E.P. 66

Thompson, Thomas 97

Thornton, Henry 76-7, 149-50

Thornwell, John Henry 361-3

'Thoughts on Death

and Immortality' (lecture) 187

Thoughts on Slavery (book) 141

Times (newspaper) 321

Ti-Yu, James 292

Tolstoy, Leo 380

Tomkins, Oliver 426

Tonga 290, 427

Totem and Tabu (book) 511

Townsend, Henry 281

Toynbee, Arnold 68

Toynbee Hall (London) 458-9

Tractarianism 254-5, 257-63, 272

'Trail of Tears' 23, 339

Transcendentalism 340

Treaty of Nanking (1842) 272, 293

Treaty of Paris (1814) 148

Treaty of Westphalia (1648) 42, 166

Trevithick, Richard 69

Truth, Sojourner 346

Tuckerman, Dr Joseph 209

Tuke, William 227

Turner, Henry M. 367

Turner, Nat 352

U

Uchimura, Kanzo 423

Uganda 408, 428-30

ultramontanism 168, 241-3, 247

Uncle Tom's Cabin (novel) 355

'Underground Railroad' (US) 350,

.... 352, 354, 356

Union Theological Seminary 494-5

Unitarian Christianity (sermon) 9

Unitarianism 9, 203, 481-2, 484

United Free Church 514

United Kingdom Alliance 225

Universalism 9

Université de France 57

urban mission

and Catholicism 464-6

and church attendance 454-5, 472-3

and Holiness Revivalism 466-9

and moral reform 453

and Settlement Movement 458-61

and social problems 439-40, 455-8

and Social Gospel 469-71

and Urban Revivalism movement ... 461-4

Urban Mission Movement (Britain) ...208-9

Urban Parochial Model (Scotland) 204-8

urban restoration schemes 439, 443,

....455-8

Urban Revivalism movement 461-4

USA

African-American Christians in ..16-22,

.... 351-2, 363, 367-8, 503-5

anti-slavery movement in 349-59

and Christian mission 114-15,

...... 118-22, 272, 275-6, 408-12, 433-4

and church attendance 10-11, 12-13,

...... 324, 341, 442, 448, 450, 472, 489

Civil War 359-65, 475

Constitution of 4-6, 9-11, 31-2, 140

and Darwinism 322-4, 333

and evangelism 11-12

expansion of 22, 339-40

formation of 21

and Fundamentalism 498-505, 513

immigration into 338, 450

industrialisation of 338-9

Jewish communities in 450

and moral reform 453

new religious movements in 476-80

population growth in 337-8, 443-4

post-Civil War mainstream theology

....480-97

post-Independence religious activity

.... 6-9, 340-3

prominence of Southern states 349-50

religious diversity in 12-16,

....475-6, 505-6

and religious expressionism 11-12,

.... 337, 476-7, 506

slave-owning states 356

urbanisation of 442, 448

voluntary bodies 29-31

War of Independence 1-6, 33, 35

Utilitarianism 228, 235-6, 335

V

Van der Kemp, Johannes 116-17

Vaughan, Robert 201-2

Veniaminov, Innokenti 378

Venn, Henry 111, 273-5, 281-3, 302, 407, 435

Venn, John 76, 111, 214, 273

Vestiges of the Natural History

of Creation (book) 315

Victor Emmanuel II, King 383

Victorian Nonconformity

Movement (Britain) 87

'vital religion' 80

Voltaire, François-Marie Arouet 8, 37

voluntary bodies 29-31, 88-91

Voortrek (Great Trek) 117

W

Wagner, Richard 171

Waifs and Strays Society (Britain) 219

Wales 81-2, 204

Wallace, Alfred Russel 315-16, 320, 334

War and Peace (novel) 380

War of Independence (US) 1-6, 33, 35

Ward, William 104, 119

Wardlaw, Ralph 209-10

Ware, Henry 9

Warfield, Benjamin Breckinridge 493

Warren, George 115

Washington, Booker T. 367

Washington, George 3, 6, 10, 11, 33

'watchword' 519-20

Watts, Isaac 126

Wayland, Francis 276

Weber, Ludwig 453

Weber, Max 441

Wedgwood, Emma 313-14, 333

Wellhausen, Julius 190-1

Wells, H.G. 459

Welsh Revival 514-15

Wesley, John

and anti-slavery movement ... 141, 143-4

and Christian mission 97, 114-15

conservatism of 65

conversion of 99

death of 82

and liberalism 250-1

and Methodist movement (Britain) ...80-2

and Moravians 71

and religious toleration 66

and US War of Independence 3

and volunteers for America 12-13

West Indies 115, 129, 152-4, 157-9

Western cultural imperialism 434-5, 521

Westminster Confession 79, 476,

.... 482-3, 490, 494

What is Darwinism? (book) 325

Whateley, Richard 74

Whewell, William 306

'White Terror' (France) 2

White, Andrew 453

White, Ellen Gould 348, 477

Whitefield, George 2, 74, 79, 82, 127

Whitman, Walt 338

Wichern, Johann Hinrich 455

Wilberforce, Samuel 327-30

Wilberforce, William

    and anti-slavery movement 143-5, 151-2

    and Christian mission 110, 113,

                 .... 149-50, 278

    death of 159

    and evolution 314

    and RSPCA 224

    and social reform 76-8

Wilhelm II, Kaiser 193, 539

Willard, Frances 464

William III, King 78

Williams, Eric 138

Williams, George 217

Williams, John 109, 290

Williams, William 82

Wilson, Sir Daniel 310-11

Wirth, Lewis 440-1

Wiseman, Nicholas 223

Witherspoon, John 4

Wöllner, J.C. 174

Woman's Bible (book) 346

women

    and anti-slavery movement ... 157, 344-6

    and 'Bible Missions' (Britain) 214

    and Christian mission 409-11, 522

    and church attendance 451

    and French Revolution 44-5, 51

    and Methodism 14

    as preachers (US) 348-9

    role in post-Independence USA 343-9

Women's Christian Temperance Union 464

women's rights.................. 28-9, 343-6, 510-12

women's voluntary bodies (US) 30-1

Woods, Joseph 147

Working People and their Employers (book)

    495-6

working-class church

    membership 450-1, 454

'World Christianity' 509-10, 521, 537

World Student Federation 520

World's Parliament of Religions (1893)

    529-30

Worldwide Evangelization Crusade 414

Wright, G.F. 499

X

Xi Shongmo 418-19

Y

Yang Wen-hui 415

Yeast (novel) 266

YMCA (Young Men's Christian Association)

    .... 217-18, 456, 519-20

Young People's Society of

    Christian Endeavour 456

Young, Brigham 479

Z

Zahm, John 325, 497

Zambezi 287-8, 427, 528

Ziegenbalg, Bartholomew 98

Zion movement (Africa) 527-8

Zollverein (customs union) 167

Zong (slave ship) 136

Christian Focus Publications

publishes books for all ages

Our mission statement –

STAYING FAITHFUL
In dependence upon God we seek to impact the world through literature faithful
to His infallible Word, the Bible. Our aim is to ensure that the Lord Jesus Christ
is presented as the only hope to obtain forgiveness of sin, live a useful life and
look forward to heaven with Him.

REACHING OUT
Christ's last command requires us to reach out to our world with His gospel. We
seek to help fulfil that by publishing books that point people towards Jesus and
help them develop a Christ-like maturity. We aim to equip all levels of readers
for life, work, ministry and mission.

Books in our adult range are published in three imprints:

Christian Focus contains popular works including biographies, commentaries, basic doctrine and Christian living. Our children's books are also
published in this imprint.

Mentor focuses on books written at a level suitable for Bible College and
seminary students, pastors, and other serious readers. The imprint includes
commentaries, doctrinal studies, examination of current issues and church
history.

Christian Heritage contains classic writings from the past.

Christian Focus Publications Ltd,
Geanies House, Fearn, Ross-shire,
IV20 1TW, Scotland, United Kingdom.
www.christianfocus.com